THE
DEMOCRATIC
DEBATE

THE

DEMOCRATIC

DEBATE

An Introduction to American Politics

Second Edition

Bruce Miroff
State University of New York–Albany

Raymond Seidelman
Sarah Lawrence College

Todd Swanstrom
State University of New York–Albany

HOUGHTON MIFFLIN COMPANY   Boston   New York

To our teachers, who taught us to take democracy seriously:

Walter Dean Burnham, Norman Jacobson, Isaac Kramnick,
Theodore J. Lowi, Grant McConnell, Michael Paul Rogin,
Sheldon S. Wolin

Sponsoring Editor: Melissa Mashburn
Assistant Editor: Lily P. Eng
Editorial Assistant: Vikram Mukhija
Project Editor: Anne Holm
Senior Production/Design Coordinator: Jill Haber
Manufacturing Manager: Florence Cadran
Marketing Manager: Sandra McGuire

Cover design: Tony Saizon
Cover image: Paul Vozdic/Photonica

Library of Congress Catalog Card Number: 97-72980

ISBN: 0-395-87542-0

456789-DH-01 00

BRIEF CONTENTS

PART ONE   FOUNDATIONS

PART TWO   PARTICIPATION

PART THREE   INSTITUTIONS

PART FOUR   POLICY

CONTENTS

PART ONE
FOUNDATIONS

Introduction: The Democratic Debate   1

The Revolution and the Constitution: Origins of the Democratic Debate   14

Public Opinion and Political Culture: Should Citizens Count?   43

The American Political Economy   75

PART TWO

PARTICIPATION

The Media: Who Sets the Political Agenda? 133

Where Have All the Voters Gone? 106

Are the Parties Over?   165

Campaigns: Organized Money versus Organized People   197

9

**Interest Group Politics:
Elite Bias   229**

10

**Mass Movement Politics:
The Great Equalizer   257**

PART THREE
INSTITUTIONS

Presidential Leadership and Elite Democracy   312

Congress: A Vehicle for Popular Democracy?   283

Bureaucracy: Myth and Reality   341

The Judiciary and the Democratic Debate   369

PART FOUR
POLICY

Economic and Social Policy: The Democratic Connections   462

Foreign Policy in the National Security State   494

Afterword: The Prospects for Popular Democracy   521

Appendix   A-1

BOXED FEATURES

FIGURES

PREFACE

When we wrote the first edition of *The Democratic Debate* we were convinced that many students and professors were looking for a different kind of textbook—one that covered the conventional topics in American politics but in an unconventional way. Specifically, we wrote a book that examined American political institutions and practices from the critical standpoint of participatory democracy. The positive response to the first edition has convinced us that our initial intuition was right.

The Democratic Debate is motivated by our dissatisfaction with existing American politics texts. Most mainstream texts claim to be objective descriptions of American politics. In fact, they present a consensus interpretation that supports the status quo and deadens students' critical sensibilities. Worse, they often make politics seem distant and boring, as if the important debates are over. We also are dissatisfied with the left-wing point-of-view texts that first emerged in the 1960s. These books raise critical issues and challenge the status quo, but after using them we noticed that they did little to counter student cynicism about politics. Most of these texts argue that American political institutions are corrupted by the structures of global capitalism. After documenting the economic forces that overwhelm democracy, the authors often turn around in the last chapter and call for radical change. As teachers, we felt the unintended consequence was to reconfirm student cynicism about all politics, even the democratic kind.

With the end of the Cold War, we felt it was time for a new critical theme text. Instead of taking our critical standard from European socialism or utopian democratic theory, we have written a point-of-view text that draws its standard from the homegrown traditions of participatory democracy in America. These traditions are rich and deep, stretching from the Anti-federalist critics of the Constitution to the Populists, the progressive unions, the civil rights movement, and more recent struggles, including the women's rights, gay rights, and environmental movements.

THEMATIC FRAMEWORK

Students can easily become overwhelmed and confused by the sheer volume of facts presented in most textbooks on American politics. They need a framework to make sense of the facts. We have developed a simple yet powerful framework for analyzing American politics. In *The Democratic Debate* the facts of American politics are organized around the theme of democracy. Specifically, each chapter examines the debate between what we call elite democracy and popular democracy, showing how that debate has impacted on the particular institution, process, or policy covered in the chapter. The overall goal is to assess the prospects and possibilities for the extension of democracy in the United States.

Our thematic framework leads us to treat the conventional topics of American politics very differently from other textbooks. Many texts, for example, treat the framers as a brilliant group of men who gave the country a Constitution that created a consensus about democracy that has persisted to this day. Because they lost the debate on the Constitution, the Anti-federalists are viewed by most textbooks as backward-looking opponents of progress who were relegated to the dustbin of history. *The Democratic Debate* is the only major American politics text to take the arguments of the Anti-federalists seriously. In our view, the founding period did not end debate but *began* a debate about American democracy between the tradition of elite democracy, as founded by the Federalists, and popular democracy, as founded by the Anti-federalists. To emphasize that point, we included an Anti-federalist paper in the Appendices of the book.

Although the basics of the democratic debate were laid down at the Founding, both the elite and popular democratic positions have evolved over the years. We define *elite democracy* as a system in which elites acquire the power to rule by a free competition for the people's votes; between elections the elites are given substantial autonomy to govern as they see fit. Elites stress that inequalities of power and economic resources are justified if they reflect real differences in ability, knowledge, and ambition. Over the years, the elite justification for rule has been buttressed by their claims to expertise and knowledge in an increasingly technically complex and competitive world.

We define *popular democracy* as a system of government in which people participate as much as possible in making the decisions that affect their lives. Popular democracy does not just mean majority rule, however, because it requires decisions that create the preconditions for democracy, including basic equality, tolerance, and respect for individual rights. Although elites have successfully used claims of expertise to buttress their rule, popular democrats have not been without resources. Since the first ten amendments to the Constitution were added, partly at the insistence of the Anti-federalists, popular democrats have succeeded in amending the Constitution in a more democratic direction, including winning the vote for women and African Americans. The inclusionary logic of democracy, based on the language of equal rights and equal participation, has been used to revive the spirit of protest that began the Revolution and to build popular democratic movements. Throughout American history, periods of elite domination and consolidation have been followed by periods of mass upsurge and democratization.

In addition to organizing the facts of American politics, the theme of the democratic debate helps students to become personally engaged in the material. The book challenges students to examine their own beliefs about democracy. At the most basic level, the democratic debate revolves around different conceptions of human nature. Elite democrats view most people as private and self-interested; with the exception of a well-educated elite, they argue, people are not well suited to make public policy decisions. Popular democrats, on the other hand, view people as political beings by nature; once involved in democratic participation, they are capable of transcending their narrow parochial interests and becoming responsible, public-spirited citizens. *The Democratic Debate* challenges students to devise their own democratic philosophy based on their view of human nature.

One final point: Although we make every effort to present both sides of the democratic debate, we make no pretense of impartiality. *In the pages ahead, we develop a popular democratic critique of American politics.* Our values are clear. We constantly ask the question: How is it possible to increase democratic participation in American politics and create a more democratic society?

N EW TO THE SECOND EDITION

In the second edition, we have tried to make the democratic debate theme even sharper and more provocative. The second edition is tighter in focus and shorter than the first edition.

Users of the first edition suggested two new chapters. First, we have written a chapter on political culture and public opinion that places the democratic debate within the context of Americans' basic beliefs. Second, the continuing devolution of policy from Washington, D.C., to the states has made clear the need for a chapter on state and local politics. We have placed this discussion within the context of our analysis of American federalism, so important for understanding contemporary American politics. Also in response to the suggestions of users of the first edition, we have combined economic policy and social policy in a single chapter.

Many new issues and developments in American politics receive extensive discussion in the second edition. Highlights include:

- The place of civil society in American democracy
- The "electronic republic"
- The campaign finance scandal of 1996
- The Republican revolution in Congress and its aftermath
- The Clinton presidency
- The progressive critique of the judiciary
- The "devolution revolution"
- The balanced budget debate
- Welfare "reform"
- Post–Cold War foreign policy strategies

ORGANIZATION OF THE BOOK

The Democratic Debate covers all the conventional topics treated in mainstream texts. One of the main purposes of a textbook, we believe, is to cover all the important institutions and processes of American politics that should be addressed in an introductory course, thus freeing the instructor to lecture on themes of particular interest that supplement the text. We do not sacrifice coverage to develop the theme but rather use the theme to draw the reader along, examining the essential facts and concepts that are covered in other texts.

We also discuss a number of unconventional topics that are not covered in most mainstream texts. We feel, for example, that a book with democracy as its central theme must have a chapter on nonvoting, probably the most serious flaw in American democracy. Chapter 5, "Where Have All the Voters Gone?" examines why so many Americans don't vote and how voters might be mobilized. We have also included a chapter (Chapter 10) on mass movements—their history, tactics, and importance to American democracy.

The book is organized in four parts. Part One deals with the foundational rules and structures of American politics. After a short introductory chapter that lays out the theme of the democratic debate, we go on to examine the Revolution and the struggle over the Constitution. In this book, the chapter on the founding is not just of historical interest in explaining the Constitution, as it is in most texts; instead, it defines the basic contours of the democratic debate that has persisted to this day. Chapter 3 examines political culture and public opinion and Part One concludes with an analysis of political economy, showing how the private system of wealth formation affects the public system of democratic governance.

Part Two covers the basic processes of participation in American politics. As befits a book that is focused on the issue of democracy, this section is longer than in most texts, spanning six chapters. Part Two is designed to acquaint students with the basic patterns of participation and the literature in political science that helps explain why some people are well represented in the political system and others are not. In the absence of strong political parties, we argue, other institutions, such as the mass media and interest groups, take over important political functions, with questionable effects for democracy. While fully documenting the phenomenon of nonvoting and other obstacles that lie in the path of democratic participation, Part Two ends on a hopeful note by examining the ability of mass protest movements to level the playing field of American politics.

Part Three covers the basic institutions of American politics—Congress, the presidency, bureaucracy, the courts, and the system of federalism. In Chapter 2, we showed how the original Constitution set up institutions that were highly elitist in nature, with the House of Representatives the only institution directly elected by the people. Since then, democratic struggles have made the major institutions more responsive to popular pressure, though they still contain many elitist elements. A theme of Part Three is that institutions have an independent effect on political outcomes and on the democratic debate.

Part Four explores the democratic debate further by looking at three policy areas: civil rights and civil liberties, economic and social policy, and foreign policy. The democratic debate concerns not just processes and rules but the distribution of rights, resources, and services. Part Four examines contemporary public policy debates through the lens of democracy, concentrating on a question usually ignored by policy analysts: Does a particular policy enhance or undermine democratic participation?

The Democratic Debate concludes with a short Afterword on the future of popular democracy. We remain guardedly optimistic about the prospects of popular democracy in the second edition. In particular, the end of the Cold War presents an opening for the extension of democracy. The main threat to popular democracy, we conclude, comes from rising economic inequality and the flood of cash that is corrupting the electoral process. Without reforms that redistribute wealth and income more equally, elite democracy will, in the long run, face little challenge. Finally, we emphasize the need to strengthen the institutions of civil society, those face-to-face organizations that lie between the individual and big government and big business. Democracy means more than voting every few years; it means getting involved in churches, schools, and neighborhood organizations that help build a more democratic society.

SPECIAL FEATURES

We have included a number of special features to help students learn from the book and deepen their understanding, but we have tried not to clutter the text with too many distractions from the central theme.

To give students a road map through the book, we have included an outline at the beginning of each chapter. Important terms are boldfaced, listed at the end of the chapter, and defined in a glossary. As a guide to further reading, an annotated bibliography follows each chapter.

A boxed feature called "A Closer Look" provides students with contemporary examples of the democratic debate. For the second edition, we have added new boxes, called "Making a Difference," that profile extraordinary individuals and groups, famous and not so famous, who have made a difference in popular democratic struggles.

We have illustrated our book's themes with cartoons instead of photographs in the second edition. The all-cartoon format is part of the second edition's attempt to be even more pointed and provocative than the first. We think students will find the cartoons funny and eye-opening.

TEACHING AND LEARNING AIDS

- An *Instructor's Resource Manual with Test Items*, written by Bruce Miroff, based on an earlier version written by State University of New York at

Albany graduate students Lance Denning and Christopher Grill, accompanies the text, providing ideas for lectures and innovative classroom exercises. The text's focus on the debate over competing versions of democracy will, we believe, help to stimulate class discussion. The manual includes a wide array of test questions, including multiple choice, identification, and essay; the test questions are available on computer disk as well.

- A set of twenty-five acetate transparencies from the illustration program is available to instructors upon adoption of the text.
- *NEW!* The **Houghton Mifflin American Government Web Site,** which can be accessed from the **Houghton Mifflin College Home Page** at **<http://www.hmco.com/college>,** contains a wide array of resources to accompany Houghton Mifflin American Government titles, including an extensive **Documents Collection;** instructor's resources; Web-based research activities; an annotated collection of links to innovative and useful Websites; and a downloadable, updated version of the award-winning **Crosstabs,** a computerized software program allowing students to cross-tabulate survey data on the 1996 presidential election and the 1994–95 voting records of members of Congress in order to analyze voter attitudes and behavior.

Finally, we note with pride that since the first edition we have published a reader called *Debating Democracy,* building upon themes in our text. Each of the sixteen chapters in the reader contains a debate between two opposing sides on an important issue for democracy, such as affirmative action, the mass media, presidential leadership, and welfare policy. The enthusiastic reception of *Debating Democracy* has made it clear that it can be used in conjunction with any American politics text. It works especially well, however, as a companion volume to *The Democratic Debate.* The two books, when purchased together, are available at a discount. Contact your Houghton Mifflin representative.

ACKNOWLEDGMENTS

Like democracy itself, this text has benefitted from the participation of many people. We were fortunate to have a series of dedicated professionals to guide the project over the years at Houghton Mifflin: Gregory Tobin, Margaret Seawell, Jean Woy, Janet Young, Merrill Peterson. Naomi Kornhauser helped select appealing cartoons and photos for the first edition. Melissa Mashburn, who took over for the second edition, was a patient and supportive editor.

Our friends and colleagues Walter Balk, Susan Christopherson, Marty Edelman, Anne Hildreth, and Steve Wasby provided insightful feedback on a number of chapters. A number of graduate students at SUNY Albany, including Martin Shaffer, David Filbert, and Christopher Price, helped us with research on the text. Michael Gizzi and Lance Denning wrote the glossary and assisted with the research. Paul Goggi updated tables for the second edition and wrote drafts of several boxes.

At Sarah Lawrence, students Joni Ang, Asia Friedman, and David G. Hill provided outstanding research assistance. The staff of the Esther Raushenbush Library—especially Charling Fagan, Bill Haines, David Nicholls, Judy Kicinski, and Barbara Hickey—showed how patient librarians can be with impatient scholars. Grants from the Julie and Ruediger Flik Travel Fund and the Hewlett-Mellon Fellowship Fund helped provide the time needed to meet publishing deadlines.

The book benefitted greatly from the comments of many political scientists across the country. Fortunately, these outside reviewers did not spare us in their criticisms, and although we squirmed, the book was ultimately much better because of their efforts.

Seven reviewers provided criticism of our original prospectus: Theodore S. Arrington, University of North Carolina at Charlotte; Jim Bromeland, Winona State University; John P. Burke, University of Vermont; Allan J. Cigler, University of Kansas; Henry Flores, St. Mary's University; Dr. Virginia G. McClamm, City College of San Francisco; M. Elliot Vittes, University of Central Florida.

The following individuals gave us valuable criticism on the first edition: Gordon Alexandre, Glendale Community College; Judith A. Baer, Texas A&M University; Sue Davis, University of Delaware; Dennis J. Goldford, Drake University; Steven Hoffman, University of St. Thomas; James Hogan, Seattle University; Robert Kerstein, University of Tampa; Kenneth Kennedy, College of San Mateo; James Meader, Augustana College; Jerome O'Callaghan, State University of New York at Cortland; Mark P. Petracca, University of California, Irvine; George Pippin, Jones County Junior College; Ted Radke, Contra Costa Community College; Leonard Ritt, Northern Arizona University; and John Squibb, Lincoln Land Community College.

An additional eight individuals gave us valuable feedback that helped us make significant improvements for the second edition: Stephen Amberg, University of Texas–San Antonio; Horace Bartilow, Jr., University of Kentucky; Gerald Berk, University of Oregon; Richard Bush, Southern Illinois University; Richard Herrera, Arizona State University; Robert Kerstein, University of Tampa; Pamela H. Rodgers, University of Wisconsin–La Crosse; and Mitchell Weiss, Charles S. Mott Community College.

We especially want to acknowledge the work of our editor for the first edition, Ann West, who improved the book immeasurably with her suggestions. Our editor for the second edition, Ann Torbert, did an excellent job working under extremely tight deadlines.

Finally, we want to thank our families for their love, support, and patience: Melinda, Nick, Anna, Fay, Eva, Rosa, Katie, Jessica, Madeleine, and little Eleanore.

B.M., R.S., T.S.

ABOUT THE AUTHORS

Bruce Miroff (Ph.D. University of California, Berkeley, 1974) is professor and chair of political science at the State University of New York, Albany. He is the author of *Pragmatic Illusions: The Presidential Politics of John F. Kennedy* and *Icons of Democracy: American Leaders as Heroes, Aristocrats, Dissenters, and Democrats*, as well as numerous articles on the presidency, political leadership, and American political theory. Along with Seidelman and Swanstrom, he is coeditor of *Debating Democracy: A Reader in American Politics*, also published by Houghton Mifflin.

Raymond Seidelman (Ph.D. Cornell University, 1979) is a professor of political science at Sarah Lawrence College in Yonkers, New York. Seidelman is the author of *Disenchanted Realists: Political Science and the American Crisis*, and the co-editor (with James Farr) of *Discipline and History: Political Science in the United States*. He instructs courses in American electoral politics, political economy, and urban and suburban history and politics. He has taught in China and South Korea and lectured extensively in many East Asian countries.

Todd Swanstrom (Ph.D. Princeton University, 1981) teaches at the State University of New York at Albany. Specializing in urban politics and public policy, he is the author of *The Crisis of Growth Politics: Cleveland, Kucinich, and the Challenge of Urban Populism* and coauthor of *City Politics: Private Power and Public Policy*, which will be out in a second edition in 1998.

Introduction:
The Democratic Debate

> Men, by their constitutions, are naturally divided into two parties: 1. Those who fear and distrust the people, and wish to draw all powers from them into the hands of the higher classes. 2. Those who identify themselves with the people, have confidence in them, cherish and consider them as the most honest and safe, although not the most wise, depository of the public interests. . . . The appellation of Aristocrats and Democrats is the true one, expressing the essence of all.
>
> Thomas Jefferson, *Writings*, vol. XVI, p. 73

Americans view themselves as a model democracy for the world. As long-time democrats, we cheer the new democratic movements struggling to overcome the entrenched elites in China, Latin America, Eastern Europe, and the former states of the Soviet Union. The media treatment of these movements has been reassuring, even self-congratulatory: Aren't these countries struggling to create the same democratic free market societies we created in this country? As this text will show, the struggle for democracy actually is taking place inside the United States *at the same time* that it is taking place outside in other countries. A democratic debate lies at the heart of American politics.

The central idea of democracy is quite simple. Democracy originated in the fifth century B.C. in the small city-states of Greece. The word *democracy* comes from the Greek words *demos*, meaning "the people," and *kratein*, meaning "to rule." Democracy, therefore, means simply "rule by the people." Defined as "rule by the people," democracy, Americans agree, is the best form of government. Americans disagree, however, about what democracy means in practice and how far democratic decision making should be extended.

One of the fundamental disagreements is over who is best suited for democratic decision making: the masses or political elites. *Elites* are small groups of people who possess extraordinary amounts of power. Throughout history, advocates of elite rule have argued that ruling is too difficult for ordinary citizens. Elites dominate many political systems—including communist, aristocratic, and even formally democratic ones. Elitism comes in various forms, with claims to rule based on different criteria. A totalitarian regime, for instance, is ruled by an elite few with unlimited power to control the daily lives of the citizens; a theocracy is a system run by religious elites. Although these are among the most extreme forms of elitism, even U.S. democracy is seen by some as controlled by a group of highly educated and wealthy elites. This was C. Wright Mills's central argument in *The Power Elite* (1956). Today, many Americans would support the representation of citizens by a well-heeled and well-educated few, who are presumably best qualified to make important decisions.

Few Americans are classical elitists, however; a strong democratic impulse pervades American culture and politics. Anyone who argued that family genes, religious training, or even wealth automatically qualified a person to rule would not be taken seriously in the United States. Americans believe in the democratic principle that political power ultimately should stem from the people. Americans also agree on certain basic principles of democratic government, including the importance of a written constitution, representative institutions, and basic rights such as freedom of speech and press. Throughout American history, political movements have risen to extend democratic citizenship to blacks, women, and other excluded groups. Political equality is a strong value in American politics.

A deep elitist strain, however, also pervades our politics. Americans believe in rule by the people, for example, but every time we cede power over war and peace to an executive elite on the grounds that "the president knows best," Americans buy into elitism. Americans generally support elitism not because they believe elites are inherently superior to the common people, but because they believe elites have the specialized knowledge and experience to make the best decisions. In a modern high-tech world, democracy must often defer to specialized expertise, whether in government or private corporations. Democracy is a fine ideal, many people argue, but to be realistic and effective, "the people" must cede much of their decision-making power to elites.

The thesis of this text is simple: American politics is characterized by a fundamental conflict between elite democracy and popular democracy. **Elite democracy** is a political system in which elites acquire power by a free and fair competition for the people's votes.[1] Once elected, elites are given the freedom to rule as they see fit. If the people do not like the results, they can vote them out at the next election and put different elites into office. Under elite democracy, the people are not expected to participate in the day-to-day affairs of governing.

Popular democracy has its roots in **direct democracy,** in which all citizens gather in one place to vote on important matters. In the Greek city-states, where democracy originated 2,500 years ago, democracy meant face-to-face debate and decision making by all citizens, with offices rotating among the citizens. Some examples of direct democracy still exist in the United States, such as the New England town meeting, where all town citizens gather in one hall to debate and decide important issues.

Popular democracy is the adaptation of direct democracy to a large country with a modern economy and society. **Popular democracy** can be defined as a political system in which the people are involved as much as possible in making the decisions that affect their lives.[2] Popular democrats maintain that ordinary citizens should be closely involved in governing and that, in the long run, they will govern more wisely than elites. In a large country, popular democrats admit, everyone cannot meet in one place to make decisions. Political representatives are needed, but they should remain as close as possible to the people who elected them, accurately reflecting their values and interests. Between elections, citizens should be involved in political affairs, holding representatives accountable and making sure that experts, who are necessary in a complex modern society, serve the needs of the people and not the needs of elites.

It is crucial to recognize that popular democracy is not the same as majority rule. Ironically, majorities have often supported elite rule and undemocratic values. Ordinary citizens, for example, often defer to corporate elites in the private marketplace, and for much of American history a majority opposed giving full civil rights to blacks and women. Popular democrats believe that basic rights, such as freedom of speech and freedom of religion, should not be subject to a vote, to the whims of the majority. The question of whether the rights guaranteed to all citizens should extend beyond basic civil liberties to include positive rights that would require action by government, such as the right to health care or a roof over one's head, is at the heart of the democratic debate today. (We examine the question of whether citizens should have the right to welfare or a job in Chapter 17.) Although majority rule should be limited by basic rights and majorities often make mistakes, popular democrats still believe that for most issues, most of the time, majority rule is best. The greatest threat to democratic values comes from minority elites, not from majorities.

At the heart of American politics lies an essential tension between two different conceptions of democracy. We are not the first to present a conflict interpretation of American politics. Marxists have long focused on the "contradictions" of capitalism, particularly the conflict between workers and capitalists. Although class inequalities have often caused deep divisions in American politics, we believe that the enduring conflict has been between elite democracy and popular democracy. The United States does have a radical political tradition, but it is rooted in homegrown ideas of popular democracy rather than in European socialism.

As we flesh out the principles of elite and popular democracy that serve as the framework of this text, we begin in the 1780s, the founding period when the U.S. Constitution was written and approved.

ORIGINS OF THE DEMOCRATIC DEBATE: THE FOUNDING

Normally, the founding period is treated as a celebration of the American consensus on democracy as embodied in the Constitution. As Chapter 2 shows, however, the U.S. Constitution was born in conflict, not in consensus. The ratification of the Constitution did not end debate but began a new debate about the meaning of democracy. The terms of this debate, which were laid down over two hundred years ago, continue to influence American politics to this day.

Our Constitution was not written by lofty statesmen who offered their eternal truths to a grateful nation. The men who wrote the Constitution were practical politicians with pressing political objectives. The framers distrusted popular democracy, especially the power of the majority. (Read James Madison's *Federalist No. 10* in the Appendix.) The supporters of the Constitution in the late 1780s, known as **Federalists,** were the founders of elite democracy in the United States. The Constitution they wrote and ratified was mixed, containing elements of both elitism and democracy. The original Constitution placed severe limits on majority rule and contained many elitist elements; neither the president nor senators, for example, were to be elected directly by the people. (In the original Constitution, senators were chosen by state legislatures and presidents were elected by an elite, the Electoral College, appointed under procedures chosen by the state legislatures.)

The ratification of the Constitution was bitterly opposed by a group known as the **Anti-federalists.** The Anti-federalists were the founders of popular democracy in the United States.[3] The Anti-federalists denounced the proposed Constitution as a betrayal of the democratic spirit of 1776 and the American Revolution itself. The new Constitution, they protested, took too much away from the states and localities and gave it to the central government. In the long run, they charged, it would erode the face-to-face participation necessary for a healthy democracy. The Anti-federalists were not a marginal group; many state conventions ratified the Constitution by only the narrowest of margins.

Federalists and Anti-federalists disagreed about the most basic questions of human nature, society, and politics (see Chapter 2). In the eyes of the Federalists, the mass of Americans were passionate and selfish creatures. In a small republic where simple majority rule prevailed, nothing would stop this mass from taking away the rights or the property of the minority. But in a national republic, where the majority could not rule directly, minority rights would be protected. Elite representatives, likely to be drawn from the wisest and most virtuous segment of society, would rise above selfish conflicts and pursue the common good. Should these elites themselves go astray, other elites would check them through the ingenious constitutional system of checks and balances.

Anti-federalists had more faith in the common people. They believed that most people could be educated into civic virtue, overcoming their selfish inclinations and learning to pursue the common good. They wanted representatives who would not claim superiority over the masses, but who would faithfully reflect ordinary citizens' grievances and aspirations. To the Anti-federalists, the main threat to democracy came not from majorities but from selfish and powerful elites. Instead of elites checking elites, they wanted ordinary citizens to check elites and hold them accountable. The best way to protect against the tyranny of an aristocratic elite was to have the people participate directly in political decisions.

The original debate between Federalists and Anti-federalists had its limitations. In contemporary terms, neither the Federalists nor the Anti-federalists were true democrats. Many on both sides owned slaves, for example, and neither advocated citizenship rights for women, African Americans, or Native Americans. Both Federalists and Anti-federalists supported property qualifications for voting.

Although the Federalists and Anti-federalists were limited by the prejudices of their times, they laid down the basic principles of the democratic debate that have animated American politics to the present. Even though the principles have remained the same, the debate between elite and popular democrats has evolved dramatically in response to the changes in American society over the past two centuries. Understanding this evolution is necessary to understand the contemporary democratic debate.

EVOLUTION OF POPULAR DEMOCRACY: THE LOGIC OF INCLUSION

The Anti-federalists are normally viewed as losers who had little impact on American politics. This is false. Although the Anti-federalists lost the initial struggle over the Constitution, their perspective has had a tremendous influence on American politics.

If the founding document of elite democracy is the Constitution of 1787, the founding document of popular democracy is the Declaration of Independence of 1776. With its bold statement that "all men are created equal" and are "endowed by their Creator with certain unalienable Rights," the Declaration laid down the basic principles of popular democracy. The Declaration of Independence proclaimed a radical idea: If the government violates people's rights, they have a right "to alter or abolish it." This "Spirit of '76"—based on political equality, rights, and rebellion—has inspired popular democrats ever since.

The democratic faith of Americans, as expressed in the Declaration of Independence, has given popular democrats an ideological advantage and has frequently placed elite democrats on the defensive. In 1791, for example, two years after the Constitution was ratified, the first ten amendments—the Bill of Rights—were added, mostly at the insistence of the Anti-federalists, who wanted to ensure protection of their political rights. (Chapter 16 discusses the importance of civil rights and civil liberties for popular democracy.) Nearly all the amendments to the Constitution since then have moved it in a popular democratic direction, including the Fifteenth Amendment, which extended the legal right to vote to blacks in 1870; the Seventeenth Amendment, which required the direct election of senators in 1913; the Nineteenth Amendment, which extended the right to vote to women in 1920; and the Twenty-sixth Amendment, which gave the vote to eighteen- to twenty-year-olds in 1971.

Popular democratic influence, however, has not been limited to amending the Constitution. It has also affected how we interpret the Constitution. Elected in 1800, Thomas Jefferson, who shared many of the beliefs of the Anti-federalists, can be viewed as our nation's first popular democratic president. As such, Jefferson could have proposed writing a new constitution. Instead he decided to infuse democratic content into the Constitution of 1789 by expanding the participation of common people in governmental decision making. Jefferson supported a narrow interpretation of the powers of the federal government, preferring that as many decisions as possible be made by state and local governments that were closer to the people. Jefferson's attempt to read popular democratic views into the Constitution was pivotal in American history and helps explain why Americans love the Constitution but disagree so vehemently about how to interpret it.

Although politicians like Jefferson, at the top of the political system, sometimes championed popular democracy, more often its impulses came from ordinary citizens. Throughout American history, popular democrats have mobilized the masses to expand democratic decision making. Periods of elite dominance have given way to periods of mass participation and popular democratic upsurge, such as the 1890s, the 1930s, and the 1960s.[4] During the last period, the civil rights, feminist, environmental, and neighborhood organizing movements, among others, challenged the power of entrenched elites and forged landmark legislation such as the 1964 Civil Rights Act and the 1970 Environmental Protection Act.

In mobilizing people for mass movements, popular democrats have appealed to the ideas of political equality and rights found in the Declaration of Independence. In 1848, for example, Elizabeth Cady Stanton used the language of the Declaration of Independence to write a women's declaration of independence. Her Declaration of Sentiments is considered the founding document of the women's rights movement, which won the right to vote in 1920 and flowered into a modern feminist movement in the 1960s. In the 1950s and 1960s, Martin Luther King, Jr., used the popular democratic language of rights and equality to energize the civil rights movement and appeal successfully to a broad white audience. The civil rights movement, examined in Chapter 10, shows how protest politics goes beyond electoral politics and uses the techniques of direct action to empower the powerless.

EVOLUTION OF ELITE DEMOCRACY: THE LOGIC OF EXPERTISE

Elite democrats have not stood still while popular democrats pushed for extending democracy. Throughout American history, elite democrats have been immensely resourceful, devising new arguments for limiting democracy. In the early years of the republic, many openly defended elite values. The democratization of American values, however, soon rendered such naked appeals to elitism illegitimate. Elitism is no longer defended on the grounds that elites are inherently superior to the masses or that certain people are destined to rule. In contemporary American society, elites profess democratic values but maintain that elite rule is necessary in many spheres of modern society. Elite democrats would not admit they are elitist; they would simply say they are realistic.

The elite democratic position cannot be easily dismissed. When we ride on an airplane, for example, we do not take a vote to see how high the plane will fly or who will serve as pilot. Everyone acknowledges that democratic decision making must defer to rule by experts, or technical elites, in particular situations. But where do we draw the line? Elite democrats believe that in a rapidly changing, technologically complex, dangerous world more and more power must be ceded to elites—elites whose power is justified not by birth or wealth, but by their knowledge, expertise, and experience. Democracy is viewed as a kind of luxury that we cannot "afford" too much of, especially given our desire for economic growth and the necessity to compete with other nations for economic, political, and military advantage.

The elite democratic position has evolved over the years, especially in response to changing economic conditions. At the time of the debate over the Constitution, few private corporations existed; those that did were small and family owned. By the late nineteenth century, huge railroad and industrial corporations controlled national markets and employed thousands of workers.

"We can't come to an agreement about how to fix your car, Mr. Simons. Sometimes that's the way things happen in a democracy."
Drawing by Handelsman; © 1987 *The New Yorker Magazine, Inc.*

These private corporations were run in a top-down fashion by wealthy elites. Elite democrats argued that the owners of capital should be free to run corporations as they saw fit. Corporations would be held accountable by market competition; by giving free rein to the corporations, government would encourage economic growth that would, in the long run, benefit everyone. This argument for elite autonomy based on free market capitalism has continued into the present period of multinational corporations. Chapter 4 examines the argument for free market capitalism that is so important for contemporary elite democrats, as well as the popular democratic response that corporations exert power over the marketplace and thus must be held democratically accountable.

In the late nineteenth century, a popular democratic movement, called *populism*, emerged, challenging the control of corporate elites over the economy. In the crucial election of 1896, however, the populist candidate, William Jennings Bryan, was defeated by the candidate of big business, William McKinley. Drawing on huge corporate contributions, McKinley is credited with having pioneered the first modern campaign using mass media techniques of persuasion. McKinley's victory ushered in a long period of weak party competition and declining voter turnout. Chapters 6, 7, and 8 document the power that money can exert over the electoral process when parties decline and their functions are taken over by the mass media.

In the political struggles produced by economic changes, elite democrats and popular democrats have reversed some of their original positions. One of the most important shifts concerns whether power should be centralized in the national government or decentralized into the states and localities. At the time of the founding of this country, elite democrats like Alexander Hamilton favored a strong national government whereas popular democrats wanted states and localities to retain most powers. The rise of powerful corporations, which helped to spawn tremendous inequalities in the private economy, caused popular democrats to reverse their position and favor expanded powers for the federal government. Beginning with President Franklin Roosevelt's New Deal, popular democrats have increasingly turned to the federal government as a counterweight to the power of private corporations and as a way of ensuring action on behalf of the disadvantaged.

Present-day elite democrats have often appealed to the popular democratic value of states' rights or local control in order to defend elite privileges. The principle of states' rights was used for many years to prevent the federal government from intervening to guarantee blacks the right to vote. The need to expand the powers of the federal government, however, has placed popular democrats on the horns of a dilemma: Although an expanded federal government is necessary to address inequalities and curb the powers of entrenched elites, the result, too often, is a government removed from popular democratic participation. Chapter 15 examines this dilemma of federalism.

Although elite and popular democrats have nearly switched positions in domestic policy, in foreign policy elites continue to favor decision making by the few whereas popular democrats remain suspicious of centralized power and its potential for elite tyranny. In the twentieth century, many have argued that trends in this country and in the world justify concentrating power in the hands of experienced elites. These trends include the increasing complexity of social relations, the mobility of capital in an international economy, and the alarming speed of modern warfare in a rapidly shrinking globe. Just as the Anti-federalists feared, presidents have gained substantial powers at the expense of Congress, which is often viewed as too slow to act effectively in the modern world. In particular, the Cold War against communism was used to justify the creation of what we call in Chapter 18 the "national security state"—a shadow government, led by an elite in the executive branch, with substantial power over American foreign policy and little congressional oversight. Popular support for the national security state demonstrates that elitism has not been supported only by elites; ironically, elitism has often enjoyed widespread popular backing.

SUMMARIZING THE DEMOCRATIC DEBATE

Americans supposedly agree that democracy is the right way to make decisions. Everyone who runs for elected office uses the myths, symbols, and rhetoric of democracy to win votes. According to the consensus view of American politics, there are no more burning debates about the rules of the game. If Americans disagree, it is over specific policies, not the rules of the game.

This consensus view of American politics fundamentally distorts reality. Americans do disagree about the rules of the game. In particular, Americans disagree about the meaning of democracy and how far democratic decision making should be extended into the economy and society. This text argues for a conflict, not a consensus, approach to American politics. American politics is best understood as embodying an essential tension, or conflict, between two different conceptions of democracy: elite democracy and popular democracy. The differences between these two approaches can be summarized in six points:

ELITE DEMOCRACY	POPULAR DEMOCRACY
1. With the exception of an educated, largely white male elite, most people are uninterested in politics and uninformed about issues; most people are more interested in their own private lives than in politics.	1. People are naturally inclined to participate in the decisions that affect their lives; if they don't participate, something must be wrong with the democratic system.
2. When the masses do get involved in politics, they tend to be highly emotional and intolerant; the main threat to democracy comes from the masses, not from elites.	2. Through democratic participation people can overcome their parochial interests and become public-spirited citizens. When their powers and privileges are

ELITE DEMOCRACY   **POPULAR DEMOCRACY**

threatened, elites often respond by curtailing democracy; the main threat to democracy comes from selfish elites, not from ordinary citizens.

3. Democracy basically means free and fair elections in which elites acquire the power to rule by competing for people's votes.

3. Democracy means more than fair elections; it means the participation of ordinary citizens in the decisions that affect their lives in an atmosphere of tolerance and trust.

4. The main goal of democracy should be to protect the rights of individuals to pursue their own interests, especially the acquisition of property. Because of varying talents and ambitions, democracies must tolerate substantial inequality.

4. The main goal of democracy should be to strengthen community; inequalities that divide the community should be minimized.

5. Political representatives should filter the views of the people through their superior expertise, intelligence, and temperament.

5. Representatives should stay as close to their constituents as possible, accurately reflecting their views in the political system.

6. Reforms in America almost always come about gradually, through the actions of elites.

6. Meaningful reforms in American politics have almost always come about because of political pressure from below by ordinary citizens.

INTERPRETING POLITICAL FACTS: THE PROBLEM OF PARTICIPATION

It is easy to become confused by the complexity of American politics. Magazines, newspapers, radio, and TV bombard us with facts about political negotiations in Congress, interest group bargaining, maneuverings of the political parties, the state of the economy and its effect on political fortunes, key decisions by the Supreme Court, and the actions of foreign countries. The sheer volume of political facts threatens to overwhelm our ability to comprehend them. Students of American politics need an organizing framework to make sense of these facts—to identify patterns, decide which facts are important, and evaluate political outcomes.

The ideas of elite and popular democracy can serve as an interpretive framework to help us make sense of American politics. To understand how this framework is used in the text, we apply it here to one example: the different ways people interpret basic facts about political participation in American politics (a topic covered in Chapter 5).

The facts of political participation in the United States are well known. Voting is the most common political act, yet less than half of the eligible electorate voted in the most recent presidential election; the turnout rate in off-year congressional elections is only about one-third.

Although these facts are straightforward, making sense of them is more difficult. For example, how do we assess the simple fact that about half of the eligible electorate votes in presidential elections? Is the glass half full or half empty? What you see depends as much on your interpretation of the facts as on the facts themselves.

For elite democrats, the glass of democratic participation is half full. According to this view, the fact that only about half the people participate in elections is a sign of a healthy democracy. People are not inclined to participate in politics; most prefer to spend their time in private pursuits: making a living, raising children, watching TV. The fact that many people do not participate in politics is a sign of satisfaction. After all, nothing is stopping them from voting—legal barriers to voting (property qualifications, poll taxes, literacy tests) have been eliminated. If the masses of nonvoters felt their interests were threatened by government, they could mobilize their slack resources, including the vote, and influence the system. Moreover, because we know that nonvoters tend to be less educated, we should be happy that many do not participate in politics. As *Newsweek* columnist George Will put it: "The reasonable assumption about electorates is: smaller is smarter."[5]

Popular democrats contest the elite democratic interpretation of the facts of participation on every count. For them, the glass of democratic participation is at least half empty. They see low levels of political participation as a sign of a sick democracy. Popular democrats believe that people are naturally inclined to participate in the governance of their societies. When they don't participate, something must be wrong. Although there are no legal barriers preventing Americans from participating in the political process, popular democrats argue, many people feel so alienated from politics that they view their own participation as meaningless. They see the decisive role of money in elections and conclude that ordinary citizens have little influence. Moreover, when they see the limited choices on the ballot, they think that it doesn't matter who wins. In short, those who fail to participate in politics are not satisfied, they are *discouraged*.

Who is right? As the example of participation shows, political facts do not speak for themselves. The same facts can be seen from radically different perspectives. Interpreting the facts of American politics is like viewing a Gestalt drawing (Figure 1.1); what you see depends on how you look at it. Do you see a vase or two faces? You can see one or the other, but you cannot see both at the same time. As with the Gestalt diagram, we must interpret the facts of American politics to give them meaning. Elite and popular views of democracy are the two frameworks we will use to interpret the facts of American politics.

FIGURE 1.1

Gestalt Drawing

There is an important difference, however, between interpreting the Gestalt diagram and interpreting political facts. What you see in the Gestalt diagram does not affect anyone's interest. In politics, interpretations of the facts are hotly contested because they directly affect people's interests. Consider the different interpretations of nonvoting. If nonvoting is an expression of satisfaction, then the system is legitimate—those in power are viewed as having the right to rule. On the other hand, if nonvoting is an expression of alienation, then the government loses legitimacy and political protests outside of normal channels, such as street demonstrations and civil disobedience, are justified. Our interpretations of political facts shape our evaluations of right and wrong, and what should and should not be done.

CONCLUSION: JOINING THE DEMOCRATIC DEBATE

We must end this introduction with a warning: The authors of this text are not neutral observers of the democratic debate. Although we present both sides, we defend popular democracy and develop a popular democratic critique of American politics. We do so to redress an imbalance that is unconsciously embedded in most treatments of American politics, both in scholarly texts and in the mass media.

Finally, we invite readers not to accept our bias but to critically examine their own views toward democracy. In short, we invite you to join the democratic debate.

KEY TERMS

elite democracy
direct democracy
popular democracy

Federalist
Anti-federalist

SUGGESTED READINGS

Robert A. Dahl, *Who Governs? Democracy and Power in an American City.* New Haven, Conn.: Yale University Press, 1961. An influential community power study arguing that plural elites govern cities, with little direct participation from the masses of ordinary citizens.

Robert A. Dahl, *Democracy and Its Critics.* New Haven, Conn.: Yale University Press, 1989. Moving in a popular democratic direction, Dahl argues here that democratic decision making should be extended into all areas of the society and economy.

G. William Domhoff, *Who Really Rules? New Haven and Community Power Reexamined.* Santa Monica, Calif.: Goodyear, 1978. A critique of Dahl's *Who Governs?* arguing that private elites dictate policy, with few democratic checks and balances.

Frances Moore Lappé, *Rediscovering America's Values.* New York: Ballantine Books, 1989. Written as a dialogue between two points of view that correspond roughly to elite and popular democracy, the book synthesizes a great deal of information on American value conflicts.

C. Wright Mills, *The Power Elite.* New York: Oxford University Press, 1956. The classic statement that America is ruled by a small elite who occupy the command posts at the top of the economy, the polity, and the military.

The Revolution and the Constitution: Origins of the Democratic Debate

When modern American politicians hope to establish their noble aspirations and to wrap themselves in the mantle of higher authority, they invariably turn to the founders of the republic—even to those whose ideas seem very different from their own. Proclaiming a new national beginning after the dark days of Watergate, President Gerald Ford, a conservative, quoted radical Thomas Paine on our revolutionary beginnings. President Bill Clinton, an advocate of an activist national government, is fond of citing Thomas Jefferson, who favored local action and feared national power. Republicans or Democrats, conservatives or liberals, American political leaders speak in hushed tones of the founders as our political saints.

Ford and Clinton drew on assumptions that most Americans hold: that the founders agreed among themselves about the fundamental premises of politics and government; that they believed in the same kind of democracy that we profess; and that they were above the desires for power and wealth that seem to drive most present-day political leaders. All of these assumptions are essentially false. The founders of the republic did not agree among themselves; they argued vehemently about fundamental issues of human nature, society, and government. Many were skeptical about democracy and its values and held to an elitist conception of government that no contemporary American politician would dare to profess openly. Struggles over power and wealth were as central to their politics as to our own.

This chapter demonstrates that the American political system was born not in consensus but in conflict. American political life at the time of our founding was characterized by a debate between popular and elite democracy—a debate that has driven our politics ever since. The two sides differed on six basic questions of politics:

1. Human nature

2. The proper scale of political life

3. Representation

4. Separation of powers and checks and balances

5. The purpose of government

6. Stability and change

Popular democratic answers to these questions produced a hopeful brand of politics that extended self-government to ordinary citizens. Elite democratic answers left ultimate sovereignty to the people but placed actual governance in the hands of a political and economic elite.

The story of the American founding that this chapter tells unfolded in three stages. It began as Americans cast off their colonial past and launched a bold experiment in republican politics. The hopeful political spirit of 1776 was expressed in the philosophy of the Declaration of Independence, the original state constitutions, and the Articles of Confederation. Popular democratic answers to the six basic questions of politics prevailed during the revolutionary moment.

But this revolutionary beginning gradually became caught up in economic conflict and political controversy. In the second stage, a conservative and propertied elite, unhappy with the emerging popular democracy, developed an alternative political philosophy that answered the six basic questions very differently. These men produced a national constitution in 1787 that reflected the new brand of elite democracy.

In the concluding stage of the story, the ratification of the new constitution provoked a fundamental and wide-ranging debate between elite democrats and popular democrats. Their conflicting answers to the six basic questions were fully developed in the ratification debate. Pages 31–40 of this chapter present the climax of the story—and an essential key for an understanding of the whole book.

The story of the American founding does not produce a final victory for either elite democrats or popular democrats. In studying the Revolution and the Constitution, we witness the origins of the democratic debate. Particularly in the argument over the new Constitution, which pitted Federalists against Antifederalists, the democratic debate was launched with a depth and passion that still echo in today's politics.

FROM COLONIALS TO REVOLUTIONARIES

In 1763, the idea that the American colonies of Great Britain would declare their independence, start a revolution, and shape a political system unlike any then known would have seemed absurd. In the first place, the colonists enjoyed their status as outposts of a glorious empire. England, their "mother country," was nurturing and permissive. The colonies flourished economically and possessed a considerable degree of liberty and self-government under the relatively lax British administration. Second, the colonists not only thought of themselves as English people but also resembled them in many respects. Historian Gordon Wood has written that colonial America was, like Britain, a "monarchical" society, hierarchical in character and dominated by a small elite of "gentlemen."[1] Americans felt a strong allegiance to the King and liked to celebrate his birthday with rousing toasts.

But in 1763, the British had just defeated the French and Spanish in the Seven Years' War and established their dominance in the New World. They needed revenues to pay off the debts incurred in this war. As beneficiaries of the British efforts, the American colonists seemed the obvious targets for new taxation. However, this assumption proved to be disastrous for the British. Colonial America responded to the first British tax levies, the Sugar Act and the Stamp Act, with spirited resistance. While American writers denounced taxes imposed by a Parliament in which the colonies were not represented, American "patriots" formed organizations known as the Sons of Liberty and mobbed stamp-tax collectors until they resigned their royal commissions.

For the next decade, a political dynamic developed that led the Americans toward independence. When the British eased their attempts at taxation, peace returned. But every time they tried to reassert their authority, the American spirit of resistance grew stronger. It was not that Americans rushed eagerly into revolutionary politics; even the leaders of the patriot forces continued to swear allegiance to the (unwritten) British constitution and to claim that they were only seeking to preserve the rights of all Englishmen. Yet the increasingly bitter conflict wore away old loyalties and fostered a growing sense of an independent American identity.[2]

After listening to a reading of the Declaration of Independence, a New York crowd of soldiers and civilians pulls down a statue of King George III. The picture dramatizes the overthrow of monarchism (rule by one) by republicanism (popular rule).

Two events epitomized the colonists' growing radicalism. One was the famous Boston Tea Party in 1773, where Boston patriots, disguised as Indians, dumped a shipload of tea into the harbor in protest of a tax on the beverage. Notable here was the colonists' militance, their reliance on direct popular action to redress a grievance. A second event was the fiery rhetoric of the most widely read pamphlet calling on Americans to declare their independence, Thomas Paine's *Common Sense*, published early in 1776. Paine poured scorn on a monarch that Americans customarily had revered. By sending his troops to enforce his taxes with bayonets, wrote Paine, George III deserved to be called the "Royal Brute of Britain." Monarchy itself, Paine thundered, was a crime; if we could trace the origins of kings, he wrote, "we should find the first of them nothing better than the principal ruffian of some restless gang. . . ."[3] A decade of resistance and protest had undermined much of the hierarchical thinking of colonial Americans; reading Tom Paine, many of them became filled with a bold and hopeful spirit that was ready to launch a grand revolutionary experiment in popular democracy.

Birth of Republicanism

To understand this revolutionary experiment, we need to look beneath questions of taxation and representation. Contemporary historians have identified a deeper level of thought that transformed loyal colonials into defiant revolutionaries. This body of thought shaped the political activities of Americans and infused them with the revolutionary "Spirit of '76." The name historians have given to this body of thought is **republicanism.** (The republicanism of the Revolution should not be confused with the ideas of the Republican party, formed in the 1850s.)[4]

What were the central ideas of republican ideology and how did they shape the thinking of the American revolutionaries? We focus on four interrelated ideas: liberty versus power, legislatures versus executives, virtue, and the small republic.

Liberty versus Power. Eighteenth-century republicans saw the struggle between liberty and power as the core of political life. *Power* meant dominion or control. Although necessary for the maintenance of order, power's natural tendency was to exceed legitimate boundaries and to invade the sphere of liberty. By *liberty*, republicans meant both private liberty—such as property rights—and public liberty—the right of the people to have a collective say in government. This view of politics made the actions of the British government especially frightening to the American colonists. The taxes imposed by London, the flood of new royal officials to rule over the colonists, and the troops eventually sent to America to support both were viewed not as limited measures but as steps in a comprehensive plot to reduce Americans to servility.

Legislatures versus Executives. Republican theory identified power largely with executives. Executives were entrusted with enforcing the laws, but they had a natural inclination to arbitrary rule and self-aggrandizement. Thus, executives were seen as the most likely threats to liberty. Legislatures, on the other hand, were the most likely defenders of liberty. Closer to the people, mirroring the people's desires, cherishing the people's liberties, the legislature was the natural adversary of the executive. This view helped Americans make sense of their quarrel with Britain. Executives—the royal governors appointed by London, the ministers of the King, and ultimately George III himself—were assailing American liberty; American colonial legislatures and later the Continental Congresses were championing it.

Virtue of the American People. Why were republicans so optimistic about the people and their representatives in the legislature? Might not the people, under some circumstances, also prove dangerous? Republicans conceded that liberty could go too far and become anarchy. But they hoped for a people characterized by virtue rather than lawlessness. By *virtue*, they meant the willingness of individuals to subordinate their private interests to the common good. Virtue was a passion for the public good superior to all private passions. Americans believed that the British effort to introduce tyranny into the colonies showed that the British government and even the British people had become corrupt; selfishness had destroyed their traditional commitment to liberty. But America—peopled by those who had fled the Old World in search of liberty—was a land where virtue still resided.

The Small Republic. What conditions encouraged virtue? As good republicans, the American revolutionaries stressed such things as simplicity and frugality. But the single most important condition necessary for republican virtue was the small republic. In a large republic, diverse economic interests and dissimilar ways of life would produce factional conflicts, encouraging selfishness and eroding virtue. In a small republic, however, a genuine common interest could be found, for the people would be more homogeneous and united. To the Americans of 1776, the British empire proved how a large republic became hostile to liberty and the common good. The revolutionaries' goal was not to build a large republic of their own but small republics that would nurture virtue and the public good. Their principal political efforts were focused on the governments of the thirteen new states, not on the national government.

Thus, the revolutionary assumptions of 1776 were the danger of power and the need to safeguard liberty, the threat of executives and the confidence in legislatures, the hope for a virtuous people, and the stress on small republics and political decentralization. On the basis of these popular democratic assumptions, Americans began shaping their own independent governments in 1776. However, each of these assumptions would be challenged in the decade that followed and debated at length in the struggle over the Constitution.

The Spirit of '76

The American Revolution exploded in 1776 with political energy and creativity. The institutions it first shaped were soon replaced by others, but the ideals it espoused were to form the base of America's democratic creed. Both the successes and the failures of revolutionary creativity are evident in the Declaration of Independence, the constitutions of the new states, and the Articles of Confederation.

The Declaration of Independence. When the Second Continental Congress finally decided that the moment had arrived for the decisive break between America and Britain, it appointed a small committee to prepare a justification for such revolutionary action. This committee of five wisely turned to its best writer, the young Thomas Jefferson of Virginia. The **Declaration of Independence,** the document that Jefferson drafted and that the Congress adopted with some revisions on July 4, 1776, has become, along with the Constitution, the most hallowed of all American political texts. Its opening words are very familiar, so familiar that we usually do not read them with the care and reflection they deserve.

> When in the course of human events, it becomes necessary for one people to dissolve the political bands which have connected them with another, and to assume among the powers of the earth the separate and equal station to which the Laws of Nature and of Nature's God entitle them, a decent respect to the opinions of mankind requires that they should declare the causes which impel them to the separation.
>
> We hold these truths to be self-evident, that all men are created equal, that they are endowed by their Creator with certain unalienable rights, that among these are life, liberty, and the pursuit of happiness. That to secure these rights, governments are instituted among men, deriving their just powers from the consent of the governed. That whenever any form of government becomes destructive of these ends, it is the right of the people to alter or to abolish it, and to institute new government, laying its foundation on such principles and organizing its powers in such form, as to them shall seem most likely to effect their safety and happiness.

Scholars argue about the sources of Jefferson's ideas in the Declaration of Independence. The most common view is that he was influenced by an English philosopher, John Locke. Several of Locke's central themes are evident in the Declaration: that the primary objective of government is the protection of life, liberty, and property, and that all legitimate political authority derives from the consent of the governed and can be taken away from rulers who betray the will of the people. These ideas of Locke's are considered central to the political philosophy of liberalism.

If Locke's liberal philosophy is found in the Declaration, the democratic Jefferson gives it a more revolutionary interpretation than the English philosopher intended. The Declaration of Independence establishes equality as the basis for American political thought and makes "life, liberty, and the pursuit of happiness" universal rights. It dethrones government as a higher power and renders it subject to the consent of the people. In its argument, and even in its form, it transforms the nature of political life, supplanting the commands of a king with the discussion and persuasion suitable to a free people.[5]

Like most great documents, the Declaration of Independence bears the marks and limits of its time. Its words about equality and rights were not meant to include women or African Americans. The American revolutionaries used universal terms but restricted them in practice to white males. Still, the Declaration created a standard to which later popular democrats would appeal in efforts to include those who had originally been excluded from its promises. Battling the spread of slavery, Abraham Lincoln grounded his opposition on the words of the Declaration, proclaiming in 1859 that the "principles of Jefferson are the definitions and axioms of free society."[6] Feminist and African-American movements for emancipation have also rested their cases on the Declaration of Independence.[7]

The Revolutionary State Constitutions. The revolutionary ideas of 1776 were also embodied in the first state constitutions. In 1776, ten states established new constitutions to replace their old colonial charters. These constitutions reflected both the struggle with Britain and the core ideas of republicanism. They provided popular democratic answers to the basic questions at issue in the democratic debate—answers that would be rejected a decade later by the elite who drafted the U.S. Constitution.

Three features of the new constitutions were noteworthy: the inclusion of a bill of rights, the weakening of executive power, and the enhancement of legislative power.[8] After years of fighting against British invasions of their rights, Americans wanted to make it clear that these rights were sacred and inviolable, beyond the reach even of the governments that they themselves were establishing. So most of the new constitutions contained a bill of rights; several, including Virginia's influential one, began their constitutions with such declarations.

Colonial experience and republican theory had identified executive power as the chief threat to liberty. Therefore, the revolutionary constitution makers sought to guard against the return of executive despotism. Revolutionary executives were, intentionally, weak executives. In the first state constitutions, executives were chosen by the legislature and held office for a term of only one year. They were stripped of the executive powers traditionally exercised by the British monarch and were left with only modest duties of law enforcement.

The revolutionary mistrust of executives did not extend to legislatures. In the eyes of the constitution writers of 1776, the legislature was not likely to threaten liberty because it would be close to the people, even an embodiment of the people. Legislators were expected to act as mirrors of the people's views and interests. American revolutionaries were not, however, completely optimistic about legislative politics. The bills of rights they wrote were designed to limit what the legislatures could do. Equally important, the revolutionaries attempted to make the state legislature, particularly the more popular lower house, genuinely representative. This required annual elections so that legislators would frequently be returned to live among the people and feel the effects of the laws they had passed. It also required a large and equal representation so that all areas of a state would be fairly reflected in the deliberations of the legislature.

The Articles of Confederation. The states, not the nation, were seen as the centers of political life in 1776. More than a holdover from colonial experience, the primacy of the states reflected the belief that republics were workable only in a small territory. Consequently, the first American system of national government was a confederation, a loose association of states that agreed to join in a compact for common ends (especially foreign relations and the conduct of war). In a confederation, the individual units remain sovereign, so each state had

A CLOSER LOOK

A Revolutionary Experiment in Popular Democracy

All of the state constitutions written in 1776 reflected the revolutionary desire to restrict the power of rulers and to place government more directly in the hands of the people. No state carried this impulse further than Pennsylvania. The Pennsylvania Constitution of 1776 was the boldest revolutionary experiment in popular democracy.

In most states the struggle for independence created a coalition between the social and economic elite and "common" folk. In Pennsylvania, however, the elite clung to the hope of reconciliation with Britain. Encouraged by champions of independence in the Continental Congress, middle class and working class Pennsylvanians—small merchants, shopkeepers, and artisans—shouldered aside this elite. Aiming to shift political control to the people and to prevent wealthy "gentlemen" from resuming their traditional rule, they drafted a constitution whose character was, for its day, remarkably democratic.

The principal institution in the new government was a unicameral (one-house) legislature. Pennsylvania democrats saw no need for an "upper" house, which would be dominated in any case by the elite. To ensure that this legislature would represent all the people, the constitution established the easiest suffrage requirement in any of the states. To ensure that it did what the people wanted (and did not become a new elite with interests of its own), it provided for annual elections and prohibited any representative for serving for more than four years out of every seven. Even more fearful of executive despotism than constitution writers in the other states, popular democrats in

Pennsylvania eliminated the office of governor, putting in its place an Executive Council of twelve, elected directly by the people and holding very limited powers.

Critics complained that this simple form of government placed no checks on the power of the unicameral legislature. Defenders of the constitution responded that it was designed to make the people themselves the check. The constitution made government in Pennsylvania more open to public knowledge and involvement than in any other state. It required that the doors of the legislature be open for public attendance and votes be published weekly for public scrutiny. Once the legislature passed a bill, it could not become law until the next session, allowing the people time to consider it and, if they chose, to reject it through their election of new representatives.

Was this popular democratic experiment in government workable? What makes the question hard to answer is that the experiment never had a clear trial. Opponents of the constitution, many from the old social and economic elite, fought from the beginning to obstruct and overturn it. Their powerful resistance gained ground as the revolutionary spirit of 1776 faded. In 1790, Pennsylvania adopted a new constitution, setting up a government similar to those in other states, and ended its revolutionary experiment in popular democracy.

Sources: The Pennsylvania Constitution of 1776; David Hawke, *In the Midst of a Revolution* (Philadelphia: University of Pennsylvania Press, 1961); Gordon S. Wood, *The Creation of the American Republic, 1776–1787* (New York: W. W. Norton, 1972).

supreme power within its borders. The **Articles of Confederation,** adopted by the Continental Congress in 1777 but not finally approved by all thirteen states until 1781, put little power in the hands of a centralized authority.

Congress under the Articles of Confederation was an assembly of delegates from the states, each of which had one vote. It had the authority to levy taxes and raise troops but had to requisition each state to supply its assigned quota; should a state fail to meet its duty, the central government could do little about it. The suspicion of the states toward national authority was displayed most dramatically in the provision of the Articles of Confederation regarding amendments: No alterations in the Articles could be made until the legislature of *every* state agreed to them.

That this first national authority was not a real central government was evident in its fundamental differences from the first state governments. The national government could not tax the people directly. There was no provision in the Articles for either an executive or a judiciary. All of this government's limited and closely watched powers were left in the hands of the Congress.

The deficiencies of the Articles of Confederation became apparent once it was put into practice. Supporters of the 1787 Constitution based their strongest arguments on the inadequacy of the Articles of Confederation to meet America's need for an effective national government. Alexander Hamilton, in particular, heaped scorn on the Articles of Confederation as weak and futile, and his sarcasm has shaped the way later generations have regarded them. Yet it should be remembered that the Articles of Confederation were not designed to create a strong national government. The framers of the Articles, adhering to the revolutionary spirit of '76, believed that local liberty—and not national power—was the true source of republican strength and virtue.

FROM REVOLUTION TO CONSTITUTION

What happened to the political institutions established by the American revolutionaries? Why did the spirit of '76, the hopeful experiment in liberty and virtue, give way to a more somber spirit a decade later, as reflected in the Constitution and in the arguments that upheld it? To answer these questions, we must look at the years between the Declaration of Independence and the Constitution, some of the most fateful years in American history.

In 1776, the American revolutionary cause attracted a broad coalition. The struggle for independence and self-government united wealthy merchants, slaveowning planters, and lawyers with yeoman farmers, urban artisans, and unskilled laborers. But during the war for independence, and even more in the years immediately following the war, major economic and social tensions emerged in the revolutionary coalition. Revolutionary unity broke down, and with the new economic and social divisions came divisions over both government policies and fundamental matters of political philosophy. The result was a sense of crisis in the new American republic that engendered a move to reconstitute American politics on a different basis than that of 1776.

Economic and social tensions in the revolutionary coalition that had begun during the war with England grew much worse after the fighting stopped. A short-lived boom in imports from England produced a depression that spread from commercial areas to the countryside. As prices for both manufactured and agricultural goods fell, money became scarce, especially specie or "hard money" (gold and silver). Hardest hit during this depression were the small farmers, who constituted the majority of Americans at the time. With falling prices and a shortage of specie, farmers could not pay off their creditors. Because many states were levying taxes to pay off wartime debts, the farmers also faced demands for payments from the tax collector. The combination of debt and taxes threatened many small farmers with foreclosure—the loss of their tools, livestock, or land. Some faced prison, for in this period one could be jailed for a failure to pay debts.

Not surprisingly, small farmers faced with such dire losses became the main source of political agitation in the mid-1780s. They wanted their state legislatures to relieve their distress. They petitioned for "stay laws" to postpone foreclosures and "tender laws" to allow payment of debts and taxes in agricultural commodities. Most of all, they sought paper money—a new and inflated currency that would make paying their debts and taxes easier.

In some states legislators were not responsive to these demands. In Massachusetts, the failure of the legislature to do anything about the plight of the rural majority led to an explosion. The counties in the western part of the state repeatedly petitioned for relief, but the legislature, dominated by the merchants and moneylenders of the coastal cities, ignored them. By the fall of 1786, conditions were ripe for rebellion. Under the leadership of Daniel Shays, a former revolutionary army officer, farmers in the western counties banded together to close down the local courts and prevent further foreclosures. When Shays and his followers marched on the state armory in Springfield, they were dispersed by the state militia. **Shays's Rebellion,** as this event came to be called, was hardly a revolution; it was a disorganized campaign by desperate farmers who felt they were losing everything that the American Revolution had promised them.

To the more conservative and propertied American republicans, Shays's Rebellion was a disturbing yet familiar phenomenon. Just as republican theory had warned that power, if not properly checked, led to despotism, so it had also maintained that liberty, if not properly contained by power, led to lawlessness. But in the 1780s, what most troubled the conservative and the propertied was not the people's rebellions against the state governments. Rather, they were troubled that the majority of the state governments, with their strong legislatures and weak executives, *were* responding to popular grievances. Seven states, for example, passed paper money legislation; stay and tender laws were also put into effect. Attempts by the agrarian majority to alter contractual obligations and to interfere with what conservatives defined as the sacred rights of property were now obtaining the force of state law.[9]

Why were the legislatures in the majority of the states so responsive to mass grievances? One reason was the popular democratic nature of these revolutionary governments. With annual elections and with large and equal representation, the legislatures were quick to grant their constituents' requests. A second reason was the character of the representatives themselves. Before the Revolution, colonial assemblies had been dominated by an upper class of merchants, lawyers, and large landowners. But the Revolution had brought new men into politics from the middle class, and the composition of the legislatures had changed. Now, when yeoman farmers petitioned their state legislatures, they were heard in many states by people like themselves.[10]

To conservative and propertied republicans, the new state laws (such as paper money legislation) and the new state legislators called into question the assumptions about politics that had been shared by all republicans in 1776. These men, looking fearfully at developments in the states, no longer believed the core ideas of 1776. In their eyes, power was no longer the problem; liberty was. Executives were no longer the major threat; legislatures were. Shays's rebels and debtors seeking paper money aroused concern about the virtue of the American people. The turmoil in the states seemed to invalidate the capacity of a small republic to arrive at a common good. Condemning the "Vices of the Political System of the United States," the young James Madison, soon to play the leading role at the Constitutional Convention, placed them at the doorstep of "the representative bodies" and "the people themselves." To Madison, the heroes of 1776 had become the culprits of 1787.[11]

The Constitutional Convention of 1787 assembled largely in response to these developments in the states. The delegates who came to Philadelphia agreed that efforts in the states to block what was happening had been unsuccessful. They also agreed that the weak national government under the Articles of Confederation, with its dedication to state sovereignty, provided no recourse. If they hoped to restore stability and protect property, the answer was in a new set of national institutions. These delegates were still republicans, but they no longer hoped to base the American republic on the virtue or public spirit of the people. As they saw it, if republicanism was to survive in America—without subverting either order or property—only a proper constitution could save it.

THE CONSTITUTIONAL CONVENTION

The Constitutional Convention of 1787 was a lengthy affair, lasting from May 25 to September 17. For nearly four months of a sweltering Philadelphia summer, fifty-five delegates from twelve states (Rhode Island refused to send a delegation) orated, debated, and negotiated the creation of a new American political system. Their proceedings were secret, and our knowledge of what took place rests mainly on notes of several delegates—particularly James Madison. In considering the Constitutional Convention, we focus on the creation of a strong national

James Madison was the leading figure at the Constitutional Convention. His essays in *The Federalist Papers* are the most brilliant exposition of the political theory of elite democracy.

government, the shaping of new national institutions, and the political values that guided the delegates.[12]

A Strong National Government

Forging a new national government was a complex process whose eventual outcome no one really anticipated. Most of the principal figures at Philadelphia—the delegates who took leading roles—wanted a far stronger national government than the Articles of Confederation provided. But the actual features of this government would emerge only gradually through the debates, votes, and compromises of four months.

As the debates commenced, the delegates were subject to conflicting pulls. On one hand, these mostly propertied and conservative men were representatives of the tradition we call elite democracy, and they were eager to end the upsurge of popular democracy that had been manifested in paper money legislation and Shays's Rebellion. Furthermore, they hoped that a lofty new national government, elevated high above local democracy, would be dominated by people like themselves rather than by the more ordinary folks who had gained prominence in the state legislatures. On the other hand, they knew that whatever they might consider the best plan of government, the new Constitution would have to obtain the approval of the American people. Frequent references were made during the proceedings to the values or "genius" of the American people, which could not be ignored or overridden. As historian Alfred Young has observed, the leading figures at the convention were "accommodating conservatives," who "made democratic concessions to achieve conservative ends."[13]

The initial agenda for the convention was set by the **Virginia Plan,** introduced on May 29 by that state's governor, Edmund Randolph, but principally the handiwork of James Madison. Where the Articles of Confederation had been based on the sovereignty of the states, the Virginia Plan made national government primary and reduced the states to a subordinate position. It envisioned the United States as a large republic—the kind of centralized political order that the American revolutionaries had opposed as inconsistent with liberty. Under the Virginia Plan, representation for each state in *both* houses of the bicameral legislature was to be based on either taxes paid to the national government or the number of free inhabitants—provisions that would favor the large states. The provision that most strongly indicated how authority was to be shifted from the state governments to the national government was one crafted by Madison that empowered the national legislature to veto state legislation.

Although the Virginia Plan dominated the initial debate, it leaned so far in the direction of the large states that the smaller states took alarm. On June 15, they countered with an alternative framework, introduced by William Paterson of New Jersey and thus known as the **New Jersey Plan.** The New Jersey Plan was essentially a reform of the Articles of Confederation rather than a wholly new constitutional order. It retained from the Articles a unicameral legislature in which each state would have equal representation. It strengthened the Articles by bestowing on Congress greater powers over revenues and commerce and by establishing a plural executive and a national judiciary. The New Jersey Plan never had enough support to gain serious consideration, but the concerns of the small states that it raised had to be addressed if the convention was to arrive at sufficient agreement to present a new constitution to the nation.

The quarrel between large and small states over representation was finally settled through a compromise proposed by the delegation from Connecticut and known as the Connecticut Compromise, or **Great Compromise.** Under the terms of this compromise, the House of Representatives would be apportioned according to the populations of the various states, while each state would have two members in the Senate. Senators would be selected by their state's legislature. The origination of revenue acts would be an exclusive right of the House. Through this compromise, the large states had the dominant position in the

House and a more favorable position with regard to taxation, yet the small states were well protected by their equal representation in the Senate.

The delegates who were most eager to build national power at the expense of the states had to make compromises that pained them. Equal representation for the states in the Senate was one blow to the "nationalist" position; another was the defeat of Madison's plan for a national veto power over state legislation. Rather than drawing clear lines of national dominance and state subordination, the constitution that began to emerge by midsummer drew uncertain boundaries between national and state powers. The Constitution of the United States is celebrated for creating a novel system of **federalism** under which power is divided between the central government and the states. Alexander Hamilton and especially James Madison applauded the virtues of this federalism in *The Federalist Papers*, considered later in this chapter. The irony is that this system of federalism was not what Hamilton, Madison, or their allies wanted. If they had not needed to compromise on representation and had not lost on the veto over state laws, we would have had a far more centralized government.

National Institutions

The Articles of Confederation had provided only a single legislative branch. But the Constitutional Convention intended to create a more complex government, possessing a bicameral legislature, a national executive, and a national judiciary. Molding these institutions and determining the appropriate relationships between them occupied much of the convention's time. In framing new national institutions, most of the delegates rejected the assumption that had dominated constitution making a decade earlier: that the legislature—the branch closest to the people—should be entrusted with the most power. Recent actions of the state legislatures had soured most of the men at Philadelphia toward the virtues of the people's representatives and made them look more favorably at traditional organs of power.

The Legislature. The House of Representatives proved to be the least complicated of the institutions to fashion. The delegates were clear that this branch would directly reflect the people's opinions and interests. But they were also clear that a legislative body so closely representing popular democratic sentiments would need strong checks. The House was seen as the most democratic part of the new system—and for that very reason the part most feared and constrained.

The nature and shape of the second legislative body, the Senate, occasioned greater controversy. Many delegates envisioned the Senate as an elite assemblage, a forum where the nation's economic, political, and intellectual aristocrats would constrain the more democratic House and supply wisdom and stability to the process of law-making. Those who wanted a cool, deliberative, elite legislative body fought hard against making the Senate a forum for state interests.

Madison bitterly opposed the Great Compromise, saying it would turn the Senate into a copy of the inept Congress under the Articles of Confederation. Yet even though the Senate that emerged, with its special protection for the small states, fell short of the elite national body that Madison and his allies urged, it was viewed by all as more selective, conservative, and stable than the House. As a consequence, it was given deliberative functions and prerogatives denied to the House: Senate consent was required for treaties and for presidential nominations to the executive branch and the judiciary.

The Executive. If the fashioning of a Senate gave the convention its share of pains, the shaping of the executive was a continual headache, not relieved until the closing days of the proceedings. The Virginia Plan had left open the question of whether the United States would have a single or a plural executive. To some delegates, the idea of a single man exercising executive powers over so vast a country as the United States conjured a disturbing likeness with the King of Great Britain. Thus, when James Wilson of Pennsylvania proposed on June 1 that "the Executive consist of a single person" who would provide "energy, dispatch, and responsibility to the office," Madison's notes observe "a considerable pause ensuing." Attacking Wilson's proposal, Governor Randolph of Virginia claimed that a single or "unitary" executive would be the "fetus of monarchy," and suggested instead that the executive consist of three men.[14]

After vigorous debate, Wilson's proposal for a unitary executive carried, but another of his proposals—election of this executive by popular vote—failed. For most of the remainder of the convention, the prevailing view was that the national executive should be selected by Congress. But the convention was moving, gradually and fitfully, to strengthen the executive office. Revolutionary fears of executive power were waning, especially among conservative and propertied republicans; a more favorable view of executives as pillars of order and stability was gaining ground. The willingness of the delegates to create the kind of powerful American executive that would have been unthinkable in 1776 was furthered by the universal assumption that George Washington would be the first president. The final key decision of the convention on the executive—selection by electors rather than by Congress—added greatly to executive independence and strength.

The Judiciary. The third branch of the new national government provoked surprisingly little debate. Given the suspicions of the smaller states, one of the few contested issues involved the relation between federal courts below the Supreme Court and the courts in the states. The idea of "judicial review"—that federal courts have the authority to judge a law by the standard of the Constitution and to declare it null and void should it be found incompatible—was not stated in the Constitution but was discussed by the delegates. Although they did not agree universally on the subject, their comments about judicial review suggest that most delegates did assume that the federal courts would have this authority.

Values, Fears, and Issues

The Constitution was gradually shaped by the convention as institutions were formed, their powers defined, and their relationships to one another determined. In this process a number of values, fears, and issues drove the work of the framers. The next sections consider the interrelationship of one value, property; one fear, democracy; and one issue, slavery, in the development of the Constitution.

Property. Ever since historian Charles Beard charged in 1913 that the Constitution of the United States was written for the direct economic benefit of its framers, a debate has ensued about the role of property in the Constitutional Convention.[15] Although Beard's specific arguments about the framers' personal economic gains have been successfully refuted by other historians, considerable evidence remains in the record of the convention debates that the general protection of property was an objective for many of the framers. The new national government was designed to make property far more secure than it had been under the state constitutions. The convention bestowed on the national government new powers that holders of substantial property desired, such as the means to pay off public debts, disproportionately held by the wealthy. Equally important, it prohibited the state governments from coining money, issuing paper money, or "impairing the obligations of contracts," thus putting an end to the popular democratic efforts of the 1780s to aid the many at the expense of the few.

The "Threat" of Democracy. In the eyes of most of the framers, democracy was the chief threat to property. When the framers talked about democracy, they usually meant the lower house of the legislature, where the people's interests and feelings were directly represented. Some delegates assailed democracy on the grounds that the people were ignorant, subject to fits of passion, and prone to pursuing their own economic interests at the expense of a minority of the most industrious, successful, and propertied citizens. Others feared the people less because of their inherent flaws than because they were so easily duped by demagogues, selfish leaders who stoked the flames of popular passion to gain power. Given this perspective, it is not surprising that the delegates aimed many of the checks and balances they were writing into the constitution at democracy. Only the House of Representatives would be directly democratic, and it would be restrained by the Senate, president, and judiciary, all of which would be selected in an elite rather than a popular fashion.

Slavery. The delegates at Philadelphia concurred on the importance of promoting property and averting the dangers of democracy. But they were sharply divided on another issue: slavery.

Four positions on slavery were advanced during the debates. Some northern delegates opposed giving slavery any protection in the Constitution on economic grounds; if slaves were property, why should this form of property alone gain special safeguards? Other delegates—from both northern states and the upper South—denounced the institution itself on moral grounds. Against these two positions, delegates from South Carolina and Georgia insisted that slavery was indispensable to their economies, and repeatedly warned the convention that if slavery was not given special protection their states would not join the Union. The fourth and ultimately decisive view was put forward by delegates from New England, who expressed dislike for slavery but suggested that the convention should not meddle with this topic and should accept the compromises necessary to keep the most southerly states in the Union. In accordance with this position, slavery was given three special safeguards in the Constitution: (1) to apportion direct taxes and representation in the House, slaves would count as three-fifths of free persons, thereby enlarging southern representation; (2) the slave trade could not be banned for at least twenty years; (3) fugitive slaves would be returned to their owners.

The framers of the Constitution compromised in this case for the sake of harmony and union, justifying their moral lapse with the belief that slavery would gradually die out without any forceful effort against it. The Civil War would show this pious hope to have been their greatest error. Remarkably, one delegate uttered a chilling prophecy of just such a catastrophe as the Civil War. In words that foreshadowed Abraham Lincoln's Second Inaugural Address at the close of the Civil War, George Mason of Virginia, an opponent of slavery (and soon to become an opponent of the Constitution itself) warned his fellow delegates that "by an inevitable chain of causes and effects providence punishes national sins by national calamities."[16]

The full text of the Constitution is in the Appendix at the end of the book. Table 2.1 summarizes the features of the Preamble and the seven articles. The final article stated that ratification by conventions in nine of the thirteen original states would be sufficient to put the Constitution into effect. It began one of the most important contests in American history—a political and philosophical struggle to determine nothing less than the basis on which all subsequent American political life would be conducted. It is to this debate that we now turn.

RATIFICATION STRUGGLE AND THE DEMOCRATIC DEBATE

Most contemporary Americans assume that the greatness of the Constitution under which we have lived for two hundred years must have been obvious from the start. In reality, the ratification of the Constitution required a long and

TABLE 2.1 **Preamble and Articles of the Constitution**	

Preamble	"We the people"—and not the states—establish the Constitution to "form a more perfect union" and to secure justice, domestic tranquility, national defense, the "general welfare," and "the blessings of liberty. . . ."
Article 1	Provides for the selection of representatives and senators, with a two-year term for representatives and a six-year term for senators. Grants seventeen explicit powers to Congress, including the powers to levy and collect taxes, to regulate interstate and foreign commerce, and to declare war. Also grants to Congress the power to make laws that are "necessary and proper" for executing its enumerated powers.
Article 2	Establishes the office of the president. The president to be selected by electors, with each state choosing as many electors as it has representatives in the House and Senate. A four-year term with no restrictions on reelection. The president to be "commander in chief" of the armed forces and chief of the executive branch. The president to have a say in legislation by informing Congress of "the state of the Union" and by recommending measures that he deems "necessary and expedient." The House can impeach and the Senate can remove the president (and all other civil officers) for "treason, bribery, or other high crimes and misdemeanors."
Article 3	Creates a federal judiciary, who hold their offices "during good behavior"—until they resign, die, or are impeached and convicted by Congress. Vests the judicial power in a Supreme Court and in lower courts to be established by Congress. Although the Supreme Court is made the highest court of appeals, Congress retains the power to alter its jurisdiction.
Article 4	Governs relationships between the states. Each state must give "full faith and credit" to the acts and records of the other states. Citizens traveling to another state are entitled to the same "privileges and immunities" as its own residents.
Article 5	Establishes two methods for proposing and two methods for ratifying amendments to the Constitution. Amendments can be proposed either by a two-thirds vote in both houses of Congress or by a convention requested by two-thirds of the states. Ratification of an amendment requires a favorable vote in the legislatures of three-fourths of the states or in special conventions in three-fourths of the states.
Article 6	The Constitution and the laws and treaties made pursuant to its authority are "the supreme law of the land. . . ."
Article 7	Ratification by conventions of nine states establishes the Constitution as the new national authority.

sometimes bitter struggle whose outcome was by no means certain. Although some states ratified the Constitution swiftly and with little dissent, in a number of the larger states the contest was close. In Massachusetts, the vote in the ratifying convention was 187 to 168 in favor of the Constitution. Virginia ratified by the narrow margin of 89 to 79; New York endorsed the Constitution by a vote of 30 to 27.[17]

The closeness of these votes becomes less surprising when we recall that the Constitution largely reversed the political verdict of 1776 by ending the revolutionary experiment in state-based popular democracy. Historians have suggested that the agrarian majority in many of the states was, at least initially, opposed to the Constitution. If the Constitution was a defeat for popular democracy and a victory for an elite democracy (moderated by concessions to the democratic spirit), how did its supporters, who called themselves Federalists, win popular approval?

The Federalists enjoyed a number of political advantages over opponents of the Constitution, who came to be known as Anti-federalists. Perhaps most important, they were united around a common and positive program. With a solution in hand to the nation's distresses (which they often exaggerated for rhetorical purposes), they possessed the political initiative. The Anti-federalists, on the other hand, could not agree among themselves either about what was wrong with the Constitution or about what should take its place. The Federalists also had an advantage in disseminating their ideas. Based largely in the cities and supported by most of the wealthy, they had better access to newspapers than the Anti-federalists.

The Federalist cause was also blessed with exceptional intellectual talent. A majority of the distinguished, learned, and articulate men in America argued for the ratification of the Constitution. Among them, none presented the case for the Constitution so brilliantly as Alexander Hamilton, James Madison, and John Jay in *The Federalist Papers*. These eighty-five papers laid out the arguments for the new constitutional order so profoundly that they transcended their immediate aim and became the most famous American work of political theory. (Some of their arguments are presented later in this chapter.)

Although a number of able writers opposed the Constitution, no single Anti-federalist writing was comparable to *The Federalist Papers*. Moreover, the Anti-federalists can be said to have lost the intellectual debate because their side lost the political contest. *The Federalist Papers* thus overshadowed Anti-federalist thought. Yet both sides were important in the debate over the Constitution. As political theorist Herbert J. Storing has written, "If . . . the foundation of the American polity was laid by the Federalists, the Anti-Federalist reservations echo through American history; and it is in the dialogue, not merely in the Federalist victory, that the country's principles are to be discovered."[18]

The dialogue Storing mentions is what we call the democratic debate. In the following discussion, we pay equal attention to both voices in the debate—Federalist and Anti-federalist, elite democrat and popular democrat. We consider six issues on which the two sides differed: human nature, the proper scale of political life, the character of representation, separation of powers and checks and balances, the purpose of government, and stability and change. The debate over these six issues deserves careful study. The arguments between the elite democratic position and the popular democratic position recur throughout this book; they form the essence of the democratic debate.

Human Nature: Its Dangers and Its Possibilities

The basic issue of the democratic debate is human nature. The Federalists held a pessimistic view of human nature. In the most famous of *The Federalist Papers*, number 10 (printed in full in the Appendix at the end of the book), James Madison wrote that people were "much more disposed to vex and oppress each other than to cooperate for their common good."[19] Alexander Hamilton's view of human nature was even bleaker; men, he wrote, are "ambitious, vindictive, and rapacious."[20] Although Madison could also write that "there are other qualities in human nature which justify a certain portion of esteem and confidence,"[21] the Federalist view was that good government could not be founded on the idea of goodness in its participants.

Any goodness in human nature, the Federalists believed, was most likely to be found in elites. Madison argued that the new national government would bring to power the relatively few citizens who were both wise and public spirited. Hamilton claimed that his favorite institution, the presidency, would be filled by men "preeminent for ability and virtue."[22] The Federalists recognized that the dangerous qualities in human nature might also show up in the governing elite. But their greater fear was the raw human nature of the masses. The history of experiments in popular democracy had, in the eyes of the Federalists, demonstrated that most ordinary people were prone to passion, selfishness, and disorder. To the Federalists, any attempt by the people to assemble and debate affairs in a face-to-face or direct democracy would inevitably degenerate into mob rule.

The Anti-federalists were not naive optimists who held a rosy view of human nature. They, too, wrote vividly of the ambition and greed that could disfigure the human character. Yet they differed profoundly from the Federalists on where virtue and vice were most likely to be found. Ordinary individuals, most Anti-federalist writers believed, had modest aspirations; they wanted to live a life of comfort, decency, and dignity. Moreover, whatever natural tendencies existed toward selfishness and quarreling could be counteracted through instruction in morality and religion. Virtue could be taught by republican institutions, laws, and customs, and it would grow as citizens participated in the politics of their communities.[23]

The Anti-federalists feared human nature among elites. Power, they claimed, was intoxicating, especially when the connection between governors and citizens grew distant and the instruments for abuse and corruption were nearby. Human nature at its worst was not a lawless people, the Anti-federalist Patrick Henry of Virginia proclaimed. Rather, it was "the tyranny of rulers."[24]

Scale of Political Life

From this initial difference between Federalists and Anti-federalists over human nature flowed a further difference over the proper scale of political life. Federalists favored a large republic (national government); Anti-federalists favored small republics (state governments).

In the view of the Federalists, the small republic brought out the worst in human nature. In the face-to-face political space of the small republic, a majority of selfish but like-minded individuals would form a "faction" or political group and try to oppress a minority, such as those who owned large amounts of property or those who held unorthodox religious beliefs. Irrational and violent passion would spread among this majority like an infectious disease, and politics in the small republic would degenerate into turbulence, injustice, and misery.

But in the large republic, the Federalists claimed, the selfish passions of the people could not have this unhappy result. There would be so much diversity in the large republic that a powerful and unjust majority faction was unlikely to form. James Madison explained the logic of the large republic: "Extend the sphere and you take in a greater variety of parties and interests; you make it less probable that a majority of the whole will have a common motive to invade the rights of other citizens; or if such a common motive exists, it will be more difficult for all who feel it to discover their own strength and to act in unison with each other."[25]

Given their view of human nature, the Anti-federalists favored the small republic and feared the large republic. The Anti-federalists saw the small republic as the home of liberty rather than oppression. It was only in the small republic, they argued, that citizens were close enough to their representatives in government to have confidence in them and to hold them accountable for their actions. Further, only in the small republic could citizens participate in political affairs and, through the practice of active citizenship, develop a broader and less selfish understanding of the common good.[26]

The Anti-federalists saw the large republic as bringing out the worst in human nature. Above all, they mistrusted the national elites on whom the Federalists were banking their hopes. As a New York Anti-federalist who used the pseudonym of Brutus (killer of the tyrant Caesar, who had destroyed the Roman republic) put it: "In so extensive a republic, the great officers of government would soon become above the control of the people, and abuse their power to the purpose of aggrandizing themselves, and oppressing them."[27]

Representation

Federalist and Anti-federalist understandings of representation also followed from their differing views of human nature. Because ordinary people were prone, the Federalists believed, to selfish, factional, and even violent passions, the task of the elected representative was to filter out these bad impulses and seek the people's true welfare. In a large republic, James Madison argued in *Federalist*

No. 10, the process of representation would "refine and enlarge the public views by passing them through the medium of a chosen body of citizens, whose wisdom may best discern the true interest of their country and whose patriotism and love of justice will be least likely to sacrifice it to temporary or partial considerations."[28] The Federalist claim was that representatives, as a distinctive elite, would both know better and do better than the people themselves.

The Anti-federalists denied that representatives should act the part of the people's superiors. Representatives, they argued, should not filter out what the people wanted; they should mirror the people's exact hopes and goals. In the words of New York Anti-federalist Melancton Smith: "The idea that naturally suggests itself to our minds when we speak of representatives is that they resemble those they represent; they should be a true picture of the people; possess the knowledge of their circumstances and their wants; sympathize in all their distresses, and be disposed to seek their true interests."[29]

Separation of Powers and Checks and Balances

Although the Federalists entertained high hopes for a talented and virtuous elite to run the new national government, they were aware that concentrated power could be abused. Their remedy was to separate the powers of government into three branches—legislative, executive, and judicial—each of which would have the constitutional weapons to check the others. Thus, the president could check the legislature with his veto, the Senate could check the executive with its power over appointments, and the judiciary could check the other two branches by its authority over the meaning of the Constitution and the laws. Members of each branch were expected to defend their rightful powers against the others, James Madison explained, less out of virtue than out of a regard for their own interests. To guard against an oppressive concentration of powers within government, he wrote in one of his most famous sentences, "ambition must be made to counteract ambition."[30]

The Federalists did not, however, see all branches as equally dangerous. They worried most about the popular democratic body, the House of Representatives. The more elite institutions were expected to hold the House in check and thereby ensure wiser and more stable governance. Madison and Hamilton preferred institutions that were more remote than the House from the pressures of popular democracy. Madison described the Senate as a select body that would provide cool deliberation even in the heat of passionate political controversies. Hamilton placed his greatest hopes on the presidency. Perhaps his most famous sentence in *The Federalist Papers* proclaimed: "Energy in the executive is a leading character in the definition of good government."[31]

The Anti-federalists viewed the institutions of government in a different light. Some preferred a simpler structure of government than that provided in the Constitution, arguing that its complex arrangement of conflicting powers would leave the people confused about whom to hold accountable for abuses.

The more common Anti-federalist perspective, however, accepted the idea of separation of powers and checks and balances but complained that the Constitution was checking the wrong people. It was not the democratic House that needed most closely to be watched, but rather the elite branches. Patrick Henry thus warned that Hamilton's energetic executive "squints toward monarchy."[32] Anti-federalist writers also denounced the constitutional alliance between a monarchical president and an aristocratic Senate in making treaties and appointing civil officers, judges, and ambassadors.

Purpose of Government

What was the purpose of government? Both Federalists and Anti-federalists agreed that government must protect and promote the liberty of the people. Yet they meant different things by *liberty*. To James Madison, liberty was primarily a private possession—private property or private convictions. Liberty in this sense needed to be protected from oppressive majorities that would take away property or force the same religious faith on everyone. If liberty was protected, individuals would, Madison believed, succeed or fail in accordance with their own abilities. A free society would inevitably be marked by a substantial amount of economic inequality that resulted from the natural differences between people, and such a society was therefore just.[33]

Alexander Hamilton thought of liberty in slightly different terms—as the freedom to acquire greater property and power. He wanted a powerful national government that would promote the economic growth and develop the military potential of the United States. The purpose of government was to steer the United States in the direction of national greatness. In the right hands, he suggested in *The Federalist Papers*, this bold young nation "might make herself the admiration and envy of the world."[34] Hamilton's vision of a prosperous and mighty America was beyond the sight of most of his fellow Federalists. But he shared with them the idea that inequality in wealth and power inevitably accompanied liberty.

To the Anti-federalists, liberty was equally precious. But they emphasized the political rights of the people as much as the people's right to property. Understood in this way, liberty was endangered less by oppressive majorities than by oppressive rulers. The most common Anti-federalist complaint against the Constitution—that it contained no bill of rights to safeguard the people against government oppression—is considered in the next section.

The Anti-federalists also disagreed with the Federalists about how liberty related to economic life and national defense. Although desiring a prosperous America, they hoped for a simpler and more egalitarian society than the Federalists. If wealth became highly unequal and Americans began desiring luxurious goods, they feared, the republic would lose its anchorage in the civic virtue of the people. The public good would be neglected once Americans cared only about getting rich. Anti-federalists also worried about the rise of a powerful military that might be used by rulers for domestic tyranny or foreign aggression.

The Anti-federalist view of the purpose of government looked back to the vision of popular democracy that had fired the hopes of American revolutionaries in 1776. Their protest against turning America away from its original democratic dream and making it more like the undemocratic governments of Europe was eloquently expressed by Patrick Henry:

> If we admit this consolidated government it will be because we like a great splendid one. Some way or other we must be a great and mighty empire; we must have an army, and a navy, and a number of things. When the American spirit was in its youth, the language of America was different. Liberty, Sir, was then the primary object.[35]

Stability and Change

The final critical area of difference between the Federalists and the Anti-federalists involved their perspectives on stability and change in American politics. Responding to the upsurge of popular democracy in the Revolution and its aftermath, Federalists looked for sources of stability in a new constitutional system. Their chief answer to the danger of radical economic and social change through popular democracy lay in the complex mechanisms of the Constitution itself. In the vastness and diversity of a large republic, majorities desiring radical change were unlikely to form; should they overcome the problem of distance and gain power in the democratic branch—the House of Representatives—the more elite branches would check their progress and protect the status quo. Federalists were not averse to all change—witness Hamilton's program for economic development—but they wanted change guided by an elite.

Among the Federalists, James Madison was particularly insightful in recognizing a more profound basis for stability. He saw that if the Constitution could prevail over its initial opposition, its status as the foundation of American politics would eventually cease to be questioned. It would gain "that veneration which time bestows on everything, and without which perhaps the wisest and freest governments would not possess the requisite stability."[36] Madison foresaw that Americans would come to love the Constitution. Forgetting the original debate over it, they would revere the document—and the ideas—produced by the winning side.

What the Federalists desired as stability looked to the Anti-federalists like the most dangerous form of change: political corruption and decay. The Anti-federalists were not worried that the people would become unruly; they feared that the people would become apathetic about public affairs. Under the new constitutional order, they predicted, arrogance and corruption would grow among ruling elites, while the people would become preoccupied with the scramble for riches. Unless ordinary citizens were called to remember their political rights and to exercise them, liberty was sure to be lost.

The Anti-federalist view continued the spirit of protest and resistance that had marked the American Revolution. No one expressed this spirit so strongly

TABLE 2.2	Issue	Federalists	Anti-federalists
Differences Between the Federalists and Anti-federalists	Human nature	Ordinary people basically selfish; capacity for virtue greater among elites	Ordinary people moderately ambitious and capable of virtue; dangerous ambitions found among elites
	Scale of political life	Favored a large republic (national government)	Favored a small republic (state governments)
	Role of representatives	To refine the public views	To mirror the people's hopes and goals
	Separation of powers	Favored checks and balances, with particular eye on the House of Representatives	Believed in checks and balances, with particular eye on the president and Senate
	Purpose of government	To protect liberty, especially private rights; expected inequality as just result	To protect liberty, especially political rights; sought to prevent large inequalities that threatened values of a republic
	Stability and change	Stability found in complexity of Constitution and in public reverence for it	Feared political decay and corruption; favored spirit of protest embodied in the Revolution

during this period as Thomas Jefferson. Strictly speaking, Jefferson was neither Federalist nor Anti-federalist; as the American minister to France during the years in which the Constitution was written and debated, he stood at a distance from the conflict over it. Yet his support for popular protest, expressed in letters to friends in America, dramatically opposes the Federalist dread of popular action. Whereas the Federalists reacted in horror to Shays's Rebellion as a signpost of impending anarchy, Jefferson wrote to Madison: "I hold it that a little rebellion now and then is a good thing, and as necessary in the political world as storms in the physical."[37] Jefferson, like the Anti-federalists, believed that only an alert and active citizenry could preserve the democratic values of the American Revolution (see Table 2.2).

THE BILL OF RIGHTS

When farmers in the back country of South Carolina heard that their state had ratified the Constitution, they "had a coffin painted black, which borne in funeral procession, was solemnly buried, as an emblem of the dissolution and interment of public liberty."[38] Such Anti-federalist fears—that the Constitution would become a monstrous mechanism for oppressing the people—strike us today as absurdly exaggerated. Yet in one crucial respect, the fears of the Anti-federalists were fortunate and productive. Without them, we would not have gained the Bill of Rights.

Among the Anti-federalists' objections to the Constitution, none was as frequently voiced, as popularly received, and as compelling in force as the complaint that the Constitution lacked guarantees of the people's basic liberties. Most of the state constitutions, Anti-federalist writers and debaters pointed out, expressly protected the fundamental personal and political rights of the people against arbitrary and invasive government. Yet this new national constitution contained no such guarantees of liberty. Anti-federalists at the state ratifying conventions thus began to propose various amendments to the new Constitution as safeguards of the people's fundamental rights.

Some Federalists resisted the call for amendments, fearing that they would weaken the new political system. But the more moderate supporters of the Constitution increasingly recognized that amendments that guaranteed the rights of the people would conciliate opponents of the Constitution and thus give the new system a better chance to survive and flourish. The leader of these moderates was James Madison. To win election to the House of Representatives, Madison had pledged to the voters in his district that he would introduce amendments in the first Congress. Fulfilling his promise, he became the principal drafter and legislative champion of what became the Bill of Rights. The greatest thinker in the American tradition of elite democracy thus became one of the greatest contributors to the American tradition of popular democracy.[39]

The Bill of Rights adds to the original Constitution a commitment to the personal and political liberties of the people. It safeguards the rights of religious conscience, free speech, a free press, and political activity; it protects the people against an invasion of their homes and papers by an intrusive government; it guarantees a fair trial and a freedom from excessive punishment. If the Constitution proved to be the great charter of American government, the Bill of Rights was the great charter of American liberty. It stands as an enduring testament to the vision and values of the Anti-federalists. Today, when Americans think of the U.S. Constitution, the Bill of Rights seems as much a part of its original composition as the seven articles drafted at the Philadelphia convention of 1787. The original democratic debate had made the Constitution a better—and a more democratic—document.

CONCLUSION: BEGINNING THE DEMOCRATIC DEBATE

The Constitution represented a victory for elite democrats in the original democratic debate. Not only did this victory lie in the creation of lofty national institutions in which elites would control most of the offices. Even more, it lay in the impediments to popular democracy that the constitutional system established. The growing size of the national republic tended, as Madison had argued, to fragment potential popular democratic movements and encourage in their place the narrower struggles of interest group politics. The complexity of national institutions tended to stalemate democratic energies for social change. The remoteness of national institutions tended to undermine the civic virtue nourished in local, face-to-face political participation.

Elite democrats also won a philosophical victory in 1787. Embodied in many of the clauses of the Constitution and brilliantly argued in the pages of *The Federalist Papers*, the premises of elite democracy have come down to Americans with the sanctity of the highest political authority.

The constitutional victory of the elite democrats did not, however, mean that the popular democrats were vanquished in the era of the American founding. Later generations of popular democrats have looked back to the founding for authority and inspiration—but to the Revolution more than to the Constitution. The American tradition of popular democratic protest and struggle finds its roots in the Sons of Liberty, the Boston Tea Party, and the revolutionary war militia. The popular democratic vision of equality and self-government rests on the opening paragraphs of the Declaration of Independence. Echoing the revolutionaries of 1776 (and the Anti-federalists as well), popular democrats balance their fears of remote and unaccountable power with hopes for democratic community and public-spirited citizens.

Popular democrats not only can claim the revolutionary heritage, they also can point to concessions obtained from elite democrats in the constitutional system itself. The framers of the Constitution had to include elements of popular democracy in order to win ratification. Subsequent to ratification, popular democrats won an even larger victory when the Bill of Rights was added to the Constitution. Later amendments have also made the Constitution more compatible with popular democracy. The Thirteenth, Fourteenth, and Fifteenth Amendments, products of the Civil War and Reconstruction era, established the rights of African Americans to participate in the American political system. The Nineteenth Amendment established women's right to the suffrage. Products of long struggles by popular democratic movements, these amendments opened doors that the founders had kept shut. They established the equal right—although not the equal chance—of all Americans to exercise the political rights and enjoy the political rewards that had originally been reserved for white males alone.

The Revolution and Constitution engendered a great democratic debate, but they did not resolve it for all time. Throughout this text, we point out how the democratic debate continues to flourish in American politics. Should large corporations, for example, be regarded as the indispensable engines of economic growth, or should we instead discourage concentrated economic power and favor smaller economic enterprises and a more equal distribution of economic resources? Do contemporary elections foster civic virtue or bury it under a blizzard of media spectacles financed by elite money? Is the modern president the "energetic executive" that Alexander Hamilton applauded or the arrogant "monarch" that Patrick Henry dreaded? In these and many other forms, the democratic debate still animates American politics. As we study its contemporary expressions, we need to recall the fundamental terms of the debate set down by the founders of the American Republic.

KEY TERMS

republicanism
Declaration of Independence
Articles of Confederation
Shays's Rebellion

Virginia Plan
New Jersey Plan
Great Compromise
federalism

SUGGESTED READINGS

Ralph Ketcham, ed., *The Anti-Federalist Papers*. New York: New American Library, 1986. An anthology of the leading Anti-federalist critics of the Constitution.

Richard K. Matthews, *If Men Were Angels: James Madison and the Heartless Empire of Reason*. Lawrence: University Press of Kansas, 1995. A provocative analysis of Madison as an elite democratic theorist.

Jack N. Rakove, *Original Meanings: Politics and Ideas in the Making of the Constitution*. New York: Alfred A. Knopf, 1996. A wide-ranging yet subtle examination of the Constitutional Convention and the major ideas that it produced.

Clinton Rossiter, ed., *The Federalist Papers*. New York: New American Library, 1961. Hamilton's and Madison's brilliant defense of the Constitution— and the foremost work in the history of American political thought.

Herbert J. Storing, *What the Anti-Federalists Were For*. Chicago: University of Chicago Press, 1981. A brief yet profound explanation of the Anti-federalists' political ideas.

Gordon S. Wood, *The Creation of the American Republic, 1776–1787*. New York: W. W. Norton, 1972. The leading work on the transformation of American political thought from the popular democracy of the Revolution to the elite democracy of the Constitution.

Public Opinion and Political Culture: Should Citizens Count?

Ordinary people's beliefs and expressions about politics and policies are called **public opinion.** Today, public opinion seems like a kind of democratic royalty, as dozens of polling organizations investigate and report minute changes in its "mood." Social movements and interest groups compete to gain its attention and support. Candidates and elected officials, as well as their policies, flourish or perish on the basis of favorable or unfavorable ratings in surveys. How could it be otherwise? In a democratic society, the public's thoughts and actions must matter.

Yet all this attention and apparent respect is tinged with fear and may disguise a deep elite skepticism about the public's capacity to understand, reason, or judge public policies. Beneath the constant monitoring is the worry that unless public opinion is carefully contained and properly educated, it may surge out of control. From the perspective of elites in politics and business, the public may be dangerous, ignorant, or stupid—or a potent combination of all three.

PUBLIC OPINION AND THE DEMOCRATIC DEBATE

Skepticism about the inherent ignorance and passions of the public has long characterized elite democratic views. Two centuries ago, Alexander Hamilton frankly called public opinion "a great beast," prone to "sudden breezes of passion." In the 1920s, the first systematic student of public opinion, Walter Lippmann, observed that the public was "a bewildered herd," driven by "manufactured images." More recently, one prominent student of contemporary public opinion wrote that public opinions are so changeable that it seemed that most citizens decided important questions by flipping a coin.[1]

These days, elite doubts about the public are rarely voiced openly, lest the public be offended. But modern skeptics have had plenty of ammunition to back up their doubts. Despite rising levels of formal education, most Americans just don't know many key political facts. A majority cannot identify the Chief Justice of the Supreme Court. While anyone who follows politics knows that the Republican party took control of Congress in 1994, as of 1996 most citizens didn't know or guessed that the Democrats still held Congress. It gets even worse when it comes to foreign matters: Even with 25,000 U.S. troops in Bosnia, most Americans couldn't point out the country on a map.

Knowledge is one problem. In addition, public opinion often seems to lack consistency. Take, for example, the wild fluctuation that George Bush's popularity experienced between 1991 and 1992. In less than a year, Bush sank from a high of nearly 90 percent popularity during the Persian Gulf War to less than half that figure. Rapid changes in public mood also suggest how easily opinion can be sidetracked by media spectacles. In 1994 and 1995, the arrest and trial of O. J. Simpson drew far more public attention and passion than the far more important debate about health care reform.

Given this apparently sad record, it is no wonder that educated skeptics have voiced concern about how much public opinion *does* matter and how much it really *should* matter as an independent force. The millions of dollars spent to influence public opinion and to understand its workings may, in this sense, be used not so much to test public opinion but to manage and control its potential excesses. Political scientist Ben Ginsberg calls this modern apparatus of public opinion management a huge effort to create a "captive public."[2]

Fears of the mass public and its opinions haven't gone unchallenged. In the 1920s, the philosopher John Dewey conceded that most Americans knew relatively little about everyday affairs and policies. He fully admitted that the public's judgment was often wrong. Yet he argued that the public was still the best judge about most long-term questions by which it was affected. Ordinary citizens, after all, have to live with the consequences of governmental actions and policies in ways that elites don't. It is ordinary citizens who bear the burdens of war, the sting of inequality, and the sacrifices of economic depressions.

Dewey argued that the major threat to intelligent and informed public opinion didn't come from any inherent defect of ordinary humans. On the contrary: Dewey held that the strength of American democratic traditions rested in strong communities of citizens who knew and conversed with each other. Democratic communities, far from being instruments of elites, stood as bulwarks against their potential tyranny. Dewey blamed government and corporate elites for constricting the ability of democratic citizens to converse with each other, to answer back to authority, and to realize their views through political participation. Through the use of propaganda, public relations, advertising, and the mass media, modern elites employed new ways to restrict debate, silence dissent, and manipulate opinion, Dewey argued. Writing in the 1950s, the sociologist C. Wright Mills extended Dewey's critique of elites and their powers over public opinion. Mills warned that a power elite was turning "publics" into "masses." The antidote to this tendency, both Dewey and Mills agreed, was the expansion of the scope and independence of public discussion. Public opinion should be freed to do more, not less.[3]

The Vietnam War era provides one of the best examples of the emergence of active and informed public opinion that popular democrats have in mind. At the war's beginnings and in the early stages of U.S. troop involvement, most Americans didn't know many details about the war. Popular majorities, egged on by government propaganda and media complicity, initially supported the war. Yet this was in part because the public was deprived of essential facts about the nature of U.S. involvement. The public, quite simply, had not thought much about the matter. As the war progressed, public opposition grew in tandem with new facts that revealed a pattern of government dishonesty, half-truths, and propaganda about the war's origins and its tragic consequences. As public discussion about the war broadened, and as a broad antiwar movement arose to protest it, informed public opinion had a chance to mature. As it did, the public turned against the war and the politicians who had originated it and began to question elite assumptions about what was at stake in Vietnam. In popular democratic terms, public opinion played a key role in exposing, and then curbing, elite delusions about the Vietnam War's "progress."[4]

The democratic debate about public opinion raises fundamental questions about contemporary political life. If the public is as ignorant, fickle, and dangerous as elite democrats believe, then the manipulation and control of public opinion by "responsible" elites can be justified. If, on the contrary, these same elites in both government and corporations possess the means to seize control of democratic politics through intimidation and propaganda, then popular democratic ideas are justified. Just how government, the media, and large corporations act to control public opinion is discussed at length in Chapters 4 and 6. In this chapter, we will address several questions: Is the public as ignorant and irrational as many elites believe? From what experiences and sources do people derive their opinions? How and when, if ever, can public opinion become what Mills called "face-to-face citizens discussing the public business"?

Answering these questions is the central concern of this chapter. To do so, we first look at whether or not ordinary Americans profess democratic beliefs about how government should operate. Second, the chapter outlines how different interpretations of common beliefs emerge. Third, we ask if Americans think consistently about public policies, and then we inquire about the circumstances that shape public opinion and how it changes. Finally, we turn to the subject of public opinion's independence and effectiveness: Who organizes public opinion today, and when is it effective in shaping governmental policies and actions?

AMERICAN POLITICAL CULTURE

More than many other countries with long histories and homogeneous populations, the United States' survival as a nation depends on the quality and scope of its democratic understandings. Common values of toleration, mutual respect, and national community need to work to forge bonds between people of diverse races, national origins, religions, and cultures. When they don't, the darkest dimension of American life emerges, whether it be in the form of African-American slavery and the persistence of white racism, the subjugation of Native Americans, or the demonization of dissent as un-American. Much of our history suggests that the association between democratic values and nationhood has never been easy. Alternatively, the brightest moments in U.S. history are those times when more and more people become included in the expanding democratic "promise" of American life.

What do citizens today understand about the meaning of being an American? The set of common rituals, stories, symbols, and habits that Americans share might be called American **political culture.** Political culture is not just a set of abstract values. It is more like a common political vocabulary, a kind of tool kit that we all use, sometimes to express very different values and aspirations for ourselves and others. As such, political culture is broad enough to include both sides in the democratic debate. Despite differences, the tradition of American

TABLE 3.1	**At least eight in ten Americans agree to the following:**
The Essentials of American Political Culture	1. Free speech should be granted to everyone regardless of how intolerant they are of other people's opinions.
	2. Freedom to worship as one pleases applies to all religious groups, regardless of how extreme their beliefs are.
	3. The private enterprise system is generally a fair and efficient system.
	4. A party that wins an election should respect the rights of opposition parties to criticize the way things are being run.
	5. Forcing people to testify against themselves in court is never justified.
	6. Our elected officials would badly misuse their power if they weren't watched and guided by the voters.
	7. A minority family that wants to move into a particular neighborhood shouldn't have to check with anyone before doing so.
	8. Everyone in America should have equal opportunities to get ahead.
	9. Children should have equal educational opportunities.

Reprinted by permission from *The American Ethos* by Herbert McCloskey and John Zaller. Cambridge, Mass.: Harvard University Press. Copyright © 1984 by the 20th Century Fund.

political protest and dissent—embodied in the civil rights, labor, peace, and feminist movements—has something in common with the ideas of those who oppose many of the specific goals of political protest and dissent. The important point about our political culture is that people agree about what to disagree about.[5] Table 3.1 details some of the essential elements of our common political culture.

Patriotism, Democracy, and the National Community

As described in Chapter 2, democracy became an honored idea in the United States soon after the founding debates. Even in periods of crisis and upheaval (such as the 1960s), public support for the basic forms and procedures of democratic government has remained overwhelming and widespread. Today, the language of democracy still stands as the essence of American political culture.

The broad requirements of democratic government are widely supported by Americans, at least when they are asked about them in the abstract. The idea that public officials should be chosen by majority vote in regular elections and that minorities and individuals maintain rights to freedom of speech, press, expression, and religion are supported by more than nine in ten citizens. The idea that defects in the American system should and can be changed through legal processes is also supported. Not surprisingly, the Constitution and the Bill of Rights receive similarly high levels of approval.

Belief in democratic values is accompanied by extraordinarily high levels of *patriotism*. More than nine in ten citizens profess pride in being an American— a cultural attribute that crosses the divides of race, class, religion, region, and gender. A similar consensus extends to the "special" character of U.S. institutions and society, with overwhelming popular support for the belief that America has a "destiny" to set a democratic example for other nations and to "expand freedom for more and more people." The national community's image is thus strongly positive for most Americans and is often experienced symbolically as reverence for the flag, for our great public buildings such as the Capitol, Washington Monument, and Lincoln Memorial, and for U.S. holidays such as the Fourth of July and Thanksgiving. Nearly three in four Americans even believe that "our system of government is the best possible system."[6]

While professions of faith in democracy and patriotism may seem vague and not very meaningful, it is significant that Americans express more of a consensus about such matters than the citizens of nearly any other country.

Individualism and Liberty

Foreign observers since the beginning of the republic until today have observed that American culture is distinctively individualistic. In contrast to the dominant cultures of continental Europe and east Asia, Americans don't generally think of their society as having an existence separate from the individuals who make it up. Americans tend to think of society as composed of independent persons, each striving for unique goals in life. Individuals are thought to be the authors of their own destinies, endowed with the capacity—even the duty—to define beliefs, thoughts, and aspirations for themselves.

Thus, individualism is often associated with the idea that U.S. citizens are born with rights to *liberty* and *freedom*. No institution, and most especially no government, can arbitrarily command us to think, speak, or act in a way that we do not believe in. For this reason, American political culture favors limits on government in order to preserve liberty of thought and action. Government can violate an individual's liberty, Americans tend to believe, only in protection of the rights of others. Even then, government coercion can occur only after strict procedures are followed. Public support for freedom and liberty, especially of speech and religion, is virtually universal in surveys taken since the 1930s.

To whom should the rights of liberty extend? The idea that all "men" are created equal is as old as the Declaration of Independence. Through a bloody Civil War and numerous movements for equal rights, *formal political equality* has been extended to all U.S. citizens, regardless of race or gender. Formal political equality does not mean that all people are born with equal talents, capacities, or intelligence. It does mean that when it comes to civil and political rights—to the vote, to free speech, to association, to a fair trial, and to religion—citizens should be treated in the same way before the law. Again, more than 85 percent of Americans support such an idea of political equality. Large majorities of Americans also believe that such basic human rights should stretch to everyone across the globe.[7]

Political and Economic Equality

Not surprisingly, a culture that values individualism is also inclined to have generally favorable beliefs about *private property*, especially if it is acquired through individual effort. Massive popular assent to the idea that the private enterprise system is generally fair has consistently been recorded in surveys.

In our political culture, favorable views of property ownership are generally associated with the broader social and political goals it supposedly helps to further. Thomas Jefferson believed that a nation of independent farmers would instill resistance to arbitrary authority; Alexander Hamilton believed that property ownership would build the nation's power and wealth. For most Americans today, owning property, especially in small or moderate amounts, is seen as a badge of achievement and a mark of character. Even most Americans who own neither a home nor a business seem to share in the political culture of property ownership—most Americans who don't own their own home want to, and many who work for others would prefer to own their own business. Most Americans rank small business entrepreneurs as one of the most respected groups.

Widespread cultural support for private property doesn't mean that most Americans support wide gaps in either wealth or income, however. In fact, in some ways cultural beliefs in property ownership are accompanied by ideas that ownership should be diffused throughout the population: Everyone should have some property, but no one should have so much that it deprives others. Thus, as we will see later and in Chapter 4, assent to private property and the free enterprise system stops short of assent for many of the practices of private corporations. Still, in comparison with the views of people in other wealthy countries, Americans are remarkable for how little they believe in **equality of condition**—leveling incomes and wealth so that nobody is either very rich or very poor.[8]

Instead of equality of condition, Americans generally support **equality of opportunity.** This belief embodies the idea that people should start their lives with the same chance to succeed or fail on their own merits. In recent years, overt racial and gender discrimination, once accepted by many Americans, has given way to the widespread idea that discrimination should not prevent people from getting an education, working at a job, or finding a home. Of course, verbal assent to such ideas is very different from practicing them. And equality of opportunity, like much in American political culture, can mean very different things to different people. For some, it means that government should help people start out with equal educational resources or compensate for disadvantages they experience because of poverty. For others, it simply is the right to succeed or fail on the basis of individual achievement alone, without government help.[9]

Community: A Country of Joiners

Except for survivalists and the Lone Ranger, Americans live in neighborhoods, families, and workplaces, where rugged individualism is neither possible nor desirable. When we care for sick relatives, work with others on a common project, or even vote, Americans express interdependence and reliance on a community for support. Even in the 1830s, the French aristocrat Alexis de Tocqueville wrote that American individualists tempered their isolation by joining numerous associations and groups. While individualism is a strong trait in our culture, so too is appreciation of and search for community.

When Americans think of community, the key element is that we join groups voluntarily. Voluntary and civic efforts at the local level are the most valued. There may be no more prized symbol of American community than the small town and its intimate, face-to-face relationships among friends and families. The New England town meeting with its equality of participation and absence of hierarchy may be the model of government that many Americans most admire.[10]

Most of us no longer live in small towns. Yet the power of American community is often evident today in the attempt to reproduce community virtues in cities and suburbs and their various neighborhoods. While Americans today are often pushed and pulled by competing obligations at work, in families, and in communities, they continue to their attachments to others as very important. Churches remain extremely popular, as do associations that help the needy, aid the schools, or organize community events.

Americans also join many associations of a more self-interested nature. More than in most other countries, state and national clubs and associations that bring together people of common lifestyles, political beliefs, or economic interests proliferate. Thus, even in a country that prizes liberty, over eight in ten Americans today say that the pursuit of the public good should be of equal or greater priority than individual freedom alone. At least in the abstract, Americans still think of themselves as a nation of joiners and participants. Positive attitudes about the idea of community and the ethics of civic responsibility are widespread.[11]

INTERPRETING POLITICAL CULTURE

The expansion and existence of a democratic political culture provides few supports for elite doubts about average Americans. It may very well be true that most Americans don't know all the players and facts about *particular* issues. But ordinary Americans do share a common vocabulary, and they reason from something like the same foundation about the basics of politics. Most support the broad outlines of a democratic system. Especially in comparison with other peoples, Americans reveal startling political commonalities. Most of us want to believe in the civic ethics and symbols of American democracy. The real question might be how well or poorly American elites and institutions embody the promise of our shared beliefs.

In the following section, three examples of divides within public opinion are presented. Each case reveals deep fractures between elite and popular democratic views of public opinion. Each shows that the apparent consensus in our political culture nonetheless leads to serious divisions when it comes to public evaluations of how well, or poorly, our economic and political institutions live up to democratic ideals. Each demands that readers consider the essential question: Are the opinions of the mass public a problem for American politics, or is the problem rather one of excessive elite power?

Civil Liberties and Political Tolerance

Ordinary people may profess support for democratic values in the abstract, but what about in practice? For the last forty years, some studies have found that rhetorical support for civil liberties simply doesn't translate into popular toleration of cultural and political minorities. These studies conclude that ordinary

Americans are intolerant of people who are culturally, politically, and racially different from the majority. In contrast, highly educated and affluent people are said to be more tolerant, expressing firm support of the Bill of Rights and its guarantee of free speech, religion, and nonconformity.[12]

Public intolerance seemed to run particularly high at the Cold War's beginnings, the so-called *McCarthy era* of the late 1940s and early 1950s. One study conducted during the era found levels of popular support of only 37 percent for freedom of speech by atheists and only 27 percent for communists. Only 6 percent believed that communists should be allowed to teach in colleges. Again, support for freedom of speech rose with level of education: Among "opinion leaders," levels of toleration were almost half again as high as they were for those with only high school diplomas. Commenting on this long-visible split between the highly educated and less educated, Thomas Dye and Harmon Ziegler argue that the "active" masses are "antidemocratic, extremist, hateful and violence prone." In contrast, political elites "give greater support to democratic values than do masses." Are these statements justified?[13]

In recent history, the notion of a split between "democratic" elites and "extremist" masses does not stand up well. It is true that elites often say they are tolerant, while ordinary citizens are more willing to restrict the speech of some. Yet in practice, ordinary people have not been the instigators or even the participants in most of the acts of recent political repression. Even during the mass hysteria of the McCarthy era of the early 1950s, surveys revealed that the public was not as concerned about communism as governmental leaders and elites were. In Senator Joseph McCarthy's home state of Wisconsin, support for his anticommunist crusade came primarily from the well-off and well-educated voters, not from working class voters with less education. In an important study, political scientist James Gibson found no evidence that the mass public favored repression of American communists. Rather, Gibson discovered that political elites in state governments were likely to push repressive legislation even when they weren't urged to do so by the public.[14]

A similar pattern was evident in the 1960s and 1970s. Then, it was the federal government and some state and local political agencies that initiated secret plans of repression against antiwar activists, the Black Panthers, and the Native American movement. The COINTELPRO (short for Counter-Intelligence and Propaganda) program during the Nixon years deployed federal agents from the FBI and CIA as plants in numerous political organizations. Few ordinary citizens were recruited in the spy network. It was the Nixon Administration, not the "great beast" of the mass public, that tried to prevent the publication of the Pentagon Papers, the secret history of governmental deception about the Vietnam War.

Because all of these operations were conducted secretly and were not subject to public debate, they could hardly have been caused, or even supported, by a tyrannical majority or a bewildered herd motivated by breezes of passion. In fact, public opinion polls taken at the time revealed widespread public opposition to such measures. Rather than underscoring the dangers of popular democracy and

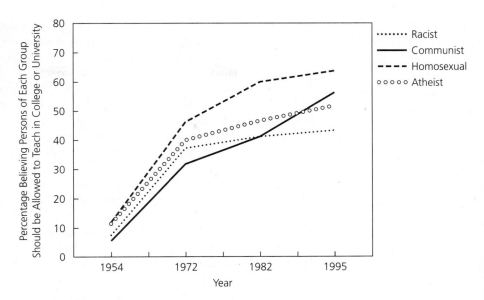

Sources: General Social Survey, 1995; Harold Stanley and Richard Niemi, *Vital Statistics on American Politics,* 5th ed. (Washington, D.C.: Congressional Quarterly Press, 1995), pp. 28–29. Copyright © 1995 by CQ Press. Used with permission.

uncontrolled public opinion, these episodes of repression seem to show that the chief dangers to democracy emerge when political elites monopolize information, spy on citizens, and narrow the range of discussion.[15]

Perhaps most important, studies of public opinion indicate how much people's attitudes can change over time. Changes in public opinion are especially common when the public is exposed to new information and to different points of view. Figure 3.1 shows that Americans are still sharply divided about the rights of specific political and cultural minorities, yet since the 1950s there has been growing support for increased tolerance. People who lived through the McCarthy era remained less tolerant of cultural and political nonconformists than younger people who came of age during and after the civil rights, feminist, and antiwar movements of the 1960s and 1970s. In the 1990s, toleration for the rights of gays and lesbians, and even popular support for special protections to prevent job and housing discrimination against them, has grown.[16]

The Confidence and Trust Gap

High levels of patriotism and support for the American form of government could indicate public support for whatever elected politicians and powerful institutions do. This, however, is hardly the case. Trust and confidence in our form of government in recent years has a healthy critical edge when it comes to the public's evaluations of elite behavior. Since the 1960s, a *confidence and trust gap* has developed around almost all government institutions and between political elites and ordinary Americans. Quite simply, the public in the last three decades is "less trusting, more cynical, more likely to perceive the government as being corrupt, and less likely to believe that the government is responsive to ordinary citizens."[17] Perhaps the greatest popular distrust is directed toward the federal government, its elected officeholders, and its personnel.

Since Richard Nixon's failed presidency, public trust in government has been high only immediately after elections, during brief military actions abroad, or in other moments when national honor seemed clearly at stake. As Figure 3.2 shows, these popularity blips hardly balance the long-term rise in political alienation.[18]

Rocked by scandal and gridlock in recent years, Congress is now the most distrusted national institution. In the wake of the "Rubbergate" check-cashing scandal of 1992, confidence in Congress sank to a record low of 18 percent. Confidence in Congress recovered only temporarily after the GOP's 1994 ascendancy. By late 1995, trust and confidence in both the Senate and House were back in the doldrums, and sank even further in 1997 in the midst of investigation of House Speaker Newt Gingrich's ethical problems. Three-fourths of Americans believed that most members of Congress were *personally* corrupt.[19]

Presidential popularity varies with particular circumstances. Yet no president since Nixon has enjoyed approval ratings above 50 percent for more than eigh-

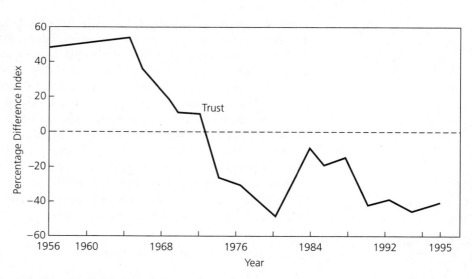

FIGURE 3.2

Individual Trust in Government, 1956–1995

Question: "How much of the time do you think you can trust the government in Washington to do what is right—just about always, most of the time, or only some of the time?" The percentage difference index is calculated by subtracting the percentage giving a cynical response from the percentage giving a trusting response.

Harold Stanley and Richard Niemi, *Vital Statistics in American Politics,* 5th ed. (Washington, D.C.: CQ Press, 1995). Copyright ©1995 by CQ Press. Used with permission.

teen continuous months. Respect for the federal bureaucracy declined steeply in the 1980s and has never recovered. Government has been tagged with spending too much on the wrong programs and too little on the right ones. It's seen as wasteful, inefficient, meddlesome, and prone to silly regulations. Republicans, and increasingly many Democrats, have tapped the confidence and trust gap for an attack on many government programs and institutions.

Although most Americans have neither trust nor confidence in the existing federal government, public opinion also indicates that Americans don't want so much to limit government in general as to restore what they see as its lost accountability to ordinary people. Even in 1994, at the height of Republican attacks on big government, the public supported increased government spending on education, health, the environment, Social Security, and even assistance to the poor and to the big cities.[20]

Why is a generally patriotic public dissatisfied with politicians and government? Drops in confidence began with the Vietnam War and were worsened by scandals such as Watergate in the 1970s, Iran-Contra in the 1980s, and the supposed financial misdeeds of President Clinton and Newt Gingrich. Dissatisfaction is also linked to the widespread popular sense that the problems of U.S. society—from homelessness to crime, drug use to declining family values—are somehow out of control.

Economic Elites and Power

The public perception that government is run for the benefit of a few big interests hints that political elites and institutions are not the only source of public disenchantment. The sense that *economic* elites and corporate America are out of touch has been extended with the decline in middle class economic security and the rise in economic inequality since the early 1970s (see Chapter 4). Widespread support for the free enterprise system cannot be mistaken for confidence in corporate America and its leaders or performance.

In 1995 and 1996, over half the public believed that the American Dream of increased social mobility, homeownership, and educational and job opportunities was a goal few could realize. By margins of 70 percent to 30 percent, the public blamed the job losses suffered in the U.S. economy on the policies of big corporations, the workings of the U.S. economic system, and the policies of political and corporate elites. Not surprisingly, by large majorities the public believed that too much economic and political power is concentrated in the hands of big business, and that corporations don't usually balance the pursuit of profit with protecting the public interest.[21]

Alongside the core belief that people who work hard get ahead, Americans nonetheless split when it comes to belief that equal opportunity actually exists in today's economy. A small majority believe that most people don't have an equal chance to succeed in life. Many jobs, including teaching, nursing, and restaurant work, are seen as socially worthy but grossly unrewarded. In contrast, according to one exhaustive study, the "average person believes that much wealth is inherited and that the wealthy receive income greatly disproportionate to their roles' contributions to society."[22]

Such results can be seen as evidence of an inconsistent public. Yet public opinion is really not contradictory on the matter of poverty. Justified or not, most Americans make distinctions between two groups: those who can work but don't versus those who seek jobs but can't find them, or who work but are not paid enough to stay out of poverty. While the first group is seen as "undeserving," Americans are empathetic and sympathetic with the far larger group—the "deserving" poor. For this group, big majorities support increased government aid for medical care, food, housing subsidies, government measures to raise wages and require employee benefits, and increased spending on education. Apparently, this distinction has been lost on the political elites in both parties who spearheaded welfare reform. The new legislation required people to work but provided no aid if people sought work but failed to find it.

What does this mix of opinions mean? For one, it confirms the idea that the confidence and trust gap between citizens and government also exists between many citizens and the owners and managers of corporate America. Most Americans voice support for the ideals of American democracy, and feel some conflict about what these ideals mean. So, too, most Americans support free enterprise, though they do not necessarily endorse corporate behavior.

IDEOLOGICAL DIVISIONS IN PUBLIC OPINION

Great turbulence exists under the placid surface of American political culture. Do Americans reason in systematic ways about politics and governmental activity, linking their beliefs about one issue with their views about another?

Specific world views that are used to form opinions about political questions are called **ideologies.** Ideologies usually originate with intellectuals and political activists, but they have often taken root in social and economic groups that forge broad political goals. In their most positive form, ideologies provide a foundation to help make sense out of apparently unrelated issues and events, bringing them together around a coherent political position. On the negative side, viewing the world "through ideological blinders" (as the saying goes) implies closed-mindedness and an unwillingness to learn from new information and experiences.

In Europe, politics has long been divided along broad ideological lines among socialists, communists, aristocratic conservatives, religious advocates, economic liberals, and even neofascists and monarchists. At least since the 1950s, scholars have claimed that these large differences don't divide Americans. It seems that European ideologies haven't traveled easily across the Atlantic.[23]

A Conservative Tide?

In place of the large ideological gulfs of European politics, American public opinion and politics are said to be divided over the lesser differences separating liberalism from conservatism. **Liberalism** features a strong belief in equality and in a government role in reducing racial, class, and gender inequities. Liberals promote government action to regulate the capitalist economy, and they defend the civil rights of cultural and political nonconformists as well as ethnic and racial minorities. In contrast, **conservatism** resists governmental spending programs that retard "natural" inequalities based on merit and achievement, generally opposes government regulation that interferes with economic growth and profit making, and calls for precise standards for private conduct. During the four decades of the Cold War, liberals were thought to be less likely to use military force and conservatives more likely to do so to fight communism, but this was not always the case.

American liberalism and conservatism share much in common despite important differences. During the Cold War, both liberals and conservatives backed the national security state and the projection of America as a supreme world power. Both have come to agree about programs like Social Security and Medicare. Both support the broad outlines of the American capitalist system and the private ownership of land, factories, and assets.

For a long time pollsters have been asking people whether they are liberals or conservatives. The responses are summarized in Table 3.2. Because the table reveals a slow but unmistakable rise in the percentage of people who identify themselves as conservatives, these results can and have been interpreted as confirmation of growing support for conservative public policies, groups, and politicians. After all, self-proclaimed conservatives have risen by 6 percent in the last two decades, while liberals are 4 percent less numerous. Combined with the election victories of conservative Republicans in the 1980s and 1990s and a public agenda hostile to big government, this interpretation seems to make sense. In addition, analysts have found that increases in the conservative ranks have been great among so-called political sophisticates—people who know what conservative ideology is and who use it in their understanding of public issues.[24]

Yet there are reasons to doubt a conservative ideological trend. When other surveys probe further, they have found that a quarter of the public declines

TABLE 3.2 Liberals and Conservatives in U.S. Public Opinion		% Liberal	% Moderate	% Conservative	% Don't Know
	1973	31	36	29	6
	1978	26	36	31	5
	1985	24	37	35	4
	1991	26	39	27	4
	1995	27	35	35	3

Harold Stanley and Richard Niemi, *Vital Statistics in American Politics,* 5th ed. (Washington, D.C.: CQ Press, 1995). Copyright ©1995 by CQ Press. Used with permission.

to identify with any ideological label. Of the three quarters who do identify themselves as liberals, moderates, or conservatives, over one-third choose the moderate label. Moreover, among people who label themselves conservatives, there is little consistency about how they define what the term means or how it applies to specific public policies. For example, a third of self-declared conservatives agree with two ideas considered "liberal": that "the government should provide more services even if it means an increase in spending" and that "abortion is a matter of choice." In 1994, a whopping 65 percent of conservatives believed that the United States "should spend less on defense." Liberals are somewhat more consistent than conservatives appear to be in their definition and support for generally recognized liberal policies and politicians. Still in all, even as identification with liberalism has waned and with conservatism has grown, the public's views of social and economic issues and policies have not changed much. Even during the conservative Reagan and Bush years of the 1980s and early 1990s, the public held to many liberal positions about foreign policy and government spending.[25]

Since there is confusion about the two terms among most citizens and there are so many self-proclaimed moderates, it might be thought that many people are centrists with views that are somewhere in between the two ideologies. But it turns out that moderates don't have consistent or similar views, either. For example, many moderates favor government health insurance (a liberal position) but also strongly favor the death penalty for capital crimes (a supposedly conser-

vative position). Being a moderate may mean mixing liberal and conservative positions. Perhaps the easiest conclusion is that, for the most part, most Americans just don't think about politics in consistent ideological terms. While most people understand something about what liberalism and conservatism mean, they largely don't use these terms themselves when they give their answers to survey questions.

There is another phenomenon at work here: Elites and the politically knowledgeable think of themselves as liberals or conservatives, but when they explain their positions to the public, they often ignore the terms or muddy their meaning. Ronald Reagan, by most accounts the most conservative president since the 1920s, presented himself to the American public as the rightful heir of Franklin Roosevelt, America's most liberal president. A self-proclaimed conservative, Reagan rolled up the biggest budget deficit in history through an enormous expansion of federal spending on the military. Against traditional conservative doctrine, Reagan lowered taxes even as the deficit grew.[26]

Beyond Liberalism and Conservatism: New Ideologies

We can draw two possible conclusions about the role of ideology in public opinion. One is that most people just don't think very systematically, consistently, or coherently about politics. This view confirms elite democratic expectations by blaming the people for ignorance and inconsistency. Elites and expert commentators are therefore needed to make sense of the real choices and issues faced in politics. Facing a fickle public with contradictory opinions, elites rightly reserve to themselves the real ideological debate and decisions. But there is an alternative, popular democratic explanation of the same phenomena: It is that ordinary people do bring systematic beliefs to real politics. It just so happens that their systematic beliefs have little to do with the traditional liberal-conservative split.

In *Why Americans Hate Politics*, journalist E. J. Dionne argues that both contemporary liberalism and conservatism distort and misrepresent the beliefs of ordinary Americans. Public opinion, Dionne states, was once less a set of abstract ideologies or random choices than an expression of the positive, concrete identities forged through debates and discussions in city neighborhoods, small towns, factories, schools, and families. Today, elites ignore these community contexts, preferring instead to appeal to citizens' fears and cynicism. According to Dionne, elite ideologues pose "false choices . . . that make it extremely difficult for the obvious preferences of the American people to express themselves. . . . We are encouraging an either/or politics based on ideological preconceptions rather than a both/and politics based on ideas."[27]

What are these ideas and preferences of ordinary Americans? Dionne is reluctant to put a new ideological label on them. But other analysts have referred to a deeply engrained **populism** in American public opinion. Populist beliefs are particularly strong in the middle and working classes. They include hostility to all concentrations of economic and political power, and a belief that institutions work best when they are simple, understandable, and accountable to the basic needs of people who work hard and play by the rules. Most Americans, according to Dionne, don't believe that either government or corporate America today operates according to such principles. They don't believe that enough people, rich and poor, really do play by the rules and take personal responsibility for their actions. And they don't believe that exclusively liberal or conservative ideas will help to resolve the central problems of U.S. society.[28]

Whether or not Dionne is entirely right, his argument raises an important issue. Most people may very well think systematically about politics. But the existing elite divisions between traditional conservatism and liberalism don't capture this reality. If Americans do indeed think systematically about politics, where do their views come from?

WHERE DOES PUBLIC OPINION ORIGINATE?

Public opinion isn't formed out of thin air. We are not born with a ready-made political culture, a distinct political ideology, or precise ideas about human nature, the individual, equality, or democratic government. Opinions develop through a complex interaction among people's life experiences—in their families, at school, at work, at leisure—and their experiences as American citizens, men or women, members of racial groups or of distinct religious or ethnic communities. Public opinion is also forged in response to national and international events—scandals, wars, economic depressions—and people's collective and individual experiences of each of them. The formation of individual opinions is thus a lifelong process, often involving choice, change, and learning.

Chapter 6 discusses the mass media's impact on people's specific opinions. Here we concentrate on the broader views of politics and public life and how they are shaped.

Political Socialization

Basic views of the political and social order and of other people are formed quite early in life through a process called **political socialization.** In the impressionable years through age eighteen, basic political orientations concerning race, class, ideology, nationhood, and democracy are formed. Most of these orientations help to form specific opinions later on in adulthood. Most children and adolescents, however, lack opinions about specific government actions and policies.

Even if politics isn't discussed around the dinner table, the family is an important shaper of people's opinions later in life. Through parents and relatives, children learn basic orientations toward neighbors, strangers, the world of work, school, and government. The learning that happens may be indirect: Observing a parent or a relative struggling with tax forms or a period of unemployment probably has important but subtle effects on later political attitudes. Religious life may teach forms of morality that are later applied by children to their views about other races, groups, and believers. Family also has an important, but not decisive, influence in the later choice of a political party. Six in ten adult Americans develop the same allegiances to a political party (or nonallegiance, in the case of independents) as their parents. However, there is reason to believe that the political views of parents do less to shape children's later attitudes than they once did. One reason may be the role of mass media, schools, and peers. In most families, politics is not discussed all that much. Even in the area of inherited party affiliation, the family is apparently a weaker influence than it used to be: in the last fifty years, party affiliations have simply become less important to people's identities (see Chapter 7).[29]

Schooling is the second shaper of political orientations, and especially of the broad features of political culture. For most people, schools provide the initial exposure to people of different races, creeds, and religions. Grade school children learn basic civic rituals such as the pledge of allegiance and are introduced to highly favorable renditions of U.S. history, complete with biographies of national heroes and heroines. Science and social studies curricula currently teach students about environmental questions and geography. In recent years, multicultural curricula have been designed to teach that America is a land of racial and ethnic diversity. Political socialization in schools also helps to reproduce the social order. For example, numerous studies confirm that noncollege-bound students are treated very differently by teachers and school authorities, reinforcing their working class status. Often, the treatment is subtle: Routines and regimens in different schools resemble the kind of workplace environment teachers believe their students will face.

Schooling's specific effects on precollege-age children is unclear. What is clear is that schools instill the core beliefs of the American creed. By the time people reach their twenties, some of their political preferences are already formed. Yet schooling is not always just a way of transmitting the status quo: The traditional ways in which future college students were "socialized" in the 1950s did not prevent widespread dissent and protest from emerging on college campuses in the 1960s.[30]

Social Differences and American Public Opinion

Political socialization occurs in families and schools. But what seems to matter even more are people's identities and their perceived place in the social hierarchy. Shared conditions, histories, and experiences generate opinion similarities and divisions. How the world works is very much linked to people's social class, race, gender, and religion.

Social Class Differences. Since the advent of mass democracy, public schooling, and the Industrial Revolution in the nineteenth and twentieth centuries, **social class** has often been the major dividing line both in public opinion and in politics in most democratic countries. Scholars and activists disagree about the definition of social class. Is *class* simply a group with higher or lower income and wealth? Or is it a broader term that includes collective experiences concerning where and how people work, how they are educated, how much schooling they have, and how much control they have over their own lives? [31]

Chapter 4 presents evidence supporting the broader definition of social class. What the upper classes of owners, managers, and many professionals do with their money and how they use their power in economic and political institutions have enormous effects on democracy, culture, and the life chances of others in society. The majority of citizens neither own nor control these institutions. That important fact influences the way they think about politics and other aspects of life. Indeed, it would be surprising if social class did not have effects on people's opinions and political orientations. [32]

As it turns out, social class does make a difference in American public opinion, more so now than at any time since World War II. People with incomes below the median, who have not completed college, and who labor in nonprofessional blue or white collar jobs feel more vulnerable to the workings of the corporate economy than wealthy professionals and managers. They are more likely to favor governmental programs that create jobs, establish standards of occupational safety and health, and prevent corporate downsizing and workplace shutdowns. They are more dissatisfied with conditions in the workplace and are generally favorable to measures that promote universal medical insurance, government aid to education, and tax rates based on the ability to pay. People with incomes and levels of formal education below the median are more concerned about high unemployment than about high inflation. They are also more likely to think favorably about labor unions and unfavorably about corporate behavior than are people with the highest incomes. The gap between working class and upper class respondents is particularly large when it comes to support for Social Security, unemployment insurance, and child care.

Class divides American public opinion. Yet it just doesn't make as much of a difference in opinions as it does in other countries. Working class people elsewhere might be surprised at the relatively high numbers of low-income Americans who oppose many measures that would redistribute wealth and power downwards, and limit corporate behavior. If American wage earners don't always think like a class, the upper classes generally do. Among owners and managers, there is scant support for measures to redistribute wealth and income.

While social class divisions about economic equality are less pronounced in America than elsewhere, the classes are very much divided in two areas: Upper-class Americans have a strong sense that their participation in politics matters, and they have high levels of *political efficacy*. They also place more trust and confidence in the rules of the political system. The contrast with poor and working class Americans is extreme. These groups have low political efficacy; they believe that their participation doesn't make much of a difference, and they tend to have much less trust in politicians and economic institutions. In Chapter 5, we explore further this class gap. Significant variations in voter turnout and power result from the class divide.[33]

Racial Differences. The prominence of racial divisions is one reason that American public opinion is less divided by social class than it is elsewhere. Low income and vulnerable Americans of all races have often been separated from each other through the promotion of racial divisions.

Nearly thirty years after the civil rights revolution, some progress has been made in limiting racial divisions in public opinion. Still, whites and African Americans differ on many, though not all, important political questions. Although the divisions between whites of European origin, Latinos, and Asian Americans are also significant, the black-white split remains more pronounced than any other in public opinion.[34]

Most prominent of all is division about the nature and remedies for racial discrimination. At one level, great strides have been made over the last three or four decades. At least in public opinion, on questions concerning equal treatment of blacks and whites in the major public spheres of life, there has been a strong and steady movement of white attitudes from denial to affirmation of equality. Less than 5 percent of whites favor racial segregation in neighborhoods, workplaces, schools, or other public facilities. Whites reject racist organizations like the Ku Klux Klan in numbers as high as African Americans, and large majorities say they would vote for qualified African Americans for the presidency and lesser offices. Very few whites say they oppose sending their own children to schools where black children attend, working in the same office as blacks, or eating in the same restaurants.[35]

Although both whites and blacks oppose segregation in principle, significant differences remain about the sources and remedies for racial discrimination. About three-quarters of whites think that African Americans are more likely than whites to prefer living on welfare. In addition, overwhelming white opposition to segregation should not be read as unqualified support for integration. Whites almost unanimously find no problem with schools, neighborhoods, and workplaces where *some* blacks are present. White support for integration decreases when blacks equal or outnumber whites.

Moreover, although big majorities of whites oppose discrimination and support general laws that do so, only a small plurality support specific governmental measures that compel integration in the workplace or in neighborhoods. Most whites are particularly opposed to so-called "race-targeted" programs such as affirmative action. Only a fifth to a quarter of white adults favor preferential admissions for African-American college applicants, and only a tenth support preferences for blacks in hiring and promotion.[36]

The views of African Americans about such matters are far different. Most African Americans, from painful personal experience, believe that racial discrimination is an everyday occurence, not a historical curiosity. As Table 3.3 shows, the racial gap is as large as 50 percent when it comes to views about

TABLE 3.3			**Whites**	**African Americans**
White and African-American Opinions about Race-Targeted Programs	Federal spending should be increased to assist blacks	Favor	19	69
		Oppose	24	2
		Stay same	57	29
	Blacks should be given preferential hiring	Favor	15	62
		Oppose	86	37
	Openings should be reserved for black college students	Favor	27	78
		Oppose	73	22

Steven Tuch and Lee Sigelman, "Race, Class, and Black White Differences in Social Policy Views," in *Understanding Public Opinion*, B. Narrander & C. Wilcox, eds. (Washington, D.C.: CQ Press, 1996), pp. 48–49. Copyright © 1996 by Congressional Quarterly Press. Adapted with permission.

race-targeted programs. Yet it is worth noting that support for race-targeted programs has even diminished somewhat among African Americans in the last twenty years. Apparently, more blacks now believe either that government hasn't been very effective or that measures to redress past racial discrimination are no longer necessary.

Apart from opinions about race and race relations, African Americans and whites differ most in their opinions about policies to reduce economic inequalities. African Americans of all incomes are much more likely to believe that many features of the U.S. political economy are unjust not only for people of their own race, but for many whites and other racial minorities as well. Unique in the American population, high-income African Americans express opinions about economic equality that are remarkably similar to those of low-income blacks. They're even as likely as low-income whites to challenge economic inequalities.[37]

Given these opinion differences and similarities, how important is race as a dividing line in public opinion? One aspiration of popular democrats has been to bridge racial gaps through greater sharing of the nation's economic resources. Yet many poor and working class whites may be less supportive of such goals because they associate some government poverty programs with favoritism towards blacks. When it comes to social programs that seem to benefit people of all races, low-income whites, blacks, and Latinos often do express similar views.[38]

Gender Differences. Since the early 1970s, the appearance of a **gender gap** in public opinion and in voting behavior (see Chapter 7) has sparked a massive amount of commentary. The birth of the feminist movement clearly has something to do with opinion differences based on gender. But much research indicates that the increasing economic independence of women and the perceived economic vulnerability of both genders have also shaped the gap. The changing role of parenting has also contributed to the gap, as men and women have developed different expectations about their obligations to children, home, and the workplace. The gender gap is thus not only about women changing their opinions, but about change in men's views of the world as well.

Perhaps surprisingly, the gender gap is *least* evident in opinions about gender equality and womens' rights. Majorities of both men and women favor legal abortions in many circumstances and oppose abortion on demand by narrow margins. Nor were there differences between men and women over the proposed Equal Rights Amendment (ERA) in the 1970s and 1980s. Although the amendment failed, similar majorities of both sexes supported it. The opinions of men and women do differ on other feminist issues, however: Women express more support for affirmative action, equal pay in the workplace, and legislation regarding sexual harassment.

The gender gap widens over policies on the use of force and violence by the military, the state, criminals, or in the family. Women are much more likely to oppose the use of military force, whether it be in Iraq, Somalia, Haiti, or Bosnia. A majority of women are in favor of the death penalty, but they are less supportive of it than men. Women favor gun control by margins of 10 to 15 percent over men. A majority of women, but a minority of men, believe that spanking a child is always wrong.

Women are also somewhat more likely to favor increased support for the weaker members of society, whether they be the ill, the elderly, the homeless, the working poor, or, most particularly, children. They are more inclined than men to favor higher governmental spending for education, the environment, health care, and social welfare. And they are more likely to favor laws that curb the use of pornography.[39]

In recent years, the gender gap has been most evident during elections. Put simply, in voting behavior men have become much more Republican over the past twenty-five years while women have become slightly more Democratic. The biggest divide separates white married men and unmarried working women; here the gap is nearly 20 percent in the 1992 and 1996 presidential contests. Similar disparities have developed in the House and Senate elections. In 1996, women favored Bill Clinton by 9 percent over Robert Dole, while men split evenly between the two.[40]

Religious Differences. If religious belief is a virtue, the United States is the most virtuous of any wealthy country. An impressive three-quarters of the American population claims that religion is very or somewhat important in their lives; nearly half of American adults pray every day. Only 10 percent of Americans profess no religious faith. American religious believers are highly diverse. Mainline, fundamentalist, and charismatic Protestants, Catholics, Jews, and Moslems create a rich mosaic and a volatile opinion mix. Given the visibility and diversity of religious life in the United States, it is no surprise that religion has an effect on people's opinions.

In current political dialogue, religion is most often seen as a battleground of what 1996 Republican presidential candidate Pat Buchanan called the "culture wars." In this view, battles between advocates of traditional family values and their secular humanist detractors have replaced the older conflicts of class and race. Is there any evidence that divisions about abortion, school prayer, homosexuality, and single parenthood dominate public opinion? To some extent, church attendance, especially if the congregation is white, fundamentalist, and Protestant, is associated with opposition to abortion, pornography, and homosexuality and advocacy of mandatory school prayer and private school vouchers. The biggest gaps on such social issues occur between active white fundamentalist Protestants on one hand, and Jews, white mainline Protestants (Episcopalians, Presbyterians, Lutherans, and Methodists), and religious nonbelievers on the other. On such hot button issues, Catholics stand somewhere in the middle of these large religious divides. Fundamentalist white Protestants remain a distinct minority in American politics, but their growing numbers indicate that they will remain a potent and generally conservative force.

When it comes to economic issues, white fundamentalist Protestants are more likely to take conservative positions as well. They register much greater resistance to domestic spending on health care and to income and wealth redistribution than do mainline Protestants, their black fundamentalist cousins, Catholics, and Jews. Evangelical Christianity is one case where religion has most decidedly acted to reduce class divisions, largely because divisions of opinion about morality are generally deemed more important than economic questions. As a result, even low-income white evangelical Protestants have provided majority support for conservative politicians and policies.[41]

Still in all, the relationship of growing evangelical Christianity with a general conservative trend in public opinion is less than clear. Catholics seem the most torn over questions of traditional family values and toleration, but they show little movement towards the positions or voting patterns of fundamentalist Christians. Catholics remain generally more liberal on both culture and economic questions than are evangelical Christians. For almost all those who are not evangelical Christians, the important point may be that the Christian Right's cultural agenda is just less important than other political questions.

Bewildered Herd or Divided Publics?

However Americans feel about each other and whatever their views about politics, the divisions detailed here contradict the idea that most Americans decide on public issues by flipping a coin. Americans are united about many questions, but their gender, class, and race do result in rational differences about policies. In real life, Americans live as members of groups and communities, not as isolated individuals. Thus, the differences they reveal are longstanding and persistent, not driven by sudden and irrational shifts in mood. What changes we do see—from the emergence of more racially tolerant attitudes among the white population to increasing divides between men and women on various issues—seem to emerge slowly. Far from the bewildered herd of elite democratic fears, the public and its opinions tend to follow the lines of power and inequality in American society.

HOW PUBLIC OPINION IS ORGANIZED

No matter how rational and rooted it may be, public opinion goes unheard if it is not expressed and is powerless if it is not organized. But who does the organizing? If opinion is organized only by elites, or if the information available to the public is narrow and limited, than public opinion is merely an echo, not a voice. On the other hand, if the public has the means to get together, deliberate, and share a wide variety of information, then it fulfills the promise of popular democracy. In Chapters 6, 7, and 8 the important roles of the mass media, political parties, and electoral campaigns are discussed with these questions in mind. Here we show that inequalities in power matter in how public opinion is organized, and that these inequalities can be overcome.

When Public Opinion Matters

Public opinion is sometimes described as a sleeping giant. On important occasions, the giant rouses itself slowly, discovers its own energy and power, and swings into action. The civil rights, women's, and antiwar movements of the 1960s at first faced formidable barriers. Participants were told that they were out of the mainstream, that their views were rejected by most Americans, that people didn't care. For a while, elites could simply ignore these movements. Yet with patience, time, and discussion, each movement came to organize public opinion, carving out for itself a limited public space where its ideas could be disseminated.

Events helped, but so too did the new information and education produced by each movement. The civil rights movement based itself on the strength of the African-American church. The antiwar movement drew from the intellectual resources of college campuses, veterans' groups, and also churches. The feminist movement developed its own networks through women's health clinics and college campuses. Ultimately, each movement experimented with new ways to bridge the gaps between itself and broader public opinion. Each movement eventually sparked change not only in public attitudes, but also in how people related to government and each other. The details of how public opinion can organize itself in these ways are revealed in the accompanying feature box about the nuclear power debate. In this case, public opinion came to be treated with respect because it overcame the barriers posed by elite democracy itself.

The Potential Tyranny of Polls

These days, polls are the most obvious way in which separate individuals are brought together to form a public. Even the most casual observer of American culture soon discovers that ours is a poll-driven society. The public's opinions on everything from the softness of toilet paper to the quality of marriages is tested. In 1996, President Clinton apparently decided to go white-water rafting because a poll revealed that it would improve his election prospects. This book is no exception. Much of the evidence in this chapter comes from public opinion

MAKING A DIFFERENCE

The Battle Against Nukes

In the 1950s and 1960s, the groups and institutions supporting American nuclear power plants seemed unstoppable. A powerful and united elite coalition dominated public opinion about the subject. In the 1950s, President Eisenhower's "Atoms for Peace" program began. By the 1960s and early 1970s, support for nuclear power stretched to succeeding presidents, the leadership of both congressional political parties, a host of scientific experts, the mass media, and America's largest private utilities and corporations.

Americans were told that nuclear power would be cheap, safe, and unlimited—that it was the "modern way." During the oil crises and energy embargoes of the 1970s, nuclear power was sold as the path to national energy independence. As late as the Nixon administration, there was no public debate about nuclear power generation. In 1972, the Atomic Energy Commission confidently predicted that by the year 2000 most of America's electricity would be generated through nuclear power plants.

A quarter of a century later, nuclear power and its elite supporters have been stopped dead in their tracks by grassroots activists and their increased ability to inform and educate the mass public. Not

a single plant has been planned in twenty years, and some existing plants failed to open even after they were built, thanks to massive public protests. How did the passive and docile public opinion of the 1950s and 1960s transform itself into a solid political consensus opposing the expansion and use of nuclear power?

The public opinion transformation started among activists fighting specific plants. In the mid-1970s, antinuke New Yorkers and Californians stopped three different plants from being constructed. Activists in many states went on to question the credentials and findings of the experts hired by government and private utilities by revealing new information about the poor safety records and expense of nuclear power plants. By 1975, antinuclear groups took their fight to the ballot boxes, proposing referenda to ban nuclear power expansion in seven states. Private utilities outspent the antinuclear groups by 50 to 1, but the battles helped put nuclear power and conservation on the national political agenda. From then on, local officials could be pressured into thinking critically about the subject.

In April 1979, the Three Mile Island (TMI) nuclear power plant nearly melted down, and radiation

surveys. A reasonable question, then, is whether polls express or distort public opinion.

George Gallup, the founder of systematic public opinion polling, wrote in 1940 that his invention "means that the nation is literally in one great room. . . . After one hundred and fifty years, we return to the town meeting. This time the whole nation is within the doors.[43] Like many of his successors, Gallup assumed that good surveys are simply a scientific tool to discover what the public really thinks and wants. As Table 3.4 shows, most surveys conducted by academics and by reputable national organizations such as the Gallup Organization or the

spewed into small Pennsylvania towns nearby. The event, combined with the disastrous accident in the USSR's Ukraine seven years later, turned American public opinion against nuclear power. But even before TMI and Chernobyl, growing public support for energy conservation and doubts about public utilities and government reports had turned support for nuclear power into a minority position. In the late 1980s, the Shoreham nuclear plant in Long Island, New York, was refused a license after months of protest by local suburbanites who pressured state and federal officials to block the Shoreham plant. Unlike Japan, France, Italy, and other rich countries, in the United States an active public opinion, infused with energy by strong grassroots movements, successfully blocked efforts in the 1980s and 1990s to build more plants.

Today, the nuclear power debate is hardly front and center in U.S. politics. But the debate rages on, especially because the nuclear plants that still operate have to find a place to dump their radioactive wastes. After years of conflict, the Federal Department of Energy picked Yucca Mountain, Nevada, as the national "repository." In response, a unique coalition of ranchers, Las Vegans, and Native American tribes such as the Shoshone and Paiute have banded together to fight the federal government's plans to locate a national radioactive waste dump in the salt domes underneath the mountain.

They've successfully convinced Nevada's congressional delegation, once solidly pro-nuclear, to become the chief critics of nuclear power in Congress. Today, the Yucca Mountain site is still subject to legal challenges—it's thought that the nation's wastes could leak, destroying most of Nevada in the process.

Opposing the dump has catalyzed a unique environmental and peace coalition that's taken on a wide range of issues, from public ownership of Nevada's electricity to accounting for high levels of radioactivity at Nevada's famed nuclear test site where generations of nuclear bombs were first exploded.

Can American public opinion be changed? Three decades ago, opposition to nuclear testing or nuclear power plants was considered odd and even treasonous. Today, in southern Nevada, it's a source of political vitality. Bill Rosse, a Shoshone and longtime antinuclear activist in "Citizens Alert," comments after twenty years of work: "I feel like the Creator [has] been keeping me here for a purpose. Probably this is what the purpose is, what I'm doing now."

Sources: William Freudenberg and Eugene Rosa, *Public Reactions to Nuclear Power* (Boulder, Colo.: Westview Press, 1984); Charles Piller, *The Fail Safe Society* (New York: W. W. Norton, 1991); *Citizens Alert: An Alternative Information Source,* August, 1996. This material compiled by Joni Ang, Sarah Lawrence College, 1997.

CBS/*New York Times* poll strive to use neutral and professional methods. Much care is taken to conform to widely accepted standards of sampling, question wording, and answer coding.

To be sure, not all polls nowadays conform to such rigorous standards. Many advocacy polls sponsored by interest groups often stretch or ignore scientific methods in order to conform to the political agenda of the people who pay for them. But for the polling industry, professional standards serve to undermine the credibility of such surveys. From this perspective, the chief problem with polling is limited to its abuses, not its uses.

TABLE 3.4

Methods and Problems in Public Opinion Sampling

Formulating the questions: Polls conducted by professional organizations and academics strive for "objectivity" in question wording. Questions cannot be vaguely worded, nor should a hidden or obvious bias be contained in them. Moreover, pollsters often err in designing questions and eliciting answers about issues that respondents neither know, care, or have thought about. In one way or another, questions must be carefully tested to avoid bias and forced choice. In practice, both problems plague many polls.

Drawing a sample: Through various means, pollsters try to select a small number of people to interview that can be said to represent the opinions of a much larger group. Population sampling is the science of developing an exact and small replica of an entire population in terms of income, education, race, gender, religion, and other social characteristics.

Selecting an interview format: Modern pollsters may contact interviewees by mail, phone, or in person. While polling by mail is the cheapest method, it is the most unreliable because it "oversamples" those people who are strongly interested in responding to questionnaires. Personal interviews used to be the major way that pollsters contacted their sample, but they are very expensive. Most political polls today are conducted by telephone through random digit dialing.

Interpreting the results: If mistakes are made in any of the above areas (and they often are), poll results are unreliable. If respondents have been forced to choose between alternatives about which they know or care little, if random digit dialing excludes poor people or people who work during certain parts of the day, or if questions are biased or vague, then poll results can be faulted.

Yet there may be a broader problem with surveys that goes beyond their scientific rigor. The very act of asking certain questions of separate and distinct individuals and then aggregating all the responses creates public opinion where it otherwise wouldn't exist. In short, polling *organizes* the public in a particular way that it wouldn't on its own. As such, polling is not only a way of recording opinions, but of shaping the political agenda.

What effects might this practice have? Gallup talked of polling as if it were a town meeting. But asking individuals their views from a questionnaire is not at all the same as a meeting. The people interviewed in a typical opinion survey don't know each other, haven't talked with each other, and thus do not necessarily share what Susan Herbst calls a "coherent group identity."[43] They can't listen to others or participate in a debate before they answer, nor can they control how their responses are recorded and used. Nor do people who are surveyed have control over which questions are asked. In most polls, they have no way of telling the sponsors that they think the questions being asked are not the right ones. Consequently, they can't give the open-ended and qualified answers that constitute independent and thoughtful public opinion in a supposedly democratic society.

Therefore, insofar as polls organize opinion by standing in for the real discussion characteristic of the democratic debate, they can be deceptive and manipulative. They become useful to elites in their competition for advantage or, as in advocacy polls, for the interests that have the money and clout to finance them. In short, polls may force people to choose between equally unacceptable alternatives. By asking a particular question and not another, polls may artificially increase what scholars call the *salience*, or priority, of what they do ask, and may reduce a strongly felt minority opinion to a marginal one.

Using the same questions as the professionals, reporter Christopher Hitchens tried to conduct his own telephone poll during the 1992 New Hampshire presidential primary campaign between then-candidate Clinton and former Senator Paul Tsongas. Here's the transcript of Hitchens's experience:

> The first three voters hung up in my face when I announced myself to be from the "New Hampshire Poll." Making contact on my fourth call, I quickly established that the respondent was over eighteen and a likely Democratic voter. As I read her the list of candidates and asked how she "leaned," she said it was equal between Clinton and Tsongas.
>
> There was no real provision for that answer.
>
> "Who do you think has the best likelihood of beating George Bush?"
>
> "Who knows? It's only January. There might be another of his wars between now and November."
>
> No designated space for that answer, either. I was trembling when I hung up, and trembling too when I thought to what mush her spirited and warm answers would be reduced.[44]

The essential power of such polls is in how, when, and in what context the results are used. In the preceding case, candidate Bill Clinton used the ambivalent responses of 1992 New Hampshire polls to claim that his candidacy had momentum and that he had overcome public doubts about his personal behavior. But all that many surveys really record are short-lived changes and spasms of mood. Instead of probing the deeper thoughts and reasons people might have, spot surveys record short-term sentiments and attitudes about hot button issues. What's missed in all the hoopla are the deeper concerns.

In response to such criticisms, University of Texas political scientist James Fishkin organized the first nationwide **deliberative poll** in 1996. Fishkin's idea was simple: gather a representative sample of Americans in one place, present to them different views on important public matters, let them discuss their views, and *then* survey the results. The results were instructive: After discussion with others, people's views about matters ranging from foreign aid to school funding altered. Exposed to participation and debate, people became more tolerant of other points of view and more inclined to seek consensus.

In a way, though, deliberative polling helps to reveal the limits of public opinion surveys and the barriers democratic public opinion faces. The public can't be reduced to a representative sample in a democracy because democracy by its nature involves *mass* participation. What kind of democracy is it that involves flying Americans to a professor's home town so that they can have a real dialogue?[45]

Manufacturing Public Opinion

The power of polls to organize public opinion is subtle. More direct are those occasions when government elites shape public opinion through lies and distortion. In such circumstances, elites literally *manufacture* public opinion. This has been particularly true when the U.S. government engaged in sudden military actions abroad. In 1983, 1989, and 1991, respectively, U.S. troops invaded the island nation of Grenada, overthrew Manuel Noriega in Panama, and mounted an attack on Iraq. In each invasion, the Pentagon tightly controlled access by the press to the battlefield. In each, the U.S. government reserved the right to censor photos. In each, U.S. victories were quick and achieved with few American deaths. In each, congressional critics were largely silent because U.S. forces were engaged in combat and had to be supported.

After each incursion, public opinion registered quick and lopsided support for the president's actions, even though (or perhaps because) most Americans knew little about the involved countries or the history of U.S. foreign policy regarding them. In 1991, George Bush broke all polling records when he achieved approval ratings of 90 percent in the wake of the Gulf War.[46] Such instances cast doubt on the democratic character of public opinion, even as they reveal the darkest side of elite democracy. In all three cases, the president and the executive branch developed initiatives in secret, insulated from a nonexistent democratic debate.

Yet the ability to manufacture public opinion and sustain it over time is limited. Public opinion tends to be much more lopsided about foreign policy than about domestic matters because the public is less knowledgeable about the former than the latter. However, given time to reflect and exposure to new facts, public opinion about military intervention can change. A year after the Persian Gulf War, people developed doubts about the venture. George Bush's popularity as commander in chief soared during the war but evaporated in its wake. Democratic public opinion needs time to mature.[47]

Distorting Public Opinion

Public opinion can become distorted when it is not well organized from the bottom up. *Distortion* means that elites are able to organize and then use favorable public opinion to achieve their own political agenda, even though the public is only dimly aware of what that agenda is.

The story of the 1994 Republican Revolution is an excellent case of distortion. In the summer of 1994, one observer summarized the prevailing mood in public opinion as "angry, self-absorbed, and politically unanchored. . . . Interviews with

American voters . . . find no clear direction in the public's political thinking other than frustration with the current system, and an eager responsiveness to alternative political solutions and appeals."[48]

Republican pollsters and strategists, using polling data and focus groups, crafted and tested a ten-point electoral program that they dubbed the "Contract with America." Almost all Republican congressional candidates endorsed the contract, pledging to implement it if elected. In the fall election, the GOP gained new majorities in the House and Senate, and new House Speaker Newt Gingrich claimed that angry voters had delivered a firm mandate for the contract's provision. Others opined that 1994 "was the beginning of the end of liberalism." Using the contract and the supposedly high public support for it, in 1995 the GOP launched initiatives to roll back the federal government's power to enforce environmental regulations, tax capital gains made from the sale of stock at a lower rate, and limit citizens' ability to sue businesses. In late 1995, claiming public support, the congressional GOP shut down the federal government in an effort to force President Clinton to agree to budget and tax cuts.

There was only one problem with the Republicans' supposed mandate, embodied in the contract: Public opinion had been distorted. On election day, 1994, seven in ten voters hadn't even heard of the Contract with America. Of those that were aware of it, more opposed than supported it. Even those who supported it could only name a few of the contract's provisions. Only by the end of 1995 did opinion congeal, generally in opposition to the contract's increasingly controversial details. By the 1996 election, the apparent popular mandate had evaporated, and nervous Republicans generally ignored it in their congressional campaigns.

The conditions necessary for the creation or distortion of public opinion reveal something about effective democracy. In the case of foreign invasions, the public was manipulated by blind appeals to patriotism and government contol of most information. The public had virtually no time to reflect and no facts or competing opinions to judge. The distorted mandate for the Contract with America is more complex. Public opinion was not well informed about the contract but remained passive and inactive even as its provisions became known. In the voting booth, those who participated in the election preferred Republicans, but not for the reasons trumpeted by winning House Republicans. When the public is not listening or not organized, a false mandate can be claimed and debate on issues can be reduced to empty clichés.

Yet in both instances, public opinion eventually woke up. Given time to reflect and subsequent access to a fuller range of information, unqualified and manufactured support for government actions dwindled. Given access to a raging debate and alternative arguments, public opinion became more informed, substantive, and divided. When there is debate and time for public opinion to get itself together, public opinion fulfills its democratic promise. Under these circumstances, public opinion can have important effects on changing and influencing governmental policies. Indeed, one study shows that the public's general policy preferences get enacted about two-thirds of the time.[49]

CONCLUSION: THE SENSIBLE PUBLIC

American public opinion is not always right, is frequently ill informed about policy details, and is especially subject to "sudden breezes of passion" when aroused by dramatic and rapid presidential acts abroad. Yet there is little evidence to support the elite democratic view of the public as a bewildered herd. Most of the public holds coherent beliefs, many of which are rooted in institutions such as families and schools, as well as in personal experiences and other identities. Moreover, public opinion responds to new information and new events by modifying its views, albeit slowly. Public opinion reveals its best qualities when it is free to organize and is exposed to many sources of information about politics. Contrary to many elite democrats' views, it is elites themselves who are the most likely to debase public opinion through manipulation and distortion of its messages.

KEY TERMS

public opinion
political culture
equality of condition
equality of opportunity
ideology
liberalism

conservatism
populism
political socialization
social class
gender gap
deliberative poll

SUGGESTED READINGS

David Croteau, *Politics and the Class Divide*. Philadelphia: Temple University Press, 1995. An interesting examination of the gulf between working class and middle class people and their views about voting, parties, political participation, and inequality.

Robert Erikson and Kent Tedin, *American Public Opinion*, 5th ed. Boston: Allyn and Bacon, 1995. An exhaustive and comprehensive account of the social science literature on the subject.

Susan Herbst, *Numbered Voices: How Opinion Polling Has Shaped American Politics*. Chicago: University of Chi-

cago Press, 1993. A fascinating account of modern polling and how it can often distort and shape public opinion.

Walter Lippmann, *The Phantom Public*. New York: Harcourt Brace Jovanovich, 1925. A classic work on the emergence of modern public opinion and the problems it presents.

Benjamin Page and Robert Shapiro, *The Rational Public*. Chicago: University of Chicago Press, 1992. Two scholars of the subject argue for the reasonableness and democratic character of American public opinion.

The American Political Economy

Less than a decade has passed since an awestruck world watched as Soviet and Eastern European communist states crumbled one by one. The fledgling democratic governments that took their place proceeded to dismember their state-owned economies. Despite their control of society, communists failed to deliver the consumer goods, economic dynamism, and political freedom taken for granted in the West. The collapse of communism, and the expansion of market economies everywhere, seem to have closed a monumental conflict in human history—the conflict between capitalism and communism. Capitalism, it seems, has triumphed.

Yet we have since learned that debates about the fundamentals of economic organization and their relationship to democracy have hardly stopped with communism's demise. Indeed, lacking a common enemy, the differences among capitalist democracies seem to be greater than ever. In Japan, Sweden, France, Germany, and Great Britain, politicians and movements try to shape peculiar forms of capitalism to national goals, democratic values, and distinctive cultural traditions. If anything, conflicts about the organization of the economy have increased in countries that claim to be both democratic and capitalist. Just how well a new global capitalist order works for most citizens is an ongoing controversy, even in the richest countries.

Americans are not immune to these debates. Historically, we've engaged in heated conflict about how our economy is organized, who controls it, and how both arrangements affect the quality of democratic life. Mostly, the debate in the United States hasn't been between advocates of Soviet-style communism on the one hand and free market capitalism on the other. For this reason, communism's demise has meant little for critics of the U.S. economic system, because few saw the former Soviet Union as a model anyway. Most Americans, even fervent critics of the economic system, have shunned a state-owned economy and believe that private goods and services in society should be distributed primarily by markets and not by government. Even critics believe that people should be allowed to accumulate private property by their own efforts.

Yet within this consensus there are important lines of division. Most Americans agree that private property is fine so long as its accumulation or use doesn't harm others. Yet where to draw the line between the private sector and the government is a subject of much contention. Debates about the proper relationship between governments and markets often focus on how to make a more efficient and productive economy. But they also hinge on how to make a better democracy—and that is our main concern here.

How far should democratic decision making be extended into the American economy? Should government policies be designed to decrease inequalities? What kind of a political economy will produce strong social institutions that will help create a vibrant democracy? Because political economy is concerned with which institutions and people exercise power over citizens' lives—over the livelihood of their communities, the conditions of their work, and the forms of their consumption—the economic debate is very much part of the larger democratic debate.

TWO TALES OF THE POLITICAL ECONOMY

Two brief tales introduce the American democratic debate about our political economy.

The Pacific Lumber Company was an economic and environmental model for the entire timber industry. Owner of some of the last remaining stands of ancient redwoods, the northern California–based company cut down its trees with an eye to maintaining the long-term health of the forest ecosystem. Despite ups and downs in the price for lumber, Pacific Lumber offered its employees relatively high wages and good benefits, established a generous pension fund, and was able to withstand bad times without laying off its employees.

The company was so good that, like many others, it became a prime target in the corporate merger frenzy that began in the l980s. In 1986, Maxxam, Inc., a Texas-based conglomerate controlled by entrepreneur Charles Hurwitz, raised $900 million in junk bonds (a high-risk form of debt financing) from an assortment of investors for a hostile takeover of Pacific Lumber. Maxxam quickly abandoned Pacific Lumber's environmental and worker-friendly strategies. It immediately doubled the timber cutting rate, shipping many of the cut logs directly to Japanese mills. In 1990, Hurwitz drained $55 million from the company's pension fund to invest in other Maxxam projects. By this point, the company was employing fewer and fewer people. Hurwitz told his employees: "There's a story about the golden rule. Those who control the gold rule."[1]

Our other tale took place across the continent and four years before the Maxxam takeover, at Weirton, West Virginia, when steelworkers were informed by National Steel Company that their town's plant was about to be closed. National, a large multinational company, did not think it worthwhile to modernize the Weirton plant because of competition from foreign steel companies. To save money on pension and severance pay commitments, National offered to sell the plant if Weirton's workers could find a way to buy it. Workers and their community held sockhops, raffles, and bake and rummage sales to raise the $2 million necessary for the legal and bank fees. Employees agreed to a 32 percent wage cut and contributed much of their life's savings to finance the required purchase price of $66 million. Aided by a 1974 federal law that created special tax deductions for employee-owned plants, Weirton's workers took over ownership of the plant in 1984. The new worker-owned steel mill was modernized, reorganized, and rebuilt, and in the very first year the new company reported a profit.

Weirton, West Virginia, had been saved. Yet worker ownership cannot shield a business from the pressures of the market. Hit by the recession of 1990–91 and needing capital for further modernization, Weirton had to cut its workforce by over 20 percent. It also offered some of its stock to the public, diluting the workers' ownership and profits. Nonetheless, Weirton continues to be a thriving concern, one of a number of companies that have become more productive and profitable once their workers became their owners.[2]

The Democratic Debate
on the Political Economy

What do these stories tell us about the American political economy? At the simplest level, they are morality plays about greed and heroism. In the first tale, Charles Hurwitz plays the villain's role; in the second, scrappy Weirton workers defy the odds. Yet these stories are more than accounts of personal greed and unusual triumph. They are about the private and public institutions, laws, and people who dominate the modern American political economy, and the odds that citizens, consumers, and workers face in the attempt to counter them.

The American corporate economy is one of the most productive and competitive economies in the world. Compared to its impressive rates of growth since the Civil War, it has sputtered over the last several decades, leading worried observers to look to the more robust economies of Western Europe and Japan for alternative capitalist models. But in the mid-1990s the United States is again outpacing its capitalist rivals, who now are looking to this country for tips on flexibility and innovation in high-tech production.[3] As an engine of prosperity, the American corporate economy today delivers the goods.

But prosperity is not the only measure of an economy. The modern U.S. economy has three other characteristics that raise troubling issues for American democracy: corporate power, inequality, and the erosion of civil society.

Corporate Power. Huge corporations, run by an economic elite, control vast resources and make decisions that affect the lives of millions. Can these corporations use their power over the private economy to shape what government does and to undermine democratic decision making? Are there any forces in the economy itself that check corporate power? Do citizens have any means to hold corporate elite accountable for their actions?

Inequality. Even though the American capitalist system generates a great deal of income and wealth, these fruits of the economy are unequally distributed. Indeed, economic inequality in the United States has grown worse in the last two decades and is now much more extensive than in other advanced capitalist democracies. Do economic inequalities translate into political inequalities? What happens to democracy when the rich get richer, the middle class is hard pressed, and the poor get poorer?

Erosion of Civil Society. Americans are working harder today in an increasingly competitive and insecure economy. Women have entered the workforce in large numbers, and employees of both sexes are working longer hours. The issue for democracy is basic: At what point does participation in the competitive market economy take away from participation in politics and from the institutions of civil society, such as religious and community organizations, that are essential for a healthy democracy?

The Marketplace: The Elite Democratic View

To elite democrats, the American economy is not really a problem for democracy. On the contrary, they argue, a market economy along American lines provides the essential underpinning for democracy.

In the elite democratic view, markets maximize freedom and minimize power. Unlike government, with its laws, police, and bureaucracy, markets don't force people to do anything. As in a yard sale or a church bazaar, people in the world marketplace act *voluntarily*—no one buys or sells unless he or she wants to. In this way, individuals are free to be the best judges of their own interests and desires.

Even though individuals pursue their own self interest in a market economy, the whole process is efficient and promotes the economic growth that fuels national prosperity. A modern market economy is less interested in the motives of the participants than the overall beneficial results. There is thus little difference between Maxxam buying Pacific Lumber Company and selling off redwood trees to Japanese consumers and Weirton workers bringing an ailing steel company back to life. In both cases, self-interest was coupled with innovation, not because either Hurwitz or Weirton's workers were forced to be innovative, but because they stood to profit by being so.

Elite democrats use the language of political democracy to explain how the free market works. Terms like "consumer sovereignty" are employed to suggest that markets are driven by the wants and needs of individuals who vote with their dollars. From this point of view, corporations resemble elected representatives; instead of voters, corporations respond to consumers who either buy or reject their products. Similarly, the market, like American government at its origins, is assumed to have its own automatic checks and balances. If a corporation doesn't perform well, then it will be challenged by new enterprises and entrepreneurs who supply superior goods to consumers.[4]

Voluntary action by self-interested entrepreneurs responsive to the demands of consumers is much preferable, say elite democrats, to economic commands by government. As economists Milton and Rose Friedman put the case: "By enabling people to cooperate with one another without coercion or central direction, [the market] reduces the area over which political power is exercised. . . . The combination of economic and political power in the same hands is a sure recipe for tyranny."[5]

Modern elite democrats do not contend that markets always work perfectly or that they can be completely self-regulating. Somewhat more than their eighteenth-century predecessors, they acknowledge that government should play an important, if limited, role in the political economy: Government should set the rules that ensure fair and honest competition in the marketplace. It should correct dramatic failures of the market system, such as depressions. It should supply public goods that the market cannot provide, such as highways, dams, and schools. It should provide military protection against countries that threaten political and economic freedom. And it should do something to take care of those who can't compete in the marketplace: the aged, children, and the disabled. Beyond these policies, elite democrats argue, government should stay out of the way of the market.

One thing government definitely *should not do*, from the elite democratic perspective, is to meddle with the inequalities that a market economy generates. Inequalities fairly reflect varying individual abilities and efforts and help to make the economy function justly and well. They provide the incentives to ensure that the most important and difficult tasks in society are performed by the most motivated and talented people. Few have the talent to be brain surgeons; fewer still have the motivation to endure six years or more of medical school and residency after college. If brain surgeons make ten times more than the average worker, it ensures that competent people will be drawn to this vital task.

Elite democrats hold that unequal economic rewards are necessary to drive individuals to work hard, save, and invest. If government taxed away wealth or high incomes, the ambitious and talented would have little reason to risk their time and resources in new enterprises. And if unskilled work produced a comfortable income, individuals would have no incentive to work harder and learn new skills. Attempting to rectify economic inequality, government would retard economic growth, eventually leaving the poor—the very people who were supposed to benefit from redistribution—even poorer.[6]

The market, elite democrats believe, is based upon a realistic view of human nature. Recognizing the way people are, as opposed to the way they are told to be, is thus one of the key strengths of a free economy. Trying to alter natural human behavior leads to authoritarian government and economic inefficiency. For example, idealists might have forced National Steel to run the Weirton mill at a loss and against its will. Eventually, the entire enterprise would have lost customers and closed down. The net impact of defying human motivations and interests would have been economic stagnation as well as a violation of private property rights.

If the market produces dislocations in people's lives—plants shutting down, jobs relocated out of communities, increased pressures on workers' time—these are the unavoidable side effects, say elite democrats, of a free and prosperous economy. This economy offers the average person an abundance of choices—more and better goods and services than ever before. It makes available to all,

regardless of religion, race, or any other factor, the objects of consumption through which individuals can fulfill their hearts' desires. What could be more democratic than that?[7]

Popular Democratic Perspectives

Popular democrats do not disagree with elite democrats about the importance of markets and private property. If economic exchanges are purely private and do not harm anyone, they should be allowed to proceed without interference from government. But the advantages of the free market of which elite democrats boast are, in the eyes of popular democrats, often contradicted in the real world of modern corporate capitalism. An economy that is supposedly characterized by voluntary exchanges between individuals has become, for popular democrats, a new economic regime where unaccountable and undemocratic power rules on a global scale.

Today, the supposedly neutral rules of the marketplace make it easy to do what the Maxxam corporation did: take over a perfectly healthy company that respected the environment, the community, and the workers and damage all of them in the name of profits. Maxxam's kind of freedom wasn't available to most people, who lack the ability to raise hundreds of millions in junk bonds and then repay investors by degrading forests and towns. In contrast, the survival of Weirton is less the positive side of the modern political economy than the exception that proves the rule. Against incredible odds and through great sacrifices, Weirton's workers saved their town and their jobs. They were helped by tax laws that came not from the market itself but from a government policy that favored citizen buyouts. In the 1990s, corporations like Maxxam, that specialize in reducing their workforces to raise their stock prices, have become more common than experiments like Weirton Steel, that benefit every member of an enterprise.

Popular democrats see power wielded through the market processes that elite democrats label as voluntary and private. Instead of individuals cooperating and competing under the impersonal laws of supply and demand, popular democrats see large organizations and rich individuals doing most of the voluntary cooperating and deciding. The rest of the population—wage workers and small businesspeople—are generally compelled to take part in a game they neither created nor benefit from. And in place of a strict separation between the freedom of the market and the potential tyranny of government, popular democrats see an increasing tendency toward connections between the politically and economically powerful in *both* arenas. Far from dispersing political and economic power, our modern political economy concentrates both. The economic elites who head large corporations are not held accountable to democratic citizens through competition, and they often prevent political elites from serving citizens as well.[8]

To popular democrats, the increasing inequalities characteristic of corporate capitalism in America reflect illegitimate power more than they do effort or ability. Popular democrats do not deny that a certain amount of inequality is necessary. The problem is that present inequalities go far beyond those required for a well-functioning capitalist democracy. Almost all other capitalist democracies have less inequality than the United States, yet most of them outperformed the American economy over the last two decades. Is it a matter of efficiency or of power that corporate CEOs sometimes make two hundred times more than ordinary workers in their companies? Is it a matter of efficiency or of power that truckdrivers, who are generally men, make far more than daycare workers, who are usually women?

Massive economic inequality, popular democrats contend, is hardly efficient. It wastes human talent and potential, erodes social trust and community bonds, and spurs social disintegration as many citizens fall into poverty or are forced to struggle in an otherwise rich society. Far from cultivating the characteristics in people that promote self-government, the modern market economy often confuses greed with virtue.[9]

Left alone, market capitalism can erode the bases for a democratic society by demeaning citizenship. In a market system, consumers vote and choose through their purchases, but their power as citizens and voters is limited. And some people, of course, have many more dollars than others. The net effect is to distort our civil society by placing profits over all other human needs. Markets produce fantastic plastic surgeons who can make the affluent look more attractive, but they are slow to develop treatments for AIDS and obesity, diseases that disproportionately affect drug users and the poor. Markets produce private cars in abundance but tear up mass transit systems that move people quickly, cheaply, and efficiently. Markets produce luxurious condos in abundance but create ghettoes and homelessness in inner cities. If we care as much for the quality and justice of the society in which we live as for the profusion of consumer goods on sale in the marketplace, say popular democrats, then we have to surround the economy with the fresh air of democratic participation.[10]

Finally, popular democrats argue that market capitalism is prone to crisis and even self-destruction. In the 1930s, our economic system collapsed in the Great Depression, throwing a quarter of the U.S. population out of work. Since then, our economy has experienced a cycle of booms and busts. The public interest, in this view, is too important to be left to the uncontrolled forces of market capitalism.

The elite democratic view of the marketplace is readily available to Americans. It floods the airwaves and fills the magazines, and it is widely taught in colleges. (Corporate advertising is even making its way into elementary school education.) The popular democratic critique of modern corporate capitalism seldom receives an equal hearing. In what follows we try to right the balance by developing a popular democratic analysis of the American political economy.

CORPORATE KINGDOMS: PRIVATE POWER AND PUBLIC EFFECTS

When the American republic was founded, the democratic debate concerned how to form and control governmental power. The Constitution was silent, however, on concentrations of economic power. With the important exception of plantation slavery, the early republic contained few economic institutions that needed to be checked. There were inequalities of income and wealth in that society, even among the free population of whites, but there also was a great degree of economic independence. The early U.S. economy was local. People grew crops and produced commodities within a web of small communities and cities. Most owned some land, or at least their own tools, and if they worked for wages they did so in small shops alongside their bosses.

Over the last century and a half, the modern corporation's rise has transformed the simple capitalism of the eighteenth century into modern **corporate capitalism.** In both eras, the means by which goods are produced—land, tools, workshops, factories, and stores—are in *private* hands. In both, entrepreneurs invest according to the *profit motive*, and **market competition** drives the system. In both epochs, *contracts* between buyers and producers are essential and protected by law. But we no longer have an economy based on small farms, artisans, and local markets. Corporate capitalism is a system within which most labor for wages, markets exist on a global scale, and the conditions of work and consumption are established by huge economic units. As Figure 4.1 shows, corporations and their wealth often dwarf the production of entire nations. The general store of 1787 and the General Electric of today may both be capitalist, but corporate

FIGURE 4.1

Worldwide Sales of the Three Largest Companies in the World Compared to the Gross Domestic Product of the Developing Countries, 1992 (in billions of $US)

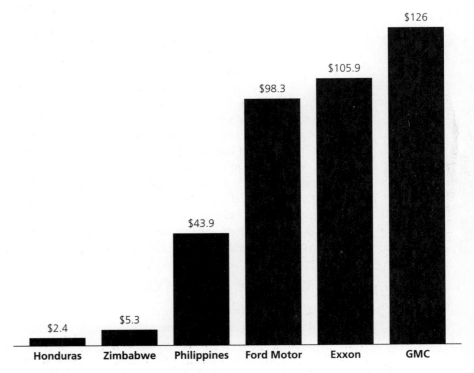

Source: Nancy Folbre, *The New Field Guide to the U.S. Economy,* (New York: The New Press, 1995).

capitalism creates hierarchies and concentrations of power on a scale utterly alien to the merchant and farmer economy.[11]

Although the rise of corporate capitalism is usually ascribed to the market itself, government policies (see Chapter 17) and Supreme Court decisions (see Chapter 14) have been central to the transformation of the American economy. Corporate capitalism borrows from the rhetoric of individual freedom and enterprise that characterized early American capitalism, but beneath its rhetorical cover lies concentrated power that would have astounded the founding generation. According to political scientist Charles Lindblom, "The corporation fits oddly into democratic theory and vision. Indeed, it does not fit."[12]

Corporate Organization: Special Privileges

Large corporations have three characteristics that set them apart from unincorporated businesses owned by individuals:

1. *Joint stock ownership.* Corporations pool the resources of a number of investors, called stockholders. The stock can be freely bought and sold.

2. *Limited liability.* Corporations can attract investment more freely because no owner is financially responsible for more than his or her own investment and can lose only that amount if the business fails.

3. *Continuous legal identity:* Corporations do not dissolve with the death of any owner. Like the Energizer rabbit, they just keep going, no matter what.

These defining legal features of corporations make corporations seem like individuals, enjoying the rights and legal protections similar to those enjoyed by all U.S. citizens. Yet corporations are not like ordinary citizens. Unlike individuals, corporations were not born endowed with rights. Corporations exist because governments license them. Unlike individual citizens, single corporations are composed of individual citizens ordered in a hierarchy. Corporate organization resembles a monarchy more than a democracy. With their own king and court, called the *chief executive officer* (CEO) and the *board of directors*, corporations also have layers of officials, called *managers,* who implement orders and monitor activities. At the bottom are the commoners—ordinary workers who usually have no power to elect either their immediate bosses (supervisors) or the distant managers.

Who Owns American Corporations?

Corporations often claim they are democratic because they take orders from large groups of shareholders. If shareholders reflected, even remotely, the U.S. citizenry, then the case for **shareholder democracy** controlling corporate hierarchy would be persuasive. But who *are* the owners of U.S. corporations?

Since the early 1950s, the number of Americans who own corporate stock has quintupled. Today, a little over a third of American families owns stock, either through retirement pension accounts, mutual funds, or directly. Pension funds alone account for a whopping $1.3 trillion in stock value; General Motors employees alone had $23 billion invested in stock through their pension funds in the early 1990s.[13]

Yet even though the number of stockholders has grown rapidly in the mid-1990s, a big majority of Americans still owns no stock at all. Three-quarters of the population owns less than $2,000 worth, and these families taken together own only 20 percent of all stocks. While owning stock has become a more popular way of saving for many Americans, the richest 5 percent of Americans still own half of all stock, with the top one-half of 1 percent owning nearly a third. Most Americans gain their income from salaries and wages, not from owning stock or property.[14]

If only about one in twenty Americans has much of a direct stake in owning corporations, the idea that shareholders "democratize" corporations falls apart. Moreover, most small shareholders have little power to control the modern corporation. The real power is held by the increasingly influential institutional investors—banks, insurance companies, universities, and the managers of mutual funds. Employees who own shares of U.S. corporations through their pension funds have as little say in what stocks are bought as how corporations are run. Most employee pension funds are entirely controlled by company management. Even if shareholders were a larger and more diverse group, management controls most of the information about companies, diluting the already small powers of most shareholders. Small shareholders dissatisfied with management generally sell their stock.[15]

Do Markets Control Corporations?

How are the powers of corporate management defended? One old defense, occasionally recycled, is that the corporation is private property and what it does is no one else's business. Yet corporate actions often have broad public effects, and most corporations today strive to defend their actions and their reputations.

The most common defense of corporate power is that corporations have the know-how to innovate and compete, while ordinary people don't. Corporations may be governed by elites, but that is because only elites can deliver the efficiency and innovation desired by consumers and demanded by the new and highly competitive international economy. In a global marketplace, corporations must act quickly to meet changing consumer demand and must implement new technologies in the most efficient manner possible. Any corporation that engaged in lengthy democratic consultations with shareholders, workers, consumers, and communities would soon be left in the dust in the competitive race. The real claim, therefore, is that corporations are controlled by the market. And although they may not be run like democracies, they serve democracy anyway by giving Americans the prosperity they desire.

Corporations may indeed respond to consumers and competitors, but how they respond reveals how much discretion and power they really have. In a system justified by the "informality" and "freedom" of market exchanges versus the "deadening bureaucratic hand" of government, it is ironic that corporations prosper by doing precisely what elite democrats don't like about government: They engage in **economic planning**.[16] Corporations and their managers seek to shape markets and control their environment. Managers must decide long in advance what to do with their shareholders' capital—where and when factories are to be built, workers employed, and research conducted. They exercise the important power of determining who has jobs, how many there are, how work is organized, and what the standards of achievement will be.

To plan also means to predict and, if possible, to mold consumer behavior. The advertising industry discovered long ago that consumer demand does not grow by itself but must be created through the manipulation and even creation of consumer desire. Corporate decisions about these matters are not automatic responses to free markets but calculated exercises of power to maximize profits.[17]

Corporate Power and the New Global Economy

The history of corporate America is less the story of a growing free market than it is a tale of the emergence of **corporate oligopoly**—markets where a few giant firms dominate and plan production. Since the formation of large industrial firms and banks in the late nineteenth century, periods of intense rivalry have been followed by periods of oligopoly. By the 1950s and 1960s, for example, a few hundred large and seemingly stable U.S. corporations dominated trade, production, and banking. The Big Three automakers dominated car sales, while General Electric and Westinghouse monopolized the electrical equipment and machine tool industry. Small entrepreneurs in the newborn computer industry were quickly gobbled up by the industry's then giant, IBM. In this period, a new form of corporate capitalism appeared in which competition from either new companies or foreign ones became severely limited. Major American corporations had achieved their central aim—power over the marketplace. Satisfied with stability through predictable profits and sales, many corporations bought peace with their workers by promises of job stability and steadily increasing wages.[18]

As it turned out, the easy life of corporate oligopoly didn't last. Since the late 1960s and early 1970s, U.S. corporate capitalism has been transformed by events both beyond and within its control. The stimulus for change *was* competition—from Western European and Japanese corporations in the mass production, research, and banking industries and from east Asian and Latin American nations in textiles, shoes, clothing, toys, and home applicances. This economic competition, based on consumer demand, initially cut into the profits of U.S. corporations.

The ways U.S. corporations have responded to the breakup of oligopoly reveal a great deal about the contours and consequences of corporate kingdoms in the new age of the globalized economy. In our political economy, the choices about how our nation responds to global competition are left to the holders of investment capital, not to ordinary Americans. U.S. corporations could have chosen to compete through investments geared toward creating new jobs and new forms of widely shared prosperity. They could have pioneered new breakthroughs by cutting down on the use of fossil fuels or through investments to upgrade the skills and productivity of American workers. Generally, however, they've made very different decisions, with huge implications for the economic and political prospects facing ordinary U.S. citizens. We will now examine three different responses to the new global economy.

If You Can't Beat 'Em, Join 'Em: Going Global. One way American corporations have responded to the new foreign competition has been to become less American. In search of larger profits, U.S. companies have built new plants in foreign countries, invested heavily in foreign corporations, replaced formerly domestic-made products with foreign-made ones, and sold their own brand names to foreign companies. Much the same thing has been happening to foreign companies, which increasingly have shed their own national characteristics as well.

These new *transnational corporations* plan, invest, produce, and market on a worldwide scale. With the aid of new technologies, they move their resources easily around the planet in search of cheaper labor and bigger profits—while workers, consumers, communities, and even nation-states have to stay where they are. Such **capital mobility** provides an important instrument by which the

modern global corporation can evade control by local communities, electorates, and governments.[19]

For American manufacturing workers—once the backbone of American middle class society—the formation of the global corporation has generally been bad news. In the 1980s, the United States lost a total of over 1.3 million manufacturing jobs. General Electric, a mainstay of upstate New York's economy, became Singapore's largest corporation. Zenith, Magnavox, and Whirlpool—proud American brand names—globalized their operations elsewhere. Job growth in the United States has shifted from manufacturing to the *service economy*, that broad swath of labor from home health care workers to gasoline attendants, hamburger flippers to paralegal assistants. The good news is that new jobs are still being produced; the bad news is that most of them are less secure and pay less than the jobs lost.[20]

Leaner and Meaner. A second and equally well-known response of U.S. corporations to international competition has been to make their new globalized companies "leaner and meaner." As Figure 4.2(a) shows, America's biggest companies have indulged in an orgy of layoffs. First in manufacturing and then increasingly among white collar workers and executives, massive **downsizing** has been a favorite corporate strategy. Between 1979 and 1996, 43 million U.S. jobs were lost. Most companies have downsized not because they are suffering from losses but because they want to make still higher profits. In fact, since 1976 the 500 largest corporations in the United States have increased their assets by 230 percent and their sales by 140 percent even as they have shed the most jobs.[21]

As Figure 4.2(b) shows, the results of such massive downsizing have been widely felt by Americans. What has happened to the workers who have been the

FIGURE 4.2	Companies with the most layoffs, 1992–1996		
Downsizing in the U.S. Economy		Jobs Cut	Share of Workforce
	ATT	123,000	30%
	IBM	122,000	35%
	GM	99,400	29%
	Boeing	61,000	37%
	Sears, Roebuck	50,000	15%
	Digital Equipment	29,800	26%
	Lockheed Martin	29,100	17%
	Bell South	21,200	23%
	McDonnell Douglas	21,000	20%
	Delta Airlines	18,800	26%
	GTE	18,400	14%
	NYNEX	17,400	33%
	Eastman Kodak	16,800	13%
	Baxter Int'l	16,000	28%

(a)

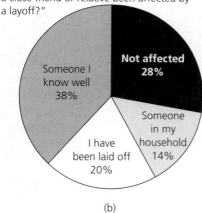

1996 Survey Question:"In the past 15 years, have you, a member of your household, or a close friend or relative been affected by a layoff?"

Not affected 28%

Someone I know well 38%

I have been laid off 20%

Someone in my household 14%

(b)

Source: New York Times, March 3, 1996, p. 26–27.

targets of downsizing? Most have found new jobs that are less productive and less well paid than the jobs they lost. To corporate spokespeople, this is merely an inescapable byproduct of necessary adjustments to a competitive market. Yet there is growing evidence that many downsized firms are in fact less productive and profitable than they were before jobs were slashed. To boost their short-term profits and raise the prices of their stocks, many corporations shortsightedly laid off the skilled and educated workers who made their firms dynamic, while the workers who survived the downsizing binges grew demoralized and mistrustful toward their employers, thus damaging productivity.[22]

Corporate *restructuring*, as it's called, also brings with it **outsourcing**—contracting out to smaller companies jobs and functions once done in house. No longer do big companies have to pay salaries and benefits to large staffs; they can hire outsourced labor from small companies that don't pay health insurance or pension benefits for part-time labor. Outsourcing has helped to shape a new economy made up of part-time and temporary workers, and this is where many of the downsized workers have found jobs. Outsourcing creates new opportunities for hundreds of small firms and startup companies who, far from competing with the corporate goliaths, serve them as labor brokers. Manpower, Inc., for example, has grown to be the biggest U.S. employer by providing benefit-free workers to downsized companies. In writer David Korten's words, "The giants are shedding people but not control over money, markets, or technology."[23]

While some corporations have gone global by downsizing and outsourcing at home while rapidly moving capital around the world, a new form of business organization has been developing: **enterprise webs,** or networks of small and large companies that feed on each other to produce new products and constant innovation. Examples include Los Angeles' entertainment industry, Silicon Valley's computer industry, Massachusetts' high-tech Route 128 corridor, and university-oriented research webs in college towns such as Madison, Ann Arbor, Ithaca, and Durham. All are part of what business advocates praise as the emergence of an **information-based economy** in which highly skilled and educated workers are brought together to think up the new products of the future. Often, corporate hierarchies in this sector have been leveled by more participatory and less bureaucratic work procedures.

Yet the formation of a less hierachical workplace in enterprise web zones may be the exception that demonstrates the general rule. At most, people who work in these areas constitute what former Secretary of Labor Robert Reich calls the "fortunate fifth" of the modern workforce, and even this group is subject to increasing job insecurity. More important, even in enterprise web capitals like the wealthy Santa Clara Valley (Silicon Valley) in northern California, a third of the workforce earns $15,000 or less a year. These are the janitors, waiters, dishwashers, hotel maids, gardeners, and construction laborers who labor for the fortunate fifth.[24]

The Casino Economy. The third corporate response to competition is the birth of what economist Susan Strange calls the **casino economy.** Money that might have been used for productive investments has instead been employed in a high-stakes crapshoot: acquiring, merging, dismantling, and rearranging companies. The mid-l980s was the high point of such merger mania. At a cost of over half a trillion dollars—nearly half the federal government's budget—over 12,000 companies changed hands or disappeared. Today, after a brief respite, the casino has reopened again with a series of megamergers in banking, telecommunications, publishing, and media.

The money changing hands in the casino economy has brought fabulous sums to the lawyers, the accountants, and especially the corporate raiders and junk bond dealers who have engineered the deals. But these mergers are also part of a larger restructuring of global corporations. They have allowed corporations to reduce potentially destructive competition among themselves, creating markets that are more predictable and controllable.

Americans today depend for their standard of living upon the prosperity of the corporate economy. Yet very few of us have thought much or had much to say about the changes erupting in the new global corporate order. U.S. corporations have generally responded to the international challenge of globalization with strategies that have slashed workforces, held down wages, decimated communities, and built new pyramids of power insulated from citizen or government controls. The point is not that corporations are led by immoral people. Rather, it is that by their very nature corporations limit democracy as they go about the process of change. Whether corporations are run by nice or nasty people, their most disturbing aspect may be that they use their power and mobility to undermine controls imposed by governments whose leaders are elected by voters.[25]

If neither the internal organization of the corporation nor the external discipline of the free market can hold corporations accountable, what can? Let us briefly consider two potential candidates: labor unions and the federal government.

Labor Unions: Can They Control Corporate Power?

Many Americans assume that labor unions today serve as a strong control over corporate power. But this image of unions is badly outdated.

During the New Deal, the **Wagner Act of 1935** guaranteed workers the right to organize unions and bargain collectively. Union membership soared, reaching a peak of 31.8 percent of the nonagricultural workforce in 1955. Union contracts negotiated with management often gave workers certain rights within the corporation—for example, to take work breaks and to refuse overtime work. Yet even at their peak, unions provided only a limited countervailing force to the power of management within the corporation. As bread-and-butter organizations, concerned mostly with obtaining higher wages and better fringe benefits for their members, unions conceded control over investment decisions and production methods to the corporation.[26]

FIGURE 4.3   Membership in Labor Unions, 1900–1996

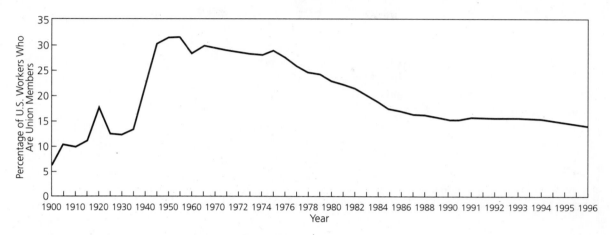

Percentages do not include agricultural workers or self-employed workers whose businesses are incorporated.
Source: Harold W. Stanley and Richard G. Niemi, *Vital Statistics on American Politics*, 5th ed. (Washington, D.C.: Congressional Quarterly Press, 1995), p. 176; *New York Times*, June 8, 1997, p. 4.

More important, as Figure 4.3 shows, the union presence in the U.S. workforce has been declining since the 1950s. Today only 14 percent of American workers belong to a union, one of the lowest rates among all the capitalist democracies. With declining numbers, the bargaining strength of unions has deteriorated rapidly. Hanging over their heads has been the threat of corporate flight abroad, automation, downsizing, and outsourcing. All these factors discourage workers from complaining, even though they have real grievances. To make matters worse, the protections of labor law have eroded in the hands of administrators appointed by pro-business Republican presidents. Since the election of Ronald Reagan in 1980, people who want to unionize have been deprived of many of the legal protections their forebears once had. As a result, most current bargaining doesn't consist of workers making demands but of management demanding concessions in the form of pay and benefit cuts.

Labor has been on the ropes, but it is far from knocked out. In 1995, an insurgency in the American Federation of Labor/Congress of Industrial Organizations (AFL-CIO) toppled the organization's conservative and bureaucratic leadership and installed a militant new president, John Sweeney. Under Sweeney's leadership, the AFL-CIO poured millions of dollars into a 1996 campaign to defeat antilabor legislators (with only moderate success). As the accompanying feature box shows, since 1995 the national AFL-CIO has been devoting many of its resources to organizing workers in the industries of the new

MAKING A DIFFERENCE

Unions and the New Economy

To the legions of gamblers and tourists that pour through McCarran International Airport annually, Las Vegas is an oasis of glitz, golf, and gambling in the middle of the Nevada desert. Yet Las Vegas, with 1 million residents, is also America's fastest-growing big city. Some call it the Pittsburgh of the 1990s because of the large numbers of workers in new factories there. But instead of making steel, today's workers make the beds, clean the toilets, shuffle the cards, and dig the ditches that make for a new service economy. In Vegas, service jobs mean gaming jobs.

All over America, but especially in Las Vegas, the new face of the service workforce is increasing female, often Hispanic, African American, Asian American, and young. But until recently, organized labor has primarily been composed of male workers in declining manufacturing industries such as autos and steel. That's one reason why union membership has been declining, and with it the wages, working conditions, and job security of millions of new service workers.

For a long time, the leadership of American unions didn't pay much attention to organizing new workers. That's why newly elected AFL-CIO president John Sweeney's 1997 visit to Las Vegas was particularly important. He came to tell a cheering throng of parking lot attendants, maids, dishwashers, nurses, and hard-hatted construction workers that the labor movement was back. He declared Las Vegas "the hottest union city in America," a test for a new union strategy to reach out to the new multicolored, heavily female workforce. Pledging hundreds of new organizers and money to a broad coalition of unions trying to organize construction laborers, hospital workers, and employees at small hotels and casinos, Sweeney declared, "If all America needs a raise, then the buck starts here."

Sweeney was telling many Las Vegas workers what they already knew from their own experience of activism. Back in 1994, the Culinary Workers Union, Local 226, began to fight for recognition at the MGM Grand Hotel—with 2,000 rooms, Las Vegas's biggest. MGM, like many companies, had wanted to outsource many of its restaurant jobs to subcontractors who paid their workers low wages and provided no medical insurance. After three

economy. Moreover, the unions are trying to bridge gender and racial gaps by concentrating on organizing women, African Americans, Hispanics, and Asian Americans. The unions face an uphill struggle—but by 1997 reforms within the AFL-CIO and the Teamsters Union seemed to be bearing some fruit. United Parcel Service (UPS) workers went on strike during the summer, and won an important victory ensuring that the shipping giant would hire more full time workers and contribute to a union-directed pension fund. As Robert Reich, former Secretary of Labor, observes: "Organized labor is an aging, doddering prizefighter still relishing trophies earned decades ago. But it's the only fighter in that corner of the ring. There's no other countervailing political force against the overriding power of business and finance."[27]

years of struggle with MGM, the 4,000 workers won management recognition of their union, and with it a contract that paid a living wage and provided important benefits. Since then, the MGM Grand has continued to reap huge profits, throwing doubt on corporate claims that economic growth doesn't go with unions or decent wages.

Can the Las Vegas model of multiracial, aggressive union organizing be successful elsewhere? There have been some failures. Long strikes at Caterpillar, Inc., and against Detroit newspapers were eventually lost because companies could so easily hire replacement workers; autoworkers, machinists, and flight attendants have often lost ground when companies have insisted that they will outsource or move abroad.

One fact is sure: The new AFL-CIO leadership is going all out to make changes. Sweeney and the AFL-CIO's new leadership have urged all the member unions to spend up to 15 percent of their dues on new organizing activities. Unions and their leadership have been revamped to include more women and people of color—those with the lowest wages in the U.S. workforce. Many of the unions in the textile, food, and office work industries have achieved notable successes organizing janitors working in Los Angeles skyscrapers and laborers

in New York City construction sites. In 1997, United Parcel Service workers won an historic new contract that made many part-time workers into full-time employees.

One new labor strategy has been to reach out to groups like students, retired people, churchgoers, and environmentalists. In 1996 and 1997, the labor confederation introduced two thousand college students to the labor cause through "Union Summer." Students worked with union organizers in boycotts and strikes and on political campaigns for pro-labor candidates. Nicole DeCrescenzo, a Sarah Lawrence College junior, wrote after her experience: "Growing up in the '80s has taught us to expect and accept greed and exploitation in business. I have never been able to accept that, but until I got involved in the labor movement, I did not believe there was recourse." Apparently, Las Vegas workers agree: At last count, unions had signed up 40,000 new workers in one year alone.

Sources: Marc Cooper, "Labor Deals a New Hand," *The Nation*, March 24, 1997; Martha Hamilton, "Labor Gets a Young Look," *Washington Post*, September 1, 1996; Nicole DeCrescenzo, "Memoirs of a Union Summer Graduate," unpublished manuscript, Sarah Lawrence College.

The Federal Government: Checking or Sustaining Corporate America?

The federal government appears to be in a stronger position than the labor unions to check the corporations. If we listen to the complaints of corporate executives or free market ideologues, it does so all too frequently and aggressively. As in the case of unions, however, prevailing images are misleading.

Since the Industrial Revolution in America, popular democrats have often looked to the federal government to cope with the injustices and instability of corporate capitalism. Alliances between popular democratic movements and progressive politicians have produced some important constraints on the corporate sector: the Wagner Act for unions mentioned earlier, the regulatory protections for workers and the environment discussed in Chapter 13, and the social welfare measures discussed in Chapter 17. Much derided today, "big government" in America had to grow big largely to counter the power amassed and the damage wreaked by big business. Yet to concentrate only on governmental policies that limit corporate power is to overlook the even more substantial policies that sustain corporate power. Today, as in the past, the federal government and large corporations are partners far more often than they are antagonists.

Chapter 17 discusses in depth the relationship between economic policy and private power. Here, two examples must suffice to illustrate the partnership between government and business. The first concerns the sizeable share of tax dollars that flow to **the military-industrial complex**—the alliance between the Pentagon and defense contractors in search of large military budgets. Constituting close to a twelfth of the modern U.S. economy, military contractors and industries have long formed a privileged island. The military-industrial complex is largely sheltered from market competition, with the Pentagon often providing a guaranteed demand—and guaranteed profits—for the corporate contractors of weapons systems. Absorbing a quarter to a third of all federal expenditures since World War II, the military-industrial complex was justified as necessary to fight world communism. Yet even in the post–Cold War era, when the threat of communism has disappeared, the military-industrial complex lives on. At $260 billion in expenditures in 1996, the Pentagon spends about the same amount of money as it did before Reagan's massive buildup in the 1980s.[28]

So-called **corporate welfare** also provides direct governmental aid to the private economy. An estimated $38 billion is provided by the federal government in direct subsidies to particular industries—more than aid to education and the food stamp program combined. The most direct forms of corporate welfare subsidize the lumber industry by building roads, at taxpayer expense, on national forest lands so that companies like Maxxam can more easily cut timber. Large farmers receive $3 billion annually to support the prices of their sugar, rice, and other commodities against foreign competition. Other programs to help particular corporations provide subsidies to advertise McDonald's Corporation hamburgers and Marlboro cigarettes to foreign consumers; fund research to university professors to develop products that corporations can use; and give direct subsidies to energy companies for new fuels and waste disposal.[29]

Why, if corporations are dominated by the few, is the federal government, as the supposed instrument of the many, so often a corporate partner? Corporate power in politics is strongly related to the ability of companies to translate their economic power into political clout. Corporate executives have a great advantage over less moneyed citizens in making the large campaign contributions that bring access to policy makers (see Chapter 8). And they have far greater resources when it comes to hiring the lawyers, academic experts, and lobbyists who influence Congress and the federal bureaucracy (see Chapter 9). By effectively deploying their superior resources to influence public policies, corporations win measures that bring them further resources, and so the cycle of economic success feeding political success continues. The result is an economic corruption of democracy.

But corporations don't always need their campaign contributions or their lobbyists to obtain favorable treatment from the federal government. They benefit almost without lifting a finger, through what Yale political scientist Charles Lindblom has called the **privileged position of business.** Because corporations possess the power to invest or not to invest in the U.S. economy as well as the power to hire or not hire more workers, policy makers defy their will only at great risk. If politicians offend investors and corporations—for example, by proposing pro-union laws or tax increases—they risk prompting a "strike" by capital. Businesses and investors can simply take their money abroad. No politician who needs favorable economic growth in order to be reelected is likely to run such a risk. As the case of President Clinton, discussed in Chapter 12, will show, even a leader elected by the votes of working people and generally opposed by corporate elites will change his tune when confronted with the privileged position of business.[30]

THE ECONOMIC RECORD OF CORPORATE CAPITALISM

A political economy composed of hierarchical corporations and largely pro-business government limits the ability of citizens to control the forces that shape their lives. Yet maybe the high price is worth it if prosperity and growth are secured for large numbers of Americans. The defenders of corporate capitalism and the new global economy stress that the entire world economy is now in a painful but necessary transition. If the United States is to lead in the competitive global economy, they say, then the price of this successful transition is adjustment to the new realities imposed by corporations and investors. In the long run, the argument goes, the new corporate capitalist economy will produce the incentives necessary for investment, and this will yield security and prosperity for most Americans—at least those who work hard and seek individual success.[31] To evaluate this argument, we need to evaluate how the corporate capitalist economy has performed.

Economic Growth

When it comes to overall economic growth, corporate capitalism has indeed produced generally high marks. Since the emergence of the modern corporation, the United States has experienced tremendous *overall* economic growth. With but 5 percent of the world's population, America has the biggest economy and ranks among the top five in *per capita GNP* (gross national product)—the amount of goods produced per person. The U.S. workforce has also achieved remarkable **productivity:** Despite some lags in the 1980s, the amount of goods and services produced for each hour of work has continually improved in the postwar years. Though both growth and productivity rates have sometimes lagged behind those of other wealthy countries in the last two decades, American corporate capitalism can claim much success. It continues to generate new wealth.

From the perspective of corporate capitalism, America at the dawn of the new millennium is better off than ever. The pain of downsizing and outsourcing and the achievement of lower taxes and less government have resulted in an increasingly successful transition to the Third Industrial Revolution, where the products of the manufacturing age are replaced by new developments in the computer, media, finance, and other innovative industries. As a result America remains a world leader in the production of the new technologies that count in the global economy. The evidence for these claims is not hard to find. From 1992 through 1997, the economy was in steady expansion, without much inflation. Millions of new jobs were created that took the place of the jobs shed through downsizing. In stark contrast to many Western European nations less friendly to the new economic globalism, the U.S. unemployment rate dipped below 5 percent in 1997. The stock market surged, buoyed by favorable reports on corporate profits. Perhaps the combination of corporate power, market competition, and generally friendly government policies works after all.

Inequality

There is only one problem with the rosy scenario just outlined: Although the transition may have helped many to amass huge fortunes and others to earn more comfortable incomes, for the majority of Americans the economy today provides less security, lower wages, and less support than it did in the 1950s and 1960s. In those earlier decades, the rewards of economic growth were distributed more equally to the different groups in U.S. society. Yet since the 1970s, the enormous new wealth and productivity has rewarded some, punished most, and left others in the same position as their parents. The United States may again be number one in high technology. But the United States is also number one in poverty and in income inequality among all the industrialized democracies.

Figure 4.4 tells the story for wages. Since 1973, real wages (controlled for inflation) for people who work in private industry have dropped steadily. The median wage, even in a time of overall prosperity, dropped by 7 percent. This has not been because America as a whole is poorer, but because economic growth has not been shared equally. Indeed, in the late 1960s the top 20 percent of wage earners made 40 percent of the national income; by the mid-1990s they were making nearly 50 percent. The figures generally get worse for the "unfortunate fifth"—the bottom 20 percent of the American workforce that receives a meager piece of the total economic pie.[32]

If income inequality has reached levels not seen since the turn of the century, the figures for wealth are even more skewed. (*Wealth* is defined as people's assets—in homes, stocks, bank accounts, or other possessions, minus what they owe to creditors.) Wealth inequality has always been pronounced in America. In the 1950s and 1960s, though, it remained steady. As the saying goes, a rising economic tide lifted all boats. Since the 1980s, however, economic tides have lifted

FIGURE 4.4   **Declining Real Wages for Americans, 1965–1996**

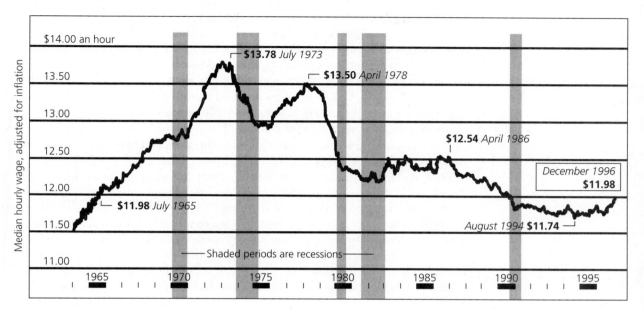

Note: Figures are in 1996 dollars.
Copyright © 1997 by The New York Times Company. Reprinted with permission.

only the yachts while swamping the small craft. Since the 1980s, the top 20 percent of the population absorbed a staggering 99 percent of the new wealth, with
the top 1 percent of the American wealthy getting more than two-thirds of that
percentage. For 200 million Americans, the economic boom years of the mid-
1980s and mid-1990s simply didn't happen. For the poorest fifth of Americans,
the boom has been a cruel joke. Their already meager share of the wealth gave
way to net indebtedness. Poor people today owe more than they own.[33]

Given these numbers, it is not surprising that the U.S. poverty rate is the
highest among the wealthy countries of Western Europe, East Asia, and Canada.
Some analysts note, too, that the U.S. government's definition of poverty seriously understates the problem. Since the 1960s the federal government has calculated the poverty level by taking the cost of a minimal diet and multiplying this
by three. This sets the poverty level way too low because food is now only about
one-sixth of the average family's budget; other expenses, like housing, transportation, and utilities have become much more expensive. By some standards,
over a quarter of all households are poor; by the government's criteria, about 14
percent of Americans live in poverty. With concerted government efforts,
poverty declined in the 1960s. Since the 1970s, however, overall poverty rates
have continued to climb slowly once again, although in 1995 and 1996 they

dipped somewhat because of both the general economic recovery and the increase in Earned Income Tax Credit for low income families passed at President Clinton's urging. Still, in 1995 close to a quarter of all U.S. children were poor, and nearly half of all African-American children were.

Most poor American adults work, and with the welfare reform passed in 1996, being poor and having a full-time job may become the major reality for more than one in five Americans (see Chapter 17). Most people who are poor are not on welfare but are paid at or near the minimum wage. Even with the rise of the minimum wage in 1996, many who received it still remained poor. A full-time minimum wage worker makes less than $10,000 annually, still far under the government defined poverty line for a family.[34]

In the last several years, and five years into the present economic recovery, the trends toward greater wage stagnation and poverty have eased slightly. Yet the amount of inequality generated in the last twenty-five years can't be made up just through recent economic growth alone. Even after five years of continuous economic expansion, the median wage still hasn't recovered to where it was in 1989, just before the last economic recession. As we've seen, the present levels of stagnation and inequality are not the result of American workers' lack of productivity. And enormous amounts of new wealth *have* been created. The problem is essentially a political one: how does a society distribute its rewards? The answer in contemporary America is clear: Today, American wealth and income inequality is more pronounced than in any other rich country, and the gap is wider than in poorer countries like Zimbabwe and Malaysia. Felix Rohatyn, a Wall Street investment banker and ambassador to France, worries that "what is occurring is a huge transfer of wealth from lower-skilled middle class Americans workers to the owners of capital assets."[35]

Are Inequalities Necessary?

Perhaps widening inequalities are "necessary" to rebuild our economy, create new jobs, and spark investment. Perhaps, also, the huge slice of national wealth consumed by the few is a just reward for work well done, while stagnant and declining wealth for the majority reflects their personal deficiencies. Earlier, we talked about brain surgeons and their salaries as examples of why inequalities might be justified in the job market.

One problem with this assumption is that the people whose income has surged the most are not research scientists, brain surgeons, innovative inventors, or others who have a big role in thinking up new products. Much of the wealth has gone to **paper entrepreneurs,** people who reap huge salaries from Wall Street investments, mergers, acquisitions, and other such deals. Another example of the rewards of jobs well done can be seen in the compensation received by the chief executive officers of U.S. corporations. Between 1990 and 1996, pay for CEOs has doubled to an average of nearly $4 million annually. Some CEOs, like Lawrence Coss of Green Tree Financial Corporation, make as much as $65 million in a single year, while other executives of major corporations grossed "only" $15 million or more.

A 1996 study by *Business Week* magazine showed that the relationship between CEO pay and the performance of the particular corporations CEOs lead is far from clear. *Business Week* discovered that the CEOs of twenty companies who had downsized the most saw their salaries and bonuses rise by a whopping 25 percent in one year. Nor was there any direct relationship between corporate profits and the salaries of CEOs. Some of the highest salary increases went to individuals who led companies where profits were way below average. Pay has risen for all CEOs, widening the gap between them and their employees, whose salaries were often being cut or their jobs eliminated or outsourced. In 1980, the boss's pay was a "mere" 42 times that of the average manufacturing worker. By 1996, it had risen to 141 times the average worker's pay.[36]

There is even less of a direct relationship between the concentration of wealth and long-term corporate health. A 1992 study of corporations with the highest levels of pay inequality found that they produced products of lower quality and that their workers were more demoralized and less productive than less unequal firms. As workers become less secure in their salaries and jobs, they become less trusting of their bosses and less committed to their companies. Workers spend much of their mental energy looking for other jobs or finding innovative ways to give the appearance that they are devoted while denying the company their full efforts.

Growing inequalities also have profound social effects that undermine the idea that they are necessary for a healthy economy. Inequality may slow the growth of a skilled workforce and produce low-wage, deadend jobs that can't support the conditions necessary for democratic life. Inequality feeds on itself, producing concentrations of poor people in communities with underfunded schools and services, which in turn produce higher levels of crime, broken families, and people with little hope. When people have to work two jobs to make ends meet, they have little time to be caring and effective parents, thereby endangering future generations. In those regions where inequalities between cities and suburbs are the greatest, a cycle of economic decline may set in that eventually effects the affluent suburbs. When city incomes decline, new industries that might move into an area locate elsewhere, or go abroad.

Economic inequality, justified by elite democrats as a natural apportionment of rewards for success and punishment for failure, thus may have profoundly negative economic costs for everyone. By making it much more difficult for new workers to acquire the skills and education they need, inequality lowers worker productivity. If workers can't afford to buy the products they produce, inequality works to lessen the very economic growth and prosperity elite democrats say it is supposed to encourage.[37]

The Prism of Race and Gender

Corporate capitalism has had a particularly big impact on women, African Americans, and Hispanics. Most people in these groups are not poor, but they bear, if for somewhat different reasons, a disproportionate weight of poverty's burdens.

Moreover, each group lags behind in wage levels, even when they work at jobs comparable to white men.

Since the late 1970s, women have made fairly large wage gains, but in the mid-1990s they still earned less than 75 cents for every dollar earned by men. Women gained on men but this was partly due to the fact that the average wage for men was falling during this period. African Americans started to close the gap with whites between 1956 and 1973, but since then they have fallen back and now earn on average 20 percent less than whites. Hispanics have lost ground since the 1970s as well, earning today 25 percent or so less than whites do.[38]

What factors account for these economic inequalities? Some argue that corporate-led economic growth will take care of the problem. Other defenders of the market economy and its essential justice argue that the problem for all these groups is that they lack the education and skills that many white men have. Employers can't be blamed if they pay higher wages to better-qualified white men.

Both explanations have real problems, however. Corporate-led economic growth has so far not changed the ratio of white to black and Hispanic earning levels and has hardly closed the gap between men and women. Moreover, all three groups have made great strides in educational and skill levels since the 1970s. If skills and education were rewarded equally in the marketplace, then the racial and income gap should be closing for African Americans and Hispanics. Instead, it seems to be widening again.

African Americans have been hard hit in the marketplace despite generally rising educational and skill levels. For African Americans with college degrees or high school degrees in the 1980s and 1990s, earnings were 17 percent less than for whites with similar skills. Working class blacks have been unevenly hit by a number of other factors, also. The decline in union membership, combined with the downsizing of many manufacturing industries, caused much pain. Jobs are moving to the suburbs, but African Americans are often stuck in the center cities, unable to reach them. And finally, outright racism persists in the job market. An Urban Institute study sent testers of both races and equal qualifications and ages to apply for the same 476 jobs in the Washington, D.C., metro area. The study concluded that "discrimination against blacks appears to be highest in types of jobs offering the highest wages and future income potential."[39]

Does the market reward women and men of equal qualifications? There is evidence that it often does not. Even in the highly skilled professions of law and computer programming, women receive about 20 percent less in their paychecks than men do. In other, less high-status jobs, gender discrimination is equally acute. Secretaries, elementary school teachers, and registered nurses—occupations where women predominate–require comparable education and involve as much responsibility as carpenters, truck drivers, and high school teachers, occupations dominated by men. Yet there are big disparities—again up to 20 percent—in how the two sets of jobs are compensated.[40]

Given the patterns of gender and racial inequality just detailed, it isn't surprising that the poorest group in U.S. society is women of color, and especially

African-American and Hispanic women with dependent children. Although women of color are in the workforce just as much as white women, their wages equaled only 86 percent of that of white women—a group whose wages already lag behind those of men.

POLITICAL ECONOMY AND CIVIL SOCIETY

American corporate capitalism has produced profound economic inequalities among citizens. Not only are these inequalities often unfair, they may even undermine the supposed prosperity that justifies them. Yet the effects of economic inequality may be felt even more on democratic politics. From Aristotle through Thomas Jefferson and Martin Luther King, Jr., thinkers have acknowledged that democracy requires a strong middle class that can reduce the class antagonisms and social disorder that accompany a society divided into rich and poor. If democracy is synonymous with participation, an economy built on growing economic inequalities isn't. As we'll see in Chapters 6–9, the wealthy can turn their money into political influence that often dwarfs the democratic dignity and voices of the less privileged. When this happens, citizens often become discouraged and begin to see politics as a distant and exclusive sport that they can't play. People insecure about their livelihoods, their jobs, and their futures are hardly in a good position to participate in politics. Current trends may trap and divide people in ways that undermine faith in the democratic character of institutions.

Combined with undue corporate power and privilege, growing economic and political inequalities also may be undermining what political theorists call a strong civil society.[41]

Civil society encompasses the voluntary associations that lie between the private realm of the family and the public sphere of politics. Alexis de Tocqueville, the French democratic theorist who visited the United States in the 1830s, argued that the great strength of American democracy lay precisely in the character of its voluntary associations. Voluntary associations, from food banks to labor unions, from Boys' and Girls' Clubs to arts associations, act like informal schools, enabling citizens to develop the civic skills necessary to participate effectively in a democracy. Civic associations can help to take the rough edges off American individualism, with its tendency to worship success and competitiveness. They help people realize that they are part of a community and that the meaning of a full life can be found in a common, shared life with others.

Since the days of de Tocqueville, Americans have continued to be joiners. A 1990 national survey found that 79 percent of Americans were affiliated with at least one organization. Americans are still more likely than citizens of other countries to be members of voluntary associations.[42] On the other hand, evidence is mounting that civil society in the United States has deteriorated in the past twenty years. According to one survey, since 1974 group memberships have declined by one-quarter.[43] Membership in the League of Women Voters, for example, is off by about 42 percent since 1969, and the number of people belonging to parent-teacher associations (PTAs) is down from 12 million in 1964 to about 7 million today.[44] The decline of civil society is thought to be a major cause of the decline in voter turnout (see Chapter 5).

The deterioration of civil society is also clearly related to changes in the economy. Ironically, the associational life of some people is harmed by having too little work, while for others the problem is too much work. As we saw earlier, the unemployed poor are increasingly concentrated with other poor people in so-called *underclass* neighborhoods that suffer from severe social problems including high crime rates, drug abuse, and family breakdown. Lacking strong institutions and voluntary associations, underclass residents experience social isolation and deep feelings of powerlessness and despair. According to sociologist William Julius Wilson, the underclass has formed precisely because of the loss of industrial jobs that allowed corporations to regain their profits and competitiveness.[45] Unable to support a family, some black males withdraw from the world of work, as well as civil society, and enter the world of part-time jobs or the drug trade. Single women, who are left to care for the children, are often too busy or fearful to participate in voluntary associations, though churches are still vibrant in many poor neighborhoods.

Economic pressures to withdraw from associational life affect the working poor as well. In general, the poor are underrepresented in voluntary associations. Only 52 percent of the poor are involved in a nonpolitical organization, compared to 89 percent of the rich.[46] The economic pressure to work overtime and *moonlight* in a second (or third) job, instead of being involved in voluntary associations, has increased. Because of deteriorating wages, production workers would have to work an additional six weeks per year just to reach their already meager 1973 standard of living.[47] Moreover, unskilled low-wage jobs, such as machine operator or laborer, teach few civic skills—such as how to run a meeting—that can be carried over to political participation.[48] Nor does the hierarchical nature of most workplaces encourage democratic problem solving. (See Chapter 9.)

The great middle class has not emerged unscathed from the corrosive effects of the present political economy on civil society, either. During the 1950s and 1960s, middle class households didn't generally suffer from the threats of downsizing, declining wages and salaries, or constant insecurities about how to balance work life with raising a family and participating in civic life. Many families could achieve homeowner status with only one wage earner, usually the male, in the workforce. Moreover, most could expect to have stable job prospects and thus could make solid plans for their children's future. But in the last twenty years middle class insecurity has increased on all these counts. By 1996, nearly three-quarters of American households had had a "close encounter" with a layoff. One in ten Americans said that a lost job had brought on "a major crisis in their lives." Workers with above-average educational levels felt the pinch, too, as layoffs for those with some college education began to outnumber layoffs for people with only high school diplomas.[49]

Since the 1960s, many women sought equality with men by entering the workforce and forming their own professional careers. But women's massive en-

try into the workforce was affected by declining wages for most workers as well. To stay even, the two-earner family became for some a choice, but for most a necessity. The percentage of married women in the workforce increased from 20 percent after World War II to over two-thirds by 1990. Even the two-income family has not bought much security, however.

For many families, the two-earner family has created a time crunch in which taking off work to care for a young child or an aging parent just isn't possible economically. The corporate workplace is generally indifferent to the needs of parents, who find it difficult to visit a child's teacher or take a sick child to the doctor—much less participate in civic life. The phenomenon of latchkey children is primarily the product of an economy that pays less money for more work. Under these circumstances, it is not difficult to understand why many parents arrive at home exhausted, too busy to participate in voluntary associations.[50]

Indeed, some of the economic pressures on free time have affected participation in civil society for all classes, even the fortunate fifth. In a late 1980s Harris poll, people reported a nearly 40 percent decline in free time between 1973 and 1987.[51] The main culprit indeed appears to be work demands in "lean and mean" corporations. Between 1969 and 1987, Americans increased their work time by an average of 163 hours, the equivalent of almost an extra month a year.[52] Because their husbands still do relatively little of the housework, employed mothers average about 65 hours of work a week on the job and at home. With this kind of harried schedule, it is not surprising that many women have withdrawn from participation in voluntary associations.

Finally, downsizing and outsourcing may have made some corporations more efficient, but their effects on community life and participation can be devastating. Consider the case of Dayton, Ohio. That city suffered from 50,000 layoffs in the 1980s. Civic leaders noticed a rapid decline in membership in churches, social service organizations, and even the Boy Scouts. According to a Dayton mother of three, the community is being pulled apart:

> Many of these kids I see are on their fifth or sixth move because the company keeps saying, "We're not making enough money; we need to downsize more." . . . It really hurts the child's ability to develop those long-term commitments. It's devastating to the sense of community.[53]

CONCLUSION: WHOM DOES THE POLITICAL ECONOMY SERVE?

Each reader must come up with his or her own assessment of human nature and how it operates to shape the political economy. What level of democratic participation is the average American capable of and inclined toward? Your assessment of human nature will determine to a great extent the level of democratic participation in the economy you deem appropriate. The organization of the political economy lays the foundation, or lack thereof, for democratic participation.

The democratic debate about these questions pits elite democratic faith in markets, corporations, and economic growth against popular democratic advocacy of equality, citizenship, and community. In the present debate, the public hears media reports that assess the democratic debate primarily from an elite democratic perspective. On the news, the political economy is assessed by indexes that gauge the stock market, the inflation rate, the number of jobs created, and the amount of goods and services produced. If all these measures are healthy, as they have been for the last several years, many assume that society is better off. If they're going down, many assume that society is worse off.

Ultimately, however, the case for popular democracy rests on imposing a different set of standards. Popular democrats argue that corporate capitalism is a drag on the potential of democratic citizenship. The inequalities generated by corporate hierarchies go beyond those necessary for the functioning of a market economy and undermine democratic civil society. Does the Dow Jones Industrial Average measure the wasted potential of ordinary workers, the insecurities at home and at work that citizens feel, the sting of inequalities spawned by corporate hierarchies and their decisions?

Historically, ordinary people have always tried to shape the political economy to their own ends. When they have succeeded in making changes, the results have hardly devastated or destroyed the nation's ability to produce economic growth or new wealth. Periods of popular democratic strength, in fact, correspond with periods of moderate economic growth and great strides toward economic equality. Given the obstacles in their way, how can ordinary citizens shape the political economy in democratic ways? Chapters 5–10 of this text examine the dilemmas and opportunities of democratic participation in American politics.

KEY TERMS

corporate capitalism
market competition
shareholder democracy
economic planning
corporate oligopoly
capital mobility
downsizing
outsourcing
enterprise web
information-based economy

casino economy
Wagner Act
military-industrial complex
corporate welfare
privileged position of business
productivity
wealth inequality
paper entrepreneur
civil society

SUGGESTED READING

Milton Friedman, *Capitalism and Freedom*. Chicago: University of Chicago Press, 1962. The now-classic defense of the relationship between economic markets and political freedom.

William Greider, *One World, Ready or Not*. New York: Anchor/Doubleday, 1997. A provocative account of economic globalization, showing how transnational corporations affect labor and consumption and weaken democratic governments.

Jeremy Rifkin, *The End of Work*. New York: Tarcher/Putnam, 1995. An account of how and why corporations eliminate jobs, and the role automation and new technology plays in downsizing and wage inequality.

Robert Reich, *The Work of Nations*. New York: Random House, 1991. The former Secretary of Labor argues that worker retraining and the creation of "symbolic analysts" and enterprise webs are the key to future economic growth and political democracy.

Juliet Schor, *The Overworked American*. New York: Basic Books, 1992. An economist examines how business and government urge Americans to work long hours in order to consume more products, with dire effects on private and public life, families, and individuals.

CHAPTER

5

Where Have All the Voters Gone?

Few would disagree that democracy is synonymous with popular participation in political and social life. Speech, protest, letter writing, petitioning, and voting—all are the basic "stuff" that makes democracy more than an abstraction. Essential, too, are the millions of less dramatic actions that make communities healthy and whole. People can volunteer their time in schools and food banks, get together to clean up neighborhoods, or work to provide summer activities for young people. Even talking with neighbors about politics across the fence or on the front stoop can count as participation, because it brings people into public life.

Participation also presents the opportunity to create a level playing field in politics. If everyone has a right to be heard, some of the economic inequalities discussed in Chapter 4 could be lessened. When participation is strong, government is less likely to float free of the popular will. Through action with others to shape public life, citizens can find their own identities and achieve dignity. This is perhaps why African Americans and women, once deprived of the right to participate fully in politics, fought so hard for voting rights.

Yet civics lessons about participation disguise a growing mystery about the whole subject. On paper, citizens have won more rights to be included in many facets of political life. Overtly sexist and racist barriers that excluded millions have fallen. Americans are more educated and more informed about national affairs than their ancestors were a hundred years ago. American politics is full of polls and reports of popular grievances. Yet the odd fact is that despite all this, Americans just don't get involved as much or as extensively as they did in most periods of the past.

In this chapter, we'll attempt to solve the mystery of participation by examining the most important clue of all. Among all the political acts citizens can do, voting stands out as the most inclusive, available, easy, and accessible. Yet the strange fact is that voting doesn't seem to engage even a majority of Americans. With a few exceptions, voter participation has been declining since 1960, and it reached a low point in 1996.

Early in the twentieth century, low voter turnout was less difficult to explain. It was directly mandated by elite control of politics and laws that consciously excluded a "dangerous" electorate. African Americans, recent immigrants, and poor whites and their demands for dignity and economic equality were seen as threats by the political elites of both North and South. Through **Jim Crow laws** in the South, African Americans were effectively deprived of voting rights. In many northern states, registration laws and other means were used to "cleanse" the electorate of urban immigrants and working class voters.

Yet it has now been over thirty years since the passage of the Federal Voting Rights Act and the abolition of Jim Crow laws. And in recent decades, registering to vote has become even easier than it once was. If citizens feel intensely about voting, they are now usually, though not always, able to do so without big obstacles. Yet despite the continuous easing of registration requirements, voter participation has continued to be very low.

Solving the mystery of nonvoting helps to explain how it affects our politics. With half to two-thirds of the U.S. voting-age citizenry absent from the polls, our leaders are chosen by an electorate that is still diverse and various, but very far from representative of the U.S. citizenry as a whole. With so many absent, can U.S. elections be legitimate expressions of the popular will? As the most obvious defect of American democracy, massive nonvoting needs to be explained.

THE MYSTERIOUS FACTS ABOUT NONVOTING

First, the facts about nonvoting need to be set out. As Figure 5.1 shows, voter turnout in U.S. presidential elections declined sharply in the early twentieth century, recovered somewhat with the onset of the Great Depression up until 1960, declined again for thirty-two years thereafter, rose again a little in 1992, and then

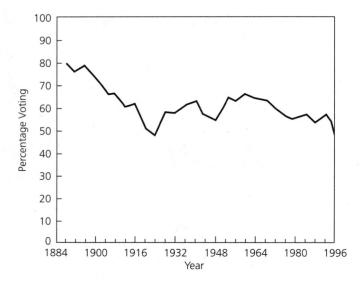

FIGURE 5.1

Voter turnout in Presidential Elections, 1884–1996

Harold Stanley and Richard Niemi, *Vital Statistics in American Politics,* 5th ed. (Washington, D.C.: CQ Press, 1995). Copyright ©1995 by CQ Press. Used with permission.

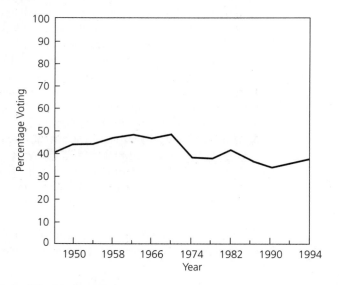

FIGURE 5.2

Voter Turnout in Off-Year Elections, 1946–1995

Source: Federal Election Commission.

dipped again in 1996. Generally, presidential elections provoke the highest turnout of any contests. Off-year congressional and state races have even lower turnout rates. Figure 5.2 displays participation rates for recent off-year elections.

Party primaries held to nominate candidates for public office draw even fewer voters. The total number of voters participating in the 1988 Republican and

Democratic presidential primaries was 35.5 million, less than a fifth of the voting-age population. Four years later in 1992, party primary totals dropped further, to 32.5 million, or less than a sixth of the voting-age population. In 1996, party primary voting was even lower.[1]

Local elections for mayor, city council, school boards, and the like are usually not held at the same time as state and national elections. For that reason, participation rates are generally the lowest of the low. An extreme case is supplied by the 6 percent turnout among registered voters for New York City's local school board elections in early 1996. More typically, about 10 percent to 25 percent of the voting age population comes to the polls in the big city elections in Los Angeles, New York, Houston, and elsewhere.[2]

The enormous size of the nonvoting population casts doubt on the mandates so often claimed by newly elected presidents and members of Congress. In 1992 and 1996, President Clinton defeated his opponents by convincing margins, but in both years never received the votes of more than one in four adult citizens. Clinton's total is far less than the votes received by 1936 Republican presidential nominee Alf Landon, who was crushed by Franklin Roosevelt in a historic victory. In 1994, Republicans took over Congress and claimed the people's support for the Contract with America. Yet the revolutionary Republicans received the votes of less than one-fifth of the voting-age population—hardly a mandate for long-term change.

What sorts of people do and do not vote? Table 5.1 (p.110) compares the voting participation rates of those Americans *most* likely to vote with those *least* likely to vote in the 1992 presidential election—a contest that featured relatively high turnout for modern times.

There are four major characteristics that capture the vast social divide between those who vote the most and least: age, income, race, and education. Table 5.2 (p.111) reports the voting participation rates of different kinds of U.S. citizens in recent presidential elections. People of non-European descent, who have less formal schooling and who are younger and poorer than the norm, tend to vote the least in America. Voting participation among Latinos has increased in recent years, but is still below average despite their enormous growth in the population. Among African Americans there have been notable increases in 1984 and 1988, but blacks still lag somewhat behind whites in national participation rates. Asian-American voting rates have risen in some cases but still don't come close to equaling rates for white Americans.

Yet age, race, education, and income aren't the whole story. Since 1960, almost *all* varieties of Americans, including highly educated and wealthy whites, vote less. And the most dramatic decline in voting turnout is among America's "new" working class—people who work in service occupations like the retail trades, as hospital orderlies, secretaries, and waiters and waitresses. Later, more will be said about why this group, so increasingly numerous in the population, is declining among the active electorate.

To sum up: People of all races, educational levels, ages, and income are voting less, and many are voting much less. At the same time, the huge gap in voting

Which Groups Vote the Most and Which the Least? The 1992 Presidential Election

Groups Most Likely to Vote	Percent Turnout	Groups Least Likely to Vote	Percent Turnout
Whites, $50,000+ income	74.3	Whites, income less than $5000	24.8
People with advanced degrees	75.9	People with less than 8th grade educations	31.6
People ages 45–64	63.6	People ages 18–24	38.4
White executives and managers	70.6	Hispanic farm workers	7.8
Homeowners	61.6	Renters	36.1
Government workers	71.2	All farm workers	32.9
The employed	62.4	The unemployed	46.2
College students 18–24	49.8	People not in college 18–24	28.6

Percentages are of voting age population, adjusted by the authors to reflect average overreporting of survey respondents.

Source: "Voting and Registration in the Election of 1992," Bureau of the Census, Series P-20. (Washington, D.C.: U.S. Government Printing Office, 1993), p. 466.

participation among races, generations, educational levels, and social classes remains.

All this translates into some odd disparities within metropolitan areas, between inner cities and outer suburbs. In America's central cities, neither the Democrats, Republicans, nor independents are a majority—the "party of nonvoters" is. In Bedford Stuyvesant, Brooklyn, 90,000 voters elected Rep. Major Owens to Congress in 1986, even though there were 348,000 potentially eligible citizens. Less than 20 miles away, in the suburbs of much wealthier and whiter Westchester County, 210,000 voters from a potential 388,000 elected a conservative Republican to office in the same year.[3]

The overall decline of voting participation nationwide also disguises some important differences among regions. Generally, southern states have witnessed a rise in voting participation since 1960. It is the northeastern, midwestern, and western states that have experienced steep drops.

Voting turnout has not always been so low. Over a hundred years ago, in 1888, voting turnout was at its highest in the republic's history. Although high turnout was sometimes the result of illegal and corrupt practices such as paying people to vote, there is still no question that citizens voted in greater numbers regardless of their race, education, social class, or age than they do these days. (In 1888, women couldn't vote). Since 1888, the proportion of nonvoters and voters has

TABLE 5.2

Participation by
Group in 1992
Election, as
Percentage of
Voting-Age
Population

Group	Percent Turnout	Group	Percent Turnout
Race		*Income (family)*	
Whites	57.2	<$5,000	24.9
Blacks	47.6	$ 5,000–10,000	32.0
Hispanic origin	22.5	$10,000–14,999	39.3
		$15,000–20,000	48.2
Gender		$20,000–25,000	55.0
Males	53.8	$25,000–35,000	62.0
Females	55.9	$35,000–50,000	67.2
		$50,000+	72.4
Age			
18–24	38.4		
25–44	51.9		
45–64	63.6		
65+	63.7		
Education			
Less than 5th grade	15.1		
5th–8th grade	32.7		
9th–12th grade, no diploma	34.8		
High school graduate	51.1		
Some college	62.3		
Bachelor's degree	72.1		
Advanced degree	75.9		

Source: Compiled from U.S. Bureau of the Census, "Voting and Registration in the Election of 1992," Series P-20 (Washington, D.C.: U.S. Government Printing Office, 1993).

fluctuated, but it has never come close to the earlier standard. Clearly, one's social class, age, race, and educational level have not always made a difference. A century ago, many very rich people worried because they voted proportionally less than the poor. Yet for some reason all these characteristics matter much more than they used to.[4]

Some say that the decline in voting is associated with increasing prosperity. As people become more satisfied with private life, they are said to have fewer reasons to get excited about politics. With the temptations of consumer items, the pressures of work and raising a family, and the diversions of vacations and the mass media, many people just don't find enough reasons to go out and vote.

Yet it seems curious that those who have the fewest reasons to be satisfied— people with low incomes or insecure jobs and the unemployed—are the most likely to stay away from the polls, while those with high levels of income and education still turn out in relatively large numbers. It also seems strange that other modern and wealthy countries—such as Japan, Sweden, France, and

TABLE 5.3

Voter Turnout in the World's Wealthiest Democracies

	Percent Turnout in Recent Elections		Percent Turnout in Recent Elections
Belgium	92	United Kingdom	78
Italy	86	Canada	67
France	85	Japan	67
Denmark	83	**United States**	**49**
Germany	78	Switzerland	46

Source: Consulates; U.S. Federal Election Commission.

Germany—have much higher participation rates than does the U.S. Table 5.3 shows that the United States in fact ranks next to last in voting participation in comparison with other advanced industrial democracies.

If history and foreign experience are any guide, the currently high rates of American nonvoting are apparently not natural. How, then, can nonvoting on such a massive scale be explained? Does massive nonvoting detract from our democracy, or doesn't it really matter all that much?

ELITE DEMOCRATIC THEORIES OF NONVOTING

There are many schools of thought about why so many Americans fail to vote and even more about its implications. They follow the lines established by the elite and popular democratic currents in American political life.

Elite democrats generally view nonvoting not as a problem of the political system, but of the people in it. Some people lack the interest that is necessary for politics, others the knowledge to participate. Some are just too busy with personal affairs, while others get easily confused by all the complexity.

Nonvoting: Why Worry?

ABC commentator and columnist George Will has captured the essentials of a key elite democratic argument. "The fundamental human right," Will claims, is not to the vote, but to "good government." To Will, there is no necessary relationship between good government, American democracy, and high rates of voting participation. Why, he asks, should people who are more interested in watching TV soap operas be urged to vote at all, and why should we be troubled if they don't? Will argues that higher voter turnout could be dangerous for democracy. Many people who now don't vote are ignorant and ill-informed, and bringing them to the polls would only worsen matters. Like Alexander Hamilton and other elite democrats, Will also fears the passions of a highly mobilized but generally ignorant citizenry.[5]

Few elite democratic explanations are as blunt as Will's. Scholarly studies, for instance, emphasize the psychology of nonvoters in order to understand their inaction. Many of these studies tend to confirm Will's views: Nonvoters are less interested in political issues, don't follow campaigns all that closely, and are less likely to believe that their participation will make a difference. Moreover, nonvoters usually have less formal education than do voters. All in all, nonvoters therefore lack a sense of **political efficacy**—the idea that they can have an impact if they did participate. Instead of just noticing a relationship between these factors and nonvoting, elite democrats argue that one tends to cause the other.

Nonvoting can thus be seen as a natural product of a person's individual attributes: Because of their lack of formal education, nonvoters can't figure out modern politics, often get contradictory bits of information, and sometimes can't figure out how to register or where to vote. For most, the argument goes, voting just isn't worth it.[6]

Nonvoting: A Crisis in Morals?

In recent years, elite democratic intellectuals have developed a related explanation for both nonvoting and what they see as immoral forces at work in popular culture. While embracing the above explanations, they also blame the "swollen government" produced by misguided New Dealers and 1960s reformers. Government, especially the welfare state, they say, has assumed too many of the functions once left to *civil society*—individuals, communities, churches, charities, and local businesses. The result is that people get lazy and expect government to do for them what they once did for themselves. Government welfare payments and other forms of aid sap the self-sufficiency that once prompted people to get involved in the kinds of local activities that lead to voting and other forms of political participation. In this account, nonvoting is just one symptom of a larger breakdown in social norms and values that used to hold the country together.[7]

Blaming Nonvoters

The logical consequence of elite democratic thinking about nonvoting is this: Though we should do what we can to encourage uneducated people to vote, if people don't vote it is no real cause for alarm or dismay—in fact, it may even have some hidden blessings. Nonvoting cannot really be blamed on defects in the basic political and economic arrangements, but on nonvoters themselves.

Scholars and commentators of the elite democratic school share many of the same assumptions about human nature with the earlier approaches of the Federalists. Then and now, elite democrats start with the premise that ordinary people are likely to be interested only in eroding liberty and engendering tyranny—and so the participation of the ignorant is not altogether welcome. Yet if people don't participate, they are blamed for their apathy or, more recently, overdependence on government aid. And, say the elite democrats, it may be just as well that more affluent and educated people are more likely to vote and participate in public affairs because they are more attuned to the subtleties of political issues. In Will's words: "Thought must be given to generating a satisfactory (let us not flinch from the phrase) governing class." Nonvoting is thus not a problem, because it allows such a governing class to form.[8]

POPULAR DEMOCRACY AND NONVOTING

However, many other analysts and activists *do* worry about the increase in non-voting. They attribute it not to human nature and the characteristics of less able people, but to specific features of U.S. voting laws.

The Registration Problem

Some scholars and many "good government" groups, such as the League of Women Voters and Common Cause, explain low turnout by criticizing the continuing difficulty citizens are said to face when they try to register and vote. Almost alone among the citizens of western nations, each American is personally responsible for the sometimes complicated process of registering. Most of us just take for granted that we are responsible for locating the local board of elections, finding a registration form, and completing it correctly. When we move, as Americans often do, or do not vote in one presidential election, we often must reregister if we want to vote again. If we are not home on election day, it's up to us to apply for an absentee ballot and fill it in.

The American system of **personal registration** favors those who aren't intimidated by the sometimes cumbersome and time-consuming registration process. To make things more complicated, each state and sometimes particular counties often have different forms and procedures for registering. In some areas and states, voter registration forms in which an *i* is not dotted or a *t* is not crossed are invalidated by elections officials.

In most other countries, the situation is quite different. National governments are responsible for making sure that citizens are registered and that they can vote. In Britain and Canada, officials monitor who has moved and who has not for the purpose of keeping voter lists up to date. In Italy, registration is not even an issue, since the possession of a national identity card is enough. And in Belgium and Australia, minor penalties are exacted on those who do not vote.

There is no doubt that duplicating these methods in the United States would raise levels of voting participation. We know that the vast majority of people in the United States who are registered to vote actually *do* vote, so making registration a governmental responsibility would boost turnout. Voter registration was originally part of an effort to depress turnout, so it makes sense that doing away with that system would boost it.

Analysts agree that changing registration laws and voting procedures (by changing election day to a Sunday, for instance) would probably also raise American turnout. At the national level and in most states, though, Republicans have generally resisted registration reform, and many, but hardly all, Democrats have generally favored it for partisan reasons. Republicans tend to believe that easing registration requirements would bring to the polls more Democrats, who predominate among low income citizens.[9]

In 1992 the Democratic Congress finally passed and President Clinton later signed a watered-down version of the so-called **"Motor Voter" bill.** It mandated that registration forms and voter assistance be available in motor vehicle and other government offices and that mail-in registration be allowed in all states. In or-der to get majority support, the original provisions calling for the *automatic* registration of all people who apply for drivers' licenses or public assistance was dropped.

Republican governors in Michigan, California, and New York initially refused to implement the law and tested its constitutionality in the courts, delaying the law's effects in key states until the spring of 1996. On the other hand, Motor Voter was successfully implemented in Indiana and Missouri because civil servants were encouraged and effectively trained to register voters. The results have been a modest but important rise in voter registration. In 1995 and 1996 the new motor voter bill helped to boost registration by at least 11 million.[10]

As a one-shot solution for massive nonvoting, registration changes have advantages but also limitations. Taken together, most analysts say that a combination of *all* measures, including automatic registration, would probably boost actual voter turnout by only about 5 percent to 10 percent. Although this would be a notable improvement, even the most optimistic predictions about voter registration would bring turnout back only to what it was in 1960, a year when registration laws were tough. Under the most radical proposals, 10 or 15 million more people would come to the polls in the election of 2000. Although this is a very significant number, it would still mean that U.S. turnout rates in the twenty-first century would be among the lowest, with affluent and better educated voters still vastly dominant.[11]

Although registration reform would help increase voter turnout, it is only a partial solution. Even as easier registration procedures have been introduced in most states and by the federal government, voter turnout in the United States outside the South has been declining. In 1988, registration laws were relatively lax, but voter turnout was far below that of 1940 and 1960, election years when voter turnout was relatively high and registering to vote was generally much more complicated. The fact remains that other explanations are needed to tell why, in the face of improved registration procedures, voting turnout continues to be so low.[12]

History Matters: Freedom Summer, 1964

The kinds of people who don't vote are often those who have the fewest economic and educational resources with which to assert themselves in political struggles. If large proportions of low- to middle-income people stay home on election day, the politics and policies are decided by people who are wealthier, less racially diverse, and older than the U.S. adult population. Changing registration laws alone does not change that fact. What would?

In America, voting and nonvoting seem to be related to the strength or weakness of grassroots democratic associations among people who are not particularly wealthy or highly educated. The civil rights movement of the 1960s is a case in point: In the late 1950s and early 1960s, African Americans organized themselves against the system of white domination and segregation that had existed in the South since the end of Reconstruction. Aided by their churches and by many young students both black and white, ordinary African Americans took on the system of racial apartheid through boycotts, sit-ins, marches, and demonstrations.

In the summer of 1964, known as **Freedom Summer,** hundreds of young civil rights workers of both races traveled to the South to assist the movement. A few of these workers were murdered. Others were met by mobs or gangs and severely beaten. Still, many of them, along with their southern colleagues, continued the work of organizing. At great personal risk, ordinary people—people who had never been political for fear of their lives, their jobs, or simply through a sense of resignation—also began to organize through their churches and neighborhoods. They held meetings and tried to persuade others to join the struggle. They held mass marches from one southern city to another, all peacefully. They talked to tenant farmers, sharecroppers, janitors, maids, and construction workers, who also began to organize themselves for freedom.[13]

People who had thought politics was not for them joined the movement. One of them, Fannie Lou Hamer, had worked as a maid for a white plantation owner in Mississippi all her adult life. Before the civil rights movement, she had thought little about politics. But after she talked to a civil rights worker, she decided to try to register to vote. After three attempts and a beating, she passed the highly biased literacy test administered by a hostile white county official. When she got back to the plantation, she told her boss what she had done. For registering to vote, he fired her. Ms. Hamer went on to become a full-time political organizer and a leader of the Mississippi Freedom Democratic Party. In 1964, her party challenged the white Democratic party of Mississippi, prompting a civil rights revolution in the national Democratic party's rules.

Hamer's experience was not very different from that of hundreds of thousands of others in the South. Civil rights activists urged people to vote, a process that before that time had been almost impossible for African Americans. Voting became an important part in a larger experiment in the political empowerment of ordinary people through the shared struggle for political and social equality. During this drama, many people changed in ways similar to Fannie Lou Hamer's experience. If you had asked the African-American farmers and workers of the South in 1950 to state their political opinions, they might have just shrugged their shoulders and said that politics and voting was for white people and that it was safer to not get involved. But the advance of democracy in the South changed people like Hamer: She learned that what she was experiencing on the plantation was not only her reality, but that of millions of others. More important, she learned that it could be changed, that one didn't have to be white or have a lot of schooling to be an active, intelligent citizen and to make a difference.

Under pressure from this movement, Congress passed and President Lyndon Johnson signed the **Voting Rights Act of 1965.** The act swept away the racist legal impediments to registration and voting by blacks that had been in force for nearly ninety years. Federal inspectors were sent to the South to supervise the registration of black voters. Literacy tests, poll taxes, and all the other mechanisms of apartheid fell. In Mississippi, the partial removal of these barriers made a tremendous difference, as thousands of blacks registered and voted who had not done so before. But it is interesting to note that even before the passage of the Voting Rights Act, people like Fannie Lou Hamer, participants in a powerful political movement, had won some of these rights themselves. Although registration laws were a barrier to popular democracy and to voting, the civil rights movement had removed a more important psychological barrier before 1965: What counted most was the political movement that gave people the courage to come together to fight the political and economic system of which registration laws were a part.

We cannot know what would have happened in the South if registration laws had been magically removed by the federal government without a strong political movement requiring it to do so. Yet we do know that in other places where registration laws were made more accommodating but where there was not a strong democratic movement present, removal of barriers did not bring torrents of new voters. Before 1965, New York City had low turnouts in the black community too, though not nearly as low as Mississippi's. But New York did not have a Freedom Democratic Party in every neighborhood, either. For many reasons, blacks in New York City were not very well organized politically in the 1960s. Because of the low level of black participation in New York, federal inspection of registration and election procedures was ordered there, too. But black turnout in New York City hardly increased at all; in fact, it began to decline in the early 1970s and did not begin an upswing until Jesse Jackson ran for president in the Democratic primaries in 1984 and 1988.[14]

In short, registration laws do matter. But overturning them made a big difference only when changing laws were accompanied by a strong political movement that conveyed the sense that registering and voting really were important as part of a larger political cause. Only when the civil rights movement established a strong connection between popular democracy and voting did registration—and voting—really increase.

Nonvoting and Grassroots Politics

People with little formal education may vote and participate less under certain conditions, but not others. Social movements like the civil rights struggle show that when grassroots associations form among ordinary citizens, the "natural" disadvantages of less-educated people can be overcome. Meetings, marches, boycotts, sit-ins, and voting seem to go together in social movements, forming a democratic political culture among people who might be otherwise isolated from one another and turned off by politics. How exactly has grassroots politics worked in American life?

Besides the civil rights movement, the farmer and labor movements of a century ago provide a vibrant instance of grassroots politics at work. In the 1880s and 1890s, the farmers of the Great Plains and South organized "alliances" whose goals were to wrest power over land and factories from eastern bankers, entrepreneurs, and Wall Street investors. Farmers' Alliances had educational, social, economic, and political functions. The strength of the Farmers' Alliances led to the greatest of all modern American political movements, populism, and its call for a "republic based on the dignity of labor" and government "by the people." In U.S. cities in the same period, workers banded together to protect themselves against the factory and wage labor system that denied them a living wage and the right to organize. Mass strikes and trade union activism abounded during the 1890s, prompted by the strength of grassroots associations like the Knights of Labor.

A significant feature of these associations is that they provided camaraderie, social services, and community. Farmers met to hear lectures about the economics of the time; they shared machinery and labor and tried to pool their resources and money to establish their own banks and credit institutions. Workers in the Knights of Labor formed clubs and associations that found them decent housing and provided legal protection when they were hassled by the police or private security guards. The Farmers' Alliances, the Populist party, and the Knights of Labor, each in their own way, helped their members to reduce the isolation of work life in farm and factory. Often, such groups sprang from what sociologist Ray Oldenburg calls "third places"—public spaces like taverns, coffee houses, clubs, and restaurants where people could be away from home and work and that "provided frequent engagement in the most basic of all political activities—*talk*." [15]

For the farmer and labor movements, grassroots politics always included voting, but as part of a much wider range of social, cultural, and economic activities. If neither farmers nor workers had much formal schooling, they nonetheless could learn the art of democracy by their own efforts to educate themselves. Leaders didn't have college degrees; instead, they had the kind of education that came from close contact with the problems and experiences of ordinary people.

In elite democratic terms, these "ignorant" workers and farmers shouldn't have been active in politics at all—they lacked the knowledge and time to understand a "complex" political world. But through their participation and collective power, numbers, energy, organization, and enthusiasm balanced the advantages of the wealthy.

Voting, Nonvoting, and Civil Society's "Decline"

If grassroots politics in the past has increased voter turnout and the political power of ordinary people, what is the situation today? Political scientist Robert Putnam has used a whimsical example to explain the dilemma of our own times:

"Americans are bowling today more than ever before . . . but bowling in organized leagues has plummeted." The broader social and political significance of
this decline, Putnam says, "lies in the social interaction and even occasionally
civic conversations over pizza that bowlers now forgo."

Putnam broadens his observations to include a greater truth about American
civil society today: ordinary people are just not as likely to engage in the activities that their ancestors in the Populist party, Knights of Labor, and the civil
rights movement once did. Though some dispute Putnam's assertions, there
does seem to be a consensus that associational life has declined among many low
and middle income groups. One consequence is the rise in nonvoting among
poor and middle income people. Nonvoting is less a product of uninformed citizens than it is of an economy and political system that make it harder for ordinary people to get together, talk, act, and vote.[16]

An important piece of evidence supporting this idea comes from the yellow
pages of any big city phone book. Under the heading "Associations" is listed an
apparently democratic array of groups from doctors, lawyers, and realtors to
chambers of commerce and sports clubs. In the biggest cities and especially in
Washington, D.C., associations of everyone from soybean and corn dealers to
financial experts and scientists and associations of different kinds of college professors might even be listed.

TOLES © 1997 The Buffalo News. Reprinted with permission of Universal Press Syndicate. All rights
reserved.

But modern associational life is biased, just like voting, towards the affluent and educated. In phone books, there are few listings for organizations of janitors, daycare workers, home health aides, or restaurant workers. The farmers' and workers' associations of the past were made up of individuals with little economic or political clout and with few resources besides their numbers, their time, and their ability to organize and educate themselves. They were based on face-to-face conversations and relationships. In contrast, many of today's associations tend to be organized from the top down, are managed by professionals, and are composed mostly of middle and upper class people. Rather than encouraging widespread talk and grassroots organization, many of our political associations are composed of members who never meet, don't know each other, and participate in politics only in the isolation of their own homes. Such **mail order politics** means that computer direct mail, post office boxes, credit cards, and checkbooks stand in for face-to-face contact between ordinary people. Professional lobbyists "do" politics "for" others.

Mail order politics, one recent study concludes, means that political activism "largely remains the province of those with higher incomes and better education" and that "money is fast replacing time as the most valuable commodity in political campaigns." The affluent and educated also possess other new resources that further their participation and political power in modern times. Perhaps the most important is their control of, and access to, the new means of telecommunications and computer technology. The affluent can afford computers and online services, e-mail, faxes, and cellular phones. Former Secretary of Labor Robert Reich call this phenomenon the "secession of the successful." Even as the affluent find new ways to talk and meet, they can wall themselves off from the problems of cities, public schools, and public streets. No wonder, then, that a prominent study of political participation finds that "when it comes to political participation, class matters profoundly in American politics."[17]

Meanwhile, the situation is far different for the new working class. Here, civil society has indeed declined. The **new working class** is largely service workers—such as home health care aides, janitors, word processors, and restaurant employees. They face low and stagnant wages, job instability, and uncertain prospects for future mobility. Many of them don't have the middle-income wages or access to the fringe benefits that America's older workforce once had. They generally work longer hours than they used to, just to stay even. Such broader changes in work patterns are accompanied by changes in consumption, family, and residence patterns that make it difficult for these people to get together. The new working class lives in homes that are often dispersed in sprawling suburbs, making close contact with colleagues more difficult. They shop in supermarkets, Wal-Marts, and strip malls where the business is strictly consumption, not informal talk and chatter. Disproportionately made up of women, the young, and people of color, the new workers have largely not, until very recently, been approached by labor unions. As a result of all these factors, members of the new working class don't participate much in social or political affairs.

With some important exceptions that will be discussed later, it is precisely among this fast-growing part of the population that voter turnout and political organization seem to have declined the most since the 1960s. Neither registration difficulties, apathy, or stupidity account for their low turnout to vote—but the new difficulties faced by ordinary people do. Instead of participating to change politics, nonvoters seem to react by "tuning out" politics, less from apathy than from a sense of resignation, impotence, and lack of time. Nonvoting is one such response, a "silent vote of no confidence" by millions of people to politics in its present form.[18]

Perhaps we have a tentative solution to the mystery of nonvoting. With dense associational life among the affluent and weak links among ordinary citizens and workers, a class divide greatly affects the character of the democratic debate. As a consequence, unaffluent nonvoters tend to see the American political debate as someone else's. With few political or social institutions to call their own, nonvoters perceive the political system and politicians as speaking an incomprehensible language, one with distinctive upper class accents and themes. Like Fannie Lou Hamer in the 1950s, modern citizens with few resources to participate in politics understandably come to believe that "politics is for someone else."[19]

Is such a situation permanent in American politics, or could popular democracy be revived on a large scale? Elite democratic explanations of nonvoting tend to neglect the rich historical experiences of grass roots democracy and the changes that have helped to isolate ordinary people from politics. In America, formal education, income, and age do indeed correlate with high participation in elections more than ever. Yet these are less causes of nonvoting than they are symptoms of elite democracy itself.

WOULD MOBILIZING NONVOTERS MAKE A DIFFERENCE?

What difference would it make if nonvoters came to the polls? One way of answering this question is to look at what nonvoters think about political issues. Such surveys have to be viewed with caution, though, because they try to predict the political actions of people who are not now very politically active. It may well be that any event or experience that would bring lots of nonvoters to the polls would also change their political perspectives, as the civil rights movement did to Fannie Lou Hamer. The processes that brought Hamer to politics and what she learned through participation made her a different person. So too is it likely that the process of making today's nonvoters into voters would change what nonvoters believe and do. Nevertheless, surveys *are* worth considering as snapshots of nonvoters as they are today.

Very few American nonvoters are committed in principle to not voting. By large majorities, current nonvoters tell pollsters that voting is an important right and a civic duty that they may and should undertake sometime in the future. Younger people are less likely to have this sense of civic duty than do older nonvoters. Still, there are many nonvoters who apparently feel guilty about not

MAKING A DIFFERENCE

Hispanic Power in the Southwest

Are people who don't vote not interested in democracy? The 1996 election featured one of the lowest turnouts in U.S. twentieth-century history. But Mexican and other Latino Americans in California, Texas, and Arizona, long underrepresented in the U.S. electorate, defied the national trend toward lower participation. In these states, Latino voter participation rose dramatically and in some cases far exceeded the national turnout rate. How did Latino voter participation set new records, and with what results for American politics?

The upsurge resulted from a number of short- and long-term factors. The first and most important has been the slow and steady growth of strong community organizations in the barrios and neighborhoods of big cities like Los Angeles and the working class Hispanic "suburbs" of Orange County. Back in the 1970s and 1980s, activist Willie Velasquez began the Southwest Voter Registration Project (SWVRP). Velasquez, a veteran leader of the farmworker movement, cajoled, lobbied, and prodded his fellow Mexican Americans to run for office and register to vote. He succeeded in reaching potential Latino voters by stressing the practical results of democratic politics. "The revolution started when we got Mexican American candidates saying 'Vote for me and I'll pave your streets,'" Velasquez once said. But the SWVRP did more: In Texas, Colorado, New Mexico, and California, it launched legal challenges to ban gerrymandering of electoral districts to dilute the power of Latinos. The result: between the early 1970s and late 1980s, the number of Hispanic elected officials doubled, to over 3,000, and Latinos gained representation in state legislatures, county governments, school boards, and city councils.

Velasquez's leadership spurred yet more efforts. By the early 1990s, Latino community groups launched an ambitious effort to register and get to the polls over 1 million new voters. The growth of

going to the polls, enough so that about 10 percent more people report voting than in fact do vote. At first glance, it would seem that nonvoters have no special attitudes about politics that distinguish them from voters.

Still, nonvoters are at the same time much more critical of the American political system than are people who vote consistently. In a 1984 University of Michigan study and a 1988 *New York Times* poll, nonvoters were much more likely than voters to agree with statements like the following: "I don't think public officials care much about what people like me think," "Things go on as before no matter who is elected," and "The government doesn't care about people like me." In a 1996 survey conducted by the League of Women Voters, nonvoters were much less likely to perceive significant differences between the parties and were also much less likely to see either of the two parties in a favorable light.[20]

More extensive evidence about the basic political beliefs of voting and nonvoting Americans are provided by other surveys. William Maddox and Stuart Lilie found that a political system dominated by the issues of most concern to the

Latino democratic power was spurred in part by Proposition 187, a 1994 California ballot initiative that proposed the shutoff of schooling to the children of "illegal" immigrants. But it was Latino *citizens* who turned out in record numbers to oppose it. Although the measure passed by a narrow margin, the high turnout gave Latinos throughout the Southwest a newfound sense of political muscle.

By 1996, the result was a massive 1.5 million increase in Latino registered voters in two years, with a 1 million increase in Texas and California alone, the places where the SWVRP was most active. Moreover, Latinos not only registered, they turned out on election day in both states. The results? In Texas, Democratic Senate candidate Victor Morales ran a surprisingly close race, losing narrowly to ultraconservative Senator Phil Gramm. In Orange County, California, once a bastion of Republican conservatism, Loretta Sanchez defeated Robert Dornan, perhaps the most conservative member of Congress. Hispanics boosted their membership in the California legislature, too. A Latino, Cruz Bustamante, became the new state assembly

speaker. And President Clinton's victory in many states, such as New Mexico, Arizona, and California itself, was made possible by the massive support he received among Hispanics.

Bob Mulholland, one of the California Democratic party's chief consultants, comments on the trend: "For all but the blind, the Hispanic vote is now an important part of the Democratic base. And it'll stay that way as long as Democrats respond to Latino concerns."

Willie Velasquez died in 1988. But some measure of his achievements came in 1996, when he was posthumously awarded the Presidential Medal of Freedom, the nation's highest civilian honor.

Sources: B. Drummond Ayres, Jr., "The Expanding Hispanic Vote Shakes Republican Strongholds," *New York Times,* November 10, 1996, p. A1; Gregory Rodriguez, "The Browning of California," *The New Republic,* September 2, 1996; George Ramos, "In Your Face Activist Group UNO Marks Two Decades," *Los Angeles Times,* July 15, 1996; Burt Folkart, "Willie Velasquez," *Los Angeles Times,* June 14, 1988.

affluent helps to sustain high levels of nonvoting. Lilie and Maddox found that about half of all American adults can be considered populists or liberals. Both groups share a deep disdain for government ties to corporate business. Both groups favor mild measures to redistribute wealth, regulate business, and provide more social services like universal health care. Only a third of those surveyed fall into either the libertarian or conservative groups, both groups who oppose government interference with private property rights.[21]

Lilie and Maddox found that people with populist and liberal views are much more likely to be nonvoters than are libertarians and conservatives. While about two-thirds of the latter regularly vote, only half of the populist-liberals report that they do. As a result, the groups most hostile to the existing distribution of power and wealth are not well represented in the voting electorate. Conversely, the groups most friendly to corporate power are overrepresented.

With their resentments of economic inequality, their prevalence in the American population, but their very low turnout, the populists could stimulate a new

American politics. What could bring them in large numbers back into the electorate? And if they came back, what kind of politics might they bring? Political scientist Kenneth Dolbeare argues that populists could indeed return to the political scene if faced with a national crisis of some sort. Which party they would favor depends on the nature of the crisis, he says: "Based on past experience, economic issues or events would bring populists to the side of the Democrats, national security threats or racial issues would send them to the Republicans."[22]

Do we really need a war or an economic depression to bring about higher turnout? Maybe, maybe not. The social makeup and opinions of many nonvoters suggest that there are powerful grievances and energies that could be tapped not only in times of war and depression, but in less dramatic circumstances, too. In the accompanying feature box, the story of one such effort is told. What is clear is that if the new energies are to be used in a democratic way, then face-to-face grassroots politics and organizations have to be rebuilt as well. Nothing less than the repair of the social and political organizations of the American citizenry is the solution to the "problem" of nonvoting. Though that's easier said than done, if we examine some cases where the mobilization of nonvoters has already occurred, we may find some valuable ideas for the future.

Chicago, 1983: A Case Study in Mobilizing Nonvoters

In some places, political life has been enlivened and nonvoters attracted to the polls, with real effects on public policies and the political agenda. In 1983, for example, something of an electoral revolution occurred in Chicago. Harold Washington, a Chicago congressman, led a coalition of African Americans, Latinos, women's rights advocates, labor union members, and white liberals into power at city hall, defeating the incumbent mayor Jane Byrne and the son of Richard J. Daley, the long-time Chicago boss, in the Democratic Party primary. In a tense campaign in which voters were polarized along racial lines, Washington later defeated Bernard Epton, the Republican nominee, in the general election. In 1987, Washington was reelected and brought with him a clear majority into the City Council. The next year, Washington died of a heart attack, and the coalition he helped to build suffered internal splits.

Washington's victory was remarkable for a number of reasons. First, it had been preceded by what might be called a transformation of political life in the city's black neighborhoods, featuring a revival of grassroots politics and associational life. Church congregations, labor unions, educational groups, community organizations, and even high school students combined their resources and got others to think about why they had been excluded from political power under the Democratic party's machine. New locally owned radio stations were formed and newspapers were started by people in the black community, balancing the news coverage of commercial TV and Chicago's daily newspapers with hard-hitting stories about the city's housing projects, social services, and education. People who were not otherwise expected to vote suddenly not only voted in large num-

TABLE 5.4

White and African-American Voters in Chicago Elections, 1975–1983

Election	Percent African-American Turnout	Percent White Turnout
Democratic Primary, 1975	34.1	46.5
Democratic Primary, 1977	27.4	44.8
Democratic Primary, 1979	31.5	48.9
General Election, 1982	55.8	54.0
Democratic Primary, 1983 (Washington vs. Daley and Byrne)	64.2	64.6
General Election 1983 (Washington vs. Epton)	73.0	67.2

Adapted from Paul Kleppner's *Chicago Divided: The Making of a Black Mayor,* © 1985 by Northern Illinois University Press. Used with permission of the Publisher.

bers, but also became participants in the political life of their neighborhoods and workplaces. Table 5.4 shows just how dramatic the mobilization of nonvoters was in Chicago elections.

The emergence of high levels of organizational activity and voting among Chicago's African-American population was remarkable for a second reason. While close to a majority in the city, Chicago's blacks cannot win a citywide race with their own votes alone. To win in a city election, they need to build coalitions in the Latino and white communities. Lest high levels of African-American voting spur fear among other races, the Washington coalition also organized heavily in the Puerto Rican and Mexican-American neighborhoods, and among the liberal and more affluent whites in neighborhoods surrounding the University of Chicago and bordering on Lake Michigan. Washington also drew many labor union activists of both races to his candidacy.[23]

The organizing vehicle for mobilizing Washington's constituencies was his populist stance on issues. The Washington forces attacked the big real estate developers and talked about decentralizing city services to neighborhood control, appointing new people to positions at City Hall, improving public housing, fighting drug dealers, and rebuilding public education. Washington's campaign also linked Chicago's problems to the national scene: His criticisms of the Reagan administration's treatment of the working class and poor, his opposition to bloated military budgets, and his pro-choice stance on abortion made his candidacy into a national crusade.

The Washington victory, in short, helped to change the political agenda in Chicago by forging a new coalition around issues that had been largely smothered in Chicago politics. Though Washington brought thousands of new voters into the electorate for the first time, his very success prompted a countermobilization among some whites. Emotions ran high in the general election campaign, perhaps the dirtiest and most passionate in Chicago's colorful political history. Thousands of white voters—in wards that were largely Democratic and had been for fifty years—abandoned their party's nominee and voted for the Republican Bernard Epton. Epton himself had been almost unknown until Washington's victory in the Democratic primary, and he did not shy away from using racist appeals in his campaign. One famous TV advertisement ended with the slogan "Epton: Before it's too late." Table 5.4 shows just how far voter turnout increased in white working class wards over previous mayoral elections. These wards overwhelmingly supported Epton.

The generally white city machine that Washington defeated had thrived off of low voter turnouts in African American and Latino sections of the city. Many in those neighborhoods had thought of white dominance of City Hall as an unchangeable fact. The Washington campaign taught people to view existing structures of political power as subject to discussion and change. But the Chicago case also demonstrates that when nonvoters are mobilized they may not all speak with one voice: Many white nonvoters, with many interests in common with their black counterparts, nonetheless came to the polls with the perception that race, rather than class, was the central political dividing line in the city. While the Washington campaign emphasized class themes and tried to appeal to voters in the white working class wards, these efforts were generally not successful.[24]

If nothing else, the case of Chicago casts doubts on the conventional explanations for nonvoting. In sharp contrast to those who believe that one's level of education and income determine levels of political participation, the case of Chicago in 1983 (and in 1987, when Washington was reelected) demonstrates that this is not necessarily so. Moreover, the Chicago case shows that the registration barriers are surmountable. With political organization, the unique barriers posed by the system of personal registration were overcome. When associational life is strong, as it was in Chicago's neighborhoods, new issues reach the political agenda. When political leaders express and articulate the needs and interests of their constituents, both nonvoters and voters respond in large number.

When people feel that politics matters, it becomes something no longer monopolized by professionals and experts. Politics is no longer something that can be ignored as an imposed, alien, or distant pursuit. Whatever else the Chicago election of 1983 was, it was a full reflection of the city's important divisions. Fundamental issues of political power were at stake.

Mobilizing Nonvoters in Recent Presidential Elections

Chicago in the 1980s is perhaps the clearest example of what happens when nonvoters *both* get organized *and* are mobilized by political leaders and organizations. Yet it is a rare example. In the presidential and congressional elections of the 1980s and 1990s, electoral history presents some revealing examples of the dilemmas, opportunities, and consequences of both low voter turnout and the attempts to change the situation.

The Rainbow Coalition: Half Full or Half Empty? The Reverend Jesse Jackson is the only presidential candidate in recent times who tied his campaigns' success explicitly to the mobilization of nonvoters. Jackson saw his campaigns as an attempt to speak for the outcasts in American life. Touring inner-city high schools, churches, factory towns in decline, and gatherings of striking workers, Jackson always accompanied his political message with efforts to register new voters. He targeted groups with high proportions of nonvoters—racial and ethnic minorities, young people, downsized and unemployed workers, and the poor, and he attempted to bring them into a "Rainbow Coalition" with feminists, environmentalists, and other groups in the liberal wing of the Democratic party. Jackson was critical of those in his party who had tilted toward support of the Republican economic policies of the Reagan-Bush years.

In the Democratic primary contests of both 1984 and 1988, Jackson gained what was seen as a surprisingly large vote. Much of it came from first-time voters. Turnout in Democratic party primaries surged in 1984 and increased by 6 million between 1984 and 1988, when Jackson's candidacy became a serious quest for the nomination. Jackson did remarkably well among young black and white voters participating in their first election, helping to bring to the polls hundreds of thousands of them.

The effects of Jackson's mobilization efforts on U.S. politics have been mixed. The long-term aims of the Rainbow Coalition were to build a solid, permanent bloc of new voters to transform the Democratic party. In the short term, some of these goals were accomplished. Jackson's candidacy, precisely because it shook up established politicians, probably pushed the party into more aggressive positions against the Republican party's social welfare and economic policies. Yet in the longer term, the Rainbow Coalition failed to build on its initial strengths at the grassroots level. After Bill Clinton's 1992 victory and after the 1994 Republican congressional victories, the agenda of politics turned less to representing outcasts than to attacks on government spending and on advocates of economic equality.[25]

The 1992 Campaign. The 1992 presidential election featured a 5 percent rise in voter participation, the biggest increase in forty years. Clinton was elected and a Democratic Congress was returned to office. The increased turnout looks less impressive when it is remembered that the previous presidential contest in 1988 featured the second lowest turnout in this century. Only 1924 had been lower.

What accounts for the moderate turnout rise in 1992? While keeping Jackson at arm's length, Clinton nonetheless appealed directly to many nonvoters. He made direct appeals to the "forgotten middle class" and concentrated on themes like universal health insurance, an increase in the minimum wage, and increased government aid for education of downsized workers. "It's the economy, stupid" was emblazoned front and center in Clinton's Little Rock, Arkansas, headquarters. Clinton's use of new media helped: He talked on MTV and on numerous nontraditional formats such as talk shows.

The presence of a third candidate, Ross Perot, also helped to raise turnout slightly. Both Perot and Clinton posed as outsiders and as reformers. They tried to fit the mood of a citizenry apparently disgusted with politics, politicians, and Washington. At the same time, both developed detailed issue positions. Like Clinton, Perot appeared on radio and TV talk shows and launched infomercials to explain his position.

Still, neither Perot, Clinton, nor Bush used their enormous campaign war chests to really go after nonvoters. They built few new grassroots associations, concentrating instead on the media to get their messages across. Perot often talked about his volunteers but spent the bulk of his campaign fortune on television advertisements. From 1992 through 1996, his organization was controlled by his own professional operatives. Potential grassroots support was discouraged by his professional hirelings, and by 1996 his "Reform Party" was greatly weakened. Actually, given the relative interest, hope, and expectations of citizens in the 1992 race, it is in some ways remarkable that the overall vote increased by only 5 percent.

Bill Clinton's campaign and the Democrats' national efforts involved few direct resources for party building at the grassroots. Clinton spent little on voter registration and spent even less time directly appealing to the people least likely to vote. Instead, Clinton's team calculated that poor and working class people would vote for him out of default or habit. His central appeal was to a middle class, who still had the voting habit.

Still, Clinton won about half of the 5 million new voters in 1992. *Twice* as many of these new voters chose Clinton over either Bush or Perot, and Clinton's appeal was greatest when it came to increasing white low-income voter support for the Democratic ticket. As we've seen, low-income whites are a growing portion of the "party of nonvoters." Sixty percent of the poorest Americans voted for Clinton. Still, turnout among the poor and near-poor was not much higher than it had been in the 1988 contest.

The real test for Clinton, and for the entire political system, would be whether the slightly higher turnout rate could be increased further in future elections. After his election, would Clinton seek to rebuild the Democratic party by mobilizing new voters? Or would he conform to the normal pattern of contemporary politics, with its emphasis on attracting affluent and more educated voters? [26]

The Lessons of 1994 and 1996. By 1994, the answer was clear. Conservative Republicans swept to power in Congress for the first time since the 1950s. They were aided by the fact that the most affluent Americans voted in even greater proportions than usual, while Americans with the lowest incomes voted even less than their already low averages. High-income whites increased their turnout, while the turnout of low-income whites, African Americans, women, Hispanics, and others dropped from the dismally low total of 1990. The already-huge class gap was further accentuated. According to a U.S. Census Bureau report, over 60 percent of voters in families with incomes above $50,000 voted in 1994, while less than 22 percent of people in families with incomes of less than $10,000 did. To be sure, Republican advances would have occurred even if turnout levels had remained unchanged from 1990. But the magnitude of GOP gains was made possible by the decreasing participation of the poor and near-poor, groups that are heavily Democratic if and when they vote. GOP victories were sealed by the 2 percent boost in turnout among the wealthiest fifth of Americans.[27]

The presidential contest in 1996 provided a further answer. With its 48.8 percent turnout rate, the 1996 election registered a steep drop from 1992, and even set some dubious historical records. The contest witnessed the lowest turnout in any election since 1924, and the second lowest in all of U.S. electoral history. Turnout dropped in all fifty states, and among nearly all demographic groups. More than three decades after the Voting Rights Act and only three years after the Motor Voter Bill, some were surprised by the dismal totals. Moreover, turnout should have been boosted by the naturalization of over 1 million new citizens between in the two years preceding the contest. What had happened?[28]

Clearly, Clinton's 1996 campaign had not capitalized on the potential of 1992. Neither he, nor Dole, nor Ross Perot excited nonvoters. Clinton, chastened by Democrats' defeats in 1994, had moved even further away from economic inequality as a theme, and had embraced many apparently Republican themes. By 1996 he had a big lead, and he was unlikely to risk it for the pursuit of an enlarged electorate. Dole was hardly an exciting campaigner, and Perot was for many a discredited figure whose lustre had tarnished since 1992. Nor did the media help: Campaign coverage dropped in depth and breadth. (See Chapters 6, 8, 9 of this book for further analysis of the 1996 election.)

But these explanations must be seen in historical perspective. After all, 1994 was labeled by everyone as an "exciting" election with momentous significance. Still, turnout was extremely low. Perhaps reaching "rock bottom" in 1996—less than half the electorate present at the polls—coincides with already noted long-term tendencies in modern politics. It may be significant, for example, that the lowest turnout election was also the highest-spending election, and that most of the money went largely for polling and TV advertising—and not for grassroots organization. Flush with cash, the parties were poor when it came to volunteers and grassroots activism. Advertising started early and dominated the airways. Media largely confirmed the image of the election as a cynical contest between competing egos and scandal-ridden individuals. Nor did the candidates really try to appeal to those least likely to vote. This is especially true on the Democratic side. In August 1996, President Clinton signed a "welfare reform" bill that ended the New Deal Democratic Party's commitment to a social safety net. In previous months, he had turned to the center and attempted to embrace such GOP themes as smaller government and a balanced budget. He spoke little about poverty, declining working class and middle class wages, or the plight of the

ROB ROGERS reprinted by permission of United Feature Syndicate, Inc.

inner cities. Instead, Clinton stressed how good the times really were. This was hardly an appeal designed to excite low-income voters.[29]

The result was a return to recent form—declining turnouts. Ironically, Clinton's concern for his own election probably cost the Democrats potential votes among the "party of nonvoters." Conversely, low turnout magnified the power of voters who observer Scott Keeter calls "hyperactive conservatives." Voters in 1996 were much more conservative and intensely partisan Republicans than were nonvoters. The two groups most likely to vote were the two groups most likely to support the GOP—born-again Christians and pro-business conservatives. Together, these two groups constitute only a quarter of the mass public. Yet on election day, 1996, they made up an impressive 37 percent of the voting electorate. Nine of ten voted for Dole and for Republican House candidates. Conversely, among nonvoters President Clinton led Dole by a 3 to 1 margin. Had they shown up, nonvoters would have preferred Democratic candidates for the House by a 59–41 percent margin, and the House would probably have been recaptured by the Democrats.[30]

The point, perhaps, is that nonvoters *don't* show up and are not likely to, given the alternatives and their own vulnerabilities in the political system. Yet even in 1996, there were notable exceptions to turnout decline. To some extent, the exceptions prove the rule: When people are organized, they shape the political system and its agenda. In the Southwest, Latino groups had been working for years to recruit candidates, encourage voter registration, and organize neighborhood-level political groups. As we saw in the feature box, their efforts paid off in 1996.

For the first time in U.S. history, Latino turnout came within a few points of matching overall voter turnout figures.

Organized labor, too, used some of its money to increase registration, political organization, and participation among its members. This strategy also paid off—among the core Democratic groups, union members were the only ones to vote in a higher proportion than their numbers in the mass public. In about a dozen key races, higher levels of union participation helped to defeat GOP freshmen. Moreover, the proportion of union members turning out in 1996 exceeded the average turnout rate for the population as a whole.[31]

CONCLUSION: WHO'S AFRAID OF NONVOTERS?

We have argued that nonvoting is so central to present-day American politics that no discussion of democracy can start without confronting it. To solve the mystery of nonvoting, we've turned to the rich history of grassroots democracy in America. Massive nonvoting, far from being a function of the "natural" ignorance or apathy of ordinary citizens, is a symptom and product of elite democracy. Nonvoting serves elite democracy by limiting political debate to the issues and alternatives most relevant to the affluent. Far from revealing the indifference of citizens to political participation, today's high levels of nonvoting expose the indifference of elite democratic institutions to the extension of democracy.

In the short term, a massive reentry of nonvoters into electoral politics is unlikely. Nor, if it did occur, would a fully participating electorate magically solve all the nation's problems. This is perhaps the point: Nonvoting is not just a bothersome blemish on an otherwise democratic system, but one of the key foundations of elite democratic dominance. The elements of popular democracy that remain in our system suggest that mobilizing nonvoters would change what we talk about. It would widen debate to include the concerns and interests of millions who fare poorly in the new global economy. The media would have to respond to new groups and their concerns. The best, as well as the worst, elements in American politics would stir electoral debate.

Who's afraid of nonvoters who might become voters? In the nineteenth century, opponents of participation barely disguised their elitism. Today, elitism is more subtle. The global political economy has helped to promote nonparticipation and nonvoting by fragmenting and dividing people with common interests. This situation makes it harder, though not impossible, for grassroots activism to start. The actions of elite politicians, interests, and institutions also have an important role in sustaining nonvoting. Concluding an exhaustive study of participation in political life, scholars Steven Rosenstone and John Mark Hansen remark that "participation in electoral politics rises when political parties contact, when competitive election campaigns stimulate, when social movements inspire." How true. The problem is that our political institutions seem to do little to contact citizens or stimulate social movements. From an elite democratic perspective, organizing takes time, money, and energy better devoted to influencing people who already do vote. And after all, elected officials have achieved their power within the *existing* electorate. So why bother with troublesome and unpredictable nonvoters and their demands?[32]

What are the prospects for a return to a fuller democratic debate? Even as elite democrats worry about too much democracy, there is every reason to believe that the problem is that there is too little. There is certainly no shortage of grievances that could bring nonvoters back into fuller participation. In future chapters, we explore at greater length the dilemmas and opportunities popular democracy faces in a world of media, parties, campaigns, and interest groups.

KEY TERMS

Jim Crow laws
political efficacy
personal registration
Motor Voter bill

Freedom Summer
Voting Rights Act of 1965
mail order politics
new working class

SUGGESTED READINGS

Michael Avey, *The Demobilization of American Voters*. Westport, Conn.: Greenwood Press, 1989. An important study demonstrating that the correspondence between low education and nonvoting can hardly be taken for granted.

Walter Dean Burnham, *The Current Crisis in American Politics*. New York: Oxford University Press, 1982. In this collection of essays by a prominent scholar of American elections, the rise of nonvoting is seen as one of the prominent features of twentieth century politics.

Frances Fox Piven and Richard Cloward, *Why Americans Don't Vote*. New York: Pantheon, 1986. Two scholars make a compelling argument about why increased voter registration is the key to increasing voter turnout and to fundamental political change.

Steven Rosenstone and John Mark Hansen, *Mobilization, Participation and Democracy in America*. New York: Macmillan, 1993. An exhaustive study of electoral and other forms of political participation, and an attempt to explain their fluctuation.

Sidney Verba, Kay Lehman Schlozman, and Henry Brady, *Voice and Equality: Civic Voluntarism in American Politics*. Cambridge: Harvard University Press, 1996. A comprehensive account of changing patterns of political and social participation.

The Media: Who Sets the Political Agenda?

Tuning in to various news stations during a busy week in the Summer of 1996, the casual listener might have heard this:

Meanwhile in Moscow, Boris Yeltsin, coasting to election victory . . . blew up a TWA jetliner over Long Island . . . amidst heavy traffic jams as the Olympics began in Atlanta . . . beginning a downward spiral into genocidal chaos in Burundi. . . . U.S. Senators challenged President Clinton by passing a welfare reform bill . . . created by the merger of Time Warner and Turner Broadcasting. . . . and followed by a steep slide in technology stocks . . . as a new outbreak of E-coli bacteria caused alarm in rural Japan.

Today, we tune in to the media to make sense out of a complex world. Yet the pace of "all news all the time" may only confirm the widespread sense that both history and the present are "just one damned thing after another." As you read this book, almost all of the "late-breaking stories" from 1996 will have disappeared, replaced by new tales of seemingly disconnected natural disasters, personal tragedies, far-off wars, touching feature stories, and political scandals. Avid media watchers seek in vain a sense of continuity and of context. Most of the millions of world events happening each week are beyond our personal knowledge and experience. For good or ill, it is the mass media that decide what is news in a confusing world. Defining news gives the mass media enormous power over politics and the political agenda.

In itself, media power shouldn't be cause for alarm in a democratic society. Thomas Jefferson, for one, said that he'd much rather live in a country with no government and many newspapers than in a nation with a government but no newspapers. To Jefferson, many newspapers meant many opinions and a spirited, educated, and diverse citizenry. A free media would embolden the people, alerting them to abuses of power and tyranny. Enshrined in the Bill of Rights, freedom of the press is synonymous with the idea that the media are powerful precisely because they represent different voices in a wide marketplace of ideas. At least in the abstract, elite and popular democrats alike support the media's freedom and independence.

Yet beyond the apparent consensus about press freedom lies the real debate. Just as in the discussion of the corporate political economy, it is important to ask: What if power is *concentrated* in the modern American media marketplace? In a true marketplace, there are many sellers and buyers. Is this true of the mass media today? Do media use their vast powers to set the political agenda in a particular way? Do a wide range of ideas and people get a hearing? Indeed, do new political ideas get as much attention as new celebrities or musicians? Are the mass media independent from other centers of power in America or connected to them?

At first glance, the answers to these questions are reassuring. One odd reason for confidence is that virtually everyone has something critical to say about the mass media. If surveys are to be believed, citizens are skeptical about what they see and hear through the mass media, even though Americans tune into the media more than ever. Political activists who otherwise despise each other come to a consensus that the mass media are "biased," even as they disagree about what the source and nature of that bias is. Ironically, media critics use media to voice their charges: Rush Limbaugh, for example, built a national radio audience precisely as an alternative to what he regarded as the liberal Washington news elite. In short, today's media seem anything but monolithic. With over 4,000 magazines, 1,500 daily newspapers, the prospect of 500 TV channels, and the brave new world of cyberspace, the mass media today seem to embody Jefferson's hope for variety. We may not like what part of the media says, but there's always the choice of turning off the television or writing an irate letter to the editor. These days, dissenters can wind up with their own Web site or as callers on a radio talk show.[1]

THE DEMOCRATIC DEBATE AND THE MASS MEDIA

Yet if America is a society of media critics, this doesn't necessarily mean that the media serve democracy all that well. From a popular democratic perspective, the modern mass media exercise a peculiar kind of freedom. Today, the mass media are less advocates for citizens than alien powers over them. Instead of being a rich idea marketplace where many voices and debates are heard, the media are criticized by popular democrats for concentrating on instant spectacles, contrived drama, "infotainment," and "eyewitless" news.

The top journalists are themselves celebrities who, in reporter William Greider's words, "have secured a comfortable place for themselves among the other governing elites." In what now passes for local news, there seems to be plenty of dollars for fancy weather maps and helicopters hovering over murder scenes, but only a few dimes for stories about how cities spend their money, schools educate their students, or employers treat their workers.[2]

In contrast, elite democrats worry little about corporate control and its attendant commercialism. The reasons are closely tied to the elite democratic idea that markets—whether they be in labor, toys, or media programming—are self-justifying. News programs succeed or fail because they give citizens or consumers what they want and so produce audiences for advertisers. For elite democrats, the basic structures of the media industry need to remain competitive and relatively free from governmental influence. Insofar as the media are free of this influence, the basic requirements of a free market, and a free press, are met.

Elite democrats, though, worry when the mass media defy established authority and tweak dominant cultural values and powerful institutions. Media messages can undermine established morality by promoting alternative lifestyles, questioning traditional families, and concentrating on abuses of power by corporations and established government institutions. Former Education Secretary William Bennett and GOP presidential candidate Bob Dole have complained about Hollywood and its supposed glorification of sex and violence; others score shows like the *Simpsons* for allegedly fostering widespread youth cynicism. For elite democrats, the mass media appear too often as irresponsible antagonists and critics of dominant American institutions and cultural beliefs.[3]

This chapter explores the varied charges against the media. The most important questions concern the media's role in the democratic debate and its definition and portrayal of public life. Has the growth in media power fulfilled the hopes of those, like Jefferson, who assumed that it would be a instrument of democratic rule? Or do the media squelch active democratic citizenship, mistaking the

sheer number of media outlets for political diversity and debate? Although critical of specific individuals in power, do the media nonetheless act to protect elite democracy?

MEDIA POWER AND U.S. HISTORY

Two fundamental historical developments help answer these questions. The media have grown in American life, but they have done so by crowding out other ways of getting information and ideas about politics and about other people. Where the family, the school, the tavern, the church, and the political party used to be the chief foci for political knowledge and conversation, most of what Americans know and think today about politics comes from TV, radio, magazines, newspapers, and the Internet. Second, media power and influence have followed the same tendencies rampant in the global political economy. Although political communications in America have almost never been owned or operated by government, private ownership of the media has passed over time from single individuals and small organizations into the hands of large corporations with a direct material stake in shaping government's economic, social, and foreign policies. Rather than acting as a check on unaccountable power, the mass media have become a source of undemocratic power themselves. How did the present situation come about? Do these trends make any difference for our marketplace of ideas?

Newspapers

American newspapers have always been published by individuals and private organizations. Yet in their early days their main purpose was not to make money. Rich or poor, American newspapers conveyed a political, usually highly partisan, version of truth. While today we'd think it odd if *USA Today* mixed its detailed weather reports and sports coverage with political treatises, the *New York Packet* printed the entire text of *The Federalist* in 1787. Frankly partisan and almost never objective, the republic's early newspapers were vehicles for political factions. Jefferson started one as an instrument of his Democratic-Republican party, just as his Federalist rival Hamilton began the *New York Post* as a political mouthpiece for his views. Financed by political loyalists or parties, newspapers were locally owned and represented the democratic debate in towns, villages, and small cities of the early republic.[4]

Although American newspapers were born partisan, they gradually lost their openly political character. By the mid-nineteenth century, the strictly partisan press began to be challenged by a new generation of owners whose aims were status, profits, and the highest possible circulation. Though politics was hardly ignored, papers like the *New York Sun* and *New York Times* redefined the news. Reporting on natural disasters, robberies, murders, society galas, and real estate transactions made newspapers longer and more popular even as it reduced their political content.[5]

Still, it was not until well after the Civil War that urban newspapers really became big businesses. They first began to increase profits by promoting advertisements. As news became a commodity to be bought and sold like any other, it was natural that newspapers like Joseph Pulitzer's *New York World* and William Randolph Hearst's *New York Journal* began to compete by *creating* news and not simply reporting it. Through **yellow journalism,** newspapers reported lurid tales of crime, scandal, and corruption, often exaggerating or even creating stories. In the 1880s, *The World* sent a woman around the world in a hot air balloon. In the 1890s, one of the most famous and frightening moments in U.S. journalism occurred. William Randolph Hearst dispatched the young painter and illustrator Frederic Remington to Cuba to report on what Hearst hoped would be an impending revolution against Spain. When Remington wired Hearst that there were few signs of war, Hearst telegraphed back: "Please remain. You furnish the pictures, and I'll furnish the War." Later, with screaming headlines and the offer of a $50,000 reward for the capture of the perpetrators, the *Journal* implicated the Spanish government in the sinking of the U.S. battleship *Maine* in Havana harbor. Soon thereafter, Hearst got his war.[6]

Newspapers at the turn of the century made money. But they still remained vehicles for the views of their colorful, buccaneer-capitalist owners. Both Hearst and Pulitzer used their newspapers for political crusades. They saw themselves as champions of the "ordinary man." Hearst nearly became governor of New York, and crusaded for the eight-hour day and woman's suffrage.

Since the beginning of the century, though, the dashing and often outrageous news reports were largely replaced by the more impersonal imprint of the corporate boardroom. Oddly, today's standard of journalistic objectivity and professionalism have their origins in the very subjective pursuit of bigger profits. The *New York Times* paved the way: For its early owners, objective reporting was a means by which to boost circulation by appealing to all readers, not just the partisan few. At the same time, profitable big city newspapers began to expand, absorb, and eliminate smaller dailies in medium-sized cities. Newspaper *chains* were born, and with them the number of individually owned and locally controlled newspapers began to decline. In 1923, 502 U.S. cities had two daily newspapers and a few had three. By the mid-1990s, only New York had three papers, and fewer than thirty cities had two. Simultaneously, newspaper readership generally declined in the 1980s and 1990s. By 1996, only about a quarter of adults under age 49 read a daily newspaper regularly. All these developments have been bad news for the newspaper business.[7]

Radio and Television

One reason for the consolidation of newspaper ownership was the stiff competition papers faced—first from radio and then from television. Both media were suited to the chain idea, rebaptized as the *network*. David Sarnoff's Radio Corporation of America (RCA), itself built with money from AT&T, Westinghouse, General Electric, and the United Fruit Company, was the pioneer in consolidating local stations. Yet when RCA began in the 1920s, news programming was not a high priority at all—radio started with amateur hours, concerts, soap operas, and Westerns.

Only with the onset of World War II did radio become a prime vehicle for news. The two men most responsible for the development were William Paley, the young owner of the new CBS Radio Network, and CBS's European correspondent, the legendary Edward R. Murrow. Through live wartime reports from London, Murrow dramatized and publicized the story of the Nazi bombardment in a way that newspapers could not. By the end of World War II, RCA's National Broadcasting Corporation, along with CBS and the newborn ABC, rivaled newspapers as a source of political information. Increasingly, papers met the challenge. They diversified their product, redefining news by feature stories about cooking, sports, weather, and entertainment.[8]

In the 1950s, the new medium of television, broadcast over the NBC, CBS, and ABC networks, captured public attention. Yet much like radio in its early days, TV in its childhood was not at all news oriented. In fact, corporations produced their own programming for networks, and news was not considered to be a big seller. This policy gave the fledgling news divisions of the networks some independence from the imperatives of profit making. Again, Murrow and CBS stood out. In a time of increasing political conformity, Murrow's *See It Now* documentaries hit hard at the tobacco industry and McCarthyism and revealed dire labor conditions on American farms.[9]

The growth and expansion of TV news as the most watched and thus most profitable form of news coverage occurred in the 1960s. Technological advances account for part of the surge. With smaller, hand-held cameras, satellite transmission, and videotape, TV journalism could move out of studios and newsreels and go where the live action was, at home or abroad. The 1960s provided plenty of lively political events to cover—and to create. The televised presidential debates between Richard Nixon and John Kennedy during the 1960 campaign perhaps began the trend. After that date, television became the central medium of influence for political candidates, and coverage from the early primaries through the November election became the most important source of impressions about campaigns. Politicians, in turn, began to realize that television was the key instrument with which to influence public opinion. In Kennedy's case, televised press conferences reflected the importance the young president assigned to TV-generated images and news. His assassination, as well as the civil rights protests, the Vietnam War, antiwar demonstrations, and urban riots were all well suited to the immediacy and drama provided by television coverage. Through television, nightly images of war, political conflict, and social unrest were all filtered through the media.[10]

The increasing importance of television news departments also began to make celebrities and political figures out of some journalists, prompting networks to notice that their news divisions could make money by drawing ever larger audiences. When the networks expanded their nightly news coverage from 15 to 30 minutes in the 1960s, Chet Huntley and David Brinkley on NBC and Walter Cronkite on CBS became the best-known and best-paid journalists in the country.

Today, the three old networks, now joined by CNN, remain the major sources of national news. Yet as Table 6.1 (p. 140) indicates, in the 1980s and 1990s TV news ratings steadily declined. The decline was particularly acute in the 1990s, and most pronounced among the young. By 1996, only a fifth of young adults watched the network news regularly. The rise of tabloid programs like *Hard Copy* and *Inside Edition* and infotainment programs like *Nightline* and *60 Minutes* provided alternatives. So too did the rise of new cable television news, led by CNN, MSNBC, C-Span, and even MTV. In the 1990s, new 24-hour "all news all the time" channels combined with the proliferation of cable channels to cut further into the traditional 6:30 P.M. audience. Some lament the decline of old-style TV news: Despite its flaws and biases, network news at its height at least provided a common link among the millions of citizens who tuned into the same programs. Moreover, network news programs were largely run by professional journalists who had worked their way up in a variety of reporting jobs and who seemed as concerned with reputation as the new programs' staffers are with ratings and audience share.[11]

TABLE 6.1			
Watching	**1993**	**1996**	**Trend**
Network, Local, and CNN	23	13	−10
Two TV News Sources	39	31	−8
*Network and Local only	(30)	(23)	−7
*Network and CNN only	(2)	(2)	0
*Local News and CNN only	(7)	(6)	−1
One TV News source only	24	31	+7
No Regular TV news watching	14	25	+11

Trends in Television News Viewing (percentage of adults using various sources regularly)

Note: Questions asked in this survey were: "For each that I read, tell me if you watch or listen to it regularly, sometimes, hardly ever, or never. . . . How often do you watch the national nightly network news on CBS, ABC, or NBC? This is different from local news shows about the area where you live. How often do you watch the local news about your viewing area . . . This usually comes on before the national news and then later at night at 10 and 11. How often do you watch the Cable News Network?"

Source: Pew Research Center for The People & The Press. Survey conducted April 19–25, 1996. Used by permission.

The Electronic Republic?

Driven by the proliferation of personal computers, online services, the World Wide Web, and shakeups in the telecommunications industry, a new technological revolution seems well underway. In the next fifteen years, the vast majority of Americans will have some access to interactive communication and the so-called information superhighway.

Much like radio and television at their beginnings, the "information superhighway's" advocates trumpet potential advantages for democratic life. In the late 1990s, those online are able to communicate with people and information sources of their own choosing and to establish Web sites of their own. They are able to access millions of sites around the globe about every possible topic. Information—and for that matter, unfounded rumors and outright falsehoods—now circulate at the speed of light around the globe. Some organizations already have "electronic town halls" and "chat rooms" that promote conversations and debates beyond the conventional one-way media.

All these changes indicate fearsome possibilities to some and awesome hopes to others. Media power could go the way of the dinosaurs, as people seize control and use the possibilities of sending into cyberspace their own versions of facts and events. Technology and democratic politics could blend together as great popular democratic revivals for the modern age.[12] What is clear is that the communications revolution has moved to a new historical stage. Yet the terms of the democratic debate about it may remain much the same as about past developments like radio and television: Who uses the new technology? Who will control the access to and communication among the citizens of cyberspace?

In the mid-1990s, personal computers and online services drew millions into cyberspace. Yet a Rand Corporation study found that interactive communications remained an activity of the affluent, and especially the affluent young and male. Surveys of online users show that hopes for a politically free and inexpensive new forum—so-called **virtual democracy**—have not been fulfilled. Direct conversations between ordinary people and political representatives were rare, replaced by e-mail sound bites and propaganda on the Web sites put out by many institutions. Moreover, corporations were beginning to move to integrate the communications networks that deliver telephone, film, television, and Internet communications into people's homes, but only at a big cost for the informality of the old Internet.

The greatest threat to public access and creative use of interactive communication came from the Internet's growing commercialization. As companies like Microsoft and AT&T went online as Internet providers, there was a tendency to turn the Net into a sophisticated, one-stop shopping mall, complete with paid advertising and subscription services. While a 1997 Supreme Court ruling outlawed government censorship, private censorship loomed, as companies like America OnLine began to monitor e-mail transmissions for offensive materials. The new corporate providers are hardly small businesses. Instead, they are media empires that do everything from selling old movies to producing TV shows, news programs, advertising, and cellular phones. The fight for wide public access and control of cyberspace remains a central issue.[13]

Powers of the Mass Media

One view of mass media history in America focuses on expanding choice and abundant technology. The other view stresses power and control. As the number of news outlets expands, the number of such outlets used by any single individual seems to shrink. Fewer people read newspapers or listen to radio and network news than they used to. People tend to choose one source of news and exclude or tune out others. The mass media today may be a marketplace, but one in which millions tune out public life and dialogue. Whether we surf the Net, watch reruns of situation comedies, or listen to a favorite music station, news is in danger of becoming a commodity produced and customized for specific consumers.[14]

Still, despite the fragmentation of the mass media into various outlets serving specialized audiences, the average American interacts with some form of media over eight hours a day. And even with declining ratings, the evening news still draws the attention of 50 million people, with another 100 million hearing some news via radio, newspapers, cyberspace, or some other way. The news media remain extraordinarily powerful.

The important question is how people understand what they read, see, and hear in the news media sources they consult. Back in the 1940s, researchers found that most people balanced what they heard through the news media with other influences—friends, coworkers, family members, and local members of interest groups and political parties. In the 1970s, scholars found that the media did little to change political opinions because people tuned out news stories they didn't care about or disagreed with and remained skeptical about what they saw and heard.[15]

Today, with the decline of political parties, trade unions, and many public associations, the mass media assume an increasingly important power as the commanding source of political information and talk. The modern mass media are **agenda setters:** Although they may not tell us exactly what to think, they do tell us what to think *about*. Out of the apparent chaos of newsworthy items, they select the stories and choose the narratives. When the media omit or bury a story, it is, in effect, censored and largely marginalized in public life. By setting the agenda, the news media can shape, limit, or expand that agenda. That's why the subject of the news media remains important. Which institutions and people influence the news media's definition of the agenda? Whose voice is reflected and whose is bypassed or distorted?[16]

CORPORATE OWNERSHIP AND CONTROL

Excluding PBS and National Public Radio, the American mass media have long been owned by private institutions and individuals, not by public authority. Just as in the rest of the economy, the private marketplace is supposed to promote competition. Competition in turn, is supposed to provide diversity, variety, and easy public access.

Yet the most dramatic changes in American news media history are prompted by the ever-increasing *concentration of ownership* in the media business, combined with the giant size and diverse activities of the corporations that control the production of news. Gone are the fierce partisans, press barons, or even colorful media moguls of the nineteenth and twentieth centuries. Disappearing are the decentralized and disparate newspapers and individually owned radio and television stations that once dotted the landscape. Instead, the modern media are increasingly folded into four or five megacorporations with vast operations that go way beyond the news and its production. The roster of corporate media mergers seems relentless. In the 1980s, General Electric absorbed NBC. In the 1990s, ABC and its parent company, Cap Cities, was gobbled up by the Disney empire. CBS was bought by Westinghouse, and Time Warner bought Turner Broadcasting and the sports teams, film production, and news network that came along with it. Meanwhile, Rupert Murdoch's News Corporation rose to prominence with a worldwide satellite network, a newspaper empire, and the Fox Channel.

Each of these corporations has holdings that span cable television, radio, newspapers, magazines, movies, book publishing, and music. Taken together, these media giants and their news divisions are linked to the international nuclear power and armaments industries, chemicals and their disposal, medical research and services, banking and insurance, theme parks, and housing developments. In Figure 6.1, the partial holdings of two such media giants—General

FIGURE 6.1 **Two Parts of the National Entertainment State**

A

General Electric
(Ranked No. 1 with GM in *Forbes* 500)
Subsidiaries in the following industries:

- Transportation (diesel and electric trains)
- Turbines for nuclear reactors and electric power plants
- Electrical equipment
- Communications
  (satellites and long-distance telephone service)
- Motors and industrial controls

- Insurance (GNA Corp.)
- Lighting
- Aircraft engines
- Appliances (GE, Hotpoint, others)
- Medical services (MRIs, X-rays)
- Plastics
- Networking software
  (GE Information Services)
- Financial (GE Capital)

NBC

- *9 TV stations, including:*
  WNBC-New York; KNBC-Los Angeles;
  WMAQ-Chicago; and WRC-DC.

- *Cable channels, including:*
  CNBC; Court TV; Bravo; American Movie Classics;
  and A&E (25% with Disney and Hearst)
- *NBC owns 25-50% of other cable channels, including:*
  History Channel; News Sport; Prime; Romance Classics;
  and seven regional sports channels.

NBC Network News

- *The Today Show*
- *Meet the Press*
- *Weekend Today*
- *NBC News at Sunrise*

- *NBC Nightly News
  with Tom Brokaw*
- *Dateline NBC*
- *Nightside*

B

Disney/Cap Cities
(Ranked No. 48 in *Forbes* 500)
Subsidiaries in the following industries:

- Crude petroleum and natural gas production
- Insurance (State Farm)
- Retail (400+ Disney stores; Childcraft Education toys)
- Motion pictures (Walt Disney; Touchstone; Hollywood;
  Miramax; Buena Vista)
- TV and cable (Disney Channel; Disney Television;
  Touchstone Television; parts of A&E, Lifetime,
  ESPN, Buena Vista)
- Theme parks and resorts (Parks in Anaheim, CA,
  Orlando, Paris, and Tokyo; others.)

- Sports entertainment (California Angels; Mighty Ducks)
- Home video (Buena Vista)
- Book publishing (Hyperion Books)
- Music (Walt Disney Records; Hollywood Records;
  Wonderland Music)
- Magazines (Fairchild Publications—*Women's Wear
  Daily;* Disney Publishing; others)
- Multimedia (Disney.com; ABC Online; Disney Interactive)
- Newspapers (eleven, including *Fort Worth Star-Telegram,
  Kansas City Star*)

ABC

- *ABC Radio* (owns 3,400 stations,
  covering 24% of U.S. households)
- *ABC Video*

- *10 TV stations, including:*
  WABC-New York; WLS-Chicago; KTRK-Houston;
  KABC-Los Angeles.
- *ABC owns 14% interest in Young Broadcasting,
  which owns stations in small- to mid-sized markets*

ABC Network News, *including:*

- *Good Morning America*
- *Prime Time Live*
- *20/20*

- *World News Tonight
  with Peter Jennings*
  (and weekend shows)
- *Nightline*
- *This Week*

Source: Adapted from *The Nation*, June 6, 1996, pp. 23–26.

Electric and Disney—are displayed. Media analyst Mark Crispin Miller calls the combined power of these companies the **national entertainment state.** Others have called media concentration the "real World Wide Web."

The national entertainment state also features a new wave of mergers and agreements between the media giants and the telecommunications and telephone industries. Here, corporations from the Baby Bells through AT&T, Sprint, America Online, and Microsoft are both struggling and cooperating to carve out monopoly control over parts of the information superhighway now under construction. If events unfold as many predict, a new media system will soon emerge in which Internet use, digital television, local and long distance telephone service and pay-per-view movies will be consolidated under the control of a few international media corporations.

Concentration of ownership in the national entertainment state has sent shock waves through the traditional newspaper and book publishing industries as well. Gannett, Inc., publisher of *USA Today*, expanded its holdings to become the largest publisher of suburban newspapers. Dozens of local newspapers either died or were bought by chains like Knight Ridder or Cox Communications.[17]

What are the effects of megacorporate ownership on the news media? Don't bite the hand that feeds you may be one lesson for working journalists and editors. Stories critical of the global corporate economy's treatment of labor and the environment were never dominant in American media. Today, they are even less likely to even get started when editors know that their livelihoods depend on companies with widespread interests in everything from nuclear waste disposal to diapers. One blatant example of the costs of the megacorporate takeover occurred after the Walt Disney Company's purchase of ABC. Back before the 1995 buyout, ABC's *Prime Time Live* ran several stories on Disney, tracing the often negative effects of its theme parks on surrounding communities. After the merger, though, ABC's *Good Morning America* became something of a showcase for Disney products. There were long segments on films and TV shows produced by Disney and favorable reviews of movies like *The Hunchback of Notre Dame.*[18]

In the emerging system, news "products" must be adjusted to fit the corporate parent's image. For ABC Radio, push came to shove in 1996 in the case of Jim Hightower, a Texas populist recruited in 1994 by the ABC Radio Network to provide some balance to rightwing talk show hosts Rush Limbaugh and Bob Grant. At that time, ABC radio responded to criticism of a right-wing bias in its talk show hosts by hiring a man who had once said of George Bush: "He was born on third base and thinks he hit a triple." In the aftermath of Disney's purchase of ABC, Hightower commented about it on the air, wondering if ABC News would become just a profit-seeking organization. He went on to criticize ABC News' cave-in during a threatened lawsuit brought by tobacco giant Philip Morris against the network. ABC had rightly claimed that the tobacco industry had knowingly manipulated nicotine levels in cigarettes to promote sales. For his frankness, and despite an expanding audience and subscriptions from over 150 stations, ABC and its new Disney owners fired Hightower.[19]

Megacorporate control is not always so blatant. In today's media, stories critical of business are not censored because they are rarely produced in the first place. Networks engage in a kind of courtesy censorship of stories that may embarrass corporate America or industries that are part of other megaconglomerates. In 1996, Project Censored, a consortium of media watchers and scholars, listed top stories that were left utterly unreported by the television news media. At the top of the list was the growing media monopoly itself and the millions of dollars that broadcasters were donating to both political parties to promote further relaxation of government regulations (see Chapter 8). Further down the list were stories that never saw the light of day—on the exploding number of workplace injuries, the $175 billion in yearly "corporate welfare" given away by the federal government, and the ties between the federal government's Department of Energy and corporations (such as network owners Westinghouse and GE) who continue to produce the materials necessary for nuclear armaments.

The effects of corporate ownership on the media's coverage of events are profound, affecting not only the character of public debate but the degree to which there is public debate at all. After Disney bought ABC, Disney CEO Michael Eisner explained that it was because of "the dramatically rising global appetite for nonpolitical entertainment and sports." Thus, corporate control not only censors the news in many ways, but it also may, according to former NBC News president Leonard Grossman, lead to the "disappearance . . . of documentaries exploring vital political, economic and social questions."[20]

Advertising for the Affluent

Corporate ownership subjects news divisions to enormous, if often unstated, pressures. But companies don't have to own networks in order to influence them. Advertising is the mother's milk of network profits. Network executives regularly review programming, including news stories, to ensure that they do not offend key advertisers. Phillip Morris, the world's largest producer of cigarettes and also a major TV advertiser through its subsidiary Kraft Foods, demanded and got an apology from Disney/ABC when its news program *Day One* showed how tobacco companies manipulated nicotine levels. Procter and Gamble, maker of everything from Crest toothpaste to the highly controversial food additive *olestra*, refuses to advertise its products on networks that "give offense, either directly or indirectly, to any commercial organization of any sort."[21]

The power of advertisers need not be blatant to have effects. Networks make their money by selling advertising, and they base the price of their ads not only on the size of the audience but its wealth and income. In news programming, the search for **upscale demographics** and higher revenues may bias the definition of the news. Stories that attract the more affluent are favored, while those that appeal to the working poor or the unemployed may be newsworthy but tend to get neglected. One obvious example of such bias towards the affluent is the proliferation of programs and newspaper space about business. Every newspaper has a business section, and most TV and radio stations run stock market reports. But

almost none of the print or broadcasting media regularly covers labor, runs stories on ethnic politics, talks about daycare for working families, or transmits systematic data about the effects of welfare reform on America's poor.[22]

GOVERNMENT INFLUENCE ON THE MEDIA

The fact that the mass media are in private hands hardly means that government has no influence on the news media. Much of television and radio, as well as the new technologies of the information superhighway, are regulated by the federal government because it has the power to grant licenses to use the public airwaves. At least in theory, the public owns and has the right to manage the radio and TV airwaves in the public interest. Even the Internet, now trumpeted as an innovation of modern capitalism, was begun by research scientists connected to the Department of Defense.

Nor has private ownership of the mass media usually meant that the media act independently of governmental power. In both the past and present, close ties between government officials and news organizations have served to hide or slant stories favorable to particular people and policies. Jefferson's hope for a free and independent press has often been disappointed by the "revolving door" by which key decision makers move between the two realms.

At the same time, the mass public has sometimes used government to achieve a measure of popular control over corporate-dominated commercial media by providing public access and mandating balance in political coverage. More often than not, periods in which popular democratic movements have been strong are also periods where the mass media's commercialism has given way to increased public access and diversity in programming.

Regulation of Broadcasting

Since the advent of radio broadcasting, elite and popular democrats have struggled over the question of how well or poorly a commercially driven media can serve democracy and the public interest. Through government, the public "owns" the airwaves by which both radio and TV signals flow. Government thus possesses an enormous power to shape the mass media's structure and character. This ongoing battle was particularly important in the 1930s, when labor, consumer, and church groups pressed government for a media system in which noncommercial, publicly owned stations would be paramount over the then-young broadcasting corporations. The broadcasting industry pressed for maximum consideration for commercial interests and against publicly owned media.[23]

In 1934, the Federal Communication Act was passed, and with it the Federal Communications Commission (FCC) assumed a central role in establishing the legal guidelines for the mass media industry. The FCC—whose commissioners are appointed by the president and approved by Congress—was mandated to regulate the airwaves "in the public interest" and to foster "public dissemination of news." It was supposed to prevent monopolies and promote competition, under the assumption that the public airwaves should present the broadest possible spectrum of views. Yet the 1934 act provided few concrete provisions for public access or control over the airwaves and none for public ownership. Since then, the FCC has granted thousands of radio and television licenses to private companies, but with only loose regulations governing the media's responsibilities to citizens in a democracy.

From the 1940s through the early 1980s, the FCC did impose some minimal obligations and rules on private broadcasters. Stations were required to reserve part of their programming for public affairs. If stations aired advertisements for one political candidate, they were required to supply the same opportunities to others. (Communists were excluded.) The **Fairness Rule** required broadcasters to provide reasonable time to opposing views on controversial topics. Monopolies in local markets were prohibited: No single corporation could own local newspapers, television, and radio stations in the same media market. In the 1960s, media activists also carved out limited public space for National Public Radio and the Public Broadcasting Service. Both were meant to be places free of commercial influence.

MAKING A DIFFERENCE

Challenging Corporate Media

Will the public interest and an enriched demo-cratic debate be produced by the new media revo-lution? Or will the information superhighway be a controlled access turnpike, full of tollbooths, bill-boards, and patrol cars? When Congress passed the Telecommunications Act in 1996, most major media hardly reported it and most members of Congress puzzled over the act's complex provisions. But regulating the media is hardly a technical ques-tion. If cable, television, computer, and publishing giants have their way, the media revolution will be a reactionary one, allowing companies to monopo-lize the standards, ownership, and huge profits from new media.

Yet the act has produced a new generation of media activists who've reacted to the threats posed with new ideas of public access, diversity of content, and diffusion of ownership. Throughout 1997, conferences have been held and letters sent to the Federal Communications Commission (FCC), the government body that makes the specific rules.

Working together, a host of groups ranging from FAIR (Fairness and Accuracy in Reporting) to the American Library Association, the Learning Alliance, and dozens of local groups have worked hard to form a kind of media Bill of Rights. Conferences sponsored by the Cultural Environment Movement and the Media and Democracy Congress have made public media more than a technical topic.

In rough form, here's what they've come up with:

1. *Fighting corporate monopolies*: The American people own the airwaves over which radio and television channels operate. If there are going to be 500 channels on the new TV dial in ten years, why not reserve some of them for commercial-free pub-lic access broadcasting? The entire Public Broad-casting System and National Public Radio could be paid for if the likes of Disney, Westinghouse, Rupert Murdoch, or General Electric paid market rates for their access to new channels. In fact, the new digi-tal technology could fund hundreds of community

Yet over time and with increasing frequency during the Reagan presidency, most of these regulations were gutted, revised, or ruled unconstitutional by the courts. The broadcasting industry, whose growth and power had been made pos-sible by lenient government licensing requirements, led the charge against reg-ulation and generally succeeded in achieving most of its aims.

In the mid-1990s, the development of new broadcast technologies combined with the increased lobbying clout of telecommunications giants to produce pres-sure for deregulation. The result was the **Telecommunications Act,** passed in 1996 with substantial bipartisan support. The ostensible goal of the bill's sup-porters was to further competition by breaking down the existing walls that pre-vented one industry from entering the market of another. For the bill's support-ers, the act was supposed to stimulate a new Information Age.

By late 1997, what was clear was that the Telecommunications Act was stim-ulating a massive giveaway of the new airwaves to private corporations. The bill

broadcasting channels, and the government has the power to improve community access to the Internet. Some people even go further: In exchange for the channels, why not insist that all Americans be hooked up to the information superhighway, that access be universal and free?

2. *Content*: In any real market, people exchange things. How about applying the same idea to the new information superhighway? Corporations are going to reap huge profits, but shouldn't they be obligated in return to provide educational programming for children, without commercials on the Internet or television? And how about the obligation to cover public affairs and news? What about using the proceeds to be gained from the new digital networks to hook up all public and private schools to the Internet and make them immune from advertising? The resources provided on the new information superhighway are enormous. Can't we take advantage of them to widen the public square?

3. *Access and affordability*: Just now, only a quarter of the American public has access to computers or the Internet. Will we build a system where people have to pay unaffordable fees to be part of the Internet? How about taxing advertising on the Internet to pay for universal access to information for all American citizens? If it's going to be impossible to work, relax, or think without access to the World Wide Web and e-mail, shouldn't everyone have access to it?

The basic message of media reform groups is this: Civic life, governed as it is by the media, is too important to be left to megacorporations. Media activist Leslie Savan believes that the new technology of telecommunications is also producing a "real World Wide Web" of democratic activists but that it "gets relatively little media attention because the big media players own the media that could tell the story. . . . And to all the choices between Coke or Pepsi, Nike or Reebok, we can give thumbs up or thumbs down. We have the power!"

Sources: Center for Media Education, "Seven Public Interest Principles of the Telecommunications Policy Roundtable" (www.cme.org); Robert McChesney, "Digital Highway Robbery," *The Nation*, April 21, 1997; "A Twelve Step Program for Media Democracy" (www.cme.org/cme.).

knocked down restrictions that once separated telephone, cable, TV, and radio companies from competing in each other's markets. At the same time, it also allowed them to combine in yet larger megacompanies that control communications in entire markets. The new law scrapped the remaining FCC regulations regarding concentrated ownership of diverse media. Companies could now own two television stations in the same market, and there is virtually no limit on the number of radio stations companies may own.

Perhaps the most disturbing aspect of the bill was the FCC's interpretation of it. In a few years, television will be transmitted through a *digital spectrum*, a new technology that will allow the multiplication of TV channels and their marriage with the Internet and the telephone. In theory, the public owns the digital spectrum. Yet by late 1997, the government was giving away digital spectrum licenses (with a market value of $70 billion) to megacorporations—at no charge and with virtually no strings attached. Companies like Rupert Murdoch's News

Corporation and Michael Eisner's Disney may use the new airwaves and cyber-space to make as much money as they want, without any obligation to broadcast news, public service programming, or even provide debating time to political candidates. In Robert McChesney's words, "The stench of corruption is so thick that the *Wall Street Journal* even ran a front page article deploring the give-away."[24]

What could government do to act in the public interest, to provide public access to the new digital spectrum? The feature box (p. 148) details popular democratic efforts to democratize the new media.

From Disinformation to Intimidation

Through its advocacy and even outright aid to media conglomerates, the federal government has largely withdrawn from imposing even minimal requirements for public affairs programming and public access to the airwaves. But as the government has spurned the democratic task of providing public access, other parts of government have not refrained from attempting to shape media content. Throughout the Cold War, the CIA organized "disinformation" campaigns to plant fabricated stories that confused and discredited domestic critics and foreign opponents of U.S. government interests. In the 1980s, for example, CIA director William Casey successfully disseminated false information about the supposed connections between Nicaragua's Sandinistas and the drug trade, leaked untrue information about Soviet missile strength, and even organized an association of newspaper owners friendly to the cause of overthrowing the Sandinista regime. During the 1989 invasion of Panama, the agency successfully disguised its long-time relationship with Panamanian dictator Manuel Noriega, who had by that time become a U.S. enemy.[25]

J. Edgar Hoover ran the FBI for nearly sixty years, and part of his longevity rested on his ability to buy, intimidate, and manipulate reporters. Hoover's agents spied on many reporters deemed unfriendly. They blackmailed some by threatening to reveal aberrant sexual behavior or alleged affiliations with leftist organizations. After Hoover died, the bureau's activities continued, this time in the Nixon "Counterintelligence Program," infiltrating left and antiwar newspapers with spies and wiretapping and leaking stories designed to discredit antiwar leaders to friendly newspapers like the *San Diego Union*.[26]

The Revolving Door

Yet in most cases, government influence over the news is not so direct. A subtler example of government influence is the **revolving door:** Often, independent journalists are picked to be government officials, and government officials find new and distinguished careers as reporters covering the institutions they recently left. When government insiders become working journalists and vice versa, the wall of separation between media and political authority may be weakened and the incentive for reporters to file objective stories is greatly lessened.

"Celebrity" journalists are particularly prone to be beneficiaries of the revolving door. Renaissance Weekends attended by Bill and Hillary Clinton include numerous guests like Cokie and Steve Roberts of ABC and reporters from the *New York Times*. George Will soared to journalistic fame with ABC and through a widely syndicated column, but in 1980 he coached Ronald Reagan for his debate with Jimmy Carter. Employed by ABC at the time, Will later praised Reagan's debate performance in front of the TV cameras. (After his dual role as coach and commentator was revealed, Will apologized.) The *New York Times* columns of William Safire, former speechwriter in the Nixon White House, reach a worldwide audience. Ted Koppel touts his friendship with Henry Kissinger, who once offered him a job as press spokesperson for the Nixon State Department. David Gergen, a former aide to Presidents Ford, Reagan, and Clinton, may be the revolving door champion, interspersing White House service with jobs as commentator on PBS and editor of the *U.S. News and World Report*. In recent years, Clinton aide George Stephanopoulos and Republican congresswoman Susan Molinari left public service to take jobs as TV journalists and commentators.

Professional journalists strive for objectivity. Yet media bias today is often revealed in the kind of "experts" that are chosen as commentators and sources on national news programs. Here, the revolving door spins rapidly. Most experts chosen tend to be fellow insiders, former government officials, academics associated with Washington think tanks closely tied to the federal government, or officials themselves. *Chicago Tribune* columnist Clarence Page has labeled this phenomenon the "Rolodex syndrome." When a dramatic story appears, the networks, including CNN, all seem to possess a similar guest list of former government officials recast as either journalists or neutral experts. A study of Ted Koppel's *Nightline* reveals that over 80 percent of his guests were professionals, government officials, or corporate representatives.[27]

The Rolodex syndrome is on particular display when it comes to military intervention abroad. During the Persian Gulf War of 1991, the Pentagon enacted the toughest restrictions on the news media in U.S. history. It controlled the movement of all journalists in Saudi Arabia, Kuwait, and Iraq, and supplied all the combat images available to the private media. Since much of the action was in the air war, the Pentagon fed to the media news videos, usually of laser-guided smart bombs hitting their targets precisely. Reporters were grouped into "pools," and the Pentagon reserved for itself the right to censor news stories. Yet at home, few experts employed by the media contested any of the government's measures or its highly censored accounts of the war's progress. Out of the 878 on-air sources used by all the networks, only one represented a national peace organization. In 1992, NBC News hired Pete Williams, director of the Pentagon's media-muzzling program, as one of its major Washington correspondents.[28]

In the years that have followed, we have discovered that much of what was reported during this war turns out to have been false, while other stories ignored by the experts have come to light. Six years after the war's conclusion, a government report revealed that the "smart bombs" shown on TV didn't work at all well. In early 1997, the high levels of disease reported by Gulf War veterans exposed to chemical warfare sparked some attention. But the Pentagon had by then conveniently lost most of the records that would have established connections between illness and American incursions into Iraqi territory.

Media Bias: Which Way Does It Go?

One common response to the charge of overzealous government influence on the media has been to deny its existence. Another has been to claim that the media are overwhelmingly liberal, prone to grinding ideological axes against government, big corporations, and established power. In recent years, conservative Republicans have led a spirited attack on the television news media for its allegedly liberal biases. In 1995, the new GOP House and Senate majority worked hard to cut funding for both National Public Radio and the Public Broadcasting System, partly because of the alleged liberalism of their journalists. Organizations like Accuracy in Media (AIM) have concluded from their studies that the media is unduly influenced by the supposed liberalism of most journalists.[29]

Such charges rest on very slim and partial evidence—for one thing, they virtually ignore the effects of corporate ownership and government influence on working journalists that we've already discussed. Still, surveys of journalists *do* indicate that they are somewhat more likely than the public at large to vote for Democrats for president and that they are slightly more liberal on issues like the environment and abortion than the public as a whole is.[30]

Yet the numbers are hardly overwhelmingly tilted in one direction. According to one study sponsored by the Freedom Forum, only 23 percent of journalists call themselves liberal, 19 percent are avowed conservatives, and the rest "middle of the road." Moreover, the journalists who define themselves as liberals have a far from radical, or even politicized, definition of the term. Journalists tend to define liberalism as "not bound by doctrines or committed to a point of view in advance." Few define liberalism as the advocacy of rights for labor, people of color, or the poor and unemployed. Only 14 percent think that "being an adversary of business" is extremely important, while only 21 percent think "being an adversary of government" is. Providing analyses of complex problems and getting news to the public quickly rank much higher for the average journalist than ideological bias. Often, as James Fallows has demonstrated in his study of the 1994 debate about the North American Free Trade Agreement, the Washington "press displays . . . an instinctive sympathy with the interests of the educated elite. . . . The press chose the 'college boy' side of the argument—apparently without realizing that it was choosing sides."[31]

Overall, the social characteristics of American journalists mirror those of other professionals. With the important exceptions of celebrity journalists and reporters for the most prestigious publications, reporters' salaries average less than those of elementary school teachers and college professors. While African Americans, Latinos, Asian Americans, and especially women have made employment gains in journalism over the last twenty years, the vast majority of reporters are white males who hold college degrees and come from upper-income Protestant homes. None of these characteristics is supportive of the idea that journalists are somehow prone to liberalism, much less to radical critiques of the American social order.[32]

MAKING (AND CREATING) THE NEWS

Earlier, we detailed some of the possible effects of corporate ownership and government influence on the mass media. Yet it is quite another thing to say how—or even if—most journalists on an everyday basis are effected by such influences.

After all, most reporters have nothing like the connections, status, or seven-figure salaries of Dan Rather, Diane Sawyer, or Peter Jennings, who are power centers in their own right. For the average reporter, making the news is about the much less dramatic daily business of gathering facts, attending press conferences, and interviewing sources. For news editors who supervise reporters, making the news is about assigning reporters to stories, ensuring that reporters' stories live up to certain professional standards, and making daily decisions about which news will appear and where. From inside the news organization, blatant pressures from advertisers, the parent corporation, or the CIA or FBI may seem pretty remote. News media professionals point to how stories exposing corporate and government shenanigans—like Watergate in the 1970s, the savings and loan debacle in the 1980s, or the campaign finance scandals in the 1990s—have been unearthed by and through adherence by news organizations to the high-minded standards of American journalism.

Thus, the professional standards of journalism are often seen by media defenders as the shield against overtly political and corporate influence. Reporters are taught to be *objective*, in that they remove from their stories their own ideological point of view, letting the facts speak for themselves and the chips fall where they may. As they seek *balance*, they report the diverse views of different spokespersons when a dispute arises. And, as news organizations compete to better inform the American public, they seek to create that wide "marketplace of ideas" that is supposed to be the major justification for media competition and press freedom in the first place.

These standards are professed by most reporters, producers, and editors, including the big-name celebrities. No doubt, most are sincere as they seek to uphold them. Yet the structure of modern news organizations makes the task difficult. Objectivity and balance are difficult to maintain in a world where elite institutions have an advantage over ordinary citizens when it comes to defining and creating news.

The Problem of Sources

News doesn't happen everywhere. Issues, facts, and events become news only when reporters report them. And to report the news, journalists must be present where something happens. Thus, where reporters are located often determines the subjects the news media select for attention. The vast majority of American political reporting comes from Washington, D.C. The White House, the Congress, the Justice Department, the Pentagon, and other governmental agencies are the major beats of political reporters. Government agencies and institutions, as well as interest groups that can afford it, have thus become not only the major objects of political reporting, but the prime sources for most political news as well. There is certainly no lack of government and corporate press relations personnel to influence the press. In Washington alone, an army of 13,000 federal employees generates publicity for several thousand correspondents. In the early years of the Reagan administration, the Pentagon alone spent $100 million on press relations, and the Air Force alone generated over 600,000 press releases.[33]

It is understandable that the doings in Washington make news. But a natural corollary of the process is that Washington reporters mostly report what they hear in Washington from their sources. Day after day, reporters travel between press briefings issued by private and public organizations who spend millions to create favorable public images for the people and institutions they represent. Thus, "balance" is sought within the restricted realm of the Washington think tanks, government agencies, and monied interests who have the resources to establish themselves as newsmakers. And almost all the sources upon which journalists rely for their information have a very direct, often personal stake in what is reported. Moreover, they have press relations bureaucracies in place to influence the press, and journalists come to rely on such staff to provide them access to the interviews, background information and inside scoops necessary to get the job done. The result, former reporter Robert Entman has claimed, is **source bias** and the fact that "the news largely consists of information supplied by sources who support democracy in the abstract, but must in specific encounters with the press subordinate that ideal to the protection of their own political interests."[34]

Given the Washington connection, it is difficult to see how journalistic objectivity can operate in practice. Some Washington beats—especially the White House, State Department, and offices of the major congressional leaders—serve as the chief sources for hundreds of reporters. The press releases, interviews, and press conferences emanating from these sources by themselves make news. Even if it is false, what the Presidential press secretary says must be reported. For "balance" or a response, yet another governmental official, probably from the opposing party, is quoted. Less likely to be quoted as part of balance are those groups without extensive clout or without Washington offices with press officers. These include most of the grassroots groups in American society that can't afford to employ the media experts, lawyers, and lobbyists that government and corporate America can. In this way, media reporting often reflects not reality but how the different representatives of the status quo construe it. Smart reporters take care not to alienate too many of their sources; if they do, they'll be cut out of the inside story. Professor Lance Bennett comments: "Cooperation between reporters and officials is so routine that officials rarely have to employ intimidation tactics."[35]

McNews

The concentration on similar sources does not mean that all news is reported in exactly the same way. Television news specializes in the dramatic and the immediate and is more likely to cover one-time events and the doings of people and celebrities. In contrast, the print media tends to report more extensively on institutions, issues, and policies and in most cases provides stories with more information and facts than does television. With the exception of National Public Radio and a few other sources like the Pacifica Radio Network, radio news consists of short bulletins and little depth. The media marketplace is also competitive: Reporters and their news organization compete to achieve better access to news sources and the inside stories and scoops.

Yet despite these important contrasts between TV and the print media, what is remarkable about "news products" is not how different they are but how similar they have become. Modern news organizations work according to routines and draw from other media sources that tend to standardize how the media define and report news. Many newspapers as well as the networks rely on the wire services of Associated Press for their stories. And the New York Times Company and other media giants supply articles that are often picked up by smaller newspapers. To save money, local news stations—now more than ever owned by media conglomerates—often depend on their parent networks to lead them to important national stories.

For TV, a premium is placed on the predictability of "where news will be happening." Camera crews and reporters must generally be prepared in advance to cover speeches, hearings, natural disasters, or the travels of politicians. Thus, those institutions and organizations that can preplan their events for the TV cameras have an advantage. Besides Washington, news beats are likely to include, in order of importance, New York City, Los Angeles, Chicago, and these days perhaps Atlanta or Houston. News happening outside the reach of the national news bureaus stationed in such cities is likely to get much less attention. For local stations, the situation is even more driven by commercialism; they find it cheaper and more profitable to cover sensational crimes, feature stories, weather, and sports. "Investigative journalism is just too expensive," explained one student of the subject.[36]

While print and TV reporters do compete for stories, they also cooperate in a phenomenon known as **pack journalism.** Most of the time, reporters covering everything from political campaigns to presidential trips travel together, receive the same press kits, attend the same press conferences, and face the same requirements to file a story by the deadline. In these interactions, they acquire a collective sense of where the story does and doesn't lie. As Timothy Crouse said in his study of the 1972 presidential race, reporters "arrive at their answers just as independently as a class of honest seventh graders using the same geometry text."[37]

The result is a remarkably similar spin on a story and a strong consensus, forged by what the pack sees and hears. The problem is that what they see and hear is limited by the nature of the beat itself and often by the public relations talents employed by the organization and persons being covered. When the pack travels with the presidential candidates, the aftereffects and prepreparation of a candidate's visit are often missed and the press can seriously misread the candidate's strength or weakness.

Conversely, where the pack *isn't* defines a news nonevent. If a reporter isn't there to cover a story about nuclear waste disposal sites in eastern Washington state, the civil war in Algeria, or rising income and wealth inequality, then a story simply won't be filed and won't appear. The big stories are often missed by hundreds of journalists assigned to cover conventional institutions and politicians. The exposure of major scandals like Watergate or Iran-Contra was hardly the result of the huge numbers of reporters stationed at the Nixon or Reagan White House. The pack remained ignorant of both stories until well after the events had occurred.

The pack is not an association of equals. Among reporters, the coverage of the *New York Times, Wall Street Journal*, and *Washington Post* possesses influence far beyond that of most other news sources, including the television networks. Stories that appear in any of these newspapers may work their way into the reporting of other news media because, if the *Times, Journal,* or *Post* reports it, it is almost by definition news. Although some reporters knew about government lies about the conduct of the Vietnam War, it took the *New York Times'* coverage of the 1968 Tet offensive and its decision to release the Pentagon Papers (a secret history of the war) in 1970 that really burst the dam of media silence on the government's war policies. Many other news outlets are reluctant to run news stories about major national institutional figures and events if they have not been covered first by one of the Big Three.

Like fast food, "McNews" is also the product of the increasingly profit-driven character of news organizations. As megacorporations come to dominate and control news organizations, the standards of professional journalism tend to erode in favor of news that is manufactured to be entertaining. In order to serve the parent company's bottom line, news must be inexpensive to produce. Keeping a costly staff of reporters who do in-depth stories is not very profitable, especially if the company can find ways to make money with fewer reporters, more pictures, human interest stories, entertaining formats, and "feeds" from network news sources. If murders, natural disasters, fires, and traffic accidents are easier to report and help to increase audience share, then they can replace more difficult-to-cover stories about politics, economics, and the effects of public policies. What passes for variety in modern media is less often about what is reported than in the formats in which news is delivered. Stations differentiate themselves through gimmicks—colorful weather reports, humorous anchorpeople, "live team coverage" of murder and mayhem, or unique feature stories about nonpolitical topics. McNews defines the important news as the entertaining news.[38]

Companies usually justify McNews by saying that news, like any other product, is simply a response to what people want. This is an interesting rationale, for it seems to mean that news is not a set of objective or even real events, but a planned and packaged contrivance manufactured for sale to consumers. Also, it may very well be that people want McNews because it is the only available choice presented to them on the news menu. Media surveys rarely ask people what they really want or need to learn about public affairs. Instead, they confine their questions to choices between such weighty matters as the clothing styles and studio decorations, or viewer preference for more sports or more weather. Alternative ways of defining and reporting the news are not options. News is less the product of consumer choice than it is the product of the limited offerings presented to consumers by media corporations.

BATTLE OF THE TITANS: JOURNALISTS, POLITICIANS, AND CAMPAIGNS

So far, we've stressed that the news media are profoundly affected by *outside* influences like government, corporations, sources, and beats. To a greater or lesser degree, each influence also makes bias toward the support of existing institutions almost inevitable, even if unintentional.

Still, it would be a mistake to see the bulk of news organizations as membranes through which the views and conflicts of other elites merely pass unfiltered. If media were simply the slaves of politicians, it would be impossible to explain the varied treatment given to such figures as Bill Clinton, Newt Gingrich, and Colin Powell. It would also be impossible to explain why virtually every elected politician seems to distrust the media. If the press is so close to powerful elites, why do elite politicians complain so much?

The way the media covers presidential campaigns helps to answer the question. Here the media appears at its most combative and independent. Scholars seem to agree that candidates of both parties get their share of positive and negative stories, and that overall there is no tremendous bias toward one party or ideology over another. Reporters grill the candidates regularly. Commentators give searing analyses of image problems, gaffes, and apparent contradictions in the candidates' statements.[39]

While campaign journalism seems hard hitting and independent, it is worth asking: Hard hitting about what, and independent from whom? Answers to these questions are provided by observing the 1992 presidential campaign between President Bush, then-candidate Bill Clinton, and Ross Perot. In comparison with the elections of the 1980s, the 1992 race is unique because the candidates spent more time answering questions posed by ordinary citizens than in any modern election. In their nationally televised debates, local town hall forums, and replies to callers on radio and TV talk shows, the three candidates were forced into the open. Most of the questions posed by ordinary citizens were about the substance of politics and public policy—they asked about the budget deficit, health care, gun control, and taxes (See Chapter 8).

Analyses by Thomas Patterson, Matthew Kerbel, and Marion Just found that the concerns of both print and TV reporters in 1992 were far different from the concerns of citizens. Reporters asked candidates about the *hows* of politics. They wanted to know what the "strategic intentions" of the candidates were as they talked about policy. They asked about campaign flip-flops, gaffes, and apparent failures to attract new constituencies. Eighty percent of the stories filed even in that most substantive of newspapers, the *New York Times*, interpreted what the candidates said in terms "of how they were calculated to advance electoral prospects." By concentrating on who's ahead and who's behind, campaign reporting has been labeled **horse race journalism.** Covering the horse race means that campaign journalists spend very little time examing the *merits* of policy proposals, their interconnectedness, or who benefits and who loses in the American population. Instead, all that matters is whether or not what candidates say affects their poll standing.[40]

Horse race journalism is coupled with journalists' self-designated role as key interpreters of the inside strategies used by modern campaigns. In 1992, TV journalists often crowded out the candidates on news reports. The average sound bite from candidates averaged only 8 seconds on the evening news, while journalists' comments swelled to over 35 seconds apiece. Journalistic independence, in this sense, often came across as covering stories of interest to the politically knowledgeable, but utterly bewildering and mostly irrelevant to those with little interest in the inside story.[41]

As Figure 6.2 shows, the 1996 race was not much different, and perhaps even magnified current trends. All three major candidates appeared in fewer "open forums" than in the 1992 race. As usual, the bulk of news coverage consisted of stories about polls and strategy. But polls and strategy were not quite as newsworthy in 1996 because Bill Clinton maintained a big and consistent lead throughout the year. Consequently, policy stories made up a slightly higher proportion of news stories on TV. Overall, however, TV time and newspaper space devoted to election coverage dropped dramatically in a campaign year the media deemed to be boring precisely because the race wasn't close. In the continuing search for drama and excitement in the 1996 race, one picture did make it onto almost all newspapers' front pages. When Bob Dole fell from a platform in Chico, California, his pained expression made big news.[42]

As usual, the two debates held between Clinton and Dole (Perot was excluded) were analyzed solely in strategic horse race terms. Postdebate commentary featured comments on who had won and lost by pundits whose criterion was style, not substance. The media consensus was that neither Dole nor Clinton said anything new, that each candidate had performed close to the expectations of his "handlers," and that Clinton had therefore won by not losing ground.[43]

A slightly new 1996 twist on horse race coverage was how it dealt with allegations about Whitewater and the Democratic Party's campaign contributors—an old potential scandal and a new one. Journalists reported little about the severity, meaning, or even substance of the alleged transgressions of the Clintons in the Whitewater affair or the Democrats in fundraising. What was important was not the substance of the stories but their potential political effects. Reporters concentrated on *how* the Republicans planned to use both in campaign strategies

FIGURE 6.2

**Focus of
TV Coverage,
1992 and 1996
Presidential
Elections,
Primary and
General Elections**

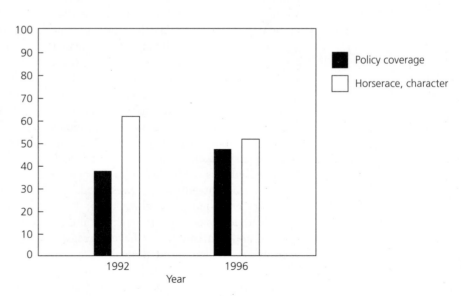

Source: Center for Media and Public Affairs, 1993, 1997.

and *how* the Clinton team attempted to "spin" a defense. Typical is NBC White House correspondent Jim Miklazewski's portrayal of Clinton's remark about *New York Times* columnist William Safire. Safire had called Hillary Clinton a "congenital liar," and Bill Clinton responded that he'd enjoy punching Safire out if he were not president. Here's how Miklazewski dealt with the incident: "It's all part of the new White House strategy to launch an aggressive counterattack against Mrs. Clinton's critics. First, deny the allegations. . . . Second, attack the investigations. . . . Then attack the accusers."[44]

Campaign journalism and its focus on the game of politics has an ironic effect. In their quest for the inside story, campaign journalists come to rely on the strategists and campaign organizations they investigate. If campaigns are just games between candidates and their staffs, reporters need to rely on insider sources who can tell them about what is "really" going on behind the public speeches and posturing. Campaign consultants, media experts, and pollsters become the sources for such information. And of course, candidates' staffs are well prepared to soothe the press and meet its daily appetite for juicy tidbits and rumors. After serving Clinton as a 1992 campaign consultant, James Carville wrote a book telling all about how the Clinton campaign cared and fed for the press corps and their demands for insider information. Dick Morris, Clinton's discredited 1996 campaign strategist, recounts a similar game in his "kiss-and-tell" tale of the 1996 campaign.[45] (See Chapter 8 for more.)

Left out of the journalistic loop are citizens, their groups, their needs, and their interests—except as they appear in the raw numbers of the continuous polling about who is ahead and who is behind. Journalists need not even visit a state to find out what its voters are thinking. Instead, they can talk to pollsters and spin doctors who give them the latest numbers from tracking polls. Thus, while campaign consultants and the media seem to detest each other, they become dependent on each other for information and publicity.

Some argue that campaign journalism is the way it is because that's what consumers—a.k.a. voters—want. Yet both public opinion polls and TV ratings indicate that the media rendition of politics as a game turns off most citizens. Voters gave the 1996 campaign press acceptable grades, and a majority of those who did vote said they thought they knew enough to make an intelligent choice. But perhaps the notable grade on the media comes from its inability or unwillingness to report matters from the standpoint of ordinary citizens. After all, half the citizenry failed to show up in the 1996 election. James Boylan, one of the founding editors of the *Columbia Journalism Review*, argues that nonvoters "fail to see in current politics, as presented by the media, any connection between their vote and their political interests."[46]

Indeed, levels of popular cynicism and indifference toward both the electoral process and the candidates have increased with modern campaign coverage, even as knowledge about the candidates and their positions has generally decreased.[47] Campaign journalists thus do achieve a kind of independence. Unfortunately, it is usually independence from ordinary citizens. By defining campaigns the way it does, journalism degrades democratic politics and citizenship.

Rather than as a horse race, perhaps campaigns are portrayed as professional wrestling matches. Voters, like wrestling fans, really know that the grunts and bluster of politicians are fake and feigned and that the makeup and costumes are designed only to titillate. We cheer or boo, but ultimately who wins and loses doesn't matter—it's just a game. The problem is that politics, because it decides who gets what, is more than a game. Real people get helped or hurt by a president. We are not fans, but citizens. And unlike sports reporters, campaign journalists have the power to shape the contest they observe.

Despite the apparent antagonism between the press and political candidates, media coverage of campaigns is thus a good example of the constraints imposed by both the media's routines and their emphasis on entertainment rather than content. Ultimately, whether it is in the media's coverage of campaigns or battles in political institutions, the mass media seem to reserve to themselves the task of shaping the political agenda. Unfortunately, the agenda that they set often bolsters elite democracy by confining citizens to the role of passive spectators and consumers.

Popular Democratic Alternatives

The examples presented here confirm the argument of political scientist Jarol Manheim, who called news a "manufactured commodity" driven by the modern media's need for "power and money."[48] Yet could the news be defined differently? Could citizens develop their own media that tell them what they need to know as citizens? Could news organizations be tranformed so that a wider definition of what matters could surface?

Alongside the dominant tendencies toward elite insulation in the contemporary media stand some rich traditions and contemporary innovations that give meaning to these questions. The richest tradition of all is perhaps the widespread popular skepticism about what the media say. Despite all the powerful tendencies toward corporate control of the news media, ordinary Americans remain unconvinced by the news media and their portrayal of events. Perhaps declining ratings for news programming reflect widespread distrust of the dominant media's portrayal of politics and events rather than public apathy. For all the vaunted power of the news media, they have lost a good deal of credibility in recent years. Declining numbers of viewers may represent a silent vote of no confidence in a media world dominated by the likes of Disney and Rupert Murdoch.

More positively, the situation is not hopeless for alternative voices—those who seek to build a different media more connected to democratic citizenship. A small but vibrant press remains alive on the margins of the corporate-dominated media (See Table 6.2 on p.162). The most important role of alternative media is to break stories and pioneer cultural and political trends that corporate media shun or ignore. On the national level, magazines like *Utne Reader*, and *Mother Jones* continue to break stories neglected by the conventional news organizations. The savings and loan scandals were largely ignored by the dominant press in the 1980s but were fully investigated by *The Nation* throughout the decade.

TABLE 6.2	Conventional Magazines	Circulation	Alternative Magazines	Circulation
Comparative Circulation of "Alternative" and "Conventional" Magazines, 1997	Time	4,095,000	Ms. (liberal feminist)	478,000
	Newsweek	3,228,000	Utne Reader (liberal-left)	260,000
	US News	2,220,000	La Opinion (LA Hispanic daily)	201,000
			Mother Jones (liberal-left)	136,000
			The Nation (liberal-left)	100,000
			The Advocate (gay-lesbian)	75,000
			2 Magazine (left)	22,500

Source: *The Standard Periodical Directory*, 20th edition, 1997.

When the story broke during the Bush administration, the groundwork for further investigation was already prepared.

Nor are all journalists working in contemporary news media muzzled or led so easily. The tradition of investigative journalism brought the American public knowledge (albeit belated) of government lying and deception during the Vietnam War, the Iran-Contra scandal of the 1980s, and covert aid to death squads and right-wing terrorists in Nicaragua and El Salvador. The tradition of investigative journalism knows no ideology and is often upheld by journalists and their own professional organizations and standards. Within news organizations, many reporters continue to fight to remain autonomous from the dual imperatives of commercialism and corporate control. One professional organization among journalists—FAIR (Fairness and Accuracy in Reporting)—publishes monthly accounts of how corporate control warps what Americans see and hear.[49]

Another sign of change within American journalism is the number of critical accounts of the contemporary news media penned by reporters themselves. Some of these criticisms have hit home via a new move towards **civic journalism** among editors, reporters, and academics. The civic journalism movement decries the trend towards entertainment over reportage and insider cynicism over coverage of issues that concern the mass public. It is not surprising that civic journalism seeks to reconnect to the people as thinking citizens, not simply as consumers. In North Carolina, the *Charlotte Observer* initiated "citizens' panels" in 1996, drawn to represent the characteristics of the state's population, that would meet and advise the paper about its coverage of the long-term issues affecting the state's economy, culture, and society. Concerned less with objectivity and more with connections to the ordinary people of the communities they serve, the civic journalism movement has spread to other papers (many of them independently owned).[50]

New media like the World Wide Web and the Internet also can serve as instruments of popular democracy. While we've said that corporate control threatens these new media, there is also some sign that they can be used to generate and disseminate information and create new networks and political communities. People concerned about toxic waste dumps in their communities have, for example, shared information on the Net about corporate misbehavior. Labor and environmental groups have established impressive Web sites that allow instant access to a host of data useful to activists. Former network executive Lawrence Grossman calls these developments the formation of a new "electronic commonwealth" that might overturn, or bypass, the old, corporate-dominated news media.

The biggest obstacle faced by those who want to expand the diversity and voices of the mass media is the shrinking public space for political and cultural debate. Public radio and television, once thoroughly uncommercial and free, have seen their budgets slashed and their mandates narrowed by advocates of market economics. In response, both have turned to corporate underwriters as new sources of revenue. Yet both struggle to remain relatively free, and the battles about them continue in Congress and in the communities they serve. In the near future, the biggest shrinkage of public media space is posed by the Telecommunications Act and its mandate for corporate mergers. But here, too, the battle is far from over, as public media activists argue for public access and participation in the information superhighway.[51]

CONCLUSION: DEMOCRATIZING THE MEDIA

In an era promising 500 TV channels, instant communication, and a periodical to suit every taste, political media have the chance to be as diverse as the public they serve.

Yet in the news media, choice of stations cannot be mistaken for diversity of news coverage. The media are not sharply partisan, but they do seem to ignore stories that defy their increasingly commercial drives. The result is conformity, though diffused through a multiplicity of news outlets. Excluded are the wealth of views of social movement activists without public relations experts, nonconforming activists and scholars, and those critical of media commercialization itself. Ultimately, today's dominant news media seem to be saying that ordinary people aren't really interested in politics and can't bring about political change.

Despite these tendencies, epitaphs for the popular democratic character of the mass media are premature. The media can and sometimes do reflect and enrich the democratic debate. For popular democrats, prompting the media to live up to their full democratic potential remains the central task.

KEY TERMS

yellow journalism
virtual democracy
agenda setting
national entertainment state
upscale demographics
Fairness Rule

Telecommunications Act
revolving door
source bias
pack journalism
horse race journalism
civic journalism

SUGGESTED READINGS

W. Lance Bennett, *News: The Politics of Illusion*, 3rd ed. White Plains, N.Y.: Longman's, 1996. A comprehensive and hard-hitting account of commercial and other factors at work in the news business.

James Fallows, *Breaking the News: How the Media Undermine Democracy*. New York: Pantheon Books, 1995. The current editor of *U.S. News and World Report* calls for a return to professional standards in U.S. journalism.

Doris Graber, *The Mass Media and American Politics*, 5th ed. Washington, D.C.: Congressional Quarterly Press, 1996. The most complete text on the media in American politics, updated to take into account new developments.

Marion Just et. al. *Crosstalk: Citizens, Candidates and the Media in Presidential Campaigns*. Chicago: University of Chicago Press, 1996. A good selection of readings on recent developments in campaign journalism.

Robert McChesney, *Corporate Media and the Threat to Democracy*. New York: Seven Stories, 1996. A critical and scholarly account of both new and old developments that threaten public access to the airwaves.

Are the Parties Over?

Dateline: Washington, Kansas, 1892

The People's party rally began with a long procession from town to the grove. Each Alliance and People's party club member carried an appropriate banner. For two days, over a thousand people heard speeches, listened to band music, and sang songs. Nearly everybody, men, women and children, wore the same kind of badge. "Equal rights to all, special privileges to none" was the favorite.

Dateline: Washington, D.C., 1997

Over four years, 938 guests stayed in the White House, many in the Lincoln Bedroom. In the year before the 1996 election, the president held scores of coffees for donors and other political supporters. Many donors who gave $50,000 to $100,000 were invited to small dinner parties with the president. The donations were made to the Democratic party, avoiding the legal limit on the size of contributions to individual candidates . . . but the Party spent most of the money on television advertisements promoting the president's policies.[1]

A century apart, these two campaign reports show that American party politics and electioneering are about the business of gaining loyal supporters and staging often-spectacular events. Whether it is Kansas in 1892, Washington in 1996, or on the road with Bob Dole and his "three-day campaign marathon" in the waning hours before the 1996 election, political parties and their candidates have to grab the people's attention if they are to win their votes. Yet despite similarities, these accounts also signify enormous changes that have transformed our political parties and the meaning of elections.

Return for a moment to 1892. Kansas farmers rallied under the banner of a political party, the "people's party," or Populists. Their loyalty to the Populist party went beyond just voting for it. Their massive, open-air rally was not only support for a political candidate but also a community festival. A thousand farmers, most probably with little schooling, put up with two days of political speechmaking. By their presence and patience, Populists testified to their intense devotion to their cause. The banners they brought testified to the larger Populist goal—economic equality and an end to Wall Street misdeeds. Not even present was the Populists' 1892 presidential candidate, James Weaver. Blending circus with seriousness, the party politics of the nineteenth century was a collective effort.[2]

For these Populists or even for their Democratic and Republican counterparts in 1892, the Democrats' 1996 strategies would have come as a shock. President Clinton's efforts appealed to loyal supporters, but most of what he and his party did to win votes required money, media, and marketing to reach the voters. The candidate himself was at center stage, not the Democratic party's grassroots supporters and activists in cities and towns. The television advertisements paid for by the Democratic party promoted the president and his record, not the party and its principles. Many of the Democratic party's donors were not Democrats but people seeking special access to whomever was in power.

These two events capture the themes of this chapter. Something has changed about what political parties mean to people and how party candidates present themselves to American voters. Today, many citizens think of the parties as corrupt and elitist clubs or don't pay attention to them, while others still feel affection for them. Historically, the competition between our parties is the most visible testament to the growth of electoral democracy. Some say our parties are stronger than ever. The Democratic and Republican National Committees raised and spent more money in 1996 than they ever had before. The parties recruit, train, and finance candidates, and partisan debate sets the agenda for Washington politics. Yet we'll explain later why parties have become weaker in the one area that may matter the most: inspiring activism or even consistent loyalty among average Americans. At the grassroots level, our political parties are not very strong. For popular democrats, rebuilding them as instruments for political participation is an urgent task.

We will explain these statements by looking at the important roles political parties can play in democracies, then exploring the peculiarities of American parties and their historical record. We will discuss when and how our parties embody popular democratic impulses and suggest why they might have persisted and even grown stronger today at the cost of many of their popular democratic features.

WHY POLITICAL PARTIES ARE IMPORTANT

What makes parties in democratic countries different from other political organizations like social movements, interest groups, or debating societies? Parties do many of the same things as all of these but have special functions as well.

Political parties are distinct because they bring together individual citizens around elections and voting. While the vote of a single individual rarely makes a big difference, blocs of voters can and do. Parties can transform individual powerlessness into the collective voice of the many. Since voting is the one political resource all adult citizens share equally, parties and their mobilizing roles further political equality. Ordinary people don't have much money, can't lobby, and have few personal connections. But parties, because they're in the business of putting together votes, can provide a public, democratic space where people can converse, debate, and come to common agreement (see Chapter 10).

Parties naturally want to win as many votes as they can, if only because more votes means more elected officials for them. Naturally, therefore, they'll want to increase turnout, especially if they face competition. Mobilizing maximum support usually requires parties to build *coalitions* among religions, regions, classes, races, and other social divisions in American public opinion. Effective coalitions slowly alter the narrow claims of groups and individuals, turning them into a vision of the public interest through compromise and discussion. This *party philosophy* becomes important as a way of holding different kinds of voters together and forming an identity that endures over time.[3]

American parties also *recruit and nominate* candidates and help them campaign for public office. In theory, strong parties can provide the resources that allow any party activist, regardless of his or her personal wealth, to stand for public office. When they are strong, parties also ensure that there is some minimal political similarity among people who run on the party's ballot line. By forming distinctive identities, parties can present clear choices to voters. As they compete, parties clarify these choices by accentuating their ideological and policy differences.

Strong political parties promote the *accountability* of elected officials to the voters who elected them. As we saw in Chapters 1 and 2, elite democrats have long wanted to free officeholders from the supposed "whims and passions" of voters. In contrast, strong political parties can discipline elected officials by making sure that there is a correspondence between what elected officials do and the *party platforms* on which they campaigned.

American parties were born in the late 1790s from the realization that chaos would result if each senator or House member represented only the interests of his or her district or state. Political parties have bridged the differences among officeholders by forcing them to consider the claims of other representatives from other districts and states. By bringing representatives together, parties can make our political institutions accountable to the electorate for their performance. At their best, parties can reduce the gridlock that can result from the separation of powers and checks and balances laid down in the Constitution.[4]

WHY AMERICAN PARTIES ARE UNIQUE

What parties *can* do is pretty abstract. Scholars of American politics, who have coined the phrase **responsible parties** to stress their potentially democratic virtues, have also long observed a gap between theory and practice. For most of American political history, our parties haven't performed many of these functions all that well.

Listing the ideal virtues of parties is useful, however, because it allows questions to be asked about how well parties serve elite or popular currents of democracy. Have, for example, American parties organized some voters while excluding or ignoring others? Do they provide the electorate with a space to debate policies and philosophies? Do the parties reflect the wide differences and commonalities of the American citizenry, or do they squelch popular participation and conflict as they seek power? Asking such questions leads to a bigger one: Do American parties work to retard or further political participation in politics?

American parties have complex histories. Next, we trace their uniqueness compared to political parties elsewhere in the democratic world.

Age and the Weight of Tradition

Americans often think of their nation as young. Yet our Republican and Democratic parties are extremely old. Born in the 1790s and already mature when

Andrew Jackson assumed the presidency in 1828, the Democratic party is one of the oldest political parties in the world. The Republicans are younger but can still trace their origins to the 1840s and 1850s and the battle to limit slavery's expansion.

It matters that our two dominant parties are aged. Both began by organizing voters around issues peculiar to preindustrial, premodern America. Both parties were up and running before the country spanned the continent. They predate the formation of great cities, an industrial working class, African-American emancipation, the Great Depression, leafy suburbs, and the new global economy. The GOP and the Democrats were competing before the modern corporation existed and before the United States was a great world power.[5]

Their longevity is an achievement, but it is also a burden. Harvard's Samuel Huntington has commented that "our parties resemble a massive geological formation composed of different strata, each representing a constituency or group added to the party in one political era and then subordinated to new strata produced in subsequent political eras." Our parties have noble traditions, but their customs can freeze practices, like racism, that many would just as soon leave behind. Many people remain loyal to parties not because of their current stances on public policy issues, their vision of the future, or their responses to current events, but merely out of habit.[6]

As a result, both parties can be tradition bound, conservative institutions that persist despite big changes in the culture and economy. Although party elites, leaders, and philosophies often change, their appeals to party loyalists often remain nostalgic recollections of past glories and conflicts. For this reason, the major American parties may mobilize some voters but can remain hostile or indifferent to newcomers of all kinds.[7]

Political Parties as Local Organizations

The age of American parties suggests the important role of tradition in American elections. But there is something else: Reflecting their nineteenth-century beginnings, parties are still organized and oriented toward particular states, regions, and locales and not toward the national and international concerns that have often come to dominate the political debate in Washington. Simply put, parties mean different things to different people depending on where they live. At the national level, both parties have often been extremely loose coalitions of groups with little in common but their desire to nominate a winning presidential candidate.

Take as an example the different social groups that supported the Republicans and Democrats in the less than memorable election of 1920. In the Republican bastion of upstate New York, the GOP appeared as a party of small-town, native-born Protestant farmers. Yet in New York City and Boston, Republicanism meant the party of big business and of the up-and-coming urban professional middle class. In the South, the descendants of African-American slaves and a few dissenting whites were the only Republicans to be found. Looking backward, we might find the 1920 Democrats even harder to comprehend. The new Irish and Italian immigrants of New York and Boston called themselves Democrats, but so too did Protestant plantation owners and businessmen of the South. Such variety sparked some perplexing divisions within party ranks: The 1920 Democratic Convention featured bitter debates about whether to support or condemn the Ku Klux Klan. One segment of the party—Irish Catholic Democrats—were victims of the Klan, while many of its southern loyalists were the Klan's founders and supporters.

How did these local parties hold themselves together? One way was through **patronage.** In their local strongholds, the parties paid off their loyal supporters. The most highly developed form of patronage in American history was the urban **political machine.** In midwestern and eastern cities after the Civil War and well into the twentieth century, machines thrived by building connections between city halls and highly developed ward (neighborhood) party organizations. In return for votes, party organizations gave aid to their supporters, rewarded some with city contracts, and provided government jobs to thousands of recent immigrants and other potential voters.

Today, machines have a bad reputation. They're seen as bastions of corrupt, cigar-smoking bosses. They were often ruthless with opponents, making scandal a normal part of urban politics. But machines had some positive features, providing minimal forms of political and cultural representation for new immigrant neighborhoods. At their best, they buffered the most vulnerable urban groups against the worst aspects of the emerging class system. The most famous political machine, New York's Tammany Hall, made the New York Police Department into a symbol of Irish control. Since machines dealt in votes, they did mobilize voters, especially when middle and upper class reformers threatened them with "anticorruption" campaigns. Today, party machines have almost completely disappeared. But they do explain how American parties survived without either clear ideologies or principles (see Chapter 5).[8]

Ideological Fuzziness

The local origins and complex social diversity of American parties present a big contrast to their European cousins. Western European political parties originally organized strong national identities and comprehensive political ideologies. Generally, European parties were born out of the class tensions accompanying the Industrial Revolution. They developed comprehensive party platforms. The first mass parties were critical of industrial capitalism and tried to advance democracy by campaigning for mass suffrage. They thrived on organization, developing party sections and branches in factories and city neighborhoods. Clearer about whom they wanted to organize than Democrats or Republicans, Europe's mass parties inspired activism, voter mobilization, and organization. More often than not, the upper and middle class parties that formed to compete with labor, socialist, and social democratic parties had to form similarly strong national identities.[9]

Today, a visitor to Berlin, London, or Rome could still find the headquarters of the major political parties in large, multistoried office buildings. There would be party offices responsible for propaganda, the press, and outreach to particular groups. The names of the parties—Labor and Conservative in Britain; Social Democratic, Christian Democratic, and Green in Germany—reveal something precise about their identities. But until recently, the headquarters of America's two cumbersome parties were small and inconspicuous. In 1972, employees of Richard Nixon's reelection campaign burglarized the headquarters of the Democratic National Committee in the Watergate complex in Washington. From a foreign perspective, what they found was puzzling. The national center of the biggest and oldest political party in the world was far smaller than the Safeway Supermarket downstairs and the luxury co-op apartments above.

While there are important differences between American parties about particular issues, the range of ideological difference is not all that great. Both parties agree about many of the central questions that have divided parties elsewhere. Democrats and Republicans both support capitalism and a powerful international role for the United States, and both oppose the redistribution of wealth. Both support a limited role for government in planning the national economy. As their rather general names imply, "Democrats" and "Republicans" are broad designations that offend nobody. In short, our parties tend to blur social differences and ideological distinctions. The range of disagreement may

seem great during election time, but it is hardly profound in comparative and historical terms.[10]

Why Only Two Parties?

All of these factors contribute to the most obvious fact about American political parties: With a few exceptions, only two major parties dominate most American elections. For over 140 years, Democrats and Republicans have fought it out, even though a two-party system is a rarity in the rest of the world. Some argue that America has two major parties because Americans don't have many political differences. But this ignores the fact that a two-party system is sustained less by popular will than by the parties themselves and their mutual control of electoral laws and campaign finance regulations. In most states, getting a new party on the ballot is so difficult that it exhausts the time and resources of third-party activists, leaving little time to make a real splash in the ensuing election. A 1997 Supreme Court ruling even made it possible for states to prohibit third parties from endorsing Democratic or Republican candidates. In a case involving the liberal-left New Party, the Court ruled that the state of Minnesota could prevent the fledgling reform party from listing Democratic or Republican candidates on their ballot line.

Third parties like the Populists, Socialists, and Progressives on the left, Ross Perot's Reform party in the center, and George Wallace's 1968 American Independent party on the right have often had important effects on the Democrats and Republicans. Yet our electoral system makes it nearly impossible to elect many of their candidates to office. Instead of dividing up representation by the proportion of the vote each party receives, (a system called *proportional representation*), in America a party's candidate must win a plurality to get any representation at all. Americans elect candidates in separate districts in which only one candidate can assume office. The **single-member district system** virtually assures a two-party system by strangling new parties in the cradle. While they may have many potential supporters, third parties flounder because they cannot grow fast enough to win a plurality.[11]

Here, the Constitution and the **electoral college** also come in handy to preserve the two-party system. The highest office in the land is not elected by a popular majority but is chosen by acquiring a majority of electoral votes. Like single-member district systems, this is a "winner-take-all" method. Presidential candidates receiving one vote less than a plurality in a given state receive no electoral votes from that state at all (with one exception, Maine, which apportions electoral votes by congressional district). The very existence of the electoral college makes presidential bids by small parties or individual candidates unlikely to succeed. In 1992, Ross Perot received no electoral votes, even though he garnered 19 percent of the popular vote; in 1996, 9 percent of the popular vote for Perot didn't yield a single electoral vote either. Many voters are deterred from voting for challengers to the two parties because they believe their votes are wasted.

CRITICAL ELECTIONS

If American parties and their unique features tell us anything, it is that their vast democratic potential is often compromised by their unique histories and identities. There is no major party in America that is specifically tied to advancing the interests of average wage earners or defending them from the power of large corporations. The localism of American parties means they've often ignored or even suppressed conflicts and debates about national and international issues in favor of defending the power structures in the areas where they've been dominant. The age of American parties makes them often resistant to social changes, whether it be the drive for women's suffrage, the civil rights struggle, or gay and lesbian rights. The two-party system may be preferable to a multiparty one, but it means that dissenters and activists are often absorbed as factions within the Democrats or Republicans, or give up in disgust if they have no effect. For elite democrats, all this distinctiveness can be a virtue. Giovanni Sartori, a prominent scholar of political parties, has praised them precisely for their ability to "control society."[12]

Yet it would be a mistake to discount parties as mere elite democratic instruments. At crucial moments, they've been indispensable agents promoting massive political change. The democratic debate within and about our political parties has been most heated before, during, and after what scholars call **critical, or realigning, elections.** Table 7.1 (p. 174) lists these important electoral moments. In the last two hundred years, the United States has had only five (a few say six) such events. During realigning periods, our parties have tried to both respond to a newly active and divided mass electorate. Walter Dean Burnham, the foremost student of realigning elections, has called them "America's surrogate for revolution."[13]

What happens during these important realigning periods? In some cases, new parties are born or achieve power for the first time, as with Andrew Jackson's 1828 Democratic victory and Abraham Lincoln's 1860 Republican ascendancy. In others, as in 1896 and 1932, the parties keep their names but succeed by altering their philosophies and appealing to the electorate with new platforms and identities. Realigning elections excite and reshuffle the electorate. Voter turnout surges, and new groups enter the electorate and voice their claims through the parties. Critical elections initiate enormous policy changes not only at the national level, but also in states and localities. Moreover, critical elections are not one-shot deals. Their effects endure. Typically, a majority party emerges to shape the agenda of national politics for several decades, while a minority party hangs on to its local and regional bases. Thus, realigning elections create new **party systems** in which voters generally retain their new party loyalties in succeeding elections, even passing on such loyalties to their children and grandchildren.[14]

The two critical elections with the most impact on today's politics were the 1896 and 1932 contests. Both are analyzed here.

TABLE 7.1

Realigning Elections
and Their
Consequences

Election	Party System	Big Issues	Partisan Consequences
1800 (Jefferson)	*First:* Democratic-Republicans over Federalists	"Privilege"; agrarian vs. urban interests; power of national government	Repudiation of Federalist Party
1828 (Jackson)	*Second:* Democrats over Whigs	Democracy of common man; state vs. federal power	First mass party system; introduction of patronage; Democratic predominance
1860 (Lincoln)	*Third:* Republicans over Democrats	Slavery; states' rights; North vs. South	Republicans as party of Union; growth of urban machines; the Solid South
1896 (McKinley)	*Fourth:* Republicans over Democrats and Populists	National depression; industrialized North vs. agrarian South and West; monopolies vs. "the People"	Republicans as party of modern business prosperity; decline of party competition; Jim Crow in South
1932 (Roosevelt)	*Fifth:* Democrats over Republicans	Depression; social rights; government responsibility for economy	Democrats as party of equality and prosperity; mobilization in North; Solid South persists
1968 (Nixon)	*Sixth:* Partisan dealignment and "split-level" rule	Race; economic decline; American strength as world power	Party decomposition at grassroots; breakup of Democratic South; candidate-centered campaigns

The System of 1896

Held in the aftermath of a severe economic depression, the 1896 election featured two contrasting visions of the nation's past and future. The first, crystallized in the Populist and Democratic presidential candidacy of the Nebraskan William Jennings Bryan, recalled the Anti-federalist and popular democratic vision of the early republic. Bryan, and most especially his followers, claimed that the growing power of banks and trusts was strangling American democracy. The Republican nominee, William McKinley, ran the first modern campaign, spending $3.5 million in a crusade promising corporate-led prosperity.

The election split the nation's regions, with the West and South siding with Bryan and his Populist-Democratic coalition, and the populous Northeast and Midwest going for the GOP. Crucial to Republican success were the swing votes of Catholic immigrant workers, repelled by Bryan's Protestant fundamentalism but also distrustful of McKinley's pro-business program. Here, McKinley's campaign money helped win the elections by a narrow margin of 3 percent. With an 80 percent turnout, the 1896 election was a dramatic battleground.[15]

The result was the **system of 1896,** thirty-six years of more-or-less uninterrupted Republican control of Congress and the White House. The system of 1896 had its ironies. Born in an election that mobilized and stimulated the elctorate, the victorious Republicans and defeated Democrats went on to suppress political participation and debate in the regions they each controlled.

In their midwestern and northeastern strongholds, the GOP's leaders disenfranchised industrial workers and immigrants whose loyalty to Republicanism was tenuous. In the South, the system of 1896 was much more brutal. Here, the potential voters to be controlled were poor, black, or both—the people who had supplied the mass support for Bryan's anticorporate leanings in 1896. The region's factory owners and big landowners moved successfully to take over the Democratic party. While race had long been a useful instrument to divide the poor in the South, the new elites instituted segregation through Jim Crow laws. In elections, the Democrats instituted all-white primaries, poll taxes, literacy tests and other forms of intimidation. Jim Crow worked to crush electoral participation.[16] (See Chapter 5.)

The important political movement of **Progressivism** was the 1896 system's second irony. A rising class of educated professionals and managers rose to challenge the dominance of both parties in their foremost strongholds. Progressives wanted strong, incorruptible government and an educated, informed citizenry. As such, they demanded controls on the parties and their control over patronage and voting procedures. More important, they sought to "purify" the electorate with the kind of difficult registration requirements detailed in Chapter 5. According to historian Samuel Hays, many Progressives simply "distrust[ed] greater political participation in making decisions about complicated and technical questions."

Intended or not, the system of 1896's legacy was steady declines in voter turnout and a gap between ordinary people and elections. By 1924, twenty-eight years after McKinley's election, only 30 percent of the working class voters of industrial Pittsburgh, Chicago, and Philadelphia were showing up at the polls. In Democratic-dominated Virginia, less than a quarter of the adult citizenry voted. With a demobilized electorate, the GOP could hold onto power at the national level, the Democrats in their southern bastions and a few Northeastern cities.[17]

Overall, the system of 1896's effect was to produce a party system friendly to corporate power. V. O. Key, a political scientist who wrote a classic work on southern politics, found that the system encouraged "debates over personalities." To become a candidate in a one-party system meant catering to the interests of industrialists, planters, and the wealthy in order to achieve success. In the North, some states still had party competition, but the 1896 system served similar interests.[18]

1932: Rise of the New Deal Democrats

There would be little reason to talk of a democratic debate at all if the system of 1896 had continued unchallenged. The labor movement, farmers, and feminists struggled under the 1896 system but achieved only marginal success within its confines.

Relying as it did on pro-business prosperity and profound social and political inequality, it is perhaps fitting that the party system imploded through the collapse of the stock market and the ensuing Great Depression. By 1930, a quarter of the American workforce was unemployed, life savings disappeared as banks failed, and the entire financial system was on the brink of total collapse. Under these pressures, not even the system of 1896 could rule unchallenged. In the elections of 1932 and 1936, the system of 1896 collapsed outside the South. Nationally, the 1932 election and 1936 landslide victory of Franklin Roosevelt and a Democratic Congress catalyzed a new realigning period. This time, the Democrats and their philosophy of active government forged a new dominant party.

The **New Deal Democratic coalition** was based on the new electoral mobilization of northern industrial workers, farmers, and the unemployed in a reformed Democratic party. Senators and House members from the highly industrialized states provided the impetus for reforms that made the federal government responsible for the national economy and for providing a minimal standard of living for all. New Deal legislation created government jobs, allowed the growth of the union movement, and established a minimum wage and the Social Security system. The revived national Democratic party, led by Roosevelt, posed as a party opposed to the "economic royalists" who hoarded the country's wealth. Working class voters both prompted, and responded to, the Democratic party's new appeals. Jews, Catholics, and industrial workers—the disenfranchised in the 1896 system—backed the reborn northern Democratic party, and they voted in much larger numbers. Middle and upper class voters moved to support the now-minority Republicans, as voter turnout surged on both sides. The realigned New Deal party system fed off renewed voter participation and party competition.

Yet voter turnout in national elections during the New Deal never reached the high levels of the 1896 election. The reason was simple: In the "Solid South," the 1896 system largely persisted and blacks and many poor whites remained disenfranchised. Some southern Democrats arose to challenge the old elites of the Democratic party and made direct appeals to tenant farmers and industrial workers (people like Alabama's Hugo Black, "Big" Jim Folsom, and Lister Hill; Claude Pepper of Florida; and Huey Long of Louisiana). Still, southern Democrats at their most radical never challenged Jim Crow segregation. Neither did Franklin Roosevelt, who depended on the certain support of the old Confederacy for four straight presidential victories. In the absence of a popular democratic revival in the Solid South, southern Democrats and Republicans in Congress became a conservative drag on the liberal, pro-labor, and pro-farmer policies of northern New Dealers. The dead hand of the segregationist South held back the full popular democratic potential of the New Deal.[19]

THE NEW DEAL AT RETIREMENT AGE

The New Deal and its conflicts are now a distant memory. Like all realigning periods, the party system it created endured. After World War II, the coalitions forged in the 1930s created what some called a "normal" politics of Democratic majorities in Congress and—Republican Dwight Eisenhower excepted—Democratic presidents from Harry Truman through John Kennedy and Lyndon Johnson. Government was now responsible for the economy and for maintaining some level of support for those in need. Many praised the New Deal party system for its seemingly happy combination of moderate democracy, limited conflict, and apparent stability and consensus. An esteemed scholar of the time called it "one of the truly conservative arrangements in the world of politics," while E. E. Schattschneider, a liberal critic of the era, could see the same New Deal system as embodying "the great moral authority of the majority."[20] However, like all previous party systems, the New Deal one was eroded both from conflicts of its own making and historical tendencies it couldn't resolve.

Explaining the Democrats' Decline

As the dominant party of the New Deal system, the Democrats have had the most to lose in recent years. From the 1960s onward, the Democratic party has been a battleground for all the big new issues and contending groups in a changing society. Race, the Vietnam War, middle class economic stagnation, and culture and lifestyle divides tore the party apart.

The Democrats and Race. New Deal Democrats always depended on the South, and its system of white domination, to gain national victories. By the 1960s, the growth of the civil rights movement meant that the party's long equivocation on the central divide in U.S. society couldn't stand. After some foot dragging, Presidents Kennedy and Johnson responded to the moral and political power of the civil rights movement. Through a series of civil rights acts, the Jim Crow system of legal segregation was dismantled through federal intervention. In the North, President Johnson and liberal members of Congress launched their War on Poverty and Great Society programs, establishing new commitments to end poverty in this otherwise wealthy country.

Confronting racist political structures in both South and North had electoral costs for the Democrats. It split off the segregationist southern wing of the party and angered many northern whites who believed that racial progress should wait for another day. The Democrats gained moral authority and African-American votes. Yet the New Deal coalition was disrupted.[21]

Vietnam, Liberals, and Communism. In the postwar period, Democrats and Republicans alike pursued a stridently anticommunist foreign policy. The New Deal party system achieved a consensus around "containing" communism through an enormous global military presence. The logical result was the Vietnam War, begun under Eisenhower but greatly expanded into a major conflict under Democratic Presidents Kennedy and Johnson. The war's expense in lives gradually spawned a huge antiwar movement. In the Democratic party, antiwar dissent crystallized in the presidential candidacies of Eugene McCarthy and Robert Kennedy in 1968. The party establishment, and many Democrats who supported the war, dug in their heels against antiwar activists and their candidates. Tensions peaked at the party's 1968 Chicago convention. While a stunned nation watched on television, Democratic Mayor Richard Daley's police force beat demonstrators, delegates, and journalists in front of the city's major hotel. The convention scene was a metaphor for a party and a nation utterly split into separate camps.

Democratic divisions and the war's unpopularity left a deep rift in the party. As a result, Republican Richard Nixon was elected in 1968 and then reelected in a landslide against Democratic peace candidate George McGovern in 1972.[22]

Culture Wars. The civil rights and antiwar crusades were the most prominent of many social movements that emerged and grew in the 1960s and 1970s (see Chapter 10). Movements among other racial minorities, feminists, environmentalists, civil libertarians, and the young questioned the conventions of American life and challenged military, corporate, political, and educational elites. Always a diverse coalition of outsiders, the Democrats were far more open to these cultural currents than were the Republicans.

Yet each battle over "liberation" produced a backlash among a wide swath of people who felt threatened by criticism of established institutions, from traditional fatherhood to military service. Each challenge to authority led to splits between new and old Democrats. Combined with the race and antiwar divides, the culture wars provided a volatile mix within the Democratic party.[23]

Middle Class Economic Stagnation. The New Deal party system's greatest strength was its ability to provide economic growth and distribute some of the resources to middle and lower income voters by means of Federal policies. Chapter 4 of this book details how the brave new world of the global economy made this accommodation all but impossible. For the Democrats, the economic stagnation that began in the early 1970s undermined their support among middle and working class voters. The only Democratic president between Johnson and Clinton was Jimmy Carter. Carter confronted something new: price inflation combined with high levels of unemployment. Succumbing to business demands, Carter sided with the inflation fighters, and during his administration unemployment soared to new highs. Traditional Democratic constituencies, especially hard-pressed wage earners, were hardly pleased.

Economic stagnation and persistent inflation in the Carter years allowed Ronald Reagan in 1980 to place blame for all economic troubles on the Democrats and their general sponsorship of higher tax rates and strong government.[24]

Republicans and the Revolution from Above

The New Deal system's demise naturally catalyzed numerous opportunities for the nation's second party, the Republicans. In the 1950s and early 1960s, the Republicans had been a diverse party. Generally pro-business, the GOP still contained in its ranks a sizable band of liberals and moderates as well.

The Democrats' troubles, however, sparked a new, aggressively conservative trend in the GOP. Writing in 1968, Kevin Phillips, a young adviser to Richard Nixon, urged him to turn the GOP into the party of the "unpoor, unblack, uncool"—a "silent majority" of voters who went to work every day, paid their taxes, didn't protest the war or racism, and accepted without criticism the promise of the American Dream and the power of a strong U.S. military establishment.

Nixon, and most of his Republican successors, listened closely to Phillips. The GOP gained ground by exploiting each and every Democratic division, "peeling" off disenchanted Democrats through **wedge issues.** Republicans generated powerful national symbols, then spoke about how the Democrats violated them. Against antiwar dissenters, Nixon promised "peace with honor" in Vietnam; a decade later, Ronald Reagan sought to restore "America as number 1" against an "aggressive" USSR. Against the claims of the civil rights movement, Republicans slowed down more progress on achieving racial equality by reducing aid to the cities and slowing policies aimed at school integration. Against such nonconformists as feminists, gays, and rebellious college students, Republicans, and the newly powerful Christian Right, talked of law and order and family values. For GOP propagandists, the divided Democrats became the party of special interests. The GOP posed as the party of the silent majority.[25]

Later, we'll see that the silent majority was more a GOP wish than an electoral reality. The real revolution in the GOP was less among the voters than among the party's elites, fundraisers, and intellectuals. Political scientists Joel Rogers and Thomas Ferguson have suggested that changes in American parties, and even realignments, are prompted less by voters than by major economic investors. In the Republicans' case, this meant turning a party with a pro-business slant into an well-oiled coalition that was an instrument of the new and aggressive agenda of corporate America.

This corporate revolution from above had a dual character. One part was intellectual. During the Carter administration, conservative business leaders launched and funded new think tanks that provided books, academic papers, and media experts for a new doctrine. It was called **supply-side economics** (see Chapter 17). Supply siders took direct aim at the legacy of the New Deal and at moderate and liberal Republicans. They attributed the country's economic woes to high taxes, big government, and excessive regulations on business behavior. At a time of both high unemployment and inflation, supply-side doctrines got a hearing. The second revolution was in the structure of campaign finance. Conservative businesses stepped up their campaign donations, increasingly targeting them against liberal Democrats in the U.S. Senate.[26]

Through the 1980s and early 1990s, Phillips's strategy bore fruit for the GOP. The GOP won five of six presidential contests and captured and reheld the Senate between 1980 and 1986. For Republicans, the 1980s seemed like a dream come true, a clear statement that the electoral system had "realigned" their way. But the GOP's successes hardly amounted to a realignment at all. Democrats still controlled Congress through most of the period. George Bush, and then Robert Dole, were defeated by Democrat Bill Clinton in 1992 and 1996. And even the GOP's triumph in 1994 was less than total—by 1996, the GOP's House majority was slender indeed.

A Sixth Electoral System?: 1968–?

The events described here did signal the demise of the New Deal system. What is less clear is whether a new realigned system has been born. Reflecting this uncertainty, most scholars agree that we have entered a *sixth electoral system* since 1968. But most stop short of saying that a full-scale electoral realignment has happened.

Scholarly caution is justified. In contrast to 1896 or 1932, the sixth system is characterized precisely by the inability and incapacity of either Republicans or Democrats to become a dominant party. The old system has eroded, but a new one wasn't born through a critical realignment. The important features of the current epoch may be the sixth system's incapacity and unwillingness to form broad-based and enduring voter coalitions. Rather than mobilizing and realigning voters, the sixth system features **electoral dealignment**.[27]

The major symptoms of electoral dealignment are the following:

- Among the mass electorate, parties hold onto pockets of strength.
  Whether it be in the form of voting or volunteering, both parties seem

weak compared to their predecessors. With only two exceptions in thirty years, elections since 1968 have featured ever-declining turnout.

- Where parties really matter in the present system is less among voters than in their various institutional power centers. In Washington and in most of the state capitals, parties bring together an array of interests, raise money, fund their candidates, and develop policy positions. Parties, in this sense, have become stronger, but only because they have become elite organizations.

- The new party elites respect and fear the mass electorate, but they really don't trust voters. When key issues arise, the public appears as an abstraction, or as a fickle, angry, and frequently irrational mass. To control the "herd," both parties increasingly employ expert professionals to raise the money, poll the voters, advise the candidates, and "guide" voter impressions and images.

- In response, many citizens have tuned out politics altogether. The confidence gap discussed in Chapter 3 is pervasive as citizens express a broad-based dislike and distrust both for government and politicians of both parties. Politicians have always been distrusted in America, but the levels of acrimony have reached historic highs. Apparently, voters feel trapped: Many want a third party, but they tend to see the biggest alternative, Ross Perot's Reform party, as part of the problem rather than a solution to it.

- Try as they might and interpret as they will, neither party today can achieve a clear mandate from the voters. Recent history since 1992 presents good cases in point. In 1992, the Democrats broke the Republican lock on the White House and kept their majority in Congress. Yet two years later, it was the GOP's turn to claim a mandate and even a revolution. But by 1996, the revolution was stymied by a Clinton reelection and a narrower majority for the House GOP. After the 1996 election, new fundraising scandals seemed to make the electorate even more cynical.[28]

THE POLITICS OF DEALIGNMENT

These general features of political dealignment have formed a political culture with some disturbing and even antidemocratic features. Dealignment has been accompanied by the profound growth in wealth and income inequality, by declining voter turnout, by the rollback of federal commitments to a safety net for poor people, and by growing corporate influence in politics. Thus, in the sixth electoral system, it is perhaps less important to "build a bridge to the twenty-first century," in President Bill Clinton's words, than to rebuild the bridges between citizens and increasingly elite-dominated parties. Let us now detail the politics of dealigned parties and voters.[29]

Generals Without Armies:
Current Party Organization

Popular democratic parties build their strength on face-to-face interactions at the grassroots. At their liveliest, American parties possessed strong local party organizations and provided for constant two-way communication between ordinary voters and officeholders. At the grassroots, party organizations were forums for citizens to meet, debate, and hold elected officials accountable for their actions and policies.

Figure 7.1 presents a pyramid of present-day party organization. On paper, the pyramid seems to represent a viable democratic structure linking millions of voters to local party activists who operate the party "machinery" in neighborhoods and precincts. In turn, the parties at the grassroots send representatives to more important county and congressional district committees, who elect a state central (or executive) committee. Each state party then sends representatives to either the Democratic National Committee (DNC) or the Republican National Committee (RNC). From the ranks of the national committees come the national chairpersons, who plan the national convention, raise funds, and coordi-

FIGURE 7.1

Pyramid of American Party Organization

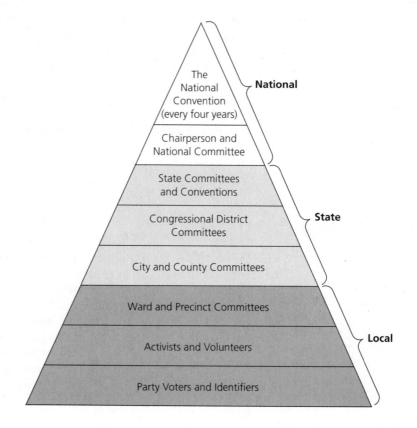

nate state races. At the national convention, a platform is drafted and developed and presidential and vice-presidential candidates are nominated.

This formal work of party organizations is still important to American political life. In fact, it may be more important than ever. Over 70 million voters who have registered as Democrats or Republicans form the base of the two-party pyramid. At the top, the national committees and related "affiliated committees" that coordinate congressional campaigns perform crucial functions. For example, national Democratic chairpersons Paul Kirk, the late Ron Brown, and Senator Chris Dodd are credited with rebuilding the Democrats' bank accounts and technical campaign expertise during the 1980s and 1990s. In the 1970s, GOP chairman Bill Brock revitalized the party after the Watergate scandal. In the 1990s, Haley Barbour engineered the 1994 GOP congressional victories.[30]

The local party organizations are supposed to hold the national parties accountable. In a dealigned system, the roles and powers of party organizations vary. Some local party groups actively recruit, fund, and coordinate diverse campaigns for public office. A few launch voter registration drives. In counties, towns, and city neighborhoods, party organizations sometimes find candidates to run for lesser offices like tax assessor, city councilperson, and county supervisor while helping the campaigns of all the candidates on the party's ballot line.

Yet while local parties still do something, they are stripped of their power to do much beyond their localities. Local party organizations have lost control of their most important resource: They can no longer even nominate their own candidates for public office. Instead, in an odd concession to "openness," the state nominees of parties can be virtually anyone with campaign dollars who claims to be a Democrat or Republican and stands for office. In presidential years, four-fifths of the states now conduct **primary elections** to select national convention delegates pledged to particular presidential candidates. In most cases, though, the task of nominating candidates for lesser offices is left to the party's registered voters through *closed primaries*. Some states have *open primaries* in which voters registered in any party (or no party at all) may cast votes to nominate candidates. Others, such as Iowa, conduct *caucuses* in which candidates' supporters meet to select delegates.

Whatever the merits of these processes, they render local party organizations powerless to control their own agendas. At the national level, they leave the nomination process completely open to millionaires like publisher Steve Forbes, who spent nearly $40 million of his own money in the 1996 Republican primaries.[31]

Besides their national committees, the existence of national parties with local roots are really only evident at the **national party convention** held every four years to nominate the presidential and vice-presidential candidates and write a party platform. The conventions were once the one event where party activists and officials from thoughout the country could debate the party's purposes and platform while bosses brokered deals in smoke-filled rooms.

Yet the party conventions no longer decide much at all. As already detailed, the delegates arrive with preexisting commitments to particular presidential candidates, so there is little suspense about the actual party nominee. The platform is generally preordained and carefully written to offend the fewest number of voters. Stripped of real power, the delegates wear colorful hats and serve as amusing backdrops for speeches. National conventions have been "professionalized," providing an arsenal of free publicity for those who plan and stage the events. Reduced to spectators and cheerleaders, delegates make few if any decisions. In 1996, the national party conventions became so contrived, and so devoid of real debate, that they drew mediocre television ratings. The major networks even threatened to cease live coverage of them in future elections.[32]

The Missing Base

All of the foregoing might be understandable if the base of each party pyramid had somehow wrested real power from the top or held the professionals accountable. Party primaries, designed by the Progressives, were supposed to do this. Today they're still important. But they involve decreasing numbers of voters even as they require growing piles of cash. Only 13 million Republicans voted in the highly competitive Republican party primaries of 1996, while only 25 million voted in the turbulent Democratic primaries of 1992. The GOP total was less than 7 percent of the eligible electorate.[33]

But more important is how even this slender slice of the party faithful is organized, and by whom. Are ordinary people active in party affairs? Consider the all-too-typical experience of a Connecticut woman who was dedicated enough to send a check to the Democratic National Committee in 1996. The woman sent in her money and said that she'd like to volunteer to work for Bill Clinton in the upcoming election. She received a dozen more computer direct-mail appeals asking for more money. But the Democratic National Committee couldn't tell her where the Democratic party in her state or community was located.

Indicative of the empty space at the base is how party leaders regard it. The modern language of party organization is more akin to the boardroom of an advertising agency than to the rough and tumble of democratic engagement. Take, for example, Representative Newt Gingrich's 1991 comparison of the modern Republican party to Bell Laboratories. "That's the closest model to what we do," Gingrich explained. "The first thing you need at Bell Labs is a Thomas Edison, and the second thing you need is a real understanding of how you go from scientific theory to a marketable product." Gingrich explained that the goal of the Republican party was to build "an improvable and relatively technical core product."

In a party of Thomas Edisons and core products, where are the party activists?[34] With some exceptions, grassroots party organizations have few members and little influence. Consider as an example the Democratic party's plans for a bicentennial birthday party in 1992. Wanting to invite all its officeholders to a grand Washington celebration, DNC leaders asked their staff to invite the party activists and regulars responsible for running the party machinery, walking the precincts, and holding the meetings. DNC workers searched their computer files for the names of all the activists. To everyone's surprise, there weren't any. The

AUTH © 1996 The Philadelphia Inquirer. Reprinted with permission of Universal Press Syndicate. All rights reserved.

largest and oldest political party in the United States hadn't found time to collect the names of its activists. What the DNC did have was lists of contributors. Consulting the state party committees, the DNC staff had somewhat better results. But many of the countywide party organizations had few activists or none at all.[35]

The top-heavy quality of modern party organization is a symptom of dealignment that is hard to measure. After all, many Americans participate in groups that are in some way affiliated with the parties. Many feminists, environmentalists, civil rights advocates, and union members contribute to the Democrats. Anti-abortion and fundamentalist Christians provide money to the Republicans. Yet increasingly, the major point of access to the parties is less social activism and more the checkbook and credit card (see Chapter 8).

To be sure, party activism at the grassroots is not completely dead. In the Republican party, Christian Right activists in recent years have been particularly adept at reviving the GOP's machinery in some states. In some places, like Chicago, the Democrats still possess neighborhood organizations. In others, union members are still active. Yet the numbers of activists are not impressive, nor are they much more than remnants of their former strength. One simple if not particularly systematic test illustrates this point. Out of all the people you know, does anyone attend meetings of the Republican or Democratic town committees? Consult the phone book yellow pages to see whether the parties have offices or even phone numbers. Ask your grandparents whether the parties are currently more organized in your town than they were in the 1930s, 1940s, or 1950s. The answers you will get will probably tend to cast doubts on the democratic future of our parties.

Survey data reflect the fact that citizen involvement and connection with the parties is low. Even in 1980, when the Reagan revolution began, overwhelming numbers of voters agreed that parties seemed to be only interested in people's votes, not in their opinions. Only 18 percent of the electorate thought that parties help government "pay attention to what people think." Almost as many thought joining a protest march would be as effective as being a party activist. A majority ranked other kinds of political action (like writing letters or giving money) as more effective. Although Americans may not always be hostile to political parties, mass indifference appears to be the norm.[36]

Candidates Without Parties

In the sixth electoral system, candidates may be avid members of political parties and have strong political philosophies. Those political philosophies and party affiliations will matter when they are in office. Yet dealigned parties and their candidates tend to hide their party affiliation during campaigns—either that, or the voters see party affiliation as generally irrelevant to their choice.

The 1994 Republican conquest of the House of Representatives is a perfect example of this phenomenon. In September, 1994, Republican House candidates pledged themselves to a "Contract with America"—a list of ten items the GOP promised to bring to a vote in their first year in power. The party's professionals had pretested in focus groups all the items of the contract. In the November election, Republicans were victorious and claimed a voter mandate for the contract. Throughout 1995, the new Republicans pressed their agenda. Yet public opinion was never really behind the contract. Voters had supported insurgent Republican candidates in 1994 not because of their party, nor because of its platform, but as a protest vote against Washington politicians. As GOP House members attempted to fulfill their self-proclaimed "mandate," public opinion turned against them. By 1996, incumbent Republicans sought reelection but largely ignored talking about a GOP agenda or even their own party affiliation. In a dealigned system, such big disconnections between parties, candidates and voters are common.[37]

At first glance, preferences for particular individuals over party affiliations seem to be an expression of thoughtful independence. Yet the result is often a gulf between what members of Congress do in Washington and voters' intentions. In the dealigned system, most voters can't evaluate the candidates in terms of even the most elementary political philosophies. (See Chapter 8 for the ways that candidates worsen the confusion.)

Retrospective and Split-Ticket Voting

Judging between competing personalities is one symptom of party dealignment and decline. Another is the voter tendency to judge candidates on the basis of the performance of the economy or feelings about the state of the nation as a whole.

When times are good, voters confirm incumbents. When things are seen as bad, voters throw them out. Political scientists label this phenomenon **retrospective voting.** Its rise helped Ronald Reagan and, more recently, Bill Clinton in 1996. In 1994, Republicans won because they were able to exploit voter perceptions that the country was on the wrong track. Retrospective voting supplies a kind of electoral judgment. But it is a very blunt instrument of voter control. For one thing, it fails to distinguish between candidates who supported, or opposed, the policies that led to "good" or "bad" times. For another, it tells officeholders nothing about what they should or might do in the future.[38]

A final symptom of dealignment is the rise of **split-ticket voting.** From the 1970s onwards, from half to two-thirds of the electorate did not vote consistently for candidates of the same party on the ballot. Since 1968, split-ticket voting has naturally resulted in divided party government, with either branch of Congress in the control of one party and the White House controlled by the other. Between 1968 and 1992, the predominant pattern was a Republican president and a Democratic Congress; after 1994, it's been the reverse.

Split-ticket voting can result in the kind of governmental gridlock that in turn promotes more voter disillusionment. In the 1980s, Presidents Reagan and Bush and a Democratic Congress couldn't agree on many matters, from taxation to foreign policy. After 1994 and the GOP's victories, Clinton and the Republican Congress faced the same dilemmas. The results have usually led to acrimony, with each party blaming the other for inaction and with both the president and Congress representing themselves as "outsiders" to politics even though they obviously aren't. To govern at all, officeholders of both parties have often engaged in backroom deals or have delegated important decisions to bipartisan commissions that are supposed to be somehow "above" politics. Alternatively, the parties engage in partisan combat by launching investigations of each other, as the Democrats did in the 1980s and the Republicans have after the 1996 election. Through it all, the voters can't tell who is really responsible for public policies.[39]

THE PARTIES IN THE ELECTORATE

A culture and politics of party dealignment ultimately produce voter cynicism. Perhaps the ultimate test of party vitality among voters is **party identification.** Most Americans still feel some remote attachment to the parties, but identification with either party is not all that strong. Then again, considering the foregoing, it remains stronger than might be expected. What is the public, democratic face of the parties?

The Democrats: Who Are They?

Since the late 1960s, the Democrats have suffered far more from the politics of dealignment than the Republicans have. As Figure 7.2 shows, the party of Roosevelt had become a pale imitation of its former self. Today, roughly a third

FIGURE 7.2

Changes in Partisan Identification, 1952–1996

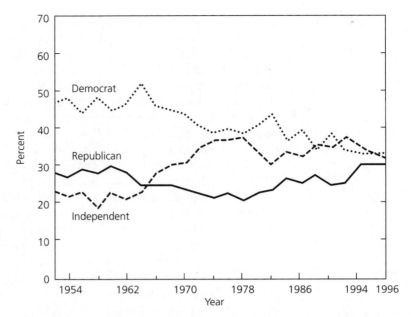

Source: National Election Data Sets, 1952–1994. Pew Research Center for The People & The Press, 1996. Used by permission.

of the electorate are still Democratic identifiers. Yet the number of self-described "strong" Democrats has been declining while the numbers who seem to merely "lean" to the party have become more numerous.

Catholics, low- to middle-income voters, and union members were at the core of the traditional Democratic party. Among all of these groups, Democratic identification has dropped since 1968. Although many still vote for Democrats for various offices, these voters don't necessarily think of themselves as Democratic loyalists. Since 1968, Catholics and middle-income voters have often abandoned the Democratic party's presidential candidates. In 1992 and 1996, Clinton recouped some support, but Democrats still can't count on the consistent support of either of these groups. Among union members, Democratic loyalty surged to nearly 60 percent in the 1996 elections after an aggressive new leadership took control of the AFL-CIO (see Chapter 4). But the union movement has its work to do: At the height of New Deal Democratic power, union members were about one-third of the entire electorate. Today, they're only one-eighth of all voters.[40]

It is not surprising that the steepest declines in Democratic identification have been among southern whites. The white exodus from the Democrats started in the late 1940s but really took off when the Republicans employed the great wedge issue of race. By 1964 and 1968, southern whites had already abandoned the presidential candidates of the Democrats. In the 1980s, indentification with congressional Democrats faded as well. By 1994, a revived GOP routed southern Democrats in Congress, with the wealthiest and most educated southern whites leading the way towards the GOP. In the rest of the nation, the Democrats have also lost white support and identification, but to a much lesser extent.

For some, the new pattern of southern racial divisions has been crystallized by a series of federal court and Supreme Court rulings that divide electoral districts along racial lines in order to increase the number of African Americans in the House of Representatives. In Georgia, North Carolina, and Texas, congressional districts were redrawn to ensure that the high numbers of African Americans in each of these states would lead to more minority members of Congress. This tactic led to new congressional districts in which up to 80 percent of voters were black; such districts duly returned liberal, African-American House members. At the same time, the new black-majority districts diluted African-American strength in other congressional districts where fewer blacks were present. These very white districts turned increasingly Republican. The GOP, with its new predominance among southern whites, would be ensured a growing number of seats as whites and blacks became more concentrated in the redrawn districts.

In the mid-1990s, a series of court rulings reinterpreted the Voting Rights Act of 1965, holding that **racial redistricting** was one of only a number of factors to be taken into account when congressional district lines were drawn. As a result of federal court judgments, several African-American and Democratic members of Congress were forced to run in racially mixed districts in 1996. Could black members of Congress win in districts with numerous whites? The accompanying feature box (p. 190) shows that it can be done, though with some difficulty.

All in all, the Democrats in recent years have lost some of their core constituents. Today, African Americans, Jews, Hispanics (with the exception of Cuban Americans), the very poor, and women are the Democrats' key supporters. Yet even among these relatively loyal Democrats, party identification has slipped. Increasingly, it is only among older voters with memories of the once mighty Democratic party where loyalists predominate, with steep dropoffs among younger voters. More important, as detailed in Chapter 5, the Democrats have largely ceased being a party that is either able or willing to mobilize the voter groups that are its strongest potential supporters.[41]

The Republicans: Feeding Off Democratic Disarray

Among southern whites, and particularly among southern white men, drops in Democratic identification have led to impressive Republican gains. As we saw above, southern white defections from the Democrats started long ago and picked up real steam in the 1960s. But, as shown in Figure 7.3 (p. 192), until the 1970s southern whites still largely identified with local Democrats and voted for them for Congress and local offices. By 1994 and 1996, however,

MAKING A DIFFERENCE

Will Whites Vote for a Black Congresswoman?

The first black woman to serve in the House of Representatives from Georgia, Cynthia McKinney was targeted for defeat by eager Republicans in 1996. The reasons were simple: A 1995 Supreme Court ruling, *Miller* v. *Johnson*, had made McKinney's African-American Eleventh congressional district illegal. The court ruled that the district lines were a "racial gerrymander," and that its meandering boundaries denied white voters equal protection under the law. "I suppose they couldn't wait to toss us out of our districts, even before our constituents had a say in the matter," McKinney commented after the decision.

Most Georgia political experts expected McKinney to retire, seek another office, or go down in flames. McKinney had other ideas. She decided instead to run uphill in the Fourth Congressional District, which included part of her old district but had one big liability: It was 84 percent white. Never before had a majority white district elected a black woman to Congress. And McKinney was not only

an African-American woman running in a white district. She was also an outspoken feminist, an unapologetic liberal, and a caustic critic of a fellow Georgian, Speaker Newt Gingrich. Moreover, she remained an ardent supporter of "majority-minority" districting, even though she now sought to represent a mostly white district. Her one potential advantage was the Democratic voting patterns of her new district. The GOP, smelling victory, nominated a moderate Republican, John Mitnick. Democratic consultants told her to moderate her message to fit the new district.

McKinney did otherwise. She bet that she could build a coalition between white and black women and that many white women had soured on Gingrich's Republican revolution and its cuts to education and child care assistance. Seeking to bridge the gaps between poor women and so-called "suburban soccer moms," McKinney got both talking about common concerns of parenting and women's relatively low wages. She got working women with union cards talking to small business owners about

southern Republicans passed an historic barrier. In 1994, the GOP won its first post-Reconstruction majority in southern congressional districts, and in 1996 continued to pick up Senate and House seats in the South.

Born-again white Christians total nearly 20 percent of the voting electorate, and here the GOP has also made impressive strides. Over time, GOP identification has grown among this group, and it translated into solid support for Ronald Reagan and George Bush in elections from 1980 through 1988. By 1994 and 1996, born-again Christians supported Republican candidates by an astounding 40 percent margin over Democrats.

Republican gains among males are also noteworthy. The GOP's presidential candidates compiled an impressive 7 percent plurality over the Democrats in the elections of the last two decades. With the partial exception of white northeast-

shared concerns, such as medical insurance coverage. And with the help of the labor movement, she was able to harness the energies of scores of young volunteers from throughout the country.

Republican Mitnick ran a classic wedge-issue campaign. He tried to tie McKinney to the Nation of Islam and anti-Semitism and labeled her a "left-wing radical." In the Fourth District, with high numbers of Jewish voters, charges of anti-Semitism could be telling. And it didn't help when McKinney's father called Mitnick a "racist Jew"—a statement that his daughter repudiated and that led to the elder McKinney's dismissal from the campaign. Cynthia responded by citing her strong support for the state of Israel and among Jewish women in the district.

To almost everyone's surprise, McKinney's coalition strategy worked on Election Day. She beat Mitnick by an impressive 58–42 percent margin and ran only slightly behind President Clinton's strong showing in the Fourth. One volunteer, elementary school principal Shirley Reams, commented: "I had a chance to stop by Cynthia's headquarters the other night. There were Jews, Gentiles, wealthy, poor—most of them women—all stuffing en-velopes. This is a coalition that's been waiting to be born for a long time. Cynthia's brought it into being, and it's not going away."

Is McKinney's experience typical? Five out of six African-American House incumbents whose "majority-minority" districts were redrawn did win reelection in new districts in 1996. Still, many—including McKinney herself—wonder if the victories had more to do with the power of incumbency than the evolution of a "colorblind" society. African-American challengers in predominantly white districts still face uphill battles. "I won because of the majority-minority district I used to represent," McKinney says. "It gave voters the opportunity to elect someone like me, who had ony $38,000 to spend." Yet given recent court decisions, black candidates will have to study McKinney's victory closely.

Sources: "Cynthia McKinney: A Profile," *Congressional Quarterly Voter '96* (www.voter96.cqalert.com); John Nichols, "Georgia's Cinderella Story," *The Nation*, November 11, 1996, p. 12; Michael Fletcher, "Is the South Becoming Colorblind?" *Washington Post National Weekly Edition*, December 2, 1996, p. 16.

ern men, the GOP acquired something like a bloc vote among affluent men in the same period. In both 1994 and 1996, the new GOP majorities in the Senate and the House were made possible by men and their lopsided support for Republican candidates.[42]

Despite impressive showings among these groups, the GOP today remains a minority party, gaining the identification of only between a quarter and a third of the electorate in the 1990s. The GOP gains have been offset by nearly equal losses elsewhere in the electorate. Low- and middle-income voters, in particular, have left the GOP as it has become more conservative. Northern Protestants, for instance, used to be the keystone of the party of Lincoln. By the 1980s, the GOP's massive lead among this huge group was erased, with many voters declaring themselves to be independents.

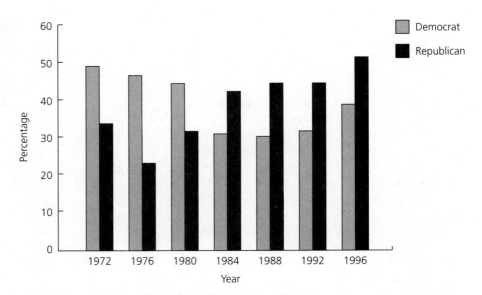

Sources: Data drawn from CBS/*NY Times* Polls, 1972–88; Voter Research and Surveys poll, 1992, Pew Research Center for the People and the Press, 1996.

Republicans have also learned that their advantage among men has been balanced by their losses among women voters. The gender gap has become institutionalized in the sixth electoral system. In the 1980s, women supported Reagan much less heartily than did men. In the 1990s, women supported Bill Clinton, and provided a majority for Congressional Democratic candidates. Nor is the GOP's advantage among men really all that solid. In 1992 and 1996, Clinton pulled even with his opponents among male voters, even as he won large majorities among women.[43]

Young voters are crucial to the future of either party. In the 1980s, the GOP boasted of an imminent "realignment" based upon its majorities among young voters who supported Ronald Reagan. Yet by 1992 and 1996, the GOP's lead among young voters was reversed. People under age twenty-nine supported Clinton and congressional Democrats by large margins. Today, neither party can rely on the consistent support of young people. In fact, one of the major symptoms of decline is precisely the inability of either party to renew itself by attracting young loyalists and activists.

Independents and a Fluid Electorate

Together, both parties can claim the broad identification of about two-thirds of the active electorate. But only about a quarter of the electorate is very loyal to either party, voting for its candidates in election after election and for office after office. As we might expect in a dealigned electorate, weak identifiers are more likely to say that they vote primarily on the basis of the candidate, and not the party label.

Another third of the electorate are **political independents**—people who spurn identification with either of the two parties and who mix and match their choices on election day. The number of independents increased most rapidly in the 1970s. They abound among younger (and now middle-aged) voters with few memories of the New Deal party system. Combined with the weak identifiers, the one-third of voters who claim "independence" signal an important feature of the sixth electoral system. Majorities of voters support the formation of a third party, and majorities believe that the two-party system is "inadequate." The problem, perhaps, is that an electorate critical of the two parties sees few alternatives in available third parties. In the end, the two-party system seems strong enough to prevent complete collapse, but too weak to sustain or stimulate strong loyalties or avoid popular hostility.[44]

Elusive Mandates: 1992–1996

Taken together, the elections of 1992, 1994, and 1996 seem to dash the hopes of both parties for a realigning mandate. In presidential elections, Democrat Bill Clinton ended GOP hopes for a future realignment. At the same time, Clinton's vote totals are not all that impressive—he did not receive a majority in either 1992 or in 1996. According to some observers, Clinton in 1996 was less a leader of a vibrant new party than a candidate adept and lucky enough to position himself as a moderate in the face of an ultraconservative, extremist GOP congressional majority. Moreover, voter support for Clinton was less a mandate for his policies than contingent approval for comparatively good economic times: In political scientist Gerald Pomper's words, "After [a] campaign without substance, Clinton's victory may have only limited meaning beyond the White House. . . . the election conveyed a mood more than a message." Table 7.2 (p. 194) indicates who voted for whom in the presidential contests.[45]

Congressional elections present an equally murky voter verdict, disguised within radical institutional results. In 1992, the Democrats appeared to be in the saddle with control of both the White House and Congress. The Democrats' inability to unite behind health care reform, and the dramatic defeat of Clinton's initiatives, combined with widespread voter anger at governmental gridlock to produce an apparent Republican revolution in the elections of 1994. Interpreting the results as a voter mandate for small government, low taxes, and political conservatism, the new GOP congressional majorities overreached. By early 1996, performance ratings for the GOP Congress were as low as they had been for the Democratic majorities three years before. The November elections preserved GOP majorities, but in the House the GOP held onto the slimmest of margins. Among the voters, the election was a draw. Table 7.3 (p. 195) tells the story among the voters.[46]

As might be expected from a dealigned electorate, voters in the 1990s seem to be sending a mixed and muddled message of anger, apathy, disgust, and even

TABLE 7.2

The Presidential
Vote in 1992
and 1996, by
Social Groups

Percent of total '96 vote	1992			1996		
	Clinton	Bush	Perot	Clinton	Dole	Perot
All 100%	43	38	19	49	41	9
Race						
83 White	39	40	20	43	46	9
10 African-American	83	10	7	84	12	4
5 Latino	61	25	14	72	21	6
1 Asian	31	55	15	43	48	8
Gender						
48 Men	41	38	21	43	44	10
52 Women	45	37	17	54	38	7
33 Married men	38	42	21	40	48	10
20 Unmarried women	53	31	15	62	28	7
Family Income						
11 <$15,000	58	23	19	59	28	11
23 $15–30,000	45	30	20	53	36	9
27 $30–50,000	41	38	21	48	40	10
39 >$50,000	39	44	17	44	48	7
18 >$75,000	36	48	16	41	51	7
9 >$100,000				38	54	6
9 First-time voters	46	32	22	54	34	11
23 Union households	55	24	21	59	30	9
Religion						
46 White Protestant	33	47	21	36	53	10
17 Born-again	23	61	15	26	65	8
29 Catholic	44	35	20	53	37	9
3 Jewish	80	11	9	78	16	3
Region						
23 East	47	35	18	55	34	9
26 Midwest	42	37	21	48	41	10
30 South	41	43	16	46	46	7
20 West	43	34	23	48	40	8

TABLE 7.3	Percent of total '96 vote	1994		1996	
		Democrat	Republican	Democrat	Republican
The 1994 and 1996 Vote for the House, by Social Group	All				
	100%	47	53	50	50
	Race				
	83 White	42	58	45	55
	10 African-American	92	8	82	18
	4 Hispanic	61	39	73	27
	1 Asian	54	46	43	57
	Gender				
	48 Men	42	58	46	54
	52 Women	53	47	55	45
	Income				
	11 <$15,000	62	38	63	37
	22 $15,000–30,000	51	49	56	44
	27 $30,000–50,000	45	55	50	50
	21 $50,000–75,000	45	55	47	53
	9 $75,000–100,000	40	60	43	57
	9 >$100,000	36	64	37	63
	23 Union household	60	40	63	37
	Age				
	17 18–29	49	51	55	45
	33 30–44	46	54	50	50
	27 45–59	47	53	50	50
	23 60+	49	51	49	51

limited contentment. Depending on the circumstances, voter targets have been both Democrats and Republicans. Officeholders and partisans in Washington, however, want to see the matter differently, as "mandates" for this or that course or policy direction. One observer calls this the "pretense of vitality on top of an electoral volcano that continues to rumble in the party system." According to one study, "each party has failed in adding to its base" and neither has a "clear advantage on key dimensions" of voter concern.[47]

CONCLUSION: THE FUTURE OF PARTIES

A dealigned electoral system is characterized by an increasing distance between elites and ordinary citizens. Is it too late for the major parties to revive as popular democratic instruments or for new parties to form? For today's Democrats and Republicans, the challenge is to draw millions of politically isolated citizens into public places where they can speak and act together. For critics of the two parties, the challenge is to reduce cynicism and despair about parties and political action in general.[48]

These are substantial challenges in the current political climate. To address this issue more fully, we need to examine modern political campaigns. Here the developments that have weakened grassroots democracy are on full display, as are the possibilities to create parties and organizations less driven by elites than by ordinary citizens.

KEY TERMS

responsible two-party system
patronage
political machine
single-member district system
electoral college
critical (realigning) election
party system
system of 1896
Progressivism
New Deal Democratic coalition

wedge issue
supply-side economics
electoral dealignment
primary
national party convention
retrospective voting
split-ticket voting
party identification
racial redistricting
political independent

SUGGESTED READINGS

Walter Dean Burnham, *The Current Crisis in American Poltitics*. New York: Oxford University Press, 1983. A collection of path-breaking essays by a noted scholar of American elections.

E. J. Dionne, *They Only Look Dead*. New York: Simon & Schuster, 1996. A journalist argues that the future of American politics belongs to progressives who address growing income and wealth inequalities.

Thomas Edsall and Mary Edsall, *Chain Reaction: The Impact of Race, Rights, and Taxes on American Politics*. New York: W. W. Norton, 1992. A compelling and controversial account

of the Democrats' decline and GOP's rise in the 1970s and 1980s.

Wilson Carey McWilliams, *The Politics of Disappointment*. Chatham, N.J.: Chatham House, 1995. A noted democratic political theorist analyzes American elections in terms of the decline of popular participation and public life and suggests alternatives.

Martin Wattenberg, *The Decline of American Political Parties, 1952–1988*. Cambridge: Harvard University Press, 1990. A political scientist traces the erosion of partisan identification and suggests many consequences.

Campaigns: Organized Money versus Organized People

For a single day every two to four years, the American people possess the awesome and direct power to determine who governs. Yet that power would be meaningless if there were no choices, no debates, and no conversations between citizens and those who would rule.

Political campaigns are supposed to provide the foremost example of the democratic debate at work. As such, they epitomize the possibilities of popular democracy. During campaigns, incumbent officeholders are directly challenged by vigorous contenders. Political elites are forced to struggle and compete with others in the public realm. Voters are at center stage because candidates must speak directly to their concerns. Campaigns provide the framework in which social and political movements can be heard and in which participation matters. In the mass media, candidates must withstand critical scrutiny of their platforms and motives. With their focus on millions of ordinary voters, campaigns deeply matter to democratic life.

Today, campaigns maintain the trappings of democratic interchange, and sometimes the substance as well. Yet while modern campaigns can expand public debate, they just as often limit it. Campaigns can elicit voter interest and participation, but they can also exploit momentary passions and generate images that have little to do with the substance of government decisions. Campaigns can fall short of their promise, turning citizens into cynical and passive spectators and candidate debates into personality contests that have little to do with the real decisions relevant to voters. While they can bolster popular democratic citizenship, campaigns in these ways can also reinforce elite democracy.

American political campaigns have always presented this mix of possibilities. Generally, however, as political parties at the grassroots have decayed, campaigns have become dominated by the individual candidates and their financial resources, concocted images, and ambitious personalities. Parties deeply matter to candidates as sources of outside money and expertise, but voters take a back seat as the contests become a professional business directed by managers. This chapter probes the effects of these developments on candidates, voters, and parties. It examines different campaigns for the ways they frame essential political questions and suggests how to bring political campaigns back to their popular democratic possibilities.

PERSONALIZED CAMPAIGNS

From Clinton and his bridge to the twenty-first century to Dole and his World War II injuries, campaigns today have become **candidate-centered.** Voters judge based on what they see, and today's campaigns feature fierce competition between apparently ambitious and driven individuals. In these battles, personalities come to matter, and just how candidates perform on television, talk to the media, produce drama, manufacture images, and handle scandals has become the staple of campaign theatrics. In today's electoral marketplace, philosophy and issues still matter, as do parties. Yet more than ever, the fate of ideas, policies, and parties depends on the merits and demerits of unique individuals. Ostensibly about voters and their thoughts, needs, and interests, modern campaigns are mostly contests between candidates struggling for center stage.

When candidates dominate campaigns, politics seems like nothing more than a high-stakes game with moments of drama, surprise, attack and retreat. Sometimes, the candidates come from nowhere and grab political attention and power. A year before Jimmy Carter and Bill Clinton were elected president, fewer than one in five Americans knew who they were. GOP presidential candidate Steve Forbes was hardly a household name in late 1995. Yet only several months later, thanks to $37 million in personal expenditures, he emerged as veteran Bob Dole's chief rival for the Republican nomination. Candidate-centered campaigns seem to confirm pop artist Andy Warhol's trenchant observation: Just about everyone in modern campaigns can be famous for at least 15 minutes.[1]

In House and Senate campaigns, where the candidates are less well known, party loyalty still serves as an important guide for many voters. But these races are increasingly candidate-centered as well, because party loyalty just matters less to voters and candidates can't rely on its working in a increasingly dealigned electorate. At least for prospective House members, the main ingredient of electoral success is personal **name recognition.** If voters don't know who you are, then they are simply less likely to vote for you, regardless of what party you're in. Achieving name recognition eludes most challengers for House seats. But if they pass this hurdle, the resulting campaign will be a battle to achieve positive images or to make negative caricatures of opponents sink in. Successful candidates set the campaign agenda through media advertising that keeps the opposition off-balance and defensive. Once elected, senators and House members can't rest. They've got to work hard to keep their names and accomplishments visible to voters. They fend off new challenges by raising formidable amounts of money that scare off potential opponents. The candidate-centered world is a topsy-turvy, insecure, and uncertain universe. Even powerful people have to work hard to gain the attention of voters, and no one can depend on voters and their loyalties.[2]

The volatility of today's campaigns is compounded by the mass media's concentration on horse race journalism and on scandals and dramatic revelations (see Chapter 6). Since voter opinion about individual candidates is rooted in thin soil, a politics of charge and countercharge often makes for effective strategy. The media are likely to cover "exciting" drama and ignore "boring" debates about issues. Seeking protection from the tempest, savvy candidates try to control information about themselves. All this is not particularly instructive for voters. Left to judge among constantly changing candidate reputations and competing negative portrayals, many voters come to distrust the truth value of all the images that politicians try to create. Yet in the end, someone has to survive the process on election day.

Wild Ambition: From Nobody to the White House

The candidate-centered world is inhospitable terrain for the timid, humble, or circumspect. The road to the White House is a good example, for it is strewn with the bodies of the financially challenged, the unlucky, the inept, and the uncertain. Presidential bids start long before election year, and the fifty separate primaries and caucuses potential candidates must face to win a major party's nomination (see Chapter 8). While incumbent presidents seeking reelection have an easier time, challengers face daunting hurdles and unpleasant surprises. Major features of the process are summarized in Table 8.1.

Long-term planning, sophisticated strategic thinking, and luck are necessary for success in the presidential sweepstakes. Take candidate Bill Clinton's struggle for the Democratic nomination and the presidency in 1992. The trip be-

TABLE 8.1 **Campaigning for President: Essential Steps**	**Two years before the election** Goal: Become a viable candidate. 1. Form an electoral base and a distinctive theme. 2. Visit key states, like New Hampshire and Iowa, where convention delegates are first selected. Visit key politicians and potential contributors. Campaign for members of Congress in these states. 3. Establish contacts with news media by appearing before key interest groups and TV programs such as *Face the Nation* and *Meet the Press*. **One year before the election [The invisible primary]** Goals: Build a competent campaign team, achieve name recognition, raise enough money to hire a permanent campaign staff. 1. Register an official campaign organization with the Federal Elections Commission. 2. Fundraise in at least twenty states to qualify for federal assistance. Fundraise in other states to acquire the maximum allowed amount of money. 3. Assemble a campaign team that includes campaign managers, lawyers, and political consultants specializing in press relations, media, fundraising, polling, speechwriting, and issue development. 4. Campaign in Iowa and New Hampshire, but include key states like New York and the many states that hold primaries the following March. 5. Announce candidacy. **Primary season, January–June, election year** Goal: Assembling a majority of delegates to your party's national convention in the summer. 1. Win or take a close second in Iowa caucuses and New Hampshire primary in late January and February. 2. Sustain momentum by winning key states in the "frontloaded" March primaries. 3. Continue to develop fundraising and staff for April and May primaries and caucuses, especially New York, Pennsylvania, Illinois, and Michigan. 4. Establish a lead over nearest contenders by late April, causing them to drop out. Pick up their supporters. 5. Begin to act like your party's nominee by unifying your party against the opposition. 6. Win last primaries by convincing margins. 7. Dominate rules, procedures, and platform deliberations preceding national convention. Interview and investigate vice presidential candidates. 8. In your acceptance speech, unite your party while addressing the broader nation.

TABLE 8.1 (continued)	**General election: Convention to November's first Tuesday**

Goal: Amass 271 electoral votes and win the presidency.
1. Develop target states where campaign and media spending will be concentrated.
2. Develop a theme that dominates your campaign.
3. Develop a coalition for electoral victory and possible later governing. Enlist members of Congress and prominent local politicians.
4. Develop a common line of attack against your opponent(s).
5. Expand your organization, especially "soft money" fundraising. (See Key Terms.)
6. Establish system for transition to presidency.

gan long before election year. Just after the 1990 congressional elections, Clinton began to try to make himself known both to the national media elite and to key fundraisers. The Arkansas governorship is a full-time job. Still, Clinton worked 18-hour days outside the state. Long before the voters even knew who he was, he raised substantial amounts of cash and a network of steady donors among the elite who follow politics closely and bet on newcomers. By 1991, Clinton had met, and impressed, some of the "great mentioners"—newspaper columnists, network news anchors, and key Washington insiders whose attention makes or breaks a candidate's early chances. And he had assembled his campaign team, a mixture of campaign consultants, young volunteers, and academic professionals who supplied money, support, and policy papers. By the time Clinton declared his candidacy in October 1991, he had already established his credentials in this so called **invisible primary** of money and media.[3]

Four years later, the invisible primary was even more important for the eventual GOP nominee, Bob Dole. Unlike Clinton, Dole's long service in the Senate had already established him as a man with connections and a predictable, reliable base of donors and supporters. As a Washington fixture, Dole and his nomination campaign were also aided by a process called **frontloading.** Individual states can determine when their caucuses or primaries are held to pick party convention delegates. In an effort to gain influence over the process and gain attention from potential presidents, many states began to schedule their primaries earlier and earlier in the election year. Dole, with his instant name recognition and national prominence, had by late 1995 raised a large amount of money and established substantial connections among officeholders in many states.

That's where frontloading helped. Dole faced a surprisingly strong challenge from right-wing columnist Pat Buchanan. To everyone's surprise, Dole came in second to Buchanan in New Hampshire, the first primary election. Dole instantly lost the media's confidence, and with it the perception that his nomination was inevitable. Yet Buchanan, Steve Forbes, and Lamar Alexander—Dole's chief opponents—hadn't organized in the large number of states that had frontloaded their primaries to March. Dole, whose early success in the invisible primary meant that he had organizations in most of these states, recovered in the

South Carolina primary and went on to win the nomination when his opponents couldn't raise money or generate momentum.[4]

At the same time, even success in the invisible primary doesn't always lead to victory. Even the favored can be tripped up by revelations and allegations of scandal. The prime example is the quick demise of 1988 Democratic frontrunner Gary Hart, who had won the invisible presidential primary only to be felled by the tabloid press and its reports of his extramarital affair. In 1992, the same thing almost happened to Bill Clinton. Unlike Hart, Clinton skillfully handled stories about draft dodging and womanizing; he and Hillary Rodham Clinton appeared on *60 Minutes* to fend off the charges. Then Clinton turned the revelations to his advantage as he turned himself into the "Comeback Kid." By the end of the 1992 campaign, almost every voter knew Clinton as the Man from Hope, who as a teenager defended his mother against an alcoholic stepfather, won a Rhodes Scholarship to Oxford, and helped a needy brother even as he won the Arkansas governorship. Candidate-centered contests are, after all, less battles between differing ideologies or principles than referenda on individuals.[5]

From the standpoint of most candidates, voters must seem like a fickle and inconsistent lot. Yet from the voters' standpoint, the candidate-centered campaign is puzzling and frustrating. Nearly a year before the general election, small numbers of primary voters can decide who the nominees are. In a personalized campaign held on a nationwide scale, voters can't really know the candidates all that well, yet they're compelled to judge between competing, flickering images. Consequently, their loyalties to specific candidates are often thin and tenuous.

In this volatile environment, the candidates who emerge as victors need to have certain key traits. First, wisdom, policy positions, or principles matter less than what journalists call "fire in the belly"—the overwhelming ambition that allows candidates to run a very long gauntlet. Second, overweaning ambition must be accompanied by extraordinary ego. With the entire process centered on you, your personality, your character, your past, your record, and your campaign performance, the modern candidate must be able to withstand critical scrutiny that would fell humbler mortals. Third, presidential candidates must gain support in the elite circles of American society, or be part of these elites themselves.

When candidates lack these qualities, they're not likely to succeed whatever their other merits. In the days before the personalized campaign, presidential candidates were likely to be less openly aggressive. But in recent years, reluctance to endure the rigors of campaigns probably prevented retired General Colin Powell from entering the 1996 race. In 1992, then New York Governor Mario Cuomo possessed the requisite ambition and ego but was seen by many as too thin skinned to withstand the campaign's challenges. Even Bob Dole, who won the GOP nomination in 1996, was tagged by commentators with various liabilities. He was said to miss the Senate; his age was a factor because he lacked the requisite drive. In his political life, Dole had come across as thin skinned and defensive. Despite his attempts to reverse all these negatives by nonstop campaigning and constant talk about his long preparation to be president, by the end of the 1996 campaign Dole learned a hard lesson in campaign cruelty. As his campaign failed to surge in the fall of 1996, some anxious GOP candidates refused to be seen on the same podium with him and the Republican party stopped mentioning him in many of their ads.[6]

THE PERMANENT CAMPAIGN GAME

The uncertain and insecure world of candidate-centered campaigns has naturally led to new strategies to provide some security. For most politicians in office, the **permanent campaign** provides an important but limited insurance policy against unpredictability. The term, coined by journalist Sidney Blumenthal, is not all that complex. It simply means that politicians become entrepreneurs and that almost everything they do is carefully gauged to prevent unexpected opponents from emerging and gaining surprise victories. A good part of their time in office is spent thinking about how to stay there. In the permanent campaign game, voter loyalty can't be relied on—much of the money spent and high technology used disguises the real insecurity of the candidates who play the permanent campaign game.[7]

Like any game, the permanent campaign has stated and unstated rules, tried and true strategies, and techniques that successful candidates learn quickly. In recent years, most voters and some politicians have become disillusioned with it. In the 1996 election, even a respected senator like New Jersey's Bill Bradley refused to play it, complaining that he couldn't be an effective and honest senator at the same time. But in the absence of new rules, the campaign game often exists by default, with enormous consequences for the democratic debate. The following sections examine the game's rules of play. Remember: The object is to win the most votes. In the process, making a point or mobilizing voters may or may not be useful. As you assess the rules, ask this: Are voters pawns, spectators, or players?

Campaign Rules: Managing Cash Flows

The essential pieces of the campaign game are the chips—the money needed to even contemplate a race for the House, Senate, or presidency. How much is necessary? Where does it come from?

Dimensions of the Cash Pile. Money has always been important in modern political campaigns. Yet no matter how the money pile is measured, its growth rate has been nearly exponential in recent years. The presidential and congressional candidates and national party organizations spent over $2 billion in 1996, with tens, perhaps hundreds of millions in additional cash—some of it undisclosed—spent by interest groups and state and local party organizations.

How much do House and Senate candidates have to raise just on their own? Together, these candidates spent $659 million in 1996, up 30 percent from 1992. On average, winning House candidates spent $700,000 in 1996, up from "only"

$550,000 four years earlier. A Senate seat cost the average victor between $4 and $5 million in 1996. Such costs create a fundraising treadmill, for it means that senators interested in reelection have to raise about $2,000 each day of their six-year terms, while House members need to raise $1,000 daily. Two decades ago, electoral victory cost only a sixth as much.[8]

The presidential nomination contests have experienced similar inflation. Back in 1992, the nomination price tag was $126 million—a figure that had doubled in sixteen years. Yet in only the four years between 1992 and 1996, the nomination campaigns nearly doubled these amounts, to $243 million. In the fall campaign, the official organizations raised and spent over $320 million, again way up from the already soaring totals reached in 1992.

These totals are only part of the story—they represent only the monies raised and spent under the direct control of candidates and their official organizations. Most remarkable about 1996 was the dramatic rise in fundraising and spending by organizations that "help" candidates but stand legally free of their control. Some of it is raised and spent by the national parties and their congressional campaign committees. More comes from so-called "independent" committees established by the parties to skirt campaign finance restrictions. A third source is the state and local parties. A fourth and even newer source is the "soft money" and "independent expenditures" that come directly from corporations, interest groups, and wealthy individuals.

The real novelty of 1996 was the radical increases in monies spent by all these associations and groups. The official national parties alone spent over $880 million in 1996, double their 1992 totals. The AFL-CIO chipped in at least $35 million for selected Congressional races, while their pro-business and Christian Right opponents probably spent over $100 million on independent efforts. Overall, the 1996 election was by far the most expensive in U.S. history, representing a quantum jump in cost.[9]

Who Money Favors. The growing size and sources of the campaign cash pile should concern anyone who cares about free elections. Yet it is just as important to see who gets the cash—and the cost for democracy from the resulting policies.

Theoretically, anyone who fits the constitutional qualifications can run for Congress. But modern congressional campaigns are not level playing fields open to any interested or active citizen. While politics is an uncertain art, what is certain is that money is the premier advantage in modern campaigns. Herewith we list three laws of modern campaign finance.

Law 1. Incumbent members of Congress almost always receive more money than their challengers. Coincidentally or not, incumbents usually get reelected.

Law 2. Challengers are able to defeat incumbents only when (a) they raise something close to the totals raised by the incumbent, or (b) when the incumbent is very unlucky, openly corrupt, or very stupid.

Law 3. The congressional campaigns that are really unpredictable are the open seat contests where incumbents have retired. There are more of these than there used to be.

The distribution of campaign cash in the last three congressional elections ('92, '94, and '96) demonstrates why and how these simple laws seem to operate. Although each election featured very different voter moods and partisan outcomes, the three laws still worked.

Take the 1992 and 1994 congressional elections as examples. On the surface, the actual results couldn't contrast more. In 1992, voters returned a Democratic majority to Congress and elected candidate Clinton to the White House. In 1994, voters seemed to switch, repudiating Democratic policies and providing the GOP with control of both houses for the first time since 1954. Both elections occurred in a climate of voter anger and even disgust with the performance and record of Congress. In both, challengers ran against incumbents by blaming Congress for scandal, corruption, and policy gridlock. How did the laws work in practice?

Law 1 held up well in both contests. Table 8.2 shows that despite all the partisan change and voter anger at Congress, the incumbents still did surprisingly well. Given voter moods, how did incumbents win? In both campaigns, successful incumbents beat their challengers and fought voter disgust by raising and spending more money. In 1992 and even 1994, Senate and House incumbents compiled something close to 3 to 1 spending advantages over challengers.[10]

What, then, explains the apparent revolution in 1994—a gain of fifty-four seats for the Republicans, and the defeat of a record thirty-four Democratic incumbents? In 1994, Law 2 applied, with many Republican challengers matching or outspending Democratic incumbents. Particularly vulnerable were Democratic freshmen—first termers who couldn't use Law 1 to their full advantage because they hadn't the time or the clout to become congressional powerhouses. Many Democratic first termers were simply outspent by Republican newcomers. Still, most Democrats returned, along with most more senior Democratic incumbents and virtually all the Republican incumbents. Still, too, while the successful Republican challengers spent $500,000 or more to gain victory, most challengers couldn't even raise a third of that amount. As a consequence, they lost.[11]

TABLE 8.2 Incumbent Reelection Rates, 1992 and 1994		Incumbent Reelection Rates (percent)	
		House	Senate
	1992 (Clinton wins; Democrats maintain control of Congress)	90	85
	1994 (Republican takeover of Congress; Newt Gingrich becomes Speaker)	90	94
	Source: Congressional Quarterly Weekly Reports.		

Law 3 also operated in 1992 and 1994. There were a large number of open seats where candidates spent lots of money in very competitive races. Not all who spent more won, but to play the open seat game at all substantial money raising was necessary. Here, GOP candidates, who outspent their Democratic rivals, also won most of the open contests.[12]

By 1996, congressional elections returned to the relative calm of incumbents almost always defeating challengers. As usual, the most competitive races were the open ones, as well as those involving many House first termers. This time, all the first termers up for reelection were Republicans elected in 1994. Bolstered by their new majority and incumbency advantages, Republican senators and House members got increased infusions of cash. The open and first-termer seats provided the most drama, and it was in these races that the most money was spent by competing candidates. The median amount received by GOP House first termers was a mammoth $850,000, whereas the median for *all* Democratic challengers was only half that amount. However, the Democrats who defeated Republican first termers conformed to Law 1. They came close to, or exceeded, the vulnerable House GOP freshmen money totals.[13]

The iron laws of campaign money don't mean that only money counts, but that money counts most of the time. Law 2 indicates that there are occasionally well-funded candidates who are corrupt, stupid, or unlucky. Take, for example, the rather sad case of former Nevada Republican Senator Chic Hecht. The senator, who had not been able to prevent the siting of nuclear waste dumps in his home state of Nevada, continually referred to them as "nuclear suppositories." A former Army intelligence officer, he continually said "overt" operations when he really meant "covert." During a debate, Hecht admitted that he had forgotten what the First Amendment was about. Hecht lost. In 1994, Democratic powerhouse Dan Rostenkowski of Illinois suffered from another variation of Law 2: No one doubted Rostenkowski's intelligence, but he had been indicted for bilking the House treasury. Rosty, despite his enormous campaign treasury, also lost.[14]

Given the three laws, it is natural to think that most incumbents are pretty secure, since most times they far outraise challengers. But the members of Congress who raise the most money don't feel secure at all. Most of them have to work extremely hard to raise the dough, and they do so precisely because they fear challengers who might outraise them. The 1994 defeat of so many Democratic incumbents was an object lesson for many incumbents—without building even bigger treasuries, they were all potentially vulnerable.

Moreover, the three laws can be broken when the campaign money is tainted. In the 1994 California Senate race, Republican candidate Michael Huffington far outspent his Democratic incumbent rival, Senator Dianne Feinstein. Yet Huffington still lost, because his immense personal fortune gave credence to charges that he was trying to buy the election. As discussed in Chapter 7, some southern Democratic incumbents are having more trouble winning reelection no matter how much they spend because of the GOP trend in that region. And, as we'll see by the end of this chapter, well-funded incumbents can be defeated the old-fashioned way, through grassroots campaigns.

Insofar as they persist, the realities of campaign finance bolster elite democracy. By making money the indispensable political resource, the equality of citizens is undermined. Those who have the resources to participate in the game can play, while those who don't are generally excluded and always handicapped. Even many successful candidates and incumbents see burdens and costs to the permanent campaign. In 1992, Pennsylvania Democrat Peter Kostmayer raised $1.2 million in a Congressional race. Kostmayer still lost to an even-better funded Republican challenger. He wasn't sad, admitting in a campaign post mortem, "Fundraising became the dominant part of my campaigns—and campaigning came to dominate my life. . . . Members of Congress despise the process but are addicted to it, terrified that change means defeat."[15]

Where do people like Kostmayer go for their cash? A simplistic view is that candidates are bribed, or that they enrich themselves while in office. While there are quite a few examples of such blatant corruption, outright bribery is pretty rare. To most members of Congress it is inappropriate and unethical. To the merely prudent, bribery can ruin a thriving political career. One powerful and popular California Democratic Senator, Alan Cranston, was censured by the Senate for such practices in the early 1990s.

Bribery and personal corruption occur, but they aren't usually necessary to raise lots of cash legally. In theory, there are many restraints and regulations on campaign finance. In recent years, however, ambitious legislation has been decimated by a series of court judgments, ignored through loopholes, and skirted through ingenious forms of "creative financing." What's left of campaign laws is now a complex legal shell that, in the hands of the professionals, promotes a sure and easy flow of large, nearly unlimited quantities of cash from private interests to cooperative Democratic and Republican candidates. Like the computer game Myst, the system is at first hard to understand. But in the end, the diligent participant figures it out.

The Tragedy of Post-Watergate Campaign Finance Reform

The laws governing campaign finance were passed with the best of intentions and on a wave of popular outrage. On paper, they are strict. Current laws are products of the revulsion following President Nixon's 1972 campaign, fueled by the revelations of the Watergate scandal. The Nixon campaign took in millions of unreported cash contributions, often handed over in paper bags or carry-on luggage directly to White House operatives. Nixon's money came from interests as diverse as the dairy industry, the ITT Corporation, and entrepreneurs like H. Ross Perot (who gave $200,000 to Nixon in 1972). Usually, the Nixon people laundered the contributions, returning them in the currency of ambassadorships, price supports for favored products, tax loopholes, or lenient interpretations of federal regulations for their clients.

The Federal Election Campaign Act (FECA) and its subsequent amendments were passed to prevent such practices. Twenty-five years later, there's not much left of them except the autopsy report. Still, it is worthwhile to describe the act's provisions and intentions, and then show how both have been subverted and by-passed. Among other laudable goals, the FECA requires disclosures of the names of campaign donors, limits the size of donations to parties and candidates, provides some measure for public financing of presidential races in return for

---

TABLE 8.3

Federal Regulations, Funding of Presidential and Congressional Campaigns, 1996

Disclosure

Campaigns must report all contributions over $100 and expenditures to the Federal Election Commission (FEC).

Campaigns may not

Accept contributions from foreigners.
Take cash contributions over $100.
Take contributions over the prescribed limits.

Individual contribution limits

$1,000 to each candidate or candidate committee for each election.
$25,000 limit to all federal candidates.
$20,000 limit to *national* party committees.
$5,000 limit to PAC or other political committee.
No federal limits on contributions to state parties (soft money).
No limits on contributions that are independent of a candidate's organization.

Political action committees (PACs): Congressional Elections

PACs must have at least 50 members, give to at least 5 federal candidates, and register six months before the first contribution.
$5,000 limit to any candidate in any one election.
$15,000 limit to any one national party committee in one year.
No regulation of PAC contributions at state party level.
No caps on absolute spending by any single PAC.
No limits on the amount of "independent" expenditures.

Presidential primary funding

Candidates running for their party's nomination may receive matching funds from the federal treasury if they raise at least $5,000 in contributions of $250 or less in 20 states.
In return, candidates must accept spending caps established by the FEC.

Presidential general election funding

The federal government pays the entire cost of the general election campaigns of the major presidential candidates. Those candidates representing smaller parties qualify for funding by receiving 5% or more of the vote in a presidential election. In return, presidential candidates accept absolute spending caps.
Money from so called "soft" sources is not counted as part of official campaign expenses.

spending limits, and bans contributions from foreigners as well as direct contributions from corporations to candidates. It establishes a bipartisan Federal Election Commission (FEC) to enforce the laws. Table 8.3 shows the general provisions of the FECA.

As Table 8.3 shows, FECA establishes different regulations for presidential and congressional elections as well as for the size of individual and organizational contributions to political parties. Presidential campaign finance laws were the most restrictive. *Public financing* was introduced into both the primary and general election. If candidates adhered to spending caps and raised small amounts of money in at least twenty states, taxpayers kicked in with matching funds in exchange. Early critics of these provisions claimed they excluded independent and third party candidates. But they haven't, or at least not entirely: 1980 independent candidate John Anderson got "matching funds," as did Ross Perot in 1996.

PACs

Unlike the presidential race, House and Senate campaigns receive no public financing. However, to hold down the size of large contributions to any one campaign, federal law limited the size of individual contributions to official campaign organizations of Congressional candidates. To prevent direct links between candidates and special interests, **political action committees** or **PACs** were established. PACs are voluntary, independent associations designed to bundle individual donations and give them to particular campaigns. The size of any particular contribution is regulated, while the overall amount PACs could spend on all political campaigns isn't. When FECA was passed, nobody expected PACs to grow so quickly. From a mere 608 in 1974, their numbers expanded to nearly 5,000 by 1996. House candidates caught on to PACs more than Senate candidates. By 1996, PACs spent $131 million.

Individual companies have formed *corporate* PACs, and whole industries create *trade association* PACs. Labor unions and professional associations form PACs as well. Any medium-sized company or trade association peddling California prunes, beer, soda, jet fighters, or American wheat is likely to sponsor a PAC. The health insurance industry increased their PAC representations and campaign contributions to defeat President Clinton's health care reforms that were proposed in 1993. Dentists, realtors, teachers, lawyers, cheese producers, exporters, importers, and other claimants on legislation all have their PACs as well. Neither college professors nor college students have their own PAC; nor do the homeless, welfare recipients, or poor children.

Ideological PACs usually have broader goals than increasing tariffs on Turkish figs or promoting tax breaks and subsidies for particular commodities. For instance, in the late 1970s and early 1980s, the National Conservative Political Action Committee (NCPAC) became famous and feared for its ability to target money to defeat liberal Democratic senators. In recent years, the National Rifle Association (NRA) contributed over $1.7 million to federal candidates in the 1992 election season.[16]

For defenders of the present system, the sheer number and variety of PACs provides evidence that they are healthy instruments of free speech. Rich bankers and working class machinists have PACs, as do environmentalists, feminists, and conservative evangelical Christians. Indeed, many PACs are small and give money to only a selected group of favored incumbents and a few challengers. Moreover, because they are regulated, the amounts of money most individual PACs give to any one candidate are unimpressive by Washington standards.[17]

Yet a closer look at PAC giving reveals a massive conservative ideological and pro-business bias in their cumulative effects. Corporate and trade association PACs consistently outspend labor union and other liberal PACs by nearly 2 to 1. Adding conservative ideological PACs to the totals, the overall effect is stunning. *Washington Post* correspondent Thomas Byrne Edsall states flatly: "the financial elites of all these groups share a common conservative economic view."[18]

Before 1994 and the GOP takeover of Congress, the PAC system seemed to favor all incumbents, including liberal Democratic incumbents and Republican conservatives. There was a simple reason why: There were more Democratic incumbents in the House and Senate than Republican incumbents. Congressional Democratic majorities made individual legislators powerful arbiters of legislation on taxation, regulation, and spending. In the attempt to influence legislation, otherwise highly conservative corporate PACs spread their money around to prominent incumbents in both parties.

Over time, the dependence of liberal Democratic senators and House members on PACs may have pushed the party to the center and the right. In the days before PACs, Democrats in Congress used to get the bulk of their money and grassroots support from unions, movements, people of color, and liberal groups and individuals. Yet in the era of growing PAC influence, Democratic incumbents became increasingly dependent on corporate and trade association contributions—everyone from oil producers through realtors, attorneys, brokerage houses, insurance companies, banks, and utilities. Even as liberal and labor PACs tried to match growing corporate PAC influence, the business PACs almost always outbid them, even in contributions to Democrats. By 1992, incumbent Democrats received three times more money from corporate PACs than from liberal and labor PACs. The effects of PAC money split the Democratic party and diluted its liberalism. Jake Lewis, a long-time Senate committee aide, comments, "We've had a lot of liberals [on the Banking Committee] who were good on housing and would take care of the banks on the other side. As long as they take care of the banks, they could be as liberal as they wanted."[19]

In contrast, congressional Republicans had few problems raising money from "purer" sources. More than the Democrats, the Republican incumbents got money from generally affluent individual contributors. In the battle of the PACs, Republican incumbents took money from conservative and business sources alone. The pristine, pro-business sources of GOP contributions created no problems for already pro-corporate Republicans. In short, while congressional Democrats and their message got fragmented through PAC contributions, the Republicans only became more united.[20]

The big break in this pattern came in 1994. Many business PACs sensed that some Democratic incumbents were vulnerable, and the party's majority in both houses was in jeopardy. Along with the Republicans, business PACs targeted some Democratic incumbents for defeat and did so by pouring contributions into the campaigns coffers of the most able Republican challengers. In the end, business PACs nearly doubled their contributions to conservative Republican challengers. Their effort bore fruit as the GOP achieved its historic majorities.[21]

By 1996, the patterns of PAC giving returned to the incumbent norm. Yet this time it was the new majority of Republicans that now benefitted in two ways. As conservatives, Republican incumbents received money from the usual corporate, trade association, and ideological sources. With more incumbents and now in control of Congress, Republican candidates got an increasing share of PAC support. No wonder, then, that PAC money flowed to GOP candidates in preponderant amounts. To compete at all in the money game, Democrats had to contain even more their historic liberal tendencies.[22]

Soft Money

PACs fuel the personal and permanent campaigns of congressional candidates. As legislators come to rely on PACs, their campaigns float free of the weakened grassroots parties. These developments have sparked the growth of a new kind of strong party. As we saw in Chapter 7, its strength lies less in organizing voters than in attracting donors.

The foundation of the new, strong parties comes from raising and spending **soft money.** Unlike the "hard" variety just described, soft money allows unlimited amounts of cash to flow from monied interests to the national parties. It is then laundered by the national parties into "independent" expenditures or "transfers" to state parties, who spend it for "party-building activities." Soft money is based on the dubious proposition that money not given directly to particular candidates shouldn't be capped or regulated. Simply put, soft money is an elaborate bipartisan scheme that utterly violates the intent of post-Watergate campaign finance regulations. National parties can raise and spend as much as they want, so long as the dough is used for "party-building" activities that "just happen" to help all of the party's candidates. The evasions are entirely legal. From a trickle in the 1970s, soft money rose to a stream in the 1980s. In 1996, soft money became the mighty Mississippi of campaign finance, sweeping all before it (see Figure 8.1 on p. 212).

A nice legal distinction gave birth to soft money, but friendly court rulings and ingenious campaign strategists helped it grow. A most helpful parent of soft money has been the U.S. Supreme Court. In the 1976 decision ***Buckley* v. *Valeo*** the court upheld many of FECA's provisions but held that any restrictions on an individual or group's ability to spend as much on campaigns as it wanted was a violation of free speech rights. In effect, free speech was equated with a unlimited ability of the wealthy to spend money. Through this ruling and others that stemmed from it, any mandatory spending limits on political campaigns, or

FIGURE 8.1

**Growth in Soft
Money, 1991–1996**

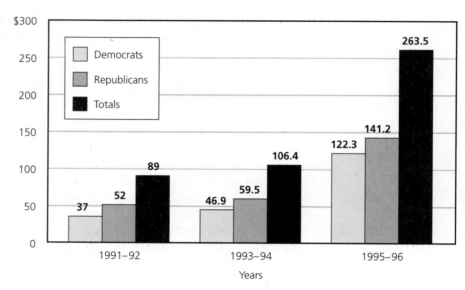

Reprinted by permission from *Congressional Quarterly,* April 5, 1997, p. 773.

limits on the amount of personal money spent by candidates, has been ruled unconstitutional. And the courts have gone on to rule that amounts spent "independently" of a candidate's official campaign organization are "free speech" and thus can't be regulated at all.[23]

Soft money got a further big boost in 1996 in the case of *Colorado Federal Republican Campaign Committee* v. *Federal Election Commission.* Here, the Supreme Court ruled that the national parties didn't even have to transfer soft money to the state parties before spending it to help candidates. Instead, the national parties could pretend that they were "independent" of their own candidates, and raise and spend unlimited and unregulated amounts of cash to help them. The caveat was that all such money had once again to be raised and spent independently of the official campaigns of particular candidates.

The *Colorado* decision was a mere legal sanction of what the parties had already started doing earlier. In 1995, the Democratic National Committee and President Clinton's advisors had already thought up an ingenious way to avoid the FECA's restriction on presidential campaign fundraising regulations. The Democrats had raised mammoth amounts of money for a new breed of "independent expenditures" called **issue advocacy ads.** These ads, which ran from 1995 through the primary season, praised Clinton and his record and attacked the Republicans. But they carefully avoided a direct appeal to "Vote for President Clinton." For this reason, the $25 million used to pay for them could come from "soft" and unregulated sources, and the Clinton campaign didn't have to curtail its expenses in order to get its taxpayer-sponsored matching funds during the election year. Not surprisingly, the GOP quickly caught on to the new challenge and opportunity. Skirting the FECA, the GOP raised $14 million in soft money for "independent" issue advocacy ads that touted Bob Dole's credentials.

The rise, maturation, and explosion of soft money is a sordid tale. Which party deserves the most praise or blame? The GOP pioneered creative uses of soft money fundraising in the late 1970s. But the Democrats responded to the challenge in the 1980s by raising an equal amount in the 1988 elections. By 1996 standards, the $45 million raised in that year looks pretty puny. Thanks to the aforementioned court rulings and the bitter acrimony between the parties following the Republican revolution of 1994, the competition for soft money became an arms race between the parties. Between 1988 and 1996, the tidal wave of soft money fundraising rose 700 percent, cresting at $263.5 million. According to Anthony Corrado, raising and spending soft money has developed from an "illness" of the 1970s and 1980s into the present "epidemic," soliciting the kind of "organized interests that are supposed to be illegal in federal elections."[24]

As this book is written, the Democrats and Clinton are taking the most heat for their feeding frenzy on soft money. In 1997, the public heard a growing set of lurid tales about $50,000 coffee klatsches in the White House, strange guests in the Lincoln Bedroom, telemarketing from the vice president's office, foreign arms merchants and felons shaking hands with the First Family. Republicans, led by Senator Fred Thompson, started investigating, and even Clinton himself apologized for some of the fundraising practices. Yet while the practices of 1996 seemed to hurt the Democrats the most, the Senate investigation showed that there were few differences between the parties when it comes to how soft money is raised or spent. The Republicans, in fact, raised and spent more soft money than the Democrats did in 1996.

How is soft money raised, and who contributes? Here, the story is similarly squalid and bipartisan. The vast preponderance of soft money doesn't come from Asian donors, but from wholly American global corporations, trade associations, and individuals. As of 1996, labor unions joined the fray as well. Yet labor, as was the case with PACs, can hardly match the onslaught of corporate America and affluent individuals. Both parties have developed new ways to make it easy and productive to give, and give generously. Ronald Reagan and the GOP were innovators in this strategy. Back in 1988, they invited prospective big donors to the White House, in the hopes that they "would make their $2,500 contribution right away." Reagan's successor and the Republican National Committee organized "Team 100," a group of donors stretching from the CEOs of ARCO to Archer Daniels Midland who had contributed over $100,000 apiece. One example of how soft money works is the $2.7 million gift given by the Amway Corporation to the Republican Party in 1994. The gift financed a "party-building activity"—actually a broadcasting center—that enabled the GOP to spread its message and televise its candidates on a new cable television station. Another example is beer magnate Adolph Coors and his $150,000 contribution to the

Colorado Republican Party. It just so happened that Colorado Republicans could use the money to support advertising for the entire Republican ticket.

In 1995 and 1996, soft money fundraising became more sophisticated. The fundraisers of both parties found new ways to trade cash for access, and pleasant occasions in which to do so. In addition to coffee sessions, a common technique became "retreats" that mixed business leaders with prominent politicians at resorts. Another technique was the sale of honorific titles. In 1996, it took a hefty $100,000 just to become "a managing trustee" of the Democratic party. This humble amount bought the possibility to "participate in foreign trade missions" organized by the Department of Commerce. For the Republicans, breakfasts got very expensive, with $45,000 netting a shared croissant with Speaker Newt Gingrich. Black tie dinners are perhaps the most common fundraising technique; tables with prominent officeholders can cost over $100,000 a plate. At two Washington black tie dinners held by the Republicans and Democrats in early 1996, more soft money was raised than in the entire 1988 election cycle—nearly $28 million in one night.[25]

Still somewhat important to voters, the parties and their candidates can also be known through their benefactors. From this standpoint, the parties represent slightly different variations of corporate and affluent America. The Republicans get more money from tobacco, drug, and oil companies, whereas the Democrats seem strongest among global entertainment and communications conglomerates, trial lawyers, and parts of Wall Street. Labor unions gave soft money to the Democrats, too, in the attempt to counter the corporate influence. But corporate soft money to the Democrats beat labor by a 7 to 1 ratio. Almost all the corporate contributors were remarkably bipartisan, giving some money to one party and much to the other.[26]

The Class Bias of Money Politics

Kentucky Republican Senator Mitch McConnell, one of the few forthright defenders of the campaign money game, argues that the whole enterprise furthers "more political speech" and as such furthers the aims of full democracy. Yet what McConnell neglects is how the money, used as a political resource, overrepresents the most powerful and affluent people and institutions in American life while excluding others.

Insofar as the search for contributions has come to dominate campaigns, an economy and society already sharply unequal in its rewards further invades the one realm where everyone is supposed to be equal—citizenship and voting. The reasons are straightforward enough. While the number of people who give money to political campaigns has been rising, about three-quarters of the American citizenry never contribute a dime to political campaigns. The likelihood of giving to candidates rises with household income. Fully 56 percent of people who make over $80,000 annually contribute something, while only 6 percent of people making under $20,000 do. Although only about one in thirty American families make $150,000 a year or more, this group contributes over a quarter of

all campaign dollars. As a form of political participation available to average citizens, giving money ranks well below voting or discussing politics.[27]

Those who contribute to candidates or parties are not only more affluent, they also think very differently than ordinary citizens about the current corporate political economy. Eighty-three percent of the mass public report agreement with the statement that "average working families have less economic security today because corporations have become too greedy," and by a 2 to 1 margin think that "government is too concerned with what big corporations want." It is not surprising that donors disagree. Only 15 percent of contributors to campaigns agree with the first statement, and only a third accept the latter. Writing in *The Nation*, Robert Borosage and Ruy Teixeira comment: "A majority of voters are open to a policy that is more nationalist, more assertive, more willing to regulate business and stand with citizens. . . . Not surprisingly, the conservative bipartisan consensus on economic policy that dominates politics reflects the views of big donors rather than majority opinion."

Yet the most pernicious effect of the money game may be its effects on other kinds of political action that ordinary people *can* fully undertake. Is it a coincidence that as campaigns become more expensive, voter turnout has dropped? Or that fewer people donate "time" to campaigns, even as "contributions" become the privileged way of participating in politics? Most studies see a direct link between the rise of money and the decline of other, less class-oriented ways people participate in politics. In this sense, money becomes equated with "speech," even though the two are very different indeed.[28]

THE RISE OF HIGH-TECH POLITICS

Why has the drive for money become the dominant goal of political campaigns, dwarfing other resources and the energies of ordinary citizens? One partial answer to this question comes from Dick Morris, Clinton's chief campaign adviser until his resignation after reported escapades with a Washington prostitute.[29] Morris is widely credited, and blamed, for moving Clinton to the center and away from the party's traditional liberalism. In his postelection book about the Clinton White House, Morris tells story after story about how his expertise and advice turned Clinton's presidential fortunes around. Nearly two years before the 1996 election, Morris reports: "To prepare for the State of the Union address, Clinton asked me take the mother of all polls. . . . The survey was 259 questions long, and had to be divided into five parts, since no one would willingly stay on the phone for the hours it would have taken to answer every question." . . . Later in the book, Morris shows how he used almost daily polling to press the new species of issue advocacy ads, designed to build support for the president long before election year. Morris proudly proclaims that "we spent thirty five million dollars . . . burying Republican proposals and building a national consensus."[30]

One of Morris's chief antagonists inside the White House was Clinton aide Harold Ickes, an unabashed New York liberal. If Morris advised on how to spend the money, Ickes was in charge of raising it. Ickes's memos and notes, released after Democratic fundraising practices came under fire in 1997, reveals a White House in which the daily balance of soft money raising had become an obsession. Ickes, like the rest of the Clinton team, raised growing amounts of money through fear that the Republicans were raising even more. In early 1996, he wrote to Clinton: "The fundraising needs of the D.N.C. will require a *very substantial* [emphasis in original] commitment of time from the President, the Vice President, the First Lady, and Mrs. Gore." He went on to suggest event after event in 1995 and 1996 to counter the growing GOP money pile. In addition to dozens of coffees and dinners, Ickes urged the president and vice president personally to raise $1.2 million by making thirty-five phone calls.[31]

Although Ickes and Morris had real political differences, they both seemed to agree that more money was the essential currency of a successful Democratic effort in 1996. Behind it all was anxiety and fear, fueled by the correct sense that the GOP was outraising the Democrats. For Morris and Ickes, only money could buy the high technology and services necessary to keep Clinton and the Democrats competitive. What, exactly, does all the money buy?

Political Consultants

One big campaign expense is the experts themselves. While modern political campaigns have always employed political experts, the modern political consultant—personified by Morris—is a different kind of animal than his party boss predecessors. Political consultants are expensive—by some accounts, Morris's fees alone exceeded $2 million in 1996, and a well-run congressional campaign employs consultants for fees of $100,000 or more. The old bosses lived in style, too, but their skills were different. The party bosses dealt in votes and as such ran operations where ward heelers, voters, and government jobs came into play along with grassroots contact with ordinary voters through a complex party organization. The old bosses didn't have college educations and were rough-talking, down-to-earth types. Most of them would have died before working for candidates of different parties.

Modern political consultants like Morris are college educated, well trained and well spoken, able to manipulate data, design surveys, and feel more comfortable with advertising executives than with ordinary voters. Unlike the party bosses, today's consultants increasingly seek work from anyone who pays them. Morris worked for candidates of both parties, including the Democrats' adversary, Senate Majority Leader Trent Lott. Their origins are often in the worlds of advertising, public relations, and communication, but in recent times political consultants have even founded their own graduate school in Washington, D.C. Unlike party professionals of the past, modern consultants know voters, but only as abstractions and numbers on a survey. The currency of political consultants is high technology as it applies to politics.

The business of professional political consulting began about four decades ago. Like many innovations, California showed the way, with the two firms of Spencer Roberts and Whitaker & Baxter pioneering the new profession. Today, no serious candidate can afford to be without consultants, if only because all the other candidates have them.[32]

What do consultants offer? Candidates have choices about whether they hire a "full-service firm" or form their own "campaign team" from the expert pool. In line with the importance of the permanent campaign, modern political consultants are not just employed during election years. Dick Morris became an informal advisor to Clinton just after the 1994 election. Others achieve fame after elections and live on as prominent advisers—Jimmy Carter's pollster Patrick Caddell and George Bush's Robert Teeter are good examples. More typical, however, are specialists of lesser fame who concentrate on polling, TV and radio advertising, direct mail fundraising, and press relations for congressional and gubernatorial candidates. The rise of political consultants parallels the growth of the permanent and personal campaign.[33]

Polling

Polling is the basis for all other modern campaign activities. It is so important that key consultants like Morris often insist that their clients hire a favored firm (Clinton hired New York City's Penn and Schoen). Surveys plumb both name recognition and voter attitudes about candidates, their opponents, and the issues of most and least concern to voters. In well-funded campaigns like Clinton's, polling provides constant, even daily tracking of voter opinion, allowing experts to monitor the campaign's success in reaching groups targeted for selective appeals. In recent years, polling has been supplemented by the use of **focus and dial groups.** A small number of people selected by the pollsters are invited to view videos of the candidate's recent public appearances and TV performances. Sometimes they are asked to push "hot" and "cold" buttons as they watch, indicating degrees of positive or negative reactions to what they see and hear. Through both polling and focus groups, campaign specialists test and refine changing campaign themes and strategies.[34]

Media Advertising

Polling is useful only insofar as the candidate's images and opponent's weaknesses are effectively accented in subsequent TV and radio advertising. Media advertising currently is the most expensive part of Senate, gubernatorial, and presidential races. In key media markets, TV ads can run over $100,000 a minute. The importance of campaign media specialists has grown accordingly. They've got to make quick choices about the themes of commercials. (Which "issues" should be presented? Should the candidate talk in the ads? When should positive images be reinforced? When should opponents be attacked?) Media consultants also decide where and when to purchase TV and radio time, how to pace the commercials during the course of a campaign, and how to respond to an opponent's attacks.

We've already seen that media advertising is no longer limited to the days immediately preceding election day. In the candidate-centered campaign, name recognition and favorable media images have to be cultivated early, if only because both will allow advertisers to set the agenda for the real campaign season. To be sure, media specialists make mistakes. Advertising can't do everything. In 1996, Dole's advertising team made a big error by focusing most of their attention on California, a state where Clinton possessed an enormous lead. Consequently, Dole lost states he might have won—Florida, Arizona, and Illinois.[35]

Media consultants for presidential candidates cannot simply manufacture images out of thin air, because the major candidates usually have established records. But in the much more numerous congressional and state races, where candidates are often unknown, the potential for consultant creativity is enormous. The consultant's dream is a pliable candidate who allows the experts to do their work unhindered.

One of the most creative ads lifted Malcolm Wallop, now retired, to a Wyoming Senate seat. A New Yorker by birth, a Yale graduate, and a polo-playing relative of Queen Elizabeth, Wallop was effectively recast as an average Western cowboy. Here's a transcript of one Wallop ad:

VISUAL:
(Wallop, dressed as a cowboy, is saddling and mounting his horse.)
ANNOUNCER:
Everywhere you look these days, the federal government is there, telling you what they think, telling you what they think you ought to think. Telling you

how to do things, setting up rules you can't follow. I think the federal government is going too far. Now they say if you don't take a portable facility along with you on a roundup, you can't go.

VISUAL:

(Wallop appears angry and disgusted, matching the announcer's sarcastic tone, as the camera pans a porta-potty strapped to a donkey tied to Wallop's horse.)

ANNOUNCER:

We need someone to tell 'em about Wyoming. Malcolm Wallop will.

POSTER:

Malcolm Wallop for US Senate.[36]

Direct Mail and Media Fundraising

Consultants, polls, and ads are expensive. The ironic result is that campaigns need a growing number of fundraising consultants to pay for all three. Soft money specialists aren't cheap. In congressional races, maintaining contacts with PACs and with the national and state parties that dispense money requires trained experts. Fundraisers who deal with ordinary citizens have pioneered the use of direct mail, toll-free numbers, and Web sites as ways to raise money. Still, computer direct mail experts handle the funding of most campaigns. Consultants in direct mail compile names from friendly political organizations, magazine subscription lists, the professions, and interest groups such as the American Medical Association or the National Association of Realtors. They tailor the text of computer-generated letters to accent themes of interest to the addressees.

Like polling and advertising, direct mail features virtually no two-way conversations between the candidates' staff and the voters. Approval or disapproval is measured solely in terms of money gained versus the fundraising costs. A bad direct mail expert, for instance, might neglect to mention a candidate's pro-gun policy to readers of *Field and Stream* or might write a letter with false claims that could be leaked to the candidate's opponents and later used to discredit its creator. Good direct mail experts are more sensitive to the limits of the possible. They may not even have contacts with the candidate's organization and may work for PACs and organizations that work independently of official campaign organizations. In 1980, NCPAC, a pioneer in direct mail, took credit for defeating four liberal Democratic senators. In 1986 alone, the Republican party used direct mail to raise $256 million.[37]

Press and Media Relations

The general relationship between campaigns and the news media is discussed in Chapter 7. Here we note some new departures. "Press relations" no longer means just handing out press kits and making the candidate available for chats with the national press.

Today's press relations techniques are much more complex than in the past. In the 1992 presidential elections, press relations specialists helped all the candidates to avoid traditional reporters and established forums. Consultants tried to find novel ways for candidates to communicate directly with voters, thereby avoiding the insider "hardball" questions often posed by the Washington media. Via direct satellite hookups to local TV stations, the campaign strategist decides where and when the candidate's valuable time can be best used in targeted media markets. Press relations can also be expressed through duelling fax machines. In 1992, the Little Rock, Arkansas, headquarters of the Clinton campaign successfully countered the Bush team's charges impugning Clinton's record by choreographing "rapid responses" to every news outlet in the country.[38] In 1996, the process spread, with the Clinton team again leading the way with responses to Republican charges sometimes delivered to the press before GOP strategists had a chance to air them.

Effects of High-Tech Political Consultants on Election Results

Many—including most political consultants—argue that high-tech politics isn't worth worrying about and that in any case it is inevitable in a nation of over 260 million people. Image makers, like all advertisers armed with marketing data, can also fail if their "product" is found wanting. Another view is that consultants represent the ultimate corruption of U.S. political campaigns. Candidates become mere commodities to be packaged and repackaged to a gullible electorate.[39] Closer to the truth, perhaps, is that the rise of high-tech politics does help individual candidates, but demeans all politicians and insults and disempowers voters.

The growth and sophistication of negative campaigning provide some support for this view. Observe, for instance, the 1988 presidential race between George Bush and Michael Dukakis. Early in the fall campaign, Bush's consultants discovered that Dukakis, despite an apparent lead in the polls, was vulnerable because he was unknown on the issues of race, crime, and patriotism. The resulting commercials created by Bush's team turned the election around. The most famous among them blamed Dukakis, then Democratic governor of Massachusetts, for the prison furlough of one Willie Horton, a black prisoner who raped a white woman after he was furloughed. In other ads, Bush was seen visiting a flag factory, with a voiceover noting that Dukakis opposed a constitutional amendment to ban flag burning.[40]

Since 1988, crudely negative personal ads haven't been quite as effective when used. As a result, they've been employed with somewhat more subtlety and caution, and usually with the attempt to link particular candidates with unpopular national politicians. In 1994 the faces of vulnerable Democratic incumbents and first termers were "morphed" into Bill Clinton's, while in 1996 the faces of Republican incumbents were often morphed into Newt Gingrich's. Many races still feature the usual servings of crude stereotypes. Perhaps a new low was reached in a California congressional race, where incumbent Democrat Vic Fazio's face was "morphed" into the condemned killer of a young girl. Fazio's "crime" was his opposition to the death penalty. In New Jersey's bitter Senate race, candidates Bob Torricelli and Dick Zimmer spent millions in negative attacks. All in all, though, negativity didn't work as well as it did in 1988, especially for Republicans intent on repeating and renewing the old "Willie Horton" charges against Democrats.[41]

One response to the negativity of modern campaigns is that it is nothing new. Democratic icons like Jefferson, Jackson, Lincoln, and FDR were accused of everything from treason to spousal abuse. While true, what this kind of argument neglects is the distinctive elite context provided by the modern professional campaign. Scholar Wilson Carey McWilliams notes that past negative attacks occurred in a polity "dense with associations," where campaigns "drew citizens into public places" and in a setting where "the vast majority of the press was local" and "judged the propriety and authenticity" of slurs and innuendo. In contrast, present-day campaign management occurs in "a context where the people are more exposed to and dependent on the mass media," where the "private, individualistic, self-protective side of American culture" is emphasized over "citizenship and public life."[42]

Voters watch negative and positive ads, and there is indeed much evidence that these ads do have some effects. They watch insider accounts of strategy shifts and attempts to repackage candidates. Ultimately and by definition, they vote. Yet it is likely to be without much enthusiasm. Instead, voters become cynical and depoliticized, unsure of the sincerity of any and all political claims and "negative" about all politicians.[43]

Equally serious is the effect of professional campaigns on a generation of grassroots organizers, people who used to train volunteers, hold meetings, and visit community groups. Writing in the *Washington Post*, grassroots activist Kenneth Weine recounts: "A friend of mine called . . . ready to be shipped to a 'battleground' state to run the party's effort to mobilize the women's vote. She's a great organizer. I asked what she would be doing—building a committee of local women leaders, running phone banks? No, she responded, her job was administering the money from Washington—securing phone bank vendors, approving scripts and reviewing direct mail scripts."[44]

Ultimately, the modern high-tech campaign benefits elite democracy. Voters, sensing manipulation, lose interest in campaign politics. "We keep pushing the button, but the public's response is no longer there," complains Democratic consultant Carter Eskew. Within the limited terms of elite democracy, a solution to Eskew's problem is more innovative ads that look "all natural." Another consultant says, "Ads won't work if they look like political ads. That's why I want to do stuff that hasn't been done, like hand-held shots." If these consultants get their way, the false alternative to high-tech politics will be more sophisticated high-tech illusions, not changes in the campaign game itself.[45]

CAMPAIGNING AND POPULAR DEMOCRACY

If the personalized, monied, and high-tech strategies were the total political campaign package, there would be little democratic debate. Campaigns in which

citizens are seen as focus groups registering hot or cold responses more closely resemble a psychology laboratory than real democracy. That the "subjects" get to vote on the success of the experiment is of little value. Left unchecked, the campaign game is a prime example of elite democracy. Citizens turn from participants into spectators, politicians from democratic leaders to image merchants.

Can ordinary voters fight back? Can politicians lose their addiction to campaign money, or is it a permanent feature of our politics? Although eliminating money and high technology from political campaigns altogether is unlikely, redirecting campaign rules toward popular democracy is possible.

1992 as a Case Study: Did Voters Take Command?

Voters can change the campaign game. When they expect and demand more, candidates are forced to respond and the elite driven process is opened up, at least somewhat, to popular democratic politics.

The 1992 presidential election is a case in point. Voters began the campaign of 1992 in a cynical mood. Yet by the fall campaign and November election, most voters felt more positive about the process, the candidates, and themselves. Even voter turnout rose. What happened to affect voter attitudes?

In 1992, voters took partial control by demanding from the candidates specific policies and proposals rather than vague images and generalities. Democratic presidential candidate Paul Tsongas was perhaps the first to respond to voter cynicism. In the early Democratic primaries, he made unexpected headway by writing and distributing long pamphlets about his policy stances. The other Democratic candidates, including Bill Clinton, soon had to follow his lead. The primaries featured an exceptionally large number of debates, in which candidates couldn't avoid tough questions. Ross Perot's entry into the race helped, for his attacks concentrated attention on the follies of Washington party politics and the absence of "straight talk" in the political debate.

In the summer and fall, the long-term future of the economy began to dominate campaign dialogue. As it did, it became more difficult for the candidates to trade personal attacks. George Bush's campaign attempted to run TV ads reminiscent of the notorious 1988 race, but they didn't work. All three of the candidates, including President Bush, were forced to give diagnoses of what had gone wrong in the 1980s. The declining quality of life of the American middle class became the lightning rod for detailed discussions of the health care crisis, the deficit, taxes, and the state of American schools and other public institutions.

Seeking answers and a wider debate, the voters demanded and to some degree got the candidates to appear in "uncontrolled" settings where real conversations occurred. In one presidential debate, Bush began a personal attack on Clinton, only to be halted by a citizen questioner who insisted that all three candidates talk about larger issues. Sources of information about the candidates broadened beyond the evening news and candidate commercials. First with Perot and his appearances on *Larry King Live* and later through numerous candidate appearances in open settings, the candidates were forced to answer hard questions and address voter concerns. Generally, the more the candidates appeared on the *new media* of talk shows, on call-in programs, and in debates, the less character was an important factor and the less campaign advertising became the central battleground of the campaign.

As the campaign shifted from advertisements and negative campaigning to issues and discussion, voters began to feel more informed about the process and more involved in it. From the summer to election day in November, more Americans than in the three previous elections were paying attention to the electoral contest. Each time a candidate appeared on a national phone-in program, over 1 million attempted phone calls were registered. Participation in such formats was particularly popular among the youngest voters, those least attached to the political parties.

Can we therefore say the voters were in control in the 1992 election? More so than in 1988 or 1996. While the campaigns all cost an enormous amount of money, the most effective media were the ones the candidates didn't pay for.[46]

Grassroots Campaigns

Are there ever campaigns in which voters are powerful from the start? Such efforts might be called **grassroots campaigns.** Grassroots campaigns value volunteer efforts and organization; downplay the role of advertising and money; and

MAKING A DIFFERENCE

Grassroots Campaigns and Minnesota's Senator Wellstone

Short, bald, disheveled and with a career as a college professor in rural Northfield, Minnesota, Paul Wellstone was hardly a political consultant's dream of the ideal Senate candidate. Moreover, in overwhelmingly white and Protestant Minnesota, he was Jewish and had led Jesse Jackson's losing effort to win the 1988 Minnesota primary. In 1990, Democrat Wellstone faced well-known Republican incumbent Senator Rudy Boschwitz. With a $7 million campaign treasury and one of the best political consulting teams in the business, Boschwitz spent more on television advertising in the campaign's last weekend than Wellstone spent in eighteen months of campaigning. Yet in 1990, Paul Wellstone beat Boschwitz to become Minnesota's junior Democratic senator. How Wellstone turned conventional "liabilities" into strengths reveals that there are popular democratic alternatives to the high-tech money campaign game.

Wellstone began his campaign in 1989 with a long list of activists everywhere in Minnesota and an old school bus customized to serve as a mobile campaign headquarters. Visiting mining towns, Native American reservations, farm hamlets, college campuses, and minority neighborhoods in Minneapolis, Wellstone left behind more volunteers pledged to contact neighbors and colleagues. To save money on billboards, Wellstone volunteers stood at major intersections with their posters. To economize on TV advertising, Wellstone appeared on local radio and cable TV stations and challenged his opponent to numerous debates. Instead of hiring a full-service consulting firm, Wellstone organized his campaign by recruiting his ablest supporters as paid workers in Minnesota's small towns and urban precincts. With the help of labor and environmental groups, Wellstone phone banks contacted 300,000 voters. Spontaneous and informal in campaign style, he refused to utter sound bites.

Wellstone's message was a simple one: Boschwitz, he claimed, was part of the inside-the-Beltway politics that had succumbed to procorporate policies. He'd lost contact with the inse-

make the candidates reliant for direction, support, and advice on organized voters. They change the campaign game by making "organized people" just as important as "organized money" and consultants. Voters' activities become as important as the candidates'.

The victory of Paul Wellstone in the 1990 Minnesota Senate race is an excellent case study of such a campaign. Wellstone bucked the incumbency advantage, defeating a popular and personally wealthy Republican senator. The accompanying feature box details how Wellstone beat the odds, building and maintaining a powerful volunteer organization and a set of commitments to a new politics.

curity felt by ordinary working families when it came to their jobs, their health insurance, and their kids' education. Without mincing words, Wellstone promised to be a different kind of senator. He proposed big cuts in the military budget, big increases in corporate taxation, and new measures from health insurance to nutritional programs to help ordinary people raise and care for their children. But his wasn't a lone crusade: Wellstone talked about how to rebuild grassroots organizations and the Minnesota Democratic party to make candidates like him accountable to people, not monied interests. As his campaign caught fire, Wellstone's campaign bus became a symbol for a new kind of amateur politics that brought together Democratic officeholders with a novel and powerful coalition of grassroots groups. Outspent 7-1 and given little chance of winning by the experts, Wellstone was the only challenger to defeat an incumbent senator in 1990.

During his Senate term, Wellstone followed through on his campaign promises. He fought hard to increase the minimum wage, ban lobbyist gifts to members of Congress, and increase environmental regulations. He cosponsored the most ambitious plan for campaign finance reform. In a risky stand, he was the only incumbent senator up for reelection who had voted against welfare reform. In 1996, Wellstone faced Boschwitz again. But he also faced the attacks of the National Republican Senatorial Committee, who targeted him for defeat. Although as an incumbent he raised much more money than he had in 1990, Wellstone was still outspent. Once again, grassroots campaigning worked. To the surprise of most observers, Wellstone defeated Boschwitz by almost 20 percentage points. He is now serving his second Senate term.

Sources: Dennis McGrath "Running Uphill: Eight Weeks Inside the Wellstone Campaign," *Minneapolis Star-Tribune*, November 11, 1990, pp. A16–20; Dirk Johnson, "The 1990 Elections: Minnesota Professor's Everyman Appeal Wins a Senate Seat," *New York Times*, November 11, 1990, p. 26; Richard Berke, "Several Won Big By Spending Less," *New York Times*, November 2, 1990, p. A9. "Minnesota," *Politics Now* (http://www.PoliticsUSA.com).

Changing the Rules of the Campaign Game

The details about money and politics provided in this chapter come as no surprise to most Americans. Various surveys indicate overwhelming agreement with the idea that the present system is rotten to the core, thoroughly bipartisan, and detrimental to democracy. By large numbers, the public supports various, even radical measures, to limit the amount of cash raised and its sources. Even the total public financing of all campaigns is supported by majorities. The problem is not the absence of public support, but rather that the public is largely not organized to make its views known. When public opinion's voice is indistinct, it leaves room for elites to confuse and narrow the issue.[47]

For most senators and House members, defining "effective" campaign reforms is full of partisan pitfalls and potentially fatal traps. The result has been that many support campaign finance reform as a symbol, but are not really serious about it. In early 1997, some House members proposed a constitutional amendment to overturn *Buckley* v. *Valeo*'s equation of free speech with unlimited spending. But the proposed amendment died. Some members used the failure of the constitutional amendment as an excuse to lie low on all reform proposals, claiming that all spending limits were unconstitutional. Others proposed legislation that would do little besides half-measures, leaving some of the channels through which private monies flow essentially unchanged, while plugging others. Some proposals limit or outlaw PACs. Others regulate or abolish soft money, while leaving much else unchanged. A few call for limited public funding of campaigns or, like the McCain-Feingold bill considered in Congress in 1996, provide for a combination of measures, including partial public financing in return for voluntary caps on campaign expenses by individual candidates. In early 1997, over fifty-seven campaign finance bills were proposed in Congress, each mixing and matching different features. On the eve of congressional investigations of the Democrats' 1996 fundraising activities, the issue of campaign finance reform was highly visible. But a coalition for real reform was unlikely to form. By fall, 1997 partisan warfare had apparently crushed hopes for even minimal changes. The reason is obvious: The entire political class was elected by playing the *existing* campaign game well. As Representative Martin Meehan admits, "Members are not going to change a system that benefits them unless they feel they have no choice."[48]

The congressional debates about campaign finance reform disguise the real issue—how to bring campaigns back to the people by stopping the flow of private money into campaigns. Only a wave of popular pressure is likely to bring about fundamental change, but what would real reform look like? Three senators, and many advocacy groups, have proposed a "Clean Money, Clean Elections" bill to regulate federal elections. Their model is a new system passed by Maine voters in a 1996 referendum. The idea is simple: establish a strong if voluntary system of public finance for federal campaigns, allowing candidates to choose the "clean" option of rejecting private money altogether. To qualify for public funding, candidates for Congress would have to raise $5 contributions from 1,000 voters within their own electoral districts. They'd have to reject all offers from PACs as well as soft money from parties, independent expenditures, and big individual donors, and they could not use their own bank account to fund their campaigns. In return for "going public," candidates who complied would get a set amount of public funds as well as matching funds that allowed willing candidates to match the dollar amounts of opponents who pursued the old route of private fundraising. The "public" candidates would get 90 minutes of free media time and reduced rates if they wanted more.[49]

Compared to existing law and many of the current proposals, the "Clean Money" bill is simple, comprehensible, and—because it is voluntary—entirely in conformity with Supreme Court rulings. As of this writing, however, it couldn't pass Congress, not because it lacks public support but because the public hasn't organized or mobilized. In the states, however, the prospects are much better because citizen groups have been at work designing referenda; eleven states have real possibilities to pass comprehensive campaign finance reform. With increasing revelations into abuses promised throughout 1997 and 1998, public opinion could get organized. If it did, than the full democratic debate could be restored.[50]

CONCLUSION: WHO WINS THE CAMPAIGN GAME?

The campaign game is often an impenetrable and vicious circle of big money, high-tech consultants, and manufactured images. When the game is played to perfection, it reinforces elite power by depriving citizens of the wherewithal to participate in and shape campaigns. Without this crucial element of citizen participation, campaigns become less exercises in popular control of government than political control of the population by existing elites. Deprived of the means to converse and debate among themselves and with politicians, citizens have two choices: to withdraw from their already limited roles in the game or to fight to reshape it.

Eventually, however, citizens reject the cramped roles assigned to them as spectators, money sources, and laboratory subjects. When they do, the campaign game cannot sustain even elite democratic power, for elections confer neither mandates to govern nor real security to officeholders. In recent years, the campaign game is showing signs of decay. Scandals, as well as the daily grind of fundraising, have led many to question the game, its rules, and its policy results. The game itself has become a campaign issue, and playing it with impunity now involves risks as well as benefits.

"The people who are running things," William Greider tells us, "are especially prone to error when they are isolated from the shared ideas and instincts of the larger community." The quest for campaign reform, for grassroots campaigns, and for new ways of bringing politicians into dialogue with voters are healthy signs that the democratic debate may be reviving. Such a revival will depend much more on the organization of citizens than on the goodwill of elites. Our next chapter focuses on the interest groups and political movements that dot the landscape of American politics and help organize citizen politics.[51]

KEY TERMS

candidate-centered campaign
name recognition
invisible primary
frontloading
permanent campaign
political action committee (PAC)

soft money
Buckley v. *Valeo*
issue advocacy ad
focus and dial group
grassroots campaign

SUGGESTED READINGS

Stephen Ansolabehere and Shanto Iyengar, *Going Negative: How Political Advertisements Shrink and Polarize the Electorate*. New York: Free Press, 1995. The authors show both why negative advertisements are effective and why campaigns use them, even though they repel large numbers of voters.

Dick Morris, *Behind the Oval Office*. New York: Random House, 1997. Once Bill Clinton's chief political strategist, Morris writes of the making of a "New Democrat" and the role of polling, advertising, and strategy in the 1996 election.

Michael Nelson, ed., *The Elections of 1996*. Washington, D.C.: Congressional Quarterly Press, 1997. A general reader on the 1996 election, particularly strong on congressional elections and the role of the media.

Gerald Pomper, ed., *The Election of 1996: Reports and Interpretations*. Chatham, N.J.: Chatham House, 1997. A stimulating collection of essays tracing changes and continuities in the 1996 presidential and congressional campaigns.

Martin Wattenberg, *The Rise of Candidate-Centered Politics*. Cambridge: Harvard University Press, 1991. A careful yet provocative look at what happens to the electoral and governing processes when both are ruled by personalities rather than party organizations.

CHAPTER 9

Interest Group Politics: Elite Bias

In 1992, Bill Clinton ran for the presidency promising to provide health insurance for all Americans. With 37 million Americans lacking health insurance and health care costs soaring way beyond the inflation rate, Clinton's promise was popular and helped him to win the presidency. Less than a year after he won office, President Clinton unveiled his proposal in a nationally televised speech before Congress. Harkening back to Franklin Roosevelt's popular Social Security program, Clinton vowed to provide a "Health Security card" to every American, that would, he promised, "guarantee you a comprehensive package of benefits over the course of your lifetime that will equal the benefits provided by most Fortune 500 companies." Two days after the speech a national poll found that 59 percent "favored" Clinton's plan to reform health care, with only 33 percent opposing it. Less than a year later the situation had changed dramatically: Support for the President's plan had fallen to 42 percent, while those opposed increased to 50 percent.[1] Lacking broad public support, Clinton's Health Security plan died in Congress. What happened?

What happened is that Clinton's health care proposal became the most heavily lobbied legislative initiative in U.S. history, with interests for and against spending over $100 million. Opponents were especially effective at carrying out a media blitz that raised enough doubts about the Clinton plan that people were no longer willing to support it. At the same time, opponents used traditional lobbying techniques that bogged down the proposal in Congress. The fate of national health insurance illustrates the theme of this chapter: interest group politics, the politics that takes place *between* elections, can be as important as electoral politics in deciding who wins and who loses.

Clearly, Clinton made tactical errors in devising his Health Security plan. He was criticized for appointing First Lady Hillary Rodham Clinton to head a massive task force to write the administration's Health Security bill. In fact, Hillary Clinton was highly knowledgeable, holding hearings around the country and consulting over 500 experts. The final bill, 1,342 pages long, was difficult to understand, however, and provided opponents with a convenient target for their charge that it would create an oppressive new federal bureaucracy. In fact, the Clinton proposal was a compromise between government and market approaches, favoring a method called managed competition.

What really killed national health insurance, however, was the furious mobilization of interest groups who would be hurt by reform. Outspending supporters of the Clinton plan by more than 4 to 1, a coalition of insurance companies, doctors, and small businesses funded a nationwide campaign that combined media attacks with the mobilization of grassroots networks in key congressional districts.[2]

A central theme of the campaign was that the Clinton plan would create a bureaucratic nightmare. Fearing restrictions on their members' salaries, the American Medical Association (AMA) attacked Clinton's proposal, charging that the plan threatened to separate the heart from the soul of American medicine by "forcing a bureaucrat or an accountant to stand between patient and physician."[3] A conservative research organization in Washington, the Heritage Foundation, printed an article in its journal *Policy Review*—ominously entitled "Clinton's Frankenstein: The Gory Details of the President's Health Plan"—that got a great deal of media attention; Clinton's plan was also attacked on moral grounds. The Christian Coalition, based partly on opposition to government funding of abortions, led a $1.4 million campaign that included 30 million postcards distributed to 60,000 churches.

The most effective attacks came from the Health Insurance Association of America (HIAA), a trade association of insurance companies that stood to lose substantial business under the Clinton plan. HIAA spent $15 million on slick ads in which a yuppie couple named Harry and Louise discovered the horrible consequences of bureaucratic domination of health care. Falsely implying that people would not be able to choose their own doctor under the president's proposal, the ads prompted an attack from Hillary Clinton, but this response only increased their visibility. The Harry and Louise ads succeeded in convincing many middle class Americans that the president's plan would force them into low-quality managed care plans.

With public support waning, the Clinton plan became bogged down in Congress, where interest groups had easy access to policy deliberations in the fifteen committees deliberating on health care reform. Clinton had made a political miscalculation by developing the bill outside of Congress. Lacking ownership in the proposal, many members of Congress found it advantageous to champion their own proposals, introducing weaker reform bills in the House and the Senate that drained support from the Clinton plan. Lacking the votes even to get out of committee, the Clinton plan died a quiet death.

The failure of national health insurance in 1994 illustrates how difficult it is to enact comprehensive reforms in the American political system. The government established by the framers, with its checks and balances, gives opponents many veto points where they can slow down and even paralyze the political process.

Lacking strong political parties, proponents of reform find their ranks fragmented into many interest groups, each pushing a narrow agenda and unwilling to compromise in order to join a broad coalition. Most important, if they have enough money, opponents can use the mass media to generate the appearance of a spontaneous grassroots movement against reform. In this chapter we examine the rise of a sophisticated and professionalized pressure group system in Washington and the troubling issues it raises for popular democracy.

INTEREST GROUP POLITICS AND THE DEMOCRATIC DEBATE

Interest group politics can be defined as any attempt by an organized group to influence the policies of government through normal extra-electoral channels, such as lobbying, letter writing, testifying before legislative committees, or advertising. Interest group politics cannot be separated from electoral politics because interest groups often try to persuade officials that supporting interest group policies will enhance their chances for reelection. Also, interest groups often contribute money to campaigns through political action committees (PACs). Nevertheless, interest group politics can be distinguished from electoral politics because interest groups, unlike parties, do not seek to win political office. They attempt to influence policy through other means.

Interest groups are held together by the shared interests or goals of their members. The goals of interest groups are varied, stretching from economic goals (limits on foreign car imports) to social goals (the right to family leave) to political goals (campaign finance reform), to humanitarian goals (shelter for the homeless). The shared interests that hold groups together can be as broad as clean air or as narrow as allowing heavier trucks to ride on interstate highways. Generally, narrow economic interests are better represented in the interest group system than broad political or moral concerns.

Although both elite and popular democrats consider interest groups to be necessary in a democracy, they differ in their evaluations of interest group politics. Interest group politics nicely suits the elite democratic conception of democracy and human nature—that most people are not interested in politics for its own sake but rather view politics as a way of protecting their own private interests. Since common people have neither the time nor the inclination to participate directly in politics, the interest group system allows people's wants and desires to be represented by political specialists called lobbyists. Moreover, because policy choices are often highly technical, interest groups hire experts to communicate complex information to decision makers.

According to one variant of elite democratic theory, called pluralism (which we examine later), the interest group system in the United States is open and accessible. Not every group has equal access, but every group can make itself heard at some point in the system.

Finally, we should note that many elite democrats criticize the interest group system as it is practiced in the United States today. Since the 1960s, they argue, the system has become "overheated," with special interests bombarding Washington and steering the policy process to benefit narrow groups at the public's expense. Later in the chapter we will examine the criticism that interest group politics has become too accessible.

Popular democrats are naturally more critical of interest group politics than elite democrats. By relying on representatives and hired experts, they say, interest group politics asks too little of ordinary citizens, who are given few opportunities for meaningful participation. Interest group politics suppresses passionate political participation by requiring that every issue be passed through an elaborate system of political representation, bargaining, and compromise. Moreover, by giving power to those who control information, popular democrats believe, interest group politics excludes the masses of ordinary citizens. In short, interest group politics is easily manipulated by elites—technical experts and political insiders who know how to play the "inside-the-Beltway" game in Washington.

Unlike elite democrats, popular democrats view the influx of new citizens' groups into the interest group system beginning in the 1960s as a healthy development. Despite this opening up of interest group politics to new groups, however, popular democrats charge that the system is still biased in favor of elites with political connections or the money to purchase them. The solution is to mobilize people at the grassroots to demand that their interests be represented. The problem with the interest group system is not too much democracy, as elite democrats maintain, but too little.

As we examine the competing claims of elite and popular democrats about interest group politics, keep the democratic debate in mind: Is the playing field of interest group politics level, giving every interest a fair chance to win, or is it tilted in favor of well-connected elites and those who have the money to hire them?

THE GROWTH OF INTEREST GROUP POLITICS

Before the New Deal of the 1930s, Washington, D.C., was a sleepy town with few diversions other than politics. Since then, Washington has become a vibrant cosmopolitan city, the center of one of the fastest-growing metropolitan areas in the country, with high-paid white collar workers spilling over the boundaries of the District of Columbia to occupy wealthy suburbs in Maryland and Virginia. The metropolitan area surrounding our nation's capital now boasts the best-educated and highest-paid workforce in the nation. This prosperity did not stem solely from the growth in government, but also from a tremendous expansion in the number of people who make a living trying to influence government.

Interest group politics is big business in Washington. Legally, in order to work the halls of Congress as a lobbyist, you must register with the U.S. House of Representatives and Senate. In 1992, 6,104 lobbyists were registered with the House; supporters of a new law that took effect in January 1996 estimate that three to ten times as many lobbyists will now have to register with the government.[4] The best information on the number of interest groups in the nation's capital is a publication called *Washington Representatives*, a directory of "persons working to influence politics and actions to advance their own or their client's interest." In 1991, more than 14,500 *interest representatives* were listed.[5]

The number of people who make a living by working to influence government is even greater. Scholars estimate that there are 50,000 or 60,000 more lobbyists and employees of law firms and trade associations. Besides trying to influence legislation, interest groups also try to influence the implementation of laws through decisions by executive agencies and the courts. When you include the lawyers, lobbyists, public relations specialists, and trade association and corporate representatives who make a living by keeping track of and attempting to change federal regulations, the number exceeds 100,000.

The Washington interest group community is large and diverse. It includes powerful business associations, such as the U.S. Chamber of Commerce, and narrow trade associations representing specific industries, such as the U.S. Hide, Skin and Leather Association. It includes organizations with millions of members, such as the AFL-CIO coalition of unions, and organizations with only one member, in particular the Washington offices of national corporations, such as IBM and GM. It includes public associations, such as the National Governors Association and the National League of Cities. It also includes lobbyists hired by foreign governments to represent their interests in Washington, a feature of our interest group system that has increasingly come under attack. Two of the best represented foreign governments are Japan and Israel. Table 9.1 lists some of the major interest groups in Washington, D.C.

TABLE 9.1		Members	Staff	Budget
Some Major Interest Groups	**Economic Interest Groups**			
	National Association of Manufacturers	14,000	180	$5,000,000
	Business Roundtable	213	18	not listed
	United States Chamber of Commerce	219,200	1,200	$70,000,000
	Trade Associations			
	American Petroleum Institute	300	400	$56,000,000
	Association of Bank Holding Companies[a]	295	15	not listed
	Labor Groups			
	American Federation of Labor– Congress of Industrial Organizations (AFL-CIO)	13,300,000	400	not listed
	American Federation of State, County and Municipal Employees (AFSCME)	1,300,000	not listed	not listed
	International Brotherhood of Teamsters	1,600,000	not listed	$1,400,000
	United Automobile Workers (UAW)	1,400,000	not listed	not listed

TABLE 9.1

(continued)

〰〰〰〰〰〰

	Members	Staff	Budget
Farm Groups			
American Farm Bureau Federation	4,000,000	not listed	not listed
National Farm Workers Association	50,000	130	$5,000,000
Professionally Motivated Groups			
American Bar Association (ABA)	375,000	800	$65,000,000
American Medical Association (AMA)	297,000	not listed	not listed
Association of Trial Lawyers of America (ATLA)	60,000	165	$19,400,000
Educational Quasi-union Groups			
American Association of University Professors (AAUP)	42,000	35	$3,646,900
American Federation of Teachers (AFT)	900,000	not listed	$65,000,000
National Education Association (NEA)	2,000,800	600	$147,500,000
Public Interest Groups			
American Civil Liberties Union (ACLU)	275,000	125	$20,000,000
Common Cause	250,000	100	$11,000,000
National Rifle Association (NRA)	2,524,000	460	$66,000,000
National Taxpayers Union	250,000	20	$3,500,000
Public Citizen	not listed	not listed	$7,000,000
Sierra Club	550,000	294	$43,000,000
American Association of Retired Persons (AARP)	32,000,000	1,200	not listed
National Association for the Advancement of Colored People (NAACP)	400,000	132	not listed
National Organization of Women (NOW)	280,000	30	not listed
Salvation Army	450,312	30,930	$1,354,000
Southern Poverty Law Center	300,000	60	$9,500,000
Public Agency Groups			
National Governors Association	55	87	$11,000,000
National Conference of State Legislators	not listed	145	$11,500,000
National Association of Counties	1,750	70	$10,000,000
National League of Cities	1,450	80	$10,500,000
U.S. Conference of Mayors	1,050	50	$8,600,000
International City Management Association[b]	8,400	125	not listed

Reprinted from Sandra A. Jaszak, ed., *Encyclopedia of Associations*, 32nd edition, Volume 1, 1997 by permission of Gale Research, Inc.

[a] Association of Bank Holding Companies now known as Banker's Round Table
[b] International City Management Association now known as International City/County Management Association.

Interest groups play a more powerful role in U.S. politics than in most other Western democracies. There are two main reasons for this. First, American political institutions stimulate interest group politics. As we know from Chapter 2, fearing tyranny of the majority in a democratic government, the Federalists wrote a Constitution that fragmented policymaking authority—including the separation of powers into three branches; the bicameral Congress (with decision making further fragmented into committees and subcommittees); the authority of the courts to intervene in administrative decisions; and the division of power among federal, state, and local governments. In this way, the Constitution created a government that provides many access points to interest groups. In addition, interest groups in the United States are able to intervene on the administrative side of government, influencing the implementation of a law after it is passed. Critics of the interest group system charge that in striving to protect the country against tyranny by majorities, the founders may have created a system that stimulates too much interest group activity, making it prone to tyranny by minorities.

The second reason for the exceptional strength of interest groups politics in the United States is the weakness of political parties, discussed in Chapter 7. In European countries interest groups normally operate through the powerful political parties, which aggregate the various interests and devise a legislative program. In the United States, some interest groups, such as labor unions and business organizations, work through the Democratic or Republican parties, but for the most part they operate as independent political entrepreneurs. The thesis that strong parties inhibit interest group politics is confirmed by research at the local level showing that cities with strong parties, such as Chicago with its political machine, have less powerful interest groups than cities with weak parties, such as New York.[6]

TRADITIONAL LOBBYING: THE INSIDER STRATEGY

Interest groups are often referred to as lobbies, as in the "gun lobby" or the "steel lobby." (The term *lobbyist* stems from the mid-seventeenth century, when citizens would plead their cases with members of the British Parliament in a large lobby outside the House of Commons.) Interest groups are also referred to as *pressure groups*. Both terms have taken on negative connotations, evoking images of pot-bellied, cigar-smoking influence peddlers prowling the halls of Congress with bags of money to corrupt legislators. In fact, lobbying is an essential function in a democracy. Interest group politics is protected by the First Amendment, which guarantees freedom of association, "or the right of the people peaceably to assemble, and to petition the Government for a redress of grievances."

Of course, corruption is a problem in interest group politics. One of the most notorious examples is the California savings and loan company that contributed $1.3 million to the campaigns of five U.S. senators in exchange for their intervention with federal regulators. In 1989, as federal regulators looked the other way, the savings and loan company went bankrupt. The bailout cost the federal taxpayers $2.5 billion. Some perfectly legal practices verge on corruption: Lobbyists frequently purchase large numbers of tickets to congressional fundraisers or pay politicians fat fees for short appearances at association gatherings. In response to abuses, Congress passed tough new lobbying restrictions that took effect on January 1, 1996, banning, for example, gifts to senators valued at more than $50. Although a certain amount of corruption and outright bribery still goes on, the image of money-toting lobbyists buying votes misrepresents the normal operation of interest group politics in the United States. Corruption of the democratic process is more subtle (and pervasive) than the conventional image suggests.

In discussing interest group politics it is important to distinguish between an insider strategy and an outsider strategy. The **insider strategy** is what we normally think of as interest group politics: face-to-face discussions in which the lobbyist tries to persuade the decision maker that the interest group's position makes sense. The insider strategy depends upon intimate knowledge of how the game is played in Washington and access to what used to be called the "old boy" network. The **outsider strategy,** by contrast, relies on mobilizing forces outside Washington to pressure decision makers. The insider and outsider strategies are often coordinated with each other, but traditional interest group politics is usually associated with the insider strategy. (We examine the use of the outsider strategy later in the chapter.)

The insider strategy takes place largely behind closed doors and is most effective when applied to issues sufficiently narrow in scope not to have caught the public's attention. Speaking about lobbying around the 1986 Tax Reform Act, Representative Pete Stark, Democrat of California, observed, "The fewer the number of taxpayers affected, and the more dull and arcane the subject matter, the longer the line of lobbyists."[7]

The effectiveness of the insider strategy stems from the fact that legislation has become so complex that neither legislators nor their staffs are able to keep up with all the relevant information. As we show in Chapter 11, most of the work of Congress now takes place in committees and subcommittees, but even the specialized staffs attached to these committees cannot keep up with the staggering growth of information that is relevant to policy making. Lobbyists therefore perform an important function in a modern democracy: They provide decision makers with detailed information on the effects of different policies.

The insider lobbying strategy applies to the executive branch as well as Congress. Political issues still remain after a bill is passed. Congress usually formulates broad policies that leave a great deal of discretion to executive branch employees. The Environmental Protection Agency (EPA), for example, has the power to set standards for particular pollutants. When agencies formulate policies, they usually do so by issuing draft regulations in the *Federal Register,* a publication of all administrative regulations issued by the federal government. Interest groups can try to influence the regulations before they are issued in final form.

Whether dealing with Congress or the executive branch, a successful lobbyist must develop relations of trust with key decision makers. Lobbyists, however, are not completely objective; they specialize in information that favors their client's cause. Members of Congress are especially interested in how a bill will affect their home districts. In opposing Clinton's Health Security plan, which would have required business to provide health insurance for their employees, lobbyists provided information to members of Congress on the number of businesses in their districts that would have been affected—implying that many businesses would have been harmed by the requirement.

From morning phone calls to afternoon golf dates to evening cocktail parties, lobbyists spend most of their time keeping up personal contacts and seeking out the latest information. Access is the key. A survey of interest groups found that 98 percent contacted government officials directly to express their views, and 95 percent engaged in informal contacts with officials—at conventions, over lunch, and so forth.[8] Eventually, skilled lobbyists make decision makers dependent on them. Policy makers begin to call on the lobbyists, who become sources of hard-to-obtain information for overworked political staffs and government officials. As one legislative aide observed:

> My boss demands a speech and a statement for the *Congressional Record* for every bill we introduce or co-sponsor—and we have a lot of bills. I just can't do it all myself. The better lobbyists, when they have a proposal they are pushing, bring it to me along with a couple of speeches, a *Record* insert, and a fact sheet.[9]

A troubling aspect of lobbying is the so-called revolving door. Many lobbyists formerly worked for Congress or for an executive agency. When they left government service, they got jobs with lobbying firms or interest groups, usually at much higher pay, exploiting their access and knowledge to the benefit of their clients. James Watt, former Secretary of the Interior under Ronald Reagan, reportedly received $250,000 from a client for a single phone call to a high-level official in the Department of Housing and Urban Development (HUD).

In 1978, Congress passed the Ethics in Government Act to deal with abuses of the revolving door. The act forbids former executive branch employees from lobbying their former agency on any issue for one year (Clinton increased it to five years for top officials) and prohibits all lobbying, with no time limits, on issues in which they were "personally and substantially involved."[10] Lyn Nofziger, former Reagan White House aide, was convicted of illegally using his contacts with the White House on behalf of various business interests and labor unions. Former members of Congress are also heavily involved in lobbying, even though the 1989 Ethics in Government Act barred former elected officials from lobbying anywhere on Capitol Hill for one year.

Since the 1960s, interest group activity has exploded in Washington. Between 1977 and 1991, the number of people representing groups in Washington more

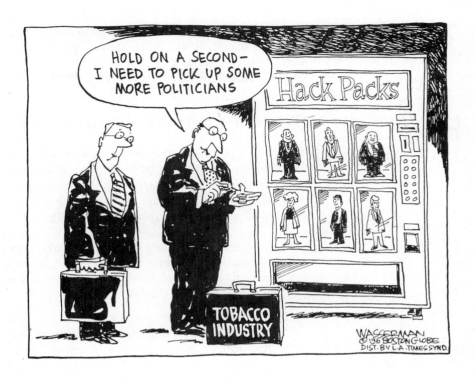

than tripled, increasing from 4,000 in 1977 to more than 14,500. Lobbyists in Washington now have their own lobbies, including the American League of Lobbyists and the American Society of Association Executives. Part of the reason for the proliferation of interest groups is the decline of political parties and the fragmentation of power in Congress. The growing federal presence in the economy and the mushrooming of federal regulations have also stimulated interest group activity.

The increase in interest group activity is also attributed to the upsurge of participation in the 1960s and 1970s that created new interest groups representing broad citizens' groups and the poor. Of interest groups that existed in 1981, fully 76 percent of the citizens' groups and 79 percent of the social welfare and poor people's organizations were formed since 1960.[11] In response, corporations countermobilized: The number of corporations with offices in Washington increased tenfold between 1961 and 1982.[12]

The tremendous growth of interest group activity in American national government raises disturbing questions: Have we created an interest group society where every group feels entitled to have its problems solved by government? Are the new interest groups genuine expressions of the needs of groups of citizens, or have they been spawned by government programs and regulations? Have some interest groups become so entrenched in government that we can no longer draw the line between public government and private interests? Answers to these questions depend on our understanding of who is represented by the expanded interest group system.

HOW REPRESENTATIVE IS THE INTEREST GROUP SYSTEM?

If the U.S. interest group system truly represents the many diverse interests of the citizenry, then it might be one of the most democratic features of our political system. This argument is, in fact, the cornerstone of a variant of elite democratic theory, called **pluralism.**[13] Pluralist theory views the interest group system as a kind of political marketplace with the following characteristics:

1. *Free competition:* Most people do not participate directly in decision making but, like consumers in the economy, are represented in the system by political entrepreneurs who compete for their support. Competition ensures that all major interests will be heard.

2. *Dispersed power:* Money is an important source of power, but other resources are equally important, including motivation, leadership, organizational skills, knowledge, and expertise. Elites who are influential in one issue arena tend not to be active in others. Thus, power is widely dispersed.

3. *Bargaining:* Success in the interest group system requires bargaining and compromise with other interests, which discourages rigid moralistic or ideological politics that threaten democratic stability.

4. *Balance:* Mobilization on one side of an issue produces mobilization on the other side; public policies thus reflect a balance of competing interests that approximates the interest of society as a whole.

An examination of the interest groups that are active and influential in the American political system indicates that pluralist theory is deeply flawed. Clearly, some groups find it easier than others to organize and gain access to power.

Business has disproportionate influence in the interest group system. Whose interests are represented by corporations? Corporate lobbies represent the interests of producers—the owners and managers of corporations—not the interests of consumers. Sometimes, as when automobile manufacturers lobby for limits on imports, corporate lobbies represent the interests of workers in the corporation, but mostly they lobby to increase the power of management to be free of government regulations and to achieve maximum profits free of taxation. A separate set of lobbies, discussed later, have grown up to represent the interests of consumers.

The interest group system is not highly participatory. A 1981 Gallup poll found that only about 20 million Americans were members of special interest organizations and another 20 million had given money to such groups during the previous year. Overall, the survey found that only about 13 percent of the adult population were members of special interest groups.[14] Moreover, membership in special interest organizations is skewed by income, as shown in Figure 9.1. A 1989–90 survey found that 77 percent of people from families with incomes over $125,000 were affiliated with a political organization, compared to only 29 percent for those from families making less than $15,000.[15] All interests are free to organize but, contrary to pluralist theory, power is not widely dispersed. As political scientist E. E. Schattschneider concluded in a well-known critique of pluralist theory: "The flaw in the pluralist heaven is that the heavenly chorus sings with a strong upper-class accent."[16]

What is perhaps most disturbing for popular democrats is that interest group participation has declined significantly in the past twenty years. Harvard political scientist Robert Putnam noted a distinct generational pattern in group participation, with those born before 1930 belonging to almost twice as many groups as those born in the 1960s.[17] (See Figure 9.2.) Political scientists are hotly debating the causes of these trends, with increased work pressures, mobility rates, divorce rates, and television watching all advanced as causes.

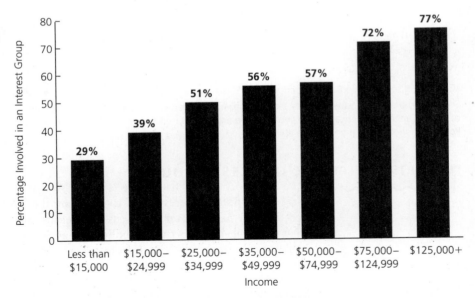

FIGURE 9.1

Interest Group Membership by Income Level

From Kay L. Schlozman, "Voluntary Organizations on Politics: Who Gets Involved" from *Representing Interests and Interest Group Representation,* edited by Crotty, Schwartz & Green, 1994, p. 76. Reprinted by permission of the University Press of America.

FIGURE 9.2 **Group Membership by Generation** [a]

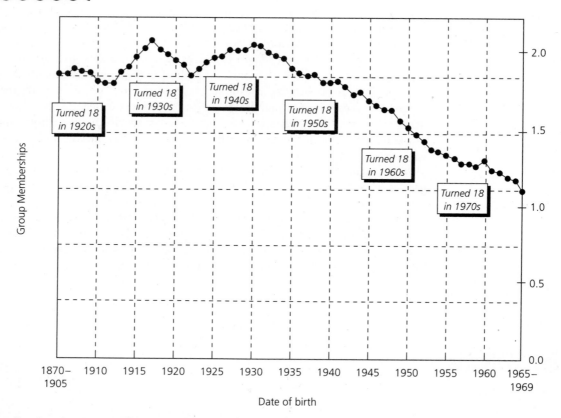

Turned 18 in 1920s

Turned 18 in 1930s

Turned 18 in 1940s

Turned 18 in 1950s

Turned 18 in 1960s

Turned 18 in 1970s

Group Memberships

Date of birth

[a]Controlling for education. Respondents aged 25–80. Five-year moving averages. Equal weighting of three educational categories.
Source: General Social Survey, 1972–1994; compiled by Robert D. Putnam, "Tuning In, Tuning Out: The Strange Disappearance of Social Capital in America," *PS: Political Science and Politics* (December 1995): 675. Reprinted by permission of the American Political Science Association and the author.

THE RISE OF PUBLIC INTEREST GROUPS

Narrow economic interests tend to dominate the interest group system not just because they have greater resources, but because they find it easier to overcome what political scientists call the **collective action problem.**[18] Assume that each member of a group will benefit from government action and that to provide the common benefit an interest group needs to be formed to pressure the government. The collective action problem is that *everyone* in the group will benefit regardless of his or her contribution to the collective action (and one individual's contribution rarely makes a difference in the outcome). Thus, most people, the so-called "free riders," will try to enjoy the benefits without contributing to the group. As a result, most groups never get off the ground.

Collective action is less of a problem for large corporations, however, when one or a few companies dominate an industry. With fewer members in the interest group, each member recognizes that his or her contribution is necessary for success. Analysis of the problem of collective action helps explain why producer groups dominated by a handful of corporations are relatively successful in organizing interest groups and obtaining collective benefits, whereas consumer groups, trying to represent the interests of millions of dispersed consumers, are more difficult to organize.

In the 1960s and early 1970s, a different species of organized interest, the public interest group, flowered. A **public interest group** can be defined as any group seeking government action that will not principally benefit the members of the group. Most interest groups seek benefits for their members; a steel producers' lobby, for example, seeks limits on imported steel to shut out foreign competition. A public interest group, on the other hand, seeks policies that, at least in the minds of the members, will benefit society as a whole. The League of Women Voters, which seeks a better informed electorate, is a classic example of a public interest group. Consumer groups that seek safer and more reliable consumer goods, as well as religious groups like the Christian Coalition, are public interest groups because everybody will presumably benefit, not just the leaders and members of the group.

Public interest groups would appear to have a difficult time overcoming the collective action problem because their benefits are so widespread. The rise of public interest groups shows that people will join groups not only to benefit from them materially, but because they believe in the purposes of the group, whether it be safer cars, cleaner air, or fewer abortions. Environmental groups, such as the Sierra Club (450,000 members) and the Environmental Defense Fund (60,000 members), have successfully attracted members even though the benefits of the collective action are widely distributed. (We should note that nearly all public interest groups also provide their members with specific benefits for joining—all the way from bumper stickers to magazine subscriptions.) People are also attracted to citizens' groups by the companionship that arises from participating with like-minded people in a political cause. Compared to special interest groups, public interest groups are more consistent with the popular democratic view of human nature, which views people as naturally inclined to participate in politics and capable of transcending their own parochial interests in favor of a broader public good.

Cultivating the Outsider Strategy

The public interest groups that burst on the scene in the 1960s cultivated an outsider strategy in which they appealed to citizens outside Washington to put pressure on Congress and the executive branch to address their issues. Instead of trying to persuade individual politicians and officials behind closed doors (the insider strategy), they took their issues to the public, dramatizing the effects of inaction and skillfully using the media to communicate their message to the

MAKING A DIFFERENCE

Defending Children

In her book, *The Measure of Our Success: A Letter to My Children and Yours,* Marian Wright Edelman, founder of the Children's Defense Fund (CDF), discusses her role model, Sojourner Truth, an illiterate yet outspoken slave woman: "One day during an anti-slavery speech she was heckled by an old man. 'Old woman, do you think that your talk about slavery does any good? Why I don't care any more for your talk than I do for the bite of a flea.' 'Perhaps not, but the Lord willing, I'll keep you scratching,' she replied." Over the last twenty-five years, Edelman has followed in her role model's footsteps, trying to "keep them scratching" in her pursuit of "putting children first."

Born in 1939, the daughter of a black Baptist minister, Marian Wright grew up in segregated Bennettsville, South Carolina. Greatly influenced by her father, who taught her the importance of both education and helping others, she graduated first in class at all-black Spelman College in 1960. Following graduation, she accepted a scholarship to Yale Law school. Active in the civil rights movement, upon completing her law degree she imme-diately traveled to Mississippi to work for the National Association for the Advancement of Colored People (NAACP) Legal Defense Fund. As the first African-American woman to practice law in the state, she undertook the dangerous work of defending civil rights workers.

Her interests gradually shifted from civil rights to the plight of poor children. In 1967, Senator Robert F. Kennedy visited Mississippi and Wright was able to show him firsthand the deplorable conditions faced by poor, mostly black, children in that state. It was on this trip that she met her future husband, Peter Edelman, an assistant to Senator Robert Kennedy. The interracial marriage produced three sons, who were given much-publicized "Baptist bar mitzvahs."

In 1968, Marian Wright Edelman, as she was now known, moved to the nation's capital, where she set up a public interest lobbying organization supporting the federal War on Poverty program. Edelman noticed that African Americans had the NAACP (established in 1909) and the elderly had a powerful interest group, the American Association

American people. By carefully documenting the facts and exposing problems, often through emotional congressional hearings and published exposés, public interest groups swayed public opinion. Politicians were forced to respond.

Public interest groups opened up the elite-dominated interest group system in Washington to an upsurge in popular democratic participation. Although the outsider strategy employed by citizens' groups succeeded in democratizing the system for a time, elites soon learned how to use the outsider strategy themselves to reassert their dominance. Nevertheless, the rise of public interest groups is instructive because it shows that the American political system is not impervious to popular democratic pressure. One person, even someone lacking wealth and political connections, can make a difference, as Ralph Nader has proved.

of Retired Persons (AARP, founded in 1958), but children had nothing. In 1973 Edelman formed the Children's Defense Fund (CDF).

Part lobbying organization and part think tank, under Edelman's leadership the CDF, with a budget today of about $13 million, has become an influential and controversial advocate for children. Conservatives argue that Edelman is simply using children to support her liberal causes. The problem, they say, is not just that children are in poverty but that their parents fail to get jobs and become hooked on government handouts.

Edelman's moral approach to the issues has been controversial even for liberals, whom she frequently attacks for being insufficiently attentive to the well-being of children. Senators reportedly hide in the bathroom whenever Edelman is sighted in the Senate Office Building. Clearly, however, her methods are effective; Senator Edward Kennedy has referred to her as the "101st Senator."

With the election of Bill Clinton in 1992, many expected Edelman to become even more influential because Hillary Rodham Clinton was both a long-time friend and former chairperson of the CDF Board of Directors. The relationship between Edelman and Clinton, however, was strained by the president's support of welfare reform. In November 1995, the *Washington Post* published her open letter to the president in which she stated that it would be a "tragic irony" for "this regressive attack on children and the poor to occur on your [Clinton's] watch." Subsequently, her husband, Peter, resigned a high post in the Department of Health and Human Services to protest Clinton's welfare policies. Edelman's access to the White House ended.

Recognizing that lobbying was not enough, Edelman has worked hard to build a broad social movement behind children's issues. On June 1, 1996, 200,000 people descended upon the nation's capital to participate in the CDF-sponsored Stand for Children rally. Endorsed by 3,541 other organizations, the rally exemplified Edelman's belief that "enough committed fleas biting strategically can make even the biggest dog uncomfortable."

Sources: Joann J. Burch, *Marian Wright Edelman: Children's Champion* (Brookfield, Conn.: Milbrook Press, 1994); "Children of a Lesser Country," *The New Yorker*, January 15, 1996, pp. 25–26; "Mother Marian," interview, *Psychology Today* (July/August 1993): 26–29; Mark Peyser and Thomas Rosenthal, "She's Taking Her Stand," *Newsweek*, June 10, 1996, p. 32. Written with the assistance of Paul Goggi.

Ralph Nader: Expanding Democratic Citizenship

Little in Ralph Nader's background suggested that he would become the scourge of corporate America.[19] The son of Lebanese immigrant parents, Nader was something of a nerd, often carrying a briefcase to school and reading late into the night. Ironically, his high school yearbook predicted he would become a corporate executive. After graduating from Harvard Law School, Nader practiced law for a number of years in a rather undistinguished fashion.

What set Nader apart from other lawyers was his interest—some called it an obsession—with automobile safety. With lethal protruding fins, dangerous dashboards, and no seat belts, cars in the early 1960s were not designed with safety foremost in mind. Nader's concern with automobile safety stemmed from an incident in 1956 when he "saw a little girl almost decapitated in an accident when the glove compartment door flew open and became a guillotine for the child as she was thrown forward in a 15-mile-an-hour collision."[20] Nader focused on the "second collision"—the collision between the human body and the car. He felt strongly that cars could be designed much more safely and that U.S. car companies irresponsibly designed them with the singular goal of increasing sales.

In 1964 Nader moved to Washington, D.C. as a consultant to the U.S. Labor Department, where he wrote a dry 234-page report with 99 pages of footnotes criticizing Detroit automakers on safety issues. Like most government reports, Nader's probably would have gathered dust on a shelf if not for other developments. First, in 1965 Nader published *Unsafe At Any Speed*,[21] an emotional indictment of the auto industry, which replaced the dry technical language of the report with vivid accounts of the mayhem caused by unsafe auto design. Singling out GM's Corvair, with its oversteering tendency and vulnerability to "one-car accidents," Nader called it "one of the greatest acts of industrial irresponsibility in the present century." *Unsafe At Any Speed* quickly became a best-seller.

Meanwhile, with over a hundred lawsuits pending against the Corvair, GM began an exhaustive investigation of Nader. The detective hired to do the job was instructed: "They [GM] want to get something, somewhere, on this guy to get him out of their hair, and to shut him up." This was not a typical background check, as further directions to the detective indicated: "Apparently he's in his early thirties and unmarried. . . . Interesting angle there. . . . They said 'Who is he laying? If it's girls, who are they? If not girls, maybe boys, who?' They want to know this."[22] The exhaustive investigation turned up nothing that could be used against Nader, who led a spartan lifestyle.

When word of the investigation became public, GM first denied it. At this time, however, Senator Abraham Ribicoff of Connecticut began hearings on auto safety and Nader became a star witness. Concerned that GM was trying to intimidate a congressional witness, Ribicoff called on GM president John Roche to testify. Unable to deny knowledge of the investigation anymore, Roche was forced to make a public apology to Nader. The image of one of the world's most powerful corporations trying to crush a lone reformer captured the public's imagination. The publicity generated public pressure that resulted in one of the first comprehensive pieces of consumer legislation, the 1966 Traffic and Motor Vehicle Safety Act.

The safety features that we take for granted today—seat belts and shoulder harnesses, head rests, collapsible steering columns, padded dashboards— grew out of the great automobile safety debate in the 1960s that Nader triggered. The government-mandated and "voluntary" safety devices that were introduced beginning in the 1960s have saved thousands of lives. Even though Americans drove many more miles each year than the year before, automobile-related deaths declined steadily in the 1970s and 1980s, only beginning to rise again in 1993.

Nader sued GM for violation of privacy and after a four-year legal battle settled out of court for $425,000. He used the profits from the lawsuit, book royalties, and fees from his many speeches to provide initial funding for a series of public interest groups that represented consumer interests. As Figure 9.3 shows, Nader has constructed a formidable network of citizens' groups.

Nader's groups rely on idealistic young people who are willing to work long hours at low pay in a public interest cause. Las Vegas nightclub singer, Connie Smith, for example, quit her job and hounded Nader until he gave her a job so she could "do something worthwhile."[23] Law students come to Washington for the summer to work on task forces investigating such issues as water pollution, food additives, and bank lending practices. Nader began *public interest research groups* (PIRGs) on college campuses around the nation, supported by student fees, to lobby and conduct research on behalf of students and consumers. In 1994 there were PIRG chapters on ninety college campuses in twenty-two states (Table 9.2).

Nader and his associates are credited with helping to enact key consumer laws, including the Wholesome Meat Act of 1967, the Natural Gas Pipeline Safety Act of 1968, and the Comprehensive Occupational Safety and Health Act of 1970. Nader has continued his frenetic work schedule on behalf of consumer issues. In 1996 he ran for president under the Green Party (an environmental organization), but he refused to solicit contributions and garnered less than 1 percent of the nationwide vote.

Nader and his citizens' consumer movements draw from the American tradition of popular democracy. Although often accused of being a communist, Nader is, in fact, a strong believer in free market capitalism in which corporations are held accountable by competition, government regulation, and consumer- and worker-owned businesses. Above all, Nader believes in an active citizenry— based upon what he has called "the average American's natural inclination to want more democracy, not less, and to instinctively distrust power that is concentrated in few hands."[24]

At the same time, Nader's vision of citizen action, of how to democratize interest group politics, is flawed. Thanks to Nader and his "raiders," the policy making process *has* become more open to information and analysis. However, the entry barriers to influencing the interest group system, as Nader did, are high; few citizens have Harvard law degrees. In addition, the consumer issues Nader has concentrated on benefit the middle class more than the working class and the poor.

Finally, Nader's example of democratic citizenship has an ironic elitist twist to it. Most of the early citizens' groups emerged out of grassroots organizing. Over the years, however, many public interest groups with offices in Washington, including Nader groups, have become staff dominated, surviving on grants from wealthy patrons or foundations. Groups in which the staff communicates with the members only through direct mail fundraising techniques are more consistent with the values of elite democracy. One study found that almost one-third of all public interest groups had no active individual members at all. Moreover,

FIGURE 9.3

The Nader Network

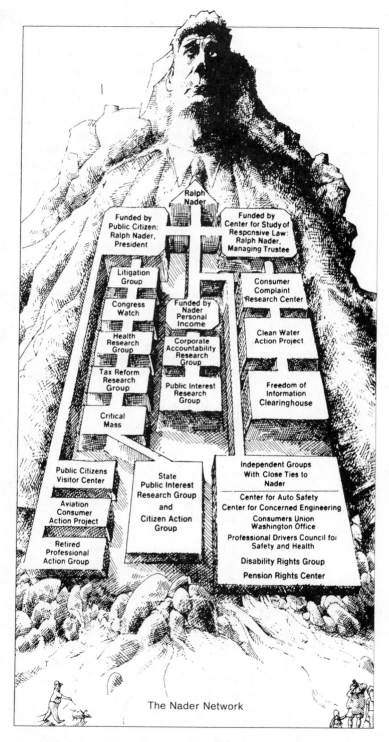

The Nader Network

"The Nader Network" from James Q. Wilson, *American Government, Brief Version,* Third Edition. Copyright © 1994 by D.C. Heath and Company. Used by permission of Houghton Mifflin Company.

TABLE 9.2	
States with Public Interest Research Groups (PIRGs) and Numbers of College Campuses with Chapters, 1994	AKPIRG (Alaska)—0 MPIRG (Minnesota)—6 AZPIRG—0 NJPIRG—6 CALPIRG—4 NMPIRG—1 CONNPIRG—2 NYPIRG—20 COPIRG (Colorado)—5 Ohio PIRG—1 Florida PIRG—4 OSPIRG (Oregon State PIRG)—5 Illinois PIRG—1 PennPIRG—0 MaryPIRG—1 PIRGIM (PIRG in Michigan)—1 MassPIRG—28 VPIRG (Vermont)—1 MontPIRG—1 WASHPIRG—2 MOPIRG (Missouri)—2 WISPIRG (Wisconsin)—1

Source: New York Public Interest Research Group.

more than half of those that had members had no way for them to influence the policy stands of the group. On the other hand, about one-third of all public interest groups do have local chapter with active members.[25] These groups function as building blocks of popular democracy.

THE NEW LOBBYING: ELITE COUNTERMOBILIZATION

The public interest movement pioneered an outsider strategy that democratized the interest group system. What had previously been a closed pressure group system dominated by white males representing dominant producer interests was suddenly thrown open to new groups concerned about a variety of issues—consumer product safety and quality, worker health and safety, environmental degradation, minority and women's issues, and corporate governance. The rise of public interest groups made the system more balanced between producers and consumers, rich and poor.

In the 1960s, corporate elites were initially taken off guard by the outsider strategies pioneered by citizens' groups and became alarmed by their success in imposing federal regulations on business. In the mid-1970s, however, corporate elites countermobilized, and by the 1980s they once again dominated the interest group system. In 1970, only a small number of Fortune 500 companies had public relations offices in Washington; ten years later, 80 percent did.[26] Between 1960 and 1980, business's share of all organizations having representation in Washington increased from 57 percent to 72 percent. Citizens groups as a proportion of all groups having representation in Washington fell from 9 percent to 5 percent, and the labor union proportion of the total plummeted from 11 percent to 2 percent. Only 2 percent of all interest groups in Washington represented issues concerning civil rights, social welfare, or the poor.[27] According to a Senate study, public interest groups were stretched so thin that they did not even show up at more than half of the formal proceedings on regulatory issues; when they did appear, they often were outnumbered 10 to 1 by industry representatives. Corporations invested 50 to 100 times more resources than public interest groups on many important issues.[28]

Corporate elites were not just engaging in a power grab. They believed that public interest politics and government regulation of business were harming the nation. In making their case they recalled the elite democratic idea that elites should filter the emotional demands of the people. Too much democracy, they said, was overloading the system with too many demands.[29] The masses were being manipulated into supporting government regulations by emotional appeals from liberal activists who would benefit from the new jobs in the expanded regulatory state. In the long run, elite democrats argued, regulatory burdens would stifle growth, hurting all Americans' living standards.

Corporate elites portrayed their views not as private interests but as a new version of the public interest: Freeing business from regulatory and tax burdens would, in the long run, benefit all Americans; "a rising tide would lift all boats." As the economy faltered in the early 1970s, ordinary citizens were receptive to the message that excessive regulations and high taxes were choking off economic growth. Using the outsider strategies pioneered by citizen groups, corporate elites mobilized grassroots pressure on Congress, greatly enhancing the power of their insider lobbyists in Washington. Moreover, the development of new communication technologies enabled corporate elites to play the game even more effectively than public interest advocates.

Corporate Image Advertising

Realizing that they could no longer rely on insider deals, corporation elites began a sustained effort to shape public opinion. Spending on corporate image advertising soared. **Corporate image advertising** does not promote a company's products but rather attempts to shape public opinion about business in general or the positive contribution of a particular industry, such as the chemical industry, to American life. In 1978, a congressional committee estimated that corporations spent $1 billion per year on this type of advertising.[30] Spending on corporate image adverstising has multiplied in the interim.

Perhaps the best known example of corporate image advertising is Mobil Oil's ads that appear regularly in business publications and prominent newspapers like the *New York Times*. Essentially paid editorials extolling big business and warning against the dangers of big government, the Mobil ads use popular democratic language to support elite democratic positions. Commenting on the environmental movement, for example, one ad stated: "We feel the need to express, from time to time, our belief that those who object to economic development on ecological grounds may often be expressing mere rhetoric and couching their real elitist motives in terms they see as popular and effective."[31]

Think Tanks: Shaping the Agenda

Control over information and ideas is crucial in policy making. Ideas especially play a crucial role by setting the policy agenda and framing the policy alternatives. Increasingly, **think tanks**—private not-for-profit research and advocacy organizations—play the role of evaluating programs and generating new policy ideas. At present there are over a thousand think tanks operating in the United States, with about a hundred in and around Washington, D.C.[32]

To maintain their tax-exempt status, think tanks must remain nonpartisan: They cannot support political parties or candidates running for office. Increasingly, however, think tanks have taken on an ideological and partisan edge. Since the 1980s, conservative think tanks, generously funded by corporations and foundations, have been extraordinarily successful at shaping the national agenda. Whereas consumer and environmental groups once dominated policy discussions by documenting the costs of private enterprise, now conservative think tanks have succeeded in focusing discussion on the costs of government regulation. Policy debates are now dominated by new ideas derived from market economics, such as supply-side economics, privatization, and deregulation.

As Table 9.3 shows, some think tanks, supported by liberal foundations and unions, do research and advocacy for workers, the poor, and minorities. The Urban Institute, one of the oldest and biggest, supports government programs for

TABLE 9.3

Influential Washington Think Tanks

	Approximate Annual Budget (in millions of $)	Main Goals
1. Heritage Foundation	$22.9	New right; antigovernment; pro-free market; culturally conservative
2. Urban Institute	20	Pro-city and minority; performs objective evaluations of government programs to improve them
3. Brookings Institution	19–20	Scholarly policy analysis often with liberal orientation
4. American Enterprise Institute	10	Advocates private enterprise over government solutions
5. Joint Center for Political and Economic Studies	5.5	Does research to improve the lot of African Americans
6. Committee for Economic Development	4.6	Corporate-oriented; favors free market solutions
7. Cato Institute	4	Libertarian; individual liberty and limited government
8. Economic Policy Institute	2	Pro-union; favors more equal distribution of wealth

Adapted with the permission of The Free Press, a division of Simon & Schuster, from *The Idea Brokers: Think Tanks and the Rise of the New Policy Elite* by James A. Smith. Copyright © 1991 by James Allen Smith.

cities and the poor, but it views itself primarily as an objective and scientific evaluator of public policies; its research agenda is driven by government contracts, not a political vision. The Economic Policy Institute, which receives most of its funding from unions, has a clear political agenda, but it is tiny compared to the large number of pro-corporate think tanks.

The most powerful think tank in Washington is the Heritage Foundation, which has a highly partisan, pro-corporate agenda. Within one year of its founding in 1973, the Heritage Foundation was receiving financial support from eighty-seven corporations. Its budget grew from $1.0 million in fiscal year 1976–77 to $22.9 million in 1993. Joseph Coors, right-wing president of the Coors Brewing Company, has been a major supporter of the Heritage Foundation, along with Richard Mellon Scaife, heir to the Mellon banking, oil, and industrial fortune. Corporate donors include Mobil Oil, Dow Chemical, Gulf Oil, and the Reader's Digest Association.[33]

With a permanent staff of 150, the Heritage Foundation generates over 200 publications per year. Devoting more than one-third of its budget to marketing, Heritage has been especially successful at gaining media attention for its publications. Most of its publications are designed to meet the "briefcase test"— short enough to be read in the time it takes to take a taxi from Washington's National Airport to a congressional hearing on Capitol Hill (about 20 minutes).[34] Senior scholars at Heritage are available to produce a paper on a policy issue for a sympathetic member of Congress in a matter of hours.

The Heritage Foundation achieved national prominence in 1980 when it delivered to President Reagan's transition team a 1,000-page volume entitled *Mandate for Leadership* that laid out the detailed steps that would be necessary for conservatives to take over the government. The book soon became a bestseller. One reporter characterized it as a "blueprint for grabbing the government by its frayed New Deal lapels and shaking out 48 years of liberal policies."[35] In 1986, at a breakfast honoring the Heritage Foundation, President Reagan acknowledged the importance of its work, stating: "Ideas do have consequences, rhetoric is policy, and words are action."[36]

Conservatives think tanks and foundations are also making efforts to shape political debates on college campuses, which they maintain have long been dominated by leftist ideas. The Madison Center for Educational Affairs (MCEA), a conservative advocacy group, helps seventy conservative newspapers on college campuses with $400,000 worth of grants and a range of valuable services. The Liberation News Service (LNS) provides editorial services for left-wing college papers, but it is not nearly as well funded or organized. Accuracy in Academia (AIA) is an explicit attempt to counter the alleged left-wing bias in American universities. Started by Reed Irvine, also founder of a similar group called Accuracy in Media, AIA recruits students to monitor college classes and report professors who fail to include the conservative point of view or who have "Marxist leanings." The results are published in AIA's monthly newspaper, *Campus Report*, that is distributed free to about 1,500 colleges and high schools. The effect of these efforts are uncertain, but they demonstrate a capacity by conservative think tanks and foundations to reach out beyond Washington.

Direct Marketing

A third method used successfully by corporate elites to seize the agenda from citizens' groups is direct marketing. **Direct marketing** is the targeted solicitation of individuals for political support, sometimes by phone but more often by mail. The advantage of direct marketing is that, much more than with radio or television, the political appeal can be adapted to specialized audiences. Pioneered by public interest groups, which often relied upon individual membership dues for funding, direct marketing has been greatly enhanced over the years by high-speed computers that maintain huge mailing lists broken down into segments for specialized appeals. By the 1983–84 election cycle, direct marketing of politics had induced 14 million people to contribute almost $1 billion to various political candidates and causes and had generated 20 million letters to Congress.[37]

Direct mail marketing begins by prospecting a large mailing list. This is an expensive task, and usually only 1 or 2 percent reply to the appeal. Respondents comprise the "house list," which can be successfully solicited again and again for support, typically with a 10 to 20 percent response rate. Mailing lists are traded and sold between organizations. One enterprising researcher enrolled her four-month-old son in six organizations to trace direct mail fundraising. Over the next year and a half the infant received 18 pounds of mail—185 solicitations from the original six organizations and 63 from thirty-two other organizations that bought or rented mailing lists.[38]

Direct mail solicitations are cleverly designed so that they will not be thrown in the wastebasket unopened. They are often addressed directly to the individual ("Dear Mr. Malone") and contain emotional appeals that evoke an exaggerated threat. A letter from Common Cause talks about "the threat posed by the torrents of special interest campaign cash," which it calls "Alarming. Outrageous. Downright dangerous." A solicitation from the Christian family right begins: "Just When You Thought Your Children Were Safe From Homosexual Advances, Congress Introduces House Resolution #427: The 'Gay Bill of Rights.'"[39]

Computers break down mailing lists into niches and specialized appeals. By a simple command, a computer can be ordered to produce letters for all those on the mailing list who live, for example, in the districts of representatives who serve on the House Banking, Finance, and Urban Affairs Committee. Lobbyists increasingly see direct mail as a way to supplement their insider strategy with an outsider strategy that carefully orchestrates grassroots pressure on Congress.

THE NEW INTEREST GROUP POLITICS: DEMOCRACY FOR HIRE

The new style of lobbying developed by the public interest movement in the 1960s and 1970s has tilted the playing field for interest groups. Instead of insider lobbyists and congressional leaders striking policy deals behind closed doors, the process is now more decentralized and public, with information and policy analysis playing more prominent roles. Congressional hearings are more important as well, with expert witnesses amassing mountains of information on each issue. The emphasis on information in the policymaking process gives the advantage to those who control information. The new regulatory laws have created more complex policy environments controlled by *issue networks* of specialists.[40] Elected representatives, even presidents, are forced to defer to the issue networks as democratic control passes from elected leaders to unelected technocrats. Few citizens possess the expertise or the free time to track complex regulations on new drugs or the latest scientific knowledge on carcinogens. On the other hand, corporations often do.

Direct mail and other technologies have helped spawn a new generation of public relations firms in Washington, D.C., that can, for the right amount of money, generate a grassroots movement for either side of just about any issue. They are so sophisticated that recognizing the difference between manufactured public opinion and genuine expressions of public sentiment is often difficult— or, as they say in the lobbying industry: "Is it grassroots or Astro Turf?"[41]

A good example of the new breed of lobbyists is Bonner & Associates, a small but sophisticated public relations firm located near the Capitol in Washington. Founder Jack Bonner emphasizes that corporate grassroots politics was borrowed from the public interest groups that perfected the technique of using factual accusations to generate emotional public responses. "Politics turns on emotion," Bonner says. "That's why industry has lost in the past and that's why we win. We bring emotion to the table."[42]

Bonner takes pride in being able to find ordinary citizens who have no financial interest in the policy but are willing to support his corporate clients' positions; "white hat" citizens, he calls them. The offices of Bonner & Associates have a boiler room with three hundred phone lines and a sophisticated computer system. Young people sit in little booths every day, dialing around the country in search of "white hat" citizens who are willing to endorse corporate political objectives. To speak out against the 1990 Clean Air Act, Bonner was able to find senior citizens, disabled Americans, and farmers who were willing to testify against the law on the basis of questionable corporate claims that tougher fuel economy standards would make manufacturing vans, station wagons, and small trucks impossible.

The success of the Harry and Louise ads in killing President Clinton's health care reform bill has taught many people that television advertising can be an effective supplement to traditional lobbying techniques. In the battle over tort reform, the effort by corporations to limit product liability lawsuits, an organization called Citizens for a Sound Economy produced ads in which an affable older man portrayed the legal system as a circus controlled by greedy lawyers and plaintiffs. Making no mention of who funds the organization (large corporations like Cigna Insurance and R. J. Reynolds Tobacco), the ads were targeted to sixty congressional districts. Representative Louise M. Slaughter (D.–NY) said she received up to sixty calls a day as a result of the ads. "There is a frenzy they whip up," she said. "And there is no countervailing message at all."[43]

In a large country like the United States, the increasing sophistication of the mass media and direct marketing has given an advantage to interests with large amounts of money. American politics is approaching "democracy for hire." Researchers found that few corporate interest representatives in Washington expressed a need for more money—only 9 percent. On the other hand, 58 percent of unions and citizens' groups said they needed more money.[44] A chemical company can deduct the cost of flying its executives to Washington to testify against the Clean Air Act; ordinary citizens must pay their own way. Corporations use tax-exempt contributions to fund supposedly nonpartisan think tanks that shape public opinion and pay for expensive advocacy ads. Most taxpayers do not itemize their deductions on their tax returns and therefore do not receive a tax deduction for interest group activities.

CONCLUSION: HOW DEMOCRATIC IS THE INTEREST GROUP SYSTEM?

Interest group politics in America is both highly accessible and highly unequal. The rapid rise to power in the 1960s of Ralph Nader and his network of public interest organizations demonstrates that determined citizens *can* penetrate the system. The interest group system provides an important safety valve in American politics that promotes democratic stability. Government elites cannot simply run roughshod over groups of citizens; ordinary citizens have a chance to be heard and if they are smart and well organized they can usually attain influence in the interest group system. By providing access, interest group politics enhances the legitimacy of the American political system. In authoritarian systems, by contrast, people know that they cannot penetrate the system, and they are forced to either acquiesce and withdraw from politics or turn to violence to achieve their ends.

Although the American interest group system is highly accessible, power overall is distributed very unequally. Large corporations and the wealthy have greater access to power than other groups. Their ability to raise money enables them to amplify their voices by exploiting the new political technologies. On the other hand, many groups are not adequately represented: The poor, minorities, and consumers are severely underrepresented; the unemployed and homemakers have no groups to represent them in Washington.

If elites are ordinarily able to use their financial resources to control the policy process, how do we account for the period in the late 1960s and early 1970s when the system was relatively open to popular democratic influences? The answer lies in the relationship between interest group politics and the topic of our next chapter, mass movement politics. Public interest groups were able to pass landmark legislation, like the Clean Air Act, not just because of tenacious and talented leaders like Ralph Nader but because mass movements like the civil rights, feminist, and environmental movements took to the streets to demand democratic rights and social justice. These movements threatened political elites, who, sensing that the alternative was radical change, suddenly became more open to reformers like Nader. We now turn to see how protest politics, the ultimate outsider strategy, periodically overcomes the inertia of American politics by giving popular democrats a weapon that money cannot buy.

KEY TERMS

interest group politics
insider strategy
outsider strategy
Federal Register
pluralism

collective action problem
public interest group
corporate image advertising
think tank
direct marketing

SUGGESTED READINGS

William Greider, *Who Will Tell the People? The Betrayal of American Democracy*. New York: Simon & Schuster, 1992. Shows how corporate elites were able to reassert their power over the interest group system after the rise of public interest groups.

Mancur Olson, *The Logic of Collective Action: Public Goods and the theory of Groups*. New York: Schocken Books, 1968. A leading statement of rational actor theory that explains why broad public interest groups have trouble organizing.

E. E. Schattschneider, *Semisovereign People: A Realist's View of Democracy in America*. New York: Holt, Rinehart and Winston, 1960. A brief but penetrating analysis of the elitist bias in interest group politics.

Kay Lehman Schlozman and John T. Tierney, *Organized Interests and American Democracy*. New York: Harper & Row, 1986. The best overall treatment of interest groups in American politics.

Theda Skocpol, *Boomerang: Health Care Reform and the Turn Against Government*. New York: W. W. Norton, 1997. Demonstrates the conservative bias of the interest group system by showing how interest groups mobilized to kill Clinton's health care reform.

Mass Movement Politics:
The Great Equalizer

In the mid-1950s, Montgomery, Alabama, like most southern cities, had laws requiring segregation of nearly all public facilities, including public transportation.[1] Blacks were required to sit in the backs of buses. Blacks could not pass through the white section at the front of a bus, which meant that after they had bought a ticket they had to get off and reenter through the back door. The ordinance in Montgomery had a special twist: Bus drivers, all of whom were white, were empowered to enforce a floating line between the races. As more whites got on, bus drivers would order a whole row of blacks to stand up and move to the back of the bus to make room. A number of black women thus could be forced to stand to make room for one white man.

On December 1, 1955, Rosa Parks, a dignified, middle-aged black woman, boarded a bus in downtown Montgomery. The thirty-six seats on the bus were soon filled with twenty-two blacks and fourteen whites. Seeing a white man standing in the front of the bus, the driver turned around and told the four blacks sitting in the row just behind the whites to get up and move to the back. Rosa Parks refused. The driver threatened to arrest her, but Parks again refused to move. Summoned to the scene, police officers arrested Parks, took her to the police station, booked her, fingerprinted her, and put her in jail.

Word of Parks's arrest swept quickly through the activists in Montgomery's black community. The local NAACP chapter had been searching for a good case to challenge the segregation laws through the courts. Parks's commitment to the cause and unquestioned character made her an ideal test case. Despite the potential for white recriminations, Parks agreed to go forward with the case. At the same time, the Women's Political Council, a group of black professional women, decided to call for a one-day boycott of the buses to protest the arrest. They distributed 35,000 copies of a simple leaflet that called for all blacks to boycott the city buses on Monday, December 5. A group of ministers agreed to spread word of the boycott in their Sunday sermons and to hold a mass meeting on Monday night to decide if the boycott should continue.

Nick Anderson
The Courier-Journal (Louisville, Ky.)

The boycott was a stunning success; few, if any, blacks rode the buses on Monday. Since blacks made up about 75 percent of the bus riders, many buses were almost empty. Rosa Parks was found guilty of violating Alabama's segregation laws. Given a suspended sentence, she was fined $10 and forced to pay $4 in court costs. Monday afternoon black leaders and preachers met to plan the mass meeting that night. They formed a new organization called the Montgomery Improvement Association. As president, the group elected the new minister in town, Martin Luther King, Jr. Only twenty-six years old, King was articulate and intelligent, having just received a doctorate from Boston University. But according to some participants, he was chosen because, having lived in Montgomery for only a few months, he was completely independent—the white establishment had not yet "put their hand" on him.

King rushed home after the meeting and had barely 20 minutes to prepare his speech. That night the Holt Street Baptist Church was jammed. Loudspeakers amplified the speeches to the crowd that spread over several acres outside. King began slowly, carefully describing the circumstances of the boycott, including the arrest of Rosa Parks, and praising her integrity and "Christian commitment." Then King paused and intoned in his resonant voice, "And you know, my friends, there comes a time when people get tired of being trampled over by the iron feet of oppression." As if releasing years of frustration, the crowd broke instantly into a flood of yeses, cheers, and applause.

After electrifying the crowd, King stepped back to examine the pitfalls of the boycott. Stressing that "we are not here advocating violence," he said: "The only weapon we have in our hands this evening is the weapon of protest." King placed their protest firmly within the American democratic tradition. "If we were trapped in the dungeon of a totalitarian regime—we couldn't do this." he declared. "But the great glory of American democracy is the right to protest for right."

Getting to the heart of the matter—the justice of their cause—King continued: "If we are wrong, the Supreme Court of this nation is wrong. If we are wrong—God Almighty is wrong! And we are determined here in Montgomery," King went on quoting the words of an Old Testament prophet, "to work and fight until justice runs down like water, and righteousness like a mighty stream!" The crowd erupted in a release of pent-up emotion.

King's rhetoric seemed to lift the crowd onto a higher level of unity and resolve. The crowd grew silent as Ralph Abernathy recited the three cautious demands the Montgomery Improvement Association had chosen for the boycott: (1) courteous treatment on the buses; (2) seating on a first-come, first-serve basis, with whites in the front and blacks in the back; (3) the hiring of black drivers for black bus routes. When Abernathy asked for the vote, people in the church slowly began standing, at first in ones and twos, until everyone in the Holt Street Baptist Church was standing in affirmation. Cheers erupted from those standing outside.

The Montgomery bus boycott was a remarkable feat of mass mobilization. It lasted more than thirteen months, with over 50,000 blacks walking to work every day, attending mass meetings, and remaining true to the principles of nonviolent resistance even in the face of extreme hostility and provocation from the white establishment. The bus company was denied 40,000 fares a day. Overcoming deep class divisions within the black community, the movement organized carpools in which middle class blacks lent their cars with little compensation so that poor blacks could get to work. Soon police began to ticket carpoolers on trumped-up charges, but the carpools continued. King's house was bombed, as were the houses of other boycott leaders.

Refusing to compromise, the white leadership in Montgomery made every effort to repress the movement, but they failed to see how these actions would play to a national audience. Eighty-nine leaders of the movement, including King and twenty-four other ministers, were indicted on charges of conspiring to boycott. The national media immediately picked up the story, creating sympathy for King and his followers by portraying them as martyrs to a just cause. The movement could not have begun to pay for the favorable news coverage that followed. The Montgomery Improvement Association began to receive contributions from all over the country and even the world, and King became a national celebrity, later appearing on the cover of *Time* magazine.

Finally, a special three-judge federal district court ruled that Montgomery's system of bus segregation violated the U.S. Constitution. Montgomery's city government appealed the case to the Supreme Court but lost. Thirteen months after the boycott began, Montgomery's blacks were able to get on buses and sit anywhere they wanted. They had triumphed in the face of incredible odds.

The "Montgomery model" of nonviolent resistance soon spread to other cities across the South. Black preachers formed the Southern Christian Leadership Conference (SCLC), which led the civil rights movement in the years ahead. Protests erupted in more than nine hundred communities, battering down the walls of segregation brick by brick. Using boycotts, sit-ins at lunch counters, marches, and massive demonstrations, the civil rights movement built national momentum, culminating in the 1963 March on Washington where King delivered his famous "I Have a Dream" speech. Feeling the pressure, Congress passed the 1964 Civil Rights Act, which prohibited segregation in public accommodations and discrimination in hiring, and the 1965 Voting Rights Act, which put the weight of the federal government behind giving blacks the right to vote.

This chapter examines the American tradition of protest politics exemplified by the civil rights movement. **Protest politics** can be defined as political actions such as boycotts and demonstrations designed to broaden conflicts and activate third parties to pressure the bargaining situation in ways favorable to the protestors.[2] Because protest politics operates outside of ordinary political institutions, it is sometimes called "extraordinary politics."[3] When protest politics mobilizes large numbers of previously passive bystanders to become active participants, it reaches the stature of a **mass movement**.

Periodically, throughout American history, mass movements have enabled poor people, minorities, and others shut out of the system to make themselves heard and acquire power. After examining the goals and tactics that distinguish protest politics from electoral and interest group politics, we explore the dilemmas that leaders of mass movements face in keeping protests alive and achieving their objectives. We also examine the criticisms by elite democrats, who view mass movements as threats to democratic order and stability. Finally, focusing on the modern mass movements that emerged in the 1960s, we present a popular democratic defense of protest movements, showing how they level the playing field and fulfill the participatory promise of American democracy.

PROTEST POLITICS: GOALS AND TACTICS

The civil rights movement is only one example of the power of protest in American politics. Like interest groups, mass movements are a form of extra-electoral politics; they try to influence government outside of elections. Interest group politics and mass politics often blend into each other. Interest groups sometimes organize demonstrations or pickets, and it is common for mass movements to lobby Congress. Over time, mass movements often spawn interest groups that become part of the pressure group system in Washington. Nevertheless, interest group politics and protest politics are distinctly different phenomena, whose primary differences have to do with (1) their goals, and (2) the means, or tactics, used to achieve those goals.

Mass Movement Goals: Beyond Material Benefits

Whereas interest groups usually focus on specific material goals, such as lower taxes or more governmental benefits, mass movements seek broad moral and ideological goals that affect the whole society, such as the "right to life" of the anti-abortion movement or ending the war in Vietnam. As a result, mass movement goals are not easily subject to bargaining and compromise. The abolitionist movement, for example, refused to compromise on its goal of abolishing slavery. For mass movements, it is not a matter of more or less, but right or wrong. Table 10.1 lists the most important mass movements in American history together with their main goals.

The Montgomery bus boycott movement started out as an interest group, asking for three reforms that would not end segregation but simply make it more humane. The refusal of whites to compromise on these issues, King later wrote, caused a shift in people's thinking.

> The experience taught me a lesson. . . . even when we asked for justice within the segregation laws, the "powers that be" were not willing to grant it. Justice and equality, I saw, would never come while segregation remained, because the basic purpose of segregation was to perpetuate injustice and inequality.[4]

TABLE 10.1

Mass
Movements in
American History

Movement	Primary Period of Activism	Major Goal(s)
Abolitionist	Three decades before Civil War (1830–1860)	Abolition of slavery
Nativist	1850s and 1890s–1920s	Restrict immigration
Populist	1880s and 1890s	Democratic control over railroads, banks, and nation's money supply
Labor	Reached peaks in the 1880s, 1890s, and 1930s	Enhance power of workers to achieve decent wages and benefits, protect jobs, and guarantee safe working environments
Women's suffrage	Late nineteenth and early twentieth centuries	Voting rights for women
Temperance	Late nineteenth and early twentieth centuries	Prohibition of alcohol
Nuclear disarmament	Late 1950s and early 1960s	End nuclear testing
	Late 1970s and early 1980s	Ban the bomb
Civil rights	1950s and 1960s	Equal rights for black Americans
Anti-Vietnam War	Late 1960s and early 1970s	U.S. out of Vietnam
Student	1960s and 1970s	Student rights and democratic governance of universities
Neighborhood organizing	1960s–present	Community control
Women's liberation or feminist	1970s–present	Equality for women in all aspects of life
Antinuclear	1970s and 1980s	Stop the construction of nuclear power plants
Environmental	1970s–present	Stop environmental destruction
Pro-life (anti-abortion)	1970s–present	Outlaw abortion
Native American rights	1970s–present	Tribal autonomy
Gay rights	1970s–present	Equal rights for homosexuals

At that moment, the goals of the Montgomery boycott shifted from better treatment for blacks within segregation to an end to segregation, or equal rights for all, a goal that could not be compromised. At that point, Montgomery's blacks made the transition from an interest group to a mass movement that could appeal to all Americans on the basis of human dignity, equality, and fairness.

Mass Movement Tactics: Protest as a Political Resource

Mass movements are differentiated from interest groups not only by their goals but also by the political means they use to achieve their goals. Mass movements have a broad array of what we might call *protest tactics* to choose from, including petitions, demonstrations, boycotts, strikes, civil disobedience, confrontations and disruptions, riots, and even violent revolution (see Figure 10.1). Unlike interest groups, mass movements do not target their efforts directly at decision makers; protests are a form of political theater, designed to educate and mobilize broader publics who in turn put pressure on decision makers. Mass movement politics attempts to broaden the scope of conflict in the hope that battles that would be lost in the narrow lobbies of Congress can be won in the streets or in the broad arena of public opinion. Mass movement politics, therefore, has more participatory potential than interest group politics. By relying on mass mobilization and the moral appeal of their cause, people with little money or political clout can use protest tactics to gain power in the political system.

Mass movement tactics vary all the way from the legal to the clearly illegal, with a large gray area in the middle. Protestors often agonize about whether to cross over the line into illegal tactics. In choosing tactics, protesters must go far enough to dramatize their cause but not so far as to alienate potential supporters—a phenomenon known as *political backlash*. Most tactics used by mass movements are legal and protected by the First Amendment guarantees of freedom of speech, press, and "the right of the people peaceably to assemble, and to petition the Government for a redress of grievances." When legal protests are ignored and produce few results, protestors become frustrated and sometimes resort to illegal methods, including violence, to dramatize their causes.

FIGURE 10.1 **Tactical Options of Protest Movements**

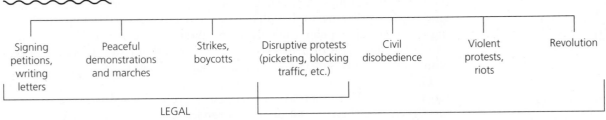

In many ways, protest movements are evidence of the failure of our democratic institutions to respond to deeply felt needs and issues.[5] Even if a democracy guaranteed majority rule, it would still need ways for minorities to make themselves heard. Blacks in Montgomery, for example, could not use electoral politics to achieve their objectives. Representing only 37 percent of the city's population, African Americans lacked the votes to control city government through elections. More important, they were prevented from registering to vote by legal obstacles and outright intimidation. In 1952, only about one in five eligible blacks in the South was registered to vote.[6] Interest group politics was also not a viable option, because whites in Montgomery were unwilling to bargain or compromise; for them, segregation was an all-or-nothing matter.

Following normal political channels, therefore, Montgomery blacks had no chance of success. The boycott, however, was a weapon they could use: By withdrawing their fares from the bus company, they could inflict fiscal pain. But it is unlikely that the boycott alone would have brought significant change. The only chance the blacks had was to appeal to a broader audience to put pressure on the entrenched white elite in Montgomery to alter the system of racial segregation. As King said in his speech, the only weapon they had was the "weapon of protest."

MASS MOVEMENTS IN AMERICAN HISTORY

American politics has been shaken repeatedly by mass movements. About once in a generation, waves of democratic participation, with strong leveling tendencies, sweep the country: the original revolutionary thrust of the 1770s; the Jacksonian era of the 1830s; the culmination of the antislavery movement in the 1850s; the Populist movement of the 1890s; the economic reform movements, including the labor movement, that rose out of the Great Depression of the 1930s; and the social movements that began in the 1960s. Mass movements have probably played a greater role in American politics than in any other Western democracy. Issues that are represented by political parties in Europe often are expressed through protest movements in the United States.

Some mass movements in the United States, such as the nativist movement and one of its offshoots, the Ku Klux Klan, have had antidemocratic goals of excluding certain groups from full democratic citizenship. Most mass movements, however, have been popular democratic in character, striving to include previously excluded groups (e.g., blacks, Hispanics, women, workers, students, gays, and Native Americans) in the full benefits of democratic citizenship. In appealing to the American people, popular democratic mass movements have called on two deeply held sets of beliefs—one rooted in politics and the other in religion—that counter Americans' well-known individualism.

First, Americans share a set of core political beliefs in liberty, equality, democracy, and the rule of law. These beliefs are embodied in sacred political texts, including the Declaration of Independence ("all men are created equal"), the Constitution's Bill of Rights (freedom of speech and press), and Lincoln's

Gettysburg Address ("government of the people, by the people and for the people"). The American political creed is by its nature inclusive and has frequently been cited by protesting groups to legitimate their causes. Thus, the women's suffrage movement asserted that liberty and equality should apply to all people and not just men. Martin Luther King, Jr., repeatedly used the language of equality and rights to legitimatize the black cause to a broader white audience. Historically, popular democrats have had an ideological advantage over elite democrats, being able to tap into a wellspring of egalitarian political beliefs.

Popular democratic mass movements have also been nurtured by American religious traditions stressing that everyone is equal in the eyes of God, that even the least of us should be treated with dignity and respect, and that morality is a force in the world. Martin Luther King's frequent use of the language of the Old Testament, comparing the liberation struggles of blacks to the efforts of the tribes of Israel to escape from exile in Egypt, is a brilliant example of the political relevance of religion in American politics. The abolitionist and temperance movements were also firmly rooted in religious traditions, as is the modern pro-life anti-abortion movement, which has adopted many of the direct action tactics of the civil rights movement.

MASS MOVEMENTS: THE NECESSARY INGREDIENTS

Protest is a political resource that can be used by disadvantaged groups lacking traditional sources of political power, such as money or connections, to influence the system. Protest, however, cannot be used by any disadvantaged group at any time to level the playing field of democratic politics. Only rarely do the necessary ingredients of successful protest movements come together. About half of the eligible voters don't even get to the polls for a presidential election every four years. Protest movements require much deeper levels of commitment than voting, as exemplified by the willingness of blacks in Montgomery to walk to work for thirteen months instead of taking the bus. Protest movements must engage the whole personalities of participants to transcend normal politics. And even when participants are engaged, remarkable leadership is necessary for movements to stay alive and achieve their goals.

For protest movements even to get off the ground, five ingredients are necessary:

1. Rising expectations. History has shown that people will endure oppressive conditions for a long time without rebelling. People do not rebel when conditions are at their worst, but when conditions have begun to improve and people begin to perceive a gap between the way things are and the way they could be. According to one theory, it is not deprivation itself that drives people to rebel, but the feeling that one's group is being deprived of resources and opportunities available to other groups in the society. This is known as the theory of **relative deprivation.**[7]

In the case of the civil rights movement, blacks had suffered under Jim Crow segregation laws since the nineteenth century, but resistance had been limited.

One event that raised black expectations was World War II. Many African-American men died fighting fascism. Those who returned were less willing to accept second-class citizenship, especially after President Truman integrated the armed forces. Urbanization of blacks following the mechanization of southern agriculture also brought many blacks into contact with new ideas and new opportunities that raised expectations. Most important, the 1954 Supreme Court decision in *Brown* v. *Board of Topeka* put the power and prestige of the Supreme Court behind the cause of integration. Black people felt they were not alone. As King put it in his Montgomery speech, "If we are wrong, the Supreme Court of this nation is wrong."

2. Social resources. Isolated individuals cannot build social movements. Social movements require networks that can spread the word and involve people in the movement.[8] Social movements need what Sara Evans and Harry Boyte call "free spaces"—organizations located between private families and large public organizations where people can learn self-respect, cooperation, group identity, and the leadership skills necessary for democratic participation.[9] Black churches provided spaces for the civil rights movement that were free from white domination, where blacks could express their true feelings and develop confidence in their abilities. Most of the leadership of the civil rights movement came out of the black churches, where traditions of commitment to the congregation and skills in sermonizing nurtured effective leaders. The national organizations of black Baptist churches formed networks that helped the SCLC spread the Montgomery model throughout the South.

All protest movements in American history have been nurtured in free spaces. Building on earlier organizations like the Grange, the Populist movement of the late nineteenth century built a vast network of Farmers' Alliances that within a few years involved 2 million families. The purpose of the Alliances was to cooperatively market crops and purchase supplies, but they also created free spaces where people could learn the skills of democracy.[10]

The feminist movement grew out of the free spaces created by the civil rights movement in the South and the anti–Vietnam War movement organized mainly on college campuses. Ironically, it was discrimination in these supposedly egalitarian movements that drove women to form their own movement. In the civil rights movement, women, who performed much of the crucial behind-the-scenes work, developed confidence in their abilities and learned the skills of political organizing. At the same time, they were excluded from decision making and public leadership roles. When women in the Student Nonviolent Coordinating Committee (SNCC, known as "snick"), the radical student wing of the civil rights movement, raised the issue of sex roles, one of the leaders, Stokely Carmichael, is reported to have said: "The only position for women in SNCC is prone."[11] Such remarks caused many black women to examine gender, along with race, as a cause of discrimination.

Shortly afterwards, the rise of black nationalism forced many white women out of the civil rights movement and into the new left, organizing against the Vietnam War. There they found that their concerns about sex roles were ignored, even ridiculed, by white men as well. The clash between the egalitarian ideas of the movement and the unequal sex roles within it was too much to bear. Women began meeting separately in small "consciousness-raising groups" where they could articulate their concerns in a supportive atmosphere. Spreading across the country, consciousness-raising groups became free spaces where women could recognize their common problems and develop the confidence to bring about change.

3. *An appealing moral cause.* Mass movements in the United States fail unless they can appeal to fundamental American values. Animal rights activists, for example, have a moral cause, but they have been unable to make the transition to a mass movement because most Americans do not believe that animals deserve the same rights as human beings. The civil rights movement, on the other hand, had an appealing moral cause because the demand for equal rights resonated with all Americans. By wrapping itself in Christian values and the rhetoric of equal rights, the movement was nearly impossible to criticize as un-American. Later, when parts of the civil rights movement shifted from a rhetoric of equal rights to a rhetoric of black nationalism and black power, appealing more to African and Muslim traditions, public sympathy for the movement swiftly eroded.

4. *Consciousness raising.* When the necessary ingredients are present for a mass movement, a sudden change of political consciousness occurs and people look at political facts differently. Reflecting on the moment at the Holt Street Baptist Church after King's electrifying speech, when Montgomery's black community voted to continue the boycott, Ralph Abernathy described just such a change in consciousness. "The fear that had shackled us across the years—all left suddenly when we were in that church together."[12]

One of the most remarkable changes in consciousness occurred in the so-called "velvet revolutions" that swept across Eastern Europe in 1989. Before then, democratic social movements were violently repressed by Soviet troops and the secret police. In 1989, encouraged by Mikhail Gorbachev's reform leadership of the Soviet Union, the people of Eastern Europe became bolder in their opposition to Soviet domination. Once they realized that the troops would not fire on peaceful demonstrators, people began to mobilize in massive demonstrations. When the fear disappeared and citizens were able to gather together to feel their collective power, people suddenly realized they had the power to overturn communism and institute democratic regimes. Overnight, the Berlin Wall tumbled and communist regimes across Eastern Europe fell to democratic movements. That same year, however, a similar democratic social movement in Bejing's Tiananmen Square was brutally suppressed by Chinese troops.

5. *Transformational leadership.* The leaders of parties and interest groups are usually **transactional leaders** who broker mutually beneficial exchanges between their followers and elites, such as votes for patronage jobs or campaign contributions for tax breaks. Mass movements, however, require **transforming leaders** who engage the full personalities of followers, teaching them to go beyond self-interest and express their commitments in direct political action.[13] Martin Luther King, Jr., was such a leader, who challenged his followers to live

up to their highest moral beliefs. Elizabeth Cady Stanton, the early leader of the women's suffrage movement, was also a transforming leader. In 1848, Stanton adapted the language of the Declaration of Independence to the cause of women's rights by writing the Declaration of Sentiments, a kind of bill of rights for women. By word and by example, Stanton encouraged women to step out of their assigned sphere of family and home and become actors in the public sphere of democratic politics. For more than fifty years she lectured, petitioned, organized, and wrote to encourage women to find their public voices.[14]

PROTEST TACTICS: WALKING A FINE LINE

Although protest tactics can be a powerful political resource, if not properly handled they can explode like dynamite in the faces of those they are designed to help. By its very nature, protest politics is confrontational and tension producing; protestors deliberately provoke those in power to get a reaction from them. Protest leaders face a tactical dilemma: They must push confrontation far enough to satisfy the needs of the protestors for direct action and dramatize the issues to a broader public. If they push too far, however, they can alienate potential supporters or even create a backlash that strengthens their opponents.

Conflict has two benefits for protest movements: First it mobilizes the protestors themselves, and it captures the attention of bystanders who are moved to support the cause of the protestors. Saul Alinsky was a master practitioner and theoretician of protest politics. In the 1930s, he organized the Back of the Yards area of Chicago, an area made famous by Upton Sinclair's exposé of the meat-packing industry in his muckraking novel *The Jungle*. Alinsky understood the necessity of conflict if disadvantaged people were to gain power. "A PEOPLE'S ORGANIZATION is a conflict group," Alinsky wrote.[15] A good fight against a common enemy unifies an organization, heightens morale, and mobilizes energies.

Second, conflict has the effect, especially if the protesters are viewed as underdogs, of drawing third parties into the fray who pressure elites to negotiate. Protest is a form of political ju jitsu; a movement with few political resources can use the strength of its opponent to its own advantage. In Montgomery the indictment of eighty-nine African Americans, including twenty-five ministers, on trumped-up charges of conspiring to boycott brought national attention to the cause. The protesters celebrated the arrests because they knew the media would paint the white establishment as the aggressors and themselves as the underdogs. Later, SCLC orchestrated Project C—for "confrontation"—in Birmingham, Alabama. "Bull" Connor, Birmingham's commissioner of public safety, played his assigned role perfectly, using powerful fire hoses and vicious police dogs against defenseless children. As the media sent out pictures of the brutality, sympathy for the civil rights movement soared.

Protest tactics can backfire, however, if they go too far. Most Americans were opposed to the Vietnam War, but when they saw protestors burning the American flag and destroying property, most people sympathized with the government not the protestors. Similarly, violence against abortion clinics and doctors did not help the pro-life, anti-abortion cause.

One method for coping with this tactical dilemma of how hard to push confrontation is **civil disobedience,** which can be defined as the deliberate violation of the law to dramatize a cause by persons who are willing to accept the punishment of the law. Civil disobedience provides a middle ground between peaceful demonstrations (which are often ignored) and violent confrontations (which can cause a backlash). Civil disobedience is not an attempt to evade the law. An act of civil disobedience, such as being arrested while blocking the shipment of arms during the Vietnam War, is done completely in the open, without any violence, and with a sense of moral seriousness.

The American tradition of civil disobedience can be traced back to Henry David Thoreau (1817–1862). Passionately opposed to slavery and to the Mexican War, which he saw as a fight for the slave masters, Thoreau refused to pay his poll taxes. As a result, he was thrown in prison. In 1849 Thoreau wrote a powerful essay, later entitled "Civil Disobedience," in which he argued that unjust laws should not be obeyed. "The only obligation which I have a right to assume is to do at any time what I think right," Thoreau argued.[16] Thoreau acted as an individual; he was not part of a mass movement. His writings, however, inspired many leaders to incorporate civil disobedience into their movements.

Mohandas K. Gandhi (1869–1948) read Thoreau and incorporated his ideas about civil disobedience into his successful movement to free India from British rule. Gandhi believed that a careful campaign of civil disobedience could mobilize *satyagraha* (pronounced sa-TYA-gra-ha) or "truth force," to persuade opponents of the justice of a cause. Gandhi stressed that movements of civil disobedience must be willing to negotiate at all times, so long as basic principles are not sacrificed.

As a college student, Martin Luther King, Jr., read Thoreau and later he adapted the ideas of Gandhi to American conditions. King did not begin the Montgomery campaign with a preplanned strategy of nonviolent resistance. Drawn to nonviolence by his religious training, King reflected on the experiences of the civil rights movement and gradually developed a sophisticated philosophy of nonviolent resistance. King was able to adapt to new conditions and learn from the experiences of others. Dissatisfied with the slow progress being made under the leadership of King and the other ministers in SCLC, college students formed SNCC to push a more aggressive grassroots approach to the struggle. King later praised the student sit-ins at lunch counters across the South for having sought nonviolent confrontations with the segregation laws. His "Letter from a Birmingham Jail," originally written in the margins of a newspaper and on scraps of toilet paper, has become a classic defense of nonviolent protest that is read the world over.

Mass movement leaders like King often find it difficult to balance the needs of protestors, who demand more and more radical action to express their moral outrage, with the need to appeal for outside support, which usually requires moderation and patience. In the civil rights movement, young blacks became frustrated watching their brothers and sisters being beaten by racist police. In the mid-1960s, the civil rights movement split, with more radical blacks joining the "black power" movement under the leadership of the Black Panther Party for Self-Defense and the Black Muslims, led by the charismatic Malcolm X. The movement never recovered from the split. The issue of integration versus separatism, or black nationalism, divides the African-American community to this day.

THE ELITE RESPONSE TO MASS MOVEMENTS

Notwithstanding repeated elite democratic warnings that mass movements threaten political order, elites have many resources for controlling mass movements. It takes as much leadership skill to deflate a mass movement, however, as it does to build one. Political elites have two basic strategies: repression (forcibly attacking the movement) or co-optation (giving in to some of the demands). Political elites face a strategic dilemma that is similar to that faced by mass movements: If they give in too readily, they risk encouraging more militancy and more demands; on the other hand, if they refuse to give in at all and attack the protestors with force, they risk creating public sympathy for the protesters. Essentially, political elites engage in a complex game of chess with mass movements and their leaders.

The accessibility of American political institutions to interest groups has enabled the demands of mass movements to be incorporated into the system. In this way mass movements are converted into interest groups. Meeting only certain demands of a mass movement deflates the moral indignation of the movement and splits reformers from the radicals. If the white leadership in Montgomery had given in to the initial demands of the boycott to humanize the system of segregation on the buses, the effect would have been to deflate, or at the very least divide, the movement. By refusing to give an inch, the white leadership in Montgomery made a serious tactical error. Their intransigence fueled the movement and caused the protestors to shift their goal from reforming segregation to ending it altogether.

Skillfully devised reforms, on the other hand, not only can divide the movement but can also draw parts of the leadership into the system to administer the new reforms. A good example is President Lyndon Johnson's War on Poverty, which was partly a response to the civil rights movement and the urban riots of the 1960s. The War on Poverty gave black activists jobs in federal antipoverty programs, deflecting their energies away from organizing the movement. Militant black leaders were co-opted by federal money.[17] Democracies are supposed to operate this way—making concessions in the face of popular pressure. As we discussed in the previous chapter, mass movements provided the pressure that enabled public interest groups to pass reform legislation in the 1960s and

1970s, including new laws on environmental protection, minority rights, and worker safety. Interest group politics, then, is a safety valve that can deflate mass movements.

In choosing a strategy of concessions or co-optation, those defending the status quo have an advantage: Time is on their side; mass movements cannot maintain a fever pitch of activism for long. Delay is one of the best weapons in the hands of elites. When a problem is brought to public awareness by a mass movement, those in power commonly appoint a commission to find a solution. This strategy gives the impression that something is being done without commitment to specific actions. By the time the commission's report comes out, the mass movement will have lost its momentum. Even if the report recommends significant reforms, there is no guarantee that they will be enacted. A good example is President Johnson's appointment of the Kerner Commission in 1967 to study the causes of the urban riots. The Kerner Commission recommended significant reforms, but very few were ever enacted.[18]

Another tactic used by elites is *tokenism*, responding with insignificant reforms or symbolic gestures to create the impression that serious action is being taken to solve the problem. These symbolic gestures quiet the protestors, but few tangible benefits are delivered. Political scientist Murray Edelman calls this "symbolic reassurance."[19] Appointing members of the aggrieved group—blacks, women, or gays, for example—to commissions or highly visible governmental posts is often used to create the impression of change. Tokenism, it is called. The leaders of student movements demanding radical changes in college curriculums in the 1960s were often appointed to committees to study the problems and come up with solutions. The opportunity to serve on committees with professors and top administrators was flattering, but the effect was often to separate student leaders from the movement and involve them in a long process of negotiation. The key to the success of co-optation is calming the confrontational atmosphere that feeds mass movements long enough for protestors to lose interest. Once they stall, mass movements are very difficult to restart.

When mass movements reach a certain momentum, the tactic of concessions loses its effectiveness and elites often turn to repression.[20] Just as protesters feel justified in using confrontation and sometimes even violence to promote their causes, elites sometimes feel justified in using repression when mass movements threaten their power or violate the law. The United States has a proud tradition of upholding the civil rights of dissenters, but as Chapter 16 shows, when elites have felt threatened by mass movements they often have resorted to repression. American labor history is especially violent. Before passage of the Wagner Act in 1935 (which guaranteed workers the right to organize a union), workers turned to strikes and picket lines that often became violent in order to gain recognition. Governments frequently intervened on the side of owners. In the Pullman strike of 1894, for example, President Grover Cleveland, at the request of the railroads, called in federal troops who, along with municipal police, put down the strike by railroad workers at a cost of thirty-four deaths and millions of dollars of property damage.

THE DEMOCRATIC DEBATE OVER MASS MOVEMENTS

As the name suggests, mass movements involve large numbers of ordinary citizens in direct political actions. The protest tactics used by mass movements are disruptive and confrontational. It is not surprising, therefore, that mass movements and their protest tactics have been the subjects of heated controversy between elite and popular democrats.

Elite Democratic Criticisms of Mass Movements

From the time of Shay's Rebellion, before the Constitution was written, to the violent demonstrations against the Vietnam War, elite democrats have always been suspicious of mass movements. Their attitude is reflected in Alexander Hamilton's statement: "The People! The People is a great beast!"[21] The direct involvement of the masses in political action is dangerous, according to elite democrats, because mass movements can quickly degenerate into lawless mobs that threaten stable democracy. It is safer for political passions to be filtered through representative institutions where elites can deliberate on the long-term interest of the country as a whole.[22]

Elite democrats maintain that the goals of mass movements in American history have often been utopian and impractical. Elites criticize mass movements for being against economic growth and progress. The Populist movement at the turn of the century, for example, was attacked as an emotional reaction against progress and industrialization, an ill-fated attempt to hold on to a doomed agrarian way of life. (The contemporary environmental movement has been attacked on similar grounds.) According to elite democrats, mass movements lack concrete programs for reform that can benefit the people involved; instead, they seek moral or ideological goals that are unrealizable and threaten to overwhelm democratic institutions. Lacking practical reforms, mass movements traffic in moral absolutes.[23]

Elite democrats criticize not only the goals of mass movements but also their tactics. In stable democracies participation is channeled through representative institutions and interest group bargaining. Protest politics brings masses of people into direct participation through confrontational tactics that threaten to divide society into warring camps, elite democrats warn, undermining the norms of tolerance and civility essential to a healthy democracy. Mass movements are not expressions of people's natural desire to participate in politics. Instead, people are drawn into mass movements by demagogues who manipulate emotions, whipping up resentment against the wealthy and the privileged.

Protest tactics can easily get out of hand, elite democrats charge. People in large crowds, or mobs, are incapable of thinking rationally and often do things that, upon reflection, they would never do. Elite democrats favor orderly interest group politics over mass movement politics. One scholar summed up the elite democratic position this way: "Mass politics involve irrationality and chaos;

group politics produce sensible and orderly conflict."[24] In short, mass movements are dangerous to democracy.

The Popular Democratic Defense of Mass Movements

The attitude of popular democrats toward mass movements is reflected in a quote by Thomas Jefferson. Remarking on Shay's Rebellion, which Federalists viewed as a sign of impending anarchy, Jefferson wrote to James Madison: "I hold it that a little rebellion now and then is a good thing, and as necessary in the political world as storms in the physical."[25] After all, popular democrats point out, the country was born in protest. The Boston Tea Party was an illegal destruction of property intended to dramatize the colonists' opposition to British rule, in particular "taxation without representation."

According to popular democrats, periodic elections and interest group bargaining are inadequate to fulfill the participatory promise of American democracy. Popular democrats see mass movements as ways for the people to communicate directly with the government, unimpeded by experts or elites. Protest tactics enable people to engage their full personality and most deeply held beliefs in the democratic process.

Popular democrats maintain that protest politics is necessary for greater equality in the American political system. Mass movement politics is one arena that is not biased in favor of wealthy elites. Throughout American history most significant reforms have come about because of pressure from below by mass movements. Protest politics is not only a way to vent emotions but also a way to overcome the inertia of the American system of checks and balances, to bring about much needed change. Far from threatening democracy, mass movements fulfill it by including more and more groups in the benefits of democratic citizenship. The primary threat to democracy comes not from mass movements but from elites who use repression to block change and hang on to their powers and privileges.

Sixties-Style Protest Movements: Elite Backlash

The democratic debate over the place of protest politics in American democracy became especially heated following the rapid rise of social protest movements beginning in the 1960s. Many of these movements are still active in various forms in the 1990s, including protests on issues such as the environment, AIDS, homelessness, migrant farmworkers, and community opposition to unwanted development. Beginning with the 1970s protests against busing in Boston, conservatives have adopted the tactics of the civil rights movement to opposed abortion and taxes. The Montana militia and other far-right groups have used violent tactics to support their antigovernment cause.

According to elite democrats, the spread of political protest since the 1960s threatens American democracy. Elite democrats criticize both the goals and the tactics of the protest movements. The goals, they maintain, are irrational and utopian. Business elites, for example, criticize the environmental movement for putting environmental goals above everything else. Instead of compromising, opponents charge, environmentalists demand an end to all ecological damage, even at tremendous cost to the American standard of living. According to elite democrats, environmental activists with secure white collar professional jobs demand sacrifice from lower-class workers in the name of environmental purity. Like earlier mass movements, the environmental movement is charged with being against progress, with wanting to turn the clock back to a simpler age. In general, social movements encourage every group—from blacks to women, from Native Americans to gays, from students to the disabled—to demand their "rights" with little concern for the general welfare of society.

Elite democrats also criticize the tactics developed by the protest movements beginning in the 1960s. The tactics of protest, elite democrats charge, began to be used by any group that wanted to "shake more benefits from the government money tree." In a biting essay satirizing the 1960s, entitled "Mau-Mauing the Flak Catchers," Tom Wolfe described how protest tactics had gotten out of hand:

> Going downtown to mau-mau the bureaucrats got to be routine practice in San Francisco. . . . They sat back and waited for you to come rolling in with your certified angry militants, your guaranteed frustrated ghetto youth, looking like a bunch of wild men. Then you had your test confrontation. If you were outrageous enough, if you could shake up the bureaucrats so bad that their eyes froze into iceballs and their mouths twisted up into smiles of sheer physical panic, into shit-eating grins, so to speak—then they knew you were the real goods. They knew you were the right studs to give the poverty grants and community organizing jobs to.[26]

According to an editorial in the *Wall Street Journal*, the murder of abortion doctor David Gunn in Pensacola, Florida, on March 10, 1993, by an anti-abortion protestor is evidence that confrontation politics is still out of control. Protest movements have created a new political culture, the elite business publication charged, that encourages every group to express its needs without concern for the overall welfare of society:

> What in the past had been simply illegal became "civil disobedience." If you could claim, and it was never too hard to claim, that your group was engaged in an act of civil disobedience—taking over a building, preventing a government official from speaking, bursting onto the grounds of a nuclear cooling station, destroying animal research, desecrating communion hosts—the shapers of opinion would blow right past the broken rules to seek an understanding of the "dissidents" (in the '60s and '70s) and "activists" (in the '80s and now).[27]

By encouraging people to pressure government, elite democrats maintain, protest movements weaken the authority of government at the same time that the demands on government are multiplying. Political scientist Samuel Huntington said the problem was caused by an excess of democracy, or what he termed the "democratic distemper."[28] In the 1960s and 1970s, as people made more and more demands on government to solve their problems, government responded with massive social programs, "overloading" the system."[29] The result was increasing fiscal deficits and a governmental tendency to cater to minority interests at the expense of the public interest.

At the same time that citizens demanded more from government, however, they were unwilling to sanction governmental authority and thus perversely rendered government less able to satisfy their demands. As a result, the public's trust and confidence in government declined. As Huntington warned: "The surge of participatory democracy and egalitarianism gravely weakened, where it did not demolish, the likelihood that anyone in any institution could give an order to someone else and have it promptly obeyed."[30] In short, as the politics of protest spread, society became ungovernable.

The Popular Democratic Response: Elite Distemper

Although popular democrats acknowledge excesses in social protest movements, they argue that overall the participatory upsurge of protest movements beginning in the 1960s strengthened American democracy rather than weakened it. Whenever long-suppressed issues are finally addressed by a political system, conflict is bound to result. Conflict is inevitable in a democracy—and healthy. The main threat to democracy comes not from a "democratic distemper"—ordinary people demanding their rights—but from an "elite distemper": Elites, fearful of losing their powers and privileges, react to protestors with repression and violence.[31]

Ironically, the civil rights movement, which was committed to nonviolence and democratic rights, had its civil liberties repeatedly violated by the government in an attempt to discredit it, and especially its charismatic leader, Martin Luther King, Jr. The Federal Bureau of Investigation (FBI) secretly planted newspaper articles alleging that the movement was manipulated by communists. Convincing evidence on this charge has never been made public. Under the direction of FBI Chief J. Edgar Hoover, the FBI treated King as an enemy, employing a campaign of character assassination using wiretaps of King's phone conversations. The FBI fed information on King's sex life and the plans of the civil rights movement to the Kennedy administration that helped it resist pressures for racial change.[32] The FBI sent a tape of King's extramarital encounters, threatening to make them public if he did not commit suicide.[33]

Another example of elite repression is the campaign of the government under presidents Johnson and Nixon against the anti–Vietnam War movement. Viewing opposition to the war almost as an act of treason, the government harassed antiwar leaders, violated civil liberties, and infiltrated antiwar organizations to spread dissension. In 1968, antiwar protestors organized a demonstration at the Democratic National Convention in Chicago. Denied permission to hold a rally near the convention, the protestors were infiltrated by the FBI and Chicago police **agent provocateurs** who spread disinformation and encouraged protestors to violate the law. When demonstrators tried to march on the convention, police attacked, clubbing not just demonstrators but journalists and bystanders as well. As outraged demonstrators chanted, "The whole world is watching!" news cameras recorded the ugly scene for a shocked TV audience.[34] The commission appointed to study the causes of the conflict put most of the blame on the city administration and concluded that the police had rioted.[35]

The Chicago riots polarized public opinion about the war. Some people, especially blacks and younger college-educated whites, sympathized with the demonstrators and felt that the police had used excessive force. Most Americans, however, were repulsed by what they saw as mobs of long-haired radicals, hurling curses at the police and waving communist flags.[36] Gradually, public opinion shifted against the war. Nevertheless, the war continued, frustrating antiwar protestors and shaking their faith in American democracy. In the so-called Days of Rage, antiwar activists launched indiscriminate acts of violence and destruction in American cities to "bring the war home." The cycle of repression and violence precipitated by the Vietnam War divided the country deeply, stretching the fabric of American democracy to the breaking point. According to popular democrats, the fault lay more with the elites responsible for the war and for repressing legitimate dissent than with the protesters.

In the past decade, corporate elites have devised a new way to suppress protest movements that oppose oil drilling and real estate developments such as shopping centers and airports. SLAPPs (Strategic Legal Action Against Public Participation) are lawsuits against protestors designed to chill protests by burdening them with expensive and time-consuming lawsuits. Thousands of protestors have been hit with SLAPPs charging them with harassment and violation of property rights.

The Achievements of Mass Movements

Perhaps the most serious charge against protest movements is that they don't accomplish anything; they simply stir people up and create conflict. Popular democrats maintain that protest movements have not been mere expressions of emotion; they have been the driving force behind reforms that made this country more egalitarian and democratic, including abolishing slavery, winning the vote for women and blacks, and regulating capitalism. Pursuing normal channels of electoral and interest group politics, many groups find it difficult even to get their issues onto the agenda for discussion. Protest movements succeeded in putting previously ignored issues, like equal rights for black Americans, onto the political agenda.

Measuring the effectiveness of protest movements is difficult because their effects are often hidden and indirect. As we noted in the previous chapter, new issues represented by public interest groups never would have made it onto the agenda of interest group politics without the threat of protest movements to goad the system into action. Protest movements have "ripple effects" that extend beyond the initial splash to affect the entire society. These ripple effects include changes in culture and the way we perceive issues.

In the controversy over protest politics, we often lose sight of the wide range of reforms enacted by mass movements. A few of their accomplishments follow.

1. The Civil rights movement. The civil rights movement began the long process of integrating African Americans into the democratic process. Largely as a result of changes in voting laws, the number of black elected officials in the United States increased from 1,472 in 1970 to 7,984 in 1993 [37] (see Figure 10.2). Critics often point out that U.S. race relations are still highly problematic. Consider, however, what race relations would be like if African Americans were still being denied basic civil rights like the right to vote.

FIGURE 10.2   **Black Elected Officials, 1970–1993**

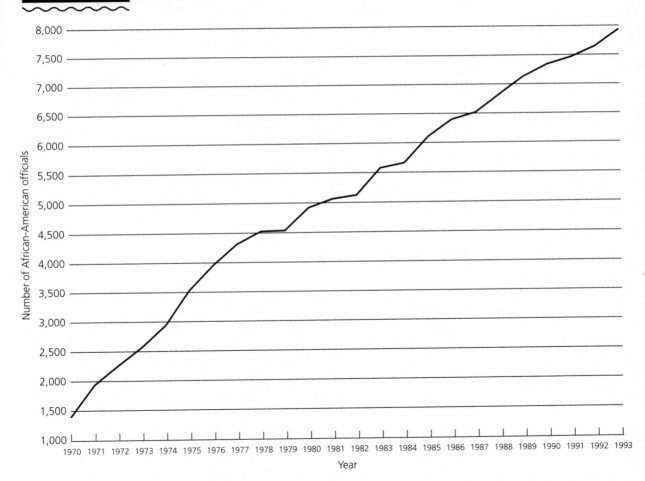

Source: *Statistical Abstract of the United States* (Washington, D.C.: U.S. Government Printing Office, various years); and *Black Elected Officials: A National Roster* (Washington, D.C.: Joint Center for Political Studies, annual).

2. The Environmental movement. As a result of the environmental movement, large construction projects must now issue environmental impact statements (EISs), giving the public a chance to comment. Substantial progress has also been made cleaning up the nation's polluted waters, with aquatic life returning to many bodies of water, and in communities across the nation recycling programs are saving energy and reducing the volume of solid waste (see the accompanying box).

3. The Antinuclear movement. The antinuclear movement succeeded in pushing the regulatory agencies to fully consider the dangers of nuclear power plants. As a result, few new nuclear power plants are constructed in the United States anymore. The chances of a Chernobyl-type disaster are low, and alternatives to nuclear energy, including solar energy and conservation, are being pursued more vigorously.

4. The Antiwar movement. Besides helping to bring the Vietnam War to a close, the antiwar movement exposed the unchecked war-making powers of the president. In 1973, Congress passed the War Powers Act, limiting the ability of future presidents to wage wars without the approval of Congress.

5. The Neighborhood organizing movement. Neighborhood protests, including lying down in front of bulldozers, have stopped highway engineers and urban renewal planners from ramming their projects through low-income and minority neighborhoods without taking into account the costs to local residents. Many cities in the country have decentralized policy-making authority to neighborhood governments, expanding the scope of democratic participation.[38]

The preceding examples illustrate that mass movements have changed American politics since the 1960s. The movement that has had the most profound effect on American politics, however, is the feminist movement, for it has influenced not only specific political practices, but also the very way we think about politics.

The Feminist Movement: The Personal Is Political

A major goal of the feminist movement was to help women enter the public worlds of work and politics that had previously been dominated by men. The movement has made progress in many fields. Interestingly, the word sex was added to Title VII of the 1964 Civil Rights Act, prohibiting discrimination in employment, not by feminists but by a southern congressman who wanted to subject the bill to ridicule.[39] Once the bill had passed, women began lobbying to ensure implementation. In 1965, President Lyndon Johnson signed Order 11246, which required that all employers holding federal contracts—covering about one-third of the workforce—agree not to discriminate in employment practices and to undertake affirmative action programs to rectify past discrimination.

The women's movement did not peak until 1970, when it began seriously influencing legislation. Whereas only ten women's rights bills passed Congress in the 1960s, in the 1970s seventy-one such bills passed.[40] One of the most

A CLOSER LOOK

The Environmental Justice Movement

According to conventional wisdom, the mass movements of the 1960s and 1970s died in the 1980s and 1990s. Although fewer mass demonstrations in Washington capture media attention, mass movement politics did not die, it simply shifted its focus. A good example is the environmental justice movement, a unique combination of the civil rights and environmental movements.

From its inception, the environmental movement was dominated by white middle class activists. In September 1982, five hundred predominantly black residents of Warren County, North Carolina, were arrested for blocking the path of trucks carrying toxic PCBs to a hazardous landfill in their community. Among those arrested was the Reverend Benjamin Chavis. Suspicious as to why North Carolina would dump its poisons in a black community, Chavis began a nationwide study, entitled *Toxic Wastes and Race in the United States*. The study concluded that "race was consistently a more prominent factor in the location of commercial hazardous waste facilities than any other factor examined." Chavis coined the term *environmental racism* to describe the phenomenon. (In April 1993 Chavis was appointed executive director of the NAACP; he was removed from the post in August 1994.)

Subsequent studies by the federal government and independent researchers have confirmed that African Americans, even after controlling for income, are exposed to more environmental hazards. According to the data, poor blacks are exposed to neurologically damaging levels of lead at almost twice the rate of the poorest whites; blacks are twice as likely as whites to live in counties with the highest levels of industrial toxins; and blacks are 50 percent more likely to die from acute exposure to hazardous materials outside the home.

A loose coalition of church, civil rights, labor, en-

vironmental, and community groups, the environmental justice movement has been led by blacks. Like the early civil rights movement, however, it has not pursued an exclusively black strategy but has articulated goals that appeal to whites as well. As Chavis expressed it: "We're not saying take the incinerators and toxic-waste dumps out of our communities and put them in white communities—we're saying they should not be in anybody's community. You can't get justice by doing an injustice on somebody else."

In fighting environmental racism, the movement has raised basic issues of popular democracy. In Kettleman City, California, residents organized themselves into "People for Clean Air and Water" in opposition to a hazardous waste incinerator. They sued the company building the incinerator, charging that it violated their civil rights by failing to provide notices about the plant in Spanish (40 percent of the residents are monolingual Spanish speakers). A California court ruled in their favor, setting a precedent that communities must be informed and participate meaningfully in environmental decisions that affect them.

Although active mostly at the local level, the environmental justice movement won an important national victory in 1994 when President Clinton signed an executive order giving federal agencies one year to address the disproportionate environmental hazards that their policies have imposed on low-income and minority populations.

Sources: "A Place at the Table: A Sierra Club Roundtable on Race, Justice, and the Environment," *Sierra* 78 (May/June 1993): 51–58, 90–91; Benjamin A. Goldman, "Polluting the Poor," *Nation,* October 5, 1992, pp. 348–49; the White House, Office of the Press Secretary, press briefing by EPA Administrator Carol Browner and Attorney General Janet Reno, February 11, 1994.

important was Title IX of the 1972 Higher Education Act, which opened collegiate sports to women.

The effect of this legislation, along with private lawsuits against sex discrimination, has been to open opportunities for women in work and politics. The numbers of women doctors and lawyers have increased significantly, as have those of mail carriers, construction workers, movie directors, and news anchors. Women's earnings have increased as well. The median salary of full-time women employees increased from 59 percent of men's salaries in 1970 to 74 percent in 1994. Moreover, women have become more active in politics. The number of women in Congress increased from eleven in 1969 (ten members of the House and one senator) to sixty-one in 1997 (fifty-two members of the House and nine senators).[41]

The effect of the women's movement has gone well beyond increasing women's rights to participate in previously male-dominated arenas. The movement has expanded the definition of politics to include relations that were previously considered cultural or even personal, especially family relations. This side of the feminist movement is captured by the slogan: "The personal is political." The effect of subjecting a range of previously unquestioned activities to political analysis has been profound. Feminism has even altered our language, with new terms such as *Ms.* and *chairperson*. Both women and men have begun to question gender roles in the family and have pressed for more male involvement in childrearing. Various forms of sexual harassment, previously tolerated, are now being challenged by women. Women have questioned the rigid ideal of beauty held over them and have demanded control over their bodies, including the right to

choose an abortion. Women have challenged the power of male doctors, especially over childbirth, and midwives have organized for more authority to deliver babies. The crimes of rape and wife beating have been exposed, and women have demanded protection from police and the courts. Thousands of battered women's shelters and rape crisis shelters have opened in communities around the country.

The politicization of male-female relations has caused a backlash in the form of a movement to defend traditional family values. In the mid-1970s, Phyllis Schlafly started a Stop ERA (Equal Rights Amendment) campaign. ERA was an amendment to the Constitution that would have outlawed discrimination on the basis of sex. Stop ERA warned that equal rights would mean that women would be drafted into the army, men would no longer support their wives, and toilets would become unisex. After passing Congress in 1972, the ERA fell three short of the required number of states to become a part of the Constitution, and opponents of feminism claimed a victory. Led by the Christian right, the anti-abortion movement applied the confrontational methods of the civil rights movement to stop abortions. Operation Rescue trained people in the practice of civil disobedience. Blocking entrances to abortion clinics, large numbers of protestors were arrested, giving valuable publicity to the movement.

The issue of family values entered the 1992 presidential campaign in an unusual way when Vice President Dan Quayle criticized an episode of the TV series *Murphy Brown* for glamorizing, he said, the decision of its lead character to have a baby out of wedlock. The Bush campaign attacked Bill Clinton as an opponent of family values. Clinton made every effort to defend traditional family values, but his positions on issues like daycare and family leave identified him more closely with feminism. Also, in contrast to the traditional image portrayed by Barbara Bush, Hillary Rodham Clinton symbolized, for many, feminist values. Not surprisingly, Clinton did better among women voters than among men in both 1992 and 1996.[42]

In short, no matter where you stand on the feminist movement, you cannot deny that it has had a profound effect on American society and politics. The movement succeeded in placing a range of new issues on the political agenda—a feat that no political party or interest group could have accomplished.

CONCLUSION: THE PLACE OF PROTEST POLITICS IN A DEMOCRACY

Protest politics provides three important benefits for American democracy. First, on those rare occasions when the proper ingredients come together, mass movements level the playing field of American politics, offering a way for minorities and the politically disenfranchised to acquire influence. Second, protest movements provide a way to overcome the inertia created by the elaborate system of checks and balances established by the Constitution. Protest politics enables political outsiders, especially those with broad political or moral concerns, to get their issues on the political agenda. Finally, participation in protest activity creates better citizens. Research shows that activists who participated in the social movements of the 1960s, when compared to nonprotesters, later participated more in politics, exhibited greater degrees of tolerance, and retained a passionate commitment to their ideals (even those who acquired fortunes).[43]

Notwithstanding the many benefits of protest politics, lines must be drawn around it. There is some truth to the elite democratic critique that to give protestors complete freedom to disrupt people's lives and to engage in civil disobedience without punishment would enable minorities to dictate terms to society. Violent protestors who injure other people should be swiftly punished. On the other hand, to outlaw nonviolent boycotts, strikes, pickets, and marches and to severely punish civil disobedience would stifle protest politics altogether. Recognizing this, the courts have given special protection to political speech designed to influence public opinion. We believe that if we err in any direction, we should err in the direction of tolerating more protest activity.

Beyond the courts, the best protection from the destructive effects of protest politics should come from the protestors themselves. Protests should never be carried out simply to vent emotions or shake people up; the purpose should be to enter into negotiations with the powers that be to institute significant reforms. As a well-known book on black political advancement in California cities, *Protest Is Not Enough*,[44] argued, the goal of protests should be to reform the basic structures of democratic governance so that they can respond to the deeply felt issues of every group in the population. Until that time, however, protest politics will be necessary to keep the participatory promise of American democracy alive.

KEY TERMS

protest politics
mass movement
relative deprivation
transactional leader

transforming leader
civil disobedience
satyagraha
agent provocateur

SUGGESTED READINGS

Saul D. Alinsky, *Reveille for Radicals*. New York: Vintage Books, 1969. A classic statement by one of the great theoreticians and practitioners of protest politics in the United States.

Samuel Huntington, *American Politics: The Promise of Disharmony*. Cambridge: Harvard University Press, 1981. A critique of mass movement politics from an elite democratic viewpoint.

Steward Burns, *Social Movements in the 1960s: Searching for Democracy*. New York: Twayne, 1990. A popular democratic reply to Huntington.

Francis Fox Piven and Richard A. Cloward, *Poor People's Movements: Why They Succeed, How They Fail*. New York: Pantheon, 1977. Argues that when poor people's movements turn into interest groups, they become coopted and cease to represent the interests of the poor.

Juan Williams, *Eyes on the Prize: America's Civil Rights Years 1954–1965*. New York: Penguin Books, 1988. A vivid account of the civil rights movement, produced in conjunction with a riveting television documentary that is available on videotape.

Congress: A Vehicle for Popular Democracy?

As the most representative branch of American national government, Congress might be expected to speak for the concerns, grievances, and interests of popular democracy. Popular democrats have often hoped that Congress would live up to its name as the "people's branch"—a branch filled with citizen-lawmakers, accessible to citizens who wished to be heard, open to citizens who wished to hear its deliberations, resistant to arbitrary action and secrecy from the executive.

Yet as we saw in Chapters 5–10, the active and assertive citizenry that might bring out Congress's popular democratic potential is undermined by many contemporary developments. With a mass media dominated by corporate interests and official sources, with parties in decline among the electorate, with "democracy for hire" for wealthy interest groups while a majority of eligible voters fails to turn out for congressional elections, the forces to which Congress responds are as likely to represent elite democracy as popular democracy.

The democratic character of Congress has, in fact, always been a matter of controversy. The Federalists designed the House to be more democratic and the Senate more elitist, but hoped that representatives in both houses would be superior men who would filter out the people's passions and promote their true welfare. The Anti-federalists, worried that legislators of this elite stripe would become arrogant and corrupt, argued for representatives who would closely resemble ordinary people. Some of the Federalists' and Anti-federalists' hopes have been realized—and some of their fears as well. Present-day Congress is a volatile mixture of elite and popular democracy.

Elite democracy, as the Federalists hoped, is reflected in a membership of well-educated political professionals whose lengthy careers produce expertise in the various fields of public policy. Elite democracy, as the Anti-federalists warned, is reflected in a membership whose continuance in office is financed by economic elites and rewarded with aristocratic "perks" of high office. Yet Congress still remains open to the pressure of popular democracy. With members of the House facing reelection every two years and senators facing the voters every six years (as a result of the 17th Amendment, adopted in 1913), representatives need to stay in close touch with their constituents if they hope to enjoy a career in Congress.

To an increasing number of Americans in the late 1980s and early 1990s, congressional elitism was more apparent than congressional populism. But could Congress be cleansed of elitist corruptions and reshaped as a vehicle for popular democratic aspirations? When the Republicans took control of Congress in 1995 after four decades in which the Democrats had always controlled the House and usually controlled the Senate, they promised just such a revolution. The leader of the Republican revolution, Newt Gingrich, claimed that he had a program to take Congress away from Washington elites and return it to the American people. Gingrich and the Republicans delivered on their pledge to bring about some remarkable changes in Congress. But did these changes result in gains for popular democracy?

This chapter examines Congress through the prism of the Republican revolution. We begin by examining Congress before the revolution. Here, we explain the enduring features of Congress but also emphasize the distinctive ways that Congress operated in the years before 1995—an era in which it was ordinarily under the control of the Democrats. Next, we turn to examine the revolution itself, the dramatic attempt in 1995 by the newly triumphant Republicans to transform how Congress works. This revolution was powerful but short lived, its limits already apparent by the end of 1995 in the showdown between the congressional Republicans and President Clinton over the budget. "After the Revolution" shows how the changes introduced by the Republicans were jeopardized by the resurgence of previous congressional habits and patterns, producing an unstable postrevolutionary Congress whose character is still unfolding. In the final section of the chapter, we examine executive-legislative relations, as Congress (before, during, and after the revolution) grapples with its sometime partner and more frequent adversary.

CONGRESS BEFORE THE REVOLUTION

Congress has some permanent elements, based in the Constitution, and some near-permanent features, such as the committee system, that go back to the nineteenth century. But much of the landscape of Congress, as unchanging as it may appear to frustrated reformers, is periodically reshaped by socioeconomic, political, and institutional tides. Above all, Congress is susceptible to partisan forces. The congressional revolution of 1995 was a *Republican* revolution. And to understand Congress before this revolution is to understand Congress during the decades when it was mostly under *Democratic* control.[1]

How did Congress work before the revolution of 1995? Four factors, in *descending order of importance*, appeared to be important:

1. Individual members and their districts

2. Committees

3. Parties

4. Leadership

As we will see, the Republican revolutionaries of 1995 attempted no less than a reversal of this order.

Individual Members and Their Districts

Most explanations of congressional behavior before 1995 placed the individual members first in importance. Individual members were extensively involved in a permanent quest for reelection that oriented them toward the interests of their own districts or states. Their voting behavior and nonlegislative activities were designed to secure individual success by pleasing the electorate back home. The decentralized structures of Congress also encouraged individualism, with members promoting their favorite policy ideas in entrepreneurial fashion. (While we use the past tense to describe activities before 1995, many of the features of Congress that we describe in this section still persist.)

Getting Elected. At the heart of congressional individualism was the electoral process. In earlier eras of American politics, the parties played a major role in recruiting congressional candidates, financing their campaigns, and mobilizing voters on their behalf. But in an era of party decline the typical congressional candidate was self-selected. Successful candidates usually shared certain characteristics: First, they were experienced public officials, having gained visibility and stature in such offices as mayors, district attorneys, or state legislators. Second, they were ambitious—running for Congress requires an ego strong enough to overcome attacks and insults and to compensate for loss of privacy, family time, and more lucrative career opportunities. Third, they were willing to work hard—a congressional race required physical and emotional energy. Amazing feats of campaigning were not uncommon. In a successful 1974 bid for a House seat in South Dakota, Larry Pressler shook an estimated 300 to 500 hands a day for eighty days.[2]

Even individuals possessing all of these qualifications faced one daunting barrier: **Incumbents** were almost always reelected in House elections, and in Senate elections challengers had only a slightly better chance. Unless there was an *open seat* (the incumbent has retired or died), the odds against the aspiring candidate winning a congressional race would scare off all but the hardiest political gamblers. In the House, incumbents regularly won over 90 percent of the contests. Sometimes, as in 1986 and 1988, incumbent reelection rates ran as high as 98 percent. Senate incumbents were often nearly as successful; in 1990, for example, 97 percent of incumbents won (only one incumbent senator was defeated). The aspiring candidate had the greatest chance to win at a moment of political turmoil, such as 1986 or 1992, when incumbents were more vulnerable.[3]

Why did incumbents do so well and challengers so poorly? Many factors favored the incumbent, including money. With years in office to stockpile campaign funds, the incumbent generally had an enormous head start in fundraising. As discussed in Chapter 8, special interests and business PACs, seeking access to legislators (and assuming that those in office are good bets to be reelected), contributed primarily to incumbents. As a result, the typical incumbent had a huge advantage over the typical challenger in campaign funds. There was a major drawback for the individual member in this system, however: the frequently demeaning and seemingly endless process of hitting up wealthy contributors for campaign dough.

Since even fundraising advantages could not guarantee reelection, members of Congress voted themselves further resources to keep their offices. Through the **franking privilege,** they sent mass mailings to constituents without having to pay postage. Newsletters, for example, publicized their accomplishments and often asked constituents to express their views on major national issues, portraying incumbents skilled in the ways of Washington yet open to the sentiments of the folks back home. Through generous travel allowances, members returned to their districts often, attending group meetings, mingling at ceremonial events, and making their faces as familiar as possible. Because of the growth of personal staff, members could deploy personal assistants to work in district offices to help constituents, a practice known as **casework.** Casework earned the gratitude of individual voters and enhanced the incumbents' reputations among their family and friends.

FIGURE 11.1

Name Recall of House Challengers and Incumbents, 1958–1994

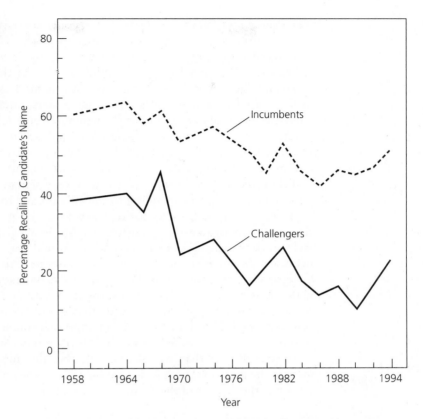

From *The Politics of Congressional Elections,* 4th ed. by Gary C. Jacobson, p. 94.
Copyright © 1997 by Addison Wesley Educational Publishers, Inc. Reprinted by permission.

All of these advantages made it more likely that on election day the voters would recall the names of incumbents while not knowing the people challenging them (see Figure 11.1). Such advantages in fact tended to scare off the kind of politically experienced challengers who might give incumbents a difficult race.

Why was incumbency somewhat less powerful in the Senate than in the House? As a more prestigious institution (and with only two positions per state), the Senate draws more prominent individuals into challenges to incumbents. Such individuals have a better chance of raising the funds to conduct a serious campaign. Statewide constituencies reduce incumbents' opportunities to mingle with them while necessitating more reliance on mass media, through which well-financed challengers can hope to match incumbents in name recognition. Finally, senators' positions on controversial national issues are more visible to constituents than those of House members, leading to greater vulnerability should the incumbent have taken unpopular stands.

The Permanent Campaign. Incumbents would not have won reelection at such impressive rates if they had not devoted so much of their time, energy, and resources to it *between* electoral campaigns. Leading scholars of congressional politics saw the ceaseless pursuit of reelection as the key to congressional behavior. They showed how legislators made themselves familiar "brand names" in their districts through visits home, newsletters, interviews on local TV, and announcements of federal projects bringing jobs and dollars to local folks. They pointed out how members of Congress took credit for creating new programs that inevitably expanded the federal bureaucracy—and then denounced the evils of bureaucracy and took credit again by assisting constituents in their problems with bureaucrats. And they revealed how representatives developed attractive personal images crafted to appeal to constituents and to win their trust.[4]

These scholars suggested that representatives devoted huge amounts of their time and thinking to wooing constituents. An aloof legislator with an aristocratic style, in the classic vein of elite democracy, would not stand a chance today. Yet because representatives had to appear to be just one of the folks did not mean that Congress had become a vehicle for popular democracy. While currying favor with voters through blatant appeals to self-interest and pleasing images, representatives did not appeal to voters' intelligence or speak to them about a larger common good. Nor did they really attempt to encourage meaningful participation in politics, as anyone knows who has filled out a survey in a congressional newsletter. Rather than stimulating a politics that increased citizens' engagement at the local level with major national issues, the politics of Congress before 1995 was the politics of the permanent campaign.

The Individualistic Legislator. Legislators who won and held onto their positions chiefly through their own extensive efforts could not be dictated to by party leaders or presidents. Individualistic motives and practices prevailed in legislative behavior prior to 1995. For example, in deciding how to cast their votes on legislation, members thought first about their own constituents: Could they explain controversial votes to the folks back home? If signals from constituents were weak or divided, members felt free to vote their own policy preferences.[5]

Reforms adopted by House Democrats in the early 1970s also fostered congressional individualism (although this was not the goal of the reforms). With power more widely dispersed under these reforms, even junior legislators became *policy entrepreneurs*, pushing their own individual policy preferences rather than uniting behind a common party program. Skilled at winning reelection, and savvy about capturing media attention, a new generation of congressmen and -women competed to see whose ideas could win majority support. Entrepreneurship was even more rampant in the Senate, where a fluid structure encouraged legislators to go their own ways.[6]

Compared to the Congress of the 1950s and 1960s, where a small corps of conservative chairs ruled in hierarchical fashion, the individualistic Congress of the 1980s and early 1990s appeared more egalitarian and open to new ideas. Yet there was a price to be paid for this individualism: It made collective action difficult. A decentralized Congress, fragmented along individual lines, frequently frustrated the popular democratic desire to see majority will at the polls translated into majority rule in the legislature.

Congressional Committees

Second in importance to individual members and their districts in Congress before the revolution was the **committee system**—the system whereby most of the work of Congress is done by smaller groups. There are several kinds of committees in the House and the Senate. *Standing committees*, the most important, are permanent bodies that perform the bulk of the work. They gather information through investigations and hearings, draft legislation (this is called the *markup*), and report it to their parent chambers for a potential vote. The majority of bills proposed by individual members of Congress never get past the standing committee that considers them; these committees thus have great negative power. *Conference committees* meet to reconcile differences when the House and Senate pass alternative versions of the same law. Composed of the members from each chamber of Congress who have been the central actors on the bill in question, they produce the final language of the law. Congress also creates *select committees* for short-term investigations and contains a few *joint committees*, with members from both houses, for the purpose of gathering information.

Because much of an individual member's legislative life is spent in committee work, obtaining an assignment to a standing committee is a matter of great importance. Party committees in each house attempt to place members in accordance with their wishes. In the Senate, with its smaller numbers, every member is assured a spot on one of the most prestigious committees. In the House, however, there is often intense competition for places on the Rules, Appropriations, Ways and Means, and Budget committees. Some legislators are less concerned about winning a spot on one of these powerful committees than on joining a committee that deals with a subject crucial to their constituents. Representatives and senators from farm states, for example, gravitate toward the agriculture committees.

Once a member has joined a committee, the usual pattern is to remain there, developing expertise and, even more important, **seniority.** Before the revolution of 1995, seniority was crucial to gaining a leadership position. Under the congressional seniority system, the member from the majority party who had the most years of continuous service on a committee became its chair. Reforms initiated by the House Democrats in the early 1970s allowed for occasional breaches in the seniority system to make committee chairs more responsive to the majority of the party, yet seniority still determined committee leadership in all but a handful of cases.

Although the committee system had long been central to the organization and functioning of Congress, its character changed considerably in recent decades. One important trend affecting the system was the growth in committee staff. As the regular workload of committees increased—and as committee leaders sought to gain media attention by initiating new and innovative legislation—large numbers of staff aides were hired. These aides came to perform many of the functions that we associate with committee leaders: developing ideas for legislation, planning hearings to promote them, lining up support for the resulting bills, and negotiating the details they contain. Legislators turned over so much of their work to their staffs that one congressional scholar, Michael Malbin, dubbed these staffs our "unelected representatives."[7]

A second trend affecting committees involved subcommittees—smaller and more specialized units of the parent committee. Although greater reliance on subcommittees, like greater reliance on staff, reflected Congress's expanded workload, the real impetus to the rise of subcommittees came during a wave of congressional reform in the early 1970s. The Democrats in the House strengthened subcommittees at the expense of committees for two reasons: to diminish the power of committee chairs and to allow newer representatives to claim a piece of the legislative "pie."

Through division of labor and specialization, the system of committees and subcommittees provided Congress with *expertise*. Faced with myriad subjects to consider, members of Congress looked for guidance to the experts on its committees and subcommittees, particularly their chairs. Committee expertise was critical in legislative-executive relations as well; without it, Congress would not stand much of a chance in conflicts with policy experts working for the president. The expertise found among long-time members of committees is important evidence for the elite democratic claim that elites bring greater expertise to the art of governance.

While the committee system divided the congressional workload and fostered expertise, it also created some of Congress's most enduring problems. One is a classic problem of elite democracy: Greater expertise is fostered, but this expertise is self-serving. Legislators often join a particular committee because they wish to serve interest groups that are important in their home districts or states. These legislators form alliances with the major interest groups and executive agencies with which their committees interact.

In the **iron triangles** that result, interest groups testify before the committee in favor of existing and potential programs that benefit them. Committee members support such programs in the bills they draft—and gain political support and campaign contributions from the interest groups. The agencies, with their missions and budgets supported by interest group and committee, implement the programs in a way that pleases the interest group and the committee (see Figure 11.2). In recent years, many iron triangles have become less rigid, with outside policy experts, public interest groups, and the press having more input. Some scholars believe that looser *issue networks* with shifting participants are now more common than the old triangular alliances. Yet the narrowly focused expertise that shapes the work of congressional committees and subcommittees remains for the most part the expertise of those whose interests are at stake.

The committee system also tended, like congressional individualism, to make collective action difficult. The more expert and powerful committee chairs were,

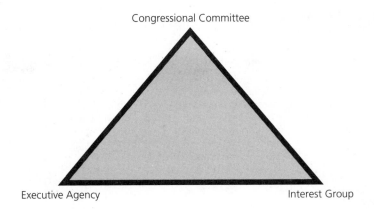

the more they tended to push their own agendas, even if these agendas conflicted with the objectives of their party and its leaders. Moreover, Congress had few mechanisms to relate or compare the bills produced by its various committees, resulting in inconsistent legislation. To take a notorious example, its agriculture committees supported subsidies for tobacco growers while its health committees supported measures to protect the public from the dangers of smoking.

By the early 1990s, committees were not as powerful as in the past. Subcommittees had taken over much of the detailed bill drafting from their parent committees. Enormous deficits had reduced the opportunities for most committees to push new programs. Committees also lost influence to party leaders, and their work was now more susceptible to alteration and rejection once it reached the floor of the House or Senate. Still, congressional scholars Steven Smith and Christopher Deering wrote in 1990, "committees remain the principal, if not always fully autonomous, players in nearly all policy decisions."[8] (For an overview of how a bill becomes a law, see Fig. 11.3.)

Parties in Congress

Third in importance in shaping congressional action before the revolution were the political parties. Independents are occasionally elected to Congress (one independent socialist, Bernard Sanders of Vermont, sits in the 105th Congress), but almost all members belong to one of the two major parties. Party is the vehicle through which the House and Senate are organized. Seats on committees and committee leadership are determined on the basis of party. Party gatherings—called *caucuses* by the House Democrats, and *conferences* by the House Republicans and both parties in the Senate—choose leaders to run their institutions and sometimes set broad policy directions as well.

Traditionally, congressional parties have been weak, at least when compared to the strong, disciplined parties found in most parliamentary democracies around the world. If legislators gain and retain their offices through their own efforts rather than through their parties, they are going to place the task of

FIGURE 11.3   How a Bill Becomes a Law

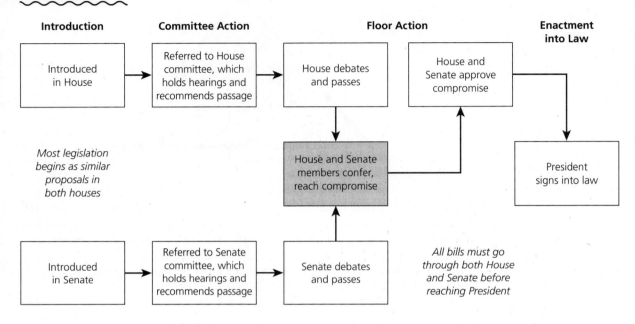

pleasing their constituents ahead of the task of cooperating with fellow partisans. Party weakness has also stemmed from the ideological diversity characteristic of America's major parties. A Republican party divided between moderates, pragmatic conservatives, and "hard right" conservatives, and a Democratic party split between northern liberals and southern conservatives, have had a hard time finding common party ground.

Beginning in the 1980s, however, the parties in Congress became more cohesive and unified. Measures of party unity in voting showed increases in both parties and both chambers. The House provided the most clear-cut example. In 1972, party unity scores (which show how frequently party members vote together) were 70 percent among House Democrats and 76 percent among House Republicans. By 1992, party unity scores were 86 percent among House Democrats and 84 percent among House Republicans. The most dramatic change came in the partisan behavior of southern Democrats, who often voted with Republicans in the past. In 1972, the party unity score for southern Democrats in the House was 44 percent; by 1992 this score had risen to 79 percent.[9]

Why did partisan unity increase if parties had traditionally been weak and were on the decline among the electorate? Several factors came together to spark a resurgence of parties in Congress. Among the Democrats, a key factor was the shrinking ideological difference between northern and southern members. Thanks to the Voting Rights Act of 1965, southern Democrats gained large numbers of African-American supporters while losing many conservatives to the

Republicans; as their electoral base came to resemble that of northern Democrats, so did their voting behavior. Among the Republicans, the electoral successes of Ronald Reagan made the party more conservative; ideological diversity within the party waned. President Reagan's effect on partisanship within Congress was not restricted to his own party. Pursuing a strong conservative legislative agenda, often in an aggressive manner, Reagan forced the Democrats to pull together as a more united opposition party. The lines of partisan conflict sharpened by Reagan continued in Congress during the Bush and Clinton presidencies.

The two legislative parties represent distinct coalitions of ideology and interests, and to understand Congress before the revolution it is particularly necessary to understand the ideology and interests represented by the majority party, the Democrats. Reflecting their heritage as the party of Franklin Roosevelt's New Deal and Lyndon Johnson's Great Society, and their electoral strongholds in the urban centers of the Northeast and Midwest, the Democratic party that controlled Congress for most of the last six decades was a party of government activism. It retained a predominantly liberal character even as the electorate became more ideologically conservative during the Reagan era.[10] Yet its liberal policy priorities in such areas as education, the environment, and Medicare retained substantial majority support.

As a coalition of interests, congressional Democrats were remarkably diverse. Despite their liberal ideology, they did not pose much of a threat to the most powerful and wealthy forces in American politics. In crafting programs for the economy as a whole, Democratic leaders of such committees as Appropriations and Ways and Means were mindful of "the privileged position of business" (see Chapter 4) and generally supported corporate priorities.[11] In crafting programs for more specific sectors of the economy, Democratic chairs and members of the other committees were influenced by the flow of contributions from business and trade association PACs that aided their reelection. Yet the forces that kept the congressional Democrats a party representative of elite democracy were balanced by more popular democratic forces. Minority groups, women's groups, environmentalists, labor unions, senior citizens, and government employees looked primarily to congressional Democrats for representation of their interests and concerns. Further, most minority and female members of Congress were Democrats. While these groups were often disappointed in the majority party's performance, they did not doubt that they would be worse off should the Republicans become the new congressional majority. (The role that women play in Congress is the subject of the accompanying box.)

Given the diversity of its coalition, the Democratic majority in Congress was often divided. It was easier to unite in opposition to a Republican president than in support for a Democratic one (witness the case of Clinton's failed health care reform in 1994). The Democrats' lack of cohesion was both cause and effect of the individualism and committee decentralization that characterized Congress before the revolution. Often ineffective in taking action to address the nation's problems, yet complacent after many decades in control of Congress, the

MAKING A DIFFERENCE

Women in Congress

Although Congress is supposed to be the "people's branch," it has resembled a men's club that excludes one-half of the people. That women become U.S. representatives and senators in growing numbers is a major concern for popular democrats. Female representatives can provide "substantive representation" for women's interests: They can bring women's distinct experiences and concerns to the legislature and promote measures that foster equality between the sexes. They also function as symbolic representatives, offering American women role models for political careers and assuring them of the democratic legitimacy of the political process.

Congress did not have any female members until 1917, when Jeannette Rankin of Montana entered the House, and the numbers of women in Congress have grown slowly since then. "The Year of the Woman"—1992—did produce dramatic gains, as the number of women in the House leaped from twenty-eight to forty-seven and the number of women in the Senate tripled from two to six. But the gains for women have been much smaller in subsequent elections. In the 105th Congress (1997–98), women hold fifty-one House seats (11.2 percent of the total) and 9 Senate seats. Research on women's membership in the legislatures of twenty-five democracies around the globe shows that even with recent improvements the U.S. still ranks in the bottom half.

Discrimination against female candidates appears, according to research by political scientists, to be a thing of the past. Voters no longer prefer male to female candidates; there may even be a small bias in favor of women as more caring and honest. The parties are eager to put forward female candidates. And women seem to do as well as men in raising money for congressional races. What has limited gains for women has not been discrimination but incumbency advantages: With so few male incumbents susceptible to defeat, opportunities for women to replace them have been scarce.

The influence of women in Congress has been limited by more than just the small size of the female contingent. On the average, women enter

majority Democrats made a fat target for public discontent in the 1990s, provided that discontent could be mobilized by a shrewd and skillful Republican leadership.

Congressional Leadership

Fourth—and least powerful—among the factors shaping congressional behavior before the revolution was leadership. Among the leadership positions in Congress, only one—**Speaker of the House of Representatives**—is specifically mentioned in the U.S. Constitution. The Speaker of the House is the most visible and prestigious congressional leader (and stands second, after the vice president, in the line of presidential succession). Technically chosen by

Congress at a later age (because of child-rearing) and have shorter careers than men; few gain the seniority that many male legislators achieve. Only a handful of women have thus become committee chairs. Regardless of whether Democrats or Republicans have been in control, the top leadership of the House and Senate has always been all male. (In recent years, both parties have provided slots for women in the second tier of legislative leadership.)

Another factor affecting the influence of women in Congress has been diversity among female representatives. Before the Republican revolution of 1994, most Republican women joined with Democratic women in a Congressional Caucus for Women's Issues. But Newt Gingrich's team included a new kind of female representative whose conservative ideology made antifeminism one of its cardinal principles. In 1995, six of the seven freshman Republican women refused to join the caucus.

Despite their limited numbers, distance from positions of power, and ideological divisions, women have made a difference in shaping the agenda of Congress. Recognizing their responsibilities as spokespersons for women in general, female legislators have taken the lead in promoting women's rights and fighting for policies of special impor-

tance to children and families. They have placed on the legislative agenda such issues as pay equity, child care, women's health, and domestic violence.

With growing numbers women have enjoyed greater successes on these issues. In the five Congresses preceding the "Year of the Woman," Congress passed an average of four bills a year on women's issues; in 1993, that number jumped to thirty! Research on state legislatures—some of which have twice as many women as does Congress—suggests that when the number of female representatives grows large enough to reach a critical mass, male representatives become more supportive of women's issues. The ability of the U.S. Congress to represent all of the people will increase substantially when women's numbers in Congress increase substantially.

Sources: Barbara C. Burrell, *A Woman's Place Is in the House: Campaigning for Congress in the Feminist Era* (Ann Arbor: University of Michigan Press, 1994); Karen Foerstel and Herbert N. Foerstel, *Climbing the Hill: Gender Conflict in Congress* (Westport, Conn.: Praeger, 1996); Sue Thomas, *How Women Legislate* (New York: Oxford University Press, 1994).

the whole House but in practice selected by a vote of the majority party in that chamber, the Speaker exercises a combination of procedural, policy, and partisan leadership.

The Speaker is the top figure in a complex leadership structure in the House. Beneath the Speaker, on the majority party side, is the **majority leader.** While the Speaker presides over the House, the majority leader runs party operations on the floor. Along with the Speaker, the majority leader shapes the legislative schedule, confers with members of the party, consults with the president (when he or she is from the same party), and promotes a party perspective through the national media. Underneath the majority leader are *whips*, who assist the party's top leaders by gathering information and "counting noses" on forthcoming votes, and by encouraging partisan loyalty through persuasion and personal attention. The minority party has a similar leadership structure. The **minority leader** runs party operations on the floor of the House, and is also assisted by an elaborate whip system.

There is no equivalent figure to the Speaker in the Senate. Constitutionally, the vice president presides over the Senate, and when he or she is absent the presiding officer is the *president pro tempore*—usually the most senior senator from the majority party. The most important leaders in the Senate are the majority and minority leaders, assisted by their whips. These Senate leaders perform many of the same functions as their House counterparts.

Before the revolution, congressional leaders were more notable for their weakness than for their strength. Because members won their seats on their own, their "bosses" were their constituents and not their party leaders. Further, congressional leaders did not have a large number of favors to bestow on legislators who provided them support or punishments to exact on legislators who frustrated their objectives. Unable to issue orders, congressional leaders had to be talented at persuasion—at finding the right mix of political and ideological arguments to craft a majority for their party's positions. Coalition builders rather than commanders, they might occasionally twist arms to achieve results but relied mostly on the arts of negotiation, conciliation, and compromise.

Beginning in the 1970s, congressional reformers began to strengthen the hand of the leadership in the hope of fostering more effective collective action. In the House, the Speaker was given several new powers. For example, the Speaker was now able to name the majority members of the Rules Committee, whose decisions determine how much time is devoted to floor debate of a bill and what kinds of amendments can be offered on the floor. Under an *open rule*, any germane, or relevant, amendment can be offered. Under a *closed rule*, no amendments can be introduced. Through their domination of the Rules Committee, Speakers could now restrict amendments offered by the minority party or dissidents from the majority party when priority party legislation faced floor action.[12]

Senate leaders faced a more difficult challenge in pushing party priorities. The Senate, less than one quarter the size of the House, offers greater freedom of action to individual members. Unlike the House, amendments to a Senate bill do not have to be germane to its subject. The ability of individual senators to attach *riders* (unrelated provisions) to bills allows them to play complex strategic games on the floor. For example, a senator who favors a measure that has been bottled up in committee can attach it as an amendment to an unrelated bill; a senator opposed to a bill may load it with amendments to draw a presidential veto.

The minority party in the Senate also has weapons to defeat the majority party leadership that are absent in the House. Senators are unrestricted in the time they can talk about a bill. Senate debate can go on as long as senators insist. The practice of trying to talk a bill to death is known as the **filibuster.** Filibusters were most commonly employed by southern opponents of civil rights legislation in the 1950s and 1960s. But in recent decades, filibusters have been often used by the minority party to block many different kinds of legislation. For example, a Republican filibuster killed President Clinton's economic stimulus program in

1993. The Senate does have a procedure, known as **cloture,** whereby debate can be terminated by a vote of three-fifths of the membership. Yet such a large majority is hard to obtain.

Along with differences in official powers between House and Senate leaders there were differences in leadership styles and abilities. Despite their relatively weak institutional position, the top Senate leaders of the late 1980s and early 1990s—George Mitchell for the Democrats and Robert Dole for the Republicans—were both effective coalition builders. Variability was greater in the House. Jim Wright, Democratic Speaker from 1987 to 1989, effectively advanced a partisan legislative agenda. Yet he was forced out of office (and out of Congress) by ethics violations, with the charge against him led by the emerging leader of the House Republicans, Newt Gingrich. Wright's successor in the speakership, Thomas Foley (1989–1994), was a more conciliatory—and a weaker—Speaker. Under Foley's loose reign, the tendency of the House Democrats to splinter once more became evident.

CONGRESS DURING THE REVOLUTION

Public anger toward Congress rose sharply during the half-decade before the 1994 elections. Congress was widely blamed for its failure to address the nation's problems, especially the enormous budget deficits. Citizens were irate about the controversies and scandals—especially sizable pay raises and widespread check bouncing in the House bank affair—that displayed members of Congress as self-serving and self-perpetuating Washington insiders. The public even seemed mad about standard congressional processes, such as haggling and compromising, which struck many as the worst of politics-as-usual.[13]

In 1994, public anger was focused entirely on the Democrats, and their majorities in the House and Senate were swept away by an electoral tidal wave. The GOP takeover culminated a decade of partisan strategizing and guerrilla actions by the new Republican hero, Newt Gingrich. Having seized majority control, Gingrich and his followers aspired to a revolution in the House—and through this a conservative transformation of American society.

As congressional scholars C. Lawrence Evans and Walter J. Oleszek write, "By the end of 1995 (the first session of the GOP-controlled 104th Congress), close observers agreed that the House, if not the Senate, was a remarkably different body compared to the years of Democratic dominance."[14] The difference in the House resulted from a striking reversal in the order of importance for the factors shaping congressional action: The last (leadership) had become first, and the first (individualism) had become last.

Leadership

Speaker Newt Gingrich was at the center of events in 1995. Everything about Gingrich appeared huge: his political skill, his ambition to transform America into a conservative country, his ego. He became the most powerful speaker since the turn of the century.[15]

At the start of the 104th Congress, Gingrich took control of the House largely into his own hands. He chose all of the committee chairs, in several cases by-passing senior members in favor of his own loyalists. He also controlled committee assignments and cemented his hold over newly elected Republicans by giving many of them slots on the most prestigious House committees. Republican rules changes reenforced Gingrich's personal assertions of prerogative. Committee chairs were subjected to a three-term limit on tenure, further reducing their independence. Subcommittees were subjected to their parent committees in a reversal of what the Democrats had done two decades earlier, adding to the centralization of power.

Gingrich held remarkable power, but knowing he could not run the House all by himself he assembled a leadership team, the Speaker's Advisory Group (SAG) (see Table 11-1). Meeting frequently, Gingrich and his SAG lieutenants defined the party's legislative direction and plotted its strategic maneuvers. The speaker entrusted day-to-day operations in the House to his principal lieutenant, majority leader Richard Armey.

Having centralized power in the House leadership, Gingrich and his lieutenants were able to focus the Republican agenda in a way that the Democrats had been unable to do when they ran Congress. The "Contract with America," the electoral platform that the Republicans had adopted for the 1994 elections, supplied the initial unifying agenda. Most Republicans in the House backed the Contract as an electoral pledge and vehicle for party success, but when a few balked at Gingrich's frantic "100 days" timetable for enacting it, the Speaker was prepared to muscle them. Informed by one chair that his committee could not meet the leadership's deadline, Gingrich responded that if it couldn't speed up its work he would find a new chair.[16] Even after work on the Contract was completed and the Republicans moved on to controversial decisions on the budget, policy and political direction continued to come from SAG.

The extraordinary degree of Republican unity in 1995 did not come about automatically. Gingrich displayed formidable skills as a negotiator and consensus builder within his party. Sometimes he leaned in the direction of the dominant

TABLE 11.1		
The Speaker's Advisory Group: Leaders of the Republican Revolution in Congress, 1995	Speaker	Newt Gingrich
	Majority Leader	Richard Armey
	Majority Whip	Thomas DeLay
	Chief Deputy Whip	Dennis Hastert
	Conference Chairman	John Boehner
	House Republican Campaign Committee Chairman	William Paxon

conservative faction; at other times he offered concessions to the much smaller bloc of moderates, whose defections on key votes could wipe out the Republicans' narrow majority in the House. In his leadership style, Gingrich was unique among House speakers. Toward fellow Republicans Gingrich often acted as the gentle "New Age" manager, preaching a mantra of "listen, learn, help, lead." Toward the Democrats, he imitated the military leaders he admired and regarded partisan legislative contests as a war for power.[17]

To advance his vision of conservative change, Gingrich aimed not only to dominate the House but to supplant the president as the nation's premier agenda setter.[18] The Speaker went well beyond his predecessors in seeking the spotlight, televising his daily conferences with the press, delivering a nationally televised address to dramatize the passage of the Contract with America, orchestrating the Republican campaign to sell the public on the party's radical budget-balancing designs. Yet in his quest for a speaker's "bully pulpit" to overshadow the president's one, Gingrich revealed his greatest weakness as a leader: The more he spoke, the more unpopular he and his agenda became. Polls showed Gingrich to be the least-liked political figure in the nation, viewed by a majority of Americans as abrasive, authoritarian, and mean spirited.[19]

While Gingrich was raising House leadership to new heights of power, Republican leadership in the Senate faced the same limitations as before. The Republican majority leader, Robert Dole, had too narrow a legislative majority (53–47) to overcome Democratic filibusters. Senate individualism also hampered Dole; while Republican moderates were few in number, the prospect that they would side with the Democrats limited Dole's capacity to pass the torrent of conservative legislation gushing out of Gingrich's House. Ironically, the most successful Senate leader during the revolution was probably the new minority leader, Thomas Daschle. After a troubled start, Daschle became effective at forging a unified Democratic opposition, turning the Senate into a major stumbling block for the plans of Gingrich and his followers.[20]

Party

Newt Gingrich's success as a revolutionary leader of the House depended in the end on an unusual experiment in party government. Under the Democrats, individualism and committee autonomy tended to be stronger than party loyalty and unity; the Republicans promised a new era of congressional government in which the party would take precedence over the committee and the individual.

It was a testament not only to the leadership skills of Gingrich and SAG but to the ideological and electoral appeal of a strong and disciplined party that House Republicans did indeed reach unprecedented levels of party unity during the revolution of 1995. Recall the high levels of party unity scores in 1992: 86 percent for House Democrats and 84 percent for House Republicans. In 1995, House Republicans easily topped these figures with a party unity score of 93 percent.[21] During the first half of the dramatic "100 days," when the easier parts of the Contract with America roared through the House, Republican support was *unanimous* in over half of the votes taken. (Party unity scores also rose impressively for Senate Republicans in 1995.)

In this experiment in party government, the Republican Conference, the body in which all House Republicans came together, took on added importance. The Republican Conference provided Speaker Gingrich and his lieutenants with a sounding board for the leadership's vision. Yet the Conference also provided a forum for sporadic party resistance to the Speaker. Concerned that Gingrich might become *too* powerful, incoming Republican freshmen won his agreement to an eight-year term limit for the Speaker. A year later, in December 1995, the conservative majority in the Conference overrode Gingrich's efforts at compromise with President Clinton over the budget and forced a shutdown of the federal government. Party was second in importance to leadership during the revolution, but it was not always leadership's docile tool.

The Republicans had greater luck with party government than the Democrats because they were a more ideologically cohesive party. Republican moderates in Congress were a dwindling band, drawn mostly from the Northeast; conservatives dominated the party's legislative ranks everywhere else. Newt Gingrich's conservative philosophy—dismantle the federal regulatory and welfare state, turn authority back to state governments and private markets—was widely shared among the Republican majority in the House and also among Senate Republicans (several newly elected senators had been Gingrich allies in the House). The fervor and energy that drove the revolution came largely from conservative ideology, especially among the seventy-three first-term Republicans swept into the House in the elections of 1994.

Republican campaigners in 1994 had capitalized on middle class and working class anger at President Clinton and the congressional Democrats. But the core of their party's active constituency were religious conservatives and economic elites. Once the less controversial elements of the Contract with America were out of the way, core Republican groups came to the fore. As a *Time* story related, "To an extent unusual even for parasitic Washington, the House GOP leadership has attached its fortunes to private lobbyists, and is relying on their far-flung influence to pass its agenda."[22] Lobbyists representing business associations as well as conservative groups met every Thursday during the "100 days" with Congressman John Boehner, chair of the House Republican Conference, to coordinate strategy for passing the Contract.

Lending their muscle to the House Republicans, business lobbyists in turn gained political authority. Republican leaders did not even bother to conceal the extent to which industry lobbyists were actually writing antiregulatory legislation on the environment. Bills passed by the House were designed to gut enforcement of important provisions in the Clean Air, Clean Water, and Endangered Species Acts. A similar process unfolded in the area of "tort reform" (torts are civil law suits claiming wrongful actions). A bill passed by the House set a cap on punitive damages in civil suits and, even more important, required that losing parties in these suits pay the legal fees of the winners. The latter provision would deter average citizens injured by products from suing the manufacturers, tilting

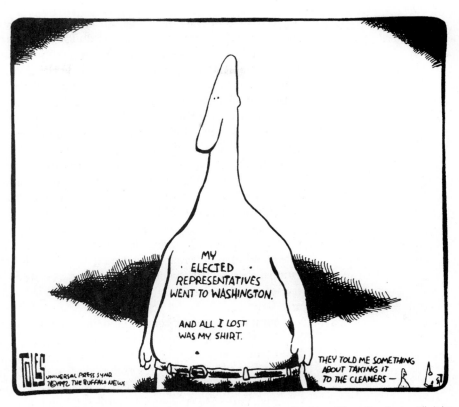

MY ELECTED REPRESENTATIVES WENT TO WASHINGTON.

AND ALL I LOST WAS MY SHIRT.

THEY TOLD ME SOMETHING ABOUT TAKING IT TO THE CLEANERS —

TOLES

UNIVERSAL PRESS SYND
7/2/1992 THE BUFFALO NEWS

the balance of power in the legal system in favor of corporations at the expense of consumers.

When critics seized upon the role of lobbyists to charge that revolutionary Republicans were just as guilty of selling out to special interests as the status quo Democrats had been, House Republican Whip Tom DeLay replied: "Our pork is freedom. Their pork is projects."[23] But many Americans could not detect a difference. The ties of the House Republicans to elite democratic interests undercut the image of a popular democratic upheaval to purify Washington. As polls showed declining support for Republicans in Congress (and increasing support for President Clinton and the Democrats), it was apparent that the ideology and interests that had brought the Republicans to power commanded less public support than their radical program required.

Committees

The power that had been gained in the Republican revolution in the House by the leadership and the party was in large part power taken away from the committees and their chairs. We have already seen how the Speaker ignored the seniority system and appointed chairs himself while also controlling key committee assignments, and how the Republican Conference adopted term limits for chairs and weakened subcommittees. In addition, House Republicans abolished three committees—District of Columbia, Merchant Marine and Fisheries, and Post Office and Civil Service—all of which primarily served Democratic constituencies. And committee staffs were slashed by one-third (since the Democrats had lost their majority status, it was their staffers who were fired).

Although the trend toward diminished importance for committees had begun with reforms adopted by the Democrats in the 1970s, the Republicans carried it much further. Consider the case of health care policy. When President Clinton's proposed health care reform was introduced in the House in 1993, Speaker Foley referred the legislation to ten different committees. By contrast, when the Republicans decided on large-scale reductions in Medicare spending in 1995, Speaker Gingrich took control of this controversial proposal. He devised the Republican approach himself with the help of ad hoc study groups he had established and then personally negotiated revisions with the most influential interest groups, such as the American Medical Association. The committees that had shaped health policy under the Democrats played only a small role on Medicare in 1995.[24]

Committees were circumvented in other ways too during the revolution. Speaker Gingrich set up *task forces* to develop priority legislation. Task forces offered him several advantages over committees: They could be stacked with supporters of the leadership, they excluded members of the minority party, and they could operate behind closed doors.[25] Even when committees did draw up bills, Gingrich and SAG frequently intervened to overrule them and alter the legislation before floor consideration.

Committee independence was also under assault in the Senate, where the conservative majority in the Republican Conference became frustrated by the persisting power of moderate chairs, such as Mark Hatfield of Oregon (Appropriations), Robert Packwood of Oregon (Finance), and John Chafee of Rhode Island (Environment and Public Works). Six months after House Republicans had voted to weaken committee chairs, Senate Republicans followed suit, establishing a six-year limit for committee chairs and ranking minority members. Republican members of a committee were given the power to select the chair by secret ballot, to be followed by another secret ballot in the party conference. These reforms made committee chairs more answerable to the party and its leaders.

Individual Members

Revolution in the House required a new type of legislator. If the individualistic pursuit of reelection defined most members during the era of Democratic dominance, the collective pursuit of a partisan and ideological agenda was supposed to define Republicans intent on revolution. The party unity scores achieved in 1995 suggested that members *were* acting differently, *were* voting their party and ideology more than their districts.

The typical legislator in the Democratic era had been a self-selected political professional. But many of the new Republican members of the House had been recruited to run, especially by Newt Gingrich's GOPAC. While they still had to raise large sums of money to have a chance at victory, more of this money now came from party sources. The huge class of Republican freshmen in 1995 particularly owed their seats to Gingrich, not only because he had trained and assisted many of them but because his strategy of nationalizing congressional elections had swept them into office in 1994.

Reflecting the antipolitician mood in the country, several of the new Republican members of the House proudly proclaimed that they had no prior political experience. They were coming to Congress, they announced, not to join the corrupt "Washington system" but to purge it.[26] The Senate too had its share of new antipoliticians, such as Bill Frist of Tennessee, a former surgeon.

Self-proclaimed political amateurs, the new Republican members professed to scorn congressional careerism. They were enthusiastic backers of a constitutional amendment to limit congressional terms—an amendment that would have guaranteed that their stay in Washington would be short. But their enthusiasm was not shared by more senior Republican legislators, and the term limits amendment became the only item in the Contract with America that failed to pass in the House.

The new class of Republican legislators normally followed the leadership and occasionally bucked it, but in either instance they acted as a group. The individual policy entrepreneurship that characterized the Democrats in power was largely absent during the Republican revolution. Resources for entrepreneurial behavior had been diminished with the reduction in committee staffs and the reining in of subcommittees. But new members had also been socialized differently, to place party unity over individualistic enterprise.[27]

CONGRESS AFTER THE REVOLUTION

At the end of 1995, when congressional Republicans failed to pressure President Clinton into accepting their seven-year plan for balancing the budget and received the bulk of the blame from the public for shutting down the government during the budget showdown, their revolution was stymied. The election results of 1996, continuing Republican control of Congress (but with an even narrower margin in the House) while returning Bill Clinton to the White House, confirmed the basic contours of a postrevolution landscape. The new Republican order in Congress still looked different than the old Democratic one. Yet Republican leadership and party unity were losing some of their force, while committee influence and the reelection drive of individual members were reasserting themselves.

Gingrich and his loyal followers had made two fundamental errors. First, they had read too much into the election results: A revolution in national policy needed greater public backing than the 20 percent of the eligible electorate who had voted Republican in 1994. Second, in disregard of the constitutional system of checks and balances they had tried to dominate the government from the House of Representatives; the Senate and especially the President blocked the fulfillment of the Speaker's agenda.

The biggest loser in the deflation of the revolution was Speaker Gingrich. Even before the defeat over the budget, some of the Speaker's first-term backers were beginning to object to the expectation that they simply take orders from SAG. Gingrich's failure in the budget showdown took much of the shine off his leadership. Especially harmful to him was the ridicule that followed his declaration that he had presented harsher budget terms to Clinton because the president had snubbed him on a plane trip to Israel for the funeral of Prime Minister Itzhak Rabin. The decline of the Speaker's power accelerated at the end of 1996, when he admitted to ethics violations—using tax-exempt money for partisan purposes and failing to provide the House Ethics Committee with accurate information about the transactions.

Gingrich was narrowly reelected Speaker in January 1997, with nine Republicans refusing to vote for him. Soon after, the House reprimanded him and ordered him to pay a $300,000 fine. As the *New York Times* commented on his reelection: "He neither looked nor sounded like the self-assured revolutionary of old, and few who watched him today believe that he will ever again wield the kind of power that he once did."[28] By the middle of 1997, Gingrich's leadership was under fire from many of his former loyalists, and tensions between the Speaker and Majority Leader Armey were increasingly evident.[29]

Jim Borgman
The Cincinnati Enquirer
King Features Syndicate

After the collapse of the revolution's momentum, the Republicans in Congress were as subdued as the Speaker. In 1996, it was hard to find congressional Republicans who were still orating about a revolution or boasting of fulfilling the Contract with America. Facing the loss of their majority in the November elections if they continued futilely to press their conservative agenda against the president's veto power, most House Republicans, overcoming protests from hardline holdouts, prudently retreated. Shifting, as a *Congressional Quarterly* headline observed, "From Revolution to Realism," they reached agreement with the Senate and the president on a conservative welfare reform, a moderate health insurance package, and a liberal minimum wage increase.[30] The party agenda was subordinated to a party record of accomplishment upon which members could successfully run for reelection.

As the centripetal forces of leadership and party ideology slackened, the centrifugal forces of committee decentralization and individualism regained some of their old strength. Gingrich's decline in power meant renewed influence for the committee chairs, especially on the crucial money panels like Ways and Means and Appropriations. Individual members who had placed their ideology over their careers reconsidered the relationship between the two. Pragmatism and compromise, two swear words during the revolution, suddenly looked appealing, if only to survive for the long revolutionary haul.[31] In the campaign of 1996, a number of the Republican legislators whom Newt Gingrich had brought to office two years earlier sought reelection by distancing themselves from the Speaker.

Ironically, while the elections of 1996 pushed the House Republicans toward greater moderation, the opposite ideological trend was detectable in the Senate. During the revolution, the Senate's cautious and deliberate pace, along with the influence of Republican moderates and the Democrats' greater institutional clout, had stalled the rush of conservative legislation emanating from the House. But when Robert Dole resigned from the Senate during his 1996 presidential bid, he was replaced by a more conservative majority leader, Trent Lott of Mississippi. In the 1996 Senate elections, in which the GOP increased its majority by two, Republican conservatives replaced moderates from both parties. With Gingrich weaker and the House Republican majority razor thin, Republican conservatism is now as likely to be championed by the Senate as by the House.

How much has the Republicans' revolution changed Congress in the end? While the unusual degree of centralization and party unity that characterized House Republicans in 1995 was bound to be eroded by the reemerging forces of committee influence and membership interests, the postrevolutionary Congress is likely to remain significantly more centralized and partisan than before. Even the Democrats seem to have awakened to the fact that a strengthening of leadership and party cohesion produces a more effective Congress.[32] On the other hand, the Republicans' sweeping experiment in party government is not likely to be repeated in the House, at least not in the immediate future. Their margin of control is too narrow, their policy disagreements are too serious, and their doubts about their leader are too deep to replay the revolution.[33]

CONGRESS AND THE EXECUTIVE

The Constitution placed Congress first among the three branches of the federal government, devoting Article 1 to the selection, organization, and powers of the legislature. During the nineteenth century, except for brief periods under strong presidents, Congress was the preeminent branch. But the twentieth century has witnessed the rise of "presidential government," with the executive seizing the lead and Congress following.

Although the overall balance of power has shifted from Capitol Hill to the White House, the dynamic of power between the two branches never remains static. From the New Deal of Franklin Roosevelt to the Great Society of Lyndon Johnson, Congress acquiesced in the rise of a strong presidency, particularly in foreign and defense policy. But the Vietnam War prodded Congress to challenge the presidency on international affairs and war making. The sweeping power plays of President Nixon compelled Congress to reassert itself in budget making and domestic policy as well. During the "divided government" of the 1980s and early 1990s, with the Republicans entrenched in the White House and the Democrats controlling Congress, warfare between the two branches was frequent.[34] It grew even more intense when partisan control of the branches was reversed after 1994.

Budgetary Politics

One of the primary elements in the rise of presidential government during the middle decades of the twentieth century was presidential capture of a preponderant share of the power of the purse. A legislature dominated by scattered committee power could not produce a coherent budget; a unitary executive, aided by a Bureau of the Budget (renamed the Office of Management and Budget in 1970), could. Congress found itself reduced to snipping budgets framed by the executive. Two developments in the early 1970s, however, propelled Congress to recapture some budgetary power. First, a fragmented congressional budgetary process generated excessive spending. Second (and probably more important), President Nixon usurped Congress's budgetary authority so aggressively that he forced legislators to develop new defensive weapons.

The vehicle Congress chose to reassert its budget-making authority was the **Budget and Impoundment Control Act of 1974.** This act established new budget committees in the House and Senate. It also created a Congressional Budget Office (CBO), a staff of budgetary and economic experts that provided members with information and analysis comparable to those supplied to the president by the Office of Management and Budget. With the assistance of the CBO, House and Senate budget committees were to draft two concurrent budget resolutions. The first, due in May each year, was to set targets for federal spending, thereby constraining other, authorizing committees. The second resolution, due in September, was to set final, binding budgetary totals for Congress. Through this new process, Congress hoped to subject the budget to a more coherent review and establish its own priorities against those of the president.

The new budget process did increase congressional power, but it also intensified conflict between Congress and the executive. It was the presidency of Ronald Reagan that turned the budget into the annual battlefield of national politics. In 1981, Reagan dominated Congress, achieving massive tax cuts and increases in defense spending. He did not, however, persuade Congress to cut domestic spending as deeply as he wished. The result was mounting federal deficits that loomed over all congressional deliberations.[35]

Unable to bring these deficits under control, Congress resorted to a desperate measure in 1985. The Gramm-Rudman-Hollings bill, named for its Senate sponsors, sought to establish an automatic mechanism for eliminating the deficit. The bill set target figures under which the deficit would decline each year until 1993, when it was supposed to disappear. If Congress and the president could not agree on a budget that hit these figures, the executive would have to reach them through across-the-board spending cuts divided evenly between defense and domestic programs. But the Gramm-Rudman-Hollings approach was a failure: Congress and the president found ways to get around it, and federal deficits grew even larger by the early 1990s.

President Clinton's 1993 deficit reduction plan finally began to produce a significant improvement in the budgetary situation. But the House Republicans' 1994 Contract with America went much further than Clinton, pledging to enact a constitutional amendment that would require a balanced budget. Although this amendment easily passed the House early in 1995, it fell short by one vote in the Senate. Republicans tried again early in 1997—and again fell a vote short in the Senate.

With the defeat of the amendment, Republican leaders in both houses devised a seven-year plan to bring the budget into balance by 2002. During the budget showdown at the end of 1995, President Clinton agreed to the seven-year concept, but his spending and taxing priorities collided with those of the Republicans.[36] No balanced budget plan was enacted in the ensuing stalemate, but both parties now were committed to the idea. President Clinton finally reached a compromise with congressional Republicans on a balanced budget in May 1997.

Foreign Policy

Foreign policy has been the preferred field of action for most presidents in the twentieth century. Presidents have substantial authority and resources in this policy arena. Preference, authority, and resources have sometimes led presidents and their supporters to claim foreign policy as almost exclusively executive in character. Yet the Constitution bestows authority and entrusts responsibility to Congress as well as the executive in shaping the relationship of the United States to the rest of the world. Through its appropriations authority, Congress funds American activities abroad. It has the sole power to declare war, and is responsible for raising and maintaining military forces. The power "to regulate commerce with foreign nations" draws it into matters of international trade. Moreover, the Senate has the responsibility to deliberate on treaties with other countries.

Despite these constitutional powers, Congress accepted presidential dominance over foreign policy from World War II to the Vietnam War, the era of the "Cold War consensus." It was the disaster of Vietnam—a presidential war—that shook Congress out of its compliant stance. Starting in the early 1970s, Congress began to reassert its role in foreign policy issues: war making, covert actions by the CIA, arms sales to foreign nations, and trade strategy. When it engaged in battles with the White House, the presidency still usually enjoyed the upper hand. Yet Congress won some notable victories—for example, instituting economic sanctions, over a veto by President Reagan, against the apartheid government of South Africa in 1986.

Unhappy with this renewed assertiveness, critics charge that Congress should not interfere with presidential conduct of foreign policy. Congress, they allege, moves too slowly, acts too indecisively, deliberates in too much ignorance, and is too obsessed with reelection pressures to handle the dilemmas of diplomacy and war. But its inadequacies in foreign policy, congressional scholar Eileen Burgin observes, are exaggerated. Congress can act swiftly if necessary, employing expedited procedures; besides, most foreign policy matters require careful consideration. Although most of its members are inexpert on matters of foreign policy, its foreign affairs and armed services committees boast many impressive students of international affairs. If Congress approaches global events with one eye on the reactions of constituents, the same is often true of the president.[37]

The real question about congressional involvement in foreign affairs is not whether it interferes too much with the presidency but whether it defers too often to presidential initiatives.[38] Perhaps because it is closer to the people, Congress has been more likely than presidents in recent decades to reflect the popular democratic tradition of fearing the engagement of the United States in overt or covert military actions abroad (see Chapter 18). Congressional resistance to President Reagan's Contra war against the Sandanista government of Nicaragua led to a cutoff of funds on several occasions. The Senate fell only five votes short of rejecting President Bush's impending war to drive Iraqi occupiers out of Kuwait. President Clinton's bid to send American troops to Bosnia as peacekeepers courted Senate disapproval until Majority Leader Robert Dole agreed to back the president's plans. In each case, regardless of party, Congress was less keen on the use of armed force. Yet in each case the executive ultimately prevailed.

Congress is not always prudent about international affairs. But its voice is welcome in foreign policy because the alternative is a presidential monologue. When presidents have dominated foreign policy, they have been inclined to secret deliberations, covert actions, and manipulative rhetoric. Congressional participation in foreign policy opens this arena, generating debate, increasing options, and allowing public input. Elite democrats admire a president who is the sole master of foreign policy. Popular democrats turn to Congress to ensure the public's voice in foreign affairs.

Congressional Oversight of the Executive Branch

The most extensive relationship between Congress and the executive involves legislative oversight of the bureaucracy. **Oversight** is the review by congressional committees of the operations of executive branch agencies. In one sense, oversight is simply a logical process—Congress must review what the bureaucracy does to see if laws are being properly implemented. In another sense, oversight is a highly political process—Congress's chief means for contesting the president over guidance of the federal bureaucracy.

Oversight can take many forms. The most visible is the congressional hearing. In an oversight hearing, top agency administrators appear before a congressional committee to report on their implementation of programs and to answer questions. Members of Congress not only elicit useful information but also signal the administrators as to who controls their statutory authority and budget resources. Informal methods of oversight are even more common, and usually less conflictive. Committees may request written reports from agencies, or committee staffers may engage in extensive communications with their agency counterparts.

Most legislators formerly gave oversight short shrift because it was routine and brought few personal payoffs in electoral terms. But oversight activities have increased during the last two decades. The rise in congressional oversight stemmed from converging factors. Voters grew unhappy with the size and cost of the federal bureaucracy, making congressional inquiries into poor bureaucratic performance more politically attractive. Deficits made new federal programs more difficult to enact, enhancing the attractiveness as an alternative of greater oversight of existing programs. Aggressive presidents laid claim to monopolistic control of the bureaucracy, making oversight a prime congressional weapon of self-defense. Moreover, increased staff resources provided Congress with the personnel and expertise to perform oversight effectively.[39]

As oversight activities have increased over the last two decades, critics have complained that Congress is interfering excessively with the executive branch and trying to "micromanage" its operations. This complaint has been justified in some instances. Yet the increase in congressional oversight has been, on balance, a welcome development, at least from the standpoint of popular democracy. Oversight is one of the chief means that Congress possesses to hold the presidency and the civil service accountable. Vigorous oversight activities prevent the bureaucracy from becoming a closed world of inaccessible experts. Some oversight is technical and dull; some is narrowly self-serving advocacy. But many oversight hearings have alerted the public to matters that otherwise would have been known only to a small circle of elites.

CONCLUSION: THE REVOLUTION IN CONGRESS AND THE DEMOCRATIC DEBATE

From the standpoint of popular democracy, Congress has critical roles to play in budgeting, foreign policy, and oversight. But how well can Congress perform these and other roles; how well can it give expression to the strengths of popular democracy? Assessing the Republican revolution in Congress whose story we told in this chapter gives us some clues into the potential for Congress to represent the public's ideas and interests.

There were many elements of genuine popular democracy in the Republican revolution in Congress. The revolution shook Congress out of its complacent "inside the Washington Beltway" habits. It brought a dramatic new emphasis on party responsibility that is essential if Congress is to take collective action and address the nation's problems. Even the striking centralization of power in the hands of the leadership, though it sometimes bordered on authoritarian methods, was helpful in producing a coherent agenda that the public could understand and debate.

But the Republican revolution also fell far short of popular democratic reform in important respects. It was based on a typically low turnout in an off-year election, with only 20 percent of the eligible electorate voting in the advocates of radical change. It tried to enact its agenda by steamrollering over the opposition, short-circuiting the processes of deliberation and debate in Congress.[40] Most important, the Republican revolution enlisted populist anger for the interests of economic elites. Too often, the popular democratic reforms of the Republicans served as a cover for an elite agenda—for example, capital gains tax cuts that mostly benefitted well-to-do investors and deregulation measures that subordinated a clean environment to industry profits.

The elite democratic side of the Republican revolution was apparent in what it omitted as well as in what it contained. With corporate PAC donations flowing abundantly into GOP coffers, once the Republicans replaced the Democrats as the dominant party in Congress the Republican leadership had no interest in campaign finance reform. Yet campaign finance reform is necessary to lessen the advantages of incumbency, restore greater electoral competition, and loosen the ties between members of Congress and special interests. A revolution that rested, at bottom, on the power of money could not really be a revolution after all.

The excesses and biases that have marred the Republican regime in Congress should not obscure the continuing importance of Congress' democratic revitalization. A strong and effective Congress is crucial to the fate of popular democracy in America. Elite democrats argue that in a complex, dangerous, and technological world, Congress, with its inefficient methods of decision making, has become outdated. They point out that in most other political systems legislative powers have receded and strong executives have become dominant. Popular democrats respond that unless legislative power balances executive power, democracy is in trouble. Only a vital Congress can ensure that government will be sensitive to the concerns of ordinary citizens and forge genuine compromises between their diverse viewpoints. Above all, whereas the executive branch makes decisions behind closed doors, in the halls of Congress citizens can hear public arguments about the public good.

KEY TERMS

incumbent
franking privilege
casework
committee system
seniority
iron triangle
Speaker of the House
    of Representatives

majority leader
minority leader
filibuster
cloture
Budget and Impoundment Control
    Act of 1974
oversight

SUGGESTED READINGS

John C. Berg, *Unequal Struggle: Class, Gender, Race, and Power in the U.S. Congress*. Boulder, Colo.: Westview Press, 1994. A radical analysis of power in Congress, stressing the clout of large and small businesses and the weaknesses of labor, women, and African Americans.

Lawrence C. Dodd and Bruce I. Oppenheimer, eds., *Congress Reconsidered*, 6th ed. Washington, D.C.: CQ Press, 1997. An anthology of original, thought-provoking articles, with many insightful analyses of the Republican revolution in Congress.

C. Lawrence Evans and Walter J. Oleszek, *Congress Under Fire: Reform Politics and the Republican Majority*. Boston: Houghton Mifflin, 1997. An incisive account of the Democrats' failures and Republicans' successes in reforming Congress.

Richard E. Fenno, Jr., *Home Style: House Members in Their Districts*. Boston: Little, Brown and Company, 1978. The classic study of how legislators present themselves to their constituents in order to win their trust and their votes.

John R. Hibbing and Elizabeth Theiss-Morse, *Congress as Public Enemy: Public Attitudes Toward American Political Institutions*. New York: Cambridge University Press, 1995. Through surveys and focus groups, the authors arrive at an intriguing account of why Congress is the least-respected of American national institutions.

Gary C. Jacobson, *The Politics of Congressional Elections*, 4th ed. New York: Longman, 1997. The leading text on how members of Congress convert their biennial exposure to popular democracy into elite longevity in office.

Presidential Leadership and Elite Democracy

Contemporary presidents present themselves to the American people as champions of popular democracy. Aided by a large public relations machine in the White House, they dramatize their status as the sole elected representative of a national majority and their commitment to battle for the public good against selfish special interests. But should we take presidential claims to the mantle of popular democracy at face value? This chapter suggests that there are circumstances in which popular democracy can indeed be furthered by a leader in the White House. But it also proposes that we be wary of prevailing presidential imagery: Most of the time, we shall see, the presidency is closer to elite democracy than to popular democracy.

In the original debate over presidential power, the most brilliant advocate of strong presidential leadership was an arch elite democrat, Alexander Hamilton. Hamilton believed that the American Revolution had gone too far in placing government directly in the hands of the people and of legislators immediately answerable to the people. A strong executive of uncommon talent and experience was needed to guide public affairs. As Hamilton put it, "Energy in the executive is a leading character in the definition of good government."[1] Only an energetic executive, Hamilton argued, could overcome the tendency of the political system to stalemate and provide creative political direction. Conditions of crisis would make executive leadership even more imperative: "Decision, activity, secrecy, and dispatch will generally characterize the proceedings of one man in a much more eminent degree than the proceedings of any greater number."[2]

To the original popular democrats, the Anti-federalists, the new presidency evoked painful memories of royal governors and British kings. They suspected that Hamilton's lofty executive office would be a breeding ground for elitism. Patrick Henry lamented that "there is to be a great and mighty President, with very extensive powers: the powers of a King. He is to be supported in extravagant magnificence."[3] Another Anti-federalist, George Mason, called upon citizens to look to their own commitment "to their laws, to their freedom, and to their country" rather than depending for their salvation upon a single leader of great power.[4] Anti-federalists placed their political hopes in the people's energies and not the executive's.

Positions in the democratic debate over the executive seemed to be reversed in the twentieth century. First with Theodore Roosevelt and Woodrow Wilson, and even more decisively with Franklin D. Roosevelt, the presidency came to be associated with popular democracy. After FDR's New Deal, which was a genuine outpouring of popular democratic energies, most journalists, political scientists, and historians came to believe that presidents were the principal agents of democratic change in the American political system. Advocates of economic reform, social justice, and racial equality began to rest their hopes on White House leadership.

These hopes were repeatedly disappointed: Presidents after FDR never seemed to bring about as much democratic change as they promised when they ran for office. And while the bond between the presidency and popular democracy was celebrated, presidents were expanding their powers in ways that threatened democratic values. With the Vietnam War, the Watergate scandal, the Iran-Contra affair, and the campaign finance scandals of the Clinton presidency, the undemocratic potential of executive power was underscored. Anti-federalist warnings, forgotten in the twentieth-century celebration of presidential power, became relevant once more.

This chapter assesses the part presidents play in the democratic debate. We explain the most important features of the modern presidency and evaluate both its powers and its limitations. We consider presidents as leaders who seek to enact their agendas and make their marks upon history. But we give equal weight to the forces that constrain and condition their leadership: Congress, economic elites, the media, the public. It is more the balance of these forces than personality, we suggest, that determines whether the president sides with popular or elite democracy.

FROM POPULAR TO ELITE DEMOCRACY: THE CASE OF BILL CLINTON

When Americans think or talk about a president, his or her personality is usually the focus of their attention. The man or woman in the White House make a more engaging subject than the institutional apparatus or policy agenda of their administrations. Media coverage reinforces this personalization of the presidency. After observing a president's portrayal in the media, citizens are more apt to know trivial details—Gerald Ford bumped his head on helicopter doorframes, Ronald Reagan liked jellybeans, Bill Clinton has a cat named Socks—than to know the name of the president's chief of staff or the substance of his or her trade policy. This preoccupation with personality would be harmless enough if it did not so often obscure from public view the systemic forces that shape a presidency. These forces can turn a president who talks like a popular democrat into one who acts like an elite democrat. Consider the case of Bill Clinton.

Running for president in 1992, Bill Clinton presented himself as a popular democrat. The Clinton of 1992 was a down-home, folksy character from one of the poorest states in the Union. He emphasized his closeness to ordinary people through town hall meetings in which he entered into a dialogue with a cross-section of Americans. Clinton's agenda was as populist as his leadership style. "Putting People First" was the title of his manifesto setting forth his campaign promises. These were mostly programs aimed to alleviate the economic problems of the middle class and the working poor.

During his first term as president, Clinton delivered on some of his populist promises. The working poor, for example, benefitted from tax relief through an expansion of the Earned Income Tax Credit. Working families in general were now able to take time off from work for new babies or medical crises through the Family Leave law. Participation in elections was boosted by easing registration difficulties through the Motor Voter law. Yet more striking than Clinton's popular democratic achievements were the ways in which he was transformed into an elite democrat.

Clinton's image as a popular democrat was battered during his first months in office when the press revealed that on a trip to Los Angeles he had gotten a $200 haircut aboard Air Force One from a Beverly Hills stylist. The incident recalled Patrick Henry's words about the "extravagant magnificence" of a president's lifestyle, but it would be too trivial to remember had it not foreshadowed Clinton's increasing immersion in the circles of the rich and famous. Clinton socialized

with elites because he liked their company but even more because he wanted some of their money. In the money-driven world of modern campaigning (see Chapter 8), ordinary citizens are priced out. Preparing for the 1996 election, Clinton no longer had time or interest in town hall meetings; presidential "face time" was now reserved for big campaign contributors.

White House coffee klatches, offering wealthy donors the chance to chat with the president, raised $27 million for Clinton's 1996 campaign. The biggest contributors were invited in for more than coffee. As a *Washington Post* story relates,

> As Wall Street deal-maker Steven Rattner and his wife checked out of the White House [on July 27, 1995], fresh from a night in the Lincoln Bedroom, Philadelphia lawyer Leonard Barrack and his wife were arriving with their suitcases. Directly across the hall in the Queens' Bedroom, Boston developer Alan M. Levanthal and his wife were penned in for one night. That evening, all three families went to the East Room for a state dinner with the president and Hillary Rodham Clinton. Together, the men and their firms contributed about $350,000 to the Democratic Party over the last two years and raised even more money from others. Their visit to the executive mansion was part of the inducement and the reward. Nor were they alone: So many big-money donors have slept at the White House in recent years that one Clinton fund-raiser likens the executive mansion to a Motel 6.[5]

Even more revealing of the pressures that move a popular democrat in the direction of elite democracy than this quest for campaign cash is what happened to Clinton's economic program. Upon taking office in 1993, Clinton had to scale back plans to "put people first" by investing in education, worker retraining, and infrastructure in order to concentrate on bringing down the federal deficit. The deficit reduction strategy was designed to placate Wall Street and the Federal Reserve so that they would lower interest rates and stimulate the economy. Having won office largely with the votes of low- and middle-income voters, Clinton had to recast policy to play to the economic elite. As journalist Bob Woodward reported the deliberations of Clinton and his economic team: "It was no longer a political campaign. They faced new economic realities and had to start all over again. Their first audience would have to be the Fed and the bond market."[6]

One of these "new economic realities" was that popular democratic rhetoric about inequality was taboo. When the populist campaign consultants who had helped Clinton to victory in 1992 suggested that the president emphasize new taxes on the top 2 percent of Americans, economic adviser Robert Rubin (a multimillionaire investment banker who now serves as secretary of the treasury) told them to avoid any language offensive to the rich. "'Look,'" Rubin said impatiently, "'they're running the economy and they make the decisions about the economy. And so if you attack them, you wind up hurting the economy and wind up hurting the president.'"[7]

Clinton was hardly happy about the forces that shoved a Democratic president into the arms of largely Republican economic elites. At one White House meeting he lashed out in frustration: "'We're Eisenhower [moderate] Republicans here, and we are fighting the Reagan [conservative] Republicans. We stand for lower deficits and free trade and the bond market. Isn't that great?'"[8] Clinton recognized that personal or partisan preferences were not a match for the economic constraints and pressures that defined his economic policy. To be sure, the policy worked largely as intended, fostering steady economic growth and positioning the president beautifully for his reelection bid. But it also helped to make Wall Street the big winner in Clinton's first term and to stifle a democratic debate about the economic anxieties and inequities that trouble ordinary Americans.

THE PRESIDENCY AS AN INSTITUTION

In our concern for presidential leadership, we focus on the individual who occupies the White House. Yet the presidency—as distinct from the president—is an institution, and we need to understand its institutional features. The institution of the presidency has expanded dramatically in the twentieth century. Although this expansion has been justified in popular democratic terms—the presidency has had to grow to fulfill public expectations of executive leadership—the consequences have sometimes been unfortunate for popular democracy. Surrounded by a sizeable staff and bureaucracy of their own, presidents can become isolated from the people that put them into office. And this staff and bureaucracy can be used to carry out actions that run counter to what Congress has legislated and the public wants.

White House Staff

The part of the institutional presidency that most directly surrounds the individual president is the **White House staff** (known officially as the White House Office). The White House staff comprises the president's personal aides and advisers along with their numerous assistants, and it has undergone dramatic growth over the last sixty years. Before Franklin D. Roosevelt, presidents had only a handful of personal aides. Abraham Lincoln had to cope with the Civil War with the help of only two personal secretaries. When a telephone was first installed in the White House, Grover Cleveland answered it himself. As late as World War I, Woodrow Wilson typed many of his own speeches.

During the Great Depression of the 1930s, as new responsibilities flooded the White House, Franklin Roosevelt recognized, in the words of the Brownlow Committee that he appointed, "the president needs help." It was Roosevelt who initiated the dramatic expansion of White House staff. But later presidents would oversee a staff far larger than Roosevelt had imagined. At its height, FDR's staff numbered around fifty. By Richard Nixon's second term, the staff had grown to over 550 people. Nixon's successors, responding to charges that the presidential staff had become dangerously bloated, cut it back, but only a little (see Table 12.1).[9]

TABLE 12.1 Size of White House Staff	President	White House Staff: Average Number of Full-Time Employees per Administration
	Truman	222
	Eisenhower	352
	Kennedy	422
	Johnson	304
	Nixon	491
	Ford	583
	Carter	412
	Reagan	371
	Bush	380
	Clinton (1993–95)	415

Lyn Ragsdale, *Vital Statistics on the Presidency: Washington to Clinton.* (Washington, D.C.: Congressional Quarterly Press, 1996), pp. 257–261. Copyright © 1996 by Congressional Quarterly Press. Used with permission.

The White House staff has not only expanded since the 1930s, it has also taken on important new functions. Before Franklin Roosevelt, presidents tended to turn for advice to cabinet members. Although presidents still consider their cabinet selections important, since the 1930s they have downgraded most cabinet heads, relying instead on their staff for assistance in decision making and even in managing federal policies. Staff members have done more than serve as the president's extra eyes, ears, and hands. Some of them—such as H. R. Haldeman under Nixon, Hamilton Jordan under Carter, Edwin Meese under Reagan, John Sununu under Bush, and Leon Panetta under Clinton—have become key decision makers in their own right.

Why have recent presidents turned to White House staff rather than cabinet members for advice? To understand this phenomenon, we must consider the differences between cabinet members and White House staffers.

A president may have had little personal contact with most members of the cabinet before assuming office. The cabinet is selected with several criteria in mind: public prestige, managerial ability, interest group or geographic representativeness (e.g., the secretary of the treasury usually is drawn from the business or financial communities, while the secretary of the interior is traditionally a westerner). Potential cabinet heads must pass Senate scrutiny and receive senatorial confirmation. Further, cabinet secretaries can be summoned to appear before congressional committees, where they may be pressed to reveal information the president would rather keep confidential.

In contrast, top White House staff do not usually come to their jobs from power positions. Rather, they are individuals personally attached to the president—men or women who have worked for the president in the past and whose loyalty is long standing. Top staff members often reflect the president's roots and political base. Bill Clinton initially drew many of his key aides, including his first chief of staff, from Arkansas. White House staff do not need Senate confirmation. Unlike cabinet heads, they cannot ordinarily be questioned by Congress because of claims of separation of powers and executive privilege.

Considering the differences between cabinet and staff presents clues about why presidents prefer to work with staff. A president has greater flexibility with staff: He or she can hire anyone, move staff members from task to task, replace ineffective or incompatible staff members with less public notice than in dismissing a cabinet member. A president can also assume greater loyalty from staff. Cabinet members must answer to many forces besides the president who appointed them: congressional committees that control the budget and statutory authority for their departments, the interest groups that are important clienteles for their departments, the civil servants who work in their departments. But White House staffers answer only to the president. Their loyalty is undivided.[10]

Offering a president greater flexibility and loyalty than the cabinet, a large and powerful White House staff seems to increase the president's reach and power. But growth of this kind of White House staff has been a mixed blessing for presidents. Members of their staffs have several potential weaknesses. Like presidents themselves, staffers can become isolated from the public. Upon leaving his position as political adviser to the president at the end of Clinton's first term, George Stephanopoulos told a reporter: "When we step inside the White House gates, we enjoy things foreign to most of the public—the Oval Office, the adrenaline buzz of high-stakes politics, and the opportunity to get things done on a national scale. But these advantages often obscure the realities of everyday American life."[11]

Isolated from the public, dependent on the president for their jobs, and highly loyal, White House staffers do not necessarily make the best advisers. Desiring to curry favor with a president, staff members have sometimes presented their bosses with distorted pictures of the reality outside the White House. Rather than enhancing presidential power, they have produced a peculiar form of presidential blindness, akin to the monarchical mentality against which Patrick Henry had warned. This blindness was especially evident in the administrations of Johnson, Nixon, and Reagan.[12]

A contemporary president requires an extensive White House staff. But the tendency of that staff to enhance the illusion of presidential rectitude and wisdom must be avoided.

Executive Office of the President

The White House Office is part of the **Executive Office of the President (EOP),** established under Franklin Roosevelt in 1939. The other most important components of the EOP are the Office of Management and Budget (OMB), Council of Economic Advisers (CEA), and National Security Council (NSC). Whereas the White House staff was designed to provide the president with personal and political assistance, the other EOP units were intended to provide institutional—that is, objective and expert—advice to the president as a policymaker (see Figure 12.1).

The largest and most important institutional unit in the EOP is the **Office of Management and Budget (OMB).** OMB prepares the annual presidential budget. It scrutinizes legislative proposals originating in the agencies of the executive branch to ensure that they accord with the program of the president. It recommends signing or vetoing legislation. In addition, it oversees the management methods of the entire executive establishment.

The **Council of Economic Advisers (CEA)** was established in 1946 to provide regular assistance of professional economists. The CEA has a chair and two other members, along with their staffs. It analyzes economic conditions, projects economic trends, and drafts the president's annual economic report.

The **National Security Council (NSC)** was established in 1947 to coordinate the military and diplomatic aspects of foreign policy in an age of American global involvement. Officially, it brings together the top national security decision makers: the president, vice president, secretary of state, secretary of defense, director of the Central Intelligence Agency, and chair of the Joint Chiefs of Staff. More important than formal meetings of the NSC, however, is the work of its staff, headed by the president's assistant for national security. (See Chapter 18 for a more detailed discussion of the NSC.)

FIGURE 12.1

Executive Office of the President— At Its Inception and Today[a]

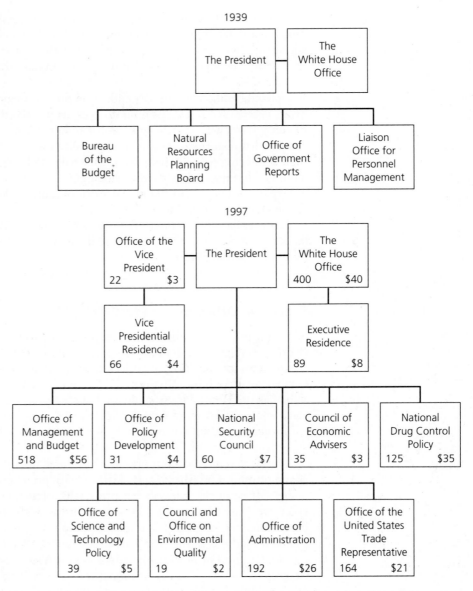

1939

The President

The White House Office

Bureau of the Budget

Natural Resources Planning Board

Office of Government Reports

Liaison Office for Personnel Management

1997

Office of the Vice President
22            $3

The President

The White House Office
400          $40

Vice Presidential Residence
66            $4

Executive Residence
89            $8

Office of Management and Budget
518          $56

Office of Policy Development
31            $4

National Security Council
60            $7

Council of Economic Advisers
35            $3

National Drug Control Policy
125          $35

Office of Science and Technology Policy
39            $5

Council and Office on Environmental Quality
19            $2

Office of Administration
192          $26

Office of the United States Trade Representative
164          $21

[a]Numbers on left indicate authorized full-time personnel. Numbers on right indicate dollar amounts in millions in proposed budget authority for the 1997 fiscal year.
Copyright © 1997. From *Presidential Leadership,* 4/e by George C. Edwards III and Stephen Wayne. Reprinted with permission of St. Martin's Press.

Although the original purpose of the EOP was to provide a president with expert institutional advice to balance the more personal and partisan advice of staff, the distinction has diminished in recent years. The White House has made the institutional components of the EOP more political, more directly responsive to the president's personal views and political needs.[13]

Recent presidents have placed trusted aides at the helm of OMB. OMB head Richard Darman was a prominent adviser to President Bush, and Leon Panetta performed a similar role for President Clinton before becoming White House Chief of Staff in 1994. The NSC was used by President Reagan to implement secret presidential policies involving arms sales to Iran and control of the Contra forces in Nicaragua. The Reagan aide in charge of these projects, Lt. Colonel Oliver North, hardly fit the profile of an objective, neutral institutional aide.

As has been the case with White House staff, the EOP has been turned into a central instrument of presidential views and politics. This extension of personal power, from the president's Oval Office outward, has been justified as an indispensable tool of leadership. But the enhancement of presidential power has not always meant the enhancement of presidential wisdom. A highly politicized OMB under David Stockman manipulated budget numbers to conceal how Reagan's tax cut of 1981 would generate a massive deficit. A highly politicized NSC helped Reagan stumble into the disaster of the Iran-Contra affair. Some scholars believe that the EOP might serve the presidency better if it were not so politicized.

Cabinet

Beyond the White House staff and the EOP lies the cabinet and the vast expanse of the executive branch. The **president's cabinet** is composed of the appointed heads of the fourteen principal executive agencies, plus a few others, such as the U.S. ambassador to the United Nations. Americans use the term *cabinet* in two ways. In the first, the cabinet is simply the collection of individuals appointed by the president to head the principal executive agencies. In the second, the cabinet is a collegial body, meeting together with the president to supply its collective advice.

Most presidents talk of using the cabinet as a collective forum. Meetings of the cabinet make excellent TV and photo opportunities, showing off the president surrounded by prestigious and weighty advisers. In actuality, cabinet meetings are routine affairs, useful for little more than symbolism. Not surprisingly, most cabinet members come to meetings to pursue the interests of their own departments. Presidents learn not to expect much from a cabinet meeting and instead solicit advice from individuals directly engaged in policy matters.

The cabinet is more accurately described, therefore, as a collection of individual department heads. In this collection, not all heads are equal. As presidency scholar Thomas E. Cronin has shown, presidents turn most often to their *inner cabinet*, composed of the secretaries of state, defense, and treasury, along with the attorney general.[14] These cabinet secretaries handle the subjects most important to the president. Until President Clinton appointed Janet Reno as attorney general and Madeleine Albright as secretary of state, all inner cabinet members had been white males.

The *outer cabinet* contains the remainder of the departments, such as Agriculture, Education, and Transportation. The business of these departments is not ordinarily central to a president's program. Presidents today are expected to select women, African Americans, and Latinos for their cabinets, but with the exceptions of Reno and Albright all from these groups have been placed in outer cabinet posts. Members of the outer cabinet often find that the prestige of their title is not matched by their proximity to the president. For example, when President Nixon's secretary of the interior, Walter Hickel, unhappily resigned in 1970, he observed that he had seen the president in private only twice in fifteen months.[15]

Managing the Bureaucracy

If presidents are to control the vast federal bureaucracy, they need the assistance of a strong cabinet. But cabinet members are subject to tugs besides the directives of the White House—pressures from Congress, from interest groups, from the staffs of their own agencies. Presidents and their White House staffers have complained about members of the outer cabinet "going native" (that is, taking on the perspectives of the departments they were appointed to head) or building personal empires.

Whatever help they receive from their cabinet appointees, presidents find the management of the federal bureaucracy arduous. Prescribed by the Constitution, it is a task that requires a president to "take Care that the Laws be faithfully executed. . . ." In traditional management theory, the executive branch should be a pyramid, with the president on top, and bureaucrats underneath carrying out decisions. But the modern administrative state diverges from this theory.

A number of factors limit a president's control over the bureaucracy. The vast size of the modern administrative state is itself a limitation, because no president, even with the help of a large White House staff, can keep track of more than a fraction of what is taking place in the bureaucracy. The historical shift from patronage to civil service also has limited presidential control. Civil servants, unlike White House staffers, do not depend on the president for their jobs and are likely to be less concerned about the success of the president than about the mission, budget, and growth of their own agencies. (The perspective of civil servants may seem narrow compared to that of the White House, but civil servants often have more experience and knowledge in their fields than White House staff.) In addition, Congress has considerable influence over executive agencies through its budgetary and statutory authority.

The capacity of executive agencies to resist directives has frustrated presidents. As President Truman prepared to hand over his office to the newly elected General Eisenhower, he predicted: "He will sit here and he'll say, 'Do this! Do that!' And nothing will happen. Poor Ike—it won't be a bit like the Army!"[16]

Frustration with managing the bureaucracy has led presidents to try to shift functions from that bureaucracy into the White House itself. More recently, it has led to determined campaigns to recast the bureaucracy in the president's ideological mold.

Reagan and the Bureaucracy

No modern president was as successful in recasting the bureaucracy as Ronald Reagan. Reagan came into office with a strong conservative agenda. His White House deployed several strategies of executive control. Most important was a personnel strategy. Presidential appointees to the bureaucracy were tightly screened by a personnel office in the White House; loyalty to Reagan and his conservative philosophy was a more important criterion for appointment than past experience or professional expertise. Another strategic weapon was the budget. In a period of large deficits, the budget was used as a tool of administrative discipline. Agencies that the Reagan White House regarded as unfriendly to its agenda saw their budgets cut and their staffs reduced. Agencies whose behavior the Reagan White House hoped to change knew that they would be fiscally hurt if they did not satisfy the White House.

Reagan's gaining the upper hand over the bureaucracy has impressed many observers. If presidents are to fulfill the public's expectations of leadership, these observers contend, they must use all available bureaucratic resources. In the view of political scientist Richard Nathan, Reagan's administrative strategy shows the way for both conservative and liberal presidents of the future. Regardless of ideology or partisanship, presidents should be sure that "politics penetrates operations," that the president controls the bureaucracy.[17]

But does this kind of presidential control over the bureaucracy serve democratic ends? Too much presidential domination may not be good for the civil service. During the Reagan presidency, many expert civil servants were demoralized (some effectively terminated) by political appointees whose main interest was undermining their agencies' missions.

More important, presidential domination sometimes can damage popular democratic achievements while serving elite democratic objectives. Many of the agencies that the Reagan White House tried to transform were carrying out laws passed by Congress and favored by most Americans. The Reagan White House undercut laws it did not like through bureaucratic methods that drew little press or public notice. For example, the Occupational Safety and Health Administration (OSHA) was created by Congress to protect Americans against unsafe conditions and toxic substances in the workplace. But the Reagan administration looked on OSHA as a harasser of businesses. Under the administrative strategy of the Reagan White House, OSHA's practices were quietly changed. Safety and health regulations were postponed or canceled, while budget cuts meant fewer safety and health inspections of factories by OSHA civil servants.[18]

The weakening of OSHA was successful presidential leadership, if leadership is measured by executives achieving their objectives. But was it good public policy and good democratic procedure? Skillful leadership is needed to prevent the bureaucracy from impeding a president's legitimate objectives. But political and ideological domination may place too high a premium on presidential leadership by slighting other values—public preferences, legislative intent, a skilled civil service—that carry weight in a democratic political order.

THE PRESIDENCY AND THE CONGRESS

The relationship between the president and Congress is seldom smooth. Conflict is more common than cooperation—as the framers of the Constitution intended. In the *Federalist Papers*, James Madison set down the theory of checks and balances: "Ambition must be made to counteract ambition."[19] The clash of presidential and congressional ambitions is constitutional theory in action.

This clash is often presented as a competition between the national viewpoint of the presidency and the localistic viewpoint of members of Congress—a portrayal that makes the president the unique champion of popular democracy at the national level. But the idea that the presidency is almost always bound to be a better servant of the public interest than Congress is not well founded. Sometimes, presidents do take a national standpoint, while Congress responds with parochial objections. Generally, however, it is more accurate to say that even though presidents speak for a broader coalition of interests than *individual* members of Congress, Congress *as a whole* may speak for an equally broad, or broader coalition.

Before accepting the claim that Congress is locally oriented and the president alone speaks for the public interest at the national level, we should remember that neither branch has a monopoly on the representation of public ends. Some public ends have been represented better by the White House at one point in time, and by the majority in Congress at another. Social welfare and civil rights legislation drew greater support from Presidents Kennedy and Johnson than from Congress between 1961 and 1969, but from 1969 to 1977 the same kind of legislation had more backing in Congress than in the administrations of Presidents Nixon and Ford. In this case, insisting that what the presidency favors is more in the national interest than what Congress favors would require us to believe that social welfare and civil rights programs ceased to be in the national interest as soon as the White House changed hands.

The image of presidents as champions of popular democracy at the national level draws upon moments when presidents achieved legislative breakthroughs: Franklin Roosevelt in 1933–35, Lyndon Johnson in 1965, Ronald Reagan in 1981. But these were moments when presidents enjoyed electoral mandates and congressional backing—that is, when they could legitimately claim to represent a majoritarian popular democratic coalition. Absent these relatively rare political conditions, presidents and Congress reflect differing coalitions, and it is often hard to tell which institution has the better claim to represent popular democratic goals.

Congressional Roadblocks

Why does Congress so often oppose the president? Perhaps the most important source of conflict is the way they are elected. Elected in districts or states, members of Congress have a different constituency than the president. To keep their jobs, they must satisfy voters who are not necessarily backers of the president. Moreover, members of Congress build their own campaign organizations and raise their own campaign funds. With different constituencies and independent political bases, they must chart their own course.

Presidential efforts to push legislation through Congress may also be frustrated by congressional structure. Prior to 1995, power in Congress was fragmented and decentralized; the legislative process presented the White House with successive barriers, tripping over any of which lost the legislative race. As we saw in the preceding chapter, the triumphant Republicans centralized the legislative process, especially in the House, in 1995, but this hardly helped a Democratic president.

Presidents are not helpless. Which factors determine their success with Congress? Political scientist George C. Edwards has argued that a president's success in securing passage of legislation depends on the partisan composition of Congress and the president's standing with the American public. Examining the years 1953 to 1994, Edwards found that the level of support for a president's program from members of his own party was usually more than 30 percentage points greater than the level of support from members of the other party.[20] A president enjoying a large partisan majority in Congress is thus primed for a successful legislative record, whereas a president facing a majority from the other party has dubious legislative prospects.

But a favorable partisan balance in Congress does not guarantee legislative success, as Bill Clinton painfully learned during his first two years in office. A president's public popularity is another important factor with Congress. A popular president is likely to have favorable ratings among constituents. Legislators will not want to appear at odds with a popular president. On the other hand, a president whose popularity is sinking can be opposed by members of Congress with little fear of electoral retribution. To be successful with Congress, a president usually needs both a favorable partisan balance and a favorable standing in the public opinion polls. Lacking the latter, President Clinton barely got his deficit reduction plan through Congress in 1993 and failed even to get his health care reform bill to the floor of Congress in 1994.

Presidential Resources

The president has resources to improve the prospects that he or she gets congressional approval. The legislative program sets the congressional agenda. By establishing a strong, well-timed agenda, a president can shape the terms in which subsequent congressional debate is conducted. Working for that agenda on the president's behalf is the **legislative liaison staff,** a portion of the White

House staff that spends its time on Capitol Hill. Members of the liaison staff keep the president informed of the political maneuvering for important bills and provide favors to members of Congress in the hopes that they will later return these favors to the White House with their votes.

The favors that the White House offers are valuable but limited. To win a few swing voters in a tight legislative contest, presidents can promise federal judgeships or positions as U.S. attorneys. Federal grants or contracts can be steered to the district or state of a crucial legislator. Minor provisions of a bill can be altered to favor interest groups. In his uphill 1993 battle to win House approval of the North American Free Trade Agreement (NAFTA), President Clinton successfully wooed several pivotal southern legislators with concessions on citrus and peanut butter imports.[21]

A resource that the White House possesses in somewhat greater abundance is the mystique of the presidency. To be photographed with the president or called to meet with the president at the White House can boost a representative's standing with constituents. Apart from political gain, few members of Congress are immune to the mystique of presidential authority. Ronald Reagan thus bestowed presidential cufflinks on numerous members of Congress and invited legislators to use the presidential box at the Kennedy Center in Washington. George Bush took members of Congress and their families on personally guided tours of the White House, highlighted by a souvenir snapshot of the visitors in the Lincoln bedroom.

If all else fails, a president retains the constitutional weapon of the **veto.** When Congress presents the president with a bill, ten days (Sundays excepted) are given to sign it into law, veto (disapprove) it and return it with a message explaining objections, or do nothing, in which case it becomes law without a signature. Should the president exercise the second option, a two-thirds vote in each legislative branch is necessary to override the veto. If Congress adjourns during the ten-day period and the president does not sign the bill, it is blocked with a *pocket veto*.

Overrides of presidential vetoes are infrequent. George Bush had only one veto overridden during his entire presidency, a record equaled by Bill Clinton in his first term (see Table 12.2). The veto is a particularly important weapon for an administration in which the opposition party controls Congress and is pursuing its own legislative agenda. Thus, Clinton used vetoes—and threats of vetoes—to stop the Republican revolution of 1995 in its tracks.

Ironically, one of the few legislative accomplishments of that revolution was the grant to the president of a **line-item veto,** a measure long sought by Republicans but also welcomed by President Clinton. Whereas before presidents had to sign or veto budgets as a whole, under the new law they can reject particular appropriations as well as tax breaks that affect 100 or fewer individuals. To restore the vetoed spending items or tax breaks, Congress must pass new legislation. Justified as a tool in the battle against excessive federal spending, this shift of authority from Congress to the executive was immediately challenged by six members of Congress on constitutional grounds. In June 1997, the Supreme

TABLE 12.2

Presidential
Vetoes
(1789–1996)

President	Regular Vetoes	Pocket Vetoes	Total Vetoes	Vetoes Overridden
George Washington	2		2	
John Adams			0	
Thomas Jefferson			0	
James Madison	5	2	7	
James Monroe	1		1	
John Q. Adams			0	
Andrew Jackson	5	7	12	
Martin Van Buren		1	1	
W. H. Harrison			0	
John Tyler	6	4	10	1
James K. Polk	2	1	3	
Zachary Taylor			0	
Millard Fillmore			0	
Franklin Pierce	9		9	5
James Buchanan	4	3	7	
Abraham Lincoln	2	5	7	
Andrew Jackson	21	8	29	15
Ulysses S. Grant	45	48	93	4
Rutherford B. Hayes	12	1	13	1
James A. Garfield			0	
Chester A. Arthur	4	8	12	1
Grover Cleveland	304	110	414	2
Benjamin Harrison	19	25	44	1
Grover Cleveland	42	128	170	5
William McKinley	6	36	42	
Theodore Roosevelt	42	40	82	1
William H. Taft	30	9	39	1
Woodrow Wilson	33	11	44	6
Warren G. Harding	5	1	6	
Calvin Coolidge	20	30	50	4
Herbert Hoover	21	16	37	3
Franklin D. Roosevelt	372	263	635	9
Harry S. Truman	180	70	250	12
Dwight D. Eisenhower	73	108	181	2
John F. Kennedy	12	9	21	
Lyndon B. Johnson	16	14	30	
Richard M. Nixon	26	17	43	7
Gerald R. Ford	48	18	66	12
Jimmy Carter	13	18	31	2
Ronald Reagan	39	39	78	9
George Bush	29	16	45	1
Bill Clinton	17	0	17	1

Source: *Presidential Vetoes. 1789–1991*, Office of the Secretary of the Senate (U.S. Government Printing Office, 1992). Updated.

Court rejected their challenge as premature, since the line-item veto had not yet been used and thus no one had suffered any personal injury. But the Court did not rule on the larger question of the line-item veto's constitutionality.

That presidents cannot ordinarily dominate Congress has been frustrating to those who assume that the executive is the only champion of popular democracy in national politics. But neither wisdom nor democratic purpose are always on the president's side. Congressional checks on the president fulfill the original constitutional concern to avert a dangerous concentration of power. That Congress represents political constituencies which may not gain a sympathetic hearing from the presidency can produce legislation that may support narrow special interests, but also legislation that may benefit weak or threatened groups, such as the poor. Rather than expecting presidents to triumph over Congress, we should accept the normality of conflict between the two branches. And we should look closely, in every contest between the president and Congress, to determine which ideologies, interests, and values each one represents.

THE PRESIDENCY AND ECONOMIC POWER

Congress is not the only powerful and independent institution with which a president must come to terms. Numerous centers of private power possess resources that presidents want and resources to constrain them. Clashes between the White House and Capitol Hill are familiar dramas in American politics. Less visible are the connections between the presidency and the reigning powers of the political economy.

The modern American economy, dominated by multinational corporations and financial enterprises, requires direction to ensure predictability. The presidency, with its Hamiltonian potential for unified will, decisiveness, and swiftness, has long been seen as the only national institution capable of such centralized direction. Presidential responsibility has thus grown with the rise of the corporate economy.

Before the New Deal, the federal government seldom tried to affect overall economic conditions. But once the Great Depression revealed the disastrous consequences of an uncontrolled economy, President Franklin Roosevelt asserted presidential responsibility. His role became a legal responsibility of every president after him, thanks to the **Employment Act of 1946.** It gave the federal government—and especially the president—the duty "to foster and promote free competitive enterprise, to avoid economic fluctuations or to diminish the effects thereof, and to maintain employment, production, and purchasing power." The act also established the Council of Economic Advisers to assist the president and required an annual economic report to Congress.

What can presidents do to promote a healthy economy? Three policy tools are available to the president as an economic manager: fiscal policy, monetary policy, and incomes policy. Fiscal policy involves federal taxation and spending to affect economic conditions. The president can, for example, propose a tax cut; such a cut will, predictably, increase economic activity. Monetary policy involves the money supply and the level of interest rates. For example, the president can, with the cooperation of the Federal Reserve, slow down inflationary pressures in the economy through higher interest rates that make borrowing money more expensive. Incomes policy is an effort to deal directly with rising prices. A president can, for instance, ask the CEA to develop wage-price guideposts and ask business and labor to adhere to them.

All these actions require the president to obtain the agreement of other powerful actors and institutions. A president can propose changes in federal taxation or spending, but Congress has the final authority over them. Presidents can suggest monetary policy, but the Federal Reserve Board has the final say. They can ask business and labor to avoid price and wage decisions that fuel inflation, but short of mandatory wage-price controls (a rarity in peacetime), little can be done.[22]

Presidential power over the economy is limited by the structural power of the corporate sector, which, as we saw in Chapter 4, plays a decisive role in determining the level of private investment in America. This investment is critical to the health of the economy. Although investment decisions are made largely on economic grounds, spokespersons for big business like to attribute lagging investment to the lack of "business confidence" in a president with whom they differ. No president wants to be viewed as undermining business confidence.

Some presidents have smooth sailing with the corporate sector. Presidents Eisenhower, Nixon, Ford, Reagan, and Bush ran administrations that pleased the corporate sector. Other presidents have had a rockier relationship. Elected in the face of corporate opposition, Presidents Kennedy, Carter, and Clinton struggled against charges that they were hurting business confidence and jeopardizing the health of the American economy.

These presidents have made herculean efforts to convince corporate America of their friendly intentions. After confronting the steel industry in 1962 over price increases that might have wrecked his administration's anti-inflation policy, President Kennedy turned around and actively wooed business executives with both substantive benefits and psychological gestures.[23] We have already seen how President Clinton played up to Wall Street with his initial deficit reduction program. Despite Clinton's efforts, a poll taken in September 1994 showed only 9 percent of business executives supporting him for reelection.[24] Only a small minority were willing to admit, in the words of the CEO of a scientific instruments manufacturer, that "Bill Clinton has been consistently supportive of the business community."[25]

Whether Republicans or Democrats occupy the White House, corporate power is a major constraint on presidential action. The business community does not have to have one of its own in the White House to benefit from presidential policy making. Its weapon of business confidence deters presidents—even ones elected primarily by the votes of ordinary working people—from pursuing a popular democratic economic agenda.

THE PRESIDENCY AND NATIONAL SECURITY

Presidential freedom of action is more extensive in foreign and military policy. Presidents enjoy greater leeway here to protect the national interest, promote democracy around the globe, and act as peacemakers. Yet if presidential dominance in foreign affairs is supposed to serve popular democratic goals, its recent history smacks more of elite democratic methods. Since World War II, presidents have made war upon their own initiative, concealed some of their actions in the deepest secrecy, and employed the agencies under their control to repress opponents. What historian Arthur Schlesinger, Jr., has labeled the "imperial presidency" of the Cold War era resembles the dangerous monarch that the Anti-federalists predicted.[26]

Presidents are not free of opposition or constraint in conducting foreign and military policy. Nonetheless, they have exceptional resources when they engage in international relations—resources that cannot be matched by any other national institutions.

The Constitution is an important source of these resources. It entrusts the president with making treaties and appointing American ambassadors, although it requires the concurrence of two-thirds of the Senate for the first and a majority of the Senate for the second. The president also receives ambassadors from other governments, and although this power may appear merely ceremonial, it has been interpreted as giving the president a unilateral power of U.S. recognition.

The Supreme Court has upheld a paramount role for the president in the conduct of American foreign policy. In *United States* v. *Curtiss-Wright Corporation* (1936), the Court gave presidents a wide latitude in foreign policy. Writing for the majority, Justice Sutherland proclaimed "the very delicate, plenary, and exclusive power of the president as the sole organ of the federal government in international relations—a power which does not require as a basis for its exercise an act of Congress."[27]

If the Constitution and the Supreme Court have bolstered the president's position in international affairs, so have the institutional resources of the executive branch. The president receives information from American diplomatic and military personnel stationed around the globe, besides secret information from the Central Intelligence Agency (CIA) and the military intelligence services. When foreign policy controversies arise, presidents claim to be the most knowledgeable actors on the scene.

Presidential Dominance in Foreign Affairs

Because the nation needs a coherent foreign policy, a strong case can be made for presidential leadership in this area. Some scholars believe that a weakness in American foreign policy making is that the president does not have enough control.[28] Congress frequently insists on an independent role in foreign policy. Even within the executive branch, different agencies—the State Department, Defense Department, Treasury Department, CIA, National Security Council staff—compete to shape foreign policy. With all the resources in this area, a president may still have a hard time ensuring that the United States speaks with one voice to other countries.

Presidential leadership is necessary in foreign policy but is not without its dangers, as U.S. history since World War II has evidenced. During this era, the United States began to intervene in the affairs of other nations around the globe in the name of anticommunism and freedom. Employing the military machinery and covert capacities of a growing national security state (see Chapter 18), presidents staked out claims of authority that were constitutionally, politically, and morally questionable. In the name of presidential leadership, there were disturbing abuses of power in the areas of war making, secrecy, and repression.

Believing that placing the decision to go to war in the hands of a single individual was dangerous, the drafters of the Constitution entrusted that decision to the assembled representatives of the people. The president was to be the commander-in-chief of the armed forces once Congress determined the need for armed hostilities. Historically, however, it proved hard to keep presidents in this secondary role. Without any congressional declaration of war, presidents began to use American forces, for example, to repulse attacks on American property abroad, to suppress domestic turmoil, or to fight small-scale wars.

The capacity of a president to employ American armed forces became controversial during the Vietnam War. Presidents Johnson and Nixon were determined to carry out their Vietnam policies against rising antiwar protests from American citizens and within Congress. Once the legal authority for their war making was questioned, they asserted that the commander-in-chief clause in the Constitution gave them vast military powers. When Nixon extended the war into neighboring Cambodia in 1970, he justified his action on the grounds that, as commander-in-chief, he had the right to take any action necessary to protect American troops. With even less justification, he ordered the continued bombing of Cambodia in 1973, even after all American ground forces had been withdrawn. Nixon became precisely what both the framers of the Constitution and their Anti-federalist critics feared: the eighteenth-century British monarch who involved the nation in war on the basis of personal whim.

Congressional Attempts to Rein in the Executive

Congress attempted to reassert its constitutional role in war making by passing, over Nixon's veto, the **War Powers Resolution of 1973.** According to this resolution, the president must, if circumstances permit, consult with Congress before sending American forces into a situation where armed conflict is anticipated. The president must also provide Congress with a written report within 48 hours of dispatching American forces into combat. After sixty days, the president must withdraw these forces from combat unless Congress has declared war or otherwise authorized continued engagement. An additional thirty days is granted to remove them from combat if the president claims that this period is needed for their safe withdrawal.

Presidents since Nixon have complained that the War Powers Resolution ties their hands and undercuts American national security. The resolution actually has had little effect. Dramatic military actions since 1973, such as the invasion of Grenada or the war in the Persian Gulf, have not been hampered by the War Powers Resolution. Because the president has enjoyed a near monopoly on information in these situations and the public has supported presidential actions, Congress has been reluctant to insist on the requirements it established in 1973.

The end of the Cold War has made little difference in the control over war making. President Clinton has been just as insistent as Cold War executives of his right to deploy American troops abroad without needing authorization from Congress. When the Senate unanimously passed a nonbinding resolution in August 1994, informing Clinton that he could not send troops into Haiti simply by citing a United Nations resolution, the president replied: "'Like my predecessors of both parties, I have not agreed that I was constitutionally mandated to obtain the support of Congress.'"[29] The following month, Clinton defied Congress—and public opinion—by dispatching the troops. As constitutional law expert Louis Fisher observes, "Clinton's interpretation of presidential war power would have astonished the framers of the Constitution."[30]

Presidential Secrecy

Inadequate though it may be, the War Powers Resolution serves as a statement that we recognize the dangerous potential for abuse in the presidential power to make war. There is similar potential for abuse in the **presidential power of secrecy.** Once the United States became involved in a worldwide Cold War against communism, revolution, and nationalism, new powers of secrecy were assumed by the White House. As we shall see in more detail in Chapter 18, the CIA, created in 1947, became a weapon of presidential policy making in foreign affairs. Through the CIA, presidents could intervene covertly in the politics of other nations, bribing politicians, financing pro-American parties, or encouraging military coups against governments the president regarded as unfavorable to U.S. interests. Clouded evidence even suggests that the CIA offered presidents means to assassinate foreign leaders.[31]

When presidents' dominant foreign policy role has been challenged, some have resorted to secret repressive tactics. The Nixon administration undertook a notorious covert campaign to destroy its critics. Journalists had their phones wiretapped. A secret White House unit, known as the Plumbers, engaged in illegal break-ins to gather damaging material on foes of Nixon's Vietnam policy. The White House compiled a large list of these critics—the Enemies List—and sought to use the auditing mechanisms of the Internal Revenue Service to harass them. Fundamental American liberties became insignificant when they stood in the way of presidential power.[32]

Secret action is enticing. It offers a president opportunity to advance foreign policy goals through methods that would raise ethical and constitutional questions if pursued openly. It allows a policy to persist even when it lacks support from majorities in Congress and the American people. Moreover, it is rationalized by the elite democratic argument that presidents have a superior vantage point and greater expertise than Congress and the public in international affairs. But secret action denies the people presidential accountability and undermines the democratic debate.

A New Era?

Can the formidable power over foreign policy amassed by presidents during the Cold War years be maintained now that the Cold War is over? Presidents have lost several Cold War advantages. There is no longer a feared and despised enemy, communism, against whom strong presidential actions could easily be justified. There is no longer a nuclear threat, which called for quick executive decisions in moments of international crisis. There is no longer a Cold War consensus on foreign policy goals, which limited partisan disagreements and enhanced popular support.

Popular support seems increasingly hard to come by for the post–Cold War presidency. In the 1990s, the American public appears little interested in global affairs and less inclined to support presidential activism in foreign policy. President Bush's specialization in foreign affairs hurt him in the 1992 election, while his challenger was helped by his pledge to concentrate on domestic affairs. In the 1996 election, neither President Clinton nor his challenger devoted much time to foreign issues.

Yet if foreign and military policy are neither as glamorous nor as easy for presidents as during the heyday of the Cold War, there are few signs that presidential dominance in foreign affairs has ended. President Bush successfully asserted presidential power during the Gulf War. President Clinton did the same by intervening with American forces in Haiti and Bosnia, even though he faced greater skepticism from Congress and the public than Bush had. Ironically, today's public inattention to foreign policy may have much the same result as public fervor for anticommunism during the Cold War: The conduct of American foreign policy is considered an elite democratic preserve run by the president and his experts in the foreign policy establishment. Popular democracy requires an open democratic debate over domestic *and* foreign policy.

THE PRESIDENT, THE MEDIA, AND THE AMERICAN PEOPLE

Rooted in the assumptions of elite democracy, the framers of the Constitution did not want a president to get too close to the American people. They placed the immediate choice of the chief executive in the hands of electors, who were supposed to be the most distinguished political elite in each state. The framers expected that the dignity of the president's office and the long duration of the president's term would provide insulation from mass passion or popular demand for economic change.[33]

Modern presidents, in contrast, claim a close bond with the American people. The voice that originates from the White House purports to be the voice of popular democracy. Cultivating public support has become a central activity of the presidency.

Present-day presidents campaign for public support because it enhances their political influence. Congress reacts more favorably to a popular than an unpopular president; bureaucrats and interest group leaders are similarly impressed by high presidential poll ratings. If the American political system possessed strong parties, a president could count on more stable support. In the absence of such parties, presidents are on their own.

To gain public support, presidents are increasingly, in the words of political scientist Samuel Kernell, "going public." A growing percentage of presidential time is spent on the road, selling presidential policy. Kernell suggests that "public speaking, political travel, and appearances before special constituencies outside Washington constitute the repertoire of modern leadership."[34]

Such presidential efforts do not necessarily succeed. As the presidency has grown in power, so have public expectations. Americans hold high and often contradictory expectations of presidents. They expect presidents to bring prosperity, peace, and prestige to the nation, while combining the qualities of a statesman and a politician.[35]

Many presidents have not been able to live up to these inflated expectations. Starting with high rates of public approval in the honeymoon period at the beginning of their administrations, they have not been able to prevent declines in popularity over the long term. Such declines are not inevitable, however. President Reagan recovered from huge declines in public approval during the recession of 1981–82 and the Iran-Contra affair to leave office as a popular figure. President Clinton hardly had a honeymoon with the public, but his popularity, approaching record lows for a president's first two years, improved in 1995–96 when he won a budget showdown with congressional Republicans and presided over robust economic growth. Despite a campaign finance scandal, Clinton's approval ratings were at their peak as his second term began.

The media play a major role in a modern president's relationship with the American people. If we listened only to presidents and their White House staffs, we might conclude that the media function as an impediment to presidential communication with the public. A huge corps of journalists is stationed at the White House to report on a president's every word and deed; when the president travels, the press corps follows. Presidential blunders or White House staff conflicts are often highlighted by the media, while the president's policy proposals are closely scrutinized by reporters and editorial columnists for hidden political motives. Some presidents' political standing has been badly damaged by negative media coverage.

White House complaints about the media, however, tell only one side of the story. The media—especially TV—provide a vehicle through which a modern president can cultivate support. The White House staff includes a Press Office and an Office of Communications; if these units are skilled at public relations, the media provide opportunities for dramatic presidential appearances, colorful photo opportunities, and engrossing human interest stories about the "first family." If the president has an attractive personality and is a skilled public speaker, the media can amplify his or her charm, wit, or eloquence in a manner that presidents living before the age of television might well have envied.[36]

The media are a two-edged sword, sometimes wielded by the White House as a potent weapon, at other times cutting a president down. President Reagan's mastery over the media is the subject of the accompanying box. In sharp contrast to Reagan's success with the media has been the stormy relationship between the Clinton White House and the press.

Clinton and the Media

It took only a few days in office for Bill Clinton's media image to change from inspiring leader of a new generation to politically inept waffler devoid of conviction. Just 30 hours after the inauguration, NBC's Lisa Meyers told the nightly news audience that the Clinton White House looked like "the Not-Ready-for-Primetime Players." A week after the inauguration, Eric Engberg of CBS said

A CLOSER LOOK

President Reagan and the Media

Among recent presidents, Ronald Reagan is unparalleled for his mastery over the media. On the surface, this mastery was all a matter of talent: Reagan, a former movie and TV actor, was hailed as the "Great Communicator." But a closer look reveals that Reagan's White House publicity machine had a great deal to do with his success and that the methods it employed were destructive to a democratic debate about the substance and meaning of his presidency.

Reagan surrounded himself in the White House with public relations (PR) experts, many of them veterans of President Nixon's pioneering efforts at news management. To these PR specialists, the key to Reagan's political success was controlling the messages the public received: The goal was to get across the administration's "spin" on events while blunting press efforts to uncover a less flattering picture of reality. A central technique of this news management was the "line of the day." Each morning, the White House PR staff would meet to discuss: "What do we want the press to cover today, and how?" This "line of the day" would be sent via computer to every part of the administra-

tion, so that every Reagan official spoke in unison. Reporters knew that this policy was designed to limit them to what the administration wanted discussed, but in their desperation for White House news they took what they were given.

Reagan's PR specialists also knew that in the age of television the eye counts for more than the ear: Appealing visual images have a greater impact than negative verbal comments. Extraordinary attention was paid by the specialists to the staging of TV and photo "opportunities" that cast President Reagan in a dramatic and glamorous light. Visiting the demilitarized zone that divides North and South Korea in 1983, Reagan was captured by the cameras as the bold commander-in-chief, dressed in a flak jacket as he surveyed the edges of the evil communist empire through binoculars. Every detail in staging this event was scripted in advance: When the president stood in a spot that did not make for the best pictures, his staff moved him to a better spot where toe marks had been drawn for him to pose.

The Reagan White House avoided the Nixon administration's tendency to attack reporters every time it disliked the tone of press coverage. Having

that the Clinton presidency had "come unstuck."[37] Throughout the opening weeks of the new administration, normally a honeymoon period between the White House and the media, reporters stressed the president's clumsiness at Washington power politics. From gays in the military to presidential haircuts, Clinton took media flak. Conservative commentators complained that he was too radical, and liberal commentators found him lacking passionate commitment. For his part, Clinton seethed in frustration at his media coverage and occasionally vented his anger in well-publicized outbursts at the press.

Why had such an articulate and charming president developed such a sour relationship with the media? During the 1992 Democratic primaries, Bill and

learned that an alienated press is more likely to be an aggressive press, Reagan's PR specialists worked to maintain relations between the White House and the media on a cordial level. At the same time, they made the president relatively inaccessible to journalists. Reagan held fewer press conferences than any of his modern predecessors, mainly because they exposed his habit of getting the facts wrong and his ignorance of what his own administration was doing. And he fended off questions at photo opportunities with a grin and a wave. It became so difficult to talk to the president that ABC's Sam Donaldson began to shout his questions at the hard-of-hearing Reagan.

Building on Reagan's personal charm and acting talent, his PR specialists aimed to make the president an icon of American ideals. On one hand, Reagan appeared through the media as strong and decisive, a leader who cited (and identified himself with) movie tough guys such as Clint Eastwood and Sylvester Stallone. On the other hand, he came across as cheerful, amiable, and humorous, an emblem of sunny optimism. As Richard Darman, one of Reagan's PR aides put it: "An attack on Reagan is tantamount to an attack on America's idealized image of itself." Reagan's carefully crafted image played well to the public, but it also obscured the consequences of his policies—for example, the increasing gap between rich and poor produced by his tax cuts and spending cuts.

Neither Bush nor Clinton have done as well with the press as Reagan. Bush lacked talent at acting the part of president. Clinton's White House staff has made many PR blunders. But Reagan's success at mastering the media could perhaps be reproduced if the same ingredients were once again combined. Considering how much the press was manipulated and the public was fed symbols instead of substance during the Reagan presidency, that would not be a healthy development for the democratic debate.

Sources: Mark Hertsgaard, *On Bended Knee: The Press and the Reagan Presidency* (New York: Schocken Books, 1989); Bruce Miroff, "The Presidency and the Public: Leadership as Spectacle," in Michael Nelson, ed., *The Presidency and the Political System*, 5th ed. (Washington, D.C.: CQ Press, 1998).

Hillary Rodham Clinton had resented the press's focus on charges of the candidate's marital infidelity, draft evasion, and marijuana smoking. Throughout the 1992 campaign, Clinton had considerable success circumventing the mainstream press and going directly to the voters with cable TV interviews and electronic town hall meetings. Entering the presidency, Clinton thought he could continue this approach. The White House closed staff offices to reporters, made it known that press conferences would be infrequent, and limited interviews with top administration officials.[38] But Clinton underestimated the power of the press. Feeling bypassed and manipulated, journalists struck back at him with negative coverage that badly tarnished his public image.

After only four months in office, Clinton was forced to reorganize his media team and alter his media strategy. Bringing David Gergen, who had been President Reagan's director of communications, into the White House as his media adviser, Clinton managed temporarily to enhance his standing with the press. But the seeds of suspicion had been planted, and the press has remained eager to investigate the series of scandals, starting with Whitewater in 1994, that have dogged the Clinton administration.

Ironically, Clinton achieved his best press coverage during the Republican revolution of 1995. With Newt Gingrich stealing the spotlight, the House Speaker was now the one who drew negative press commentary, while the president, contrasted with the highly unpopular Gingrich, was able to come across in the media as both compassionate and strong. Clinton enjoyed relatively good press coverage during his reelection campaign, only to see his relationship with the media again deteriorate with his campaign finance woes at the beginning of his second term.[39]

Developments in White House–media relations transcend personalities. With the end of the Cold War, presidents have a diminished capacity for foreign policy drama. Whereas Ronald Reagan could go to the Berlin Wall, Korea, and numerous summits with the Soviets, all of which provided heroic TV, Bill Clinton had to face Bosnia, Somalia, and Haiti, hardly colorful photo opportunities. The proliferation of cable channels has also hurt Clinton. With the mass audience fragmented into multiple media markets, a president can no longer dominate the airwaves as Reagan did.[40]

Clinton's rocky press relationship may be distinctive to his presidency, or it may herald a new era in which presidents have a tougher time using the media to communicate. The latter would be unfortunate if a president wanted to educate the American people about new problems and policies. But it also may reduce White House manipulation of the public through the media. From the standpoint of popular democracy, the diminishing ability of a president to dominate the media is welcome. A vital democratic debate is not monopolized by the occupant of the White House.[41]

THE PRESIDENCY AND DEMOCRATIC MOVEMENTS

Presidents try to sway public opinion through the media. Can members of the public directly sway the president? What impact can popular democratic movements have on presidential policies?

Some of the finest presidential moments have come when the chief executive responded to citizens and moved the nation closer to fulfillment of its democratic values. When Abraham Lincoln responded to mounting abolitionist pressures by emancipating slaves, when Franklin Roosevelt supported mobilized labor for collective bargaining rights, when Lyndon Johnson endorsed the civil rights movement by voicing its slogan, "We shall overcome," the presidency became an instrument of popular democratic leadership. These presidents were moved in the direction of popular democracy by the force of popular pressures, which compelled them to rethink their previous political calculations. But their popular democratic leadership was not simply a matter of gaining new support or attracting new voters. Mass movements educated these presidents, giving them a new understanding of democratic responsibilities.

Earlier in the chapter, we noted how President Kennedy responded to pressure from big business. But big business was not the only group to influence him; the civil rights movement also changed where Kennedy stood.[42]

Kennedy was sympathetic to the movement for racial equality. But civil rights did not hold a high priority for him. He wished to concentrate on the Cold War struggle against communism. He worried that strong backing for black equality would cost him support among southern members of Congress and southern voters. So he refused to push civil rights legislation or make statements about the immorality of racial discrimination, settling instead for quiet and gradual administrative actions.

The civil rights movement refused to settle for Kennedy's token gestures. The issue of racial equality was too central to democracy to permit the continuance of an unjust status quo. Movement organizations began dramatic campaigns of civil disobedience (see Chapter 10), designed not only to compel action from local white elites but also to pressure the president. In his first two years in office, Kennedy was able to resist this pressure. But in 1963, when civil rights demonstrators led by Martin Luther King, Jr., in Birmingham, Alabama, were savagely attacked with dogs and fire hoses, a horrified nation looked to the president.

Kennedy did respond, offering an example of popular democratic leadership. Having been educated himself by the Birmingham demonstrations about the depth of the racial crisis, he was ready to sweep aside his previous caution and take bold action. He proposed a major civil rights law (see Chapter 16). Equally important, he spoke to the nation with words that captured the moral urgency of the civil rights struggle: "We are confronted primarily with a moral issue. It is as old as the Scriptures and is as clear as the American Constitution. . . . This nation, for all of its hopes and all its boasts, will not be fully free until all its citizens are free."[43]

CONCLUSION: THE ELITE DEMOCRATIC PRESIDENCY

The story of Kennedy and the civil rights movement shows that presidents sometimes act as popular democratic leaders. It also suggests requirements of the role. If presidents are genuinely concerned to promote popular democracy, they should respect the capacities and intelligence of the people they claim to lead. Rather than manipulating public opinion, they should engage in a dialogue with citizens. Rather than aiming only to boost their own power, they should recognize their responsibility to empower ordinary citizens.

Presidents will not play the part of popular democratic leader very frequently. More often, the presidency is an instrument of elite democracy. Surrounded by a huge staff and living like monarchs, presidents tend to be cut off from ordinary Americans. Elitist attitudes and secrecy further distance the president, while making accountability difficult. Connections to and pressures from organized private interests, especially from the corporate sector, contradict the presidential claim to represent popular democracy. Presidents may cloak themselves in the symbols of popular democracy, but the modern presidential drama, featuring larger-than-life chief executives and passive citizens, is a far cry from the authentic American tradition of popular democracy.

KEY TERMS

White House staff
Executive Office of the President (EOP)
Office of Management and Budget (OMB)
Council of Economic Advisers (CEA)
National Security Council (NSC)

president's cabinet
legislative liaison staff
veto
line-item veto
Employment Act of 1946
War Powers Resolution of 1973
presidential power of secrecy

SUGGESTED READINGS

Terry Eastland, *Energy in the Executive: The Case for the Strong Presidency*. New York: Free Press, 1992. A Reagan conservative's forceful case for a contemporary version of Alexander Hamilton's strong presidency.

Charles Jones, *The Presidency in a Separated System*. Washington, D.C.: The Brookings Institution, 1994. An important argument that we should look less to the success of the president than to the success of the political system.

Bruce Miroff, *Icons of Democracy: American Leaders as Heroes, Aristocrats, Dissenters, and Democrats*. New York: Basic Books, 1993. Portraits of both elite democratic and popular democratic leadership.

Michael Nelson, ed., *The Presidency and the Political System*, 5th ed. Washington, D.C.: CQ Press, 1998. A lively anthology of original articles on the presidency.

Richard E. Neustadt, *Presidential Power and the Modern Presidents*. New York: Free Press, 1990. The classic work on how presidents can gain—or lose—personal power in the White House.

Stephen Skowronek, *The Politics Presidents Make*. Cambridge: Harvard University Press, 1997. An illuminating historical theory that relates presidential success or failure to the rise and fall of political regimes.

Bureaucracy: Myth and Reality

On March 1, 1995, the U.S. House of Representatives debated "regulatory reform," one of the items in the Republicans' Contract with America. Republican after Republican took the floor to lambaste the evils of bureaucratic regulation. Congressman George Gekas of Pennsylvania leveled a common charge against regulation: "Mr. Chairman, for too long, burdensome and complex rules coming out of Washington have strangled small business. . . . What we are about here today is to slay that dragon, to bring about sanity in the rulemaking process of the national bureaucracy." But the most colorful denunciation came from a Democrat, Congressman James Traficant, Jr., of Ohio, in a blast at the Environmental Protection Agency: "Mr. Chairman, I am one Democrat who believes regulations have gone too far. . . . It is so bad that if a dog urinates on a side lot, it may be declared a wetlands." March 1, 1995 was a field day for one of America's favorite political sports, bureaucracy bashing.[1]

Bureaucracy comprises the units of the executive branch organized in a hierarchical fashion, governed through formal rules, and distinguished by specialized functions. This chapter concentrates on bureaucracy at the national level. Although all federal bureaus have hierarchy, rulebound behavior, and specialization, they vary considerably in how they are organized, who staffs them, and what work they do. The employee of the Social Security Administration in Washington processing checks for Social Security recipients and the forest ranger checking on wildlife in the remote reaches of a national park are both bureaucrats. Thus, bureaucracy is not the drab monolith that the stereotypes present.

Bureaucracy is indeed a problem for a democratic political order, but it is also a necessity. It is a problem because bureaucratic hierarchy, expertise, and insulation from direct accountability can produce government operations that ignore the concerns of ordinary citizens. It is a necessity because our modern complex society, including the programs and policies that a democratic majority wants, requires skilled public administration.

This chapter neither bashes nor praises bureaucracy. Rather, it explains the democratic debate over bureaucracy in American politics. Two sets of key questions characterize this debate. First, how much bureaucracy do we need? Can bureaucracy be drastically cut back—for example, by turning to the alternative of economic markets, as some elite democrats now propose? Second, where bureaucracy is necessary, whose influence shapes its behavior? Are bureaucratic agencies predominantly influenced by elites? Or are these agencies responsive to popular democratic forces?

The chapter begins with a short history of the democratic debate over bureaucracy and then examines the size and scope of the modern administrative state in America, clearing away in the process some common myths about bureaucracy. Bureaucracies are inevitably entangled in politics, and the next two sections look at the internal and external political worlds of bureaucracy. Regulation of the economy by government—the principal preoccupation of conservative critics of bureaucracy—is the subject of the fifth section of the chapter.

Finally, the chapter discusses competing proposals for reforming bureaucracy: technocratic, market oriented, and popular democratic.

THE DEMOCRATIC DEBATE OVER BUREAUCRACY: A SHORT HISTORY

Bureaucracy has been one of the principal battlegrounds between elite democrats and popular democrats, both of whom have approached the issue with mixed emotions. Elite democrats have usually been the ones building up bureaucratic capacity in the federal government, but sometimes they have feared that what they have built might be transformed into an instrument of popular democratic control. (This fear is central to the contemporary elite reaction against bureaucracy.) Popular democrats have usually resisted the growth of bureaucracy, but sometimes they have needed it to turn popular democratic objectives into reality.

The Beginnings of American Administration

The Constitution says very little about how the president, as chief executive, will delegate the actual enforcement of the laws. When the first administration was formed under George Washington, there was not much of a bureaucracy. Befitting the aristocratic perspective of the Federalists, national administrators were recruited from the class of "gentlemen," and it was assumed that their personal character and reputation would ensure their good conduct without the need for impersonal rules and institutional checks.

However, Alexander Hamilton saw that a more systematic, impersonal, *bureaucratic* organization of government could achieve some of the central goals of elite democracy. In the *Federalist Papers*, he wrote that the people's "confidence in and obedience to a government will commonly be proportioned to the goodness or badness of its administration."[2] Associating popular democratic politics with disorder, Hamilton thought that efficient administration would pacify the people, turning them from active citizens into satisfied recipients of government services. As secretary of the Treasury, he made his own department into a model of bureaucratic organization and efficiency.[3]

The first major challenge to the rule of gentleman administrators came from Jacksonian Democracy. Speaking the language of popular democracy, President Jackson proclaimed, "The duties of all public officers are, or at least admit of being made so plain and simple that men of intelligence may readily qualify themselves for their performance."[4] Although Jackson seemed to be saying that ordinary citizens should fill most of the federal posts, in practice he removed only about 10 percent of the civil servants who had labored under his predecessors and replaced them mostly with well-connected lawyers. Jackson's presidency was notable, however, for relying less on trust in the personal character of administrators and more on formal rules and procedures to supervise their behavior. In this regard, political scientist Matthew Crenson writes, "the chief administrative legacy of the Jacksonians was bureaucracy."[5]

The Spoils System and Civil Service Reform

Jackson's successors followed his rhetoric more than his practice, turning out large numbers of officeholders and replacing them with supporters. Under this **spoils system,** the victor in each presidential election considered federal employment mostly as an opportunity for political patronage. In one sense, the nineteenth-century spoils system was democratic: It allowed ordinary people, through their work in a political party, to achieve government positions previously reserved for elites. But the periodic shuffling of civil servants made for inefficient administration, and the close ties of civil servants to local party machines opened the door to corruption.

The system's defects sparked a reform movement after the Civil War that aimed to institute a different basis for selecting national administrators. Reformers demanded that federal employment be based not on party service but on competitive examinations and other measures of competence. Their cause was given a boost when a disappointed office seeker, crazed by his failure to get a patronage position, assassinated President James A. Garfield in 1881. With public attention now fixed on the evils of the spoils system, Congress passed the Pendleton Act in 1883, establishing a civil service commission to administer a merit system for federal employment. Civil service reform, although an important step toward a more efficient and honest federal bureaucracy, was also a victory for elite democrats: Reformers were mainly from the upper class and expected that their class would regain its once-dominant role in administration through examinations that favored the highly educated.

As industrialization transformed American life in the closing decades of the nineteenth century, the problem of regulating the giant business corporations that were emerging gave a further impetus to builders of bureaucracy. Allied with upper-class civil service reformers seeking to expand the administrative capacities of the federal government was a new class of professionals, especially lawyers and social scientists. These state builders were largely elite democrats whose goal was a more rational, expert-dominated administrative order insulated from the partisan strife of popular politics. They were stalemated, however, by foes of a federal bureaucracy. Some were genuine popular democrats afraid of new institutions beyond the people's reach. Others, however, were concerned mainly with preserving local party machines and their pork barrel prizes.[6]

It was in the first decades of the twentieth century—the Progressive era—that the bureaucratic state in America first assumed its modern form. The Progressives hoped to combine popular democracy and elite democracy. They sponsored reforms, such as the initiative, referendum, and recall (which allow citizens to vote on legislation and to remove elected officials), that aimed to take power away from party bosses and return it directly to the people. They also proposed to staff an expanded administrative order with scientifically trained and politically neutral experts. As political scientist James Morone has written, "At the heart of the Progressive agenda lay a political paradox: government would simultaneously be returned to the people and placed beyond them, in the hands of the experts."[7] But the Progressives succeeded neither in restoring power to the people nor in achieving scientific administration. The agencies of government they created to regulate an industrial economy generally found it impossible to devise truly scientific standards that furthered the public interest. Even worse, the elite economic interests that were supposed to be the subjects of regulation generally became the most powerful influence on the regulators.

The New Deal and Bureaucracy

The Great Depression led to an expansion of the federal bureaucracy beyond even the hopes of the Progressive reformers, and the New Deal changed the attitudes of popular democrats toward bureaucracy. Just as in the case of federalism (Chapter 15), the need to achieve control over the corporations compelled popular democrats to accept a more powerful and bureaucratic federal government. Yet elite democrats still retained considerable influence within this government. The hastily built administrative apparatus of Franklin Roosevelt contained both popular democratic and elite democratic elements.

Harry Hopkins, a leading administrator, was one example of the New Deal's success in reconciling popular democracy and bureaucracy. President Roosevelt placed Hopkins in charge of federal efforts to aid the unemployed. Hopkins took charge of these efforts in a fashion that led biographer George McJimsey to dub him "democracy's bureaucrat."[8] Putting a public works program for the unemployed into operation with remarkable speed, Hopkins proclaimed, "The only thing that counts is action . . . and we are going to surround [the program] with as few regulations as possible."[9] Determined to avoid bureaucratic red tape, Hopkins was equally determined to avoid the bureaucrat's reliance on a formal hierarchy of superiors and subordinates. He ran his Washington office through group discussion and kept in close touch with administrators in the field who were working with the unemployed.

Hopkins's values, as much as his methods, made him a popular democrat as bureaucrat. When critics complained of waste and confusion in the public works programs that Hopkins headed, he conceded that he had made mistakes. But he would not apologize for them because they had been made "in the interests of the people that were broke."[10] To Hopkins, administration was not primarily a matter of scientific expertise but an opportunity to practice civic virtue. "One of the proudest and finest things that ever happened and ever can happen to me," he said, "is the opportunity to work for this government of ours and the people who make it up. . . . I wouldn't give this last two years of my life for a life work done in another type of endeavor. I have learned, as I never knew before, what it means to love your country."[11]

Unfortunately, much of the bureaucratic machinery created by the New Deal did not reflect either Hopkins's methods or his values. To cope with the emergency conditions of the Depression, the New Deal tied many of the new administrative agencies to the industrial and agricultural interests with which they dealt. Allowing private interests to play a powerful role in public agencies was supposed to be a temporary measure. But when the Depression passed, the tight bonds between private interests and public agencies remained. The bureaucratic state became, to a disturbing degree, a special interest state in which administrative expertise was placed in the service of economic elites.

The next major expansion of American bureaucracy came during the 1960s and early 1970s, with new administrative units established to carry out popular democratic goals such as environmental protection, consumer safety, and the elimination of poverty. Yet while the bureaucracy was becoming a more complicated mixture of elite and popular democratic elements, its image was becoming more simplistic and negative. Bureaucracy—with a capital *B*—became a bogeyman for critics of every political persuasion. Conservatives saw a swollen and monstrous Bureaucracy as the chief threat to individual freedom. Liberals and radicals saw an arrogant and stifling Bureaucracy as the chief barrier to social change. It was the conservatives, with the election of Ronald Reagan in 1980, who had the chance to act on their ideological hostility to bureaucracy.

From Reagan to Clinton: Attack or Reinvent Bureaucracy?

President Reagan entered office as an avowed enemy of bureaucracy, and during his eight years as chief executive he presided over an unprecedented assault on federal administration. Because Congress blunted many of his attacks, Reagan was not able to enact drastic cuts in the federal bureaucracy. But he did manage to heap scorn on bureaucracy and to broadcast negative stereotypes of it to the public.

Big government, the president told Americans, best served the public by "shriveling up and going away."[12] White House chief of staff Edwin Meese showed off a doll he named "the Bureaucrat"; he put the doll on a pile of papers and pointed out how it just sat there and did nothing.[13] In this hostile climate, many civil servants felt undermined and demoralized. The bureaucracy managed to survive Ronald Reagan, but a serious democratic debate over bureaucracy, based on a recognition of its true features, had been obscured by scornful stereotypes.

President Clinton has tackled the topic of bureaucratic reform. Even though Clinton hopes, like Reagan, to cut down the size of the bureaucracy, his goal is different: He wants the federal government to work better, not to shrivel up and go away. Meanwhile, the congressional Republican majority of 1995–96 renewed President Reagan's assault on the bureaucracy. The conflicting plans for the bureaucracy of Clinton and the Republicans are considered later in the chapter.

THE MODERN ADMINISTRATIVE STATE IN AMERICA

The present-day federal government is largely an **administrative state.** It is involved in regulating or supporting almost every imaginable form of social activity by means of a large, complex, and diverse bureaucracy. In this section, we present a snapshot of the contemporary federal bureaucracy depicting its most important features. We also set these features against some prevailing myths about bureaucracy.

The Civil Service

About 3 million Americans work as civil servants in the federal bureaucracy. (About 1.5 million more serve in the armed forces—a number that has declined with the end of the Cold War.) Contrary to the image of a centralized bureaucratic machine, approximately 90 percent of these federal employees work outside Washington, D.C. Most bureaucrats deliver services where the people are—whether as Social Security branch workers, air traffic controllers, or civilian employees at military installations. Although the federal bureaucracy draws the most attention from critics, it is actually smaller in terms of personnel than state and local governments. The states employ about 4.5 million workers, and local governments employ about 11 million.[14] When all levels of government are taken into account, one out of six employed people in the United States can be called a government bureaucrat[15] (see Table 13.1)!

TABLE 13.1

Governmental Employment, 1992

Government	Full-time and Part-time Employees (in thousands)
Federal civilian	3,047
State	4,595
Local	(11,103)
County	2,253
Municipalities	2,665
School districts	5,134
Townships	424
Special districts	627
Total	18,745

Source: Harold W. Stanley and Richard G. Niemi, *Vital Statistics on American Politics,* 5th ed. (Washington, D.C.: CQ Press, 1995), pp. 292. Copyright © 1995 by CQ Press. Used with permission.

A majority of federal bureaucrats hold their positions in accordance with the General Schedule, a merit-based personnel system in which there are eighteen pay grades. At the bottom of the General Schedule, GS-1, are the most menial tasks. At the top, GS-18, are executive positions of considerable responsibility and high pay. Competitive examinations and formal education are the two principal determinants of merit in the General Schedule. But other factors may be taken into account, with preference given to armed forces veterans and affirmative action programs for minorities.

Most civil servants spend their entire career in the same agency. Congress attempted to change this situation with the passage of the Civil Service Reform Act of 1978, which created the Senior Executive Service (SES). The SES (which is above the General Schedule) was supposed to enable presidents to choose from a pool of the most talented career executives and shift them to whatever agencies required their particular skills. The SES would also make federal service more challenging to top bureaucrats. As political scientist B. Guy Peters observes, "The managers were supposed to have the opportunity for substantial bonuses, sabbaticals, and more important positions, but ran a greater risk of being fired for poor performance than if they had remained members of the General Schedule system."[16] Contrary to these objectives, President Reagan manipulated the SES to fulfill his ideological goals.

At the highest reaches of the bureaucracy are the president's political appointees. Their merits are not necessarily the same as those of career civil servants. Certainly, managerial competence is valued for political appointees, but so are loyalty to the president and agreement with his political program. Presidential appointees are sometimes called "in and outers" because their tenure in public service is usually short; most, in fact, do not last for the four years of a president's term.

Types of Federal Agencies

The administrative state in America is made up of a bewildering variety of bureaucracies (see Figure 13.1). Federal agencies differ from one another on many scores: form of organization, type of leadership, breadth or narrowness of function, political dependence on or independence from the president, financial dependence on or independence from Congress.

Cabinet departments are the bureaucratic agencies most familiar to Americans. When the federal government was formed, its first agencies were the Departments of State, Treasury, and War (along with the individual position of attorney general). Today, there are fourteen cabinet departments, each headed by a secretary appointed by the president: State, Treasury, Defense, Interior, Agriculture, Justice, Commerce, Labor, Health and Human Services, Housing and Urban Development, Transportation, Energy, Education, and Veterans Affairs. The fourteen departments vary enormously in size and complexity. But each is responsible for a broad area of governmental operations whose administration is divided up among specialized bureaus within the department.

FIGURE 13.1 The Government of the United States (As of July 1, 1993)

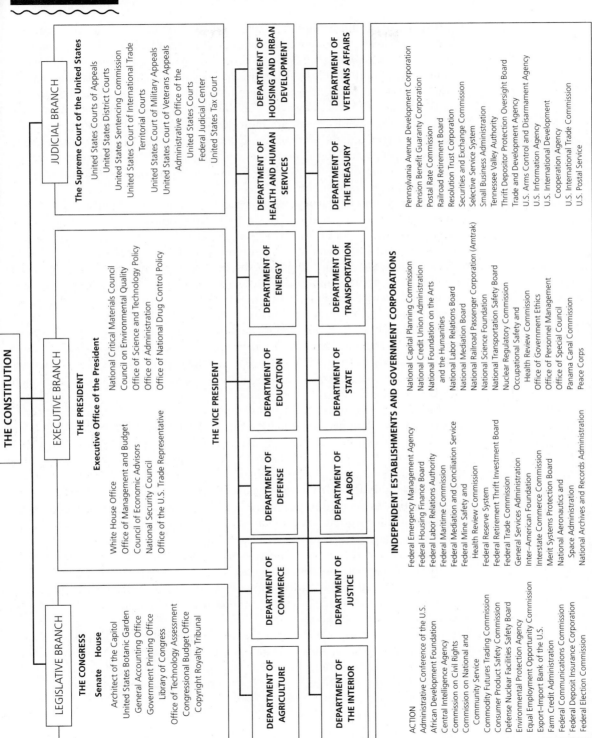

Source: Chart prepared by U.S. Bureau of the Census.

Independent agencies stand outside the cabinet departments and generally handle narrower areas of government operation. Examples are the Environmental Protection Agency (EPA), the National Aeronautics and Space Administration (NASA), and the Central Intelligence Agency (CIA). Like cabinet departments, most independent agencies are headed by a single individual appointed by the president. Some, however, like the Merit System Protection Board that governs federal employment, are multiheaded. Congress sometimes creates independent agencies, rather than simply establishing new bureaus within existing cabinet departments, in the hope that a new agency will be more innovative if it is free of the bureaucratic routines and intraorganizational conflicts that typify existing cabinet departments.

Independent regulatory commissions are designed to regulate various sectors of the economy. Examples are the Interstate Commerce Commission (ICC), which regulates ground transportation; the Nuclear Regulatory Commission, which regulates the nuclear power industry; and the Securities and Exchange Commission (SEC), which regulates the stock market. By creating multimember commissions drawn from both parties and by giving the commissioners long terms and exemption from presidential removal, Congress has tried to distance these agencies from political pressures and make them neutral and expert regulators. In practice, however, the independent regulatory commissions have not been able to separate administration from politics. Presidents are able to exert some influence by their choice of a chair for the commission. The regulated industry itself is a constant source of political pressure as it lobbies the commission for favorable decisions.

Public corporations are government agencies that engage in business activities. The most familiar of these is the Postal Service (until 1971, the Post Office was a cabinet department). Others are the Tennessee Valley Authority (TVA), which generates and sells electric power; Amtrak, which operates passenger railroads; and the Corporation for Public Broadcasting, which sponsors public television and radio. Public corporations have been created largely to carry out economic activities deemed unprofitable by private businesses. The organizational form of public corporations protects them from most political influences. Further, they enjoy far greater financial independence than other kinds of federal agencies, such as the ability to borrow money on their own rather than relying solely on appropriations from Congress.

Federal foundations and endowments allow the government to sponsor scientific and cultural activities that otherwise might languish for lack of funds. The National Science Foundation (NSF) is a major donor to scientific research in the United States. The National Institutes of Health (NIH) funds research on dangerous diseases, such as acquired immune deficiency syndrome (AIDS). The National Endowment for the Humanities (NEH) and the National Endowment for the Arts (NEA) support the creative projects of scholars, writers, and artists.

Myth and Reality in the Administrative State

To its many detractors, the federal bureaucracy is a bastion of elite privilege and irresponsibility. The expertise and power wielded by bureaucrats lend some credence to these criticisms. But myths about bureaucracy exaggerate its elitist character; in reality, the federal bureaucracy is a complex mix of elite and popular democratic features.

Probably the most powerful of the myths about the modern administrative state concerns the identity of the typical bureaucrat. The faceless bureaucrat of myth is inefficient and lazy on one hand, aggressive and hyperactive in meddling in people's lives on the other. But in truth bureaucrats are ordinary people. Compared to presidents and members of Congress, bureaucrats as a group are more representative of the American population.

Even if bureaucrats do resemble other Americans, proponents of the bureaucratic myth contend that the rigid rules of bureaucracy attract people with authoritarian personalities and that the tedious nature of bureaucratic work makes civil servants frustrated and irritable. In this view, bureaucrats, however average they may be, are afflicted with a "bureaucratic mentality." Yet empirical studies by social psychologists have found that public employees are at least as open minded and flexible as those who work in private businesses. As for the image of the miserable and angry civil servant, studies of bureaucratic attitudes show, according to public administration scholar Charles Goodsell, "relatively high levels of motivation, job satisfaction, and pride."[17]

But if bureaucrats are ordinary people with regular personalities and a positive attitude toward their work, why do most citizens have a negative attitude toward bureaucracy? Actually, this view has more to do with bureaucracy in the abstract. It reflects constant bureaucracy bashing by politicians and the media. When questioned about contact with civil servants, a large majority report satisfactory experiences.[18]

The myth of bureaucracy rests not only on stereotypes of the individual bureaucrat but also on stereotypes of the organizations that make up the federal bureaucracy. According to these stereotypes, federal agencies are gigantic in size, aggressively growing larger all the time, and immensely powerful. In reality, federal agencies come in many sizes and shapes. The Department of Defense, with approximately 830,000 civilian employees, supports the image of a gigantic bureaucracy. But most other cabinet departments and independent agencies are much smaller. The Department of Education, for instance, has fewer than 5,000 employees (see Table 13.2).

The mythical bureaucratic agency is power hungry, eagerly grasping for ever-larger functions, programs, and budgets. But real bureaucratic agencies are hesitant about growth if it threatens their identity. Most agencies have a **mission,** a central task to which its members are committed. They welcome more authority and money in pursuit of this mission. But they are not eager to take on divergent missions even when these would bring growth to the agency. Thus, the Department of Agriculture, which defines its mission as assisting America's farmers,

TABLE 13.2	Department	Personnel
	Agriculture	113,321
Size Of U.S. Government Executive Departments: Civilian Personnel, 1995	Commerce	36,803
	Defense	830,738
	Education	4,988
	Energy	19,589
	Health and Human Services	59,788
	Housing and Urban Development	11,822
	Interior	76,439
	Justice	103,262
	Labor	16,204
	State	24,859
	Transportation	63,552
	Treasury	155,951
	Veterans Affairs	263,904

Source: *Statistical Abstract of the United States 1996* (Washington, D.C.: U.S. Government Printing Office, 1996).

has been unhappy with—and tried to get rid of—its role in the welfare area as administrator of the food stamp program.[19]

Most bureaucratic agencies are not as large or as imperialistic as believers in the bureaucratic myth presume. Neither are they as powerful. Subject to many constraining forces, federal agencies tend to be defensive rather than offensive, to placate other holders of power more than assert their own power.[20]

In criticizing the prevalent myth about bureaucracy, we do not mean to claim that all is well with the American administrative state. Many problems of rigidity, inefficiency, and promotion of bureaucratic goals over public needs deserve attention. The prevalent myth, however, focuses attention on bureaucracy simply to turn it into a scapegoat. Bureaucracy is a convenient scapegoat for elected politicians who wish to divert attention from their own inability to carry through on the promises they make to voters. It is a convenient scapegoat for citizens who resent both the taxes they pay and the social ills that never seem to get cured by federal spending.

BUREAUCRATS AS POLICY MAKERS

Understanding bureaucracy in a realistic way requires, above all, a recognition that it is a *political* institution. The scholars who founded the study of public administration in the United States (one of them a future president, Woodrow Wilson) sought to distinguish administration from politics. Bureaucracies existed, they claimed, only to provide the technical means for carrying out ends that political (i.e., elected) officials had decided.[21] Today, few believe in the politics-administration dichotomy. Administrators operate in an intensely political environment, and they must make key political decisions themselves. They are policy makers, not just technicians.

Administrators are politically influential because they possess **expertise.** Bureaucrats tend to know more than anyone else about their particular areas of responsibility. Expertise may come through a combination of specialization and experience. Compare the career civil servant, who has spent many years dealing with a single policy area, to the elected official, who must tackle many different policy areas with a shorter base of experience. An even more formidable ground of expertise is professional training. "A variety of highly trained elites," writes political scientist Francis Rourke, "practice their trade in public organizations— physicists, economists, engineers."[22] The arguments of these elites carry special weight because they are presumed to draw from professional knowledge. Elected officials are the bosses of civil servants but often defer to their expertise (see the box on p. 354).[23]

Bureaucratic expertise is central to the democratic debate over bureaucracy. In the eighteenth and nineteenth centuries, it was elite democrats who were most enthusiastic about bureaucratic expertise. Since the New Deal, however, many elite democrats have come to favor the market mechanisms of the private sector and have grown skeptical about expertise in government.

Popular democrats are also troubled by the claims of expertise. They recognize that when bureaucrats invoke technical criteria to address a problem, the concerns of ordinary citizens may be shunted aside. For example, highway planners have sometimes ravaged communities in the name of engineering criteria. Yet popular democrats also recognize that their political agenda requires the help of experts. How, for example, can we clean up the environment without the efforts of environmental scientists?

Administrators are also politically influential because they exercise considerable **discretion.** Handed broad and vague policy guidelines by elected officials, administrators give policy substance through numerous, more concrete decisions. For example, Congress directs the Occupational Safety and Health Administration (OSHA) to protect employees from cancer-causing chemicals in the workplace. It is up to OSHA to set allowable exposure levels for various carcinogens. In determining these levels, OSHA administrators make decisions about which companies and unions are likely to disagree; inevitably, the decisions will be political and not just technical.

MAKING A DIFFERENCE

Dr. Helene Gayle and the Battle Against AIDS

Stereotypes about the kind of people who work in the federal bureaucracy can blind us to the talent and dedication that many civil servants bring to their jobs. One individual who explodes the stereotypes is Dr. Helene Gayle of the U.S. Government's Center for Disease Control and Prevention (CDC). This young African-American woman has played an instrumental role in the federal government's domestic and international efforts to combat the horrors of AIDS.

The federal government was, in fact, slow to adopt measures to cope with the AIDS epidemic, which began in the early 1980s. The Reagan and Bush administrations never placed much of a priority on combatting AIDS. Perhaps this was because AIDS in the United States was initially perceived as a disease confined mostly to gay men. But indifference at the top did not lead to inaction among public health professionals in the federal bureaucracy. Government scientists and health officials

have been devoted to finding ways to prevent, treat, and eventually cure AIDS. Dr. Helene Gayle, an epidemiologist, has taken a leading role in these efforts.

Dr. Gayle was born in 1955 in Buffalo, New York. Her parents were activists in the civil rights movement and instilled in her a commitment to seek a better world. She received her medical degree from the University of Pennsylvania and, interested in the social uses to which her training could be put, went on to obtain a master's degree in public health from Johns Hopkins University. At the age of twenty-nine, she joined the CDC and began training as an epidemiologist.

Upon completing this training, Dr. Gayle joined the CDC's Divsion of HIV/AIDS. She conducted research on how HIV is transmitted from mothers to children and within communities of young people—populations groups that have been, contrary to the image of AIDS as a "gay disease," increasingly at risk of contacting it. This research

Legislation can be so precise and detailed that it reduces bureaucratic discretion to a minimum. But for both political and technical reasons, such precision is usually not possible. In certain cases, a legislative majority can be constructed only through ambiguous language that leaves contending parties satisfied that their concerns have been heard. As a result, political conflict in Congress is displaced into the bureaucratic domain. In other cases, Congress may lack the time, expertise, or foreknowledge to write precise legislation and counts on bureaucratic discretion to fill in the blanks. Extensive discretion is disturbing to popular democrats, who generally prefer Congress to shape the details.

Expertise and discretion make administrators influential in policy making. They employ that influence indirectly and directly. Administrators exercise *indirect influence* over policy in their capacity as advisers to elected officials. When a president, for example, faces a major policy decision, he or she turns to the per-

drew her into federal programs aimed at preventing the spread of AIDS. In these programs, her personal and political skills proved to be as valuable as her medical skills. She recognized that given the poor initial record of the federal government in the fight against AIDS, gay and minority groups were understandably suspicious. So she bent her efforts to improving communications between public health officials and community groups in order that the two might become allies instead of adversaries in battling AIDS. She even welcomed the protest campaigns of the gay movement "as extremely important catalysts for pushing the government forward in its response to AIDS."

After her highly successful efforts to bring organizations representing gays, minority communities, and drug addicts into productive involvement in federal programs of AIDS prevention, Dr. Gayle became a leading figure in the international struggle against AIDS. Although most Americans think of AIDS as a disease affecting gay men and drug addicts in the United States, about 80 percent of HIV and AIDS cases globally are found in developing countries, where heterosexual intercourse is the primary source of new infections. Dr. Gayle helped to shape AIDS training programs that enlist doctors and scientists from countries in Africa, Asia, Latin America, and the Caribbean in research and prevention efforts. Through these programs, local expertise on AIDS has been developed and tailored to each country's distinct medical and cultural issues in the fight against AIDS.

Working in the federal bureaucracy, with all of its administrative rules and political conflicts, has carried its share of frustrations for a public health activist like Dr. Gayle. With her exceptional talents, she could easily have found a lucrative career in the private sector. Yet she has chosen to work at CDC because, she says, "the potential within the federal government to have an impact at a very broad level is very compelling." Dr. Gayle has found a place where she can make a difference in the lives of many suffering people.

Source: Norma M. Riccucci, *Unsung Heroes: Federal Execucrats Making a Difference* (Washington, D.C.: Georgetown University Press, 1995), pp. 201–25.

tinent bureaucratic agency for data, analysis, and recommendations. The agency cannot determine what the president will decide, but it may be able to shape how he or she thinks about the decision. Bureaucratic advice may be couched in the language of technical expertise, but it is seldom neutral and purely technical. An agency is likely to tell the president to achieve a desired end by giving it, rather than another agency, the resources and the responsibility to do the job.

Administrators exercise *direct influence* through the **rule-making authority** that Congress delegates to the bureaucracy. When agencies give specificity to vague congressional mandates by issuing rules, these rules carry the force of law. And since they are far more precise than the legislation under which they were drafted, they shape policy in important ways. Each year, the bureaucracy issues a far larger number of rules than Congress passes laws, and these rules are published in the *Federal Register*. Limits to arbitrary rule making are established in the Administrative Procedures Act of 1946, which all agencies must follow. Before a new rule can be put into effect, for instance, interested citizens and groups must receive advance notice and be permitted to comment on it.

Rule making by administrators is considered *quasilegislative*. The bureaucracy also possesses *quasijudicial* authority in the form of **administrative adjudication.** Whereas rules govern a large number of parties and cover future behavior, adjudications affect only the individual parties in a case and cover past behavior. Adjudication is the province of administrative law judges. Cases in administrative law must follow the rules of due process, but the requirements of due process are not as strict as in the regular courts; thus, there is no right to a jury trial in administrative law. Administrative law judges handle far more cases than federal court judges do.

American citizens most often come into contact with federal authority through rules issued by administrators and decisions handed down by administrative law judges. Indeed, bureaucrats make many of the policy decisions that affect our lives. Much of this is inevitable, and some of it may even be desirable for the advancement of democratic goals. Yet these people are not elected or necessarily visible in their exercise of power. How to hold administrators, with their expertise and their discretion, their rule making and adjudicatory authority, accountable to the people and their elected representatives is an enduring problem for a democratic society.

THE POLITICAL ENVIRONMENT OF BUREAUCRACY

Bureaucracy is a political institution not only because administrators possess political influence but also because they operate in a highly political environment. A formal, hierarchical, technically focused bureaucracy could wait passively for elected officials to order it into action. But real bureaucratic agencies exist in an environment where policies reflect political, rather than technical, values; where resources are scarce; and where rivals seek to encroach on cherished turf. Thus, agencies actively seek to mobilize political support from others—the public, interest groups, Congress, the White House—and these same political forces seek to shape what agencies do.

Seeking Political Support

Some administrative agencies, such as the Federal Maritime Commission, function largely out of sight of the general public. Other agencies, however, are highly visible to the public and take steps to ensure favorable citizens' impressions—the more favorable the public is, the better the agency is likely to be treated by Congress and the president. Agencies can inform the public about their work while casting that work in a positive light through free booklets, public service ads on television, and Washington headquarters tours. Agencies can attempt to wrap their activities in the mantle of mysterious expertise and glamorous risk taking—these have been favorite tactics of both the armed forces and NASA. To be visible, however, is to be vulnerable should things go wrong. When the space shuttle *Challenger* exploded after takeoff in 1986, killing all seven crew members, including a schoolteacher, NASA suffered a public relations disaster as well as a human tragedy.

The public is too inattentive, and its backing too fickle, to provide most agencies with all the political support they need. "Hence," Francis Rourke observes,

> it is essential to every agency's power position to have the support of attentive groups whose attachment is grounded on an enduring tie. The groups an agency provides tangible benefits to are the most natural basis of such political support, and it is with these interest groups that agencies ordinarily establish the firmest alliances.[24]

The immediate masters of bureaucratic agencies are Congress and the president, so their political support is indispensable. Congress determines the statutory authority of an agency and holds the purse strings for its annual appropriation. The leadership of an agency must therefore take care to cultivate goodwill on Capitol Hill. Political support is obtained from the key legislative and appropriations committees by respectful, even deferential treatment and by more tangible promises. As political scientist James Q. Wilson notes, "Whenever an agency sends up a budget request it makes certain that there will be projects in it that will serve the districts represented by the members of the appropriations subcommittees (as well as members of certain key legislative committees)."[25] The goodwill of the president is also a goal of bureaucratic chiefs, who do not want the White House staff or the Office of Management and Budget (OMB) frowning on their legislative and budget requests. Yet presidents, as we saw in Chapter 12, often complain that bureaucrats are insufficiently loyal and take steps to bring the bureaucracy under tighter White House control.

The more successful an agency is in gaining political support from the public, interest groups, Congress, and the president, the greater **autonomy** it will enjoy in the sense of freedom from control by external forces. Autonomy allows a bureaucracy to pursue its mission unhindered. Although this can be desirable, too much autonomy may also prove dangerous.

Probably the extreme case of an autonomous federal agency was the Federal Bureau of Investigation (FBI) under J. Edgar Hoover. By cultivating public support through highly publicized captures of criminals and by courting presidents with inside information on their political rivals, Hoover won extraordinary autonomy for his FBI. This autonomy led to autocratic uses of power. During the early years of the Cold War, Hoover was a fanatical anticommunist and employed the FBI to destroy the careers and lives of numerous individuals suspected of "subversive" activities. When the civil rights movement rose to its zenith in the 1960s, he developed a personal loathing for Martin Luther King, Jr. and set out to destroy him.[26] Under Hoover, the FBI became a nightmare bureaucracy.

Constraints on Bureaucracy

Fortunately, the kind of autonomy that Hoover achieved at the FBI is rare. Agencies struggle to mobilize political support not only to increase their autonomy but also to fend off threats to already established autonomy. The political environment that most agencies face is filled with potentially constraining forces: other agencies, Congress, the president, the courts, interest groups, and the public. These checks and constraints are double edged. On one hand, they prevent most agencies from becoming the arbitrary and oppressive bureaucracies that prevailing myths depict (and that occasionally exist, as with Hoover's FBI). On the other hand, the existence of such "potent centrifugal forces," political scientists Charles Levine, B. Guy Peters, and Frank Thompson write, "frequently makes it difficult for officials to design and implement coherent public policies."[27] As is also the case for Congress and the president, checks and balances in the bureaucracy yield greater safety but lesser effectiveness.

An agency seeking to carry out its core mission may be threatened by another agency promoting *its* core mission. A classic illustration of such conflict between agencies, which scholars call **bureaucratic politics,** is the feud between the Air Force and the Navy over bombing. Since the end of World War II, there has been a belief among Navy officers that the Air Force seeks to control all aviation and a conflicting belief among Air Force officers that the Navy, with its aircraft carriers, tries to encroach on the Air Force speciality of strategic bombing. The services have competed to promote their core missions. During the Vietnam War, former NSC official Morton Halperin writes, this competition "probably led each service to exaggerate the effectiveness of its bombing to outshine the other."[28]

In the competitive world of bureaucracy, agencies look for allies on Capitol Hill and in the White House. But friends in high places can sometimes turn into bosses, interested less in supporting the agency's agenda than in advancing their own. Both Congress and the president have in recent years intensified their efforts to shape bureaucratic behavior. Congressional oversight of the bureaucracy has increased, with legislators using formal hearings and informal contacts to signal how they want programs implemented. Presidential efforts to control the bureaucracy through personnel and budgetary strategies have been even more notable, especially during the Reagan presidency. The struggle between Congress and the presidency over the bureaucracy has become more visible, but it is an old struggle rooted in the Constitution. As James Q. Wilson comments, "That document makes the president and Congress rivals for control of the American administrative system. The rivalry leads to struggle and the struggle breeds frustration."[29] This frustration grows out of the requirement that federal agencies serve two different—and often opposed—masters.

A third master has entered the picture in recent decades: the federal courts. For most of American history, judges did not intervene in the actions of bureaucrats, believing that administrative discretion was not subject to the same judicial scrutiny as legislation. But since the New Deal, the federal courts have been more willing to take up cases of agency decision making. The courts have enabled citizens to bring suits against agencies and have required agencies to justify their discretionary actions. Judges have even ordered federal agencies to change how they implement policy. Administrators now must worry not only about how a congressional committee or a White House staff member may respond to their behavior but also about how a district court judge may rule on its legality.

BUREAUCRACY AND THE POLITICAL ECONOMY

How much bureaucracy do Americans need? The initial answer of a popular democrat would be, "Far less." Many citizens complain that the administrative state stifles individual freedom with excessive forms, rules, and personnel. Yet the most influential advocates of bureaucratic downsizing have been not ordinary citizens but members of the business community, and their unhappiness with bureaucracy has less to do with freedom than with profits. In the face of business assaults on bureaucracy since the 1970s, popular democrats have found themselves in the unexpected position of having to defend it.

Popular democrats historically opposed the bureaucratization of American politics and remain worried about the reign of unaccountable elites in the administrative state. Nevertheless, they have also had to acknowledge that their past victories in extending protections to ordinary people against the abuses of private power can be preserved only with the help of administrative agencies. Hence, the historical roles of elite democrats and popular democrats have been reversed: Elite democrats largely built the administrative state but now want to shrink it, while popular democrats defend an administrative state they once feared.

The contemporary debate over bureaucracy has focused primarily on those agencies that regulate the economy. **Regulation** is "a process or activity in which government requires or proscribes certain activities or behavior on the part of individuals and institutions . . . and does so through a continuing administrative process, generally through specially designated regulatory agencies."[30] Understanding the contemporary struggle over regulation means distinguishing two different types. **Economic regulation** is usually conducted by an independent regulatory commission; covers a specific industry; and focuses on matters of prices, quality of services, and ability to enter or leave the industry. **Social regulation** is usually conducted by a single-headed agency answerable to the president; covers all industries; and focuses on such matters as environmental protection, safety, health, and nondiscrimination. It is the latter type that has generated the most controversy.

Economic Regulation

Economic regulation has the longer history in American politics. As industrialization strained the capacities of a weak national state, Congress created independent regulatory commissions to bring the changing economy under some measure of control. The prototype of the new regulatory agency was the Interstate Commerce Commission (ICC), formed in 1887 to regulate the railroad industry. Industrial abuses paved the way for the development of economic regulation, which has often been portrayed as a victory for popular democracy over economic elites. Revisionist historians, however, have shown that industrialists themselves sometimes pushed for federal regulation, hoping to limit competition or to avert public ownership.[31]

Regardless of whether independent regulatory commissions sprang into existence to serve popular or elite interests, many of them entered into a cozy relationship with the industries they were supposed to oversee. According to the "capture thesis," once a regulatory commission was established and the public and its elected officials turned their attention elsewhere, the only political force exercising constant leverage on the commission was the regulated industry, which captured the commission and made it an ally rather than a check. Although this thesis still has some validity, recent scholarship has pointed out its flaws. In the past few decades, Congress and the presidency have exercised greater influence over the independent regulatory commissions. And public interest groups have turned their attention to the commissions, bringing pressure to bear as a counterveiling force against the regulated industries.[32]

Although most economic regulation has not been very burdensome to business, there has been a movement in recent years, promoted by economists and backed by business elites, to scale down the role of the government in the economy. Advocates of such **deregulation** argue that market forces will promote the interests of producers and consumers alike far more efficiently than the intrusive hand of government. Deregulation began during the presidencies of Gerald Ford and Jimmy Carter and accelerated during the presidency of Ronald Reagan, with the most notable changes in the fields of transportation, communications, and banking. Existing regulatory controls were relaxed, and private economic forces were trusted to serve the public interest by engaging in market competition.

How well has deregulation worked? In the case of the airline industry, the positive effects of deregulation (air fares in general have declined, and the number of passengers has increased) have outweighed the negative.[33] The situation is different, however, in the case of savings and loans companies (S&Ls). When Congress and the president took controls off this industry in the early 1980s, savings and loan operators went wild. Poorly conceived real estate loans, financial gimmicks that bilked small investors, and outright looting by operators sent many S&Ls into massive debt. Thanks to government insurance of deposits up to $100,000, the federal government and ultimately the taxpayers have had to pick up the tab of $132 billion. In this case, the assumption that the market automatically promotes the public good has been shown to be mistaken.

Social Regulation

Debates over economic regulation versus deregulation center on which approach has a more beneficial effect on people's pocketbooks. Debates over social regulation versus deregulation tend to pit the physical, moral, and aesthetic well-being of the American people against considerations of economics. Whereas economic regulation goes back to the late nineteenth century, social regulation has largely been a product of the 1960s and 1970s. Examples of social regulation include consumer safety, worker safety and health, antidiscrimination protection, environmental protection, and wildlife protection.

When contemporary foes of bureaucracy rail against "overregulation," it is principally social regulation that they have in mind. Businesses have learned to live comfortably with economic regulation, but they are adamant about the ill effects of social regulation. Social regulation draws so much fire from the business community in part because in such areas as worker health and safety, clean air and water, and nondiscrimination, it touches almost all businesses, unlike the more narrowly targeted approach in economic regulation. Social regulation also imposes costs on businesses that cut into profits.

The origins of social regulation hold another clue to business hostility. The social regulation measures of the 1960s and 1970s were supported by Congress and the president in response to the civil rights movement, the environmental movement, and the consumer safety movement. Social regulation, in other

words, has been a potent political vehicle for popular democrats in their struggle against economic elites.

A major assault on social regulation was launched during the presidency of Ronald Reagan. The intellectual justification for this assault was the damage regulation was supposedly doing to the American economy. Overregulation, opponents charged, was imposing such massive costs on American businesses as to prevent them from investing in productive new technologies, a crippling practice in an era where they faced mounting international competition.

To cut back on social regulation, the Reagan administration adopted a variety of tactics. Budgets for the social regulatory agencies were slashed. Political appointees were selected who were known to be hostile to the missions of the agencies they were to head; Anne Gorsuch Burford, a vehement opponent of environmental regulation, thus became Reagan's first head of the Environmental Protection Agency. New social regulation had to clear the hurdle of a mode of analysis with a built-in bias against such regulation. The Reagan administration claimed that it was using **cost-benefit analysis** as a neutral tool, determining if the dollar benefits of proposed regulation were greater than the dollar costs. The problem was that no clear dollar value could be placed on such intangible benefits as the worth of a human life or the beauty of a natural setting, whereas the costs incurred by an industry were readily quantifiable. Consequently, many new regulations were bound to fail the test of cost-benefit analysis.

The success of the Reagan administration's attack on social regulation was limited, however, by the countermobilization of friends of social regulation. They fought with increasing success to preserve their earlier victories. Supporters of social regulation turned to the courts and to Congress to blunt the Reagan administration's efforts.

Reagan's attack was revived by the new House Republican majority in 1995. House Republicans passed legislation establishing even more stringent cost-benefit analysis, as well as a new form of risk assessment analysis that subjected proposed regulations to time-consuming scientific and economic tests. Opponents of the legislation charged, in the words of *Congressional Quarterly*, that the goal of these measures was "to wreck, not fix, the agencies by tying them up with huge, costly paperwork requirements."[34] A filibuster by Senate Democrats eventually blocked the Republicans' "regulatory reform."

The issue of how much bureaucracy Americans need is also a matter of what citizens want from government. Certainly, bureaucratic agencies can be too big, inefficient, or wasteful. And agency accountability remains a pressing issue. But much of the present-day administrative state is necessary to protect the public and provide it with services. As we saw at the end of Chapter 4, popular democrats seek to democratize private corporate bureaucracies, making them more accountable to consumers, workers, and communities. If powerful corporations were limited in these ways, much regulatory bureaucracy would not be needed. Short of such fundamental reforms, however, modern government cannot be "debureaucratized" without major costs to the public.

Bureaucracy, with all of its flaws, is part and parcel of modern American democracy. Thus, the question of whose influence shapes bureaucracy's behavior becomes all the more important. That question lies at the heart of the contemporary debate over bureaucratic reform.

THE DEMOCRATIC DEBATE OVER REFORMING THE BUREAUCRACY

Bureaucratic inefficiency, irrationality, and arrogance are perennial targets for reform. But reformers of bureaucracy do not all necessarily share the same assumptions or seek the same ends. Elite democrats struggle against popular democrats over who will influence the workings of the administrative state.

There are three major prescriptions for reform in this struggle. The technocratic perspective on reform aims to find some rational, comprehensive, technical device for overcoming bureaucratic self-seeking and inefficiency. Developed by academic experts and sponsored by chief executives, technocratic schemes try to control bureaucracy from the top down. They resemble Alexander Hamilton's vision of a wise executive creating a more systematic administrative machine to serve his ends. A second approach to reforming bureaucracy has proposed to measure bureaucratic performance by the yardstick of economic efficiency and to turn to nonbureaucratic alternatives when private economic forces can do better than government agencies. This school of reform believes that markets are superior to governments in securing both individual freedom and economic efficiency. Finally, there is a popular democratic approach to reforming bureaucracy that focuses on citizen understanding and influence—control from the bottom up. This approach assumes that ordinary citizens are individual consumers of government services who also can deliberate intelligently about the public interest.

"Reinventing Government"

The most recent in a long line of efforts to reform the bureaucracy borrows from all three of these approaches. Vice president Al Gore heads the Clinton administration's National Performance Review (NPR), popularly known as the **"reinventing government" plan.** The Clinton administration launched this comprehensive plan for a bureaucracy that "works better and costs less" with great fanfare in September 1993. In a classic photo opportunity, Clinton and Gore posed before huge stacks of bureaucratic regulations to dramatize the necessity of transforming the federal bureaucracy. Gore followed up this session with an appearance on the *David Letterman Show*, where he smashed an ashtray for which the government, following outmoded procurement practices, had paid a ridiculously high price.

The technocratic quality of the "reinventing government" plan is evident in its Hamiltonian hope that the White House can reshape the bureaucracy with a comprehensive top-down plan. But the language of the market approach is even more evident in the Clinton-Gore scheme. Government agencies are instructed by the NPR to become more "entrepreneurial" and to begin treating citizens as "customers." They are told that the key to shaking off the hidebound practices of bureaucracy lies in "injecting the dynamics of the marketplace."[35]

Alongside the market ideas in the Clinton-Gore plan are ideas more typical of the popular democratic approach: "All federal agencies will delegate, decentralize, and empower employees to make decisions. This will let front-line and front-office workers use their creative judgment as they offer service to customers and solve problems."[36] By "empowering employees," especially at the lower levels of the bureaucracy, the civil service will be made more participatory and egalitarian. Cutting red tape means trusting federal workers to have more of a say in how they perform their jobs.

Observers have been divided over how well the "reinventing government" initiative has worked since its inception. A sympathetic commentator, political scientist Donald Kettl, writes that "the NPR has proven one of the most lively management reforms in American history. It has helped reorient the federal bureaucracy toward a far more effective attack on problems that it must learn to solve."[37] Yet Kettl finds some disturbing contradictions in the Clinton-Gore plan. For example, the NPR has promised to create a more empowering and encouraging culture within the federal bureaucracy, with civil servants motivated

to use greater personal initiative and take more personal responsibility for their work. But to sell the plan to Congress and the public, the Clinton administration has also stressed its aim of downsizing the federal workforce, sending a chilling message to civil servants that their jobs are in jeopardy.[38]

The Market Alternative

To supporters of the market approach, the flaw in the Clinton-Gore NPR is its continuing reliance on bureaucracy. Government agencies may become more entrepreneurial, say market-oriented reformers, but they still cannot match the efficiencies of private firms subject to the competitive discipline of the market. Supporters of this approach suggest that public purposes can often be served best by replacing programs run by government agencies with vouchers that allow individuals to decide what kind of education or housing they prefer. And where private companies can perform functions more cheaply than government agencies, government should contract out these functions—an idea known as **privatization.**[39]

In the desire to enhance individual freedom of choice, the market approach is compatible with popular democracy. Yet popular democrats are suspicious of claims that markets are the panacea for the problems of bureaucracy. As we have seen, competition in the American market place is imperfect, with large and wealthy corporations often in a dominant position. To substitute private businesses for government agencies is to trust too much in such imperfect markets and to rely for the fulfillment of public needs on those interested only in profit.

What ultimately places advocates of market reforms in the elite democratic camp is the same assumption that guided the Federalists: that self-interest and the acquisition of property are the people's overriding concerns and that the good society results from a proper channeling of self-seeking motives. With this assumption, market forces deserve a larger scope. But popular democrats since the Anti-federalists have also cared about equality and active citizenship, and these values are not fostered by markets. Private businesses may be more efficient (i.e., cost less) than government agencies in many areas. But this is true in part because government agencies, far more than private businesses, are expected to reflect democratic values of openness, universal service, and equity. Popular democrats are not indifferent to measures of efficiency in evaluating bureaucracy, but they do not make efficiency the sole and sovereign test.

Popular Democratic Reforms

For reasons quite different than those of the market reformers, the popular democratic perspective also perceives inadequacies in the Clinton-Gore approach to bureaucracy. Popular democrats seek to make bureaucratic decisions more open to public scrutiny. Just as the Anti-federalists sought a government that would mirror the people's concerns, so contemporary popular democrats seek a bureaucracy that is in touch with ordinary citizens.

Government agencies can evade accountability by using secrecy. Therefore, the first requirement for greater citizen influence is greater openness in the bureaucracy. The most positive step in this direction has been the Freedom of Information Act of 1966, amended (and improved) by further legislation in 1974. This act requires government agencies to make available their records (exempting certain sensitive materials) when citizens and citizen groups request them. Thanks to the Freedom of Information Act, citizens have been alerted to such bureaucratic secrets as inspection reports from the Department of Agriculture on the sale of unhealthy meat, Nuclear Regulatory Commission reports on inadequate security at nuclear power plants, and widespread injuries and deaths caused by defective automobiles that the government had refused to recall.[40] Another step toward a more open bureaucracy is the Government in the Sunshine Act of 1976, which requires regulatory commissions to open their meetings to the public.

Once citizens are better informed about federal agency activities, the second requirement for popular influence is greater public input into bureaucratic decision making. In the past two decades, Congress has frequently mandated that administrative agencies hold public hearings before taking action. Lobbyists have always been able to register their views with agencies; public hearings give citizens and citizen groups a chance to do the same. Some critics disparage hearings as symbolic gestures that appease the public but have little real effect. Yet in some areas—especially environmental protection—hearings have had a significant impact on policy.

Popular democratic reforms of bureaucracy have not been a cure-all, but they have made significant strides. As public administration scholar William Gormley, Jr., comments, "By broadening and improving public intervention in administrative proceedings, reformers helped to create a more humane, more responsive, and more innovative bureaucracy. This was no small accomplishment."[41]

Greater popular control of bureaucracy also requires involving citizens in policy implementation. Rather than trusting bureaucratic experts to carry out policies alone, citizens directly affected should cooperate in enforcement. (To the extent that citizens have been involved in the past, they have often been locally powerful ones—for example, large farmers and ranchers determining water and grazing rights.) The case of safety and health codes for the workplace illustrates what happens when ordinary people are shut out of the implementation process.

When Congress established OSHA, political scientist Charles Noble points out, the legislation "did not require employers to establish in-plant health and safety committees that might require worker participation."[42] Thus, workers had no part in the implementation of safety and health rules, which was left to factory inspectors from OSHA. The inspectors were far too few in number to provide vigorous enforcement, so the chance that a firm would be inspected in a year was approximately 1 in 100.[43] Matters worsened when President Reagan, hostile to OSHA's mission, further reduced the agency's efforts. As a result, hostile businesses and an unfriendly administration gravely weakened the workplace protection promised by the legislation. The Clinton administration has proposed an

OSHA reform bill that would require all but the smallest businesses to set up safety and health committees composed of both employees and management.[44]

Although bureaucracy can be reformed from the bottom up, ordinary citizens are limited in the time and resources they can devote to influencing bureaucratic behavior. Furthermore, the narrow, technical nature of many agency decisions shuts out all but the affected interest groups and the bureaucratic experts.

Popular democratic influence can, however, be furthered without requiring direct, sustained citizen involvement. Here, the role of elected representatives is crucial. When citizens and citizen groups are inattentive, legislators enter into mutually rewarding alliances with agencies and interest groups. When citizens and citizen groups are watching legislators, Congress often prods bureaucratic agencies to be more responsive to the public. The pressures that push Congress toward popular democracy lead it to push the bureaucracy in the same direction.

CONCLUSION: BEYOND MONSTER BUREAUCRACY

In contemporary American political discourse, Bureaucracy—with a capital *B*—is a monster. This Bureaucracy is composed of massive and ponderous organizations staffed by authoritarian drones. It smothers individual freedom under a blanket of unnecessary rules. And it grows more powerful all the time, not in the interest of the American people but in the service of its own voracious appetites. What is wrong with American government today, most people think, is mostly the consequence of Bureaucracy.

Monster Bureaucracy is a mythical creature—a hobbyhorse for irate citizens and a scapegoat for calculating politicians. When we look at real American bureaucracies, we see their diversity: They come in different organizational forms and sizes and pursue an enormous variety of missions. The people who staff them are not a perverse bureaucratic breed but rather a cross-section of the American people. And the interests that bureaucrats further range from the narrowest and most selfish to the loftiest and most communal. Some agencies are entangled with economic elites in cozy, mutually rewarding alliances. Others try to put into practice the most important legislative victories that popular democrats have won against such elites.

Bureaucracy is one of the most important arenas for political struggle in modern America. The political character of bureaucracy stems in part from the expertise and discretion that administrators possess, which make them key policy makers in their own right. It results from the attempts of federal agencies to mobilize external political support in their search for greater autonomy. And it is underscored by the efforts of every other political force—interest groups, public interest groups, Congress, the president, the courts—to direct these agencies in accordance with their preferred course of action. These political forces recognize that bureaucratic agencies, operating at the point where government directly touches the lives of the American people, are worth fighting over.

Monster Bureaucracy has to be hit with a bludgeon. Real bureaucracies may need reform. But how we approach such reform depends on where we stand in the democratic debate. If we follow the tradition of elite democracy initiated by Alexander Hamilton, we should place our trust in new forms of expertise, deployed by a wise chief executive, that will coordinate and reshape bureaucracy from the top down. If we follow the newer school of elite democracy, which claims the superiority of private markets to public agencies, we should make efficiency our standard and let business do much of what government is accustomed to doing. And if we follow the popular democratic tradition, with its commitments to citizen action, civic virtue, and an egalitarian society, we should open up the world of bureaucracy wherever possible to the grievances, opinions, and democratic hopes of ordinary people.

KEY TERMS

bureaucracy
spoils system
administrative state
cabinet departments
independent agency
independent regulatory commission
public corporation
federal foundation or endowment
mission
expertise
discretion

rule-making authority
administrative adjudication
autonomy
bureaucratic politics
regulation
economic regulation
social regulation
deregulation
cost-benefit analysis
"reinventing government" plan
privatization

SUGGESTED READINGS

Charles T. Goodsell, *The Case for Bureaucracy: A Public Administration Polemic*, 3rd ed. Chatham, N.J.: Chatham House, 1994. A lively polemic that takes on the prevailing myths about a Monster Bureaucracy.

William T. Gormley, Jr., *Taming the Bureaucracy: Muscles, Prayers, and Other Strategies*. Princeton, N.J.: Princeton University Press, 1989. A thoughtful account of the varied strategies that have been adopted to reform bureaucracy.

Kenneth J. Meier, *Politics and the Bureaucracy: Policymaking in the Fourth Branch of Government*, 3rd ed. Pacific Grove, Calif.: Brooks/Cole, 1993. A brief but comprehensive text on bureaucracy.

James A. Morone, *The Democratic Wish: Popular Participation and the Limits of American Government*. New York: Basic Books, 1990. An ironic argument about how the democratic desire to bring government back to the people results instead in more bureaucracy.

James Q. Wilson, *Bureaucracy: What Government Agencies Do and Why They Do It*. New York: Basic Books, 1989. A wide-ranging, insightful treatise on bureaucracy in the United States.

CHAPTER 14

The Judiciary and the Democratic Debate

As a nation with a tradition of transforming myriad issues into legal matters, the United States has an extensive judiciary at both the federal and state levels. The federal courts are organized in a three-tier system, which we describe later in the chapter. But our primary focus in this chapter is on the highest tier, the Supreme Court of the United States.

The nine justices of the Supreme Court form a unique elite. Appointed rather than elected, for tenures that run on "good behavior" until retirement or death, the justices have carved out for themselves the formidable role of serving as final arbiters of the Constitution. Their authority is strengthened by powerful symbolism, as they hand down decisions wearing their black robes in their marble temple, and protected by the cloak of expertise, as they pronounce their judgments in the esoteric language of the law. In all these ways, the judiciary is the least democratic branch of the federal government. Indeed, it can be said, as political scientist David O'Brien writes, that "the Court wields an antidemocratic power."[1]

Yet the Court's relationship to elite democracy and popular democracy is not this simple. The Supreme Court may be (and has been in its history) a pillar of elite democracy, upholding the interests of the powerful and privileged in the name of authority, expertise, or private property. But the Court also may be (and has been in its history) a champion of the fundamental rules of democratic politics in the face of intolerant and repressive majorities. And the Court may be (and has been in its history) the last hope for the weakest citizens—racial minorities, the poor, persons accused of crimes. Elitist in form and character, the Supreme Court is nonetheless a vital participant in the democratic debate.

This chapter begins with a consideration of contemporary debates over the proper role of the judiciary in a democracy. Next, the chapter looks back at the history of the Supreme Court, noting how the Court's relationship to democracy has changed from one era to the next. Subsequent sections cover judicial selection, the lower federal courts, the processes through which the Supreme Court functions, and the politics that divides it. Finally, the chapter examines the place of the Supreme Court in the broader political system and sums up its role in the democratic debate.

JUDICIAL POWER AND THE DEMOCRATIC DEBATE

What is the place of an unelected judiciary in a democratic republic? Answers to this question begin with a recognition of the Supreme Court's fundamental power: **judicial review.** This is the power of courts to invalidate the actions of legislatures and executives on the grounds that these actions conflict with the Constitution. This power was first asserted by the Supreme Court in the landmark case of *Marbury* v. *Madison* (1803). Although the *power* of judicial review remained controversial for much of the nineteenth century, almost no one today would question it. But questions do arise about the proper *extent* of judicial review. How far should the Court go in overturning the actions of the other federal branches or the state governments? In setting these actions against the language of the Constitution, how should the Court interpret the Constitution? Can the Court, despite its elite composition and procedures, advance the goals of popular democracy?

The Judiciary and Democracy

There are several ways in which the Supreme Court is *not* a democratic institution. First, members of the judiciary are not elected; they are nominated by the president and confirmed by the Senate. Second, federal judges serve during good behavior—that is, until they retire, die, or are impeached by the House and convicted by the Senate. No justice of the Supreme Court has ever been removed through impeachment and conviction. Consequently, members of the Court are held accountable only indirectly—by Congress through its power over jurisdiction, by presidents through their appointment power, and by members of the public through their decisions on complying with judicial rulings.

Third, justices wield their power of judicial review by striking down actions taken by elected officials at the federal or state level. The exercise of judicial review is thus *countermajoritarian*, meaning that majority rule has to give way if the Court believes that the actions of the majority conflict with the Constitution.

Fourth, the federal judiciary historically has been even less representative demographically than Congress and the executive branch. Almost all justices have been white, male, and affluent. (Women and African Americans have finally won some representation on the federal bench in the past three decades.) Equally important, they have all been lawyers, which means that one of the most powerful branches of the national government is the exclusive domain of the legal profession.[2]

There is, it seems, a potent democratic case to be made against a strong and active judiciary. Yet judicial power in America has sometimes played an essential part in preserving democratic values and rules. Nowhere is this role more apparent than in the areas of individual and minority rights. Majority rule can be used to impose unwelcome beliefs on individuals and to prohibit the expression of unconventional views. Majorities can repress and exploit minorities, whether of race, creed, or color. A democracy with unrestrained majority rule would eventually undermine the very conditions of personal and political freedom that gave it life. It would be like a sports league in which the team that won the first game was able to set the rules for all succeeding games. The democratic case for a countermajoritarian judiciary, therefore, is that it stands as a guardian for the abiding values and conditions that democracy requires.[3]

The Court serves democracy not only when it protects individual and minority rights from infringement by majorities but also when it publicly explains its actions. The Court's impact on public thinking may be limited by its legal language, yet no other branch of government offers such extensive and reasoned accounts of its decisions or elaborates on so many fundamental democratic principles. It was the Supreme Court, for example, that explained to Americans why segregated schools denied African Americans the equal protection of the laws and why coerced confessions denied criminal defendants the right to a fair trial.

The Conservative Critique of the Judiciary

Questions about the role of the judiciary in American democracy are not merely of academic interest. A politically important debate has been waged in recent decades about the courts and democracy. What generated this debate was the liberal activism of the Warren Court (discussed later in this chapter and the next). There have been three major positions in this debate: the conservative critique of an active judiciary, the liberal defense of an active judiciary, and the progressive (or radical democratic) skepticism toward a democratic judiciary.

The conservative critique has been voiced by such prominent figures as Supreme Court Justices William Rehnquist and Antonin Scalia and failed Supreme Court nominee Robert Bork. But it was given its greatest public visibility by President Reagan's attorney general, Edwin Meese. Unhappy with many of the Supreme Court's liberal decisions of the preceding decades, Meese argued that it was meddling with the affairs of the other federal branches and especially the state governments. This overreaching, he charged, arose not from constitutional duty but from an exaggerated sense of the Court's own powers and a loose reading of the Constitution. Meese believed that the Court conveniently construed the Constitution "as an empty vessel into which each generation may pour its passion and prejudice."[4] As a result, the Court's decisions represented "more policy choices than articulations of constitutional principle."[5] Yet nobody had authorized the justices of the Supreme Court to make policy choices and impose them on elected officials.

According to Meese, the Court could return to its legitimate—and more restrained—role through a **jurisprudence of original intention.**[6] By this, he meant that "the text of the document and the original intention of those who framed it would be the judicial standard in giving effect to the Constitution."[7] The standard of original intention, Meese argued, would make judges into faithful servants of the Constitution. "Any other standard," he warned, "suffers the defect of pouring new meaning into old words, thus creating new powers and new rights totally at odds with the logic of our Constitution and its commitment to the rule of law."[8]

In seeking to restrict the role of the federal judiciary, Meese's case emphasized the Court's nondemocratic aspects. His critique of the judiciary echoed the complaints of popular democrats in the past. One of Meese's allies in the debate, Robert Bork, spells out this argument succinctly: "We are increasingly governed not by law or elected representatives but by an unelected, unrepresentative, unaccountable committee of lawyers applying no will but their own."[9] In Meese's version of democracy, judges should not impede other officials unless their acts clearly violate the original intention of the framers.

The Liberal Defense of the Judiciary

This attack on judicial activism drew a swift retort from Supreme Court Justice William Brennan, Jr., one of the most influential figures in crafting the decisions of which Meese was complaining. Brennan's liberal defense of the judiciary presented a dramatically different understanding of the Court's proper role. To Brennan, a jurisprudence of original intention was "arrogance cloaked as humility."[10] It was, he argued, impossible to recover the founders' precise intent for each phrase of the Constitution. The records of their era are incomplete and ambiguous, and what they do reveal are disagreement, rather than consensus, over meaning. Brennan detected a political motive beneath the claim of fidelity to the intentions of the founders: The jurisprudence of original intention was a conservative philosophy that required the Supreme Court to "turn a blind eye to social progress."[11]

Brennan's alternative to original intention gave the judiciary a far broader role in reading the Constitution—and in affecting American life:

> We current Justices read the Constitution in the only way that we can: as Twentieth Century Americans. We look to the history of the time of framing and to the intervening history of interpretation. But the ultimate question must be, what do the words of the text mean in our time? For the genius of the Constitution rests not in any static meaning it might have had in a world that is dead and gone, but in the adaptability of its great principles to cope with current problems and current needs.[12]

To Brennan, the Constitution "embodies the aspiration to social justice, brotherhood, and human dignity that brought this nation into being."[13] His jurisprudence (judicial philosophy) used the means of elite democracy to advance the ends of popular democracy. Judges—indisputably an elite in terms of occupation and expertise—should advance the goals of social justice, brotherhood, and human dignity by serving as forceful advocates for a democracy of inclusion, equality, and fairness. Reading the Constitution as a charter for such popular democratic values, they could not be bound by the fuzzy notion of original intention—especially since the original intenders, the Federalists, were elite democrats! Although popular democrats might naturally mistrust the judicial elite, Brennan wanted them to recognize how this elite might sometimes be their ally.

Progressive Skepticism Toward the Judiciary

Although less publicly visible than the views of a Meese or a Brennan, a third position in this debate—which we label *progressive skepticism*—deserves consideration. According to proponents of this position, the judiciary's role in American democracy has varied enormously, depending on politics—on who nominates and who approves selections to the highest court. The Court's championing of

popular democratic values, which Brennan emphasized, has in fact been the exception in its history. As law professor Mark Tushnet observes: "In the long view, the Warren Court was an unusual and brief instance in which the Court happened to come under control of progressive interests."[14] With the departure of Brennan himself from the Court, along with his ally Thurgood Marshall, the last traces of the era of liberal activism have vanished. The conservative justices of the 1990s are reasserting the Court's more traditional role as a pillar of property and order.

We should not be surprised, progressive skeptics argue, when the Court sides with elite democracy over popular democracy. The great nineteenth-century observer of American politics, Alexis de Tocqueville, wrote that lawyers were the one remaining aristocratic class in an otherwise egalitarian society. To progressive skeptics, Tocqueville's argument still holds true for the modern legal profession. They point out how law students are socialized in elite democratic values as they are prepared for lucrative careers in elite democratic institutions. Almost all law schools, writes law professor Duncan Kennedy, provide their students with "ideological training for service in the hierarchies of the corporate welfare state."[15]

The progressives' skepticism extends even to the landmark liberal decisions of the Warren Court. Unlike the conservatives, they agree with the substance of what the Warren Court decided. But they argue that the gains for popular democracy were much smaller than liberals like Brennan suggested. Even when the Court called for significant social reform, it lacked the power of implementation that would turn decisions into realities. For example, court orders for school desegregation had almost no impact until the civil rights movement compelled Congress and the presidency to force change on the recalcitrant South.[16]

If popular democrats have gained little from Court victories, say these skeptics, they have paid a price for banking their hopes on friends in the judicial elite. As political scientist Gerald Rosenberg points out, when popular democratic movements look to law suits to reform society, "there is the danger that litigation by the few will replace political action by the many and reduce the democratic nature of the American polity."[17] Law suits siphon off money and other resources that mass movements need for political mobilization. They lead popular democrats to speak in the limited and generally conservative language of lawyers. Even when the litigation is successful, it deludes popular democrats with victories that are more symbolic than substantial. Progressive skeptics make a powerful argument that the struggle for popular democracy must depend on political actions by ordinary citizens rather than legal actions by a sympathetic judicial elite.

THE SUPREME COURT IN HISTORY

For an institution that derives much of its authority from its role as sacred guardian of a timeless text, the Supreme Court has been profoundly shaped by its history. The Court's relationship to history is, however, double edged. On one hand, the Court treats history with reverence, claiming to follow past decisions as **precedents** and apply them to new circumstances. On the other hand, the Court has engaged in some dramatic historical shifts. For most of its history, the Supreme Court was a pillar of elite democracy, a champion of national authority and private property against the popular democratic forces struggling for greater equality. Beginning in the 1930s, however, the Court largely abandoned its stance as the protector of economic elites, adopting instead a new focus on civil liberties and civil rights. The 1990s have witnessed another shift: the expression (by a narrow majority) of a conservative jurisprudence that favors federalism over national action.

John Marshall and Judicial Power

The Supreme Court did not become a major force in the American political system immediately on ratification of the Constitution. Article III of the Constitution, establishing the judicial branch, was brief and vague, leaving the role of the

Court an open question. During its first decade under the Constitution, the Court was relatively weak. Nonetheless, popular democrats feared its potential as a home for a judicial aristocracy. During the ratification debates, Alexander Hamilton, the arch elite democrat, had championed a judicial branch that could invalidate the actions of the other branches or the states as contrary to the Constitution. Anti-federalist writers, such as Brutus, had warned that this judiciary might promote the powers of a remote federal government while diminishing the powers of state governments closer to the people. With the triumph of Jeffersonian democracy over the elitism of the Federalists in 1800, the more radical Jeffersonians hoped that the power of the federal judiciary could be severely curtailed. Legal historian Kermit Hall observes, "Radicals distrusted lawyers and believed that local democracy in an agrarian society based on 'common sense and common honesty between man and men . . .' offered the surest road to justice."[18]

But it was the fears, not the hopes, of the more radical popular democrats that were to be realized. For as Jefferson was assuming the presidency, John Marshall was taking over as chief justice of the Supreme Court. Appointed by President Adams in the waning days of his administration, Marshall, a Federalist, was gifted with great intellectual force, rhetorical grace, and political shrewdness. And he had a vision for the Court: to establish it coequally with the other branches and turn it into a sponsor of national authority and economic development (a vision that he shared with Alexander Hamilton). Marshall dominated the Supreme Court for thirty-four years, serving from 1801 until his death in 1835. The Marshall Court, more than the words of Article III, established the judicial branch as the powerful political force that later generations of Americans came to regard as a key part of the constitutional design.

Marshall's agenda for the Court depended on establishing the power of judicial review. But he wanted to avoid a head-on collision with the Jeffersonian majority that controlled the executive and legislative branches. In a stroke of judicial genius, he found the perfect vehicle for judicial review in the case of ***Marbury v. Madison*** (1803). William Marbury had been appointed by President Adams to a position as justice of the peace for the District of Columbia, but the papers for his commission had not been delivered by the time Jefferson supplanted Adams in the White House. Jefferson's secretary of state, James Madison, refused to hand over the papers. Marbury asked the Supreme Court to order Madison, through a *writ of mandamus* (a court order directing an official to do something), to give him his commission.

Marshall's opinion in *Marbury* v. *Madison* held that the secretary of state had wrongfully withheld the commission. But the Supreme Court, he went on, could do nothing to rectify this injustice because the authority to issue *writs of mandamus*, mandated by the Judiciary Act of 1789, was unconstitutional—it expanded the original jurisdiction of the Court beyond what was specified in Article III. In bold rhetorical strokes, he crafted the doctrine of judicial review. It was evident, he argued, that "a law repugnant to the constitution is void" and that "it is emphatically the province and duty of the judicial department to say what the law is."[19] Notice how shrewdly Marshall bolstered the power of the Supreme

Court. He avoided a confrontation with the Jefferson administration by ruling that the Supreme Court was powerless to reverse the action toward Marbury. But he advanced the Supreme Court's power in the long term by making it, and not the other branches, the final arbiter of constitutionality.

Once Marshall had established the Court's power of judicial review, he moved gradually to further his vision of a powerful national government promoting capitalist economic development. Striking down Maryland's attempt to tax the Bank of the United States in *McCulloch* **v.** *Maryland* (1819), he emphasized the constitutional supremacy of the federal government over the states (see Chapter 15). And then in *Gibbons* **v.** *Ogden* (1824), the Marshall Court ruled that the Interstate Commerce Clause, under which Gibbons held a federal coasting license for his steamboat line, was superior to the steamboat monopoly granted to Ogden by the state of New York. As the *Gibbons* case indicates, Marshall was able to advance his goal of economic development in conjunction with his goal of national authority. He read the Constitution, legal historian Robert McCloskey writes, "so as to provide maximum protection to property rights and maximum support for the idea of nationalism." [20]

The Taney Court

When John Marshall died, and Andrew Jackson, a frequent foe of Marshall's, appointed Roger Taney as chief justice, supporters of the Court as the champion of nationalism and capitalism shuddered. Surely, they thought, the Court would now become a supporter of states' rights and egalitarian attacks on property. But Marshall had set the Court on a course that was not easily altered. Historians now find more continuity than change between the Marshall and the Taney Courts. Although Taney was more sympathetic to state governments, he upheld national authority and capitalist development. The Taney Court's most important economic decision came in *Charles River Bridge* v. *Warren Bridge* (1837). In ruling that the Massachusetts legislature could charter a new bridge even when it undercut the profitability of a previously chartered bridge whose owners claimed that their monopoly rights had been violated, the Taney Court fostered a more competitive capitalist system.

Taney's most notorious decision, however, came in *Dred Scott* **v.** *Sandford* (1857). The *Dred Scott* decision is universally regarded as the worst in the history of the Supreme Court. In a remarkable bit of political miscalculation, Taney thought that the Court could solve with one decision the brewing crisis between North and South over slavery. His solution took the southern side on every burning question of the day: Slaves were held to be a form of property protected by the Constitution, and Congress was told it had no power to forbid or abolish slavery in the western territories. Taney went even further, almost taunting northern champions of the antislavery cause with his vicious racist remark that blacks were regarded by the founders "as beings of an inferior order" who "had no rights which the white man was bound to respect." [21] Taney's ruling and rhetoric incensed the North and increased sectional tensions, helping to lead to a civil war that would obliterate his fateful misuse of judicial power.

From the Civil War to the Roosevelt Revolution

The Civil War confirmed on the battlefield what John Marshall had claimed on the bench: the supremacy of the federal government over the states. After the Civil War, the Supreme Court became preoccupied with Marshall's other major concern: the rights of property. For seventy years, the Court played a critical, activist role in the development of corporate capitalism in America. The Court reread the Constitution, turning the eighteenth-century founders into proponents of the free market capitalism worshipped by business elites of the late nineteenth century. Legal expertise and judicial authority were weapons that elite democrats fired repeatedly—and successfully—to shoot down the cause of popular democracy.

The industrial capitalist order that was growing rapidly in the years after the Civil War imposed heavy costs on workers, farmers, and owners of small businesses. Popular democratic forces, such as the agrarian Granger movement and the Populist movement, gained power in some states and passed legislation to protect ordinary people against capitalist exploitation, especially by the railroads. As the popular democratic forces mobilized, legal historian Michael Benedict writes, "the justices became convinced that the Court must serve as the bulwark of property rights against threatened radical legislation."[22] The Court set up a roadblock against state efforts to regulate the railroads in *Wabash, St. Louis & Pacific Railway Co.* v. *Illinois* (1886). Striking down Illinois's popular democratic legislation, the Court ruled in *Wabash* that states had no power to regulate rail rates for shipments that crossed their borders. The Court said in effect that only the federal government could regulate commerce.

A Court dominated by the doctrine of laissez faire (i.e., government should not interfere in the free market) was not, however, favorably disposed toward federal regulation either. When the government attempted to use the new Sherman Antitrust Act to break up the monopolistic "sugar trust," the Court overturned that action through a narrow interpretation of the Commerce Clause. In *United States* v. *E. C. Knight Co.* (1895), the Court ruled that manufacturing was a local activity and thus not covered under the Commerce Clause, even when the goods produced were destined for shipment across state lines.

The Court stretched the doctrine of laissez faire the farthest in redefining the meaning of "due process of law." The drafters of the Fourteenth Amendment had included this phrase to protect newly freed African Americans from arbitrary actions by state governments in the South. But the Supreme Court ignored the plight of blacks and turned the Fourteenth Amendment instead into a protective shield for corporations. It was a violation of due process, the Court often ruled, when a state interfered with the contractual freedom of employers and employees to make whatever "bargains" they wished. Thus, in *Lochner* v. *New York* (1905), the Court struck down a New York law setting maximum hours for bakery workers. "Freedom of contract" was the watchword of the Court, and popular democratic legislation to protect working people from oppressive conditions was declared unconstitutional.

In the face of popular democratic criticism during the Progressive era, the Supreme Court pragmatically allowed some federal and state regulation of the economy. But as Progressivism faded and a new conservative era set in after World War I, the majority of the Court hardened in its laissez faire dogma. It was this majority that fought the most bitter battle in the history of the Court—against Franklin Roosevelt and the New Deal. Once Roosevelt and his Democratic majority in Congress passed far-reaching measures to revive an economy mired in the worst depression in its history, the question of power over the economy was joined by the Court. It invalidated the two linchpins of the New Deal: the National Industrial Recovery Act and the Agricultural Adjustment Act. The 1936 election gave Roosevelt the largest mandate in presidential history, but the Supreme Court now seemed an impassable barrier to his efforts to improve the economy and reform it in popular democratic fashion.

Early in 1937, Roosevelt unveiled a program to smash through this barrier. He claimed (in deceptive fashion) that he was acting only to enhance the efficiency of a Court dominated by elderly judges. His proposal was that the president be given the authority to add an additional justice each time a sitting justice over the age of seventy refused to retire. (The size of the Supreme Court is not set by the Constitution.) Popular though Roosevelt was, his **court-packing plan** was a political fiasco. Public opinion sided with the Court, and Roosevelt suffered a major defeat in Congress. He lost because the public revered the Supreme Court despite its unpopular recent decisions. He also lost because his plan was viewed as a vehicle to advance his own executive power.

Yet Roosevelt won the larger battle with the Court in the end. While the debate raged over the court-packing plan, the Court narrowly approved two key New Deal measures—the National Labor Relations Act and the Social Security Act—during the spring of 1937. And in the next few years, deaths and resignations of the conservatives who had stymied the president permitted him to name a New Deal majority to the Court. Roosevelt's appointees ended seventy years of laissez faire doctrine. In one of the most important shifts in the history of the Supreme Court—a "Roosevelt revolution"—they took the Court largely out of the business of economic policy.

A signpost of the Roosevelt revolution was the case of *Wickard* v. *Filburn* (1942), in which a unanimous Court said that the federal government could extend the Interstate Commerce Clause even to regulate wheat consumed on the same farm on which it was grown. A Supreme Court that read federal authority this broadly was a Court that no longer wished to question the economic judgments of the elected branches. It would no longer champion property rights and elite democracy. But what would its new role be?

The Modern Court

Since the Roosevelt revolution, the Court's role has largely centered on civil liberties and civil rights (see Chapter 16). This constant preoccupation with questions of civil liberties and civil rights has not meant a consistent pattern of rulings, however. Responding to changing issues and public moods, and profoundly affected by changing personnel, the Court has gone through several distinct eras in its treatment of civil liberties and civil rights.

Several of the key Court decisions in the fifteen years after 1937 sided with governmental authority over civil liberties and civil rights. Thus, the Court upheld the wartime incarceration of Japanese Americans and the early Cold War conviction of leading American communists. It was only with the emergence of the Warren Court (1953–1969) that it blazed a strong path in support of individual liberties and the rights of racial minorities. But its activism on behalf of the rights of dissenters, criminal defendants, and African Americans won it many vocal enemies, including successful presidential candidate Richard Nixon in 1968.

Nixon had the opportunity to name four new justices, among them Warren Burger as replacement for the retiring Earl Warren. (For membership changes on the Supreme Court since 1960, see Figure 14.1.) The Burger Court (1969–1986), however, did not carry out the conservative counterrevolution that Nixon had advocated. Holdovers from the Warren Court and Nixon appointees who proved more moderate than expected made the Burger Court a transitional body, cutting back on some of the Warren Court landmarks, especially in matters of criminal procedure, but also announcing a fundamental new right in the area of abortion.

It is only in the current era of the Rehnquist Court (1986–present) that a new conservative jurisprudence, shaped by the appointees of Presidents Reagan and Bush, is crystallizing. Often by 5–4 votes, a conservative majority, led by Chief Justice Rehnquist, has partially shifted the Court's focus from questions of rights back to older questions of authority. For the first time since the Roosevelt revolution, the ability of the federal government to exercise broad regulatory authority has been challenged by the Court. In *United States* v. *Lopez* (1995), a federal law making it a crime to carry a gun within 1,000 feet of a school was struck down, with the conservative majority arguing that the law was unrelated to interstate commerce and intruded on the police powers of the states. In *Printz* v. *United States* (1997), a portion of the Brady gun control law was invalidated because it required local law enforcement officers to run background checks on prospective handgun purchasers, with the same conservative majority stating that Washington cannot command state officials to administer a federal regulatory program. The states' rights philosophy of the Rehnquist Court majority carries profound implications for both federal regulations and civil rights.[23]

FIGURE 14.1 Membership of the Supreme Court, 1960s–1997

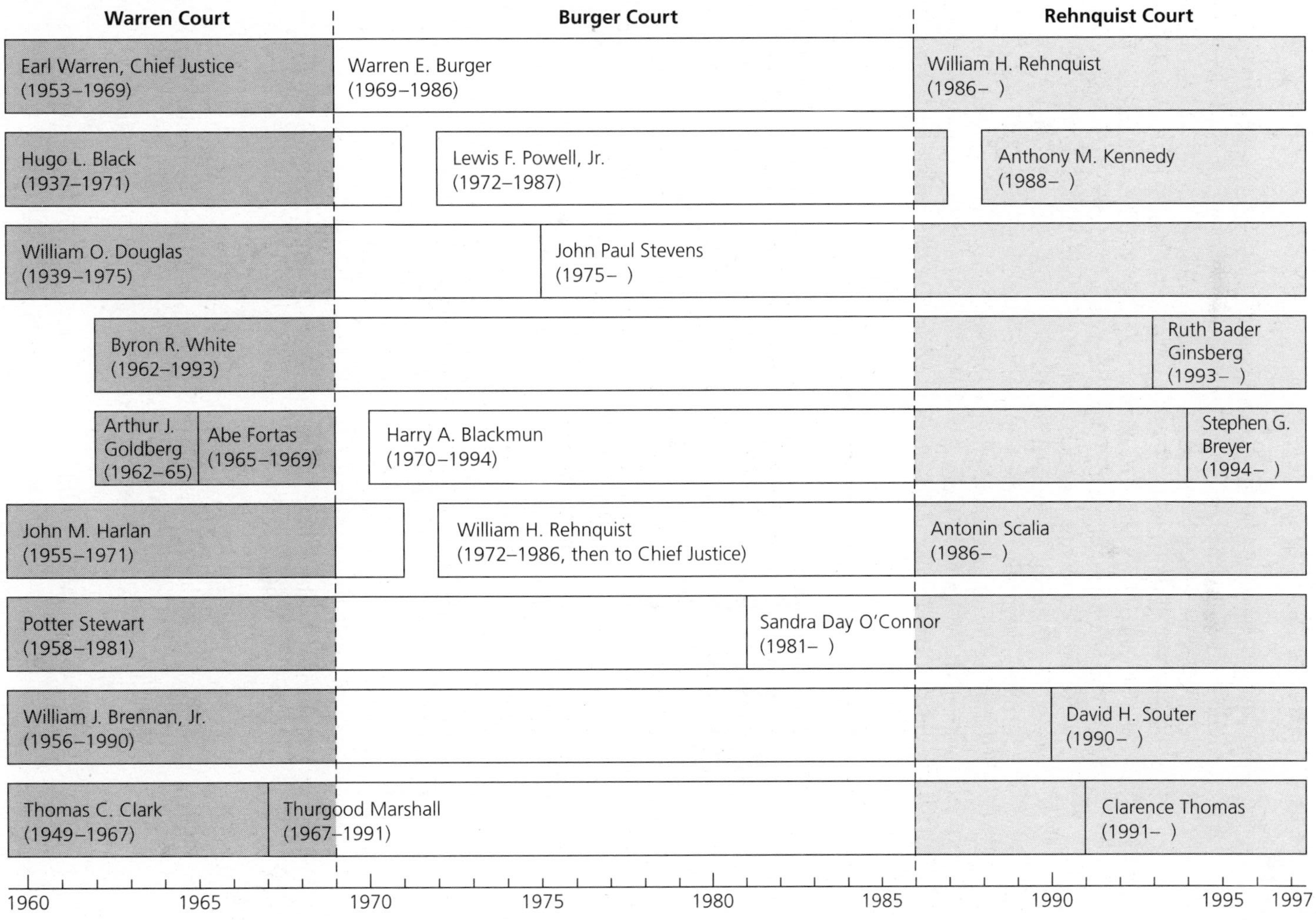

	Warren Court	Burger Court	Rehnquist Court

Earl Warren, Chief Justice (1953–1969)

Warren E. Burger (1969–1986)

William H. Rehnquist (1986–)

Hugo L. Black (1937–1971)

Lewis F. Powell, Jr. (1972–1987)

Anthony M. Kennedy (1988–)

William O. Douglas (1939–1975)

John Paul Stevens (1975–)

Byron R. White (1962–1993)

Ruth Bader Ginsberg (1993–)

Arthur J. Goldberg (1962–65)

Abe Fortas (1965–1969)

Harry A. Blackmun (1970–1994)

Stephen G. Breyer (1994–)

John M. Harlan (1955–1971)

William H. Rehnquist (1972–1986, then to Chief Justice)

Antonin Scalia (1986–)

Potter Stewart (1958–1981)

Sandra Day O'Connor (1981–)

William J. Brennan, Jr. (1956–1990)

David H. Souter (1990–)

Thomas C. Clark (1949–1967)

Thurgood Marshall (1967–1991)

Clarence Thomas (1991–)

1960 1965 1970 1975 1980 1985 1990 1995 1997

Based on Stephen L. Wasby, *The Supreme Court in the Federal Judicial System*, Fourth Edition. Copyright © 1993 by Nelson-Hall Publishers. Used with permission.

JUDICIAL SELECTION

Article II, Section 2 of the Constitution states that the president "shall nominate, and by and with the advice and consent of the Senate, shall appoint . . . judges of the supreme court." The same clause applies to judges in the lower federal courts, which were created by acts of Congress. These few words did not specify the processes by which a president would pick judicial nominees and the Senate consider them or what advice and consent comprised. Should the Senate defer to the president's judgment, rejecting a nominee only when that individual was found lacking in judicial competence or personal integrity? Or should the Senate's judgment be equal to the president's, allowing the Senate to reject a nominee of unquestioned competence and character on political or ideological grounds? With so little settled by the language of the Constitution, judicial selection has become, for presidents and senators alike, an intensely political affair.

Lower Federal Court Nominations

The politics of judicial selection operates differently for the lower federal courts than for the Supreme Court. Judges of the district courts (described in the next section) serve only in a district within one state, and the senators from that state are closely involved in their selection. According to the tradition of **senatorial courtesy,** if the senior senator from the president's party objects to a district court nominee for his or her state, the Senate as a whole will withhold consent. As a consequence, presidents consult closely with senators on district court nominations and may turn the choice over to them in exchange for future political support on other matters. Senatorial courtesy was weakened under Presidents Reagan and Bush, who insisted on having more of a say on district court appointments, but again became the norm during the Clinton administration. Individual senators have always had less power—and presidents have had more leeway—in appointing judges to the U.S. courts of appeals (also described in the next section), whose jurisdiction extends over several states.

Although presidents have to share power over lower federal court nominations, they have much to gain by taking a strong interest in judicial selection at this level. Since the Supreme Court hears only a handful of cases, the vast majority of federal court decisions are rendered by the district courts and courts of appeals. Since retirement rates are higher on the lower courts than on the Supreme Court, and since Congress periodically creates new judicial positions to keep up with the expanding workload of a litigious society, a president can exercise more influence through lower court nominations than through Supreme Court nominations. During Reagan's eight years as president, he appointed approximately half of all lower court judges (372 out of 736), giving the lower federal courts a more conservative slant.[24] Rather than countering Reagan (and Bush) conservatives with liberal appointees, Clinton has so far opted for moderates.[25] By the end of his second term, nearly half of lower court judges will likely be his appointees and the federal bench will have a more centrist cast.[26]

Clinton's principal legacy for the lower federal courts will be diversity and not ideology. In his first term, he far surpassed his predecessors in appointing women and people of color to the courts. Jimmy Carter was the first president to respond to the challenge by the civil rights and women's movements to the historic domination of the federal courts by affluent white males; 35 percent of his nominees were women and minorities. Ronald Reagan preferred white males; only 14 percent of his nominees were women and minorities. Seeking a more moderate image, George Bush raised this figure to 27 percent. Clinton made diversity the centerpiece of his judicial selection strategy, with women and minorities comprising 53 percent of his first-term nominees.[27]

Supreme Court Nominations

Most presidents have less of an opportunity in the course of a four-year term to reshape the Supreme Court than the lower federal courts. Nonetheless, any presidential nomination to the Supreme Court today is likely to initiate a high-stakes political drama, for every new member may make a major difference in determining what the Constitution and the laws mean. Some of the Court's landmark decisions have come in 5–4 votes; a replacement of only one justice would have produced a different outcome. And some new appointees influence the Court with more than just their votes. They may prove to be a catalyst for the formation of a firm voting bloc, as was the case with the liberal Justice William Brennan. Or they may bring to the Court a forceful ideological perspective, as is the case with current conservative Justice Antonin Scalia.[28]

The appointment process for a new justice of the Supreme Court begins when an existing justice retires or dies. In deliberating over a replacement, contemporary presidents tend to rely heavily on the Justice Department and legal counselors on the White House staff for advice on prospective nominees. The elite of the legal profession also plays a regular role in the selection process. The American Bar Association's Standing Committee on Federal Judiciary rates candidates as "well qualified," "qualified," or "not qualified," and a president is likely to back away from a prospective nominee who has not obtained the highest rating. (More informally, prominent law professors tend to line up for or against nominees.) Viewing Supreme Court decisions as critical to the constituencies they represent, many interest groups also are involved in the politics of judicial selection. Thus, several of the nominees of Presidents Reagan and Bush were vigorously opposed by civil rights and women's groups, which feared that these nominees would roll back the egalitarian gains of recent decades.

The drama of Supreme Court nominations reaches its apex in the hearing room of the Senate Judiciary Committee. In this televised forum, senators are able to question nominees directly about their legal experience and judicial philosophy. Although questions about controversial issues currently before the Court, such as abortion, are supposed to be off limits, senators usually find means to probe these matters. Some recent nominees, such as Robert Bork, have entertained these questions. Others, such as David Souter, perhaps learning from Bork's rejection, have fended them off with bland generalities.

In announcing the nomination of a new justice, the president is likely to highlight the legal expertise of the nominee. Less will be said about the real criterion that governs most selections: politics. As David O'Brien observes, "The presidential impulse to pack the Court with politically compatible justices is irresistible."[29]

Presidential nominations are influenced by important political forces in the nation. In the past, geographic considerations were significant, as presidents tried to ensure that each region of the country was represented on the Court. Geographic considerations have faded in the face of issues of gender, race, and religion. Thus, when Thurgood Marshall, the only African-American justice in the history of the Supreme Court, retired in 1991, President Bush found an African-American conservative, Clarence Thomas, to replace him. When given a first opportunity to appoint a Supreme Court justice, President Clinton chose a woman, Ruth Bader Ginsburg. An even more important political factor is ideology. Presidents' impacts on public policy depend not only on the legislation they sponsor or the executive actions they take but also on the decisions of the Court that reflect the ideological difference that their nominees have made.

Do presidents get what they want from their appointments to the Supreme Court? Do justices, with the independence of a lifetime tenure, continue to hold to the ideological path that the presidents who appointed them anticipated at the time of nomination? Legal scholar Laurence Tribe says yes. Tribe debunks what he calls "the myth of the surprised president." Presidents who have set out deliberately to alter the ideological direction of the Court, he shows, have generally succeeded in their strategies.[30] Nevertheless, counterexamples suggest that presidents don't always predict the future correctly. For instance, President Nixon's second appointee, Harry Blackmun, surprised everyone by becoming one of the Court's most liberal members.

Given the political basis of Court nominations, presidents are sometimes unsuccessful with them in the Senate. About 20 percent of nominees have failed to win confirmation, with rejection rates running particularly high in the mid-nineteenth century and the past twenty-five years (both periods of intense partisan conflict). Four factors seem to explain these defeats. First, the partisan composition of the Senate is crucial: A president is more likely to be defeated if the opposition party has a majority in the Senate. Second, timing is important: A president is less likely to succeed if a vacancy on the Supreme Court occurs during the fourth year of the term, as senators hold off to see what the new election will bring. Third, ideology has become central: Nominees face tougher sledding in the Senate if they are perceived as ideologically extreme or likely to tip a precarious ideological balance on the present Court. Fourth, presidential management is significant: A president can seriously harm the chances of a nominee through political blunders during the selection process.[31]

Even though the process of judicial selection has always been political, politicization recently has intensified as the stakes in controlling the Supreme Court on issues like abortion, affirmative action, and criminal procedure have grown. When President Reagan proposed Robert Bork for the High Court in 1987, political forces on both the left and right mobilized to do battle over the nomination. But it was Bork himself who was the star of the drama. A prominent conservative jurist and an adherent of the same original intent school of constitutional interpretation as Attorney General Meese, Bork tried to paint himself as more of a moderate during the Senate Judiciary Committee hearings. But a majority of the committee deemed this an unconvincing "confirmation conversion," and Bork was rejected by both the committee and the full Senate. Clarence Thomas narrowly avoided Bork's fate after President Bush nominated him in 1991.

Some recent nominations have drawn little opposition. President Clinton's moderate nominees, Ruth Bader Ginsburg and Stephen G. Breyer, easily won Senate approval. But the acrimonious politics that swirled around the Bork and Thomas nominations has led to widespread complaints that the selection process has become a political circus. Yet would it be better to go back to the quiet elite proceedings of the past, in which political and legal insiders chose justices of the Supreme Court while the public remained in ignorance until the final outcome? The American people have much at stake in the matter of who will be sitting on the Court for decades to come. From the standpoint of popular democracy, they should welcome a process that, despite its occasional excesses, opens up judicial selection to their scrutiny.

THE FEDERAL COURT SYSTEM

Presidential appointees to the judicial branch serve in a three-tiered federal court system: district courts, courts of appeals, and Supreme Court. (In addition, there are a number of specialized federal courts, such as bankruptcy and tax courts.) The Constitution only specified "one Supreme Court," leaving it to Congress to create "inferior courts" as it deemed necessary. Since the creation of the Courts of Appeals in 1891, the basic structure of the federal court system has been set. Figure 14.2 outlines the current structure of the federal court system.

U.S. District Courts

On the bottom level of the three-tiered federal court system are the U.S. district courts. The district courts are courts of **original jurisdiction,** meaning the courts where almost all federal cases begin. And they are the trial courts for the federal system, resolving both criminal and civil cases, sometimes with judge and jury and sometimes with judge only. There are currently 94 U.S. district courts; each state has at least one, and the larger states have as many as four. As of 1997, there were 649 district court judgeships.

The caseload of the district courts is large and rapidly expanding—one reason that Congress periodically enlarges the number of judgeships. In the great majority of these cases, the district courts have the final say: Decisions are not

FIGURE 14.2 Basic Structure of the Federal Court System

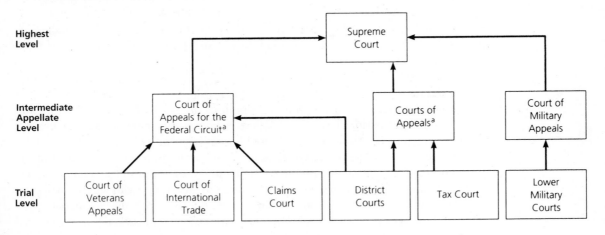

Note: Arrows indicate most common routes of appeals. Some specialized courts of minor importance are excluded.
[a]These courts also hear appeals from administrative agencies.

appealed, are settled before any higher court rulings occur, or are affirmed by the courts of appeals.

U.S. Courts of Appeals

The U.S. courts of appeals, the middle tier of the federal court system, hear appeals of decisions rendered by the district courts, specialized courts, and federal regulatory agencies. As **appellate courts,** the courts of appeals bear some resemblance to the Supreme Court and have sometimes been called "mini-Supreme Courts." Yet there are some major differences in the appellate role of the two. Whereas the Supreme Court can choose the cases it hears, courts of appeals must hear every case brought to them. Whereas the Supreme Court is interested in large questions of constitutional and statutory interpretation rather than the fate of the particular parties to a case, courts of appeals seek to correct errors in lower court decisions to ensure that justice is done to the individuals involved. Because the Supreme Court is too busy to consider many types of federal cases, however, the courts of appeals do effectively decide policy in a number of areas of law.

There are twelve courts of appeals with general appellate jurisdiction—one in the District of Columbia and eleven numbered circuits that cover several contiguous states plus associated territories. The circuits vary in size; the First Circuit (Maine, New Hampshire, Massachusetts, Rhode Island, and Puerto Rico) has only six judges, whereas the Ninth Circuit (nine western states plus the territories of Guam and the Northern Marianas) has twenty-eight judges. There are a total of 167 appeals court judges to handle a huge caseload.

Courts of appeals hearings do not retry cases; new factual evidence is not introduced, and no witnesses appear. Lawyers for the two sides in a case make oral arguments and present written briefs to the judges. Ordinarily, a three-judge panel will hear a case (and decisions are sometimes made by 2–1 vote). In especially important cases, a court of appeals may sit *en banc,* with all of its members participating. What makes the courts of appeals so significant a force in the federal court system is that few of their decisions are ever overturned.

U.S. Supreme Court

The highest tier of the federal court system is the Supreme Court of the United States. Not only does it take cases that originate in the lower federal courts; it also hears cases that originate in state courts if these cases raise constitutional issues (see Figure 14.3). That the Supreme Court is "the highest court in the land" invests it with great authority. Justice Robert Jackson once wryly observed of the Court, "We are not final because we are infallible, we are infallible only because we are final."[32]

The Supreme Court has both original jurisdiction and appellate jurisdiction. The Constitution limits original jurisdiction to "all cases affecting ambassadors, other public ministers and counsels, and those in which a State shall be party."

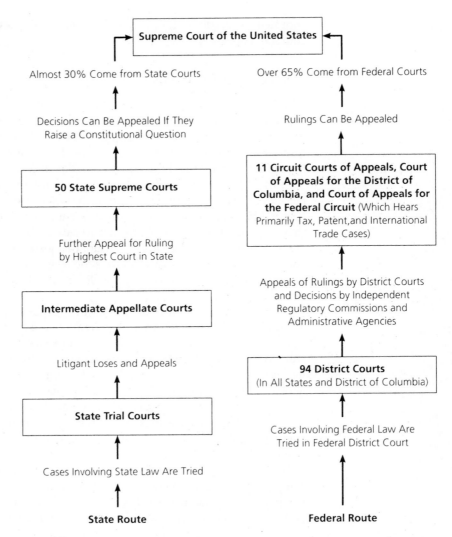

FIGURE 14.3

**Avenues of Appeal:
The Two Main
Routes to the
Supreme Court**

Supreme Court of the United States

Almost 30% Come from State Courts

Over 65% Come from Federal Courts

Decisions Can Be Appealed If They
Raise a Constitutional Question

Rulings Can Be Appealed

50 State Supreme Courts

**11 Circuit Courts of Appeals, Court
of Appeals for the District of
Columbia, and Court of Appeals for
the Federal Circuit** (Which Hears
Primarily Tax, Patent, and International
Trade Cases)

Further Appeal for Ruling
by Highest Court in State

Appeals of Rulings by District Courts
and Decisions by Independent
Regulatory Commissions and
Administrative Agencies

Intermediate Appellate Courts

94 District Courts
(In All States and District of Columbia)

Litigant Loses and Appeals

Cases Involving Federal Law Are
Tried in Federal District Court

State Trial Courts

Cases Involving State Law Are Tried

State Route

Federal Route

Note: In addition, some cases come directly to the Supreme Court from trial courts when they involve reapportionment or civil rights disputes. Appeals from the Court of Military Appeals also go
directly to the Supreme Court. A few cases come on "original jurisdiction" and involve disputes
between state governments.

Few cases arise that qualify under these terms. Almost all of what the Supreme
Court does falls under its second constitutional role as an appellate court.

Supreme Court decisions are powerful not only because they are the final judicial rulings in a case but also because they establish precedents that bind the
lower federal courts and the state courts. Once the Supreme Court has spoken,
judges at lower levels are supposed to bring their decisions into line with its in-

terpretation of the Constitution and the laws. But guidance to lower courts is imperfect when the language of Supreme Court decisions is vague or when new circumstances arise that differ from those of the case used to establish a precedent. Consequently, decision making in a complex area such as criminal procedure or affirmative action may shuttle back and forth for years between the lower courts and the Supreme Court.

THE SUPREME COURT: PROCESS

We turn now to a more thorough examination of the Supreme Court as an institution. First, we look at the processes through which the Court hears cases and arrives at its decisions. Second, we look at the politics of those decisions. As shall be seen, the Court is an institution in which the logic and rules of the law genuinely matter, as do the personalities and political beliefs of the human beings who pronounce the law.

Choosing Cases

Each session of the Supreme Court begins on the first Monday in October and concludes in late June or early July of the following year. At present, about eight thousand cases are filed per year; of these, the Supreme Court will grant a review and produce a written opinion in less than 2 percent! Disgruntled parties in lawsuits often swear that they will appeal the verdict "all the way to the Supreme Court." Obviously, the chance that the Supreme Court will hear their appeal is minuscule. The only party that has a high rate of success in having its appeals heard before the Supreme Court is the federal government itself. The solicitor general, the third-ranking official in the Department of Justice, determines which cases involving the federal government should be appealed to the Supreme Court, and the Court regards petitions from the solicitor general with a favorable disposition, accepting approximately 80 percent of them.

In the past, several categories of cases had to be reviewed by the Supreme Court. Since Congress passed the 1988 Act to Improve the Administration of Justice, the Court has been free in all but a few areas to choose the cases it wishes to hear. Today, about 99 percent of the Court's cases arrive through a *writ of certiorari.* The losing party in a lower court proceeding petitions the Supreme Court for this writ; should the Court choose to "grant cert" (shorthand for *certiorari*), it orders the lower court to send the records of the case.

The mountain of cert petitions that arrives at the Supreme Court by the beginning of its fall term has to be sifted to find the few worthy of the Court's full attention. Because the number of petitions has risen, justices have turned over the work of screening them to their law clerks, recent graduates of the nation's elite law schools. Armed with memos from clerks, the justices meet to decide which cases to hear. According to the informal **rule of four,** at least four justices must agree that a case deserves consideration.

Since almost all cases reach the Court through writs of certiorari, the justices have considerable latitude in setting their own agenda. In each year's session, they can accept cases that allow them to grapple with a constitutional or statutory issue that they deem ripe for determination and reject cases if they wish to sidestep some other controversial issue. Even when the Court agrees to take a case, it may choose to decide it without full consideration, a process known as *summary disposition*. After denying the vast majority of petitions for certiorari, and handling some of the remainder through summary dispositions, the Supreme Court leaves itself less than a hundred cases each year for full consideration.

Deciding Cases

When a case is granted full treatment, attorneys for the two sides are given several months to prepare *briefs*—written statements that argue their respective legal positions to the justices. Additional briefs may be filed by individuals or groups that are not parties in a lawsuit but have an interest in the issues it raises; these are known as *amicus curiae* (friend of the court) briefs. Having read these briefs, the justices allow attorneys for the contending litigants to appear in **oral argument.** Each side has only half an hour to present its strongest arguments to the Court. Oral argument often proves to be a battle for the attorney—but less with opposing counsel than with the justices themselves. Lawyers are not allowed to read from prepared texts, and some justices have a habit of asking barbed questions during oral arguments.

The justices meet in conference twice a week (Wednesdays and Fridays) to discuss the cases they have just heard in oral argument. The chief justice begins the discussion by presenting his or her views on how the case should be resolved. The other eight justices follow with their comments in order of their seniority on the High Court. Formal votes ordinarily are not taken since the positions of the justices have been made clear in their comments. After all nine justices have spoken, one is selected to write a majority opinion for the Court. If the chief justice is in the majority, he or she assigns the opinion. If the chief justice is in the minority, the senior justice on the majority side makes the assignment. The voting alignment at this stage is tentative. Justices may still switch their votes—which makes the next stage, the writing of opinions, all the more crucial.

The crucial test of a majority opinion is not whether it sparkles in style but whether it wins the necessary votes. The justice assigned to write the opinion for the Court must hold on to the votes that constituted the initial majority and, if he or she is persuasive enough, perhaps pick up additional votes. The risk is that an opinion may lose votes along the way; in a closely divided Court, a majority opinion may thus become a minority one as a justice or two switches sides. This happened, for example, in *Bowers* v. *Hardwick* (1986), an important case regarding homosexual rights (see Chapter 16).

The majority opinion announces the position of the Court. Justices who do not want to add their names to this opinion have two options. If they agree with the result announced in the majority opinion but not with the reasoning that justifies this result (or if they simply want to make additional points not found in the majority opinion), they can write a **concurring opinion** that sets out their alternative course of argument. If they disagree with the result, they can write a **dissenting opinion** that challenges the majority's view of what the law should be. Other justices may then sign these concurrences or dissents. In recent years, heated ideological differences and a growing preference for individual expression over institutional loyalty have led to a marked increase in concurrences and dissents

Once all opinions have been drafted, the justices make their final decisions about whether they will "join" the majority opinion, concurring opinions, or dissents. The Court is now ready for a public announcement of its holding in a case.

THE SUPREME COURT: POLITICS

Throughout the process of decision, from screening cases to announcing opinions, the procedures and precedents of the law are central to the work of the Supreme Court. But the process is political as well as legal. Three political factors influence the Court in this regard: the leadership of the chief justice, the strategic action of other justices, and the central role of ideology in shaping judicial results.

The Chief Justice and Leadership

The chief justice has certain special prerogatives during the decision process, such as speaking first in conference and assigning opinions for the Court when in the majority. The chief justice also has unique administrative responsibilities, both over the Court's own building and personnel and over the federal judicial system as a whole. Nevertheless, the chief justice is only "first among equals"; when it comes to votes, he or she has only one. Whether a chief justice is a leader depends on intellectual talent, interpersonal skills, and ability to manage the business of the Court. A comparison of the three most recent chief justices shows how widely varying their leadership styles and impact can be.

The most influential chief justice in modern times was Earl Warren, who held the position from 1953 to 1969. Appointed by President Eisenhower, Warren was a former governor of California, and he brought his exceptional political talent to the role of chief justice. Although not a legal scholar, he developed a clear vision of the Court as a champion of individual liberties and equal rights and was increasingly effective in marshaling a majority to advance that vision. Warren's personal warmth and moral conviction won him the love and respect of most of his colleagues. Perhaps his greatest feat of leadership came early in his tenure, when he convinced several wavering justices that the Court should speak to the nation with unanimity when it took the historic step of declaring racial segregation to be unconstitutional.

It was one of Warren's sharpest critics, President Nixon, who appointed his successor, Warren Burger. Burger served as chief justice from 1969 to 1986. With a rugged face under a full mane of white hair, he looked every inch the part

MAKING A DIFFERENCE

Justice William J. Brennan, Jr.

In a 1990 survey conducted by the *National Law Journal,* only 3 percent of Americans recognized the name William Brennan, Jr. Yet few public figures in the last half of the twentieth century have had as great an impact on the lives of Americans as this remarkable associate justice of the U.S. Supreme Court.

The son of Irish immigrants, Brennan grew up in Newark, New Jersey. His father began as a coal heaver but quickly rose to become a labor union official and local political leader. Despite his ascent, he never forgot his origins and bequeathed to his son a commitment to activism on behalf of society's have-nots. Brennan maintained this commitment even as he, in turn, ascended into the higher ranks of the judicial elite. Appointed to the U.S. Supreme Court by President Eisenhower in 1956 (an appointment that Eisenhower later regretted), Brennan served until 1990. He died in 1997.

During his thirty-four years on the Court, Brennan was a leading force for judicial activism. No other justice of modern times matched his record for penning landmark decisions. In area after area—reapportionment, the law of libel, obscenity, school prayer, the rights of criminal defendants, equal rights for minorities and women—Brennan crafted decisions that reshaped the rules by which Americans live.

Brennan's influence stemmed as much from his skills at strategic action as from his popular democratic convictions. Unlike his fellow giants of liberal jurisprudence, Hugo Black and William O. Douglas, who were combative and uncompromising, Brennan was adept at building coalitions and molding consensuses. In *New York Times v. Sullivan* (1964), the most conservative members of the Court wanted to retain the existing standard of libel law, by which a newspaper could be sued for an erroneous statement injuring the reputation of a public official, while the most liberal members insisted that the right of free speech barred any judgments for libel in such cases. Brennan found a middle

of a chief justice as a Hollywood movie would portray him. To his fellow justices, however, Burger was distinguished only in appearance. Most found him pompous in personal relations, poorly prepared for cases before the Court, and deficient in legal analysis. Burger had a passion and a talent for the administrative duties of the chief justice, but when it came to influencing the opinions handed down by the Court, he was a weak leader.[33]

When Burger retired in 1986, President Reagan elevated Associate Justice William Rehnquist to the position of chief justice. Since his appointment by President Nixon in 1971, Rehnquist had been the most conservative member of the Court. Although his views mark him as more extreme than Burger in ideological terms, he has proven to be a more effective leader. He has more intellectual firepower, winning him grudging respect even from his liberal adversaries. In personal style, he is unpretentious and good humored, and he runs conferences efficiently. Rehnquist also has a critical advantage in leadership that Burger lacked: A majority on the current Court shares his conservative judicial philoso-

ground: to win a libel suit, a plaintiff must show that falsehoods printed about her or him are intentional and motivated by "actual malice." Patiently rewriting his opinion to satisfy colleagues on both sides—it took eight drafts!—Brennan revolutionized libel law and expanded the freedom of the press.

The height of Brennan's influence came during the Warren Court revolution. But he continued to use his intellectual and political talents to shape the law even during the years in which the Burger and Rehnquist Courts sought a counterrevolution. Brennan mounted a powerful defense of the essential achievements of the Warren Court and frequently frustrated conservative ambitions. He was even able to extend Warren Court departures in several areas. Adept as always behind the scenes, he played a major role in shaping the Court's support for abortion rights in *Roe v. Wade* (1973). And he wrote new landmark decisions on women's rights (*Craig v. Boren*, 1976) and symbolic speech (*Texas v. Johnson*, 1989).

Yet the conservative trend on the Court pushed Brennan frequently into the role of dissenter, particularly on the issue of capital punishment. Here, the usually affable and pragmatic Brennan was passionately unyielding. To him, the core of the Constitution and the Bill of Rights was a commitment to human dignity. The death penalty, in his view, was totally inconsistent with this commitment: "The fatal constitutional infirmity of capital punishment is that it treats members of the human race as nonhumans, as objects to be toyed with and discarded." Unlike famous Supreme Court dissenters of the past, Brennan did not relish this role; he much preferred being the strategic actor who could find the common ground upon which a majority could be built. Yet his stance on the death penalty was in keeping with his commitment to justice for the most unpopular and powerless of Americans.

Sources: Kim Isaac Eisler, *A Justice For All: William J. Brennan, Jr., and the Decisions that Transformed America* (New York: Simon & Schuster, 1993); Charles G. Curtis, Jr., and Shirley S. Abrahàmson, "William Joseph Brennan, Jr.," in Kermit L. Hall et al., eds., *The Oxford Companion to the Supreme Court of the United States* (New York: Oxford University Press, 1992), pp. 86–89; Owen Fiss, "A Life Lived Twice," *The Yale Law Journal* 100 (March 1991): 1117–29.

phy. The Rehnquist Court is emerging in the 1990s as a powerful force for a conservative realignment of American law.[34]

Strategic Action

The chief justice is not the only member of the Court who can exercise leadership. Any of the other eight justices can use *strategic action* to win a majority for a legal doctrine they favor. Justices who engage in strategic action calculate the mix of tactics that will likely win over enough votes to their preferred position. Such tactics may include (1) persuasion on the merits—intellectual arguments to change minds; (2) ingratiation—using personal warmth to woo potential supporters; (3) sanctions—threats to write a stinging concurrence or dissent; and (4) bargaining—negotiation over the argument and language of a decision.[35] (The accompanying box features a master of strategic action, Justice William Brennan, Jr.)

That the Supreme Court is the most elite domain in American politics hardly frees it from internal conflict. Indeed, the Court's elite nature may exacerbate conflict. Protected by lifetime tenure, justices may bring strongly held opinions and large egos to "battles on the bench." These battles are ordinarily kept from getting out of hand, however, by prudent calculations (you may need your current adversary's vote in a future case) and considerations of authority (too much visible conflict undermines the legitimacy of the Court).[36]

Ideology

Although the leadership abilities of a chief justice or the strategic action of other justices may significantly affect the work of the Court, the most powerful political factor is ideology. In deciding how to cast votes and frame opinions, justices are profoundly influenced by their own convictions about society. Changes in the doctrines announced by the Supreme Court stem less from developments internal to the law than from the arrival of new justices with differing ideological perspectives.[37]

The most common ideological distinction among justices is that between liberals and conservatives. Liberal justices tend to favor individual rights (e.g., of political dissenters and criminal defendants) when they clash with governmental authority, to support measures toward greater equality for such previously excluded groups as African Americans and women, and to validate government regulation of the economy. Conservative justices are more inclined to cherish the peace of the existing social order and the authority of the officials (executives, bureaucrats, police, prosecutors) who maintain it and to look with greater reverence at the rights of property owners. Some justices fall midway between these ideological poles; in a closely divided Court, these "centrists" may hold the balance of power.[38]

Students of the Supreme Court look not only at the ideology of individual justices but also at the formation of **ideological blocs.** An ideological bloc is a group of two or more justices who vote the same way with a high degree of regularity. Thus, we can speak of liberal blocs, conservative blocs, or moderate blocs, such as the bloc of four conservatives who frustrated Roosevelt's New Deal or the bloc of five liberals who spearheaded the expansion of civil liberties in the later years of the Warren Court. Members of an ideological bloc may directly coordinate their actions or may simply vote the same way out of shared beliefs even in the absence of close personal relations.

THE SUPREME COURT AND THE POLITICAL SYSTEM

Ideology is the single most potent force shaping the decisions of the Supreme Court. But other factors enter in, among them concern for how decisions will be received by other political actors. A Supreme Court decision must take into account multiple audiences: the lower courts that must apply the decision to other cases, the government officials who must enforce the decision, and the segment of the public that must abide by the decision. Lacking the power of the purse (financial power) and the power of the sword (executive power, including the use of force if necessary), the Supreme Court is dependent for its power on the reaction to its decisions. As political scientist Stephen Wasby remarks, "The Supreme Court may make law, or the law may be what the Supreme Court says it is, but *only after all others have had their say.*"[39] During the process of implementing the Court's decisions, it may be checked or held accountable by other institutions or political forces.

When Supreme Court decisions require federal action, the response of the president is most important. Usually, presidents back up the Court's actions, regarding the enforcement of its decisions as a requirement of their oath of office. Sometimes, though, they drag their feet on implementation or repudiate a decision altogether. Believing that the decision in *Brown* v. *Board of Education* (1954) was forcing racial desegregation too rapidly on the South, President Eisenhower refused, despite repeated requests from others, to encourage southern compliance by placing his enormous prestige behind the Court's ruling. President Bush sharply criticized the Supreme Court's decision in *Texas* v. *Johnson* (1989), which upheld the right of a protester to burn an American flag as a form of symbolic speech protected under the First Amendment. He proposed a constitutional amendment to ban flag burning—implying that he, and not the Court, stood for patriotism. But Bush failed to get the amendment through Congress. (Congress did pass a law against flag burning—and the Court struck it down as well.)

Congress has power to chastise or discipline the Supreme Court since the legislative branch determines the appellate jurisdiction and even the size of the High Court. Congress sometimes altered the size of the Court during the nineteenth century. Since Roosevelt's court-packing fiasco, however, it has been politically unwise to propose adding or subtracting members, and the figure of nine justices seemingly has become sacrosanct. Supreme Court decisions based on the Constitution can be overturned only through the difficult process of constitutional amendment, so the ability of members of Congress to reverse specific decisions is far greater when the Court has been engaged in statutory interpretation. Thus, the Civil Rights Act of 1991, placing the burden of proof on employers in job discrimination lawsuits, overturned a dozen recent Supreme Court holdings.

Even though the justices don't face the public in elections, they know that compliance with their decisions depends ultimately on public opinion. Public views on the judicial branch tend, however, to be less clear than views on the other two branches. General public support for the Supreme Court is higher than for Congress or the presidency. On the other hand, public knowledge about the Court is lower. For example, surveys indicate that a majority cannot name even one sitting justice. The public is more attuned to controversial Court rulings than to the Court as an institution. Public support for the Court thus fell in response to decisions that favored the rights of criminal defendants. But it rose during the Watergate era, when the Court ordered President Nixon to hand over the tapes that revealed his participation in a criminal coverup, thereby forcing him to resign.[40]

Respect for law and the Supreme Court inclines most Americans to abide by judicial decisions, even those they disagree with. When the Court treads in the most sensitive areas, however, it may face major problems of evasion or resistance. Its ruling in *Engel* v. *Vitale* (1962) forbade prayer in the public schools as a violation of the First Amendment, yet decades later many public schools still conduct various forms of religious observance.

Dependent on others for the implementation of its decisions, the Court cannot help but take heed of the political environment. Its conservative critics wish it was even more deferential to elected officials and public opinion. Its liberal defenders praise it for disregarding political pressures when the fundamental values of democracy are at stake. Both, progressive skeptics suggest, tend to exaggerate the boldness of the justices, whose conservative training and cautious legal instincts place them most often on the side of elite democracy.

CONCLUSION: LAW, POLITICS, AND THE DEMOCRATIC DEBATE

In our examination of the federal judicial system, and especially in our treatment of the Supreme Court, law and politics are separate yet intertwined. The judicial branch is fundamentally different from the other branches in that it is a legal order. Its business is resolving lawsuits or criminal cases. It follows legal procedures and rules for determining how cases are brought to and then handled by the High Court and gives considerable weight to past decisions as precedents on the grounds that law should be, as much as possible, settled and known. The impressive symbolic power of the Supreme Court—the black robes, the marble temple, and the confidential deliberations—rests on the mystique of the rule of law as something that transcends politics.

Yet politics shapes appointments to the Supreme Court, as presidents try to fill the Court with justices who will carry out the presidents' political and ideological agendas. Politics is found within the internal processes of the Court, as chief justices attempt to exercise leadership and other justices engage in strategic action. Political values influence the Court, with ideology the paramount factor in determining how different justices will vote on cases. Political sensitivity to other institutions and to public opinion characterizes a judicial branch aware of its dependence on others to carry out its decisions. Finally, the Court is political because its decisions set national policy on some of the issues that matter most to Americans.

It is because the judiciary is political, and indeed so important a policymaker, that there has been an intense democratic debate in recent years over its proper role in American life. Popular democrats of the past generally mistrusted the Court as a nondemocratic defender of elite privileges. Their arguments have been taken over by conservatives such as Edwin Meese, whose very different policy agenda also requires a Court that practices self-restraint and does not interfere much with other institutions. In contrast, liberal jurists such as William Brennan, Jr., want popular democrats to reexamine their attitude toward the judiciary, arguing that only an activist Court that adapts and modernizes the Constitution can bring out its popular democratic character. Progressive skeptics question both the conservatives' fear of the Court and the liberals' hope for it. In their thinking, the Court can be of only limited value in the struggle for popular democracy. Citizens who seek popular democratic reform must rely on their own political activities rather than looking for salvation from the judicial elite.

KEY TERMS

judicial review
jurisprudence of original intention
precedent
Marbury v. *Madison*
McCulloch v. *Maryland*
Gibbons v. *Ogden*
Dred Scott v. *Sandford*
court-packing plan

senatorial courtesy
original jurisdiction
appellate court
rule of four
oral argument
concurring opinion
dissenting opinion
ideological bloc

SUGGESTED READINGS

Robert H. Bork, *The Tempting of America: The Political Seduction of the Law*. New York: Free Press, 1990. A rejected Supreme Court nominee's conservative attack on the judicial selection process and on liberal jurisprudence.

Kermit L. Hall et al., eds., *The Oxford Companion to the Supreme Court of the United States*. New York: Oxford University Press, 1992. Everything you want to know about the Supreme Court is presented in superb detail.

David Kairys, ed., *The Politics of Law: A Progressive Critique*, rev. ed. New York: Pantheon Books, 1990. An anthology of articles, most by law professors, expressing the view of progressive skeptics that the courts and the legal profession generally serve elite interests.

David M. O'Brien, *Storm Center: The Supreme Court in American Politics*, 4th ed. New York: W. W. Norton, 1996. A leading text on the Supreme Court that makes engaging use of historical anecdotes.

Gerald N. Rosenberg, *The Hollow Hope: Can Courts Bring About Social Change?* Chicago: The University of Chicago Press, 1991. A provocative argument, with case studies, that casts doubt upon the ability of the courts to advance social reform.

Laurence H. Tribe, *God Save This Honorable Court: How the Choice of Supreme Court Judges Shapes Our History*. New York: New American Library, 1986. A Harvard Law professor's account of the history and politics of judicial selection, written in a popular style.

CHAPTER

15

State and Local Politics: The Dilemma of Federalism

The United States has a system of government called *federalism* that divides power between a central government and state and local governments. Popular democrats have always favored decentralizing power as much as possible, putting policymaking authority in the hands of state, or even better, local governments. Decentralizing power brings government closer to the people, enabling citizens to participate more meaningfully in the decisions that affect their lives. It would seem, then, that the popular democratic position on federalism would be simple: shift as much policymaking authority as possible from the federal government to the states and localities. There are problems, however, with simply moving power down the federal ladder, as we can see in the case of homelessness.

When homelessness emerged as a visible problem in the 1980s, homeless policy was handled like a hot potato, shunted from one level of government to another with no one willing to take full responsibility. The Reagan administration (1981–1989) stressed that homelessness was best addressed by localities, and it was not until 1987 that Congress passed the Stewart B. McKinney Act providing federal monies for temporary emergency shelters. Funded at less than a billion dollars annually, McKinney Act monies, once distributed across the entire country, were stretched paper thin. A 1988 survey found that 89 percent of the nation's governors thought the federal government was doing an inadequate job on homelessness. By 1987, states were spending an estimated $500 million annually on the homeless, but governors knew their policies were weak as well: In the same survey, 81 percent of the governors doubted the adequacy of their own services for the homeless.

Almost by default, much of the responsibility for dealing with homelessness was left to local governments, especially big cities. But the ability of local governments to enact and implement effective homeless policies varied greatly. Consider the responses of two major American cities, Boston and Miami.

Boston, with a long tradition of active government, probably did more to help the homeless and near-homeless than any city in the country. Boston's populist mayor Ray Flynn (1983–1993) was one of the few mayors in the country to side openly with the homeless and champion local homeless policies. Under Flynn's leadership, Boston enacted a linkage policy that required downtown developers to contribute to low-income housing, raising over $70 million by 1992. The city also enacted an inclusionary housing ordinance that required housing developers to set aside units for low-income families. The city not only aggressively sought federal grants, it also committed millions of dollars of its own money to fund low-income housing. To prevent people from becoming homeless, condominium conversions were regulated and evictions of renters who could not afford to buy their units were banned. Those who did become homeless were provided with extensive services, and the number of shelter beds increased from 972 in 1983 to 2,754 in 1989.[1]

Miami's response to homelessness was very different. The city spent no money of its own on the homeless. As a result, there were only about 400 shelter beds in the city, with another 500 added in the winter—for a homeless population estimated at 15,000. Homeless people on the street, however, presented a problem for Miami, which advertises itself as a carefree tourist destination. To address the image problem, Miami implemented aggressive policies to get the homeless off the streets, arresting nearly 7,000 homeless people in 1986, for example, for such offenses as drunkenness and sleeping in public. In 1991, a federal judge ordered Miami to stop kicking the homeless out of public parks in the daytime and destroying their belongings. Miami, it should be noted, was not the only city that shunned the homeless.[2] Los Angeles city officials devised a "bum-proof" park bench; shaped like a barrel, it was so uncomfortable no one would want to sleep on it. The city also installed sophisticated park sprinklers that went off at random times to discourage sleeping.[3] Some smaller cities simply gave the homeless a one-way bus ticket to the nearest big city and told them never to return.

The contrast between Boston and Miami shows the problems with simply turning responsibility for social policies over to local governments. Many local governments are dominated by elites. Preoccupied with economic prosperity in a competitive federal system, they deliberately underfund social services in order to discourage the poor and the homeless from moving in. On the other hand, if policy making is controlled by the federal government, the result is inevitably a great deal of bureaucracy and red tape, allowing little room for meaningful participation by ordinary citizens. In short, popular democrats are faced with what we call the *dilemma of federalism:* Either alternative—centralizing power in the hands of federal authorities or decentralizing power into states and localities— seems to have unsatisfactory implications from the viewpoint of democracy.

In this chapter we explore the dilemma of federalism and look for a popular democratic way out of it. We begin by examining the evolving federal system over the years from the founding to the present, showing how power has moved among the federal, state, and local levels. In the last part of the chapter we will examine the operation of state and local governments today, focusing on the question of their potential for popular democratic participation.

FEDERALISM AND THE CONSTITUTION

The debate over federalism began with the controversy over ratification of the U.S. Constitution. The framers of the Constitution favored moving power from the states to a national government with a strong executive. Under the Articles of Confederation, the state legislatures had great power that the framers feared would be used by envious majorities to confiscate the wealth of the rich. As James Madison maintained in his famous "extended republic" argument in *Federalist No. 10*, a large democracy, like the United States as a whole, would be less vulnerable to majority tyranny than a small democracy because of the greater obstacles to coordination and communication. Moreover, by electing representatives from larger districts, Madison maintained, voters in an extended republic would favor educated and wealthy elites.

Led by Madison and Alexander Hamilton, the framers of the Constitution initially favored a **unitary government** in which all significant powers would rest in the hands of the central government and state and local governments would derive their authority from the central government. (Over 90 percent of all countries in the world today, including France and the United Kingdom, are governed by unitary systems.) The founders knew, however, that most citizens, and especially the rank-and-file soldiers who had fought in the Revolution, would not vote for a unitary government that reminded them of their subservience under the British monarchy. To aid in ratification, the Federalists were forced to compromise with Anti-federalist sentiment, creating a mixed system that gave some powers to the federal government and left others to the states. Federalism was born in compromise.

Reluctant to admit that one of the primary characteristics of the new Constitution was the result of a tactical political compromise, the framers put their best "spin" on the new Constitution in order to boost its chances of ratification. They argued that the federalism of the new Constitution arose not from a compromise but from a general theory of government that carefully balanced the powers of the central government and the state governments. Protection for the states, the Federalists argued, would come from the way the that the new Constitution divided power into two spheres, a theory that we have come to call **dual federalism.** Under dual federalism, the national government and the states each have separate spheres of authority, and "within their respective spheres the two centers of government are 'sovereign' and hence 'equal.'"[4] Each level of government relates directly to the citizens, and the other level of government cannot interfere within its legitimate sphere of authority.

Under dual federalism, the federal government has only those powers specifically granted in the Constitution, called **enumerated powers** (see Table 15.1). Seventeen such powers are given to the national government, or Congress, in Article I, Section 8, including the power to "regulate commerce with foreign nations and among the several States," "coin money," and "provide for the common defence." All powers not given to the national government are **reserved** to the states by the Tenth Amendment. (Dual federalism is sometimes called *Tenth Amendment federalism.*) With the powers of the federal government clearly spelled out in the Constitution, Federalists maintained, the Supreme Court would act as a neutral umpire making sure that the federal government does not go beyond its enumerated powers and invade the powers reserved to the states. In cases where both levels of government possess the power to act—so-called **concurrent powers**—the **Supremacy Clause** (Article VI) states that the national laws supersede the state laws.

TABLE 15.1	Power	Definition	Example
Principles of Dual Federalism	Enumerated	Powers specifically granted to Congress	Coin money, national defense
	Concurrent	Powers exercised by both Congress and the states	Taxation
	Reserved	Powers not mentioned in the Constitution and therefore left to the states	Police powers (e.g., land use regulation)

Anti-federalists opposed the Constitution primarily because it gave too much power to the national government. The Anti-federalists argued that Madison's extended republic was a contradiction in terms; democracy was possible only in small homogeneous republics. The principal threat to our liberties, they said, comes not from tyrannical majorities in the state legislatures but from selfish elites in the national government.

The Anti-federalists did not buy the theory of dual federalism—the idea that the states would be protected because the Supreme Court would prevent the federal government from extending its powers beyond those clearly enumerated in the Constitution. To begin with, they cited the vague language in the Constitution describing the division of powers, which was written in broad terms to facilitate agreement. In shaping this compromise, even the framers disagreed about the division of powers between the national and state governments. As a result, the Constitution is full of imprecise language that papers over disagreements, especially on the issue of federalism. In the words of Supreme Court Justice William J. Brennan, Jr., the framers "hid their differences in cloaks of generality."[5]

Anti-federalists attacked specific clauses in the Constitution that they felt could be used to expand the power of the federal government. They were suspicious of the so-called **Necessary and Proper,** or **Elastic, Clause** (Article I, Section 8) that gave the national Congress the power "to make all Laws which shall be necessary and proper for carrying into Execution the foregoing Powers." In *The Federalist Papers* Alexander Hamilton maintained that the necessary and proper clause did nothing but state the obvious: "Though it may be chargeable with tautology or redundancy, [it] is at least perfectly harmless."[6] The Anti-federalists, however, smelled a rat here: If this were the case, they asked, then why was it included at all? The Anti-federalists also observed that the institution that would interpret the vague language of the Constitution was itself a part of the national government and would therefore favor the national government over the states. Appointed by the president for life, with the advice and consent of the Senate, the justices of the Supreme Court would not be democratically accountable.

On the surface, the debate between the Federalists and Anti-federalists was based on principle: Each side claimed it was only trying to create a more perfect representative democracy. In fact, however, both had practical political purposes behind their positions. Fearing the radicalism of the state legislatures, the Federalists thought that they would be able to dominate a national government with a strong executive that could protect their property from radical movements. Conversely, the power base of the Anti-federalists was in the state legislatures, and they feared that the new Constitution would weaken them politically.

In fact, throughout American history federalism has been a political football. Political conflicts over federalism are not surprising because the division of powers between levels of government is not politically neutral. *Where* decisions are made determines the scope of conflict, and the scope of conflict, in turn, helps determine who wins and who loses. From the beginning in American politics, struggles over policy have been transformed into struggles over federalism.

Regardless of whether you favor popular or elite democracy, understanding federalism is essential for understanding American politics. In our political system, disagreements over *what* policies should be enacted are frequently played out as disagreements over *where* policy decisions should be made—at the national, state, or local level. The reason for this is that state and local political systems are not simply miniature versions of the national political system; there are essential differences among the different levels of government.

The Slavery Issue: Reaffirming National Authority

After the Constitution was ratified, elite democrats continued to champion a powerful national government while popular democrats emphasized states' rights. A Federalist, John Marshall, Chief Justice of the Supreme Court from 1801 to 1835, was a brilliant advocate of national power. Perhaps his most important decision, *McCulloch* v. *Maryland* (1819), used the Necessary and Proper Clause to expand the powers of the federal government. In 1836, the popular democrat Andrew Jackson appointed Roger B. Taney, a strong advocate of states' rights, to succeed Marshall as Chief Justice. Led by Taney until 1864, the Court chipped away at federal powers by upholding state laws that probably would have been struck down by the Marshall Court.

Popular democratic support of states rights came up against a contradiction with the issue of slavery. Southern states used states' rights to defend the institution of slavery. Led by South Carolina's John C. Calhoun, southern states resisted tariffs that protected northern industries and raised prices for manufactured goods. They also opposed efforts by the federal government to restrict slavery. Calhoun argued for the doctrine of **nullification**—that states have the right to nullify, or refuse to obey, laws they consider unconstitutional. In the infamous *Dred Scott* decision (1857), the Supreme Court under Taney ruled that the federal government had no power to prohibit slavery in the territories.[7] By striking down the Missouri Compromise as unconstitutional, the Supreme Court helped precipitate the Civil War. The Civil War finally settled the federalism issues raised by slavery: The federal union is indissoluble, and states do not have the right to declare acts of the federal government unconstitutional or secede from the union.

Federalism and Corporations

During the period of rapid industrialization after the Civil War, a new threat to popular democracy arose: the rise of giant national corporations and the wealthy elites who ran them. Popular democrats had power in many state legislatures and they used that power to regulate corporations. These efforts were frustrated by the Supreme Court, however, which often ruled against the states when they threatened the rights of private property. Angry about rate discrimination against areas not served by competing railroads, for example, popular democrats in the early 1870s passed laws setting maximum rates. In the celebrated Granger cases of 1877, the Supreme Court upheld the constitutionality of these laws.[8] In 1886, however, the Supreme Court reversed itself and ruled that the Constitution placed power to regulate railroad rates exclusively in the hands of the federal government, even for segments of the journey lying entirely within one state.[9]

The Court's blocking of state action provided an impetus for the creation by Congress in 1887 of the Interstate Commerce Commission (ICC), the first attempt by the national government to regulate the economy through means other than general control over money and credit. Additional support for the ICC came from the railroads, who feared the rising power of popular democrats in the state legislatures. They saw federal railroad regulation "as a safe shield behind which to hide from the consequences of local democracy."[10]

In short, elite and popular democratic forces tried to shift policymaking authority to the federal or state level, depending on how they saw their advantage. In the late nineteenth and early twentieth centuries, the Supreme Court generally acted to protect private property and was suspicious of governmental efforts, at all levels, to regulate private property. From a late twentieth-century viewpoint, the Court construed the powers of the federal government quite narrowly. It struck down the federal income tax, for example[11]; restricted the powers of the ICC to set railroad rates[12]; and declared federal laws to regulate child labor unconstitutional.[13]

For almost the first hundred and fifty years of the U.S. Constitution—until the New Deal in the 1930s—something like dual federalism prevailed in American government. The powers of the federal government were construed narrowly, and Congress did not legislate in many domestic policy areas that we now take for granted. In domestic policy, state and local governments raised more revenues, spent more money, and provided more services than the federal government. There were important exceptions to this pattern of federal reluctance, particularly the assertion of federal power following the Civil War during Reconstruction in the South and federal regulation of corporations during the progressive era. Nevertheless, until the New Deal the federal government was the junior partner in domestic policy. It was not until the Great Depression of the 1930s that the glaring weaknesses of state and local governments were dramatically exposed.

THE FAILURE OF DUAL FEDERALISM

It is difficult for Americans today to imagine the depth of the economic and political crisis the nation faced during the Depression. It began with the stock market crash on October 24, 1929—Black Thursday. The effects of the crash rippled out from Wall Street to paralyze the entire nation. The unemployment rate soared from 3 percent in 1929 to over one-quarter of the workforce in 1933.

Those who were lucky enough to have jobs saw their average incomes fall 43 percent from 1929 to 1933. The collapse of the economy spread to the financial system; by the end of 1932, more than 5,000 commercial banks had failed. The political situation was tense. Frequent and violent street confrontations broke out between police and communist-led demonstrators as well as workers trying to organize unions.

The initial response of the political system to the Depression was halting and inadequate. Under the system of dual federalism, almost all social welfare functions were left to the states and localities. In 1929–1930, local governments provided 95 percent of the costs of general relief for the destitute.[14] The American welfare state was incredibly fragmented; the state of Ohio, for example, had 1,535 different poor relief districts.[15] Burdened by a crazy quilt of jurisdictional responsibilities, welfare was poorly administered and inadequately funded. Local welfare policies had other weaknesses: Able-bodied men were generally excluded from receiving any aid; strict residency requirements excluded many others; and those who did qualify for help were usually required to live in almshouses under wretched conditions and were forced to work.[16]

Even though donations to private charities increased when the Depression hit, the system was incapable of keeping up with soaring needs. In 1932, less than a quarter of the unemployed got any relief at all. For those who did, relief payments were usually inadequate. In New York City, families received an average grant of $2.39 per week.[17] The cities with the worst problems had the fewest resources to deal with them. With nearly one-third of its industrial workforce unemployed, Detroit made a heroic effort to provide relief, spending more per capita than any other city in the country. Detroit's compassion, however, soon surpassed its tax base. Under pressure from the city's creditors, Detroit was forced to cut already inadequate relief appropriations in half in 1931–1932.[18]

Adhering to the principle of dual federalism, President Herbert Hoover refused to expand federal relief efforts. Speaking in 1932, Hoover asserted:

> I hold that the maintenance of the sense of individual responsibility of men to their neighbors and the proper separation of the functions of the Federal and local Governments require the maintenance of the fundamental principle that the relief of distress rests upon the individuals, upon the communities and upon the states.[19]

Hoover, who remained in office until 1933, held steadfastly to the position that capitalism would right itself, so long as the federal government did not interfere.

Roosevelt's Dilemma

When Franklin Delano Roosevelt assumed the presidency on March 4, 1933, he faced a difficult dilemma. The situation cried out for decisive federal action, but he knew that any attempt to expand federal power into areas that had previously been reserved for the states would meet crippling opposition in Congress, which strongly represented local interests. More important, the Supreme Court would simply declare such expansions of federal powers unconstitutional. A Supreme

Court veto was no idle threat because the Court was dominated by conservative justices who accepted the tenets of dual federalism. In 1935, for example, the Supreme Court struck down the National Industrial Recovery Act, asserting that the regulation of wages and hours fell outside the powers of Congress to regulate interstate commerce.[20] Emboldened by Supreme Court rulings, by late 1935 lower court judges had issued 1,600 orders to prevent federal officials from implementing acts of Congress.[21] In perhaps the biggest blow to the New Deal expansion of federal power, in 1936 the Supreme Court struck down the Agricultural Adjustment Act that would have enabled the federal government to restrict production in order to increase the prices farmers received for their crops. Rejecting an expansive definition of the General Welfare Clause, Justice Owen Roberts gave a classic reaffirmation of dual federalism.

> From the accepted doctrine that the United States is a government of delegated powers, it follows that those not expressly granted or reasonably to be implied from such as are conferred, are reserved to the states or to the people. . . . None to regulate agricultural production is given, and therefore legislation by Congress for that purpose is forbidden.[22]

Frustrated by the Supreme Court's opposition, Roosevelt attempted to "pack the court" by adding justices friendly to the New Deal. He failed. Although most Americans opposed Supreme Court limitations on the New Deal, they also opposed tampering with the checks and balances of the Constitution. Roosevelt was caught on the horns of a dilemma: Congress and the Court prevented him from using the federal government to address the problems of the Depression, but if the federal government did nothing, the people would continue to suffer (as would Roosevelt's re-election prospects). How Roosevelt resolved this dilemma would revolutionize federalism in the United States.

Roosevelt's Solution: Grants-in-Aid

Roosevelt gradually embraced a compromise approach that used the powers of the federal government to initiate action but gave the states and localities considerable leeway in running the programs. This solution was advocated by Louis Brandeis, a Roosevelt supporter on the Supreme Court. In a famous dissenting opinion in 1932, Brandeis praised the federal system for allowing a state to "serve as a laboratory, and try novel social and economic experiments without risk to the rest of the country."[23] Brandeis recommended to Roosevelt that the federal government encourage the states to assume more active policy roles in addressing the crisis. The Brandeis approach was essentially a "third way" that attempted to slip between the horns of the dilemma of federal domination and state inaction.

Roosevelt implemented the Brandeis approach through **grants-in-aid** that combined federal funding with state administration. Grants-in-aid are funds provided by one level of government to another for specific purposes. Usually states are required to put up some of their own money (these are called **matching grants**), and they have to meet minimal federal standards for the program.

Grants-in-aid had been in existence for many years, and as early as 1923 the Supreme Court had declared them constitutional on the ground that they were not obligatory but simply offered "an option which the state is free to accept or reject."[24] Federal grants-in-aid expanded rapidly during the New Deal, from $217 million in 1932 to $744 million in 1941.[25]

The Death of Dual Federalism

In 1937 the Supreme Court, with no change of membership, approved the New Deal's expansion of the federal government into areas previously reserved for the states. The Anti-federalist fears of federal expansion turned out to be well founded, but in ways they would have found ironical: Vague words in the Constitution, such as the Necessary and Proper Clause and the Interstate Commerce Clause, were used to justify expansions of federal power, but these expansions were opposed by elites and favored by masses of common people who needed help from the federal government against the ravages of the Great Depression. Expanded federal powers were used to redistribute wealth and opportunity from elites to the common people. Supreme Court decisions in 1937 signaled the demise of dual federalism. Within a few years, the federal government was allowed to legislate in almost all areas of domestic policy.

The New Deal revolutionized American federalism, moving the federal government into domestic policy functions previously reserved to the states. At the same time, state and local governments retained a great deal of power over these functions because they controlled the details of policy and who was hired to run the programs. As Figures 15.1 and 15.2 show, although federal spending has soared, most public employees work for state and local governments.

FIGURE 15.1

Government Spending as a Percentage of GNP, 1929–1994*

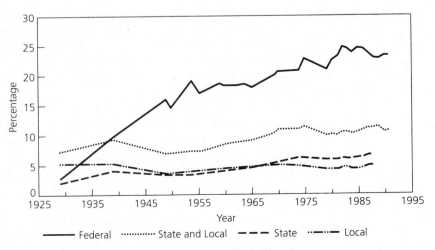

*Note: Shown as "own-source" spending, i.e., before intergovernmental transfers.
Source: Harold W. Stanley and Richard G. Neimi, *Vital Statistics on American Politics,* 5th ed. Copyright © CQ Press. Used with permission.

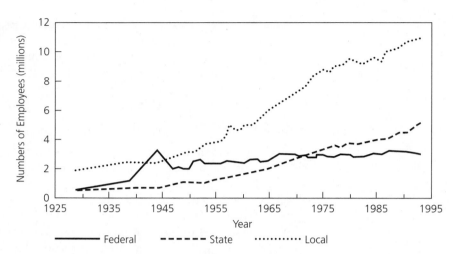

FIGURE 15.2

Number of Federal, State, and Local Government Employees, 1929–1992

Source: Harold W. Stanley and Richard G. Neimi, *Vital Statistics on American Politics,* 5th ed. Copyright © CQ Press. Used with permission.

INTERGOVERNMENTAL RELATIONS

Beginning with the New Deal, dual federalism was replaced with a new federal system called **intergovernmental relations.** Under the new system, relations among federal, state, and local governments are worked out by specific legislation and negotiations, not by judicial rulings on separate spheres of authority. Two aspects of the system help preserve a balance of power between the national government and state and local governments: (1) The states remain as separate governments with independent taxing and spending powers, and (2) the states play a crucial role in the selection and orientation of federal officials.[26] Members of Congress are elected from individual states and congressional districts, imparting a "local spirit" to the national government. Under intergovernmental relations, the powers of states and localities are protected more by political processes than by the courts.

What is true of federal-state relations is also true of state-local relations. Local governments are not mentioned in the U.S. Constitution. According to what has come to be known as "*Dillon's Rule,*" local governments have no independent powers of their own; they acquire all their powers from the states.[27] In reality, the situation is more complex. There is a strong tradition of local control in the United States. In colonial times, local governments had a great deal of autonomy; the American Revolution is best understood as a defense of local liberties, not state liberties, against incursions by the British Crown and Parliament. Notwithstanding Dillon's Rule, many states have granted cities *home rule*, the right to organize their own governments as they see fit. Local governments set their own taxing and spending policies and play a role in the composition of state governments. As with federal-state relations, state-local relations are managed mostly by political negotiations, not by judicial fiat.

Johnson's Creative Federalism

The system of grants-in-aid put in place by the New Deal expanded slowly until the 1960s. The first Republican president since the New Deal, Dwight Eisenhower, did not roll back the welfare state established by FDR, but, with the exception of interstate highways, he initiated few major new grants. By the end of Eisenhower's presidency in 1960, grants-in-aid totaled only $7.0 billion.

Massive expansion of the grant-in-aid system occurred in the 1960s under Democrat Lyndon Johnson. By 1970, federal grants had more than tripled, to $24.1 billion, representing 19 percent of total state and local outlays (see Figure 15.3). Johnson's expansion of the grant system was motivated both by a sincere desire to target social problems and by political considerations. During his presidency (1963–1969), Johnson created hundreds of **categorical grant** programs—which required recipients to apply for funding under specific categories, detailing how the money would be spent and subjecting themselves to strict federal rules. The detailed conditions attached to the grants helped ensure that the monies would go to those who needed them the most and not to the most powerful political interests.

Johnson was also motivated by a desire to tie restive urban blacks to the national Democratic coalition. In his famous War on Poverty Johnson did an end

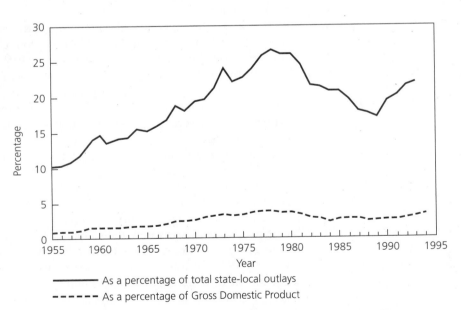

FIGURE 15.3

Federal Grants-in-Aid in Relation to State and Local Outlays and GDP, 1955–1994

——— As a percentage of total state-local outlays

- - - - - As a percentage of Gross Domestic Product

Source: Adapted from Advisory Commission on Intergovernmental Relations, *Significant Features of Fiscal Federalism*, 1994, vol. 2 (Washington, D. C.: Author, 1994), p. 9.

run around white-dominated city governments and gave money directly to community and nonprofit organizations in the inner cities. Johnson called his solution **creative federalism.** The Economic Opportunity Act of 1964, for example, created expensive new categorical grants to fight urban, largely black, poverty and included programs such as Head Start (an early education program for disadvantaged children), the Job Corps, and community action agencies. Approximately 75 percent of the community action agencies were nongovernmental.[28]

Nixon's New Federalism

Johnson's creative federalism provoked a backlash, especially among suburban whites, who viewed federal grants as biased toward inner cities and blacks.[29] Welfare especially became an issue. The number of families on welfare (AFDC) soared 237 percent from 1965 to 1975.[30] Although most welfare recipients were white, a disproportionate percentage were black, and the public viewed welfare as a black program. The expansion of welfare took place at a time of rising racial tensions worsened by the urban riots of the 1960s. During this period, federal courts began to require busing to achieve integration in the schools and affirmative action to correct historical bias in the workplace. Busing was to the North what the Voting Rights Act had been to the South: It provoked a white backlash against federal intervention.

Republicans were in a position in the 1960s to take advantage of this backlash and appeal to working and lower middle class white voters who perceived that their hard-earned tax monies were going, under Democratic-sponsored federal grants, to inner city poor and minorities. Direct opposition to the objectives of these programs, however, would risk alienating traditional Republican voters repelled by any taint of racism. Richard Nixon found a brilliant way out of this dilemma that helped him win the presidency in 1968: He supported the goal of racial equality but opposed federal intervention to achieve it in education, employment, and voting rights. Advocating decentralization of power to states and localities provided a way for Republican (and sometimes Democratic) politicians to appeal to white voters, who felt threatened by racial change, while not explicitly voicing racist views.[31]

Besides appointing judges who opposed policies like busing, Nixon also advocated changes to the grants-in-aid system. In 1969, President Nixon proposed what he called the "first major reversal of the trend toward ever more centralization of government in Washington. . . . It is time for a New Federalism in which power, funds, and responsibility will flow from Washington to the States and to the people."[32] Nixon's **new federalism** shifted the grant-in-aid system from categorical grants to grants giving more discretion to state and local governments. In 1972, Nixon won passage of **general revenue sharing,** which provided for the distribution of about $6 billion a year in federal grants to state and local governments with few strings attached. The distribution of funds was weighted to give more money to governments that had poor tax bases and were already taxing themselves heavily. General revenue sharing was popular with governors and mayors, who felt that the federal government should share its superior taxing ability. It was not popular with members of Congress, who had little control over how the money was spent compared to traditional categorical grants.

Nixon also proposed a series of **block grants**—grants in which federal involvement is midway between the tight controls of categorical grants and the minimal controls of general revenue sharing. Under this method, a number of related categorical grants are consolidated into one block grant. Instead of competing for the funds, governments are allocated monies according to a formula based on need. The recipients spend the grant as they see fit within the broad purposes of the block grant.

Nixon's new federalism was politically appealing because it weakened the power of Washington-centered liberal lobbies which now had to divide their attention among fifty state and hundreds of local governments. Republicans were powerful in many states where suburban voters were coming to power. It is important to note, however, that Nixon did not reject the social welfare goals of the grants-in-aid system originated by FDR. Nixon did not aim to shrink government but to make it more flexible by shifting responsibilities within the intergovernmental system.

THE CONTEMPORARY DEBATE ON FEDERALISM

Since the Nixon presidency, the conservative attack on the expanded powers of the federal government has intensified. Compared to Nixon, Ronald Reagan was a radical on federalism issues. His goal was to go back to the system of dual federalism that had existed before the New Deal. As Reagan put it in his First Inaugural Address (January 20, 1981):

> It is my intention to curb the size and influence of the Federal establishment and to demand recognition of the distinction between the powers granted to the Federal government and those reserved to the states or the people.

Reagan's rhetoric against federal grants invoked popular democratic values, including making government more democratically accountable and returning power to the grassroots.

Opposition to federal power, however, has not always been motivated by popular democratic values. Sometimes the conservative rhetoric of states rights and local control has been a cover for racist practices. Southerners criticized the 1965 Voting Rights Act as interference by the federal government in the internal affairs of states. The act, however, precipitated a democratic revolution in southern politics, enabling millions of blacks to vote for the first time. In this case, federal "interference" clearly increased freedom and democracy.

Conservative criticisms of the system of federal grants, however, had more than a grain of truth. The federal government funded grants for every conceivable purpose—from rat control to crime control, from urban gardening to home

A CLOSER LOOK

Linkage Policies: Robin Hood Responses to the Reagan Cuts

It wasn't just the states that became laboratories of democracy in the 1980s in response to the federal cuts. Cities also responded with innovative programs, proving that popular democracy is still alive at the grassroots.

One of the areas in which cities became the most innovative was housing. Of all the major federal policy areas, housing suffered the deepest cuts, falling from $30 billion in authorized spending in 1981, at the start of the Reagan administration, to less than $10 billion by 1986.

At the same time as the federal cuts, housing problems were worsened by a boom in downtown office construction. The high-income professionals who occupied the gleaming new office towers competed with low-income inner city families for available housing, driving up rents and displacing the poor. The process was called *gentrification*. Fur-

ther evidence of a housing crisis was the dramatic rise in homelessness in the 1980s.

To make up for the federal cuts, many cities began to experiment with innovative ways to link downtown commercial development to the provision of affordable housing. The reasoning behind "linkage" policies was simple: New downtown office buildings bring additional office workers into the city who compete with city residents for existing housing, driving up rents for low-income families, often forcing them to move. Thus, downtown office developers should be required to contribute to affordable housing; office development should be linked to housing.

San Francisco was the first city to pass a linkage policy in 1981. By 1990, 10 percent of a sample of 133 major American cities had enacted linkage policies.

insulation. Every grant required detailed regulations that became increasingly burdensome to the recipients. The pages in the *Federal Register*, which prints new regulations for administering grants, increased from 14,479 in 1960, to 20,037 in 1970, to 71,191 in 1979.[33] Red tape, it was called. Implementation became complicated because each program required the cooperation of different agencies and governments. One study of a federal program in Oakland, California, concluded that it required seventy separate agreements between different agencies, making successful implementation nearly impossible.[34]

The expanding system of federal grants was criticized not only for being inefficient but also for undermining democratic accountability. With hundreds of grants, each involving numerous actors at the federal, state, and local levels, the voters had difficulty pinpointing responsibility. Complex federal grant programs, critics argued, took power away from elected representatives and gave it to staff experts, issue specialists, and bureaucrats. *Grantsmanship*—the ability to write successful grant applications—biased the allocation of funds. Members of Congress began to ignore state and local needs and favor national lobbies situated in Washington, D.C. Every special interest seemed to have its own cate-

Corporate elites attacked linkage policies as unfair and ineffective. An article in *Fortune*, entitled "Robin Hood Subsidies: A Dubious New Fad," faulted linkage policies for "making builders scapegoats for forces beyond their control." In addition, developers warned that linkage fees would discourage investment in downtowns, "killing the goose that lays the golden eggs."

There is little evidence, however, that linkage policies have hurt investment. They are simply too small a factor in the overall costs of development. "We've checked with economists and real estate people," said Dean Macris, Director of San Francisco's Planning Department, "and we can't find any evidence that it's been harmful."

Announcing Boston's expanded linkage program in 1984, populist mayor Ray Flynn stated: "The paradox of prosperity in our downtowns and poverty in our neighborhoods can now be addressed." By the end of 1992, Boston's linkage policies had raised almost $70 million, helping to provide ten thousand affordable housing units.

Linkage policies can contribute to affordable housing, but they cannot make up for the huge federal cuts.

More important than the economic contribution is the symbolic message that linkage sends: Those who draw on the commonwealth of the city have an obligation to help those who are hurt by their profit-making activity. As a report on linkage by the Boston Redevelopment Authority put it: "The critical issue is economic justice."

Source: Edward G. Goetz, *Shelter Burden: Local Politics and Progressive Housing Policy* (Philadelphia: Temple University Press, 1993); Douglas Porter, ed., *Downtown Linkages* (Washington, D.C.: Urban Land Institute, 1985); Gurney Breckenfeld, "'Robin Hood' Subsidies: A Dubious New Fad," *Fortune*, March 21, 1983, pp. 148–52.

gorical grant, benefitting narrow constituencies, sometimes at the expense of the public interest.

Although the conservatives' critique of the bloated system of federal grants was valid in many respects, their approach of decentralizing government was designed not so much to revitalize state and local democracies as to shrink government across-the-board. Reagan had a firm ideological commitment to the market as a better allocator of goods and services than government. He thought that decentralizing power to states and localities would achieve the goal of shrinking government. Three reasons were cited for this belief: (1) Liberal lobbies, which had been centered in Washington, D.C., for a generation, would be less influential at the state and local levels; (2) because they were closer to the voters, state and local governments would be less inclined to increase taxes to pay for social programs; and (3) economic competition among states and localities for mobile investment would force them to cut taxes and limit spending.

Reagan's basic approach to federalism was to cut federal grants, especially grants to state and local governments (as opposed to grants to individuals). Reagan's popular tax cuts in 1981 and 1986 undermined the revenue base of the federal government. Facing serious deficit problems, Congress was generally receptive to his proposed cuts in intergovernmental grants. Federal spending on payments to individuals, like Social Security, increased 22 percent from 1980 to 1987 after controlling for inflation. At the same time, total grants-in-aid to state and local governments declined 15 percent.[35] (See the box on p. 412 for some of the ways that local governments responded to these cuts.) In 1986, Congress killed general revenue sharing. The Reagan cuts in intergovernmental grants hurt poor people the most, especially minorities and those living in cities.

When the Reagan administration's new federalism goals came in conflict with its goals of enhancing private decision-making power, the federalism goals were sacrificed. Businesses have trouble keeping track of regulations in fifty different states and thousands of local governments, and therefore they generally oppose shifting regulatory authority from the federal government to state and local governments. Moreover, states sometimes pass more restrictive regulations than the federal government. To forestall these limits on business, the Reagan administration advocated pro-business federal regulatory expansion in many areas, including trucking, nuclear power, offshore oil exploration, and coastal zone management.

Violating his commitment to decentralization, Reagan frequently supported federal preemption of state and local regulatory powers. **Preemption** is the ability of the federal government to assume total or partial control in areas subject to concurrent federal and state responsibility. Under the Supremacy Clause of the Constitution, federal regulations preempt, or supersede, state laws. Reagan signed 106 bills in which the federal government preempted the powers of states or local governments; he vetoed only two preemption statutes.[36]

The Devolution Revolution

The debate over federalism continued under Reagan's successors, Presidents Bush and Clinton. Since the 1960s confidence toward all levels of government has declined, but the drop in confidence has been more severe for the federal government than for state or local governments.[37] By 1995, 48 percent of respondents felt the federal government had "too much power," whereas only 6 percent felt the states had too much.[38]

Following in the footsteps of Ronald Reagan, many conservatives have called for a return to dual federalism. When he ran for President in 1996, Bob Dole frequently told audiences that he carried a copy of the Tenth Amendment in his pocket as a reminder of his commitment to rein in the federal government. In fact, conservative appointees to the Supreme Court have issued decisions that for the first time in decades restrict the powers of the federal government. In 1995, in the first decision in sixty years ruling that Congress had exceeded its authority under the interstate commerce clause of the Constitution, the Court declared the Gun-Free School Zone Act of 1990 unconstitutional.[39] In 1997, the Court struck down a provision of the Brady gun law that required state or local authorities to do background checks on buyers of handguns (*Printz* v. *United States*).

Other decisions demonstrate the resolve of the Court, under the leadership of Chief Justice William Rehnquist, to place limits on national power.[40]

Although it is doubtful that the United States will ever go back to dual federalism, clearly there is a "devolution revolution" in progress that is shifting powers to state and local governments.[41] After President Clinton lost decisively on a health care proposal that opponents painted as a massive federal intrusion into people's lives, he declared that the era of big government was over and joined the movement to decentralize programs from the federal government to states and communities. The question for popular democrats is whether this decentralization of power is good or bad for democracy.

The most controversial federalism issue during Clinton's first term was welfare reform. Clinton ran for office in 1992 promising to "end welfare as we know it." In August 1996, Clinton signed a bill passed by the Republican Congress that ended the sixty-one-year federal entitlement to welfare. In place of a federal guarantee that everyone who met certain criteria would be helped under programs administered by the states, the federal government now turns the money over to the states in the form of block grants with few restrictions. The bill will cut federal spending on welfare by an estimated $55 billion over six years.

The debate over welfare reform is fundamentally a debate on federalism: Can states be trusted to do the best thing for poor people, especially children? Proponents argue the states will become laboratories of democracy, experimenting with programs that will help people to get jobs and become self-reliant as well as self-respecting. Critics charge that the goal of welfare reform is not to empower state-level democracies but simply to cut welfare costs and force the poor to take minimum-wage jobs. They warn that states will engage in a "race to the bottom": Fearful of becoming "welfare magnets," states will cut benefits to poor people. We examine the welfare debate in more detail in Chapter 17.

Popular Democracy and Federalism

For popular democrats, the standard for judging federalism issues should be what division of powers best enhances democracy. Other things being equal, this will mean that the original Anti-federalist position should prevail: Democracy prospers best in a small setting. In local settings people more readily see the relationship between their own well-being and the well-being of the group, and they feel their participation can make a difference. Although popular democrats believe in empowering local majorities, they also believe in setting limits on what local majorities can do. Local majorities should not have the power, for example, to take away the rights of minorities, as southern states did for many years. Federal power in this case was necessary to ensure democratic rights. In a true democracy, basic rights, like the right to vote and speak freely on issues, should not be subject to a vote.

Although there is widespread agreement on federal guarantees of basic rights, there is considerable disagreement when it comes to the question of whether there should be a federal right to welfare or health care, even for children. State-level democracies have been empowered by welfare reform, but has this empowerment come at the expense of what should be a national right to minimal welfare benefits? Clearly, democracy is harmed if more people become hungry, homeless, or alienated from the system. Some popular democrats argue that a national entitlement to a basic standard of living is a necessary condition for all people to be able to fully participate in the system. Whether states have the ability, under the new welfare block grants, to devise programs to end poor people's dependence on welfare and integrate them into the economy remains to be seen. Much depends on the capabilities of state and local democracies.

Ironically, from the viewpoint of popular democracy, state and local governments today often seem to be less democratic than the federal government. Some scholars argue that state and local governments are more prone than the federal government to domination by elites.[42] Sometimes, a handful of corporations dominate the local economy, giving their owners extraordinary power. For example, for many years the Anaconda Copper Company practically owned Montana state government, and there are many documented cases of "company

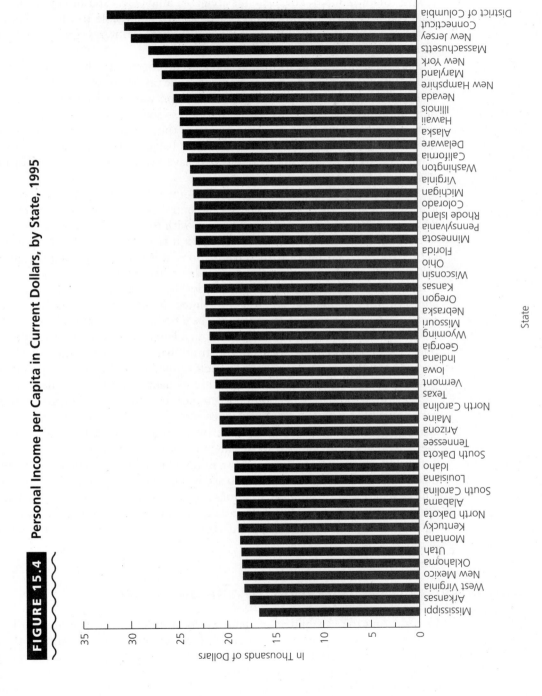

FIGURE 15.4   Personal Income per Capita in Current Dollars, by State, 1995

In Thousands of Dollars

State

Source: U. S. Bureau of the Census, *Statistical Abstract of the United States 1996* (Washington, D.C.: U. S. Government Printing Office, 1996), p. 453.

towns." State and local governments are given much less exposure by the media than the national government. When issues are not visible to the public, the scope of conflict is narrowed and it is easier for narrow interest groups to dominate policy making behind the scenes.[43]

Another factor that weakens state and local democracies is the tremendous inequalities in resources among governments. The taxable resources of states vary widely. During the 1992 campaign, Bill Clinton was criticized for not having done more as governor of Arkansas to address social ills. But, as Figure 15.4 shows, if Arkansas applied the same tax *rate* to the income of its citizens as Connecticut, it would raise only a little more than half as much revenue. Perversely, states like Arkansas and Mississippi, which have the greatest poverty problems, possess the fewest resources to address them.

Among local governments the gaps in resources are even greater. In 1989, for a sample of sixty-two cities, the ratio of central city to suburban income was 84 percent. For many central cities the gap with the suburbs is even greater: In Cleveland the ratio is 53 percent; in Newark it is 43 percent.[44] Facing pressing demands from their impoverished populations, it is hardly surprising that many cities find themselves perpetually on the edge of fiscal crisis.

Schools face the same problem. Run by locally elected school boards, primary and secondary public education in the United States seems remarkably democratic. Democratic control, however, can be a hollow prize for very poor school districts. The California Supreme Court, in a landmark case that declared local financing of schools in California unconstitutional, called local control of education a "cruel illusion" because poor districts cannot achieve excellence no matter how high they raise taxes.[45] Geographical inequalities cripple local democracy.

The longstanding connection between local control and democratic participation, coupled with the aforementioned flaws in local democracy, raises once again the dilemma of federalism: Either way popular democrats turn—toward the federal government or toward state and local governments—has powerful drawbacks. In the pages that follow we examine the popular democratic potential of state and local governments to see if there is a way out of this dilemma. The goal of self-governing communities is still an attractive vision. But the question remains: In an age of global markets, instantaneous communications, and rapid mobility, is local participatory democracy a viable alternative or simply pie in the sky?

STATES AND CORPORATIONS: SURVIVAL OF THE UNFIT?

In evaluating the capabilities of state and local governments, we need to look beyond their legal powers and examine their actual abilities to exercise those powers. A case in point is the relationship between states and private corporations. States have the legal power to charter and regulate private corporations, but too often they have failed to exercise that power. The story behind that failure is instructive.

Corporations are not mentioned in the Constitution, but it has been assumed that both the federal government and the states have the right to charter them. In the nineteenth century state charters were used by popular democrats, who controlled state legislatures, to limit the powers of private corporations. State charters prevented corporations from holding stock in other corporations, for example, and guaranteed shareholder democracy (those who own stock in the company choose the board of directors who in turn hire executives to run the day-to-day affairs of the company.)[46]

In the late nineteenth century, in blatant violation of state incorporation laws, a series of trusts were formed to achieve monopoly control over markets. One of the most notorious was Standard Oil of Ohio. John D. Rockefeller set up Standard Oil by placing controlling interest of the stock of supposedly competing companies in a trust run by a single board of directors. The Standard Oil trust enabled Rockefeller to control 95 percent of all refined oil shipments in the nation. Charging a monopoly price for his oil, Rockefeller became fabulously wealthy. Trusts were soon organized in other industries: the Cotton Oil Trust in 1884 and the Whiskey Trust, the Sugar Trust, and the Lead Trust in 1887.

A furious popular democratic movement rose to break up the trusts, using state incorporation laws to declare them illegal. In 1892, the Supreme Court of Ohio ruled that the Standard Oil Trust was "organized for a purpose contrary to the policy of our laws" and was therefore "void."[47] Standard Oil simply refused to obey the ruling. When Ohio threatened to revoke its charter, Standard Oil skipped to New Jersey, which had passed a permissive incorporation statute that legalized trusts. Ohio could do nothing because, according to the Constitution (Article IV), states must give "Full Faith and Credit" to the laws of other states. With incorporation statutes that gutted shareholder democracy and gave corporate executives the right to do as they wished, corporations flocked to New Jersey, which became known as the "Traitor State." By 1902, the resulting incorporation fees enabled New Jersey to abolish all property taxes and pay off its entire state debt.[48]

Elite democrats defended permissive incorporation laws on the grounds that they encouraged competition. In the words of John D. Rockefeller, "The growth of a large business is merely the survival of the fittest. . . . The American Beauty Rose can be produced in the splendor and fragrance which bring cheer to its beholder only by sacrificing the early buds which grow up all around it."[49] The irony, of course, is that permissive state incorporation laws allowed anticompetitive practices to flourish, enabling corporate elites to accumulate vast fortunes that they often used to corrupt the political process. According to one commentator, state competition for corporate charters promoted not the best state laws but the "survival of the unfit."[50]

State and Local Competition for Investment

The case of state incorporation laws illustrates that states can possess formal constitutional powers—for example, to regulate corporations—and yet be unable to exercise those powers effectively. As capital has become more mobile in the twentieth century, governments have moved beyond competing for chartering fees to competing for corporate investment of all types using special subsidies. Increased capital investment provides jobs and fattens the tax base, proponents argue, enabling governments to either reduce taxes or take in additional revenues at the same tax rates. If states and cities do not create favorable "business climates," the argument goes, they will experience a downward spiral of disinvestment and fiscal crisis.

After World War II, southern states pioneered the use of subsidies to attract industry. When northern states began to suffer from extensive deindustrialization (the loss of industrial jobs) in the 1970s, they began a fierce competition with Sunbelt states for industrial investment. *Business Week* called the spread of business incentives "a counterattack in the war between the states."[51] By 1986, one source reported that states offered fifty-nine different incentives, including property tax abatements, investment tax credits, loan guarantees, and land write-downs (purchasing and clearing land for private investors at public expense).[52]

A good example of how far states and localities will go to compete for investment is illustrated by the reaction when General Motors announced in 1980 that it was closing down two of its older factories in Detroit and replacing them with a new, more efficient factory on a "greenfield" site in another part of the country. In order to persuade GM to build the $600 million factory in Detroit, the city government agreed to purchase and clear a 500-acre site in the city, "the largest land-assemblage and clearance program in United States history."[53] A viable neighborhood known as Poletown was gutted, with 3,200 people forced from their homes, many churches torn down, and 160 community businesses eliminated. In addition, the city invested over $250 million of its own money and offered tax breaks worth hundreds of millions of dollars.

The benefits of such **smokestack chasing** are highly questionable. Most studies conclude that public subsidies have only a minor impact on industrial location decisions. And if they do succeed, it is a "beggar thy neighbor" situation, where one government benefits at the expense of another. Like an out-of-control arms race, the dollar amount of subsidies has soared, reaching the point in many states where the costs exceed the benefits. The authors of a major study on Poletown concluded that "the project has not paid for itself"—it cost the city more than it gave back in additional tax revenues.[54] In 1994 the state of Alabama offered Mercedes Benz $325 million in incentives, approximately $216,000 per job. Remarkably enough, the state of Kentucky even outdid Alabama, handing out a $140 million incentive package to a steel firm that amounted to $350,000 per job.[55] Why do states continue to engage in smokestack chasing when, studies show, it is often ineffective or costly? The answer is politics. Handing out subsidies enables mayors and governors to claim credit for economic growth and improve their image. Alabama's Governor Jim Folsom proudly announced that the successful landing of Mercedes was evidence that "Alabama must be doing something right."[56] In fact, the Mercedes deal included $1.5 million for a five-year advertising campaign to promote Mercedes' decision to locate in Alabama.

Political credit taking is facilitated by the way the costs of smokestack chasing are hidden from the public. Some scholars argue that this secrecy is deliberate.[57] Deals are cut behind closed doors and facts are released to the public only afterwards. Unlike direct expenditures, which must be approved by the legislature, most business incentives are in the form of future revenues forgone, which are less visible to the public. In the long run, smokestack chasing erodes states' tax bases; the result is less money for education and infrastructure.

The Growth Machine: Local Elite Democracy

Popular democrats place most of their hopes for meaningful participation in local governments. Too often, however, local governments don't live up to their participatory potential. The main reason is not that local governments are structured undemocratically. In fact, most city charters are thoroughly democratic, with all citizens over the age of eighteen given the right to vote for the mayor and city council—and sometimes many other offices, as well as judges. The problem, for the most part, is not the formal rules, but the way that economic elites are able to dominate local governments.

For many years scholars engaged in a spirited debate about the distribution of power in U.S. cities. The dominant theory of community power in political science was pluralism. The most influential pluralist analysis was Robert Dahl's *Who Governs?*, an examination of community power in New Haven, Connecticut. According to Dahl, in New Haven there were many different competing elites, each influential in a different arena. Money was a source of political power, but other resources, like political skills, leadership, and organization, were equally important. Most importantly, elections forced elites to be responsive to the wishes of average citizens.[58] Dahl concluded that urban renewal in the 1950s, for example, was guided by Mayor Richard Lee, who pushed business to participate in a program that benefitted the city as a whole. Although it was far from a perfect participatory democracy, Dahl concluded that pluralism salvaged fundamental democratic values.

Over the years, many scholars have challenged the pluralist analysis of local politics. A re-examination of Dahl's study of New Haven, for example, concluded that urban renewal was not initiated by Mayor Lee responding to the needs of the voters but was pushed by business interests to benefit their commercial interests at the expense of average voters.[59] Shockingly, between 1956 and 1974, nearly one-fifth of the population of New Haven was uprooted by urban renewal. Blacks suffered the most. Besides the disruption of community networks, urban renewal destroyed 5,636 more units of low- and moderate-income housing than it built.[60] Urban renewal benefitted mostly business owners, not local residents.

Dahl himself later admitted that pluralism was flawed for failing to note that business is not just another interest group. Because government officials must be concerned about the local economy, and business decisions have such an impact on it, they constantly cater to the needs of business even without business lobbying. Dahl and his co-author Charles Lindblom called this the "privileged position of business," noting that "the relation between government and business is unlike the relation between government and any other group in society."[61]

Business power takes a special form in cities. The distinctive power of local governments is their power over land use, through zoning laws, and building codes. Moreover, cities gain a great deal of their revenue from property taxes. For these reasons, as Stephen Elkin has noted, "The battlefield of city politics is not flat but is tilted toward an alliance of public officials and land interests."[62] City officials often do everything in their power to enhance real estate values, arguing that what is good for city landowners is good for all citizens. The goal is to attract development that pays more in taxes than it takes back in city services. Usually that means commercial expansion over residential growth, especially housing for low-income families whose children are expensive to educate in public schools. The tight alliances between local elected officials and real estate interests have been aptly termed **growth machines**.[63]

The growth machines that dominate many cities pursue what one scholar dubbed the **corporate center strategy,** a focus on development of the downtown service-sector economy with "an orientation toward luxury consumption" that appeals to young educated professionals, convention goers, and tourists.[64] One successful example of the corporate center strategy is Baltimore, Maryland, under the leadership of Mayor William Donald Schaefer (1971–1987), who based a successful run for governor partly on his revitalization of downtown Baltimore. The jewel of Schaefer's string of downtown development projects was the Inner Harbor. Formerly a bustling port, by the 1960s it was an eyesore of rotting, rat-infested piers, abandoned buildings, and desolate parking lots—

The elite-dominated growth machine model of city politics. (Richard Hedman)

perched on a harbor that smelled in H. L. Mencken's words, "like a million polecats."[65]

Schaefer's audacious idea was to transform the Inner Harbor into a national tourist destination—and he did it. The centerpiece of the $270 million 240-acre Inner Harbor project was Harborplace, a festival marketplace. Completed in 1980, it attracted 18 million visitors the first year, more than Disneyland.

Even though the Inner Harbor provided jobs and taxes, it produced surprisingly few benefits for the city's poor black neighborhoods. The fact is, inner city residents do not qualify for most jobs in the downtown corporate service sector and those they do qualify for tend to be low wage, with few benefits. Not surprisingly, between 1970 and 1980, when the downtown boomed, the poverty rate increased in 90 percent of Baltimore's black neighborhoods. As Kurt Schmoke, who succeeded Schaefer as Baltimore's first black mayor in 1987, noted: "If you were revisiting Baltimore today after a twenty-year absence, you would find us much prettier and much much poorer."[66]

Downtown-oriented growth machines are also notoriously elite dominated. Schaefer's was no exception. He created a kind of shadow government—twenty-four quasi-public development corporations that contracted with the city to direct downtown development. Because they were not part of government, these development corporations could operate behind closed doors and did not have to provide information to the city council or the public. The rationale was that these entities took the politics out of urban development, speeding up the process and making it more efficient. It is impossible, however, to take the politics out of development decisions. Investing in downtown areas is a decision not to invest in small businesses and housing in the neighborhoods. Not surprisingly, many of Mayor Schaefer's biggest campaign contributors received contracts or loans for downtown development.

REFORMERS AND THE ATTACK ON PARTY GOVERNMENT

The effort to "take the politics out" of state and local government has a long lineage. Indeed, state and especially local politics have been characterized by a clash between two contrasting philosophies of government—one of which reflects this antipolitical stance. This clash reverberates with many of the same issues as the Federalist and Anti-federalist debate.

The popular democratic, or *partisan*, model traces its roots back to Andrew Jackson, president from 1833–1841. Jacksonian democrats were suspicious of strong executives and favored dispersing power among many elected offices. (This belief was tinged with irony since Jackson substantially enlarged the powers of the presidency at the national level.) Jackson contended that ordinary citizens could perform most functions of government. He believed in the political adage "to the victor go the spoils." By handing out patronage jobs to its supporters, the victorious party ensured that the government would be responsive to the needs of common people, not to highly educated elites and experts.

Reformers derided Jackson's idea of party government as the *spoils system*. The reform, or *nonpartisan*, model traces its roots back to the Federalist Alexander Hamilton, who argued that most people did not want more democracy but better services, provided by strong executives and expert administrators.[67] The reform model contrasts the efficient administration of experts with corrupt and inefficient rule by party hacks. The reform movement grew in reaction to the excesses of urban political machines, whose corrupt practices were exposed by muckraking journalists in the late nineteenth century. It wasn't just that the parties hired political supporters but that job recipients were often unqualified for the job. The public also lost out when excessive payments were made to politically connected contractors.

In the late nineteenth and early twentieth century, the good government reformers—or "goo goos," as they sometimes derisively are called—aimed to weaken the influence of political parties and their political bosses and put more power in the hands of well-educated experts. The reform program included:

1. Nonpartisan elections so that the party label would not appear on the ballot.

2. Election to the city council from at-large districts, preferably the entire city, instead of from individual wards. (Remember Madison's extended republic argument.)

3. Civil service appointment procedures for city workers so that municipal jobs could not be used as patronage by political parties.

4. Switching from party conventions to open primaries, taking the power to nominate out of the hands of party bosses.

5. Making the chief executive in cities an appointed, professional city manager.

The reformers were remarkably successful in instituting their reforms, and they still have a significant impact, especially in city governments (although there has been a movement away from many of these reforms in the past thirty years). Other than civil service systems that are almost universal (though they vary in coverage), nonpartisan elections are the most widespread reform still in place today, with 72.6 percent of all cities prohibiting party designation on the ballot. The council-manager form of government is used in about half of all cities but in only 20 percent of cities over 500,000. About 60 percent of U.S. cities elect their council members from citywide districts, although that number has fallen in recent decades.[68]

The nonpartisan reform model is an attempt to take the politics out of government and run it like an efficient business. It is impossible to take the politics out of governing, however; no matter how hard you try, politics ends up coming in through the back door. Focusing on efficiency, nonpartisan reformers often overlooked problems of unequal distribution. Reformers are fond of saying things like: "There is no Republican or Democratic way to build a sewer—just a right way and a wrong way." This ignores the crucial question, however, of *where* the sewers will be built. San Antonio, Texas, for example, had long been ruled by business-dominated reformers when, on August 7, 1974, large parts of the Mexican-American neighborhoods were flooded by the runoff from Anglo-American highlands. The reason was simple: The Mexican-American neighborhoods lacked storm and sanitary sewers. A coalition of neighborhood organizations, Communities Organized for Public Service, or COPS, protested vigorously, and within months San Antonio passed a $47 million bond issue to implement a drainage plan that had been sitting on the shelf since 1947. In 1977, COPS successfully campaigned for a new city charter with an elected mayor and district elections for city council. The first election under the new charter resulted in the election of five Mexican Americans.[69]

The nonpartisan reform model is biased toward the upper class. This is not surprising given the upper-class background of most reformers.[70] Research has shown that nonpartisan elections lead to more elected officials coming from the upper class. Reformed cities, with nonpartisan elections and/or city manager forms of government, suppress the expression of class, racial, and religious conflicts in the political system, thus reducing turnout, especially among working class voters. At-large elections give an advantage to middle- and upper-income professionals who have the money and contacts to successfully wage a citywide campaign.[71] Perhaps the best-documented finding is that at-large elections underrepresent minorities. Blacks, in particular, feel they have a greater say in cities with district elections. Using the 1965 Voting Rights Act, minorities have successfully challenged at-large voting methods, forcing cities to institute district elections, resulting in greater minority representation.[72]

Cities run by strong political parties are seldom models of popular democracy. Nevertheless, as we discussed in Chapter 7, parties are necessary institutions for organizing large numbers of people into politics and representing their issues. Parties provide resources, apart from money, for getting elected. Therefore, the movement to take the politics out of state and local governance is doomed to failure. Reformed governments do not eliminate politics, they simply channel it into new arenas, largely hidden from public view and dominated by elites. From the viewpoint of popular democracy, it is encouraging that many cities are changing from appointed city managers to elected mayors and from citywide to district elections for city council.

STATES AND CITIES AS LABORATORIES OF DEMOCRACY

The prospects for states and localities to become laboratories of democracy are dim, indeed, if they are dominated by elites, if people are excluded from participation, and if they become locked in destructive competitions for corporate investment. Many states do succumb to smokestack chasing and cities are often dominated by growth machines. A survey of state and local policies, however, reveals that there are enough exceptions to elite rule to keep our hopes for popular democracy alive. In the present period, in fact, much like the period before the New Deal, state and local governments often lead the federal government in experimenting with popular democratic policies. Before Congress increased the national minimum wage in 1996, for example, seventeen states were considering increases in their minimum wages, and at least thirty cities had "living wage movements" to increase minimum wages for workers on city contracts.[73]

In 1932, when Justice Brandeis called for the states to become laboratories of democracy, states had glaring political weaknesses that limited their capabilities. These included antiquated elections laws that excluded blacks and systematically underrepresented city dwellers, as well as weak administrative structures. Since then, states have strengthened their representative and administrative capacities by instituting a number of reforms:

1. Governors now have more control over state bureaucracies, which themselves have been made more representative and professional. State legislatures now meet annually and have professional staffs to help them write legislation.[74]

2. Following Supreme Court mandates, beginning with *Baker* v. *Carr* (1962), state legislatures have been reapportioned to reflect population, making them more responsive to metropolitan and minority interests.

3. Following the Voting Rights Act of 1965, legal barriers to minority voting have been eliminated (see Figure 10.2 on p. 277).

Notwithstanding these political reforms, we would expect little room for democratic choice if states were tightly constrained by competition for investment. Recent research has shown, however, that state policies are not simply driven by economic forces; state elections and policies reflect the distinctive political beliefs of their citizens. Based on surveys of 170,000 individuals over thirteen years, researchers classified states according to the liberalism or conservativism of their voters.[75] They found that even after controlling for socioeconomic factors, such as class and race, public opinion made a significant difference in policies: States with liberal voters enacted more liberal policies than states with conservative voters. Oregon and Oklahoma, for example, are similar socially and economically, but Oregon has liberal policies while Oklahoma has conservative ones. States have different political cultures which are expressed through elections. Although states are hardly model popular democracies, the research shows that public opinion and elections do make a difference.

Political institutions also make a difference. States without party competition tend to be politically unresponsive to public opinion. For many years the one-party Democratic South enabled a minority of whites, especially wealthy planters, to dominate state politics and kept blacks and many poor whites powerless.[76]

The variety of state political responsiveness explains why the Reagan strategists were wrong when they concluded that the decentralization of federal policy would automatically lead to an overall reduction in government activism. The actual record was mixed. Some states and localities aggressively filled the gaps in social programs hurt by Reagan cuts; others did little. Neither conservative hopes nor liberal fears were confirmed. Generally, states with strong fiscal conditions and liberal political traditions, like Massachusetts and New York, were assertive in replacing the Reagan cuts; California, on the other hand, limited by a powerful tax revolt, did little.[77]

Beyond Smokestack Chasing

Smokestack chasing undermines democracy by giving power over policy to business elites, thereby increasing inequalities. Many states and localities have begun to compete by providing a better educated and trained workforce and higher quality public infrastructure. Instead of trying to attract factories away from neighboring states, in the 1980s states began to focus on new business formation in emerging markets and on helping local industries to find new markets for their goods.[78] In what are called "Third Wave" economic development policies, resources are concentrated on industry clusters that are highly efficient and innovative and have the potential to create not just more jobs but jobs at a living wage.

Many cities have begun to link economic development with community development. Shortly after he was elected Chicago's first black mayor in 1983, Harold Washington issued an economic development manifesto, entitled "Chicago Works Together," that could serve as a model for popular democratic development policies. The plan called for balanced growth between downtown and neighborhoods, a preference for local residents in city hiring and contracting, support for neighborhood planning, and increased opportunities for citizen involvement in economic development planning. Instead of concentrating on downtown and tourism, Washington's administration made a concerted effort to retain industrial jobs in the neighborhoods.[79]

Another encouraging development is efforts by regions to avoid the destructive competition for investment between cities and suburbs. Increasingly, it is becoming clear that success in the global marketplace requires *regional* cooperation. Destructive competition between cities and suburbs causes excessive suburban sprawl, high commuting costs, and depressed central cities. Recognizing this, fact, regions are cooperating instead of competing for investment. The Minneapolis–St. Paul region enacted tax base sharing many years ago. When a new factory is built in the region, all governments share in the additional tax base. Portland, Oregon, has placed a greenbelt zone around the city to discourage sprawl and preserve the environment and is building rail lines to encourage more compact development and reduce traffic congestion.

Experiments in Grassroots Democracy

Most people first participate in politics at the local level. Indeed, there are almost half a million local elected officials in the United States. If popular democracy is going to be meaningful, however, it must rest on something more than going to the polls every two or four years or even running for office. In the early years of the country, many local governments were run by direct democracies, town meetings in which all citizens gathered together to make the laws. Alexis de Tocqueville, author of the classic *Democracy in America*, said of these training grounds of democracy: "Town meetings are to liberty what primary schools are to science. . . . A nation may establish a free government, but without municipal institutions it cannot have the spirit of liberty."[80]

Elite democrats, of course, maintain that direct democracy in the modern world is unrealistic—and dangerous. They often cite Lyndon Johnson's War on Poverty as a case in point, in which federal money was given directly to community groups with the goal of "maximum feasible participation" by local residents. Daniel Patrick Moynihan, now a Democratic Senator from New York, skewered the program in a book cleverly titled *Maximum Feasible Misunderstanding* (1969) in which he argued that the poor were simply not ready to govern themselves. In fact, the War on Poverty was not the abysmal failure it is often portrayed as.[81] The program was beset by nasty conflicts, but conflicts must be expected when long ignored problems such as racial discrimination are finally confronted. Most important, the War on Poverty was not a fair test of participatory democracy because poor people were never given power to run their own programs.[82] In many cities, mayors quickly took control of the programs from community groups.

Even with all its faults, the War on Poverty had many benefits. It gave many low-income minorities their first experience in politics, which they used to launch their political careers. And it nurtured the formation of *community-based organizations* (CBOs) that involve low-income people in improving their own neighborhoods.

Since the 1960s there has been a veritable "backyard revolution," with neighborhood organizations springing up in city after city.[83] These organizations have spun off thousands of CBOs that rehabilitate housing and provide services like day care and job training. Many cities have begun to decentralize control over city policy to neighborhood governments, encouraging neighborhood planning. St. Paul, Minnesota, for example, has District Councils governed by representatives elected from each area. The District Councils have power over zoning, some city services, and infrastructure spending. Many issues are fully discussed at neighborhood meetings before action is taken.

A team of social scientists studied the new forms of participatory grassroots democracy in five cities—Birmingham, Dayton, San Antonio, St. Paul, and Portland, Oregon.[84] Thousands of residents in these cities were surveyed and their attitudes compared with residents of cities without institutions of neighborhood participation. The results contradict the fears of elite democrats. The people who participated in neighborhood associations did not become more selfish and intolerant. In fact, participation increased tolerance. Participation did not make people less selfish and more committed to citywide concerns, but it did increase knowledge of politics and fostered the attitude that participation can make a difference, especially among low-income people.

The growth of neighborhood associations and their recognition by government is encouraging for popular democrats. But the limits of localism must be recognized. In the five cities with extensive structures of neighborhood participation, business still dominated the economic development agenda with large downtown development projects. Neighborhood organizing is effective at protecting communities from unwanted development and improving housing, but it is much less effective at addressing issues like environmental destruction and rising income inequality.[85]

CONCLUSION: IS THERE A WAY OUT OF THE DILEMMA?

Notwithstanding the many successful examples of local democracy, federalism presents a dilemma for popular democrats today. Ever since the Anti-federalists criticized the Constitution for putting too much power in the hands of a distant central government, popular democrats have favored decentralizing power as much as possible. At the same time, popular democrats recognize the limits of localism. Local communities can maximize participation, but they lack the resources to tackle important issues like economic inequality and environmental pollution, which cross jurisdictional boundaries. All too often, states' rights have been used as a cover-up for racist policies and city governments have been dominated by growth machines that exclude citizens from meaningful participation.

Which way should popular democrats turn? Is there a way out of the dilemma of federalism? First, the issue should not be framed in an either/or manner: Either we give power to the federal government or we turn power over to states and communities. An active federal government does *not* necessarily mean the decline of local democracy. When federal judges ordered southern states to give blacks the right to vote under the 1965 Voting Rights Act, local democracy was enhanced, not undermined. Basic rights, like freedom of speech, press, and assembly, must be protected by a vigilant federal government.

The problem becomes more difficult, however, when we move from basic rights to questions of powers over social and economic policies. In all cases, the goal of federal policy should be, as much as possible, to empower people in states and communities. This is not always possible, however. Clearly, states and localities are in no position to regulate giant multinational corporations. Concentrations of power in the marketplace require countervailing concentrations of power in government. The federal government must curb the powers of corporations both in the economy and in politics. By doing this, the federal government can empower states and communities. In 1988, Congress passed plant closing legislation that required companies to give sixty-day notice before closing down a factory that employed more than five hundred workers. This law gives communities the time to come up with plans to save their jobs. Until private corporations are made more democratically accountable to shareholders, workers, consumers, and especially their communities, we will need powerful federal bureaucracies, such as the Environmental Protection Agency (EPA) and the Securities and Exchange Commission (SEC), to regulate them in the public interest.

Federal programs to promote greater equality among different jurisdictions would also go a long way toward empowering state and local governments to address their own problems. Most federal grants distribute money on the basis of population, not need. Other federal systems, including Germany, Australia, and Canada, have well-funded national laws designed to equalize the tax capacities of subnational governments.[86] In the United States, a general revenue-sharing program distributed on the basis of need would significantly reduce fiscal constraints on state and local governments. Even more important, many nations have national programs to equalize economic conditions in different areas of the country. A federal program to reduce economic inequalities among regions and between central cities and suburbs would help to revitalize our federal system.

In short, the dilemma of federalism is not inevitable. Democratizing corporations and reducing inequalities among jurisdictions would free state and local governments for democratic experimentation. We should not wait for the federal government to act, however, before acting ourselves to strengthen state and local democracies. Revitalizing state and local governments requires internal political reforms, such as reducing the power of money in elections, strengthening local political parties, and increasing voting turnout. Together, economic and political reforms can help realize the popular democratic dream of making state and local governments true laboratories of democracy.

KEY TERMS

unitary government
dual federalism
enumerated powers
reserved powers
concurrent powers
Supremacy Clause
Necessary and Proper (Elastic) Clause
nullification
grant-in-aid
matching grant

intergovernmental relations
categorical grant
creative federalism
new federalism
general revenue sharing
block grant
preemption
smokestack chasing
growth machine
corporate center strategy

SUGGESTED READINGS

Timothy Conlan, *New Federalism: Intergovernmental Reform from Nixon to Reagan.* Washington, D.C.: The Brookings Institution, 1988. The best treatment of the new federalism initiatives, arguing that Nixon and Reagan actually had very different goals and politics.

Grant McConnell, *Private Power and American Democracy.* New York: Vintage Books, 1966. An influential statement that the decentralization of power under American democracy leads to tyranny by private elites.

David B. Robertson and Dennis R. Judd, *The Development of American Public Policy*. Glenview, Ill.: Scott, Foresman, 1989. Argues that American federalism biases the policy process in a conservative direction, favoring the status quo.

Robert S. Erickson, Gerald C. Wright, and John P. McIver, *Statehouse Democracy: Public Opinion and Policy in the American States*. New York: Cambridge University Press, 1993. Argues that states are distinct political communities and that these differences are expressed through elections.

Jeffrey M. Berry, Kent E. Portney, and Ken Thomson, *The Rebirth of Urban Democracy*. Washington, D.C.: The Brookings Institution, 1993. A thorough study of the effects of grassroots participation and neighborhood government.

Civil Liberties and Civil Rights

Some of the most stirring words in the history of American democracy have been penned by judges in support of the civil liberties and civil rights of unpopular individuals and groups. "If there is any fixed star in our constitutional constellation," wrote Supreme Court Justice Robert Jackson, upholding the right of young Jehovah's Witnesses not to salute the American flag in school, "it is that no official, high or petty, can prescribe what shall be orthodox in politics, nationalism, religion, or other matters of opinion or force citizens to confess by word or act their faith therein."[1] "If there is a bedrock principle underlying the First Amendment," wrote Justice William Brennan, upholding the right of a citizen to express political dissent by burning an American flag, "it is that Government may not prohibit the expression of any idea simply because society finds the idea itself offensive or disagreeable."[2] Against the grim background of intolerance and repression that has characterized most political systems around the globe, such affirmations of fundamental liberties and rights stand as one of the proudest accomplishments of democracy in the United States.

However, civil liberties and rights have been a focus of bitter conflict, not a subject of comfortable consensus, throughout American history. What strong supporters of civil liberties consider to be basic freedoms have appeared to many other Americans to be threats to order, morality, or community. The right of persons accused of crimes to the multiple protections of due process of law strikes many Americans as favoritism toward criminals at the expense of their victims. The right of authors, photographers, or filmmakers to portray sexual activity with only minimal restrictions strikes many as the protection of filth that corrupts society in general and degrades women in particular. The right of revolutionaries to call for the overthrow of our constitutional order strikes many as a denial of society's right of self-defense against its worst enemies. Struggles over civil liberties and civil rights often pit unpopular minorities or individuals against the popular majority and its elected representatives.

Civil liberties refer to the freedoms that individuals enjoy and that governments cannot invade. **Civil rights** refer to the powers and privileges that belong to us by virtue of our status as citizens. Freedom of speech and the free exercise of religion are liberties that need protection from government; voting and nondiscriminatory treatment in education and employment are rights that need protection *by* government. Such familiar civil liberties and civil rights are in fact a recent accomplishment. Despite the grand words of the Bill of Rights and despite the historic breakthrough of the Civil War amendments, for most of American history free speech was repressed, individual privacy invaded, and African Americans and women treated as second-class citizens. The flowering of civil liberties and civil rights has taken a long time and required a fierce struggle. And some of the advances that have been made remain precarious, with forces both outside and inside the current Supreme Court striving to roll them back. Civil liberties and civil rights remain one of the central arenas for the continuing democratic debate in America.

The ultimate voice in this debate has been that of the courts. Many social, political, and intellectual forces have battled over the definition of American liberties and rights. Since these liberties and rights are rooted in the Constitution, however, it has largely been the province of the federal judiciary to have the decisive say on their meaning and scope. Consequently, our focus in this chapter is mainly, though not exclusively, on Supreme Court cases.

The chapter begins with a perplexing issue in the democratic debate: how elites and ordinary citizens respond to controversial questions of civil liberties and civil rights. Next, the discussion turns to the historical bases for liberties and rights in America: the Bill of Rights, the Civil War amendments, and the constitutional revolution of the 1930s. The remainder of the chapter examines the major areas of civil liberties and civil rights: the First Amendment rights of expression, a free press, and religion; the rights of persons accused of crimes; the right of privacy; and the right of racial minorities and women to equality in every aspect of American life.

CIVIL LIBERTIES AND CIVIL RIGHTS: FOES AND FRIENDS

It has often been argued that elite democrats are supportive of civil liberties and civil rights, whereas the ordinary citizens in whom popular democrats trust are intolerant and repressive. Chapter 3 cited social science surveys indicating that support for civil liberties increases with education and political status. The conclusion frequently drawn from these studies is that civil liberties and civil rights have to be safeguarded from the authoritarian masses by democratically spirited elites.

Unfortunately, elite support for civil liberties and civil rights is less impressive in practice than in theory. The major attacks on civil liberties in recent times were spearheaded by decidedly elite figures: Senator Joseph McCarthy, Director of the FBI J. Edgar Hoover, President Richard Nixon. Therefore, when it comes to opposition to civil liberties and civil rights, the blame must be shared by elite democrats and popular democrats alike.

Where, then, are the friends of civil liberties and civil rights to be found? Focusing on court cases, as this chapter does, may give the impression that it has been justices of the Supreme Court who have singlehandedly advanced liberties and rights out of the depths of their own conscience and democratic faith. This is not the case: Ordinary citizens and democratic social movements also have played a key part in the struggle. Landmark advances in this area have been produced by a collaboration between elites and popular democratic forces. Thus, the credit for progress in civil liberties and civil rights, like the blame for hostility to them, must be shared by elite democrats and popular democrats.

Certainly, any account of progress in civil liberties and civil rights must highlight the beliefs, decisions, and arguments of their judicial champions. An honor roll for civil libertarians on the Supreme Court would include such great figures as Oliver Wendell Holmes, Louis Brandeis, Hugo Black, William O. Douglas, and Earl Warren. Probably the greatest civil libertarian on the High Court in recent years was William Brennan, who retired in 1990. (Recall the profile of Brennan in Chapter 14.)

Whereas the justices who have championed civil liberties and civil rights in landmark cases are famous, the petitioners who brought these cases to the Supreme Court are obscure. Yet these ordinary citizens have made significant contributions to the struggle for civil liberties and civil rights. One such citizen, Daniel Seeger, is profiled in the accompanying box.

The popular democratic contribution to civil liberties and civil rights has not been limited to the courageous stands of individuals like Seeger. Popular democratic movements have been a source of key cases that reached the Supreme Court. The Legal Defense Fund of the National Association for the Advancement of Colored People (NAACP), the pioneer civil rights organization, was the leading force behind the long campaign for desegregated schools. The contemporary women's movement, which sprang up in the 1960s, also played a pivotal role in reshaping the Court's agenda. As women pressed their case for equality with new vigor, the Court responded by considering the issues of abortion and gender discrimination.

The **American Civil Liberties Union (ACLU),** formed to defend free speech against government repression of dissenters during World War I, has taken the Bill of Rights as its cause ever since. The ACLU has fought for civil liberties and civil rights in many different areas, arguing more cases before the Supreme Court than any other organization save the federal government. The ACLU prides itself on upholding the liberties of the most unpopular and obnoxious groups. Its clients have included not only communists but also Nazis and Ku Klux Klan members.[3]

CIVIL LIBERTIES AND CIVIL RIGHTS: HISTORICAL BASES

Americans regard civil liberties and civil rights as their birthright. After all, the great charter of our freedom, the Bill of Rights, is almost as old as the nation itself. Yet the ringing words of the Bill of Rights took on a powerful meaning *in practice* only through a long struggle waged mainly by popular democratic forces. This section concentrates on three critical moments in this struggle: (1) the establishment of the Bill of Rights, (2) the Civil War amendments to the Constitution, and (3) the constitutional revolution of the 1930s.

The Bill of Rights

The Constitution drafted at Philadelphia in 1787 gave only limited recognition to civil liberties and civil rights. Provisions were incorporated to guarantee individuals the right of *habeas corpus* (persons placed under arrest must be promptly brought before a judge), except under dangerous circumstances of insurrection or invasion, and to prohibit the federal government from passing *bills of attainder*

MAKING A DIFFERENCE

Daniel Seeger and Conscientious Objection to Military Service

From the late 1940s to the early 1970s, young men between the ages of eighteen and twenty-six were subject to the draft. Service in the military was compulsory unless a deferment was obtained. Many young men were deferred because they were full-time college students, but for a smaller number, religious objections to the use of violence brought deferment as a "conscientious objector" (CO). To qualify for CO status, the Selective Service law required that a young man profess his belief in a "Supreme Being." Daniel Seeger, a physics major at Queens College in New York City, could not in good conscience make this profession yet felt a spiritual aversion to taking up arms against other human beings. Risking prison, Seeger challenged the draft law and won a Supreme Court decision that expanded the meaning of conscientious objection just as the Vietnam War was escalated and large numbers of young men were drafted for a cause in which many did not believe.

Seeger grew up in Queens. His parents were conservative in their politics and devout in their Ro-man Catholic faith. As an adolescent, Seeger grew increasingly rebellious toward the strict Catholicism in which he was raised; by the time he entered Queens College, he had abandoned his parents' faith. In college, he began to develop his own spiritual and philosophical perspective. Through his extensive reading, especially of Mahatma Gandhi, John Dewey, and Henry David Thoreau, he decided that his conscience forbade him to serve in the armed forces. So, even before he was eligible for the draft, he requested a CO form from his local draft board.

The form Seeger received read: "Do you believe in a Supreme Being? Check box Yes, check box No." Unable to give a simple answer, Seeger drew in a third box and asked his draft board to read a statement he had prepared about his spiritual and ethical convictions. Following the letter of the law, the draft board turned him down and ordered him to appear for a preinduction physical exam. At this point, Seeger sought counseling from the American Friends Service Committee (AFSC), an organization representing the pacifist religious sect known as

(laws that inflict punishment on individuals without trials) or *ex post facto laws* (laws that make an act committed in the past a punishable offense). But the Constitution left out most of the fundamental rights that had been incorporated in the bills of rights of the revolutionary state constitutions. The Federalist argument was that the Constitution was the charter of a limited government, so written restrictions on nonexistent powers to invade the people's liberty were unnecessary.

Anti-federalists were unpersuaded by this argument. Correctly observing the potential for an enormous concentration of power in the federal government, they insisted that the Constitution be amended to guarantee explicitly the basic liberties and rights of the people. Heeding this protest, the first Congress,

the Quakers. Although he was not a Quaker, the AFSC supported Seeger and asked him whether he would serve as a test case by challenging the draft law.

Seeger was indicted by a federal grand jury and tried for draft evasion in a district court in Manhattan in 1963. Unsympathetic to his claim that his opposition to war was religious even if he could not profess a belief in a Supreme Being, the judge found him guilty and sentenced him to a year and a day in prison. The U.S. Court of Appeals in New York reversed this conviction on First Amendment grounds, and the federal government appealed the case to the U.S. Supreme Court.

The Supreme Court's decision, handed down in March 1965, was unanimous in reversing Seeger's conviction and sparing him from prison. Perhaps because the Vietnam War was heating up and it did not want to construct a large barrier in the way of the draft system, the Court disappointed Seeger, his lawyer, and the AFSC by refusing to rule that the Supreme Being question was unconstitutional. What it did establish was a more narrow yet still significant modification to the law on CO status: If the beliefs of a religiously unconventional CO play a similar role in his life that the belief in a Supreme

Being plays in the life of the conventionally religious CO, the former should be exempted from military service.

Eventually, Seeger became a Quaker and took a position as the executive secretary of the New York AFSC office. In this capacity, he counseled young men who refused to fight in the war in Vietnam. As he relates: " 'Many people have been through the Selective Service system in the shadow of my case and have used it. I often meet people who say, "Oh, *you're* Dan Seeger, and they seem thrilled because my case was crucial to the government's recognition of their conscientious-objector claim.' " By taking a principled stand and following his conscience all the way to the Supreme Court, Daniel Seeger made a difference for many others who shared his abhorrence of war.

Source: Peter Irons, *The Courage of Their Convictions: Sixteen Americans Who Fought Their Way to the Supreme Court* (New York: Penguin Books, 1990), pp. 153–78.

sparked by the leadership of James Madison, drafted and passed ten amendments to the Constitution, collectively known as the Bill of Rights.[4] This monumental victory for the popular democrats of the founding era was, however, restricted to white males. The Bill of Rights did not address the issue of equality for racial minorities or women.

Civil liberties in America in the decades after passage of the Bill of Rights were much more precarious than its words would suggest. The impact of the Bill of Rights was limited by two factors. First, the meaning of its words would be determined only as specific cases reached the Supreme Court—whose members would not necessarily be civil libertarians. Second, the Supreme Court ruled, in the case of *Barron* v. *Baltimore* (1833), that the Bill of Rights applied only to the federal government and did not impose any restraints on state governments. Because political activity in nineteenth-century America was mostly at the state and local levels, the Bill of Rights lacked much practical impact in this era.

The Civil War Amendments

Civil liberties and civil rights in America had a second founding: the three constitutional amendments passed during the Civil War and Reconstruction era. The Thirteenth Amendment abolished the institution of slavery. The Fourteenth Amendment protected the freed slaves against discrimination or repression by their former masters. Its key provision stated, "No state shall make or enforce any law which shall abridge the privileges or immunities of citizens of the United States; nor shall any state deprive any person of life, liberty, or property, without due process of law; nor deny to any person within its jurisdiction the equal protection of the laws." The Fifteenth Amendment extended the right of suffrage to the freed slaves—but only if they were male.

The **Civil War amendments,** an accomplishment of popular democratic struggle by abolitionists, radical Republicans, and African Americans, extended the Bill of Rights in two respects. First, to the emphasis of the first ten amendments on liberty, they added a new emphasis on equality. At least one previously excluded group—African Americans—was now promised equality under the Constitution. Second, they aimed to prohibit invasions of rights by state governments rather than by the federal government. Contrary to the decision in *Barron*, the Civil War amendments seemed to safeguard liberty against infringement by government at any level.

But the promises of the Civil War amendments were not kept for several generations. As the passions of the Civil War cooled and as the northern industrial elite made its peace with the southern agricultural elite, the protection of the former slaves ceased to be of importance to persons in positions of power. The Supreme Court validated this change, ruling—in a painful historical irony—that the Fourteenth Amendment protected corporations, but not African Americans, from hostile state actions. Nevertheless, the Civil War amendments remained part of the text of the Constitution, available for a later generation that would reclaim their words and redeem their promises. Indeed, the modern flowering of liberties and rights has been based in large part on the just-quoted words of the Fourteenth Amendment.

The Constitutional Revolution of the 1930s

For most of its history, the Supreme Court was more concerned with questions of property rights than with issues of civil liberties and civil rights. Yet when the Court backed down from further confrontation with President Franklin Roosevelt in 1937, and when Roosevelt had the subsequent opportunity to name a majority of justices, the Court was poised for a profound historical shift. The constitutional revolution of the 1930s, an expression of the popular democratic spirit of the New Deal, made civil liberties and civil rights for the first time the principal business of the Supreme Court.

This constitutional revolution was clearly enunciated in the case of *United States* v. *Carolene Products Co.* (1938). Writing for the Court, Justice Harlan Fiske Stone upheld congressional authority over commerce in this seemingly routine lawsuit. But Stone added a footnote to his opinion that pointed out how differently the Court might view governmental authority if civil liberties or civil rights, rather than commerce, were at issue.

Probably the most famous footnote in Court history, Stone's **footnote 4** set out three conditions under which the Court would not grant government actions the "presumption of constitutionality." First, government actions would be questioned by the Court if they fell within the prohibitions of the Bill of Rights or the Fourteenth Amendment. Second, they would be questioned if they restricted "those political processes which can ordinarily be expected to bring about repeal of undesirable legislation" (e.g., free elections). Third, they would be questioned if they were directed at "particular religions, or national or racial minorities."[5] With footnote 4, Stone signaled that the Court would now have as its priority the safeguarding of the Bill of Rights, of political freedoms, and of the rights of religious or racial minorities subjected to discriminatory treatment by an intolerant majority.

Footnote 4 articulated what scholars call the "double standard" of the modern Supreme Court. Legislation aimed at regulating the economy is subject only to "ordinary scrutiny" by the Court; the Court presumes that such legislation is constitutional so long as the government can show that the legislation has a "reasonable" basis. In contrast, legislation that might impinge on civil liberties and civil rights must meet the test of **strict scrutiny,** meaning the Court will strike the law down unless the government can demonstrate that a "compelling interest" necessitates such a law. This double standard has been justified on three grounds: that the freedoms protected by strict scrutiny are the basis of all other freedoms, that civil liberties and civil rights are explicitly guaranteed by the Bill of Rights and the Civil War amendments, and that courts themselves are ill-equipped to determine economic policy but well-equipped to handle the definition of fundamental liberties and rights.[6]

Footnote 4 did not make clear whether the Court intended to apply strict scrutiny to actions by state governments as well as by the federal government. In 1925, the Court had announced, in the case of *Gitlow* v. *New York*, that the right of free speech limited state governments as well as the federal government since free speech was part of the liberty protected from state invasion by the Due Process Clause of the Fourteenth Amendment. In 1937, the Court went further, stating in *Palko* v. *Connecticut* that several parts of the Bill of Rights applied to the states, through the mechanism of the Fourteenth Amendment, because these rights "represented the very essence of a scheme of ordered liberty."[7]

Since the constitutional revolution of the 1930s, the Supreme Court often has been divided about how much of the Bill of Rights is incorporated in the Fourteenth Amendment and therefore applies to state governments. Some strongly

civil libertarian justices have argued for total **incorporation**—that is, every clause in the Bill of Rights applies to the states as well as to the federal government. But the dominant position has been selective incorporation, with the Court deciding one case at a time whether to apply each provision of the Bill of Rights to the states. The practical difference between total incorporation and selective incorporation diminished in the 1960s, however, as the Warren Court separately incorporated almost all of the provisions of the Bill of Rights. Today, the combination of the Bill of Rights and the Fourteenth Amendment protects civil liberties and civil rights from both the federal and state governments.

THE FIRST AMENDMENT

The words of the First Amendment, though few in number, establish the foundation of constitutional liberty in the United States: "Congress shall make no law respecting an establishment of religion, or prohibiting the free exercise thereof; or abridging the freedom of speech, or of the press; or the right of the people peaceably to assemble, and to petition the government for a redress of grievances."

This promise of liberty was more easily set down on paper than fulfilled in practice. For much of American history, the First Amendment was a frail barrier to repression. Consider the guarantee of freedom of speech. Less than a decade after the adoption of the Bill of Rights, the ruling Federalists passed a sedition act and dispatched several of their Jeffersonian opponents to jail for criticizing the administration in power. Later, when socialists and anarchists denounced the new capitalist elite, their meetings were frequently broken up and their publications suppressed. The free speech of which we are so proud is a very recent phenomenon.[8]

Free Speech

The original proponents of a constitutional guarantee of free expression were most concerned with protecting *political speech*, such as criticism of the government or its officials. The prohibition on government interference was thus set down in absolute terms: "Congress shall make *no law* . . ." (emphasis added). But no Supreme Court majority has ever regarded the First Amendment as conferring an absolute protection for speech. The Court has had to grapple repeatedly with where to draw the boundary line dividing free speech from unprotected, and therefore punishable, speech.

The Supreme Court was first moved to draw such a boundary line in response to prosecutions of dissenters to World War I. Charles Schenck, a socialist, was prosecuted under the wartime Espionage Act for a pamphlet that urged young men to resist the draft. In *Schenck* v. *United States* (1919), the Court upheld the constitutionality of the Espionage Act and thus of Schenck's conviction. In the decision for the Court, Justice Oliver Wendell Holmes explained, in words that became famous, that speech was subject to the **clear and present danger test:**

> The most stringent protection of free speech would not protect a man in falsely shouting fire in a theater and causing a panic. . . . The question in every case is whether the words used are used in such circumstances and are of such a nature as to create a clear and present danger that they will bring about the substantive evils that Congress has a right to prevent.[9]

Fear of political radicalism lay at the heart of the repression of free speech during World War I and its aftermath. This same fear fostered a new repressive climate after World War II, as Americans became obsessed with an external threat from the Soviet Union and an internal threat from domestic communists. Fueling anticommunist hysteria during the early years of the Cold War were demagogic politicians, preeminent among them Senator Joseph McCarthy of Wisconsin. The senator gave his name to the phenomenon of **McCarthyism** by his tactics: waving phony lists of supposed communists in the government before the press, hauling individuals before his congressional committee and tarring their reputation for no other end than publicity, labeling any who opposed him conspirators against American freedom.

Influenced by the sour climate of McCarthyism, the Supreme Court went along with the effort of the executive branch to put the leaders of the American Communist party in prison. In *Dennis* v. *United States* (1951), the Court upheld the convictions of eleven top officials of the Communist party for violating the Smith Act, which made it a crime to advocate the violent overthrow of government in the United States, even though the puny American Communist party scarcely posed a present danger to the government. It was only after McCarthy and his methods came into disrepute and Cold War hysteria began to ease that the Supreme Court backed away from this repressive stance. The case of *Yates* v. *United States* (1957) also involved Smith Act prosecution of communist officials, but this time the defendants' convictions were reversed. Abstract advocacy of Communist party doctrine about revolution, the Court ruled, was protected speech. Only advocacy of immediate action to overthrow the government could be punished.

During the 1960s, radical political dissent was not restricted to communists. Many Americans began to engage in vocal political protests, especially against the war in Vietnam. It was at the end of this turbulent decade that the Warren Court, in *Brandenburg* v. *Ohio* (1969), finally gave a broad interpretation to the right of free speech. Clarence Brandenburg, a Ku Klux Klan leader, was convicted under an Ohio law for advocating racial conflict at a televised Klan rally. Overturning Brandenburg's conviction, the Court stated that government could punish an individual for advocating an illegal act only if "such advocacy is directed to inciting or producing imminent lawless action, and is likely to incite or produce such action."[10] Under such a test, only a few utterances—such as a speech that called for a riot and actually helped begin it—were still punishable. Political speech in the United States was at last given broad protection—nearly one hundred eighty years after the adoption of the Bill of Rights!

In recent decades, the Court has brought **symbolic speech**—political expression that communicates with visual symbols instead of words—under the protection of the First Amendment. Several high school and junior high school students in Des Moines, Iowa, were suspended after they wore black armbands to school as a way of protesting the war in Vietnam. Voiding the suspensions, the Court stated in *Tinker* v. *Des Moines Independent Community School District* (1969) that wearing an armband as a silent form of protest was "akin to pure speech."[11] More controversial than the *Tinker* decision was the Court's defense of symbolic speech in *Texas* v. *Johnson* (1989). Johnson had burned an American flag outside the 1984 Republican convention in Dallas, Texas, to protest Reagan's policies. Five justices—an unusual coalition of liberals Brennan, Marshall, and Blackmun and conservatives Scalia and Kennedy—voted to overturn Johnson's conviction on the grounds that the Texas statute against flag burning violated the First Amendment by punishing the communication of a political message.

Should supporters of civil liberties be in a celebrating mood because of these recent decisions? Popular democrats point out that speech can be restricted not only by punishment but by exclusion from the forums where sizeable audiences gather. Ordinary citizens or dissenting groups may now be free to say almost anything on the proverbial street corner, law professor Owen Fiss observes, but they are seldom heard in the mass media, where speech reaches large numbers. And what happens when the street corner as local gathering spot has largely been supplanted by the shopping mall? According to several decisions issued by the Burger Court during the 1970s, speakers and pamphleteers can be forbidden in these public spaces because they are private property.[12]

Indeed, even public property can sometimes exclude public speakers. In *United States* v. *Kokinda* (1990), the Rehnquist Court upheld a ban on political groups distributing literature and soliciting funds on the grounds of a post office in suburban Maryland. The majority argued that when a government agency is operating in a "proprietary capacity," it can prohibit political speech that interferes with business.[13] The space for free speech by those without wealth and power has begun to contract. It will not expand again, Fiss writes, until free speech is guaranteed in public places, even those that are private property, as an essential condition for popular democracy: "a public right—an instrument of collective self-determination."[14]

Unprotected Speech

Not all speech has been granted broad protection by the Supreme Court. Some kinds of expression are considered by the Court to be **unprotected speech**—speech unworthy of full First Amendment protection either because its social value is insignificant or because it verges on conduct that is harmful to others. Commercial speech, unlike political speech, can thus be regulated, as in bans on false advertising. *Fighting words*, such as derogatory names shouted at a police officer, can be punished on the grounds that they do not express any ideas or contribute to any search for truth (*Chaplinsky* v. *New Hampshire* [1942]). And *libel*—written communication that exposes the person written about to public shame, contempt, or ridicule—is subject to lawsuits for monetary damages. However, the Court ruled in *New York Times Co.* v. *Sullivan* (1964) that for a public official to win a judgment against a writer, the official must prove not only that the charge in question was false but also that it had been made with malice.

Drawing the line between protected and unprotected speech has been hardest for the Supreme Court in the area of **obscenity.** Probably no other term has been as difficult for the Court to define. The Court first entered the thicket of sexual expression in *Roth* v. *United States* (1957). In this case, Justice Brennan, declaring obscenity to be unprotected by the First Amendment, defined it as sexual material that appealed to "prurient interest"—that is, excited lust. Confronted by a book, magazine, or film about sex, the Court would decide "whether to the average person, applying contemporary community standards, the dominant theme of the material taken as a whole appeals to the prurient interest." Attempting to protect the free expression of ideas, even about sex, Brennan added that a work should be judged obscene only when it was "utterly without redeeming social importance." [15]

Despite Brennan's valiant effort to define obscenity, observe how many ambiguous terms dot his opinion: "prurient interest," "average person," "contemporary community standards," "redeeming social importance." After the *Roth* decision, obscenity cases became a headache for the Supreme Court. Perhaps their most ludicrous feature was that to study the evidence in a particular obscenity conviction, the mostly elderly justices had to sift through the pages of a sex magazine or sit through the screening of a porno film. It was little wonder that they lost the stomach for these cases.

As sexually explicit material became a booming market for enterprising pornographers, the more conservative justices appointed by Richard Nixon tried to tighten the definition of obscenity in *Miller* v. *California* (1973). Chief Justice Burger's opinion made two significant changes in obscenity doctrine. First, a sexually explicit work could no longer simply claim minimal social importance (for example, by including a brief scene on some social or political theme); now, the work had to possess "serious literary, artistic, political, or scientific value." [16] Second, prurient interest could be measured by local, rather than national, standards, which permitted a bookseller in a small town, for example, to be prosecuted for selling a work that could be legally sold in a more cosmopolitan city. But the *Miller* decision did little to stem the tide of pornography. And the Court soon had to back away from granting local communities a wide latitude to define obscenity after a Georgia town attempted to prosecute *Carnal Knowledge*, a popular Hollywood film, because it contained a simulated sexual act.

Conservative moralists have long decried the scope that the Supreme Court has given to the production of sexually explicit materials. In recent years, they have been joined by some feminists who regard pornography not only as degrading to women but also as contributing to their social subordination.

Freedom of the Press

If the right of free speech promotes an open debate about political matters, the right of a free press provides democratic citizens with the information and analysis they need to enter intelligently into that debate. In authoritarian political systems, the government openly owns or covertly controls the press. In a democracy, the government is expected to keep its hands off the press. (Yet as we saw in Chapter 6, both governmental and economic elites in America possess special influence over the media.)

The landmark case defining freedom of the press was *Near* v. *Minnesota* (1931). J. M. Near was the publisher of the *Saturday Press*, a Minneapolis weekly that denounced a wide array of targets: corrupt officials, racketeers, Catholics, Jews, blacks, and labor unions. Minneapolis officials obtained a court injunction to close down Near's paper under a Minnesota law that allowed the banning of scandal sheets. The Supreme Court struck down the Minnesota law as a violation of freedom of the press because the law imposed **prior restraint.** A publisher like Near could still be sued for libel, but he could not be blocked from printing whatever he chose in the first place. The Court recognized that prior restraint, by allowing government officials to determine what information could be kept from publication, would effectively destroy freedom of the press.

Prior restraint was also at issue in a case involving the *New York Times;* this time the issue was government secrecy and deception during the Vietnam War. When a disillusioned Defense Department official, Daniel Ellsberg, leaked a copy of a classified department study of the war's history, known as the Pentagon Papers, to the *New York Times,* the Nixon administration obtained a lower court order temporarily halting the paper's publication of excerpts from the study. The Supreme Court's decision in *New York Times Co.* v. *United States* (1971) voided the order and permitted publication of the Pentagon Papers. But the six justices in the majority were divided in their reasoning. Justices Black, Brennan, and Douglas were opposed to prior restraint under any circumstances. Justices White, Marshall, and Stewart voted to allow publication because the Nixon administration had failed to make a convincing case for the disastrous consequences it claimed would follow once the Pentagon Papers became public. Freedom of the press again won a victory—but a majority of the Court seemed willing to accept prior restraint if the government could make a better case on possible harm to national security.

Even though broadcast media (radio and television) enjoy much the same freedom as print media (newspapers and magazines), they are subject to certain special constraints. Because broadcast frequencies are limited, the federal government regulates broadcast media through the Federal Communications Commission (FCC). And since messages broadcast through the media, unlike messages set in print, often reach audiences for which they were never intended, the FCC may ban words over the air that could not be kept out of print. In *F.C.C.* v. *Pacifica Foundation* (1978), the Court upheld a ban on further radio broadcasts of a monologue by comic George Carlin about Americans' obsession with "seven dirty words"—which Carlin used freely as part of his routine.[17] The issue here was not obscenity—Carlin's monologue did not excite lust and clearly had artistic value—but the harm done to children who might accidently hear the seven offensive words.

Is the Internet, the new medium of the computer age, to be treated like print or like broadcast media? In its first major decision about the Internet, *Reno* v. *American Civil Liberties Union* (1997), the Court struck down the Communications Decency Act of 1996, which criminalized the transmission of "indecent" materials that minors might view, as an infringement of the First Amendment. The Court announced that the Internet, like print media, deserves the highest level of constitutional protection.

Separation of Church and State

The opening words of the First Amendment bar Congress from passing any law "respecting an establishment of religion." At the time the Bill of Rights was adopted, these words were aimed mainly at preventing the federal government from bestowing on any religious denomination the special privileges enjoyed by the official Anglican Church in England. But in modern times, the Supreme Court has given a far broader meaning to the **Establishment Clause,** reading it as requiring an almost complete separation of church and state. Religion and government are kept apart—even though America is one of the most religious nations in the world. Public opinion surveys, notes scholar Garry Wills, show that "eight Americans in ten say they believe they will be called before God on Judgment Day to answer for their sins" and that the same percentage "believe God still works miracles."[18] This religious majority sometimes has difficulty understanding why the Supreme Court believes that government is not supposed to be in the business of supporting God.

School prayer cases illustrate how the Supreme Court, flying in the face of majority sentiments, has insisted that government stay out of religion. The Court has struck down the daily reading of a nondenominational prayer in New York public schools (*Engel* v. *Vitale* [1962]), Bible reading in Pennsylvania public schools (*Abington School District* v. *Schempp* [1963]), and even a moment of silence for meditation or prayer in Alabama public schools (*Wallace* v. *Jaffree* [1985]). School prayer, the Court has reasoned, represents a government endorsement of religion that inflicts psychological injury on students (and their parents) who are not religious believers. The Establishment Clause of the First Amendment mandates government neutrality toward religion.

The Court has not been quite as strict about government approval for religious symbols where school-age children are not involved. For example, in *Lynch* v. *Donnelly* (1984), the Court approved of a nativity scene erected by the city of Pawtucket, Rhode Island, during the Christmas season—but only because it was accompanied by a Santa's house, a Christmas tree, and colored lights that indicated the city's secular purpose (attracting shoppers to downtown stores). Such breaches in the "wall" separating church and state have so far been small.

The Establishment Clause also has been central to the issue of government financial aid to religious schools. The Supreme Court's decisions in this area have not been as unpopular, however, as in the area of school prayer because Protestants and Jews do not favor aid that would go mostly to Catholic schools.

Beginning in the 1940s, a long series of cases established the principle that government could not financially support religious schools, even in the name of secular educational purposes, although it could provide direct aid to their students (e.g., bus transportation). Chief Justice Burger summed up the Court's approach in *Lemon* v. *Kurtzman* (1971)—a ruling invalidating state payments for the teaching of secular subjects in parochial schools. According to the **Lemon test,** government aid to religious schools would be constitutional only if (1) it had a secular purpose, (2) its effect was neither to advance nor to inhibit religion, and (3) it did not entangle government and religious institutions in each other's affairs. Few forms of government aid to religious schools can survive the Lemon test.

Free Exercise of Religion

The Establishment Clause in the First Amendment is followed by the **Free Exercise Clause**—the right to believe in whatever religion one chooses. The Free Exercise Clause is a legacy of America's colonial past, as many of the original white settlers had fled religious oppression and persecution in England and other parts of Europe. It is also a practical necessity in a nation where the diversity of religious faiths is staggering.

The landmark free exercise case is *West Virginia State Board of Education* v. *Barnette* (1943). At stake was the right of schoolchildren to refuse to salute an American flag because their religious faith—Jehovah's Witnesses—forbade it. Three years earlier, in *Minersville School District* v. *Gobitis*, the Court had approved of expelling Witness children from school for refusal to salute the flag. But that decision led to brutal physical assaults on the Witnesses in many towns and also became an embarrassment as the United States entered a war against Nazi tyranny in the name of democratic freedom. With the powerful words of Justice Jackson (quoted at the beginning of this chapter), the Court changed its mind and gave a firm endorsement to the free exercise of religion even when it offended the most cherished sentiments of the majority.

Although the Free Exercise Clause protects any form of religious belief, the matter of religious conduct is more complicated. What happens when a religious order prescribes practices for its adherents that violate local, state, or federal laws having nothing to do with religion? The Court first struggled with this dilemma in *Reynolds* v. *United States* (1879), when it approved the outlawing of polygamy (where a man takes several wives), a key practice of the Mormon faith. A recent case, *Employment Division* v. *Smith* (1990), upheld the same distinction between belief and conduct. The Court denied the claim by two followers of the Native American Church that smoking the drug peyote, for which they had been fired from their job, was a religious sacrament protected by the Free Exercise Clause. The position of the Court was different, however, in *Church of Lukumi Babalu Aye* v. *City of Hialeah* (1993). When the Florida city passed an ordinance to stop the practitioners of *Santería*, an Afro-Cuban religion, from engaging in animal sacrifice as a ritual, the Court overturned it as a blatant attempt to restrict the free exercise of religion.

THE RIGHTS OF PERSONS ACCUSED OF CRIMES

The constitutional bases for the rights of persons accused of crimes are the Fourth, Fifth, Sixth, and Eighth Amendments, applied to the states through incorporation in the Fourteenth Amendment. Application of these amendments to the criminal justice system at the state and local levels, where the vast majority of criminal proceedings takes place, is a recent phenomenon. The Warren Court of the 1960s set down most of the critical precedents in the area of criminal procedure. The Burger (1969–1986) and Rehnquist (1986–present) Courts, appointed by "law-and-order" presidents and responsive to the public outcry about crime, carved out numerous exceptions to these precedents.

Criminal Procedure: The Warren Court

Clarence Earl Gideon, a penniless drifter with a criminal record, was convicted for the felony offense of breaking and entering a poolroom and sentenced in a Florida court to five years in prison. Unable to afford an attorney, Gideon had to defend himself after the judge refused to appoint professional counsel for him. The Supreme Court accepted Gideon's petition (appointing a prominent lawyer to argue his case before it) and ruled in *Gideon* v. *Wainwright* (1963) that the Sixth Amendment right of counsel is so essential to a fair trial that the state must pay for a lawyer for indigent defendants charged with a felony. Gideon won the chance for a second trial, at which he was acquitted after his court-appointed counsel convincingly demonstrated that the prosecution's star witness, who had fingered Gideon for the break-in, was probably the culprit.[19]

Cleveland police officers forced their way into the home of Dolree Mapp without a search warrant in the belief that she was hiding a man wanted for a recent bombing as well as illegal gambling paraphernalia. Their search of the house turned up neither a fugitive nor gambling materials—but they did discover sexual books and pictures. On the basis of this evidence, Mapp was sent to jail for possession of obscene literature. In *Mapp* v. *Ohio* (1961), the Warren Court reversed her conviction, holding that material seized in an illegal search could not be introduced as evidence in a state court, a doctrine known as the **exclusionary rule.** This rule, based on the Fourth Amendment, had been applied since 1914 to defendants in federal prosecutions. But its extension from the tax evaders and other white collar defendants typically tried in federal courts to the wider range of defendants tried in state courts, including violent criminals, made the *Mapp* decision controversial.

Ernesto Miranda was arrested by Phoenix police on suspicion of rape and kidnapping. At first, Miranda maintained his innocence, but after two hours of police interrogation he signed a written confession to the crime. At no point had

"This is my kid—as part of his school's civics project, he's gonna read your Miranda rights."

the police advised Miranda that he had a right to have an attorney present during the interrogation. In *Miranda* v. *Arizona* (1966), the Warren Court ruled the confession to be inadmissible as evidence in court, a violation of Miranda's Fifth Amendment right not to incriminate himself. The Court's majority, in this 5–4 decision, argued that police custody and interrogation tended to create such an intimidating atmosphere that individuals felt pressured to incriminate themselves in the absence of a lawyer's counsel. With the confession thrown out, Arizona retried Miranda for the same crime and convicted him on the basis of other evidence.

The effect of the decision was that police had to change their behavior and provide suspects with what came to be known as the **Miranda warnings.** Criminal suspects must be advised that (1) they have the right to remain silent, (2) anything they say can be used against them, (3) they have the right to speak to an attorney before police questioning and to have him or her present during interrogation, and (4) if they cannot afford to hire an attorney, one will be provided at state expense before any questioning can take place.

The *Mapp* decision, and even more the *Miranda* decision, fueled widespread attacks on the Warren Court for crippling law enforcement at a time of rampant crime. Actually, these Warren Court decisions did not free many criminals. A prominent study of the exclusionary rule later estimated that less than 2.5 percent of felony arrests were undermined by the operation of this rule.[20] After initial grumbling, the police adapted to the requirement of providing *Miranda* warnings. Numerous studies found that criminal confessions continued to be made in large numbers even after suspects were informed of their rights.[21] Nonetheless, critics of the Warren Court convinced many Americans that the justices had in effect taken the handcuffs off criminal suspects and put them on the police.

Presidential candidate Richard Nixon seized on crime as a campaign issue in 1968, lambasting the Warren Court for coddling criminals and promising that his administration would appoint only law-and-order judges. Nixon's success with the issue encouraged other candidates, including his Republican successors in the White House. Supreme Court justices appointed by Nixon, Reagan, and Bush thus have been less likely than were justices of the Warren Court era to emphasize the constitutional rights of criminal suspects or defendants and more likely to emphasize the practical needs of police and prosecutors.

Criminal Procedure: The Burger and Rehnquist Courts

Of the three landmark Warren Court decisions on criminal justice just described, only the *Gideon* decision was received without controversy. No one seemed to doubt the proposition that there could not be a fair trial where the state was represented by a professionally trained prosecutor and the defendant had to represent himself or herself. So it is not surprising that the Burger Court went beyond the *Gideon* ruling in *Argersinger* v. *Hamlin* (1972), holding that the right of court-appointed counsel for the indigent should be extended from felony defendants to defendants facing misdemeanor charges that carried a jail sentence.

In the more controversial areas of the exclusionary rule and the *Miranda* warnings, however, the Burger and Rehnquist Courts have trimmed back the Warren Court precedents—without, up to now, explicitly disavowing them. Thus, in *United States* v. *Calandra* (1974), Justice Lewis Powell's majority opinion argued that illegally obtained evidence, although still barred from a trial because of the exclusionary rule, could be admitted before a grand jury considering whether to indict a suspect and thus bring him or her to trial. And in *United States* v. *Leon* (1984), Justice Byron White wrote that if police use a search warrant that later proves to have been invalid, the evidence seized is still admissible during the trial. So many exceptions have been approved by the Burger and Rehnquist Courts that legal scholar Thomas Davies calls the exclusionary rule a "shadow" of its former self.[22]

The Burger and Rehnquist Courts also have made it easier for police to obtain confessions by loosening up the requirements for *Miranda* warnings. For example, in emergency situations such as a threat to the safety of the arresting officer, the warnings are not required (*New York* v. *Quarles* [1984]). Nor do arresting officers have to notify suspects of the specific offense with which they are charged (*Colorado* v. *Spring* [1987]).

The ultimate issue in a criminal justice system—imposition of the death sentence—was not tackled by the Supreme Court until 1972 in the case of *Furman* v. *Georgia*. With all four of President Nixon's appointees in dissent, the Court struck down existing death penalty laws in every state because the random and arbitrary fashion in which juries decided on capital punishment violated the Cruel and Unusual Punishment Clause of the Eighth Amendment. In response to this decision, state legislatures and the federal government revised their criminal laws to provide juries with explicit sentencing guidelines. The Court ratified this approach in *Gregg* v. *Georgia* (1976), and prison "death rows" reopened for a new cohort of the condemned.

The criminal procedure decisions of the Burger and Rehnquist Courts have been more congenial to public opinion than those of the Warren Court. Critics of these decisions point out, however, that constitutional rights—even for the most despicable citizens—should not be decided by a popularity test. They argue that the Bill of Rights does not prevent us from putting criminal offenders behind bars, but it does require that we do so in a fair manner. This philosophy is well expressed by Justice Brennan: "The interest of . . . [the government] is not that it shall win a case, but that justice shall be done."[23]

THE RIGHT OF PRIVACY

The controversy surrounding constitutional rights spelled out in the Bill of Rights has been extended to the issue of whether other rights can be legitimately derived from the text of the Constitution even if they are not spelled out there. A **right of privacy** is at the center of this debate. Civil libertarians have long contended for this right. In a 1928 dissent, Justice Louis Brandeis wrote, "The makers of our Constitution conferred, as against the government, the right to be let alone—the most comprehensive of rights and the right most valued by civilized men."[24] But what words in the Bill of Rights established the right to be let alone—the right of privacy?

The Supreme Court finally answered this question in 1965 in *Griswold* v. *Connecticut*. At issue was a Connecticut law that made it a crime for any person to use a drug or device for birth control. The Court invalidated this law as an invasion of the constitutionally protected right of privacy of married persons. Writing for the majority, Justice William O. Douglas argued that the enumerated guarantees of constitutional rights in the First, Third, Fourth, Fifth, and Ninth Amendments had "penumbras" (shadows) that extended beyond their specific words. These penumbras suggested the existence of "zones of privacy" that the government could not invade. In an important concurring opinion, Justice Arthur Goldberg took a different tack. He based a right of privacy on the words of the Ninth Amendment, which reads, "The enumeration in the Constitution, of certain rights, shall not be construed to deny or disparage others retained by the people." To the dissenters in *Griswold*, Justices Hugo Black and Potter Stewart, the right of privacy, whether found among penumbras or read into the Ninth Amendment, was a concoction of the justices lacking any basis in the Constitution.[25]

The *Griswold* case generated a heated controversy on the Court over the idea of a constitutional right of privacy. But few outside the Court paid attention to a decision striking down an antiquated law that even the dissenters in the case considered to be "silly." The right of privacy generated a major public controversy only when it was extended from a couple's freedom to choose contraception and avoid pregnancy to a woman's freedom to choose an abortion and terminate an unwanted pregnancy.

Abortion

The abortion issue was brought before the Supreme Court by two young lawyers, Sarah Weddington and Linda Coffee, who were inspired by the new feminist movement that had emerged in the 1960s. Their client in **Roe v. Wade** (1973) was Norma McCorvey, a twenty-one-year-old woman who had carried an unwanted pregnancy to term because Texas, like most other states at that time, forbade abortions except to save the life of the mother. (McCorvey's identity was protected from publicity by the pseudonym "Jane Roe.") By a 7–2 vote, the Court struck down anti-abortion statutes in Texas and all other states on the grounds that they violated a woman's right of privacy, located in the Due Process Clause of the Fourteenth Amendment.

Authored by Justice Harry Blackmun, the decision for the Court divided pregnancy into three trimesters. During the first trimester, a state cannot interfere with a woman's right to choose an abortion in consultation with her doctor. During the second trimester, when abortions pose more of a medical risk, states can regulate them to safeguard maternal health. Only during the final trimester, when a fetus may be capable of surviving outside the womb, can a state impose severe restrictions or prohibitions on abortion. To the dissenters in the case, Justices Byron White and William Rehnquist, this trimester scheme was an arbitrary invention of the Court. They argued that the Court was enforcing on the states a right that had neither been enumerated in the Bill of Rights nor envisioned by the drafters of the Fourteenth Amendment.

Hailing the decision on abortion as a great victory for women's rights, the women's movement shifted its attention to other issues. But as supporters of *Roe* grew complacent, opponents of the decision mobilized to fight its results. The initial "right-to-life" movement was spearheaded by Catholic organizations. Later, they were joined by fundamentalist Protestant groups, such as the Reverend Jerry Falwell's Moral Majority. The religious fervor of right-to-life supporters was captured for political purposes by the conservatives of the New Right, whose candidate and hero was Ronald Reagan. Once in the White House, Reagan made abortion a litmus test for his nominees to the federal judiciary. By the end of his two terms, he had named three new justices to the Supreme Court, and *Roe* was at risk of reversal.[26]

Awakening to the peril to *Roe*, the "pro-choice" forces mobilized their supporters at last. After the Court announced early in 1989 that it would consider the restrictive laws on abortion passed by Missouri, a massive Washington rally attempted to show the justices that a majority of Americans wanted to preserve a woman's right to choose. Right-to-life forces girded for battle as well. The Court's decision in *Webster* v. *Reproductive Health Services* (1989) favored the right-to-life side. Missouri's restrictions on abortion, such as a ban on the use of public hospitals or employees to perform abortions except when the woman's life was in danger, were upheld by a 5–4 majority. But the Court stopped short of overturning *Roe* itself. One member of the majority, Sandra Day O'Connor, the only woman on the Supreme Court, was not willing to go that far.

Closely allied with the right-to-life movement, President Bush replaced two retiring supporters of the original *Roe* decision, Justices William Brennan and Thurgood Marshall, with David Souter and Clarence Thomas. The stage seemed set for the demise of *Roe* when the Court heard the case of *Planned Parenthood of Southeastern Pennsylvania* v. *Casey* (1992). But in a surprise twist to the historical drama of abortion rights, *Roe* survived. Most of Pennsylvania's restrictions were sustained by the Court, imposing new obstacles to women seeking an abortion. Yet even though four justices wanted to overturn *Roe*, restoring to the states the power to prohibit abortions, the critical fifth vote was still lacking. Justice O'Connor was now joined by Justice Anthony Kennedy (a Reagan appointee) and Justice Souter in a moderate conservative bloc willing to uphold restrictions on abortion but not willing to disclaim the constitutional right of a woman to choose an abortion. In an unusual joint opinion, the three argued that *Roe* was an important precedent deserving of respect and that overturning it would diminish both the legitimacy of the Supreme Court and the public's belief in the rule of law.

For right-to-life supporters, legal disappointment in the *Casey* decision was followed by political disappointment as the first pro-choice president in twelve years, Bill Clinton, was elected in 1992. When Justice Byron White, one of the two original dissenters in *Roe*, retired in 1993, Clinton replaced him with one of the pioneer legal advocates for women's rights, Ruth Bader Ginsburg. The landmark *Roe* decision, even though partially weakened in the *Webster* and *Casey* decisions, is thus likely to remain the law on abortion for the immediate future. Nevertheless, abortion engages deep passions on both sides, and it is not likely to disappear any time soon as one of the most heated and divisive issues in American public life.

Sexual Orientation

Is the right of privacy equally enjoyed by all Americans? In *Bowers* v. *Hardwick* (1986), the Supreme Court said no. Michael Hardwick was arrested after an Atlanta policeman, entering his bedroom to serve an arrest warrant for not paying a fine, found Hardwick engaged in homosexual conduct. Charges against Hardwick under Georgia's sodomy law were not prosecuted, but he brought a civil suit in federal court challenging the law as an invasion of his constitutionally protected right of privacy. A 5–4 majority rejected his challenge and upheld the sodomy law.

What distinguished Hardwick's claim to privacy from those in the *Griswold* or *Roe* decisions? Justice Byron White, writing for the majority, stated that those decisions involved "family, marriage, or procreation."[27] In other words, the right of privacy belongs to heterosexuals but not to homosexuals. Law professor Sanford Levinson writes that "*Bowers* is, in its way, almost as offensive as *Dred Scott*, with its notorious emphasis that blacks simply were not part of the American political community."[28]

A decade after the *Bowers* decision, the Court undid some of its damage to equal rights. In *Romer* v. *Evans* (1996), a 6–3 majority struck down an amendment voters had added to the Colorado Constitution that nullified existing local ordinances prohibiting discrimination against homosexuals and barred the state or any of its municipalities from enacting any new antidiscrimination measures on behalf of gays and lesbians. Justice Kennedy's majority decision argued that the Colorado amendment singled out homosexuals in an unconstitutional fashion: "A state cannot so deem a class of persons a stranger to its laws."[29]

CIVIL RIGHTS

Although this chapter highlights legal and legislative victories in the struggle for civil rights, primary credit for progress in the struggle belongs to the civil rights movement. The decades-long struggle by African Americans and their allies for civil rights not only prodded the white majority to act but also inspired similar movements for equality among Hispanic Americans, Native Americans, Americans with disabilities, and women. These groups' victories, such as the Americans with Disabilities Act of 1990, have redeemed a basic promise of popular democracy: respect for the dignity of every citizen.

Civil rights achievements of the 1950s and 1960s, establishing the objective of a racially just and equal society, are now applauded even by those who originally opposed them. The methods devised to attain that objective, however, have generated intense controversy since the end of the 1960s. As we shall see when we consider the practices of busing and affirmative action, many have come to argue that measures taken in the name of civil rights for racial minorities discriminate against the white majority. To the story of the heroic past of the struggle for civil rights must be appended the story of its painful present.

Fighting Segregation: From *Plessy* to *Brown*

Despite the constitutional amendments drafted during the Civil War and Reconstruction to protect blacks, they soon found themselves in a position of economic, political, and legal subordination. The commitment of the Fourteenth

Amendment to equal protection of the laws for former slaves was mocked by a series of Supreme Court decisions refusing to enforce the amendment in the face of the southern states' new system of "Jim Crow" segregation. The last of these decisions, *Plessy* v. *Ferguson* (1896), established a legal justification for racial segregation that African Americans would have to combat for more than half a century.

The Supreme Court had to consider in the *Plessy* case whether a Louisiana law requiring railroads to provide **separate but equal** facilities for whites and blacks violated the equal protection of the laws. All but one of the justices found the practice legal, arguing that separation of the races did not imply that either race was unequal. If there was a stigma of black inferiority in segregation, the majority said, it was only because blacks viewed it that way. Repudiating this reasoning, the lone dissenter in the case, Justice John Marshall Harlan, offered a powerful and prophetic alternative: "The Constitution is color-blind, and neither knows nor tolerates classes among citizens."[30]

A little more than a decade later, in 1909, the **National Association for the Advancement of Colored People (NAACP)** was founded to take up the battle against racial segregation and discrimination. In the 1930s, its legal arm developed a careful, long-term strategy to demolish the separate but equal doctrine. Rather than a head-on assault on Jim Crow, which the Court was likely to rebuff, NAACP lawyers would chip away at segregation in the area of education, showing in case after case that separate facilities could not possibly be equal.[31]

The NAACP campaign finally reached fruition in ***Brown v. Board of Education of Topeka*** (1954), probably the most famous Supreme Court decision of the twentieth century. Thanks to skillful leadership by the new chief justice, Earl

Warren, the Court was unanimous in rejecting the separate but equal doctrine in the field of education. The claim in the *Plessy* decision that segregation did not stamp blacks as inferior was repudiated in Warren's opinion for the Court: "Segregation of white and colored children in public schools has a detrimental effect upon the colored children. . . . A sense of inferiority affects the motivation to learn." The chief justice's concluding words marked a historic watershed for the Court and for the nation: "In the field of public education the doctrine of 'separate but equal' has no place. Separate educational facilities are inherently unequal."[32] Although the case dealt only with public schools, the *Brown* decision, reclaiming the original promise of the Fourteenth Amendment, inflicted a mortal wound on racial segregation in America.

But the death of segregation would not be swift. And the Supreme Court had to share a portion of the blame for its agonizingly slow demise. When the Court considered how to implement its decision in a second *Brown* case a year later, it was fearful of a hostile and potentially violent response by southern whites. So rather than setting a firm timetable for school desegregation, the Court returned the problem to the lower federal courts with the instruction that desegregation proceed "with all deliberate speed." These ambiguous words did not accomplish the goal of heading off southern white hostility and violence; instead, they only seemed to invite southern strategies of delay. The stage for the historic drama of civil rights now shifted from the Supreme Court to the cities and small towns of the South, where the civil rights movement, encouraged by *Brown*, would have to finish off a dying—but still powerful and violent—segregationist system.

Ending Segregation

Up to the *Brown* decision in 1954, the primary focus of the civil rights movement had been litigation, and its leading group had been the NAACP. After *Brown*, new civil rights groups emerged and intensified the pace of the struggle for equality by turning from litigation to direct action. Chapter 10 described the first great direct action struggle, the Montgomery bus boycott. Subsequent direct action struggles were risky, both in their use of civil disobedience to break unjust segregation laws and in the violence with which they were met by southern mobs and southern police. But these struggles were increasingly effective in riveting the attention of the North on the brutal injustices of southern segregation and in pressuring northern politicians to do something about them.

The legislative triumphs for civil rights in the mid-1960s can be traced directly to the movement campaigns that inspired them. In response to the direct action campaign of Martin Luther King, Jr.'s Southern Christian Leadership Conference in Birmingham, Alabama, President Kennedy proposed major civil rights legislation in 1963 (see Chapter 12). Passed only after his death, the **Civil Rights Act of 1964** struck a powerful blow at segregation in many areas. Its most important provisions outlawed racial discrimination in public accommodations (such as hotels and restaurants) and in employment. In response to another direct action campaign led by King and his organization in Selma, Alabama, President Johnson proposed landmark voting rights legislation early in 1965. Responding more promptly this time, Congress passed the **Voting Rights Act of 1965.** This act, removing the barriers that southern officials had placed in the way of potential black registrants, finally gave effective enforcement to the Fifteenth Amendment.[33]

As the pace of the struggle against segregation picked up in other areas, school desegregation lagged behind. A decade after the *Brown* decision had mandated an end to segregated public schools, less than 2 percent of previously segregated school districts had changed their practices. By the end of the 1960s, the Supreme Court had had enough of all deliberate speed and was ready to order immediate desegregation. Given residential patterns that separated the races, however, significant desegregation could be accomplished only by busing schoolchildren. In the case of *Swann* v. *Charlotte-Mecklenburg Board of Education* (1971), a unanimous Court approved a massive busing plan for a sprawling urban/rural school district in North Carolina.

Ironically, court-ordered busing to end the perpetuation of all-white and all-black schools was more controversial in the North than in the South. Angry white parents in the North asked why their children should be bused to remedy patterns of discrimination for which they were not responsible. Despite widespread protests, federal judges ordered busing for such cities as Boston, Denver, and Los Angeles. But the limitations of busing as a remedy for racially separate schools became evident in a case from Detroit.

The phenomenon of "white flight" to the suburbs to escape an increasingly black city, combined with economic changes, left too few white children remaining in Detroit to achieve racial balance in the schools. So a federal judge ordered a busing plan that would have incorporated the city's suburbs as well as the city itself. In *Milliken* v. *Bradley* (1974), a 5–4 majority rejected the plan, arguing that suburban school districts that had not engaged in segregated practices could not be compelled to participate in a remedy for Detroit's segregation problem. Since only interdistrict desegregation plans like that in Detroit could ever achieve racial balance in the schools, the long-term result has been that African-American children are now more likely to attend an all-black school in a big city in the North than they are in the once-segregated South.

Affirmative Action

As the bitter controversy over busing receded, it was supplanted by an equally bitter debate over affirmative action. **Affirmative action** involves taking positive steps to award educational opportunities or jobs to racial minorities or women because these groups have been the victims of prior discrimination.

Supporters of affirmative action argue that simply adopting a color- or gender-blind approach won't overcome discrimination. Economist Barbara Bergmann observes: "From the 100-member U.S. Senate (92 percent male, 99 percent white, through 1996) to the nearest construction site, it is obvious that white males continue to predominate in the best positions by a wide margin."[34] Only a deliberate policy of preferential treatment for groups victimized by discrimination, supporters of affirmative action insist, can eliminate racial and gender inequities from our society. Affirmative action will open the door of opportunity for those previously excluded, allowing them at last to show what they can do.

Opponents of affirmative action argue that it goes beyond "equal protection of the laws" to promote equal results regardless of merit. Affirmative action, they say, is "reverse discrimination" against white males. Affirmative action is also accused of worsening, not improving, race relations in the United States. Former Reagan administration official Terry Eastland writes that it perpetuates "the very tendency the civil rights movement once condemned: that of regarding and judging people in terms of their racial and ethnic groups."[35] Instead of preferences for anybody, he suggests, we should insist on laws and practices that are blind to a person's color or gender.

The Supreme Court has often seemed as divided and uncertain about affirmative action as the rest of American society. The first and most famous affirmative action case to reach the Court, *Regents of the University of California* v. *Bakke* (1978), had an inconclusive outcome. The University of California Medical School at Davis set aside 16 of the 100 slots in its entering class for members of racial minorities. Denied admission to the medical school although his grades and test scores were higher than those of the minority students admitted, Alan Bakke sued, claiming a violation of his civil rights. A split Court rejected the idea of a fixed quota of positions for minorities and ordered Bakke's admission to the medical school. Yet the Court also ruled that taking race into consideration as part of a school's admission process was legitimate as a way of enhancing diversity in the student body.

Subsequent decisions sometimes advanced and sometimes cut back affirmative action for African Americans. Affirmative action for women was first considered by the Supreme Court in the 1987 case of *Johnson* v. *Santa Clara County*. Two employees of the Santa Clara County Transportation Agency, Diane Joyce and Paul Johnson, sought promotion to a better-paying craft position as a road dispatcher. Both passed an agency test, with Johnson achieving a slightly higher score. Since women held none of the agency's 238 craft positions, Johnson was passed over, and the promotion was given to Joyce on affirmative action grounds. The Court upheld the agency, establishing that voluntary affirmative action plans can operate to end the underrepresentation of women in job categories traditionally dominated by men.

Since the *Johnson* decision, affirmative action has been losing ground on the Supreme Court. In *Adarand Constructors* v. *Peña* (1995), a 5–4 majority ruled that government programs specifying preferential treatment based upon race are unconstitutional unless a pattern of prior discrimination against minorities can be demonstrated. Although the case involved a "set-aside" of 10 percent of Department of Transportation contracts for firms owned by minority businesspeople, the decision cast a legal cloud over most affirmative action programs, announcing that racial classification by government agencies is "inherently suspect and presumptively invalid."[36]

Equal Rights for Women

The struggle for equal rights for women has taken a different course than the civil rights struggle of African Americans. During Reconstruction, drafters of the Fifteenth Amendment excluded women on the grounds that there was not enough political support to enfranchise both black males and all females, an argument that infuriated pioneer feminist leaders Elizabeth Cady Stanton and Susan B. Anthony. It took several generations of struggle by the women's movement before women won the vote in 1920 with the Nineteenth Amendment. Having attained a goal denied for so long, the women's movement faded in strength for almost half a century.

Energized by the civil rights and New Left movements, a second women's movement sprang up in the 1960s. Modeling its strategy after the NAACP's historic campaign that led to the *Brown* decision, legal advocates from the new women's movement began to press test cases on women's rights on the Supreme Court in the early 1970s. They won some important victories. Yet there was no women's rights equivalent to *Brown*, no landmark case that established full-fledged equality for women. (The most important victory for women in the Supreme Court—*Roe* v. *Wade*—was decided on the grounds of a right of privacy rather than equal rights for women.)

The first women's rights cases were the easiest. In *Reed* v. *Reed* (1971), argued before the Court by future justice Ruth Bader Ginsburg, the unanimous justices struck down an Idaho law favoring men over women as executors of estates. In *Frontiero* v. *Richardson* (1973), all but one justice voted to strike down a federal statute on military pay that discriminated against women. Blatant instances of discrimination against women, the Court was now saying, violated their right to equal protection.

But what test should the Court apply in cases of less blatant gender discrimination? Recall our earlier discussion of the double standard: Most legislation is subject only to ordinary scrutiny, with government merely needing to present a reasonable basis for it, but legislation that infringes upon civil liberties and rights is subject to strict scrutiny, with the Court voiding it unless the government can prove a compelling interest. Women's rights advocates hoped that the Court would apply the same strict scrutiny in cases of discrimination against women that it used in cases of discrimination against racial minorities. But advocates were pressing this argument before the Burger Court, not the Warren Court.

In *Craig* v. *Boren* (1976), the women's movement fell short of its objective. At issue was an Oklahoma law that allowed women to buy beer at age eighteen but required men to wait until age twenty-one. The Court struck down the law as a violation of equal protection. But Justice Brennan could not get a majority of the Court to base this holding on strict scrutiny toward gender classifications. The best he could obtain was the creation of a new, intermediate category: *heightened scrutiny*. A statute that classified by gender would pass muster with the Court, according to this new form of scrutiny, only if it aimed at an important government objective and substantially furthered that objective. Women's rights now had more constitutional protection than before but less than the protection enjoyed by racial minorities.

Because the women's movement has shifted its resources to defend the *Roe* decision and abortion rights, fewer sex discrimination cases are now pressed on the Supreme Court. The Rehnquist Court has unanimously struck down a "fetal protection policy" through which a business excludes women from certain jobs on the grounds of hazards to pregnancy. And by a 7–1 vote it has ordered the all-male Virginia Military Institute, financed by the state, to admit women. But the conservative majority is not inclined to expand the scope of civil rights for women. Nevertheless, for the first time in history two women sit on the Supreme Court. It will take the combined efforts of an effective women's movement and supporters of women's rights on the Court itself for further gains to be made on behalf of equality for women.

CONCLUSION: THE STRUGGLE OVER LIBERTIES AND RIGHTS

Americans can legitimately take pride in the civil liberties and civil rights they enjoy today. Yet these liberties and rights are the result of long struggles and only recent landmark advances: free speech (1960s), rights of persons accused of crimes (1960s), right of privacy (1960s and 1970s), equal rights for blacks (1950s), and equal rights for women (1970s). The newness of the critical Supreme Court precedents and the political backlash that has trimmed back several and tried to overturn others indicate that the struggle over the definition of American liberties and rights is far from ended.

Both elite democrats and popular democrats have a checkered past in the area of civil liberties and civil rights. Elite democrats in positions of power, while mouthing rhetorical support for American liberties, have moved to limit them in times of crisis and challenge. Popular democrats have often backed and applauded the repressive measures that elites have instituted. Yet some elite democrats and some popular democrats have done better. Judicial champions of civil liberties and civil rights have understood how fundamental these freedoms and powers are to the creation and maintenance of a democratic society. Popular democratic forces (Anti-federalists, abolitionists, New Deal populists, blacks, and feminists) have fought to establish civil liberties and civil rights in the first place as well as to bring before the courts the cases that will broaden their definition and scope.

Given that a majority of ordinary Americans may not support civil liberties and civil rights when they protect unpopular individuals or groups, individuals committed to the values of popular democracy must recognize the responsibilities of democratic education. In the spirit of the tradition initiated by the Anti-federalists, they must remind others of the importance of an open and tolerant society, where new and unconventional ideas can circulate freely, where reigning elites can be challenged, where that spark of protest that launched the American revolutionary experiment can enlighten and revitalize American democracy. And with an emphasis on the importance of citizenship, popular democrats cannot rest content merely with the defense of American liberties and rights. They also must encourage other citizens to make active use of them.

KEY TERMS

civil liberties
civil rights
American Civil Liberties Union (ACLU)
Civil War amendments
footnote 4
strict scrutiny
incorporation
clear and present danger test
McCarthyism
symbolic speech
unprotected speech
obscenity
prior restraint

Establishment Clause
Lemon test
Free Exercise Clause
exclusionary rule
Miranda warnings
right of privacy
Roe v. *Wade*
separate but equal
National Association for the Advancement of Colored People (NAACP)
Brown v. *Board of Education of Topeka*
Civil Rights Act of 1964
Voting Rights Act of 1965
affirmative action

SUGGESTED READINGS

Paul Berman, ed., *Debating P.C.: The Controversy Over Political Correctness on College Campuses*. New York: Dell, 1992. This anthology presents conflicting essays in the debate over speech codes on college campuses.

James MacGregor Burns and Stewart Burns, *A People's Charter: The Pursuit of Rights in America*. New York: Vintage Books, 1993. A vivid chronicle of the struggles that have attempted to turn the words of the Bill of Rights into realities.

Barbara Hinkson Craig and David M. O'Brien, *Abortion and American Politics*. Chatham, N.J.: Chatham House, 1993.

A thorough account of the political and legal battles over abortion that *Roe v. Wade* initiated.

Peter Irons, *The Courage of Their Convictions: Sixteen Americans Who Fought Their Way to the Supreme Court*. New York: Penguin Books, 1990. Portraits of ordinary Americans who tested the meaning of civil liberties and civil rights.

Nicolaus Mills, ed., *Debating Affirmative Action: Race, Gender, Ethnicity, and the Politics of Inclusion*. New York: Dell, 1994. Lively essays present both sides in the debate over affirmative action.

CHAPTER 17

Economic and Social Policy: The Democratic Connections

POLICY DEBATES: THE DEMOCRATIC DIMENSION

THE RISE AND FALL OF THE KEYNESIAN CONSENSUS

REAGANOMICS: THE SUPPLY-SIDE EXPERIMENT

THE POLITICS OF THE DEFICIT
How Important Is It to Balance the Budget?

THE DEMOCRATIC DEBATE OVER THE MONEY SUPPLY
The Experiment with Monetarism
Monetarism: Winners and Losers
The Issue of Fed Reform

THE DEMOCRATIC DEBATE ON WELFARE
Challenging the Stereotypes
Ending Welfare as We Know It
America's Two-Tiered Welfare State
Growing Entitlements
Tax Expenditures: Welfare for the Middle and Upper Classes
The Political Backlash Against Welfare

CONCLUSION: DEMOCRATIC CONNECTIONS

We often think of economics and politics as separate. "Free markets" supposedly operate independently of government. In fact, as we saw in Chapter 4, economics and politics are so closely intertwined that it is impossible to speak of a free market apart from government. The same could be said of economic and social policies. They are implemented by separate government agencies and have different goals: Economic policies are designed to increase economic efficiency and growth, whereas social policies are intended to help those who cannot make it on their own in the private sector. Clearly, however, the two are closely connected: Failed economic policies increase the need for social welfare spending, and poorly designed social policies harm the efficiency of markets (as when welfare policies discourage recipients from entering the labor market).

462

The connections between economic and social policy have been raised with special force in the recent effort to require that welfare recipients get a job—a policy that we will explore in depth in this chapter.

This chapter examines economic policy through the lens of popular democracy. A central theme of the chapter is that economic and social policies have widespread political effects. These effects cannot be toted up as costs and benefits in some kind of policy equation. Ultimately, our evaluation of policies is based on our values. It is for this reason, we believe, that economic and social policy making should not be left to the so-called experts but should involve all those affected by such policies. The values we bring to our policy analyses in this chapter are the values of popular democracy. As we go through different domestic policy debates in this chapter, we constantly ask the question: What will be the effects of different policies on the quality of our democracy, and in particular will they enhance democratic participation and inclusiveness?

POLICY DEBATES: THE DEMOCRATIC DIMENSION

Many Americans think that markets, if not distorted by government intervention, are the most efficient allocators of goods and services. Consumers drive the marketplace by their changing preferences, and corporations must meet the needs of consumers in the most efficient manner possible or be driven out of business by competitors. The policy implications of this belief are clear: Economic policy makers should strive to interfere with market dynamics as little as possible; policy makers should not be telling consumers what they want or corporations what or how they should produce.

Free market economics is the foundation of the elite democratic approach to economic policy. According to this view, economic policy should be left in the hands of experts, with only broad guidelines coming from ordinary citizens and their political representatives. Economic experts are viewed as those with business experience and especially those with training in economics. Economics claims to be, like physics, a value-free and objective science. Consistent with the elite democratic view of human nature, it views modern economies as driven by the private interests of consumers and producers whose behavior can be predicted with precision. But, motivated by material self-interests, most economic actors are not well suited to guide economic policy making. Like Plato's guardians who rise above private interests through training in philosophy, economists are able, through disciplined study of the laws of economics, to transcend private interests and see what is necessary to make the economy as a whole function effectively. Economically trained policy makers can be compared to expert watchmakers who, having studied how all the various gears in the market mechanism are interrelated, understand what needs to be done to ensure that it runs smoothly. Expert economic policies do not make political choices that determine winners and losers; instead, they simply set the general conditions that enable people and businesses to compete fairly in the marketplace.

Elite democrats view social policies very differently from economic policies. With social policies there is more room for democratic decision making because our values for compassion and equality will vary. Most Americans believe government should help those who cannot help themselves. However, if free market economists are right and economic progress is driven by private interests, then there is an unavoidable tradeoff between equality and efficiency. Too much equality lowers the incentive to work and invest, thereby damaging efficiency. Responding to mass pressure, politicians will be tempted to massively redistribute wealth, thus killing the engine of investment, or to spend money on popular programs without raising taxes, resulting in ruinous inflation. Thus, elite democrats conclude, popular control over social, and especially economic, policies should be limited.

Popular democrats view economic policy very differently, and this difference is rooted in how they view markets. They reject the free market view that economic progress is driven solely by self interest. Instead of viewing the economy as a mechanism, popular democrats view it more as a plant with its roots deeply embedded in social and political relations. The mechanistic treatment of the economy, they say, ignores the human factor. Economies are not giant machines that can be managed by supposedly nonpolitical experts. Economic policies have social and political implications: They determine which investments are profitable and which are not, and they affect the life chances of different groups in the population, the viability of whole communities, and, most important, the prospects for democratic participation and community control.

The popular democratic view implies that power over economic policy should be taken away from so-called experts and given to ordinary citizens and their political representatives. The tradeoffs of economic policy should be debated in an open, democratic fashion—not hidden behind the veil of economic "science." Popular democrats do not believe that expanding democracy into economic policy making will lead to incoherent policies, causing problems for the economy. They do believe that people are capable of overcoming their parochial interests through democratic participation. On the contrary, they say, it is the isolation of economic policy in the hands of selfish elites, who are removed from the pain caused by their policies, that results in destructive economic policies. More democratic economic policy making would be better economic policy making.

Popular democrats also view social policy very differently from elite democrats. Whereas elite democrats blame most poverty on the poor themselves, popular democrats tend to blame poverty on conditions in the environment. Popular democrats assume that given the proper circumstances, everyone wants to work and contribute to society. If some people are excluded from their fair share in the economy, it must be because of structural defects in the economic system. Popular democrats deny that there is a steep and unavoidable tradeoff between equality and growth. In fact, too much inequality can hurt growth by demoralizing those at the bottom and undermining the belief that anybody can get ahead through hard work. Too much inequality also causes social problems that ultimately all of us must pay for.

According to popular democrats, the goal of social policies should not just be to provide a minimum standard of living but to provide everyone with the resources necessary to become full and equal participants in society. People who are worried about where their next meal will come from are hardly in a position to become active democratic citizens. Poverty is a problem in a democracy not just because some people lack resources, but because the gap between the rich and the poor widens to the point that it undermines political equality. Too much inequality threatens democracy because it gives the rich the resources to dominate and demoralize the poor, distorting democracy.

In short, popular democrats aim to subject economic and social policies to democratic standards. The goal should not be just greater GNP per capita or even the alleviation of poverty, but a more inclusive democracy in which no group feels excluded or dominated.

THE RISE AND FALL OF THE KEYNESIAN CONSENSUS

Governments are responsible for establishing the basic conditions for smooth-functioning markets; the decisions that establish these conditions are called **macroeconomic policy.** These policies are designed to fine-tune the national economy as a whole but not to alter the distribution of economic activity across different sectors, classes, or places. Macroeconomic policies are designed to moderate the booms and busts of capitalism, making sure that the economy does not grow too fast (causing high inflation) or too slow (causing high unemployment). There are two basic kinds of macroeconomic policies: **Fiscal policy** uses the government's taxing and spending policies to speed up or slow down the economy; **monetary policy** uses government's control over the money supply (the amount of money in circulation) to achieve the same results.

Historically, capitalist economies have always been subject to booms and busts. English economist John Maynard Keynes (1883–1946) promoted the idea of using fiscal policy—having the government deliberately engineer a deficit—spending more than it received in tax revenues—to pull the economy out of a depression. His classic work, *The General Theory of Employment, Interest, and Money* (1936), argued that capitalist economies do *not* have a natural tendency to employ all the nation's workers and achieve full productive capacity because consumers cannot buy all the products that a fully operating economy would produce. At a certain stage of the business cycle, Keynes argued, the savings rate is too high, leaving too little money for consumption. Keynes's solution was for the government to use fiscal policy, its control over taxing and spending, to make the economy perform at maximum capacity. When the economy begins to fall into a recession, the government stimulates consumer demand by spending *more* than it takes in through taxes. Deficit spending heats up the economy, putting people and productive capacity back to work. When demand is too high and an over-heated economy begins to cause inflation, the government deliberately spends *less* than it takes in, cooling off the economy. (Keynes did not endorse, as some have attributed to him, a string of budget deficits, even in prosperous times, such as the United States has had for many years.)

Keynesianism dominated economic policy making in the major industrial countries after World War II. Although Keynes's theory encouraged governments to take an active role in smoothing out the business cycle, it did not require any direct interventions in markets. Keynes called for manipulating the overall level of consumer demand, but he said nothing about how that consumer demand should be distributed. Thus, Keynesianism was a theory that could be embraced at various times by both the left and the right. European governments used Keynes's ideas to justify redistributing wealth through progressive taxes and welfare spending, a scheme based partly on the notion that giving more resources to those at the bottom would result in immediate increases in consumer demand because poor people save little.

In the United States, Keynesianism was applied in a less egalitarian manner to justify what has been called "military Keynesianism" and "business Keynesianism." Deficits were created by boosting military spending and by cutting taxes on business. The Kennedy tax cuts for investors, passed in 1964, were sold to the public, Congress, and the business community on explicitly Keynesian grounds. With the economy doing well in the 1960s, there was a broad consensus behind Keynesianism and an optimistic feeling that fiscal policy could be used to fine-tune the economy to prevent disastrous economic downturns. In a 1971 *Newsweek* cover story, President Nixon proclaimed, "We are all Keynesians now."

REAGANOMICS: THE SUPPLY-SIDE EXPERIMENT

With the economic troubles of the 1970s, the Keynesian consensus began to crumble. The problems of the U.S. economy did not appear to be the result of too much saving. Indeed, the savings rate was tumbling, and the soaring trade deficit seemed to be caused in part by inadequate savings and investment in the latest production technologies. For the first time, increases in the productivity of American workers lagged behind those of other countries. The problem seemed to lie not in underconsumption but in underinvestment.

Many economists began to move from a demand-side explanation of these economic troubles to a supply-side analysis. *Supply-side economics* argued that the cause of the economic problems was a capital shortage—that we needed to reduce consumption and put more of our resources into productive investment. Supply siders especially stressed that we were consuming too much in the way of government services and that a bloated public sector was serving as a drag on economic growth. High levels of taxation reduced the incentive to work harder and to invest, and government regulations on the economy stifled private initiative.

Paradoxically, supply siders stressed that the best way to reduce the federal deficit was to *reduce* taxes, not increase them. This idea was based on the **Laffer curve,** which economist Arthur B. Laffer first drew in 1974 on a cocktail napkin

FIGURE 17.1

Laffer Curve

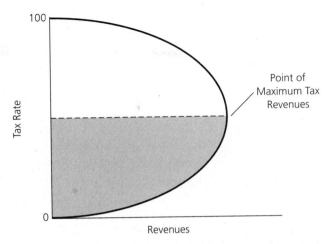

As the tax rate increases, tax revenues eventually fall because of the disincentive effects of high taxes.

in a Washington restaurant (see Figure 17.1). Laffer argued that above a certain point, increasing tax rates actually decreased total tax revenues because of the disincentive effects on productive effort. Tax rates were so high in the United States, Laffer argued, that by decreasing tax rates the country could move down the Laffer curve, unleashing an explosion of productive effort that would increase tax revenues. Laffer's ideas were popularized by Jude Wanniski, an editorial writer for the *Wall Street Journal*. Wanniski later remarked that after seeing the Laffer curve on the cocktail napkin, "it hit me as a wonderful propaganda device" for persuading policy makers to cut tax rates.[1]

As candidate for president in 1980, Ronald Reagan enthusiastically embraced the tenets of supply-side economics. To illustrate the disincentive effects of high taxes, Reagan was fond of telling the story that when the marginal income tax rate hit 94 percent during World War II, he stopped making movies. Four weeks after his inauguration, Reagan presented Congress with a "Program for Economic Recovery," which contained four key elements:

1. Cutting the growth of federal spending.

2. Reducing personal income rates by 30 percent over three years and cutting the tax rate on capital investments in plant and equipment.

3. Slashing government regulation of the economy.

4. In cooperation with the Federal Reserve, limiting the growth of the money supply to control inflation and restore faith in the financial markets.[2]

Inspired by supply-side economics, Reagan succeeded in enacting massive tax cuts in his **Economic Recovery Tax Act of 1981.** Individual tax rates were cut 23 percent over a three-year period, the marginal tax rate on the highest income group was cut from 70 percent to 50 percent, and a series of tax breaks for investors was written into law.

Reagan also enacted significant budget cuts during his first year in office. Following a shrewd political strategy, he succeeded in persuading each house of Congress to vote on an overall package of cuts before voting on the individual cuts. Since surveys show that the public wants less total federal spending but more spending on specific programs, by first requiring a vote on a total budget ceiling Reagan succeeded in getting a favorable vote and postponing the tough choices of which programs to cut. After 1981, however, the Reagan administration was not nearly so successful at enacting its program, as the Democratic-controlled Congress and the administration bogged down in political trench warfare over taxes and spending.

How successful was Reaganomics? Its biggest success was in reducing the inflation rate, which tumbled from 13.5 percent in 1980 to 1.9 percent in 1986. Much of this effect is credited to the tight money policies of the Federal Reserve, which we examine later in the chapter.

But Reaganomics did not work as expected to decrease the federal budget deficit by reducing taxes. Shortly after taking office, Reagan promised that his economic policies would balance the budget by 1984, but lower tax revenues combined with significant increases in defense spending resulted in the largest budget deficits in history (see Figure 17.2). Ironically, the Reagan administration, which was officially opposed to Keynesianism, engaged in massive deficit spending that pulled the country out of the 1982 recession. When the economy heated up, however, the government did not generate budget surpluses, as Keynes had recommended, but continued massive deficit spending. Most economists believe that the United States was not so far out on the Laffer curve that reducing tax rates would increase total revenue. (Indeed, as we saw in Chapter 4, as a proportion of the overall economy, taxes in the United States are significantly lower than in almost every other advanced industrial country.) The massive deficits of the 1980s helped sustain the second longest period of continuous peacetime expansion since World War II. But this prosperity was bought at a high price: a huge cumulative deficit ($4 trillion by 1993) that future generations of taxpayers will be required to pay back.

There is little evidence that the supply-side tax cuts significantly increased work effort, the savings rate, or investment.[3] In fact, the savings rate *fell* from an average of about 7 percent of income in the 1970s to only 2 percent in the 1980s.[4] That change would not have been so harmful if the government had borrowed extensively to finance productive investments, such as education or infrastructure, but instead the money was used to pay for tax cuts and a military buildup.

Defenders of supply-side economics argue that it was never given a fair chance. If the budget cuts Reagan asked for had been enacted by Congress, they

| **FIGURE 17.2** | **Federal Budget Surpluses and Deficits, 1950–1997 (in Billions)** |

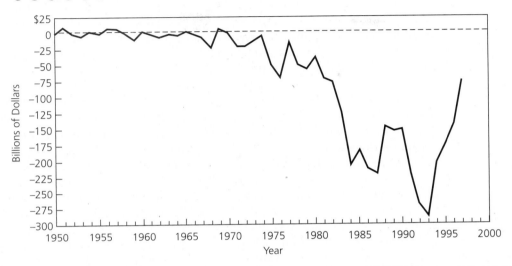

Source: *Economic Report of the President* (Transmitted to Congress February 1991) (Washington, D.C.: U.S. Government Printing Office, 1991); and U.S. Bureau of the Census, *Statistical Abstract of the United States 1996* (Washington, D.C.: U.S. Government Printing Office, 1996), p. 330.

argue, the deficit would have been much lower and productive investment higher. Certainly, Congress was partly to blame for the soaring budget deficits, but the amount of *discretionary spending* that Congress has the power to control is relatively small. About three-fourths of the budget is locked in by past commitments that politically and sometimes legally cannot be changed. Social Security payments, for example, are guaranteed by law. When Reagan cut taxes and increased the military budget, one of the few areas of discretionary spending, rising budget deficits were easy to predict.

Both Reagan's tax cuts and his spending cuts increased the gap between the rich and the poor. In the beginning, Director of the Budget David Stockman expressed the hope that "weak claims rather than weak clients" would be the targets of federal spending cuts. But middle class entitlements were protected, while most of the cuts fell on low-income groups, especially the working poor. Budget authority for low-income housing programs, for instance, fell from $30 billion in 1981 to $10 billion in 1986. Public service jobs for the poor were eliminated, and federal grants to central cities, community development, schools serving low-income students, and social services for the poor were cut. When eligibility standards for many social benefits were tightened, many working poor were excluded from government benefits. As we saw in Chapter 14, states and localities made up some, but by no means all, of these cuts.

THE POLITICS OF THE DEFICIT

When Reagan took office in 1981, the national debt was less than $1 trillion; after twelve years of the Reagan-Bush presidencies, it was $4 trillion. In the 1992 presidential election, Texas billionaire Ross Perot, pointing to graphs and charts in his infomercials, succeeded in getting the deficit on the political agenda. Bill Clinton ran in 1992, however, promising a middle class tax cut and an ambitious program to "put America back to work" that would cost the federal government an additional $50 billion per year.[5] Thwarted by a Senate filibuster, in his first few months in office Clinton was forced to scale back his economic stimulus package from $16 billion to $1 billion. Under the influence of conservatives in his administration, including Wall Street financier Robert Rubin, who became Clinton's Secretary of the Treasury, Clinton eventually sacrificed most of his domestic agenda in order to reduce the deficit.[6] Giving up his promised middle class tax cut, in 1993 Clinton enacted a tax hike on families earning $140,000 or more. Indeed, Clinton succeeded in reducing the annual deficit from a record $290 billion in 1992 to $203 billion in 1994.

In 1994, after Newt Gingrich and the Republicans took over the House of Representatives for the first time in forty years, the Republicans sought to pass the first item in their Contract with America: a Balanced Budget Amendment, which would amend the Constitution to require Congress to balance the budget each year. With public opinion firmly behind it, the Balanced Budget Amendment passed the House easily but failed by one vote in the Senate. Undaunted, in 1995 the Republicans shifted their strategy from amending the Constitution to focusing on the budget itself, calling for large cuts in domestic programs, including a plan to cut the growth of Medicare, government-funded health insurance for the elderly.

Republican efforts to reduce the deficit by cutting government spending on programs dear to liberals set in motion a complex chess game between Clinton and Gingrich. With the Republicans unable to pass a budget by start of the fiscal year on October 1, the government was forced to operate under continuing resolutions that basically extended the previous year's fiscal arrangements. The Republicans kept sending Clinton bills to keep the government running and to raise the debt ceiling, but these bills had attachments that Clinton objected to and he vetoed them. Meanwhile, Clinton began a national advertising campaign attacking the Republicans for cutting Medicare. Republicans objected that they were only slowing the *increase* in Medicare spending, but clearly the Clinton attacks began to hit home. Several times the government was forced to shut down.

The weakness of the Republican strategy was that they had no plan of action if Clinton called their bluff. Gingrich was convinced that Clinton, faced with the prospect of closing down the government, would cave in and sign the Republican budget. Sensing that the public would blame the Republicans for the government shutdown, Clinton refused. When people began complaining because they could not get passports or other basic government services, the pressure on the Republicans began to mount. They were forced to give in and pass a continuing resolution. The 1996 budget was not passed and signed by the president until April 1996, seven months late.

Having retained control of Congress in 1996, the Republicans continued to press for deficit reduction. Clinton agreed to the goal of achieving a balanced budget by 2002. In May 1997, Clinton and the Republicans finally agreed upon a plan, in principle, to balance the budget. Liberal Democrats complained that the plan balanced the budget on the "backs of the poor" while giving tax breaks to the rich, including cuts in capital gains and estate taxes. Clinton, however, could claim some victories, having won money for some of his favorite programs, including tax credits for college education and expanded health coverage for children. The deal was made easier by the fact that a booming economy had reduced the deficit for the 1997 fiscal year to an estimated $75 billion, or less.

How Important Is It to Balance the Budget?

Clearly, Americans want the federal government to balance its budget. In 1989, for example, by a 59–24 percent margin, Americans favored a balanced budget amendment.[7] However, many people argue that requiring a balanced budget would be dangerous.[8] One criticism is that if the government is forced to balance its budget each year, it will not be able to engage in deficit spending to pull the economy out of recessions.[9] Moreover, critics say, the burden of government debt should be measured not in dollars but by its size *relative* to the U.S. economy. From this point of view, the debt burden reached a peak at the end of World War II, fell until the late 1970s, increased rapidly in the 1980s, and has fallen again during the Clinton years.

Perhaps most important in judging the deficit is what the borrowed money is used for. The U.S. budget makes no distinction between operating expenses and capital expenses. It makes sense to borrow money for investments that will increase productivity (capital expenses), but it does not make sense to borrow money to pay for increased consumption (operating expenses). The problem with the huge increase in debt in the 1980s was that much of it went for a military buildup and increased consumption, not productive investments.

In fact, the debate over the deficit is as much a debate about distribution as it is a debate about economic rationality. The Republicans have successfully used public concern about the deficit to cut discretionary spending programs for the poor. Bill Clinton adopted deficit reduction not because he favored cutting programs for the poor but because he bought the logic of moderates in his administration that deficit reduction was necessary for the economy. However, deficit reduction, as Clinton has been forced to implement it, has basically benefitted the middle and upper classes. Deficits can overheat the economy, requiring the Federal Reserve Board (which sets the government's monetary policy) to raise interest rates to prevent runaway inflation. This reduces the profits of those who hold stocks and bonds. To please Wall Street, Clinton abandoned most of his domestic agenda that was designed to help displaced and undereducated workers. When questioned by one of his consultants about why he had changed allegiances from "putting people first" (the title of his book co-authored with Al Gore) to putting deficit reduction first, Clinton replied: "We can't do anything for people unless we reduce the deficit."[10] By putting the interests of Wall Street ahead of all other interests, Clinton essentially opted to ignore other deficits in education, housing, and the environment.

THE DEMOCRATIC DEBATE OVER THE MONEY SUPPLY

Throughout U.S. history, elite and popular democrats have debated the money supply. Elite democrats favor a *tight money policy*. With fewer dollars "chasing" a fixed or expanding supply of goods, prices remain stable or even fall. Falling prices—*deflation*—characterized most of the late nineteenth century.[11] Deflation is good for those who are owed money (bondholders and bank lenders) because they are paid back in more valuable dollars. Falling prices are not good for those who are in debt because they find it more and more difficult to pay back their debts. Farmers in the nineteenth century found themselves squeezed between falling prices for their crops and rising interest rates for the money they had to borrow to buy land and finance spring planting. Farmers agitated to increase the money supply by having the federal government issue "greenbacks" or use silver, in addition to gold, to back up the currency. To this day, the conflict between wealthy investors and the mass of debtors and business people needing credit remains at the heart of the democratic debate over the money supply.

The main institution responsible for regulating the money supply is the **Federal Reserve** system created in 1913. President Woodrow Wilson compromised with the bankers by creating a unique institution that combined the private powers of bankers with the public powers of government. In 1935, after criticism that contraction of the money supply had contributed to the Great Depression, the Federal Reserve—or "Fed," as it is called—expanded its mission and took full charge of controlling the nation's money supply.

The Federal Reserve is run by a seven-member board of governors appointed by the president for fourteen-year terms with the advice and consent of the Senate. The chair serves a four-year term. Because of the Fed chair's leadership position setting monetary policy, which is crucial to the performance of the economy, he has been called "the second most powerful man in the United States" (so far, all have been men.) To carry out its policies, the Fed relies on twelve regional banks, which are private institutions owned by the approximately 6,000 commercial banks that participate in the Federal Reserve system.

The most important policymaking body at the Fed is the *Federal Open Market Committee* (FOMC), which basically determines the nation's money supply and powerfully influences interest rates. The FOMC is made up of the seven members of the Board of Governors, appointed by the president, and the presidents of five regional banks, which are appointed by the commercial banks. The key decision-making body, then, is a mixture of private interests and public authority. As Representative Lee H. Hamilton, an Indiana Democrat, put the matter in 1991, "Nowhere else in the Government are private individuals permitted to participate in decisions which have such an enormous influence over the prosperity and well-being of millions of Americans."[12]

The basic mechanisms by which the Fed controls the money supply are quite simple: The American economy can be thought of as a gigantic plumbing system, with money circulating through the pipes at various rates and pressures. The Fed is the hydraulic engineer, who by turning various valves can either expand or contract the flow of money in the system. Three basic valves control the amount of money in circulation:

1. *The discount rate:* Banks that are members of the Federal Reserve system can borrow money from one of the twelve regional banks when they need additional reserves. The discount rate is the interest rate at which member banks can borrow. Lowering the discount rate makes it less expensive for banks to make new loans, thus increasing the money supply.

2. *Reserve requirements:* The Fed specifies what proportion of a bank's deposits must be held in reserve and cannot be loaned out. Increasing the reserve requirement restricts the ability of banks to make new loans, essentially reducing the money supply.

3. *Open market transactions:* The Fed can buy or sell U.S. government securities, which are Treasury bonds originally sold by the U.S. government to finance the budget deficit. When the Fed buys Treasury bonds, the money is simply credited to the accounts of the former owners of the bonds in one of the Federal Reserve banks. These funds are counted as additions to the reserves of the bank, which is now free to make more loans, increasing the money supply.

Under the Federal Reserve system, the money supply in the United States is firmly under the control of elites, with little democratic accountability. Proponents of this system argue that control over the money supply must be left in the hands of experts who understand how to protect the long-term interests of the American economy. If politicians controlled the money supply, elite democrats argue, they would be tempted to increase the money supply to stimulate the economy right before an election and benefit the mass of debtors. The result would be runaway *inflation*, rising prices. Fearing that their returns on investments would be eroded by inflation, people would pull their money out of productive investments and put it into consumption, foreign investments, or speculation in gold or other commodities. Lacking productive investment, economic growth would stagnate, hurting everybody.

Popular democrats reply that the interests of Wall Street are different from the interests of Main Street. The Fed's tight money policies help only a small financial elite. According to a study by the Federal Reserve itself, in 1983 the top 10 percent of American families owned 86 percent of the net financial assets. The majority of American families (55 percent) held no financial assets at all; overall, most Americans were debtors.[13] Tight money, popular democrats argue, acts like a regressive tax, shifting resources from debtors to creditors. The shortage of credit curbs business expansion, especially hurting small businesses and farmers who depend on credit to see them through tough times. Finally, tight money damages sectors of the economy, like home and auto sales, that are dependent on the easy availability of credit.

Popular democrats especially object to keeping unemployment high to fight inflation. Many economists argue that there is a *nonaccelerating inflation rate of unemployment* (NAIRU). If the unemployment rate falls below a certain level—say, 6 percent—tight labor markets will enable workers to demand higher wages, causing inflation. Critics like University of Texas economist James Galbraith argue that no one knows what the NAIRU is. NAIRU simply enables the Fed to shroud its political choices in technical mumbo jumbo.

The democratic debate over the money supply was played out with special intensity in the conflicts over a shift in Federal Reserve policy beginning in the late 1970s.

The Experiment with Monetarism

In 1979, President Jimmy Carter was considering appointing Paul Volcker as chairman of the Federal Reserve. A fifty-one-year-old graduate of Harvard and Princeton, Volcker was well known in Washington and on Wall Street as a man of disciplined intellect and personal frugality. Bert Lance, a Georgia banker and personal friend of the president, warned that Volcker, if appointed, would raise interest rates to fight inflation and the president would be "mortgaging his reelection to the Federal Reserve."[14] Ignoring Lance's warning, Carter appointed Volcker. The reason was clear: As Stuart Eizenstat, the president's domestic policy advisor, put it, "Volcker was selected because he was the candidate of Wall Street. This was their price, in effect."[15]

During Volcker's tenure, the Federal Reserve came under the influence of an economic doctrine called **monetarism.** Led by Nobel Prize–winning economist Milton Friedman, monetarists argued that if the money supply grows only as fast as the productivity of the economy, the result will be steady growth and stable prices. A staunch defender of free markets, Friedman argued that government should interfere as little as possible in the economy.[16] Following an economic philosophy of small government, monetarists portrayed themselves as a conservative alternative to Keynesians, who, they charged, pushed an economic philosophy of big government.

In the fall of 1979, under Volcker's leadership, the Fed officially adopted monetarism. This meant policy makers would look only at the money supply, attempting to achieve a moderate steady growth; interest rates would be allowed to fluctuate in response to the money supply targets. Using monetarist formulas, the Fed embarked on a series of swift policy shifts that sent the U.S. economy on a rollercoaster ride. The Fed began by severely restricting the growth of the money supply, driving interest rates up to record levels. The prime rate, the rate paid by the best commercial borrowers, peaked at 20 percent. The Fed lowered interest rates in the summer of 1980, but just before the 1980 election the Fed drove interest rates up again.

Campaigning for re-election that fall at a town meeting in Pennsylvania, Carter vented his frustration with the Fed:

> I don't have influence on it [the Fed], but that doesn't mean I have to sit mute. My own judgment is that the strictly monetary approach to the Fed's decision on the Discount rate and other banking policies is ill-advised. I think the Federal Reserve ought to look at other factors and balance them along with the supply of money.[17]

Despite this "Fed bashing," high interest rates were a major factor in Carter's defeat.

Although the Fed abandoned monetarism a few years later, it continued its tight money policies through the 1980s, with devastating consequences for many Americans. The Fed's policies did succeed in licking inflation: The increase in the *Consumer Price Index* (what consumers pay for goods and services) fell from 13.5 percent in 1980 to 1.9 percent in 1986 and remained low into the late 1990s. This victory was acquired at great cost, however; in the early 1980s the country suffered the worst recession since the Great Depression, with unemployment reaching 9.7 percent in 1982. Even though monetarists claimed that the costs of Fed policies were fairly distributed by free markets, in fact the costs fell unequally on the American people.

Federal Reserve policies had a devastating effect on American industry. As foreign investors flocked to take advantage of the high interest rates in the United States, the value of the American dollar rose to new highs compared to foreign currencies. As a result, U.S. manufactured products became more expensive for foreigners (it took more German marks or Japanese yen to buy one dollar's worth of goods), and foreign goods became cheaper in the United States. During a four-year period in the 1980s, U.S. exports declined by 16 percent while imports surged by 66 percent.[18] The result was soaring trade deficits.

Most big businesses could generate funds internally from profits, but small businesses were much more vulnerable to high interest rates and the limited availability of credit. Bankruptcies soared. Farmers had been encouraged to go into debt by the high inflation rates before 1980. When a delegation of state legislators from thirteen distressed farm states visited Volcker in Washington, D.C., to plead for relief from high interest rates and price deflation, the Fed chair gave them a chilly response. "Look," Volcker said, "your constituents are unhappy, mine aren't."[19]

If Volcker's constituents were financial investors, they had every reason to be happy. According to investment banking firm Shearson Lehman, returns on bonds from 1981–1984 averaged 18.5 percent, the most profitable era for bondholders in the twentieth century.[20] Income from capital (interest and dividends) increased dramatically compared to income from working (wages and salaries). In five short years, returns on capital nearly doubled as a proportion of total income, from 11 percent in 1979 to 20 percent in 1984.[21] Inequality soared.

A CLOSER LOOK

Alan Greenspan: Elite Democrat in Action

On December 5, 1996, the chairman of the Federal Reserve Board, Alan Greenspan, gave a speech in Washington referring to the recent upsurge in stock prices as an instance of "irrational exuberance." Based on fears that this phase signaled the Fed's intention to raise interest rates in order to slow down the economy, stock markets around the world were sent reeling. This incident demonstrates the incredible power of the Fed chair, as well as the problem with putting so much power into one person's hands.

The son of a New York stock broker, Greenspan was endowed with precocious mathematical abilities; at the age of five, he could reproduce the batting averages of major league ballplayers. After attending graduate school in economics, Greenspan helped found a prosperous economic consulting firm, finally earning his Ph.D. in 1977. He entered government in 1974 when President Nixon nominated him chair of the Council of Economic Advisers, a post he assumed the day Nixon left office and continued in under President Ford. In 1987, President Reagan appointed him chair of the Federal Reserve Board.

Greenspan has been a politically shrewd and powerful Fed chair. A close friend and protege of Ayn Rand, the libertarian philosopher and novelist, Greenspan is deeply conservative and hostile to government. In public, however, he rarely discusses his political ideology. Instead, using the classical legitimating device of modern elite democrats, Greenspan stresses his expertise and knowledge of obscure economic statistics that supposedly enable him to predict the economic future. In testimony before Congress, Greenspan drones on about economic statistics in what one journalist called "soporific syntax," leaving committee members drowsy, befuddled, or both.

Greenspan has been frequently attacked for being more concerned about fighting inflation, which is good for banks and stockholders, than about increasing jobs and wages, which is good for ordinary workers. Many argue that Greenspan's slow-growth policies contributed to the defeats of President Ford in 1976 and Bush in 1992.

Ironically, Republican Greenspan has become especially influential under a Democratic president. A month after Clinton's 1992 victory, Greenspan met

The Issue of Fed Reform

The democratic debate about the money supply continued under Volcker's successor, Alan Greenspan, appointed by President Reagan in 1987. As the nation's premier inflation fighter, Greenspan is popular on Wall Street, but he has come under increasing attack for sacrificing job growth to fight inflation. In 1994, Greenspan and the Fed raised interest rates several times even though there were few indicators of inflationary pressure. Critics, who range from investment bankers to left-wing academics, argue that global competition makes it more difficult to raise prices, and the fear of layoffs has broken workers' expectation

with the president-elect in Little Rock, Arkansas. Taking advantage of Clinton's well-known policy "wonkism," Greenspan spent two and a half hours deploying his incredible knowledge of economic statistics to persuade Clinton that the first priority of his administration should be deficit reduction. Only this way could long-term interest rates be brought down, Greenspan argued, boosting investment and growth. To the disappointment of liberals in his administration like Robert Reich, Clinton gave up his campaign promise for massive new public investments in areas like job training and infrastructure in favor of a deficit reduction package that included spending cuts and tax increases.

A month after he assumed office, Clinton announced the plan in a speech before a joint session of Congress. Seated in the audience, right between Hillary Clinton and Tipper Gore, the vice president's wife, was Greenspan. The media widely reported this fact as a symbol that Greenspan, and Wall Street, approved of Clinton's plan. Subsequently, Greenspan testified in Congress in favor of Clinton's deficit reduction package, which ultimately passed the Senate by one vote. No one was surprised when Clinton reappointed Greenspan to a third term in 1996.

Greenspan's career is a classic study of how elite democrats use claims to expertise to insulate deci-

sion making from democratic input. Congress has tried numerous times to give elected officials more control over the Fed or simply require that it release a transcript of its discussions. Each time, Greenspan has successfully argued that doing this would "politicize" the Fed.

Clearly, expertise must play an important role in regulating the money supply. But Greenspan's implication that his decisions are based on nothing but the facts hides the basic fact that they involve unavoidable tradeoffs between inflation and unemployment that have no technical solution. Greenspan has presided over one of the longest sustained economic expansions in American history, but it has also been an expansion characterized by ever widening gaps between the rich and the poor.

Sources: Bob Woodward, *The Agenda: Inside the Clinton White House* (New York: Simon & Schuster, 1994); Keith Bradsher, "The Art and Science of Alan Greenspan," *New York Times*, January 4, 1996.

that they should enjoy annual pay raises.[22] Therefore, it is possible for unemployment to fall much lower, even lower than it was in 1997, before we need to be worried about inflation. Greenspan, thus, is relegating hundreds of thousands of workers to the ranks of the unemployed in order to fight the inflation bogeyman. (See the accompanying box for more about Alan Greenspan.)

The controversy over interest rates has prompted calls for reform of the Fed, which is hardly a democratic institution. First, five of the twelve voting members of the FOMC, which sets monetary policy, represent private banks and have no democratic accountability. Moreover, FOMC's deliberations are secret; only

summaries of the meetings are released six weeks later. The independence and power of the Fed depend, in part, on effective political leadership by the chair of the Board of Governors.[23] But Congress and the president have always hesitated to put greater controls on the Fed for fear they will be accused of undermining the confidence of financial markets.

In 1993, Representative Henry B. Gonzalez (D.–Texas) held hearings to democratize the Fed. He proposed a bill that would have required the president to appoint the twelve regional bank presidents, forced more timely and detailed records of the meetings, and expanded opportunities for women, minorities, and nonbankers to serve as regional bank directors. Having the president appoint the regional presidents would end the practice of having representatives of the private banks make public policy. Studies have shown that the private bankers on the FOMC vote for tighter money more than do the presidential appointees.[24]

Not surprisingly, Greenspan vehemently opposed the reforms, arguing that they would subject the Fed to undue political pressure. With interest rates in 1993 at thirty-year lows, President Clinton had little reason to oppose the Fed and came out against Gonzalez's reforms, which died in committee. In 1997, Congressman Dick Gephardt (D.–Mo.) joined sixty-three other members of Congress in signing a letter urging the Fed not to raise interest rates, saying that the need for job growth was especially acute at the time because thousands of people would soon be forced off of welfare and into the job market.[25]

THE DEMOCRATIC DEBATE ON WELFARE

Economic policies affect the need for social, or welfare, policies, a topic to which we now turn. The system that came to be known as welfare was established in the midst of the Depression under the 1935 Social Security Act. Designed primarily to help children in families without a male breadwinner—so-called dependent children—the program became known as Aid to Families with Dependent Children (AFDC), but it is commonly referred to (often pejoratively) as welfare. The program set up a system of matching grants to the states to help families which could not support themselves. AFDC was a **means-tested benefit,** which meant that in order to obtain benefits a person had to prove that he or she lacked adequate means of support. But it was also an **entitlement,** which meant that any family in the nation meeting the federal means test was entitled to help; states could not deny an eligible person benefits. In the 1960s, welfare was supplemented with other means-tested benefits, including food stamps and Medicaid (government health insurance for the poor).

From the 1980s on, welfare has come under increasing attack from both Republicans and Democrats. In the 1992 presidential race Bill Clinton put out an ad attacking welfare that stated: "For so long, Government has failed us, and one of its worst failures has been welfare. I have a plan to end welfare as we know it."[26] Once he was in office, however, welfare reform took a back seat to Clinton's health care reform package, and the Democratic-controlled Congress failed to pass welfare reform prior to the 1994 congressional elections. The Republicans who took over Congress that year proceeded to pass welfare reform that was more radical than anything Clinton had proposed. Twice Clinton vetoed welfare bills because he objected to certain provisions.

As the 1996 election approached, Clinton saw the need to fulfill his 1992 promise and take an issue away from the Republicans. In August 1996 Clinton signed the **Personal Responsibility Act,** ending the federal government's sixty-one-year-old entitlement to aid for the poor. The new law replaced welfare with a system of flexible block grants to the states that requires them to place 50 percent of welfare recipients into private sector jobs by 2002. Welfare reform represents one of the biggest social experiments in American history. Riding on welfare reform is not just the economic prospects of the poor but their social and political prospects as well.

Challenging the Stereotypes

Over the years, three stereotypes have formed about welfare, that, for the most part, do not stand up to the facts. The prevailing stereotype of welfare is that *generous welfare benefits: (1) undermine the incentive to work, (2) encourage women to have babies out of wedlock, (3) create a permanent dependent class*. It is important to examine welfare stereotypes critically because they affect not only our evaluation of the old welfare system but also of the new system of state block grants.

Critics of welfare argue not only that welfare does not solve the problem of poverty but also that welfare actually *caused* poverty. Charles Murray's influential 1984 book *Losing Ground* contended that high welfare benefits made it more attractive for women to collect welfare and have babies out of wedlock than to work.[27] As Milton and Rose Friedman put the matter, "Those on welfare have little incentive to earn income."[28]

In fact, welfare benefits were never very generous. For one thing, they varied tremendously among the states. Even though popular democratic pressure in the 1930s goaded the president and Congress into action, southern elites in Congress shaped how the political system responded to those pressures, exacting concessions that later crippled public assistance. Most important, although the legislation called for the federal government to pay for part of the cost of public assistance through matching grants, program benefits were determined by the states (within broad guidelines set by the federal government). This was a concession to southern representatives, who did not want the South's economic system, based on cheap, largely black labor, disrupted by high welfare payments. Powerful southern representatives on the House Ways and Means Committee, for example, were able to eliminate the "decency and health" requirements of the original law, giving states more leeway in setting benefit levels.[29] As a result, in 1994 average monthly AFDC payments to families varied from $123 in Mississippi to $740 in Alaska.[30] Benefits levels were held down by states' fears that if they set benefit levels too high they would become "welfare magnets."[31]

Overall, welfare benefit levels were not generous. The official poverty line in the United States in 1994 was $7,547 for a single individual and $15,141 for a family of four.[32] Anyone who has tried to live on such low incomes, especially in areas with high housing costs, knows how difficult it is to make ends meet. Public assistance payments did not even raise incomes up to the poverty line. Even when noncash benefits, such as food stamps and Medicaid, were included, most families on welfare were still below the poverty line. And the situation has gotten worse in recent decades. Between 1972 and 1991, average benefit levels for public assistance and food stamps fell 27 percent in inflation-adjusted dollars.[33] No other group in American society suffered such a painful drop in income. Notwithstanding media stereotypes of "welfare queens," welfare recipients did not live in the lap of luxury. Moreover, because the process of applying for welfare was so demeaning, many poor people did not even apply. In 1991, only 43.6 percent of the poor received any cash assistance; 27 percent received no assistance at all, including food stamps, Medicaid, or housing subsidies.[34]

Researchers estimate that the effect of welfare on workforce participation rates is small. One detailed study of 214 welfare mothers found that all but one had unreported income needed to make ends meet, and most of them worked at under-the-table jobs.[35] Another study found that if all public assistance programs for people under the age of sixty-five were completely eliminated, the number of hours worked by Americans would rise only about 1 percent.[36] Finally, nearly all of the women who received welfare already worked taking care of children.

The second stereotype is that *generous welfare benefits encouraged women to have babies outside of marriage and led to family dissolution.* The argument here is that welfare encouraged families to break up because a woman usually lost her welfare benefits if she lived with a man. Although welfare does make it easier for women to establish independent households, the correlation between welfare and single-parent families is weak.[37] The number of out-of-wedlock births increased in the 1970s and 1980s even as welfare benefits fell. States with lower benefit levels did not have lower rates of out-of-wedlock births. The incentive for having another baby on welfare was, and still is, low; the per capita welfare grant falls with more children. In fact, between 1972 and 1992, the number of children in the average welfare family fell from three to two.[38]

Welfare is only a small part of the problem of out-of-wedlock births. Such births, divorce, and female-headed households have increased rapidly among middle class whites as well, suggesting that there are broader cultural and economic forces behind these phenomena. Among the inner city poor, a much more important cause of family dissolution, according to sociologist William Julius Wilson, is the inability of men to find jobs that can support a family.[39]

The third stereotype is that *welfare creates a permanent dependent class*. According to this argument, people became hooked on welfare, like a drug, staying on the dole for a long time and even raising the next generation to become welfare dependents. The research shows that two-thirds of recipients left welfare within three years or less.[40] There is, however, a minority of welfare recipients who stayed on public assistance for a long time, absorbing a disproportionate share of the resources and thereby lending some truth to this stereotype.

In short, the research on welfare does not support the stereotype that welfare is a major cause of poverty and poverty-related behaviors. In fact, the major cause of poverty is shortage of good paying jobs, not just for women but for men, so that they can support a family.

Having said all this, it is clear that the incentives of welfare all worked in the wrong direction and that welfare did not help recipients to achieve self-sufficiency. Therefore, welfare, rightly so, was not perceived as an effective program. Perhaps most damning, it was not even popular among welfare recipients themselves. Listen to the description of a former welfare mother: "Unlike Social Security, AFDC is distributed on a case-by-case basis, with enough strings to hang an elephant. It is meanly administered, hard to qualify for, hard to keep; it provides niggardly benefits and is tough to stomach with all its invasive attempts at behavior modification."[41] With the program disliked even by its supposed beneficiaries, it is not surprising that welfare came under political attack.

Ending Welfare as We Know It

During the 1960s, welfare expenditures grew rapidly, partly because of a militant welfare rights movement that encouraged people to apply for welfare.[42] As expenditures on welfare soared, taxes increased, and industrial jobs declined, a welfare backlash developed, especially among working class white ethnics. A book on the flight of Jews and Italians of Brooklyn from the Democratic to the Republican party quotes an enraged city worker: "These welfare people get as much as I do and I work my ass off and come home dead tired. They get up late and they can shack up all day long and watch the tube. With their welfare and food stamps, they come out better than me. . . . Let them tighten their belts like we have to."[43]

In the late 1960s, politicians began to exploit this resentment against welfare to mobilize votes. Former Alabama governor and segregationist George Wallace led the way in the 1968 presidential election, attracting a surprisingly large number of votes among northern white ethnics. Richard Nixon began to speak out for what he called the "silent majority" against government giveaways like welfare. Ronald Reagan built his political career partly by attacking welfare, saying that we could not solve problems by "throwing money" at them. In 1992, George Bush attacked welfare, promising to "make the able-bodied work," and Clinton promised to "end welfare as we know it."

Failing to pass his own welfare reform bill, Clinton was under tremendous pressure to deliver on his campaign promise. Welfare reform was highly popular with the voters. A national survey found that 81 percent of Americans agreed that the welfare system needed "fundamental reform," and 92 percent supported welfare reform that would "require all able-bodied people on welfare to work or learn a job or skill."[44] With the 1996 election approaching, Clinton signed the Republicans' Personal Responsibility Act even though he had reservations. The main provisions of this bill are summarized in Table 17.1. The basic idea is to give states the leeway to experiment with programs to get people off welfare and into jobs.

Experience with welfare reform is just beginning to accumulate in the states, and debates about its effectiveness are heating up. President Clinton trumpeted a nationwide 18 percent decline in welfare rolls from 1994 to 1996, but he admitted that about half of the drop was the result of an improved economy. In fact, the three states that pushed welfare recipients into jobs most vigorously—Wisconsin, Oregon, and Indiana—saw their welfare rolls decline more than 40 percent.[45] Those who succeed in finding a job often report enhanced pride and self-esteem. Marla Spencer, a thirty-seven-year-old mother of two in Milwaukee, after spending nineteen years on welfare landed a job folding sheets in a laundry for $5.25 per hour. "My whole family's happy," she said. "Now my son can tell his friends at school that his mother works."[46]

| **TABLE 17.1**

Main Provisions of the Personal Responsibility Act of 1996: Temporary Assistance for Needy Families (TANF) Replaces Aid for Families with Dependent Children (AFDC) | 1. Ends federal entitlement to welfare; eligibility now determined by the states.

2. Block grant to the states; cuts federal spending on welfare $55 billion over six years.

3. States must place 50 percent of welfare recipients in jobs by 2002 or lose funding. No person can be on welfare for more than five years in a lifetime or two years in any one stretch.

4. States must end payments to unmarried teenage mothers who do not live with their parents (or other supervised situation) and may refuse to give additional benefits to women who have children while on welfare.

5. Legal immigrants are not eligible for any means-tested federal benefits for five years after entering the country. |

For every success story, however, there are stories of deprivation and frustration. Soup kitchens and homeless shelters are reporting increased demand since the beginning of welfare reform. The most telling criticism of welfare reform, however, is that there is simply not an adequate supply of jobs capable of supporting a family. In fact, because of work-related expenses, women who take a job often end up worse off than when they were on welfare. Moreover, the influx of welfare recipients into the job market is driving unskilled wage rates even lower—by an estimated 10 percent.[47] Critics worry especially about the effects on children. One study estimated that the bill would move 1.1 million children into poverty.[48] Most experts agree that the supply of affordable day care that will be needed as welfare women enter the workforce is inadequate; as a result, children will either be left alone or in makeshift arrangements with family and friends.

Making welfare temporary and forcing welfare recipients to become self-sufficient clearly represents the will of the vast majority of Americans. And moving control over welfare policy to the states, which are presumably closer to the people, also seems to be the epitome of popular democracy. Critics, however, argue that states face structural pressures that will prevent them from unbiased action on this issue. Not wanting to become "welfare magnets" or to discourage investment with high taxes, states, especially when the national economy goes into a recession, will engage in a "race to the bottom," competing to provide the least attractive package of welfare benefits possible.

A plausible argument can be made that welfare reform, far from being the epitome of popular democracy, is in fact a violation of democratic norms. As we have argued in this book, democracy means more than following the will of the majority; it means creating a society where everyone has the resources to participate in the political process. From a popular democratic point of view, it is plausible to argue that certain benefits should not be subject to majority rule. For example, we do not vote on whether we have a right to free speech or free exercise of religion. Similarly, majorities should not be able to vote on whether families will have roofs over their heads or food on the table. Meeting basic needs should be a national right or entitlement; it should not depend on which state you happen to live in. What makes this popular democratic critique of welfare reform more compelling is the realization that self-sufficiency is a myth: Most Americans enjoy a vast array of entitlements that are rarely questioned by majority rule.

America's Two-Tiered Welfare State

The attack on welfare assumes that one group in society is "getting something for nothing." In fact, the United States has two welfare states: one for children and the poor, which has been under continual attack in recent years, and one for the elderly and middle class and above, which has largely been immune from attack. The two-tiered welfare state began with the 1935 Social Security Act, which created social insurance for the unemployed and the elderly and public

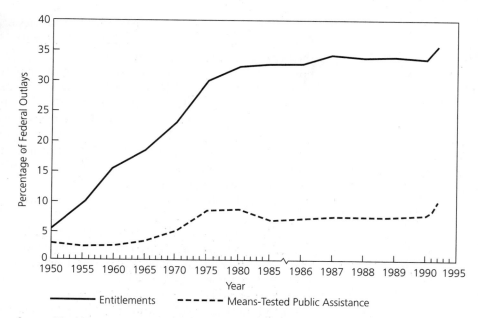

Source: Harold W. Stanley and Richard G. Niemi, *Vital Statistics in American Politics*, 4th ed. (Washington, D.C.: Congressional Quarterly, 1994), p. 384; U.S. Bureau of the Census, *Statistical Abstract of the United States 1996* (Washington, D.C.: U.S. Government Printing Office, 1996) pp. 332, 375.

assistance for the blind, the disabled, and single mothers with children. The social insurance programs are called entitlements because everyone who pays into the system is entitled to the benefits regardless of income. Even though we stated earlier that welfare was an entitlement, welfare was different because it was always means tested. As Figure 17.3 shows, over the years social insurance entitlements have fared much better than means-tested public assistance.

Growing Entitlements

Social Security started out modestly, but over the years it has expanded rapidly, both in benefit levels and in number of people covered. Social Security was originally intended to be a mandatory insurance system in which retired persons would receive benefits according to how much they paid in. As people lived longer and longer, however, the benefits paid out far exceeded the taxes paid in. In addition, coverage was significantly expanded on three occasions: In 1939, widows were included; in 1956, the disabled were added; and in 1965, health insurance for the elderly was enacted. The system is paid for by a payroll tax designated as FICA (Federal Insurance Contributions Act) on your paycheck.

The Social Security tax is *regressive* because it is a flat rate (7.65 percent) up to $61,200 in income (1996); above that amount, people pay nothing. The benefits paid out for Social Security, however, are *progressive:* Although related to the amount workers pay into the system, formerly low-income workers are given proportionately higher benefits. More important, the benefits far exceed the amount each worker paid into the system. In fact, most people exhaust the funds they paid into the system within a few years. After that, their pension is essentially paid for by the present generation of workers.

With Social Security now including over 90 percent of the work force, it has become a classic case of **majoritarian politics,** in which both the costs and the benefits are widely spread. Social Security is supported by a broad coalition uniting the poor and the middle class, blacks and whites, city dwellers and residents of small towns and suburbs. Politicians fall over each other defending Social Security. Contemplating a run for the presidency in 1972, for example, Democrat Wilbur Mills, chair of the powerful House Ways and Means Committee, proposed a 20 percent increase as well as indexing payments to inflation—all without a tax increase! To obtain partial credit for the changes, President Nixon endorsed Mills's proposal, and it became the law in 1972. The result was soaring expenditures on Social Security (see Figure 17.3) and a crisis in the Social Security fund.

TOLES © 1994 The Buffalo News. Reprinted with permission of Universal Press Syndicate. All rights reserved.

FIGURE 17.4

The Effects of Social Policies on Children and the Elderly, 1965–1986

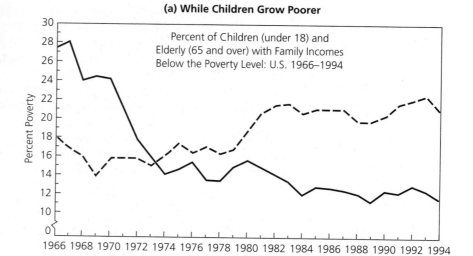

(a) While Children Grow Poorer

Percent of Children (under 18) and Elderly (65 and over) with Family Incomes Below the Poverty Level: U.S. 1966–1994

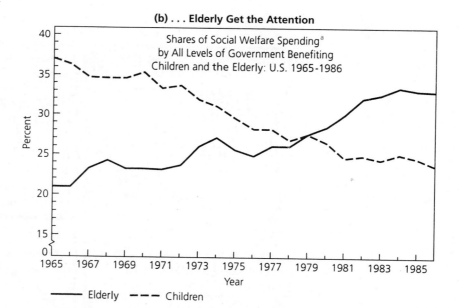

(b) . . . Elderly Get the Attention

Shares of Social Welfare Spending[a] by All Levels of Government Benefiting Children and the Elderly: U.S. 1965-1986

—— Elderly   - - - Children

Source for 17.4(a): U.S. Bureau of the Census. 1995a. *Income, Poverty, and Valuation of Noncash Benefits: 1993*. Current Population Reports, Series P60–188. Washington, D.C.: U.S. Government Printing Office. February.

U.S. Bureau of the Census. 1995b. "Press Briefing on 1994 Income and Poverty Estimates." Washington, D.C.: U.S. Bureau of the Census. October 5.

[a] Includes primary and secondary education, welfare, health programs, food stamps, Social Security, Medicare, and Medicaid.

Source for 17.4(b): *Washington Post Weekly Edition*, March 4, 1991, p. 31. Copyright © 1991 The Washington Post. Reprinted with permission. Based on research by A.E. Benjamin, Paul Newacheck, and Hannah Wolfe.

Social Security has become so politically popular that politicians refer to it as the "third rail" of American politics: Like the third rail on an electrified railway, anyone who touches it will die. Most politicians are afraid to even talk about cutting Social Security benefits. The evolution of Social Security has made it, in the words of Harvard's Theda Skocpol, "America's most effective antipoverty program."[49] As Figure 17.4 shows, the poverty rate among the elderly fell from 28 percent in the late 1960s to 11.7 percent in 1994.[50] Increased Social Security retirement benefits were responsible for pulling many of the elderly out of poverty.

Tax Expenditures: Welfare for the Middle and Upper Classes

Besides social insurance entitlements for the elderly, there are a wide range of entitlements, embedded in the tax code, known as **tax expenditures.** Tax expenditures are provisions in the tax code that reduce people's taxes in order to promote a worthwhile public objective. Calling them "tax expenditures" highlights the fact that tax exemptions are essentially the same as spending programs. The government can either exempt certain income from taxes, or it can tax income equally and write a check to the recipient for the value of the exemption. Either way, the government is spending resources to subsidize certain taxpayers. In an effort to subject tax expenditures to public scrutiny, the Treasury Department in 1968 published the first budget for the United States that included tax expenditures. The Congressional Budget Act of 1974 made the concept of tax expenditures an integral part of the budget process. Misunderstood by most Americans, tax expenditures disproportionately benefit the middle class and especially the wealthy.

The growth of tax expenditures has been astounding, far outpacing the growth of conventional spending programs. Tax expenditures soared from $36.6 billion in 1967 to $253.5 billion in 1982, rising from 20.5 percent of federal outlays to 34.6 percent.[51] In 1997, tax expenditures totaled $471 billion.[52] (See Table 17.2 for the costs of the most expensive tax expenditure programs.)

Tax expenditures go disproportionately to middle class and wealthy households. A Treasury Department study for 1977 found that the top 1.4 percent of

TABLE 17.2 **Major Tax Expenditure Programs, Estimated Cost to the U.S. Treasury in 1997**		
Homeowner tax breaks		$ 97.0 billion
Exclusion of employer contributions to health insurance		72.3 billion
Exclusion of employer contributions to retirement		<u>59.5 billion</u>
Total		$ 228.8 billion

Source: U.S. Bureau of the Census, *Statistical Abstract of the United States, 1996* (Washington, D.C.: U.S. Government Printing Office, 1996), p. 336.

taxpayers received 31.3 percent of the benefits delivered through tax expenditures. Those with the highest incomes (above $200,000) received an average tax subsidy of $535,653. At the same time that Congress debated the merits of the welfare state and cut most programs for the poor, tax expenditures for the middle class and upper classes—what one author called "fiscal welfare"—soared.[53] Between 1980 and 1997, for example, when federal spending on all low-income housing programs increased by $17 billion, homeowner tax expenditures increased by $40 billion. Almost 82 percent of the tax expenditures went to the top 20 percent of the income range; the bottom 20 percent received almost nothing.[54] The exclusions of employer contributions to health insurance and retirement benefit mostly higher-income workers. Low-wage workers often get no health insurance or retirement benefits from their companies. Tax expenditures are essentially subsidizing a privatized welfare state for the middle class.

Even though tax expenditures are expensive, they have distinct political advantages over conventional spending programs. First, they are buried in the tax code and therefore have low political visibility. Second, once enacted they do not require congressional approval each year, as conventional spending programs do. Third, there are no congressional committees with oversight responsibilities for tax expenditures, and hearings are rarely held to scrutinize their effectiveness—as happens for spending programs.

The Political Backlash Against Welfare

Overall, the United States devotes less of its public spending to social policies than any other developed nation. But this overall figure obscures the fact that the United States actually has a generous welfare system for the middle class and the elderly. Entitlement programs provide almost universal coverage for the elderly, with benefit levels comparable to those in other developed countries. On the other hand, means-tested welfare programs, which mostly benefit children, provide spotty coverage and inadequate benefits. In 1986, public policies succeeded in lifting fewer than 4 percent of poor children in single-parent families out of poverty.[55]

Most other developed countries have broad entitlement programs to address the needs of the nonelderly poor. The most important of these is health insurance. Other countries also have a system of child allowances in which every family, regardless of income, is entitled to a payment each year from the government for each child. These allowances are politically popular and have played a major role in reducing poverty rates.[56]

The only exception to America's poor showing next to other developed countries is education. The United States provided universal public education at the primary and secondary levels well before Europe did and today enables more people to pursue higher education than in Europe. The American tradition of public education played a major role in expanding popular democracy, giving citizens the skills necessary to participate in the democratic process and in the economy.

FIGURE 17.5

Spending on Social Security and Welfare as a Percentage of Total National Government Expenditures, 1991–1995

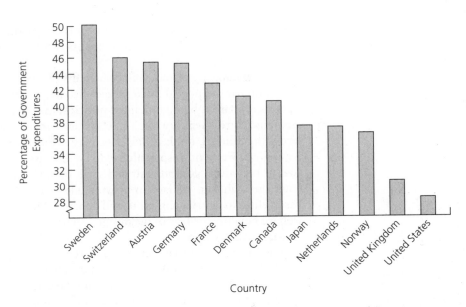

Our tradition of equal educational opportunity, however, is threatened today by unequal funding. Since funding for primary and secondary schools comes mostly out of local property taxes, children who happen to grow up in poor inner city school districts suffer from inferior education.[57] With education being the key to good jobs in an information-based economy, inferior schools can doom children to a life of poverty and exclude them from full participation in the democratic process.[58]

Expenditures in 1994 on Social Security ($317 billion), Medicare ($169 billion), and the tax expenditures noted earlier ($229 billion) total $715 billion. Of course, some of this was contributed by the recipients in taxes, but most was not contributed. Nor does this figure include other government programs that primarily benefit the middle class, such as public universities. In 1994, the total for *all* means-tested programs for the poor by *all* levels of governments equaled $345 billion.[59] (This includes thirty-three separate programs providing cash and noncash benefits.) But this total overstates aid to the poor. Over $161 billion of that is for Medicaid, and most of the money spent on Medicaid goes to hospitals and doctors. More important, although you must be poor to qualify for Medicaid, many middle class households draw down their parents' savings so that they can go on Medicaid to cover nursing home costs. A major part of Medicaid benefits the middle class. Subtracting Medicaid means that in 1994 all cash and noncash benefits for the poor totaled $184 billion. The question this arithmetic raises is: Why have politicians gone after the relatively small benefits for the poor while leaving alone the huge entitlements for the middle class and rich, who obviously need them less?

Basically, means-tested welfare benefits evolved in such a way as to generate little popular support. Unlike Social Security, which is based on majoritarian politics, welfare is based on **client politics,** in which the benefits are targeted to a narrow constituency, while the costs are widely distributed over the public at large. In addition, unlike Social Security, which is administered entirely by the federal government, responsibility for public assistance programs is divided between the federal government and state and local governments. This has weakened the ability of welfare to provide adequate benefits and has enabled state-based elites to restrict eligibility and benefits. Moreover, states hesitate to expand welfare benefits for fear of becoming "welfare magnets" or frightening away investors with high taxes.

The main reason that welfare has fared so poorly, however, is that it violates deeply held American values. Americans believe in individual and family responsibility: All able-bodied persons should take care of themselves. Welfare has the reputation of rewarding lazy people who do not want to work and encouraging women to have babies without any means of supporting them, even though this reputation is not well substantiated by the facts. Most important, welfare violates the American belief that people should not be given "something for nothing."

The two-tiered American welfare state is based on the distinction between the deserving and undeserving poor. Welfare is reserved for the undeserving poor and therefore must be rendered an unattractive option to discourage people from seeking it. Social Security, on the other hand, goes to the deserving poor because it is based on contributory insurance in which people get out what they put in. (As we have seen, however, this is not true: Social Security recipients exhaust their contributions within a few years and so, like welfare recipients, are getting something for nothing.)

Clearly, the resentment against welfare is not based only on economic factors; as we have seen, welfare is a relatively small part of federal and state budgets. This resentment is motivated partly by racism and sexism. Even though a majority of those on welfare are white, blacks represent a disproportionate share of recipients. In the public's mind, welfare is identified with blacks. Politicians have taken advantage of these sentiments. In 1991, for example, former Ku Klux Klan leader David Duke received a majority of the white vote in his race for governor of Louisiana by, among other things, mobilizing white resentments against black welfare recipients with such statements as, "Middle-class families have difficulty affording children of their own right now and yet we are financing a very high illegitimate birth rate."[60] In fact, in 1991 in Louisiana each baby qualified the mother for only $11 extra per week—hardly a great incentive for having babies.

Another issue in the welfare debate concerns the role of women. When critics say that women on welfare do not work, they are ignoring the fact that raising children is work. The disapproving judgments about women on welfare seem to suggest that it is okay to stay home with children only if a woman is part of a traditional family with a male breadwinner. The reason for keeping welfare so unattractive, some feminists say, is to discourage women from leaving bad marriages, even if the husband is abusive.[61] In the public's mind, welfare is wrapped up in the cultural debates that began in the 1960s about permissiveness—promoting a lifestyle attuned to immediate gratification and sexual promiscuity. In fact, permissive values have spread throughout society in the past thirty years, driven by corporate advertising that uses immediate gratification to stimulate consumption. Hard-working Middle Americans raised with a strong work ethic find themselves bombarded by advertising that stresses pleasure-driven consumption. Fearing a loss of control, they project their own fears onto others, including blacks on welfare.[62]

Welfare has come under attack because it has become a powerful symbol of the failure of government, the failure of liberalism, and fears about shifting race, gender, and cultural relations. After a brutal triple murder in Chicago in which a baby was ripped from his mother's womb, House Speaker Newt Gingrich said the tragedy was the result of the "welfare state," which had produced "a drug-addicted underclass with no sense of humanity, no sense of civilization and no sense of the rules of life."[63]

In fact, the old system of welfare did not work. It stigmatized welfare recipients and made them feel alienated from society. It did not encourage them to become full participating members of society. As more and more women with young children have been forced to enter the job market, public opinion will simply not support letting some women stay home on welfare. On the other hand, simply throwing welfare recipients to the private job market will not work either. In order to succeed, they need all of the supports, many subsidized by government, that middle class people take for granted, including good education, health insurance, day care, adequate retirement systems, and stable, safe communities to grow up in.

CONCLUSION: DEMOCRATIC CONNECTIONS

In recent years, the United States has had one of the strongest economies in the world. American workers are still the most productive in the world and are beating the Germans and the Japanese in many export markets. But economic policies should not be evaluated only by economic standards. Economic policies have widespread social and political effects. That is why economic policy in a democracy should not be left in the hands of isolated experts. Economic policy involves complex tradeoffs among economic, social, and political outcomes. Although the American economy has performed well in accumulating wealth, it has performed poorly from the standpoint of equality, community, and participation. Inequality has widened dangerously in the past twenty years, and large campaign contributions threaten the integrity of the electoral process. In addition, as we noted in chapter 4, many workers are forced to work overtime, leaving little time to participate in the civic life of their communities.

The rise of a permanent underclass of Americans, largely minority, trapped in inner city ghettos, divorced from the world of work, presents one of the greatest challenges to American democracy. Clearly, traditional welfare did little to solve this problem and in many ways contributed to it. By treating welfare recipients as undeserving, forcing them to go through a demeaning application process, welfare stigmatized the poor and made them feel different from the rest of society. Welfare helped to make many single mothers and minorities feel like outcasts, decreasing their ability for independent political action.

Welfare reform, if it means simply throwing welfare recipients to the private market, is not the solution. Mean-spirited welfare reform is based on the myth of the self-made man (or woman). In fact, in our highly interdependent, complex society, no one is self-made anymore. As we saw, government provides crucial social supports to the middle class. Our social policies toward the elderly have been one of the great success stories of the twentieth century. Social Security and Medicare have helped elderly people cope with the vulnerabilities of old age without making them feel stigmatized or separated from the larger community. This result has certainly contributed to the ability of the elderly to defend their interests and participate in politics.

All of us are dependent on government to achieve a high quality of life and to participate fully in political life. Public education, the most successful entitlement program of all, demonstrates that we do not need to choose between greater economic efficiency and greater equality, because public education promotes both at the same time. Try to imagine what American democracy would be like without the massive system of public education that imparts the skills necessary to debate public policies and organize political associations to defend people's interests.

Beyond education, however, the most effective way of integrating the poor into society would be to guarantee them jobs. According to a 1992 poll, 70 percent of the public favors replacing "welfare with a system of guaranteed jobs."[64] The most important entitlement that popular democrats could enact would be the right of every American to a job at a salary that could support a family.

KEY TERMS

macroeconomic policy
fiscal policy
monetary policy
Laffer curve
Economic Recovery Tax Act of 1981
Federal Reserve
monetarism

means-tested benefits
entitlement
Personal Responsibility Act of 1996
majoritarian politics
tax expenditure
client politics

SUGGESTED READINGS

Donald L. Barlett and James B. Steele, *America: What Went Wrong?* Kansas City, Mo.: Andrews and McMeel, 1992. A critique by two Pulitzer Prize–winning investigative reporters of how economic policy has benefitted the rich and the powerful—at the expense of everyone else.

William Greider, *Secrets of the Temple: How the Federal Reserve Runs the Country*. New York: Simon & Schuster, 1987. Penetrates the veil of expertise that surrounds the Federal Reserve to expose the politics behind its decisions to regulate the money supply.

William A. Niskanen, *Reaganomics: An Insider's Account of the Policies and the People*. New York: Oxford University Press, 1988. A largely sympathetic account of the implementation of supply-side economics, from a member of Reagan's Council of Economic Advisers.

Theresa Funiciello, *Tyranny of Kindness: Dismantling the Welfare System to End Poverty in America*. New York: Atlantic Monthly Press, 1993. A hard-hitting critique of the welfare system by a former welfare mother, who argues for eliminating the current system and replacing it with a guaranteed income.

Christopher Jencks, *Rethinking Social Policy: Race, Poverty, and the Underclass*. New York: HarperCollins, 1992. A skillful synthesis of existing material on which social policies work and which don't. Follows neither the liberal nor the conservative line.

Charles Murray, *Losing Ground: American Social Policy 1950–1980*. New York: Basic Books, 1984. Argues that welfare policies not only fail to cure poverty, they actually create poverty.

William Julius Wilson, *When Work Disappears: The World of the New Urban Poor*. New York: Alfred A. Knopf, 1996. An update of his influential book, *The Truly Disadvantaged*, in which Wilson argued that the main cause of ghetto poverty is not welfare but the loss of industrial jobs, especially among black males.

Foreign Policy in the National Security State

In the early 1960s, the Central Intelligence Agency (CIA), following the wishes of Presidents Eisenhower and Kennedy, was determined to get rid of Fidel Castro, the communist leader of revolutionary Cuba. Since coming to power in 1959, Castro had seized property in Cuba belonging to American corporations and had drawn his nation closer to the Soviet Union. An invasion force of Cuban exiles organized and trained by the CIA was smashed by Castro's forces at the Bay of Pigs in 1961. But behind the scenes, the CIA was plotting an even more dire fate for Castro: assassination.[1]

The first undercover plot against Castro aimed merely to destroy his popularity. CIA officials were fearful that the charismatic Castro, most famous for his bushy black beard, would become a hero to the impoverished and the discontented throughout Latin America. So they cooked up a scheme to dust the Cuban leader's shoes with thallium salt, a powerful hair remover that would make his beard fall out. The plot was to be carried out when Castro was on a trip outside Cuba and would leave his shoes to be shined at the hotel in which he was staying. But Castro canceled the trip.

Foiled in this prank, the CIA began to plot murder. It laced a box of Castro's favorite cigars with a botulism toxin, a poison so lethal that Castro would die just from putting the cigar in his mouth. The cigars were delivered to an unknown agent; it is not known what happened to him or to the cigars, but they never reached Castro.

Foiled again, the CIA became even more serious. To kill Castro, it hired experts: the Mafia. Castro had shut down Mafia gambling and prostitution operations in Cuba, so the mob had its own reasons for wanting Castro dead. The CIA paid three Mafia gangsters (two of whom were on the attorney general's list of most wanted criminals) $150,000 in taxpayers' money for the attempt on Castro's life. Mafia agents in Cuba tried to slip poisoned pills, supplied by the CIA, into Castro's drink. But like the previous assassins, they could not get close enough to Castro to carry out the deed.

By now, CIA planners were desperate. They considered the possibility of depositing an exotic seashell rigged with explosives in an area where Castro liked to go skin diving. When this idea proved impractical, they tried to have an unwitting American diplomat offer Castro the gift of a diving suit. The suit was to be dusted with a fungus that would produce a chronic skin disease; its breathing apparatus was to be contaminated with tuberculosis germs. This idea, too, had to be discarded as impractical. Castro survived this—and several further—CIA plots.

What does this bizarre tale of CIA efforts to assassinate Castro, which sounds more like a bad made-for-TV movie than a true story about an agency of the U.S. government, have to do with the democratic debate about American foreign policy? Elite democrats have long claimed that foreign policy, even more than domestic policy, requires the superior expertise and talent of elites. Ordinary citizens, they argue, are generally ignorant about events in other nations and are prone to emotional and fickle responses inconsistent with a realistic and stable foreign policy. Foreign policy, therefore, should largely be left in the hands of the president and the diplomatic and military experts who advise him. The tale of the CIA and Castro should lead us to question this conventional wisdom about wise elites and ignorant masses. When foreign policy decisions are made in secret chambers by a handful of elite actors operating free of public scrutiny (and, in the case of the CIA, public accountability), the result can be folly rather than wisdom. And the cost can be great, both to America's true national security and to its most cherished democratic values.

This chapter considers the democratic debate over foreign policy that has been waged since the nation's founding. The discussion begins with the original debate between Federalists and Anti-federalists, with elite democrats arguing for the necessity of expert guidance in a dangerous world of powerful adversaries and popular democrats warning of the threat to the maintenance of republican institutions posed by secret diplomacy and aggressive militarism. Briefly tracing the debate through American history, the chapter focuses on the era of the Cold War, when elite democrats succeeded in building a national security state to run the affairs of a global superpower. Next, the chapter describes the diplomatic, military, and intelligence agencies that conduct American relations with other nations and examines the impact that economic elites and public opinion have on foreign policy. The final section of the chapter considers the current democratic debate about what American foreign policy should be in a post–Cold War world and examines the record of the first post–Cold War president, Bill Clinton.

BEGINNINGS OF THE DEMOCRATIC DEBATE OVER FOREIGN POLICY

Elite democrats and popular democrats of the founding generation differed not only on how Americans should govern themselves but also on how the American nation should relate to the rest of the world. The former favored executive control and promoted professional armies, while the latter sought public control and favored citizen militias.

The strongest proponent of the original elite position on foreign policy was Alexander Hamilton. In the *Federalist Papers*, Hamilton called on Americans to recognize that they lived in a dangerous world, where nations would fight regularly over power, territory, and commerce. Hamilton argued that the new United States needed professional armies and navies like those of the great European powers, England and France. These forces would be required for defense and for the establishment of America as a great power, extending its influence throughout the western hemisphere.[2]

In Hamilton's conception of foreign and defense policy, the president was the dominant figure. Members of Congress lacked the information and experience to make wise decisions in foreign policy; furthermore, they could not act swiftly or keep diplomatic secrets. In contrast, the executive had the proper qualities for controlling foreign policy and using military might—in Hamilton's words, "decision, activity, secrecy, and dispatch."[3]

During the war between Great Britain and revolutionary France, Federalists boosted the primacy of the executive in foreign policy, using as their instrument President Washington's Proclamation of Neutrality of 1793. Later in that decade, they seized on the prospect of an American war against the French to create a professional army. It was Hamilton and his faction of Federalists who created the first American military establishment.[4]

The Anti-federalists feared just such an establishment. A standing army might overturn republican institutions and seize power for its commander (the example of Julius Caesar in ancient Rome was frequently cited). Or it might become a dangerous tool for the executive, tempting him to crush his domestic opponents or launch aggressive military adventures abroad. As an alternative to a professional military in times of peace, the Anti-federalists wanted to rely on state militias composed of armed citizens. (The Second Amendment reflects the importance the Anti-federalists gave to militias.) As historian Richard H. Kohn observes, popular democrats of the founding era associated the militia "with liberty, freedom, and colonial virtue—the standing army with European militarism, corruption, and tyranny."[5]

That citizen militias were capable only of defensive military operations reveals a great deal about the Anti-federalist view of foreign policy. The Anti-federalists did not want the new republic to become like the reigning great powers of the day. Rather than playing power politics, America should relate to the rest of the world as an example of how a people could flourish in freedom and self-government. A peaceful, commercial relationship with other nations could be governed as much by the people's representatives in Congress as by the executive. Foreign and defense policy of this kind would, the Anti-federalists believed, provide Americans with genuine security without threatening the republic's institutions and values.

In today's world of massive military forces and awesome technological destructiveness, some of the Anti-federalists' arguments sound old fashioned. Yet the fundamental questions of the original democratic debate endure: Should American foreign and military policy be determined largely by a small elite acting often in secret and be directed toward the projection of American power abroad? Or should American foreign and defense policy be subject to greater popular democratic control and seek a form of national security that violates as little as possible the nation's professed values as a democratic society?

ISOLATION AND EXPANSION

For much of American history, elite democrats who shared Hamilton's vision of the United States as a great power were frustrated. **Isolationism,** not power politics, was the core principle of American foreign and defense policy. Apart from commercial relations, the United States sought to stay isolated from the political and military quarrels of the rest of the world. Protected by two vast oceans, the young republic concentrated on its internal development. Since military threats were remote, the standing army remained small. Only when the United States actually became engaged in a war did the military swell in size; once war was over, the citizen-soldiers who composed the bulk of the forces were rapidly demobilized.

Even though isolationism characterized American relations with other nations until well into the twentieth century, American foreign policy was neither as defensive nor as passive as the term seems to imply. The American republic from its inception was engaged in a process of **expansion,** first on a continental scale and later into Latin America and even Asia. American expansion drove the European powers from their remaining holdings on the continent. But it had a dark side: Expansion also drove Native Americans from their ancestral lands, often in brutal fashion. And later it extended American power over Latin Americans and Filipinos, speaking the language of benevolence but employing the instrument of armed force. The responsibility for this dark side of American expansion belonged both to elite democrats and popular democrats.

Removal of indigenous peoples, the initial pillar of American expansion, was the work of popular democrats. The central figure in this removal was popular democratic hero Andrew Jackson. He understood that many ordinary Americans hungered for the fertile lands that the Native American tribes occupied—and he shared their incomprehension at Indians' refusal to give up their way of life and adopt the white man's economic and social practices. Under Jackson's leadership, Native Americans were driven from their homes in the southeastern states. As historian Richard Barnet notes, "In 1820, 125,000 Indians lived east of the Mississippi; by 1844 there were fewer than 30,000 left. Most had been forcibly relocated to the west. About a third had been wiped out."[6]

If popular democrats had their shameful moments in the history of American expansion, so, too, did elite democrats. Consider, for example, the clique of elite expansionists in the 1890s, led by such avowed admirers of Hamilton as Massachusetts Senator Henry Cabot Lodge and Assistant Secretary of the Navy Theodore Roosevelt. It was these elite expansionists, eager to project American power abroad, who prodded a wavering President William McKinley to fight a Spanish-American war and to extend the war from its ostensible focus, Cuba, halfway around the world to the Philippine Islands. The same men guided the subsequent American military campaign to crush Filipino nationalists, who wanted independence rather than American rule. A forerunner to the Vietnam conflict, the American war in the Philippines produced as many as 200,000 Filipino deaths.[7]

Although expansion drew support from both elites and masses, it always had its critics, who echoed the original Anti-federalist fear that America could become a great power only by violating its republican principles. America's role in the Mexican War, the war in the Philippines, and World War I was denounced by those who wanted the nation not to follow the path of European militarism and imperialism. These critics, among them Abraham Lincoln, were especially outraged by claims that American expansion was motivated by a desire to spread liberty to other lands; they detected the real desire for wealth and power that such rhetoric disguised.[8]

Even as the United States expanded across the continent (and into Latin America and the Philippines), even as it became the greatest industrial power in the world, the doctrine of isolationism remained strong. America came late to World War I—and recoiled after the war from the slaughter on the battlefield and the power politics of the victorious allies. Only with World War II did the nation begin to change its traditional foreign and defense policy, and it was in the immediate postwar years that the great transformation in American international relations occurred. Then, in the Cold War era, some of Hamilton's dreams were finally fulfilled, and some of the Anti-federalists' fears finally came true.

THE DEMOCRATIC DEBATE OVER THE COLD WAR

The **Cold War** was a forty-year struggle (lasting from the late 1940s to the late 1980s) between the United States and its allies, championing the cause of democracy and capitalism, and the Soviet Union (USSR) and its allies, championing the cause of communism. It was called a "cold" war because the two principal adversaries, the United States and the Soviet Union, armed themselves to the teeth yet never actually engaged in direct combat with each other. But the Cold War became a "hot" war in many places, with major armed conflicts in Korea and Vietnam and numerous smaller armed conflicts around the globe. It was also waged with nonmilitary weapons ranging from political manipulation and economic pressure to propaganda and espionage.

The Cold War remains essential to study because it fundamentally transformed American foreign policy. With the Cold War, the United States became an active and interventionist global superpower. It developed an enormous peacetime military establishment, armed with weaponry of previously unthinkable destructiveness. Presidents became the overwhelmingly dominant factors in

policy making and came to possess, among other resources, the capacity to operate in secret, employing new agencies of covert action like the CIA. Meanwhile, Congress and the public were reduced to a marginal role, expected to support but not to question American actions abroad. These developments gave rise to a **national security state,** a complex of executive, military, and secret powers previously unknown in the American republic. Even though the Cold War has now come to an end, this national security state remains.

For roughly the first half of the Cold War, almost all Americans believed in its ideas and institutions. But this "Cold War consensus" cracked during the Vietnam War of the 1960s and early 1970s. It was during the protests against American policy in Vietnam that the popular democratic tradition of opposing a foreign and defense policy based on unchecked executive power, militarism, and secret, unaccountable institutions was revived. This opposition was expressed chiefly through mass movements, first against the war in Vietnam and later against President Reagan's policy in Central America and his nuclear arms buildup. These movements were supported by some sympathetic political elites, such as Senators George McGovern (the Democrats' 1972 presidential candidate) and Edward Kennedy. During the last half of the Cold War, the debate over foreign policy was intense. In the following sections we consider more fully the perspectives of both sides in the democratic debate over the Cold War.

The Elite Democratic View of the Cold War

Most elite democrats admitted that the Cold War contained some unpleasant features and unfortunate episodes, but they insisted that it was a necessary, even heroic struggle. The advance of international communism had to be halted, they believed, if freedom and democracy were to survive in the world. And only a prudent and tough-minded elite could guide the complex and often nasty enterprise of containing communism until it collapsed of its own contradictions. Secretary of State Dean Acheson, one of the original architects of American Cold War policy, remarked that "the limitation imposed by democratic political practices makes it difficult to conduct our foreign affairs in the national interest."[9] For Acheson and other elite democratic managers of the new national security state, deviations from democracy were acceptable if needed to win the Cold War.

The elite case for the Cold War argued, first, that American policy had to have as its priority an opposition to aggression. The mistake of the Western allies before World War II—appeasing Adolf Hitler at Munich in 1938—must never again be repeated. The United States organized a European alliance, the **North Atlantic Treaty Organization (NATO),** to block any Soviet expansion in Europe. Aggression by Soviet allies and clients in the Third World also had to be halted, a rationale that involved the United States in wars in Korea and Vietnam. In this view, the United States had built a national security state not to secure military supremacy but to keep peace in the world.

Second, elite democrats saw the American effort in the Cold War as a defense of freedom around the globe. In advocating a global American struggle for the

containment of communism, President Truman declared, "I believe that it must be the policy of the United States to support free peoples who are resisting attempted subjugation by armed minorities or by outside pressures."[10] The strategy of containment, proclaimed in what came to be known as the Truman Doctrine, formed the basis of American policy throughout the Cold War.

Third, the American Cold War policy was a prudent combination of force and diplomacy. The presidents who shaped this policy had to engage in a frightening arms race, but they always kept one eye on peace. President Eisenhower sought "peaceful coexistence" with the Russians, President Kennedy negotiated a ban on the testing of nuclear weapons in the atmosphere, President Nixon restored American ties to the People's Republic of China, and even President Reagan, the harshest critic of the Soviet Union among Cold War executives, agreed to an intermediate nuclear forces treaty with Soviet leader Mikhail Gorbachev.[11]

Fourth, the Cold War had the support of the American people. The Cold War necessitated a shift of power from Congress to the president, a huge and expensive military establishment, and agencies of secret action outside the constitutional system of public accountability. Yet, elite democrats argued, Americans understood that they were in a difficult struggle with a dangerous, undemocratic enemy, and they accepted the fact that this struggle could not always be conducted in accordance with democratic political practices.

The Popular Democratic View of the Cold War

Popular democrats agreed with elite democrats that communism had to be opposed. But they believed that the threat posed by the communists to the freedom of other nations and to the United States itself was often exaggerated by elite democrats in the presidency, the military, and the CIA because such exaggerations increased their own power and resources. Further, popular democrats favored more peaceful and open methods to block communism, methods more in keeping with democratic practices and values. In the eyes of popular democrats, American Cold War policy as run by elite democrats purchased whatever successes it achieved at a high price.

The most haunting price of Cold War policy, in the eyes of popular democrats, was the war in Vietnam. In the name of containing the aggressive expansionism of the Soviet and Chinese communists, elite democratic managers of the national security state plunged the United States into what was actually a Vietnamese civil war. By the time the United States pulled all of its troops out of Vietnam, almost 60,000 Americans had died, along with hundreds of thousands of Vietnamese soldiers and civilians. The Vietnamese countryside bore terrible ecological scars, as did Vietnamese society and economy. Americans, too, were scarred by the war, especially in psychological traumas that persist to this day.[12]

Vietnam was an unparalleled disaster for America, but it was not, popular democrats insisted, an aberration for American foreign policy. A second price of Cold War policy was American backing of dictators and military regimes that repressed their own people in the name of anticommunism. Although President

Truman had promised to assist "free peoples" resisting communism, the policy of containment he initiated led the United States to support some rather dubious representatives of freedom. Thus, the CIA overthrew a nationalist government in Iran in 1953 and restored the autocratic shah to power. For the next twenty-five years, the shah was the recipient of lavish American aid, including CIA training of his ruthless secret police, SAVAK. When he was overthrown in 1979—by Islamic fundamentalists rather than communists—Iran became a bitter foe of the United States.[13]

A third price of Cold War policy was that the United States, the global sponsor of democracy, schemed to overthrow democracies abroad if they infringed on American political and economic interests and to replace them with authoritarian governments that would do what the national security managers wanted. The most important case of this type was Chile in the early 1970s. Employing the CIA, President Nixon and his national security adviser, Henry Kissinger, tried to block the election of socialist Salvador Allende as president of Chile. When this failed, they worked secretly to disrupt Chile's economy and to foment political opposition to the Allende government. They also courted the Chilean military, which finally undertook a coup in 1973 in which Allende was killed and his supporters were arrested.[14]

Claiming to champion democracy in a global campaign against communism, American Cold War policy damaged democracy at home as well as abroad. In the popular democratic view, a fourth price paid for the Cold War was the damage done to the constitutional values of open debate and checks and balances. With the emergence of a national security state, a government that was supposed to be open and accountable to the people began to classify massive amounts of information as secret and to hide numerous operations from public view. As facts were concealed, democratic debate was also stifled by Cold War taboos. No political figure who aspired to high office dared question fundamental Cold War premises lest he or she appear "soft on communism." Meanwhile, executive power swelled to previously unknown proportions in international relations, taking on the character of an "imperial presidency." Two major threats to the Constitution, the Watergate affair under Nixon and the Iran-contra affair under Reagan, could be traced to the mentality of the imperial presidency during the Cold War.

A final price paid for American Cold War policy, in the eyes of popular democrats, was the damage done to economic progress and social justice in America. The Cold War arms race introduced distortions into the economy, leaving the United States at a disadvantage in many areas of civilian production compared to the nonmilitarized economies of West Germany and Japan. Equally damaging was the impact on spending for social needs. The arms race was often used to justify the country's failure to address adequately the needs of its own poor and disadvantaged. The one extensive effort to meet these needs, President Johnson's War on Poverty and Great Society programs, was cut back because of the mushrooming costs of the war in Vietnam. President Eisenhower, the Cold War president who best understood the tragic cost of the arms race, eloquently made the popular democrats' point: "Every gun that is made, every warship launched, every rocket fired signifies, in the final sense, a theft from those who hunger and are not fed, those who are cold and are not clothed."[15]

The End of the Cold War

The Cold War came to a sudden and surprising end in the late 1980s. In an attempt to reform the decrepit structure of the Soviet state, Gorbachev only managed to expose its fatal weaknesses. The global power of the Soviet Union slipped away in 1989 when Gorbachev refused to respond with force as popular upheavals toppled communist regimes in Eastern Europe. The Soviet Union itself crumbled in 1991 after a botched coup against Gorbachev by hard-line communists. Soon Gorbachev himself was swept from power in peaceful fashion, and the Soviet state was dismantled, with Boris Yeltsin and other leaders of the Soviet republics proclaiming their independence in a loosely knit federation.

The United States and its allies exulted in the Cold War's demise. Indeed, the whole world breathed easier now that the frightening prospect of a third world war and a nuclear holocaust had been removed. Yet celebration was bound to be brief, for the post–Cold War world already contains new problems and violent conflicts. Nonetheless, there are new opportunities as well, new openings to address fundamental issues of economic progress, human rights, and environmental protection. At the same time, the institutions of the national security state are groping to redefine their roles in an era that lacks the simplifying assumption of a global communist enemy.

FOREIGN AND DEFENSE POLICY: INSTITUTIONS

The presidency is the dominant institution in the making of foreign and defense policy, and in the first half of the Cold War era it controlled this area with few checks from anywhere else. But the disastrous presidential war in Vietnam sparked Congress to reassert its constitutional role in shaping American policy abroad. Since Vietnam, foreign and defense policy has often been the subject of struggle between presidents and Congress (see Chapters 11 and 12).

Agencies of the executive branch are central to the formulation and implementation of national security policy. Presidents have considerable latitude to use these agencies as they see fit, so the role of each agency and the structure of the foreign policy process itself have varied from one administration to the next. National security agencies are subordinate units that advise and assist the president, yet they shape how the United States understands and operates in international affairs.

The National Security Council

The **National Security Council (NSC)** was created in 1947, at the dawn of the Cold War, to serve as a coordinating mechanism for foreign and defense policy

TABLE 18.1 **Composition of the National Security Council**	**Statutory Members of the NSC** President Vice president Secretary of state Secretary of defense **Statutory Advisers to the NSC** Director of central intelligence Chairman, Joint Chiefs of Staff **Other Attendees** Chief of staff to the president Assistant to the president for national security affairs Secretary of the treasury Attorney general Others as invited U.S. Army War College, Carlisle Barracks, Pennsylvania, December 1989 and, "National Security Council Organization," National Security Council mimeo, April 17, 1989; as reprinted in James M. McCormack, *American Foreign Policy and Process,* Second Edition, (Itasca, IL: Peacock Publishers, 1992), p. 371.

at the highest level. The president, vice president, secretary of state, and secretary of defense are statutory members of the NSC; the director of central intelligence and the chair of the Joint Chiefs of Staff are statutory advisers (see Table 18.1).

Presidents have found NSC meetings to be a ponderous instrument. The importance of the NSC has come to reside, instead, in the head of its staff, the president's **national security adviser.** President Kennedy was the first to transform this position from bureaucratic assistant to the council to personal adviser to the president; his national security adviser, McGeorge Bundy, came to overshadow his secretary of state, Dean Rusk, in influence. Subsequent national security advisers expanded on Bundy's role. None dominated American foreign policy so thoroughly as Henry Kissinger. Under Presidents Nixon and Ford, Kissinger was the basic architect of American foreign policy and its most celebrated spokesperson in the media.

National security advisers are in a strong position to exert influence. They have an advantage over secretaries of state in physical proximity to the president, working in the White House and briefing the president frequently on developments around the globe. National security advisers and their small staffs filter the massive amounts of information flowing into the White House from American diplomatic, military, and intelligence personnel throughout the world and can tailor what they report to fit the president's interests more effectively than the larger and more bureaucratic State Department can.[16]

However, criticism in the media and among foreign policy experts that NSC advisers had grown too powerful has led recent presidents to downgrade the adviser's role somewhat. Occupants of the position are now expected to act mainly as coordinators and facilitators and *not* to compete with the secretary of state for public attention. Brent Scowcroft, national security adviser to President Bush, and Anthony Lake and Samuel Berger, national security advisers to President Clinton, have operated in this manner.

Department of State

The **Department of State** is the oldest department in the president's cabinet and the traditional organ of American diplomacy. For most of American history, the secretary of state was the president's principal foreign policy adviser. State Department personnel, stationed in embassies and consulates in nations with which the United States maintained diplomatic relations, were America's principal point of contact with the rest of the world.

During the Cold War, however, the Department of State was eclipsed in influence by other institutions. The national security adviser often had greater influence with the president than did the secretary of state. The Department of Defense grew vastly larger than the Department of State in budget and personnel and played a more central role in overseas conflicts. The Department of State also suffered from its reputation as a rigidly bureaucratic institution whose recommendations to the president were overly cautious and uncreative.[17]

Even State's role as the American representative to the world was partially undermined during the Cold War. In countries where Cold War struggles were aggressively waged, representatives from the military and from CIA "stations" frequently played a more important role than Foreign Service officers from the State Department.

With the end of the Cold War, the Department of State has been making a comeback. President Bush selected his closest political friend and counselor, James Baker, as secretary of state. President Clinton employed his first secretary of state, Warren Christopher, as his principal foreign policy adviser. As Christopher's successor, Clinton selected the first female secretary of state, Madeleine Albright, and she quickly made a splash as a global diplomat. In the post–Cold War era, the standing of the Department of State has benefitted from the fact that diplomatic, rather than military, approaches to international problems usually seem more appropriate.

Department of Defense

The end of the Cold War has not been so beneficial to the **Department of Defense.** During that era, this umbrella organization for the armed forces, symbolized by its massive headquarters, the Pentagon, was the most powerful agency of the national security state.

The Department of Defense has a dual leadership structure: civilian and military. The secretary of defense heads the department and maintains the American tradition of civilian control of the military. Below the secretary on the civilian side are several assistant secretaries for specialized functions, along with civilian secretaries for the army, navy, and air force. Secretaries of defense have varied considerably in their approaches to the military. Some, such as President Kennedy's secretary, Robert McNamara, have seen their role as imposing organizational rationality on the military, especially by setting limits to the services' unceasing request for costly new weapons systems. Others, such as President Reagan's secretary, Caspar Weinberger, have been zealous advocates for rapid increases in defense spending.

Each of the military services also has a commanding officer from among its ranks. The top uniformed leaders come together in the **Joint Chiefs of Staff (JCS),** headed by a chair. The JCS conveys the military's point of view to the president and the secretary of defense. The JCS's influence with civilian officials often has been diminished by the perception that its advice is biased toward military priorities. But it did reach a peak of prestige after President Bush appointed as its chair General Colin Powell, the highest-ranking African American in the history of the armed forces.

The enormous expansion of the American military during the Cold War was built on claims, at times deliberately exaggerated, of a communist campaign to take over the entire planet. Concealed beneath the rhetoric about the communist threat was a different fuel for military expansion: interservice rivalry. Each branch of the services was eager to grow larger, more powerful, and better armed; each was fearful that the others would encroach on its central missions (see Chapter 13 for an example). Each service pushed for its own preferred new weapons system, even when the result was overlap and duplication in weaponry. Every time the Air Force developed a new model fighter plane, for instance, the Navy had to have a new fighter plane to match, and vice versa.

Cold War expansion of the military was facilitated by the growth of the *military-industrial complex*. Coined by President Eisenhower, the term refers to the potentially dangerous influence of the political alliance between the Pentagon and the corporations that manufacture its arms. Expensive new weapons systems are mutually rewarding to the armed forces and to companies, especially in such fields as aircraft, electronics, and shipbuilding, for which defense contracts can bring in several billion dollars a year in guaranteed sales. Defense contractors thus place their financial muscle and lobbying resources behind Pentagon budget requests.

Throughout the Cold War, the Pentagon was always eager to obtain costly new weapons. It was not, however, always eager to use them. Vietnam was a searing experience for the American military, which felt angry that it had not been allowed to go all out and embarrassed that it had lost a war for the first time in American history. After Vietnam, Pentagon officials tended to oppose the use of American troops abroad unless first assured of congressional and public support and promised that massive force could be employed.

The Persian Gulf War showed the American military at its most impressive and provided a shot in the arm for its prestige. But the euphoria of a high-tech military machine faded quickly, especially after the grim realities of the federal deficit came back into view. Now the Pentagon is engaged in a battle to hold down cuts in its force levels and termination of funding for its new weapons systems. In a nation that no longer feels militarily threatened, the Department of Defense is struggling to define new roles for a standing army in the post–Cold War world.

The Intelligence Community

One of the central features of the national security state is a large and diverse *intelligence community*. A number of U.S. agencies gather intelligence (information) about military, political, and economic developments in other countries (see Figure 18.1). Some of the institutions in this community specialize in high-tech intelligence gathering: among these is the National Security Agency, which employs the most advanced computer technology and spy satellites to monitor communications around the world. Each branch of the armed forces maintains

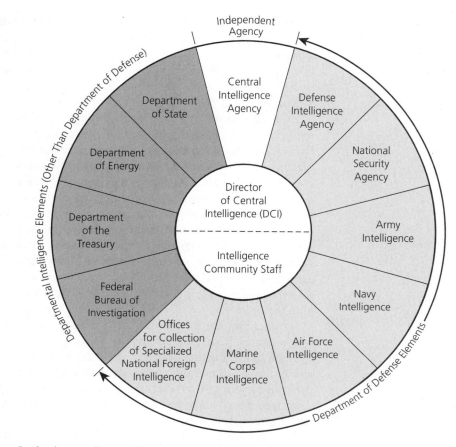

FIGURE 18.1

The Intelligence Community

Factbook on Intelligence (Washington, D.C.: Central Intelligence Agency, September 1987, p.20; as reprinted in James M. McCormack, American Foreign Policy and Process, Second Edition, (Itasca, IL: Peacock Publishers, 1992), p. 407.

its own intelligence unit. But the preeminent force in the intelligence community is the **Central Intelligence Agency (CIA).** The head of the CIA is also director of central intelligence for the entire government and the most influential figure in the highly secretive world of intelligence.

When Congress created the CIA, it thought it was establishing an agency to gather intelligence by various means ranging from analyses of foreign newspapers to espionage. Yet a vague phrase in the 1947 law referring to "other functions and duties" was seized on by the CIA to establish a unit that had little to do with intelligence gathering.[18] This was the **covert action** wing of the CIA, which specialized in clandestine operations that could not be traced to the U.S. government. Covert action became a secret weapon for presidents, allowing them to conduct a hidden foreign policy by, for example, bribing foreign politicians, stirring up economic unrest in other nations, or pushing for military coups to overthrow governments considered unfriendly.

Covert action became the hallmark of the CIA and was usually supported by the argument that the nation's communist enemies were employing the same kinds of "dirty tricks" to advance their sinister objectives. Few covert operations, as it turned out, actually hurt the communists or furthered American national security. Many backfired, making more enemies than friends in the long run; the Iranian people's continuing hostility to America is a prime example.[19]

It is not the ineffectiveness of covert action, however, that has made the CIA the national security agency that most disturbs popular democrats. They are even more worried about the incompatibility of covert action with American democracy. Political scientist Loch Johnson notes that whereas democracy requires open government, public debate, the rule of law, and ethical behavior, covert action requires "the use of tactics or 'dirty tricks' that are far removed from the accepted philosophical tenets of democratic theory—lying, sabotage, even clandestine warfare and assassination in times of peace."[20]

Revelations in the mid-1970s of CIA abuses, including spying on American citizens as well as assassination plots, led to the formation of intelligence committees in the House and Senate to monitor and occasionally veto covert operations. Through these congressional committees, there is now at least some measure of CIA public accountability.[21] Yet the CIA has found ways to evade accountability. President Reagan's director of the CIA, William Casey, misled the congressional committees about the agency's covert actions against the government of Nicaragua. When Congress later prohibited the Reagan administration from using the CIA to fund and direct the Contras, who were fighting to overthrow that government, Casey turned to the NSC staff and Lieutenant Colonel Oliver North to carry out this mission—a covert action that led to the Iran-Contra scandal.

The post–Cold War CIA has been shaken by a new crop of embarrassing revelations. Two CIA officials, Aldrich Ames and Harold Nicholson, were arrested for selling U.S. secrets to the Russians. And the agency's habit of collaborating with the most unsavory of foreign allies survived the end of the Cold War, as an expose of its activities in Guatemala documented. The CIA kept on its payroll Guatemalan military officers known to be engaged in kidnapping, torture, and assassination. When these officers covered up the murders of an American citizen and a guerrilla leader married to an American lawyer, the CIA hid the information from the congressional intelligence committees.[22] The CIA is ripe for a renewed debate on the place of a secret agency in a democratic society.

FOREIGN POLICY AND ECONOMIC POWER

Although military concerns were uppermost for American foreign policy makers during the Cold War, economic concerns were by no means forgotten. The United States emerged from World War II as an unchallenged economic giant, its superiority all the greater because its rivals had been physically or economically devastated by the war. To restore the shattered economies of Europe as trading partners (and to prevent European nations from falling prey to communist subversion), the United States undertook a massive program of economic aid, the Marshall Plan. During the first several decades of the Cold War, the United States was the hegemonic (predominant) power in the capitalist part of the world, setting the rules on international economic relations. American overseas investments and trade boomed during these decades.

But this hegemonic power finally weakened, eroded both by the economic resurgence of Western Europe and Japan and by the heavy burden of the arms race against the Soviet Union (a burden that America's capitalist competitors largely escaped). Starting in 1971, the United States began to run up a trade deficit, importing more from other countries than it sold to them. This deficit grew to huge proportions, and by the mid-1980s the U.S. had become the world's largest debtor. Rather than being able to set the rules, America now had to engage in extended—and frequently frustrating—multinational negotiations to bring down tariff barriers or open up foreign markets.[23]

Private interests play a significant role in American foreign economic policy. Labor unions are active, especially in seeking to restrict imports from low-wage nations because they eliminate American jobs. Farm groups press for greater government efforts to promote agricultural exports. The most influential private force is the corporate sector. Individuals in the top decision-making echelon of the national security state often have been recruited into temporary government service from large corporations, investment banks, and corporate law firms.[24] Regardless of economic background, American foreign policy makers have generally subscribed to the proposition that what advances the interests of American corporations and banks abroad advances the American national interest. In the globalized economy of the 1990s, business interests have become even more important players in American foreign policy than before.

It is difficult at times to disentangle economic interests from political interests in the history of U.S. foreign policy. Consider two cases already mentioned concerning the CIA: Iran and Chile. In Iran, the CIA's role in putting the shah in power not only established an anticommunist bastion in the Middle East; it also opened up Iran as a profitable field of operations for American oil companies. In Chile, American-owned corporations were just as zealous as Nixon and Kissinger in getting rid of President Allende. Fearful that Allende might nationalize their properties, the International Telephone and Telegraph Corporation and other American businesses offered the CIA $1.5 million for its covert campaign against him.[25]

FOREIGN POLICY AND PUBLIC OPINION

Until recently, scholars presented a picture of American public opinion in foreign policy that was closely in line with the perspective of elite democracy. Their studies suggested that the mass of Americans lacked interest in or knowledge of foreign affairs, were subject to emotional reactions to foreign events, and tended to defer to elites, especially presidents, in the determination of foreign policies. This view implied that it was fortunate for U.S. foreign policy that elites had the upper hand and that ordinary citizens had relatively little influence.

New and more extensive research by political scientists has altered this picture substantially.[26] The view of public opinion that has emerged is more favorable to the perspective of popular democracy. Although public knowledge of foreign affairs may fall short of the standard held by foreign policy experts, the newest research shows public opinion about foreign policy to be sensible and stable. The public responds rationally to the information it receives. It rallies behind a president who monopolizes the dissemination of information in a foreign crisis. But it may turn against the White House when alternative sources of information become available.

According to the new research, the public seldom has a direct impact on *specific* foreign policy decisions. But it can establish a climate of opinion that policy makers have to take into account. During the era of Cold War consensus, elites enjoyed a permissive climate for dispatching American troops to overseas conflicts. In the 1970s and 1980s, however, the majority of Americans were affected by a "Vietnam syndrome," an apprehension about sending troops abroad that constrained decision makers. President Reagan tried to overcome this syndrome with a guaranteed military victory in Grenada. Yet his efforts were not very successful: Public opinion constrained the Reagan administration from sending troops to attack the Sandinista government of Nicaragua and pressured the president to resume arms control negotiations with the Soviet Union.[27] President Bush claimed that he had finally vanquished the Vietnam syndrome in the Persian Gulf War. (See the accompanying box on the Persian Gulf War.) Yet public fears about sending American forces "in harm's way" continue to restrict President Clinton's options abroad.

Rather than always deferring to foreign policy elites, public opinion can, if it becomes strong and intense, compel elites to change their policies. Neither the president nor Congress is likely to hold out long once public opinion moves sharply in a new direction. Political scientists Robert Shapiro and Benjamin Page found that when public opinion changed significantly, American foreign policy subsequently changed with it about two-thirds of the time. The more that public unhappiness over American casualties in the war in Vietnam mounted, for example, the faster the president withdrew American forces from the conflict.[28]

That public opinion on foreign policy is rational *and* influential is encouraging to advocates of popular democracy. Also encouraging is what the new research has demonstrated about the content of popular beliefs. In the words of Shapiro and Page, "A strong aversion to using U.S. troops and a preference for negotiated settlements, arms control, and cooperative relations run through decades of public opinion data. The American public is willing to fight when it perceives a clear threat to U.S. interests but is very reluctant to do so unless there is no alternative."[29]

A CLOSER LOOK

Selling the Persian Gulf War

Since the war in Vietnam, the American people have been fearful of becoming involved again in a large-scale military conflict. So how did the 1991 Persian Gulf War, during which the United States led a multinational coalition in a rout of the Iraqi invaders of Kuwait, become so popular?

The popularity of the Gulf War stemmed, in part, from the kind of dramatic moral contrasts that have traditionally appealed to Americans. In Saddam Hussein, the Iraqi dictator, the United States faced a genuinely ruthless and brutal foe. With the Iraqi invasion of tiny, oil-rich Kuwait, the United States was opposing a case of naked aggression. The impressive ability of President Bush to rally a multinational coalition to drive Hussein out of Kuwait demonstrated both American leadership and international commitment to deny aggressors the object of their crimes.

But even these appealing elements were not enough, in the eyes of the White House and the military, to persuade the American people to fight a war in the Persian Gulf. The Gulf War had to be sold to the American people, they believed, with hype and myth. Consider the uses of babies and bombs to sell the war.

A shocking story of Iraqi brutality helped convince many Americans that the country had to go to war to rescue the suffering people of Kuwait. A fifteen-year-old Kuwaiti girl, identified only by her first name, Nayirah, appeared before a congressional caucus and related in a tearful voice how she had witnessed Iraqi soldiers take Kuwaiti babies out of their hospital incubators and leave them on the floor to die. The incubator story was widely repeated by President Bush and others. After the war, it was revealed that Nayirah was in fact the daughter of Kuwait's ambassador to the United States and that the incubator story had been devised by an American public relations firm in the pay of the Kuwaiti government. Reporters seeking evidence of the incubator tragedy found none and concluded that this notorious Iraqi atrocity had never happened.

Once the war began, the White House and the Pentagon kept a tight control over independent reporting by the press while feeding the media dramatic footage of military triumphs. The undisputed favorite for most Americans were Pentagon videos of laser-guided "smart" bombs homing in on Iraqi targets with incredible accuracy. Watching these videos on TV, viewers could easily believe that the war was a marvel of American technological genius and was humane to boot since smart bombs hit only military targets and spared civilians. After the war, however, the air force revealed that only 7 percent of the explosives it dropped were smart bombs. The rest were conventional dumb bombs, which landed off target 75 percent of the time, sometimes in areas populated by civilians.

There is an old saying: "In a war, truth is the first casualty." The American people had less than the truth to go on when they responded enthusiastically to the Persian Gulf War. They were skillfully manipulated by political and military elites that wanted unquestioning support. The selling of the Persian Gulf War should teach both journalists and citizens that in the face of wartime secrecy and propaganda, they must struggle to keep alive a democratic debate.

Sources: John R. MacArthur, *Second Front: Censorship and Propaganda in the Gulf War* (New York: Hill and Wang, 1992); Cecil V. Crabb, Jr., and Kevin V. Mulcahy, "The Elitist Presidency: George Bush and the Management of Operation Desert Storm," in Richard W. Waterman, ed., *The Presidency Reconsidered* (Itasca, Ill.: Peacock, 1993), pp. 275–300.

POST-COLD WAR FOREIGN POLICY AND THE DEMOCRATIC DEBATE

International relations specialist Ronald Steel captured the uncertainty and confusion of U.S. foreign policy in the post–Cold War world in these words:

> During the Cold War we had a vocation; now we have none. Once we had a powerful enemy; now it is gone. Once we had obedient allies; now we have trade rivals. Once we used to know how to define our place in the world and what our interests were; now we have no idea. Once we fretted about what critics called our arrogance of power. Now we wonder whether we are too timid and cautious. The world we knew has collapsed around us.[30]

Yet there is no shortage of proposals to provide new guideposts for this bewildering new world. In this section we consider competing strategies for the reorientation of American foreign policy. In light of these strategies, we examine how foreign policy has been conducted by the first post–Cold War president, Bill Clinton.

Strategies for a Post–Cold War World

The demise of the Cold War as the defining framework for American foreign policy sent international relations analysts scurrying to find a replacement. Among the many candidates for a new foreign policy strategy, we focus on four major ones. Two seek to continue the global activism of Cold War foreign policy while substituting new missions for the completed task of containing communism until it collapsed. The other two aim to reorient foreign policy away from the global interventionism of the Cold War era.

The first strategy, in the tradition of elite democracy pioneered by Alexander Hamilton, emphasizes the maintenance of America's preeminent leadership in a world whose challenges are more diffuse and complex than Cold War competition ever was. To foreign policy analysts who support this strategy, the primary task facing the U.S. is a tough-minded and unsentimental calculation of American interests. Foreign policy makers must learn to project power actively but carefully in the support of America's long-term interest in global stability while not becoming distracted by lesser concerns, such as the promotion of democracy and human rights abroad.[31]

Like Hamilton, these strategists place as much emphasis on economics as on military might. By itself, this is not unusual: Almost everyone in the debate over post–Cold War foreign policy agrees that America's role in the global economy has grown in importance as the threats to its military security have receded. What is distinctive about the elite democratic strategy is its insistence that even when the subject is the global economy the real issue is power. Political scientist Samuel Huntington, a prominent elite democrat quoted earlier in the book as a critic of mass movements, argues that "in the coming years, the principal conflicts of interests involving the United States and the major powers are likely to be over economic issues." To Huntington, the United States must recognize that its international primacy is endangered once again—but now the threat comes not from Soviet communism but from Asian capitalism.[32]

A second foreign policy strategy shares a belief in continuing American global activism but wants to make its mission the promotion of democracy. Adherents of this strategy believe that American power, even when wielded by elite democratic managers of the national security state, can and should serve popular democratic values around the world. They see the collapse of communism as creating an unprecedented opening for democracy in previously authoritarian states. Yet the movement toward democracy is precarious, likely to be stalled or even reversed without American involvement. Supporters of the "promoting democracy" strategy thus call for American political aid to assist fledgling democratic institutions abroad and American economic aid to cushion the difficult transition from bureaucratic socialism to free market democracy.

Promoting democracy abroad, its supporters say, satisfies a moral impulse deeply rooted in the American character. But this strategy is also claimed to be in America's best interest: Democracies abroad are less likely to pose a military threat and more likely to be reliable trading partners for the U.S. than are dictatorships. For both reasons, argues political scientist Larry Diamond, "The United States must continue to lead the democratic front. . . . The global future of democracy is intimately bound up with Americans' own global vision and daring."[33]

The third strategy, which can be termed the *new isolationism,* is increasingly advocated by conservative Republicans in Congress; its best-known champion is media commentator and two-time Republican presidential contender Patrick Buchanan. While supporters of this strategy favored an activist stance against communism, they view international involvement in the post–Cold War era with suspicion. Mistrustful of foreign policy elites, they are even more hostile to international organizations, especially the United Nations. The new isolationists want to continue American military supremacy and thus favor large defense budgets, but they want the spending directed mainly to air and naval forces and a space-based defense against missile attacks while bringing American ground troops home from their Cold War positions in Europe and Asia.

New isolationists view American society as threatened by numerous global forces. They seek to cut off foreign aid to allegedly ungrateful recipients abroad, to establish tariff barriers that will protect American workers against the competition of cheap foreign labor, and to stem the flow of immigration to the United States from Latin America, Asia, and Africa. For too long, they complain, Americans have been asked to sacrifice their interests to foreigners. "What we need," writes Patrick Buchanan, "is a new nationalism, a new patriotism, a new foreign policy that puts America first, and, not only first, but second and third as well."[34]

The fourth strategy shares with the third a skepticism about American global activism in the post–Cold War era. But it is more respectful of other societies, more generous in its concerns for their problems—and in this sense is more reflective of the best in the popular democratic tradition in American foreign policy. Supporters of this strategy warn American citizens about the pronouncements of the foreign policy elite: This elite became used to running the world in the heady days of the Cold War and is loath to give up its grip on power. And they warn of "the temptations to intervene everywhere that go along with the self-definition of superpower."[35] The Cold War is over, they say, but the habits of the Cold War continue: Thus the defense budget remains bloated even while the Defense Department is hard pressed to come up with military threats to justify it. Another enduring Cold War habit is to preach democracy but not to push for it where, as in the case of Saudi Arabia, economic or strategic interests take precedence.

According to this strategy, the United States still may have to act in global crises, to forestall extraordinary mass suffering or genocidal crimes, as well as to protect vital American military and economic interests. But recognizing the fact that the United States has never been more militarily secure than today, the new American foreign policy should be cautious and selective. And global commitments should no longer be made into an excuse for neglecting domestic problems of economic insecurity and racial conflict. As Ronald Steel has put it, we "cannot afford to indulge in lingering Cold War conceits of military omnipotence and unlimited global responsibilities. . . . Our task now is . . . that of recognizing our limitations, of rejecting the vanity of trying to remake the world in our image, and of preserving the promise of our own neglected society."[36]

Bill Clinton and the Post–Cold War World

Campaigning for president in 1992, Bill Clinton pledged to restore domestic concerns to primacy and to move American foreign policy beyond Cold War preoccupations. His criticisms of President Bush's policies toward China, Haiti, and Bosnia suggested that to the extent Clinton continued the practices of Cold War global activism, it would now be on behalf of democracy, human rights, and humanitarian relief of suffering.

Once in office, however, Clinton's approach to post–Cold War foreign policy has changed. The most common criticism of Clinton is that he has never articulated a clear, coherent vision of American purpose and strategy in the new global politics.[37] Valid as it might be, the criticism slights two important developments in Clinton's foreign policy. First, over the course of his presidency, as his domestic initiatives have been blocked and then supplanted by the agenda of the congressional Republicans, he has become increasingly involved in foreign policy, much like presidents of the Cold War era. Second, from a campaign perspective that sounded most like the cautious approach of the fourth strategy we have described, he has moved toward the first strategy of American primacy, tempered by occasional forays into promoting democracy as advocated by the second strategy.

The Size and Role of the Military. Many of those who supported Bill Clinton in 1992 anticipated that with the disappearance of the communist threat there would be a "peace dividend": Military spending could be substantially slashed and the funds freed up could be redirected to domestic needs. But from the start of his presidency, Clinton, embarrassed by revelations of his efforts to avoid the draft during the war in Vietnam, has been on the defensive in military matters. Moreover, the military-industrial complex could not be cut back rapidly without threatening large numbers of jobs, especially in the state richest in electoral votes, California. So Clinton's proposed cuts in the defense budget have been modest, barely distinguishable from the figures favored by his Republican critics. As *New York Times* journalist Tim Weiner observed during the 1996 campaign: "Mr. Clinton's Pentagon has spent more than $1 trillion, about $30 million an hour, more than the rest of the world's top 10 armies combined. It provided no real peace dividend save the uneasy prevailing peace."[38]

For the first year and a half of his presidency, Clinton was reluctant to use all this military might. Public opinion was opposed to the dispatch of American troops to global hot spots and Congress, where the new isolationists were increasingly noisy, repeatedly threatened to block American engagements abroad. But with Haiti in the fall of 1994 and Bosnia in the fall of 1995, Clinton overrode objections (some of them constitutional—see Chapter 12) and sent in American forces. Both military missions proved successful in large part and, contrary to the warnings of critics, avoided the loss of American lives. So, by the time he ran for reelection in 1996, Bill Clinton had grown comfortable in an unlikely role: commander-in-chief. In military spending and military uses, the activist strategy for maintaining American primacy in the world has been dominant.

Trade. During the 1980s, the United States rolled up huge trade deficits and saw large numbers of jobs go overseas. Bill Clinton promised a new activism in foreign economic policy, and this campaign pledge *was* fulfilled: The promotion of American trade has been the most distinctive feature of Clinton's foreign policy. His most prominent achievement in this area was congressional passage of the North American Free Trade Agreement (NAFTA) in 1993. Allying himself with large corporations, Clinton overcame opposition to the treaty, spearheaded by labor and environmental groups who argued that NAFTA would keep wages low and environmental regulations unenforced on both sides of the border with Mexico. NAFTA was only one of many multilateral trade agreements that Clinton promoted; another was Asia Pacific Economic Cooperation (APEC).

Less widely noticed than NAFTA or APEC have been the efforts of Clinton's Commerce Department, under the leadership of Secretary Ron Brown and his successors, to push American exports in the 10 "Big Emerging Markets" (BEM): China, India, Indonesia, Brazil, Mexico, Turkey, South Korea, South Africa, Poland, and Argentina. Commerce Department experts predict that in ten years U.S. trade with BEM countries may surpass its trade with Europe and Japan combined. "Clinton's BEM policy," writes international economics specialist John Stremlau, "recollects 'dollar diplomacy' as the economic and strategic interests of business and government once again run parallel. But the objectives today are far more diverse . . . and more likely to enjoy popular political support at home and abroad."[39]

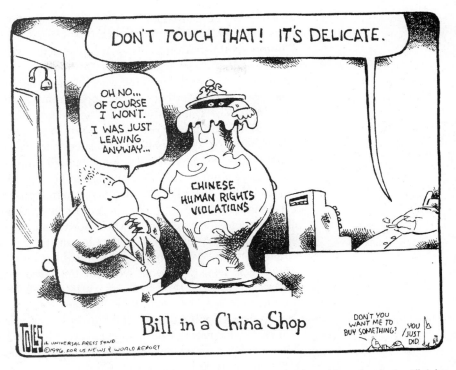

Presented chiefly as a means for increasing American jobs, Clinton's aim of expanding U.S. trade has indeed been popular. But it has also drawn him more fully into the elite democratic strategy for maintaining American primacy. Even as business leaders continue to complain about the Clinton administration and to provide ample funding for its Republican opponents, Clinton's Commerce Department has been going to bat for American businesses by helping them win contracts in the BEM.[40] As trade interests have accelerated in influence during the Clinton presidency, human rights concerns have all but disappeared. Violating his campaign promise to punish China unless it improved its sorry record on democracy and human rights, Clinton renewed China's **most-favored-nation (MFN)** trading status in 1994 and again in 1997 and overlooked numerous Chinese rights abuses. Human rights has remained a subject of concern for the Clinton administration mainly in countries such as Cuba, where "dollar diplomacy" does not apply.

Intervention in Haiti. President Clinton's strongest claim to "promoting democracy" in the post–Cold War world is his intervention in Haiti. In Haiti, the poorest nation in the western hemisphere, a democratically elected president, Jean-Bertrand Aristide, had been overthrown and forced into exile in 1991 by a military uprising. Holding down Aristide's supporters through acts of murder and terror, Haiti's military dictators brushed off the diplomatic efforts of the Clinton administration to bring Aristide back to office.

Haiti became a growing problem for Clinton, not only because the dictators' snubs made the president look weak but also because Haitian refugees, fleeing their island on rickety boats, were flooding into Florida. There was little support in Congress or among the public for military action to restore democracy in Haiti. But Clinton was passionately lobbied for stronger action against the dictators by the Congressional Black Caucus and was put into a difficult moral position by the hunger strike of activist Randall Robinson. By September 1994, the president seemingly had no choice left but bucking Congress and public opinion by using force or backing down at maximum embarrassment to his presidency.[41] Clinton chose force, and with an American invasion imminent Haiti's military dictators agreed to relinquish their power and go into exile. American troops peacefully took over the island and began the arduous task of dismantling the structure of repression that had terrorized the Haitian people. Aristide returned a few weeks later to a joyous welcome by Haiti's masses. He served out the remainder of his term, and in February 1996 he transferred power to his elected (and handpicked) successor, René Preval.

Critics have pointed out that Clinton's intervention in Haiti has done little to overcome the nation's desperate poverty. Important constitutional questions have also been raised about the president's defiance of Congress in dispatching troops to Haiti. In both respects, Clinton's intervention in Haiti recalls the Cold War heyday of the "imperial presidency." Yet there is a difference between this intervention and previous ones in Latin America: In Haiti it was democracy, not American corporate interests or anticommunist oligarchs, that was served by the arrival of American troops.[42]

Bosnia: "The Problem from Hell." No foreign policy issue so bedeviled the Clinton presidency as Bosnia—the "problem from hell," in the words of Secretary of State Warren Christopher.[43] Bosnia evoked all the uncertainties of American foreign policy in the post–Cold War World.

The civil war in Bosnia, which began early in 1992, reflected the new post–Cold War landscape in which nationalist and ethnic hatreds exploded once the old superpower conflict vanished. In the former Yugoslav republic of Bosnia-Herzegovina, ethnic Serbs battled ethnic Muslims for control. Aided by neighboring Serbia, the Bosnian Serbs had the upper hand militarily and followed their victories with "ethnic cleansing" (driving Muslims from their villages) and the mass rape of Muslim women.

As a presidential candidate, Bill Clinton blasted President Bush for standing by while human rights and democracy were violated on a massive scale in Bosnia. But once he took office, Clinton found himself standing by as well, even as the horror of Bosnia deepened. Clinton periodically talked tough, threatening to lift an arms embargo that hurt the Muslims and to employ air strikes against the Serbs. But everyone else—Congress, the Pentagon, America's European allies—was opposed. So Clinton's words were not followed by action. The president, and U.S. foreign policy generally, appeared vacillating and passive—in the stinging words of one critic, "like a cork bobbing about on the waves."[44] The Bosnian problem was left to the Europeans, who proved no more successful than Clinton in finding a solution.

Finally, in the summer of 1995, Clinton seized an opening and took strong action. A new American diplomatic mission, backed up by large-scale bombing of Serb positions, brought the warring parties to a peace conference in Dayton, Ohio. The agreement hammered out by American diplomats at Dayton maintained the legal integrity of Bosnia but effectively partitioned the country between a Muslim-Croat Federation and a Serb Republic. A NATO peacekeeping force, including 20,000 American troops, took military control of Bosnia, separating the warring ethnic factions while the political and economic reconstruction of the nation began. With a quarter of a million dead and 2 million driven from their homes, a fragile peace came to Bosnia.[45]

To a skeptical American public, President Clinton proclaimed America's idealistic motives in sending troops to Bosnia: "There are still times when America and America alone can and should make the difference for peace."[46] Clinton could legitimately claim the mantle of peacemaker, for he was also promoting peace in the Middle East and Northern Ireland. But he had other reasons finally to intervene forcefully in Bosnia: He had to remove the embarrassing stigma of his Bosnian inaction before the 1996 election and to quiet mounting criticisms that America had abdicated its global position of leadership. With his successful intervention in Bosnia—American troops encountered no military resistance—Clinton was again staking the American claim to leadership. Elite democratic strategists had urged foreign policy makers to downplay democratic and humanitarian concerns and keep their focus on global primacy in the post–Cold War world. Ironically, a humanitarian intervention in Bosnia became Bill Clinton's vehicle for realizing their agenda.

CONCLUSION: A MORE DEMOCRATIC FOREIGN POLICY?

In the confusing new world of the post–Cold War era, many Americans, echoing the old popular democratic strain, wish to cut back on international involvement and turn inward. This impulse may be taken too far when it advocates a new isolationism. The United States is too intertwined with the rest of the world, and has too much at stake in international economic, military, political, and environmental issues, to return to the isolationism of the past. In upholding their traditional standard of internationalism as against isolationism, foreign policy elites have an important case to make to the American people.

Nevertheless, the popular democratic tradition has much to offer American policy for a post–Cold War world. Popular democrats have long argued that American strength in the world depends, above all, on a healthy economy and society at home. They have believed that America should seek peaceful commercial relations with other nations and support democratic progress around the globe. They have warned of a large, expensive, and aggressive military and emphasized the distortions it introduces into the economy and political system.

Popular democrats seek to widen the democratic debate over foreign policy. To open up this debate, the secretive habits of the national security state, including excessive classification of information and covert action, must be terminated. Foreign policy experts in the executive branch and the Pentagon must not monopolize the discussion; voices in Congress and in citizen groups also must be heard. Because the United States must speak to the rest of the world in a clear and coherent fashion, presidential leadership in foreign policy will remain necessary. But in the post–Cold War world, presidents should not be the sole masters of foreign policy. Their approach to the world should emerge from a democratic dialogue over the goals and instruments of American foreign policy.

KEY TERMS

isolationism
expansion
Cold War
national security state
North Atlantic Treaty Organization (NATO)
containment
National Security Council (NSC)

national security adviser
Department of State
Department of Defense
Joint Chiefs of Staff (JCS)
Central Intelligence Agency (CIA)
covert action
most favored nation (MFN)

SUGGESTED READINGS

Richard J. Barnet, *The Rockets' Red Glare: When America Goes to War—The Presidents and the People.* New York: Simon & Schuster, 1990. A narrative history of American decisions to fight abroad, told from a popular democratic perspective.

Loch K. Johnson, *America's Secret Power: The CIA in a Democratic Society.* New York: Oxford University Press, 1989. Focuses on congressional efforts to hold the CIA accountable for its covert activities.

Henry Kissinger, *Diplomacy.* New York: Simon & Schuster, 1994. Diplomatic history as viewed by a central figure in the elite democratic tradition.

Michael H. Shuman and Hal Harvey, *Security Without War: A Post–Cold War Foreign Policy.* Boulder, Colo.: Westview Press, 1993. Provocative proposals for an American foreign policy that relies on military force less than we have in the past.

Ronald Steel, *Temptations of a Superpower* (Cambridge: Harvard University Press, 1995. One of the most prominent critics of American foreign policy during the Cold War warns that its arrogant mind-set still persists among the foreign policy elite and goes on to offer suggestions for an alternative foreign policy in the popular democratic tradition.

Afterword: The Prospects for Popular Democracy

A s political scientists, we wrote this book to explain how American politics can be understood as a debate between elite democracy and popular democracy. As citizens who came of age politically through our activism in the mass movements of the 1960s and 1970s, we wrote this book because we care particularly about the fate of popular democracy. These days, as both citizens and teachers, we sense in our communities and hear from our students that a stronger democracy is impossible, and that what we call elite democracy is destined to rule. To be sure, it is easy to become resigned about the fate of democracy today. Indeed, much of this book is written to promote student understanding of the obstacles ordinary people face.

Ultimately, is the democratic debate heading towards nearly total domination of the public square by elite democrats? Is elite democracy likely to predominate in the world of high-tech economics and politics? Given what we've said, what are the prospects for popular democracy?

Almost by definition, the forces of elite democracy are indeed powerful. Nowhere is this truer than in the structure of the political economy. Given their enormous monetary resources, central role in capital investment, and ideological status as the champions of the free market, corporations hold a privileged position in the political economy. With the onset of intensified global competition, they present themselves as America's front line in the defense of our standard of living. Global corporations warn that attempts to impose popular democratic controls over private economic forces will undercut our competitive standing and injure us all in the long run.

Insofar as they play the corporate tune, political elites look almost as powerful. They are closely connected to economic elites through campaign contributions and lobbying. And they have found numerous methods to insulate themselves from democratic accountability. Members of Congress are the most accountable, but many have mastered the fundraising and image-making techniques that practically guarantee them reelection and preserve their status as a privileged elite. Presidents must also respond to public opinion, but their royal lifestyle, engagement in elite decision-making circles, and powers of secrecy link them more to elite than to popular democracy. Although bureaucrats and judges sometimes uphold important democratic values, neither are directly accountable to the public.

The many points of connection between private power and political power create a policy process that works, more often than not, to favor elite democracy.

521

This process demeans citizenship, for it is the result not of debate but of unaccountable power stemming from money and its direct and indirect effects. Government policies tend to reflect the existing, unequal, and unjust distribution of power and political resources. Rather than fostering greater equality in resources and opportunities, they promote further economic inequality.

Elite democracy in the United States is of course sustained through many powerful institutions. This is so even though the caretakers of these institutions advertise their affection, and even infatuation, with public opinion. It is so even as elites disguise their links to money, position, or techniques of manipulation. Elite democracy rules through the idea that the world is too complex for ordinary people to understand and therefore requires elite guidance of democratic politics. In an era when change is rapid, many-sided, and often bewildering, ordinary citizens, it often seems, cannot hope to control their own fates directly. Even though citizens should hold ultimate authority through the electoral process, elite democrats assert, actual decision making must remain in the hands of the sophisticated. An ill-informed public only sidetracks the intelligent management of "necessary" decisions. Elite democracy has been, and is sure to remain, a strong force in American political life. In normal times, elites have most of the political advantages.

Yet while elite power seems overwhelming, we wrote this book because of the obvious and continued vibrancy of the popular democratic tradition in the United States. If there is continuity in American politics, it is in the strength and continued eruption of popular mobilizations that weaken and constrict the power of seemingly invulnerable elites. Our history shows that few political choices are inevitable or foreordained. When popular democratic forces become active, as in the movements of the 1960s, elite democracy suddenly becomes vulnerable. Why is elite democracy so susceptible to criticism and challenge? What are the strengths of popular democracy?

Elite democrats build their best case on their superior expertise. Yet they often make colossal mistakes. Usually, it is ordinary citizens who pay for these mistakes, and most ordinary people are fully aware of this fact. It was the elite managers of the national security state who planned the Vietnam War—and American soldiers who were its physical and psychological casualties. It was the secretive White Houses of Richard Nixon and Ronald Reagan that undermined democratic accountability in the Watergate and Iran-Contra scandals, respectively. It was corporate elites, with their short-sighted pursuit of profit, who polluted the environment and devastated communities through plant closings and layoffs in the 1980s and 1990s. Revelations of Cold War experiments in which government officials and scientists exposed unwitting Americans to atomic radiation are only one more demonstration that the people are not served well when elites make important decisions without democratic controls.

The campaign finance scandals of 1996 remind us of another weakness of elite democracy: Its power is often based not on the sophisticated operations of expertise but on the crass operations of money. To collect the votes of the many, both parties competed in 1996 for massive infusions of "soft money" from the few. Ordinary citizens could not hope to voice their concerns personally to President Clinton or to Speaker Gingrich, but wealthy campaign donors could, with the amount of access calibrated to the size of the contribution. When wealth plays this powerful and flagrant a role in elections—the core of the democratic process—elite democracy starts to look like a contradiction in terms.

Perhaps most important, elite virtue, wisdom, and power are called into question by American political values. The idea that concentrated power is dangerous to liberty and damaging to ordinary citizens is central to the American political tradition. The American Revolution was a grand experiment in bringing government under popular control. Although elite power made a comeback in the Constitution, it was tempered by concessions to popular democracy and limited by the Bill of Rights won by the Anti-federalists. Throughout the course of American history, mass movements have revived the revolutionary spirit of protest and reasserted the popular democratic doctrine that ordinary people are more than capable of running their own affairs.

Today as yesterday, the foundation for popular democracy remains a democratic civil society. In this book, we've dedicated much discussion to the forces that sustain and nurture political participation. Political participation comes in many forms, some that don't seem political at all. Still, nurturing participation—in the workplace, schools, communities, cities, and even the corporation—is the major feature of a democratic society. In recent years, a democratic civil society has been threatened. But it still stands, in churches, labor unions, and neighborhoods, as a testimony to the importance of popular democratic political values.

Last but not least, there is the language, or vocabulary, of democracy and inclusiveness. Not only in the United States but around the globe as well, the logic of democracy has become increasingly difficult for elites to resist. This inclusionary logic—the strongest advantage that popular democrats enjoy in the democratic debate—holds that every citizen, regardless of class, race, gender, or specialized education, has a rightful say in the processes of public decision making. The popular democratic emphasis on equality and the popular democratic commitment to the dignity and competence of ordinary citizens have largely won the battle for rhetorical and symbolic preeminence. Even elite democrats have to pay at least lip service to them. When these popular democratic values are put into political action, elites are put on the defensive. Accustomed to mass apathy, they are surprised and even frightened by instances of popular democratic activism.

Popular democrats cannot hope to match elite democrats in money or privileged access to the inner councils of government. Yet popular democracy in America has enduring strengths. The American tradition is rich in ideas and activities that show, contrary to the assumption of elite democrats, that people can get beyond a narrow self-interest when they participate in the affairs of society. There is the republican tradition, with its ideal of virtuous citizens deliberating together on how to advance the common good. There is the diversity of religious faiths, almost all of which teach service to others over self-seeking. There is the experience of countless neighborhoods and communities in which people have joined together to bring improvement and harmony. There are the inspiring efforts of racial minorities and women to claim their equal share of the democratic promise. And there is the experience of workers, who labor to achieve economic justice and social equality.

All of these rest on—and sustain—the most fundamental assumption of popular democracy: that people can be sociable rather than self-centered and can make their lives better and more meaningful when they are involved in public life. Against the elite democratic claim that mass apathy is natural, popular democrats argue that given the opportunity, people will participate in public affairs and will learn from their participation how they can gain in both power and dignity. Evidence for this argument can be found in the major policy victories won by popular democrats in such areas as collective bargaining for labor, civil rights, women's rights, and environmental protection.

Popular democrats concede that the complexity of modern society requires experts to play some role in the political process. They do not concede that the role of expertise must be as great as elite democrats would have it. Our modern high-tech society may in fact make possible a diffusion of expertise to citizens that will enhance popular democracy. With the rise of more diverse and interactive media, with the spread of personal computers, and with other new developments that place almost every conceivable kind of information within the public's grasp, the gap between elites and ordinary citizens can be narrowed. The end of the Cold War also favors popular democracy by reducing the need to keep so much information about the world secret in the name of national security.

Too often, we believe, elite democrats have sold American democracy short. And sometimes they have persuaded ordinary Americans of the need to accept the guidance of a "superior" few. In writing this book, we join an enduring American tradition, stretching back to the revolutionaries and Anti-federalists, that calls on ordinary citizens to have confidence in their capacity for self-government. We hope that the book stimulates thought and action on your part about the meaning of American democracy.

APPENDIX

THE DECLARATION OF INDEPENDENCE IN CONGRESS   JULY 4, 1776

The unanimous declaration of the thirteen United States of America

When, in the course of human events, it becomes necessary for one people to dissolve the political bonds which have connected them with another, and to assume, among the powers of the earth, the separate and equal station to which the laws of nature and nature's God entitle them, a decent respect to the opinions of mankind requires that they should declare the causes which impel them to the separation.

We hold these truths to be self-evident: That all men are created equal; that they are endowed by their Creator with certain unalienable rights; that among these are life, liberty, and the pursuit of happiness; that, to secure these rights, governments are instituted among men, deriving their just powers from the consent of the governed; that whenever any form of government becomes destructive of these ends, it is the right of the people to alter or to abolish it, and to in-stitute new government, laying its foundation on such principles, and organizing its powers in such form, as to them shall seem most likely to effect their safety and happiness. Prudence, indeed, will dictate that government long established should not be changed for light and transient causes; and accordingly all experience hath shown that mankind are more disposed to suffer, while evils are sufferable, than to right themselves by abolishing the forms to which they are accustomed. But when a long train of abuses and usurpations, pursuing invariably the same object, evinces a design to reduce them under absolute despotism, it is their right, it is their duty, to throw off such government, and to provide new guards for their future security. Such has been the patient sufferance of these colonies; and such is now the necessity which constrains them to alter their former systems of government. The history of the present King of Great Britain is a history of repeated injuries and usurpations, all having in direct object the establishment of an absolute tyranny over these states. To prove this, let facts be submitted to a candid world.

He has refused his assent to laws, the most wholesome and necessary for the public good.

He has forbidden his governors to pass laws of immediate and pressing importance, unless suspended in their operation till his assent should be obtained; and, when so suspended, he has utterly neglected to attend to them.

He has refused to pass other laws for the accommodation of large districts of people, unless those people would relinquish the right of representation in the legislature, a right inestimable to them, and formidable to tyrants only.

He has called together legislative bodies at places unusual, uncomfortable, and distant from the depository of their public records, for the sole purpose of fatiguing them into compliance with his measures.

He has dissolved representative houses repeatedly, for opposing, with manly firmness, his invasions on the rights of the people.

He has refused for a long time, after such dissolutions, to cause others to be elected; whereby the legislative powers, incapable of annihilation, have returned to the people at large for their exercise; the state remaining, in the mean time, exposed to all the dangers of invasions from without and convulsions within.

He has endeavored to prevent the population of these states; for that purpose obstructing the laws for naturalization of foreigners; refusing to pass others to encourage their migration hither, and raising the conditions of new appropriations of lands.

He has obstructed the administration of justice, by refusing his assent to laws for establishing judiciary powers.

He has made judges dependent on his will alone, for the tenure of their offices, and the amount and payment of their salaries.

He has erected a multitude of new offices, and sent hither swarms of officers to harass our people and eat out their substance.

He has kept among us, in times of peace, standing armies, without the consent of our legislatures.

He has affected to render the military independent of, and superior to, the civil power.

He has combined with others to subject us to a jurisdiction foreign to our constitution, and unacknowledged by our laws, giving his assent to their acts of pretended legislation:

For quartering large bodies of armed troops among us;

For protecting them, by a mock trial, from punishment for any murders which they should commit on the inhabitants of these states;

For cutting off our trade with all parts of the world;

For imposing taxes on us without our consent;

For depriving us, in many cases, of the benefits of trial by jury;

For transporting us beyond seas, to be tried for pretended offenses;

For abolishing the free system of English laws in a neighboring province, establishing therein an arbitrary government, and enlarging its boundaries, so as to render it at once an example and fit instrument for introducing the same absolute rule into these colonies;

For taking away our charters, abolishing our most valuable laws, and altering fundamentally the forms of our governments;

For suspending our own legislatures, and declaring themselves invested with power to legislate for us in all cases whatsoever.

He has abdicated government here, by declaring us out of his protection and waging war against us.

He has plundered our seas, ravaged out coasts, burned our towns, and destroyed the lives of our people.

He is at this time transporting large armies of foreign mercenaries to complete the works of death, desolation, and tyranny already begun with circumstances of cruelty and perfidy scarcely paralleled in the most barbarous ages, and totally unworthy the head of a civilized nation.

He has constrained our fellow-citizens, taken captive on the high seas, to bear arms against their country, to become the executioners of their friends and brethren, or to fall themselves by their hands.

He has excited domestic insurrection among us, and has endeavored to bring on the inhabitants of our frontiers the merciless Indian savages, whose known rule of warfare is an undistinguished destruction of all ages, sexes, and conditions.

In every stage of these oppressions we have petitioned for redress in the most humble terms; our repeated petitions have been answered only by repeated injury. A prince, whose character is thus marked by every act which may define a tyrant, is unfit to be the ruler of a free people.

Nor have we been wanting in our attentions to our British brethren. We have warned them, from time to time, of attempts by their legislature to extend an unwarrantable jurisdiction over us. We have reminded them of the circumstances of our emigration and settlement here. We have appealed to their native justice and magnanimity; and we have conjured them, by the ties of our common kindred, to disavow these usurpations, which would inevitably interrupt our connections and correspondence. They too, have been deaf to the voice of justice and of consanguinity. We must, therefore, acquiesce in the necessity which denounces our separation, and hold them, as we hold the rest of mankind, enemies in war, in peace friends.

We, therefore, the representatives of the United States of America, in General Congress assembled, appealing to the Supreme Judge of the world for the rectitude of our intentions, do, in the name and by the authority of the good people of these colonies, solemnly publish and declare, that these United Colonies are, and of right ought to be, FREE AND INDEPENDENT STATES; that they are absolved from all allegiance to the British crown, and that all political connection between them and the state of Great Britain is, and ought to be, totally dissolved; and that, as free and independent states, they have full power to levy war, conclude peace, contract alliances, establish commerce, and do all other acts and things which independent states may of right do. And for the support of this declaration, with a firm reliance on the protection of Divine Providence, we mutually pledge to each other our lives, our fortunes, and our sacred honor.

JOHN HANCOCK
and fifty-five others

THE CONSTITUTION OF THE UNITED STATES OF AMERICA*

Preamble

We the people of the United States, in order to form a more perfect union, establish justice, insure domestic tranquillity, provide for the common defense, promote the general welfare, and secure the blessings of liberty to ourselves and our posterity, do ordain and establish this Constitution for the United States of America.

Article I

Section 1 All legislative powers herein granted shall be vested in a Congress of the United States, which shall consist of a Senate and a House of Representatives.

Section 2 The House of Representatives shall be composed of members chosen every second year by the people of the several States, and the electors in each State shall have the qualifications requisite for electors of the most numerous branch of the State Legislature.

No person shall be a Representative who shall not have attained to the age of twenty-five years, and been

seven years a citizen of the United States, and who shall not, when elected, be an inhabitant of that State in which he shall be chosen.

Representatives and direct taxes shall be apportioned among the several States which may be included within this Union, according to their respective numbers, *which shall be determined by adding to the whole number of free persons, including those bound to service for a term of years and excluding Indians not taxed, three-fifths of all other persons.* The actual enumeration shall be made within three years after the first meeting of the Congress of the United States, and within every subsequent term of ten years, in such manner as they shall by law direct. The number of Representatives shall not exceed one for every thirty thousand, but each State shall have at least one Representative; *and until such enumeration shall be made, the State of New Hampshire shall be entitled to choose three, Massachusetts eight, Rhode Island and Providence Plantations one, Connecticut five, New York six, New Jersey four, Pennsylvania eight, Delaware one, Maryland six, Virginia ten, North Carolina five, South Carolina five, and Georgia three.*

When vacancies happen in the representation from any State, the Executive authority thereof shall issue writs of elections to fill such vacancies.

The House of Representatives shall choose their Speaker and other officers; and shall have the sole power of impeachment.

Section 3 The Senate of the United States shall be composed of two Senators from each State, *chosen by the legislature thereof,* for six years; and each Senator shall have one vote.

Immediately after they shall be assembled in consequence of the first election, they shall be divided as equally as may be into three classes. The seats of the Senators of the first class shall be vacated at the expiration of the second year, of the second class at the expiration of the fourth year, and of the third class at the expiration of the sixth year, so that one-third may be chosen every second year; *and if vacancies happen by resignation or otherwise, during the recess of the legislature of any State, the Executive thereof may make temporary appointments until the next meeting of the legislature, which shall then fill such vacancies.*

No person shall be a Senator who shall not have attained to the age of thirty years, and been nine years a citizen of the United States, and who shall not, when

* Passages no longer in effect are printed in italic type.

elected, be an inhabitant of that State for which he shall be chosen.

The Vice-President of the United States shall be President of the Senate, but shall have no vote, unless they be equally divided.

The Senate shall choose their other officers, and also a President *pro tempore*, in the absence of the Vice-President, or when he shall exercise the office of President of the United States.

The Senate shall have the sole power to try all impeachments. When sitting for that purpose, they shall be on oath or affirmation. When the President of the United States is tried, the Chief Justice shall preside: and no person shall be convicted without the concurrence of two-thirds of the members present.

Judgment in cases of impeachment shall not extend further than to removal from the office, and disqualification to hold and enjoy any office of honor, trust or profit under the United States: but the party convicted shall nevertheless be liable and subject to indictment, trial, judgment and punishment, according to law.

Section 4   The times, places and manner of holding elections for Senators and Representatives shall be prescribed in each State by the legislature thereof; but the Congress may at any time by law make or alter such regulations, except as to the places of choosing Senators.

The Congress shall assemble at least once in every year, and such meeting *shall be on the first Monday in December, unless they shall by law appoint a different day.*

Section 5   Each house shall be the judge of the elections, returns and qualifications of its own members, and a majority of each shall constitute a quorum to do business; but a smaller number may adjourn from day to day, and may be authorized to compel the attendance of absent members, in such manner, and under such penalties, as each house may provide.

Each house may determine the rules of its proceedings, punish its members for disorderly behavior, and with the concurrence of two-thirds, expel a member.

Each house shall keep a journal of its proceedings, and from time to time publish the same, excepting such parts as may in their judgment require secrecy; and the yeas and nays of the members of either house on any question shall, at the desire of one-fifth of those present, be entered on the journal.

Neither house, during the session of Congress, shall, without the consent of the other, adjourn for more than three days, nor to any other place than that in which the two houses shall be sitting.

Section 6   The Senators and Representatives shall receive a compensation for their services, to be ascertained by law and paid out of the treasury of the United States. They shall in all cases except treason, felony and breach of the peace, be privileged from arrest during their attendance at the session of their respective houses, and in going to and returning from the same; and for any speech or debate in either house, they shall not be questioned in any other place.

No Senator or Representative shall, during the time for which he was elected, be appointed to any civil office under the authority of the United States, which shall have been created, or the emoluments whereof shall have been increased, during such time; and no person holding any office under the United States shall be a member of either house during his continuance in office.

Section 7   All bills for raising revenue shall originate in the House of Representatives; but the Senate may propose or concur with amendments as on other bills.

Every bill which shall have passed the House of Representatives and the Senate, shall, before it become a law, be presented to the President of the United States; if he approve he shall sign it, but if not he shall return it with objections to that house in which it originated, who shall enter the objections at large on their journal, and proceed to reconsider it. If after such reconsideration two-thirds of that house shall agree to pass the bill, it shall be sent, together with the objections, to the other house, by which it shall likewise be reconsidered, and, if approved by two-thirds of that house, it shall become a law. But in all such cases the votes of both houses shall be determined by yeas and nays, and the names of the persons voting for and against the bill shall be entered on the journal of each house respectively. If any bill shall not be returned by the President within ten days (Sundays excepted) after it shall have been presented to him, the same shall be a law, in like manner as if he had signed it, unless the Congress by their adjournment prevent its return, in which case it shall not be a law.

Every order, resolution, or vote to which the concurrence of the Senate and House of Representatives may be necessary (except on a question of adjournment) shall be presented to the President of the

United States; and before the same shall take effect, shall be approved by him, or being disapproved by him, shall be repassed by two-thirds of the Senate and House of Representatives, according to the rules and limitations prescribed in the case of a bill.

Section 8 The Congress shall have power

To lay and collect taxes, duties, imposts, and excises, to pay the debts and provide for the common defense and general welfare of the United States; but all duties, imposts and excises shall be uniform throughout the United States;

To borrow money on the credit of the United States;

To regulate commerce with foreign nations, and among the several States, and with the Indian tribes;

To establish an uniform rule of naturalization, and uniform laws on the subject of bankruptcies throughout the United States;

To coin money, regulate the value thereof, and of foreign coin, and fix the standard of weights and measures;

To provide for the punishment of counterfeiting the securities and current coin of the United States.

To establish post offices and post roads;

To promote the progress of science and useful arts by securing for limited times to authors and inventors the exclusive right to their respective writings and discoveries;

To constitute tribunals inferior to the Supreme Court;

To define and punish piracies and felonies committed on the high seas and offenses against the law of nations;

To declare war, grant letters of marque and reprisal, and make rules concerning captures on land and water;

To raise and support armies, but no appropriation of money to that use shall be for a longer term than two years;

To provide and maintain a navy;

To make rules for the government and regulation of the land and naval forces;

To provide for calling forth the militia to execute the laws of the Union, suppress insurrections, and repel invasions;

To provide for organizing, arming, and disciplining the militia, and for governing such part of them as may be employed in the service of the United States, reserving to the States respectively the appointment of the officers, and the authority of training the militia according to the discipline prescribed by Congress;

To exercise exclusive legislation in all cases whatsoever, over such district (not exceeding ten miles square) as may, by cession of particular States, and the acceptance of Congress, become the seat of government of the United States, and to exercise like authority over all places purchased by the consent of the legislature of the State, in which the same shall be, for erection of forts, magazines, arsenals, dockyards, and other needful buildings;—and

To make all laws which shall be necessary and proper for carrying into execution the foregoing powers, and all other powers vested by this Constitution in the government of the United States, or in any department or officer thereof.

Section 9 *The migration or importation of such persons as any of the States now existing shall think proper to admit shall not be prohibited by the Congress prior to the year 1808; but a tax or duty may be imposed on such importation, not exceeding $10 for each person.*

The privilege of the writ of habeas corpus shall not be suspended, unless when in case of rebellion or invasion the public safety may require it.

No bill of attainder or ex post facto law shall be passed.

No capitation, or other direct, tax shall be laid, unless in proportion to the census or enumeration herein before directed to be taken.

No tax or duty shall be laid on articles exported from any State.

No preference shall be given by any regulation of commerce or revenue to the ports of one State over those of another; nor shall vessels bound to, or from, one State, be obligated to enter, clear, or pay duties in another.

No money shall be drawn from the treasury, but in consequence of appropriations made by law; and a regular statement and account of the receipts and expenditures of all public money shall be published from time to time.

No title of nobility shall be granted by the United States: and no person holding any office of profit or trust under them, shall, without the consent of the Congress, accept of any present, emolument, office, or title, of any kind whatever, from any king, prince, or foreign state.

Section 10 No State shall enter into any treaty, alliance, or confederation; grant letters of marque and reprisal; coin money; emit bills of credit; make anything but gold and silver coin a tender in payment of debts; pass any bill of attainder, ex post facto law, or law impairing the obligation of contracts, or grant any title of nobility.

No State shall, without the consent of Congress, lay any imposts or duties on imports or exports, except what may be absolutely necessary for executing its inspection laws: and the net produce of all duties and imposts, laid by any State on imports or exports, shall be for the use of the treasury of the United States; and all such laws shall be subject to the revision and control of the Congress.

No State shall, without the consent of Congress, lay any duty of tonnage, keep troops or ships of war in time of peace, enter into any agreement or compact with another State, or with a foreign power, or engage in war, unless actually invaded, or in such imminent danger as will not admit of delay.

Article II

Section 1 The executive power shall be vested in a President of the United States of America. He shall hold his office during the term of four years, and, together with the Vice-President, chosen for the same term, be elected as follows:

Each State shall appoint, in such manner as the legislature thereof may direct, a number of electors, equal to the whole number of Senators and Representatives to which the State may be entitled in the Congress; but no Senator or Representative, or person holding an office of trust or profit under the United States, shall be appointed an elector.

The electors shall meet in their respective States, and vote by ballot for two persons, of whom one at least shall not be an inhabitant of the same State with themselves. And they shall make a list of all the persons voted for, and of the number of votes for each; which list they shall sign and certify, and transmit sealed to the seat of government of the United States, directed to the President of the Senate. The President of the Senate shall, in the presence of the Senate and House of Representatives, open all the certificates, and the votes shall then be counted. The person having the greatest number of votes shall be the President, if such number be a majority of the whole number of electors appointed; and if there be more than one who have such majority, and have an equal number of votes, then the House of Representatives shall immediately choose by ballot one of them for President; and if no person have a majority, then from the five highest on the list said house shall in like manner choose the President. But in choosing the President the votes shall be taken by States, the representation from each State having one vote; a quorum for this purpose shall consist of a member of members from two-thirds of the States, and a majority of all the States shall be necessary to a choice. In every case, after the choice of the President, the person having the greatest number of votes of the electors shall be the Vice-President. But if there should remain two or more who have equal votes, the Senate shall choose from them by ballot the Vice-President.

The Congress may determine the time of choosing the electors and the day on which they shall give their votes; which day shall be the same throughout the United States.

No person except a natural-born citizen, *or a citizen of the United States at the time of the adoption of this Constitution,* shall be eligible to the office of President; neither shall any person be eligible to that office who shall not have attained to the age of thirty-five years, and been fourteen years a resident within the United States.

In cases of the removal of the President from office or of his death, resignation, or inability to discharge the powers and duties of the said office, the same shall devolve on the Vice-President, and the Congress may by law provide for the case of removal, death, resignation, or inability, both of the President and Vice-President, declaring what officer shall then act as President, and such officer shall act accordingly, until the disability be removed, or a President shall be elected.

The President shall, at stated time, receive for his services a compensation, which shall neither be increased nor diminished during the period for which he shall have been elected, and he shall not receive within that period any other emolument from the United States, or any of them.

Before he enter on the execution of his office, he shall take the following oath or affirmation:— "I do solemnly swear (or affirm) that I will faithfully execute the office of the President of the United States, and will to the best of my ability preserve, protect and defend the Constitution of the United States."

Section 2 The President shall be commander in chief of the army and navy of the United States, and of the militia of the several States, when called into the actual service of the United States; he may require the opinion, in writing, of the principal officer in each of the executive departments, upon any subject relating to the duties of their respective offices, and he shall have power to grant reprieves and pardons for offenses against the United States, except in cases of impeachment.

He shall have power, by and with the advice and consent of the Senate, to make treaties, provided two-thirds of the Senators present concur; and he shall nominate, and by and with the advice and consent of the Senate, shall appoint ambassadors, other public ministers and consuls, judges of the Supreme Court, and all other officers of the United States, whose appointments are not herein otherwise provided for, and which shall be established by law: but Congress may by law vest the appointment of such inferior officers, as they think proper, in the President alone, in the courts of law, or in the heads of departments.

The President shall have power to fill up all vacancies that may happen during the recess of the Senate, by granting commissions which shall expire at the end of their next session.

Section 3 He shall from time to time give to the Congress information of the state of the Union, and recommend to their consideration such measures as he shall judge necessary and expedient; he may, on extraordinary occasions, convene both houses, or either of them, and in case of disagreement between them, with respect to the time of adjournment, he may adjourn them to such time as he shall think proper; he shall receive ambassadors and other public ministers; he shall take care that the laws be faithfully executed, and shall commission all the officers of the United States.

Section 4 The President, Vice-President and all civil officers of the United States shall be removed from office on impeachment for, and on conviction of, treason, bribery, or other high crimes and misdemeanors.

Article III

Section 1 The judicial power of the United States shall be vested in one Supreme Court, and in such inferior courts as the Congress may from time to time ordain and establish. The judges, both of the Supreme and inferior courts, shall hold their offices during good behavior, and shall, at stated times, receive for their services a compensation which shall not be diminished during their continuance in office.

Section 2 The judicial power shall extend to all cases, in law and equity, arising under this Constitution, the laws of the United States, and treaties made, or which shall be made, under their authority;—to all cases affecting ambassadors, other public ministers and consuls;—to all cases of admiralty and maritime jurisdiction;—to controversies to which the United States shall be a party;—to controversies between two or more States;—*between a State and a citizens of another State;*—between citizens of different States;—between citizens of the same State claiming lands under grants of different States, and between a State, or the citizens thereof, and foreign states, citizens or subjects.

In all cases affecting ambassadors, other public ministers and consuls, and those in which a State shall be party, the Supreme Court shall have original jurisdiction. In all the other cases before mentioned, the Supreme Court shall have appellate jurisdiction, both as to law and fact, with such exceptions, and under such regulations, as the Congress shall make.

The trial of all crimes, except in cases of impeachment, shall be by jury; and such trial shall be held in the State where said crimes shall have been committed; but when not committed within any State, the trial shall be at such place or places as the Congress may by law have directed.

Section 3 Treason against the United States shall consist only in levying war against them, or in adhering to their enemies, giving them aid and comfort. No person shall be convicted of treason unless on the testimony of two witnesses to the same overt act, or on confession in open court.

The Congress shall have power to declare the punishment of treason, but no attainder of treason shall work corruption of blood, or forfeiture except during the life of the person attainted.

Article IV

Section 1 Full faith and credit shall be given in each State to the public acts, records, and judicial proceedings of every other State. And the Congress may by general laws prescribe the manner in which such acts, records, and proceedings shall be proved, and the effect thereof.

Section 2 The citizens of each State shall be entitled to all privileges and immunities of citizens in the several States.

A person charged in any State with treason, felony, or other crime, who shall flee from justice, and be found in another State, shall on demand of the executive authority of the State from which he fled, be delivered up, to be removed to the State having jurisdiction of the crime.

No person held to service or labor in one State, under the laws thereof, escaping into another, shall, in consequence of any law or regulation therein, be discharged from such service or labor, but shall be delivered up on claim of the party to whom such service or labor may be due.

Section 3 New States may be admitted by the Congress into this Union; but no new State shall be formed or erected within the jurisdiction of any other State; nor any State be formed by the junction of two or more States, or parts of States, without the consent of the legislatures of the States concerned as well as of the Congress.

The Congress shall have power to dispose of and make all needful rules and regulations respecting the territory or other property belonging to the United States; and nothing in this Constitution shall be so construed as to prejudice any claims of the United States, or of any particular State.

Section 4 The United States shall guarantee to every State in this Union a republican form of government, and shall protect each of them against invasion; and on application of the legislature, or of the executive (when the legislature cannot be convened), against domestic violence.

Article V

The Congress, whenever two-thirds of both houses shall deem it necessary, shall propose amendments to this Constitution, or, on the application of the legislatures of two-thirds of the several States, shall call a convention for proposing amendments, which, in either case, shall be valid to all intents and purposes, as part of this Constitution, when ratified by the legislatures of three-fourths of the several States, or by conventions in three-fourths thereof, as the one or the other mode of ratification may be proposed by the Congress; provided *that no amendments which may be made prior to the year one thousand eight hundred and eight shall in any manner affect the first and fourth clauses in the ninth section of the first article*; and that no State,

without its consent, shall be deprived of its equal suffrage in the Senate.

Article VI

All debts contracted and engagements entered into, before the adoption of this Constitution, shall be as valid against the United States under this Constitution, as under the Confederation.

This Constitution, and the laws of the United States which shall be made in pursuance thereof; and all treaties made, or which shall be made, under the authority of the United States, shall be the supreme law of the land; and the judges in every State shall be bound thereby, anything in the Constitution or laws of any State to the contrary notwithstanding.

The Senators and Representatives before mentioned, and the members of the several State legislatures, and all executive and judicial officers, both of the United States and of the several States, shall be bound by oath or affirmation to support this Constitution; but no religious test shall ever be required as a qualification to any office or public trust under the United States.

Article VII

The ratification of the conventions of nine States shall be sufficient for the establishment of this Constitution between the States so ratifying the same.

Done in Convention by the unanimous consent of the States present, the seventeenth day of September in the year of our Lord one thousand seven hundred and eighty-seven and of the Independence of the United States of America the twelfth. In witness whereof we have hereunto subscribed our names.

GEORGE WASHINGTON
and thirty-seven others

AMENDMENTS TO THE CONSTITUTION*

Amendment I

Congress shall make no law respecting an establishment of religion, or prohibiting the free exercise

* The first ten amendments (the Bill of Rights) were adopted in 1791.

thereof; or abridging the freedom of speech, or of the press; or the right of the people peaceably to assemble, and to petition the government for a redress of grievances.

Amendment II

A well-regulated militia being necessary to the security of a free State, the right of the people to keep and bear arms shall not be infringed.

Amendment III

No soldier shall, in time of peace, be quartered in any house without the consent of the owner, nor in time of war, but in a manner to be prescribed by law.

Amendment IV

The right of the people to be secure in their persons, houses, papers, and effects, against unreasonable searches and seizures, shall not be violated, and no warrants shall issue but upon probable cause, supported by oath or affirmation, and particularly describing the place to be searched, and the persons or things to be seized.

Amendment V

No person shall be held to answer for a capital, or otherwise infamous crime, unless on a presentment or indictment of a grand jury, except in cases arising in the land or naval forces, or in the militia, when in actual service in time of war or public danger; nor shall any person be subject for the same offense to be twice put in jeopardy or life or limb; nor shall be compelled in any criminal case to be a witness against himself, nor be deprived of life, liberty, or property, without due process of law; nor shall private property be taken for public use without just compensation.

Amendment VI

In all criminal prosecutions, the accused shall enjoy the right to a speedy and public trial, by an impartial jury of the State and district wherein the crime shall have been committed, which district shall have been previously ascertained by law, and to be informed of the nature and cause of the accusation; to be confronted with the witnesses against him; to have compulsory process for obtaining witnesses in his favor, and to have the assistance of counsel for his defense.

Amendment VII

In suits at common law, where the value in controversy shall exceed twenty dollars, the right of trial by jury shall be preserved, and no fact tried by jury shall be otherwise reexamined in any court of the United States, than according to the rules of the common law.

Amendment VIII

Excessive bail shall not be required, nor excessive fines imposed, nor cruel and unusual punishments inflicted.

Amendment IX

The enumeration in the Constitution, of certain rights, shall not be construed to deny or disparage others retained by the people.

Amendment X

The powers not delegated to the United States by the Constitution, nor prohibited by it to the States, are reserved to the States respectively, or to the people.

Amendment XI   *[Adopted 1798]*

The judicial power of the United States shall not be construed to extend to any suit in law or equity, commenced or prosecuted against one of the United States by citizens of another State, or by citizens or subjects of any foreign state.

Amendment XII   *[Adopted 1804]*

The electors shall meet in their respective States, and vote by ballot for President and Vice-President, one of whom, at least, shall not be an inhabitant of the same State with themselves; they shall name in their ballots the person voted for as President, and in distinct ballots the person voted for as Vice-President, and they shall make distinct lists of all persons voted for as President, and of all persons voted for as Vice-President, and of the number of votes for each, which lists they shall sign and certify, and transmit sealed to the seat of government of the United States, directed to the President of the Senate;—the President of the Senate shall, in the presence of the Senate and House of Representatives, open all the certificates and the votes shall then be counted;—the person having the greatest number of votes for President shall be the

President, if such number be a majority of the whole number of electors appointed; and if no person have such majority, then from the persons having the highest numbers not exceeding three on the list of those voted for as President, the House of Representatives shall choose immediately, by ballot, the President. But in choosing the President, the votes shall be taken by States, the representation from each State having one vote; a quorum for this purpose shall consist of a member or members from two-thirds of the States, and a majority of all the States shall be necessary to a choice. And if the House of Representatives shall not choose a President whenever the right of choice shall devolve upon them, before *the fourth day of March* next following, then the Vice-President shall act as President, as in the case of the death or other constitutional disability of the President.

The person having the greatest number of votes as Vice-President shall be the Vice-President, if such number be a majority of the whole number of electors appointed; and if no person have a majority, then from the two highest numbers on the list the Senate shall choose the Vice-President; a quorum for the purpose shall consist of two-thirds of the whole number of Senators, and a majority of the whole number shall be necessary to a choice. But no person constitutionally ineligible to the office of President shall be eligible to that of Vice-President of the United States.

Amendment XIII   *[Adopted 1865]*

Section 1   Neither slavery nor involuntary servitude, except as a punishment for crime whereof the party shall have been duly convicted, shall exist within the United States, or any place subject to their jurisdiction.

Section 2   Congress shall have power to enforce this article by appropriate legislation.

Amendment XIV   *[Adopted 1868]*

Section 1   All persons born or naturalized in the United States, and subject to the jurisdiction thereof, are citizens of the United States and of the State wherein they reside. No State shall make or enforce any law which shall abridge the privileges or immunities of citizens of the United States; nor shall any State deprive any person of life, liberty, or property, without due process of law; nor deny to any person within its jurisdiction the equal protection of the laws.

Section 2   Representatives shall be apportioned among the several States according to their respective numbers, counting the whole number of persons in each State, excluding Indians not taxed. But when the right to vote at any election for the choice of Electors for President and Vice-President of the United States, Representatives in Congress, the executive and judicial officers of a State, or the members of the legislature thereof, is denied to any of the male inhabitants of such State, being twenty-one years of age and citizens of the United States, or in any way abridged, except for participation in rebellion, or other crime, the basis of representation therein shall be reduced in the proportion which the number of such male citizens shall bear to the whole number of male citizens twenty-one years of age in such State.

Section 3   No person shall be a Senator or Representative in Congress, or Elector of President and Vice-President, or hold any office, civil or military, under the United States, or under any State, who, having previously taken an oath, as a member of Congress, or as an officer of the United States, or as a member of any State legislature, or as an executive or judicial officer of any State, to support the Constitution of the United States, shall have engaged in insurrection or rebellion against the same, or given aid or comfort to the enemies thereof. Congress may, by a vote of two-thirds of each house, remove such disability.

Section 4   The validity of the public debt of the United States, authorized by law, including debts incurred for payment of pensions and bounties for services in suppressing insurrection or rebellion, shall not be questioned. But neither the United States nor any State shall assume or pay any debt or obligation incurred in aid of insurrection or rebellion against the United States, or any claim for the loss of emancipation of any slave; but all such debts, obligations, and claims shall be held illegal and void.

Section 5   The Congress shall have power to enforce, by appropriate legislation, the provisions of this article.

Amendment XV   *[Adopted 1870]*

Section 1   The right of citizens of the United States to vote shall not be denied or abridged by the United States or by any State on account of race, color, or previous condition of servitude.

Section 2   The Congress shall have power to enforce this article by appropriate legislation.

Amendment XVI   *[Adopted 1913]*

The Congress shall have power to lay and collect taxes on incomes, from whatever source derived, without apportionment among the several States, and without regard to any census or enumeration.

Amendment XVII   *[Adopted 1913]*

Section 1   The Senate of the United States shall be composed of two Senators from each State, elected by the people thereof, for six years; and each Senator shall have one vote. The electors in each State shall have the qualifications requisite for electors of [voters for] the most numerous branch of the State legislatures.

Section 2   When vacancies happen in the representation of any State in the Senate, the executive authority of such State shall issue writs of election to fill such vacancies: Provided, that the Legislature of any State may empower the executive thereof to make temporary appointments until the people fill the vacancies by election as the Legislature may direct.

Section 3   This amendment shall not be so construed as to affect the election or term of any Senator chosen before it becomes valid as part of the Constitution.

Amendment XVIII   *[Adopted 1919; Repealed 1933]*

Section 1   After one year from the ratification of this article the manufacture, sale, or transportation of intoxicating liquors within, the importation thereof into, or the exportation thereof from the United States and all territory subject to the jurisdiction thereof, for beverage purposes, is hereby prohibited.

Section 2   The Congress and the several States shall have concurrent power to enforce this article by appropriate legislation.

Section 3   This article shall be inoperative unless it shall have been ratified as an amendment to the Constitution by the legislatures of the several States, as provided by the Constitution, within seven years from the date of the submission thereof to the States by the Congress.

Amendment XIX   *[Adopted 1920]*

Section 1   The right of citizens of the United States to vote shall not be denied or abridged by the United States or by any State on account of sex.

Section 2   The Congress shall have power to enforce this article by appropriate legislation.

Amendment XX   *[Adopted 1933]*

Section 1   The terms of the President and Vice-President shall end at noon on the 20th day of January, and the terms of Senators and Representatives at noon on the 3rd day of January, of the years in which such terms would have ended if this article had not been ratified; and the terms of their successors shall then begin.

Section 2   The Congress shall assemble at least once in every year, and such meeting shall begin at noon on the 3d day of January, unless they shall by law appoint a different day.

Section 3   If, at any time fixed for the beginning of the term of the President, the President-elect shall have died, the Vice-President-elect shall become President. If a President shall not have been chosen before the time fixed for the beginning of his term, or if the President-elect shall have failed to qualify, then the Vice-President-elect shall act as President until a President shall have qualified; and the Congress may by law provide for the case wherein neither a President-elect nor a Vice-President-elect shall have qualified, declaring who shall then act as President, or the manner in which one who is to act shall be selected, and such persons shall act accordingly until a President or Vice-President shall have qualified.

Section 4   The Congress may by law provide for the case of the death of any of the persons from whom the House of Representatives may choose a President whenever the right of choice shall have devolved upon them, and for the case of the death of any of the persons from whom the Senate may choose a Vice-President whenever the right of choice shall have devolved upon them.

Section 5   Sections 1 and 2 shall take effect on the 15th day of October following the ratification of this article.

Section 6   This article shall be inoperative unless it shall have been ratified as an amendment to the Constitution by the Legislatures of three-fourth of the several States within seven years from the date of its submission.

Amendment XXI   *[Adopted 1933]*

Section 1   The eighteenth article of amendment to the Constitution of the United States is hereby repealed.

Section 2   The transportation or importation into

any State, Territory, or Possession of the United States for delivery or use therein of intoxicating liquors, in violation of the laws thereof, is hereby prohibited.

Section 3   This article shall be inoperative unless it shall have been ratified as an amendment to the Constitution by conventions in the several States, as provided in the Constitution, within seven years from the date of submission thereof to the States by the Congress.

Amendment XXII   *[Adopted 1951]*

Section 1   No person shall be elected to the office of President more than twice, and no person who has held the office of President, or acted as President, for more than two years of a term to which some other person was elected President shall be elected to the office of President more than once. But this article shall not apply to any person holding the office of President when this article was proposed by the Congress, and shall not prevent any person who may be holding the office of President, or acting as President, during the term within which this article becomes operative from holding the office of President or acting as President during the remainder of such term.

Section 2   This article shall be inoperative unless it shall have been ratified as an amendment to the Constitution by the legislatures of three-fourths of the several States within seven years from the date of its submission to the States by the Congress.

Amendment XXIII   *[Adopted 1961]*

Section 1   The District constituting the seat of Government of the United States shall appoint in such manner as the Congress may direct:

A number of electors of President and Vice-President equal to the whole number of Senators and Representatives in Congress to which the District would be entitled if it were a State, but in no event more than the least populous State; they shall be in addition to those appointed by the States, but they shall be considered for the purposes of the election of President and Vice-President, to be electors appointed by a State; and they shall meet in the District and perform such duties as provided by the twelfth article of amendment.

Section 2   The Congress shall have the power to enforce this article by appropriate legislation.

Amendment XXIV   *[Adopted 1964]*

Section 1   The right of citizens of the United States to vote in any primary or other election for President or Vice-President, for electors for President or Vice-President, or for Senator or Representative in Congress, shall not be denied or abridged by the United States or any State by reason of failure to pay any poll tax or other tax.

Section 2   The Congress shall have the power to enforce this article by appropriate legislation.

Amendment XXV   *[Adopted 1967]*

Section 1   In case of the removal of the President from office or of his death or resignation, the Vice-President shall become President.

Section 2   Whenever there is a vacancy in the office of the Vice-President, the President shall nominate a Vice-President who shall take office upon confirmation by a majority vote of both Houses of Congress.

Section 3   Whenever the President transmits to the President pro tempore of the Senate and the Speaker of the House of Representatives his written declaration that he is unable to discharge the powers and duties of his office, and until he transmits to them a written declaration to the contrary, such powers and duties shall be discharged by the Vice-President as Acting President.

Section 4   Whenever the Vice-President and a majority of either the principal officers of the executive departments or of such other body as Congress may by law provide, transmit to the President pro tempore of the Senate and the Speaker of the House of Representatives their written declaration that the President is unable to discharge the powers and duties of his office, the Vice-President shall immediately assume the powers and duties of the office as Acting President.

Thereafter, when the President transmits to the President pro tempore of the Senate and the Speaker of the House of Representatives his written declaration that no inability exists, he shall resume the powers and duties of his office unless the Vice-President and a majority of either the principal officers of the executive department[s] or of such other body as Congress may by law provide, transmit within four days to the President pro tempore of the Senate and the Speaker of the House of Representatives their written declaration that the President is unable to discharge the powers and duties of his office. Thereupon Congress shall decide the issue, assembling within forty-eight hours for that purpose if not in session. If the Congress, within twenty-one days after receipt of the latter written declaration, or, if Congress is not in session, within twenty-one days after Congress is required to assemble, determines by two-thirds vote of both Houses that the President is unable to discharge the powers and duties of his office, the Vice-President shall continue to discharge the same as Acting President; otherwise, the President shall resume the powers and duties of his office.

Amendment XXVI   *[Adopted 1971]*

Section 1   The right of citizens of the United States, who are eighteen years of age or older, to vote shall not be denied or abridged by the United States or by any State on account of age.

Section 2   The Congress shall have power to enforce this article by appropriate legislation.

Amendment XXVII   *[Adopted 1992]*

No law, varying the compensation for the services of the Senators and Representatives, shall take effect, until an election of Representatives shall have intervened.

FEDERALIST NO. 10   1787

To the People of the State of New York: Among the numerous advantages promised by a well-constructed union, none deserves to be more accurately developed than its tendency to break and control the violence of faction. The friend of popular governments, never finds himself so much alarmed for their character and fate, as when he contemplates their propensity to this dangerous vice. He will not fail, therefore, to set a due value on any plan which, without violating the principles to which he is attached, provides a proper cure for it. The instability, injustice, and confusion introduced into the public councils, have, in truth, been the mortal diseases under which popular governments have everywhere perished; as they continue to be the favorite and fruitful topics from which the adversaries to liberty derive their most specious declamations. The valuable improvements made by the American constitutions on the popular models, both ancient and modern, cannot certainly be too much admired; but it would be an unwarrantable partiality, to contend that they have as effectually obviated the danger on this side, as was wished and expected. Complaints are everywhere heard from our most considerate and virtuous citizens, equally the friends of public and private faith, and of public and personal liberty, that our governments are too unstable; that the public good is disregarded in the conflicts of rival parties; and that measures are too often decided, not according to the rules of justice, and the rights of the minor party, but by the superior force of an interested and overbearing majority. However anxiously we may wish that these complaints had no foundation, the evidence of known facts will not permit us to deny that they are in some degree true. It will be found, indeed, on a candid review of our situation, that some of the distresses under which we labour have been erroneously charged on the operation of our governments; but it will be found, at the same time, that other causes will not alone account for many of our heaviest misfortunes; and, particularly, for that prevailing and increasing distrust of public engagements, and alarm for private rights, which are echoed from one end of the continent to the other. These must be chiefly, if not wholly, effects of the unsteadiness and injustice, with which a factious spirit has tainted our public administrations.

By a faction, I understand a number of citizens, whether amounting to a majority or minority of the whole, who are united and actuated by some common impulse of passion, or of interest, adverse to the rights of other citizens, or to the permanent and aggregate interests of the community.

There are two methods of curing the mischiefs of faction: The one, by removing its causes; the other, by controlling its effects.

There are again two methods of removing the causes of faction: The one, by destroying the liberty which is essential to its existence; the other, by giving to every citizen the same opinions, the same passions, and the same interests.

It could never be more truly said, than of the first remedy, that it was worse than the disease. Liberty is to faction what air is to fire, an ailment without which it instantly expires. But it could not be a less folly to

A-14 Appendix

abolish liberty, which is essential to political life, because it nourishes faction, than it would be to wish the annihilation of air, which is essential to animal life, because it imparts to fire its destructive agency.

The second expedient is as impracticable, as the first would be unwise. As long as the reason of man continues fallible, and he is at liberty to exercise it, different opinions will be formed. As long as the connection subsists between his reason and his self-love, his opinions and his passions will have a reciprocal influence on each other; and the former will be objects to which the latter will attach themselves. The diversity in the faculties of men, from which the rights of property originate, is not less an insuperable obstacle to an uniformity of interests. The protection of these faculties is the first object of government. From the protection of different and unequal faculties of acquiring property, the possession of different degrees and kinds of property immediately results; and from the influence of these on the sentiments and views of the respective proprietors, ensues a division of the society into different interests and parties.

The latent causes of action are thus sown in the nature of man; and we see them everywhere brought into different degrees of activity, according to the different circumstances of civil society. A zeal for different opinions concerning religion, concerning government, and many other points, as well as of speculation as of practice; an attachment to different leaders ambitiously contending for preeminence and power; or to persons of other descriptions whose fortunes have been interesting to the human passions, have, in turn, divided mankind into parties, inflamed them with mutual animosity, and rendered them much more disposed to vex and oppress each other, than to cooperate of their common good. So strong is this propensity of mankind, to fall into mutual animosities, that where no substantial occasion presents itself, the most frivolous and fanciful distinctions have been sufficient to kindle their unfriendly passions and excite their most violent conflicts. But the most common and durable source of factions, has been the various and unequal distribution of property. Those who hold, and those who are without property, have ever formed distinct interests in society. Those who are creditors, and those who are debtors, fall under a like discrimination. A landed interest, a manufacturing interest, a mercantile interest, a moneyed interest, with many lesser interests, grow up of necessity in civilized nations, and divide them into different classes, actuated by different sentiments and views. The regulation of these various and interfering interests forms the principal task of modern legislation, and involves the spirit of the party and faction in the necessary and ordinary operations of the government.

No man is allowed to be a judge in his own cause; because his interest will certainly bias his judgment, and, not improbably, corrupt his integrity. With equal, nay, with greater reason, a body of men are unfit to be both judges and parties at the same time; yet what are many of the most important acts of legislation, but so many judicial determinations, not indeed concerning the right of single persons, but concerning the rights of large bodies of citizens? And what are the different classes of legislators, but advocates and parties to the causes which they determine? Is a law proposed concerning private debts? It is a question to which the creditors are parties on one side, and the debtors on the other. Justice ought to hold the balance between them. Yet the parties are, and must be, themselves the judges; and the most numerous party, or, in other words, the most powerful faction, must be expected to prevail. Shall domestic manufactures be encouraged, and in what degree, by restrictions on foreign manufactures? are questions which would be differently decided by the landed and the manufacturing classes; and probably by neither with a sole regard to justice and the public good. The apportionment of taxes, on the various descriptions of property, is an act which seems to require the most exact impartiality; yet there is, perhaps, no legislative act, in which greater opportunity and temptation are given to a predominant party to trample on the rules of justice. Every shilling, with which they overburden the inferior number, is a shilling saved to their own pockets.

It is in vain to say, that enlightened statements will be able to adjust these clashing interests, and render them all subservient to the public good. Enlightened statesmen will not always be at the helm: nor, in many cases, can such an adjustment be made at all, without taking into view indirect and remote considerations, which will rarely prevail over the immediate interest which one party may find in disregarding the rights of another, or the good of the whole.

The inference to which we are brought is, that the *causes* of faction cannot be removed; and that relief is only to be sought in the means of controlling its *effects*.

If a faction consists of less than a majority, relief is

supplied by the republican principle, which enables the majority to defeat its sinister views, by regular vote. It may clog the administration, it may convulse the society; but it will be unable to execute and mask its violence under the forms of the constitution. When a majority is included in a faction, the form of popular government, on the other hand, enables it to sacrifice to its ruling passion or interest, both the public good and the rights of other citizens. To secure the public good, and private rights, against the danger of such a faction, and at the same time to preserve the spirit and the form of popular government, is then the great object to which our inquiries are directed. Let me add, that it is the great desideratum, by which alone this form of government can be rescued from the opprobrium under which it has so long laboured, and be recommended to the esteem and adoption of mankind.

By what means is this object attainable? Evidently by one of two only. Either the existence of the same passion or interest in a majority, at the same time, must be prevented; or the majority, having such coexistent passion or interest, must be rendered, by their number and local situation, unable to concert and carry into effect schemes of oppression. If the impulse and the opportunity be suffered to coincide, we well know that neither moral nor religious motives can be relied on as an adequate control. They are not found to be such on the injustice violence of individuals, and lose their efficacy in proportion to the number combined together; that is, in proportion as their efficacy becomes needful.

From this view of the subject, it may be concluded, that a pure democracy, by which I mean a society consisting of a small number of citizens, who assemble and administer the government in person, can admit of no cure for the mischiefs of faction. A common passion or interest will, in almost every case, be felt by a majority of the whole; a communication and concert, results from the form of government itself; and there is nothing to check the inducements to sacrifice the weaker parts, or an obnoxious individual. Hence, it is, that such democracies have ever been spectacles of turbulence and contention; have ever been found incompatible with personal security, or the rights of property; and have in general been as short in their lives, as they have been violent in their deaths. Theoretic politicians, who have patronized this species of government, have erroneously supposed, that by reducing mankind to a perfect equality in their political rights, they

would, at the same time, be perfectly equalized and assimilated in their possessions, their opinions, and their passions.

A republic, by which I mean a government in which the scheme of representation takes place, opens a different prospect, and promises the cure for which we are seeking. Let us examine the points in which it varies from pure democracy, and we shall comprehend both the nature of the cure and the efficacy which it must derive from the union.

The two great points of difference, between a democracy and a republic, are, first, the delegation of the government, in the latter, to a small number of citizens, elected by the rest; secondly, the greatest number of citizens, and greater sphere of country, over which the latter may be extended.

The effect of the first difference is, on the one hand, to refine and enlarge the public views, by passing them through the medium of a chosen body of citizens, whose wisdom may best discern the true interest of their country, and whose patriotism and love of justice, will be least likely to sacrifice it to temporary or partial considerations. Under such a regulation, it may well happen, that the public voice, pronounced by the representatives of the people, will be more consonant to the public good, than if pronounced by the people themselves, convened for the purpose. On the other hand the effect may be inverted. Men of factious tempers, of local prejudices, or of sinister designs, may by intrigue, by corruption, or by other means, first obtain the suffrages, and then betray the interest of the people. The question resulting is, whether small or extensive republics are most favourable to the election of proper guardians of the public weal; and it is clearly decided in favour of the latter by two obvious considerations.

In the first place, it is to be remarked that, however small the republic may be, the representatives must be raised to a certain number, in order to guard against the cabals of a few; and that however large it may be, they must be limited to a certain number, in order to guard against the confusion of a multitude. Hence, the number of representatives in the two cases not being in proportion to that of the constituents, and being proportionally greatest in the small republic, it follows, that if the proportion of fit characters be not less in the large than in the small republic, the former will present a greater option, and consequently a greater probability of a fit choice.

In the next place, as each representative will be chosen by a greater number of citizens in the large than in the small republic, it will be more difficult for unworthy candidates to practice with success the vicious arts, by which elections are too often carried; and the suffrages of the people being more free, will be more likely to centre in men who possess the most attractive merit, and the most diffusive and established characters.

It must be confessed, that in this, as in most other cases, there is a mean, on both sides of which inconveniences will be found to lie. By enlarging too much the number of electors, you render the representatives too little acquainted with all their local circumstances and lesser interests; as by reducing it too much, you render him unduly attached to these, and too little fit to comprehend and pursue great and national objects. The federal constitution forms a happy combination in this respect; the great and aggregate interests being referred to the national, the local and particular to the state legislatures.

The other point of difference is, the greater number of citizens, and extent of territory, which may be brought within the compass of republican, than of democratic government; and it is this circumstance principally which renders factious combinations less to be dreaded in the former, than in the latter. The smaller the society, the fewer probably will be the distinct parties and interests composing it; the fewer the distinct parties and interests, the more frequently will a majority be found of the same party; and the smaller the number of individuals composing a majority, and the smaller the compass within which they are placed, the more easily will they concert and execute their plans of oppression. Extend the sphere, and you take in a greater variety of parties and interests; you make it less probable that a majority of the whole will have a common motive to invade the rights of other citizens; or if such a common motive exists, it will be more difficult for all who feel it to discover their own strength, and to act in unison with each other. Besides other impediments, it may be remarked, that where there is a consciousness of unjust or dishonorable purposes, communication is always checked by distrust, in proportion to the number whose concurrence is necessary.

Hence, it clearly appears, that the same advantage, which a republic has over a democracy, in controlling the effects of faction, is enjoyed by a large over a small republic,—is enjoyed by the union over the states composing it. Does this advantage consist in the substitution of representatives, whose enlightened views and virtuous sentiments render them superior to local prejudices, and to schemes of injustice? It will not be denied that the representation of the union will be most likely to possess these requisite endowments. Does it consist in the greater security afforded by a greater variety of parties, against the event of any one party being able to outnumber and oppress the rest? In an equal degree does the increased variety of parties, comprised within the union, increase the security? Does it, in fine, consist in the greater obstacles opposed to the concert and accomplishment of the secret wishes of an unjust and interested majority? Here, again, the extent of the union gives it the most palpable advantage.

The influence of factious leaders may kindle a flame within their particular states, but will be unable to spread a general conflagration through the other states; a religious sect may degenerate into a political faction in a part of the confederacy; but the variety of sects dispersed over the entire face of it, must secure the national councils against any danger from that source: a rage for paper money, for an abolition of debts, for an equal division of property, or for any other improper or wicked project, will be less apt to pervade the whole body of the union than a particular member of it; in the same proportion as such a malady is more likely to taint a particular county or district, than an entire state.

In the extent and proper structure of the union, therefore, we behold a republican remedy for the diseases most incident to republican government. And according to the degree of pleasure and pride we feel in being republicans, ought to be our zeal in cherishing the spirit, and supporting the character of federalists.

JAMES MADISON

FEDERALIST NO. 51   1788

To the People of the State of New York: To what expedient then shall we finally resort for maintaining in practice the necessary partition of power among the several departments, as laid down in the constitution? The only answer that can be given is, that as all these exterior provisions are found to be inadequate, the defect must be supplied, by so contriving the interior structure of the government, as that its several constituent parts may, by their mutual relations, be the means of keeping each other in their proper places. Without presuming to undertake a full development of this important idea, I will hazard a few general observations, which may perhaps place it in a clearer light, and enable us to form a more correct judgment of the principles and structure of the government planned by the convention.

In order to lay a due foundation for that separate and distinct exercise of the different powers of government, which to a certain extent, is admitted on all hands to be essential to the preservation of liberty, it is evident that each department should have a will of its own; and consequently should be so constituted, that the members of each should have as little agency as possible in the appointment of the members of the others. Were this principle rigorously adhered to, it would require that all the appointments for the supreme executive, legislative, and judiciary magistracies, should be drawn from the same fountain of authority, the people, through channels, having no communication whatever with one another. Perhaps such a plan of constructing the several departments would be less difficult in practice than it may in contemplation appear. Some difficulties however, and some additional expense, would attend the execution of it. Some deviations therefore from the principle must be admitted. In the constitution of the judiciary department in particular, it might be inexpedient to insist rigorously on the principle; first, because peculiar qualifications being essential in the members, the primary consideration ought to be to select that mode of choice, which best secures these qualifications; secondly, because the permanent tenure by which the appointments are held in that department, must soon destroy all sense of dependence on the authority conferring them.

It is equally evident that the members of each department should be as little dependent as possible on those of the others, for the emoluments annexed to their offices. Were the executive magistrate, or the judges, not independent of the legislature in the particular, their independence in every other would be merely nominal.

But the great security against a gradual concentration of the several powers in the same department, consists in giving to those who administer each department, the necessary constitutional means, and personal motives, to resist encroachments of the others. The provision for defense must in this, as in all other cases, be made commensurate to the danger of attack. Ambition must be made to counteract ambition. The interest of the man must be connected with the constitutional rights of the place. It may be a reflection on human nature, that such devices should be necessary to control the abuses of government. But what is government itself but the greatest of all reflections on human nature? If men were angels, no government would be necessary. If angels were to govern men, neither external nor internal controls on government would be necessary. In framing a government which is to be administered by men over men, the great difficulty lies in this: You must first enable the government to control the governed; and in the next place, oblige it to control itself. A dependence on the people is no doubt the primary control on the government; but experience has taught mankind the necessity of auxiliary precautions.

This policy of supplying by opposite and rival interests, the defect of better motives, might be traced through the whole system of human affairs, private as well as public. We see it particularly displayed in all the subordinate distributions of power; where the constant aim is to divide and arrange the several offices in such a manner as that each may be a check on the other; that the private interest of every individual, may be a sentinel over the public rights. These inventions of prudence cannot be less requisite in the distribution of the supreme powers of the state.

But it is not possible to give to each department an equal power of self defense. In republican government the legislative authority, necessarily, predominates. The remedy for this inconvenience is, to divide the legislature into different branches; and to render them by different modes of election, and different principles of action, as little connected with each other, as the nature of their common functions, and their common dependence on the society, will admit. It may even be necessary to guard against dangerous encroachments by still further precautions. As the weight of the legislative authority requires that it should be thus divided, the weakness of the executive may require, on the other hand, that it should be fortified. An absolute negative, on the legislature, appears at first view to be the natural defense with which the executive magistrate should be armed. But perhaps it would be neither altogether safe, nor alone sufficient. On ordinary occasions, it might not be exerted with the requisite firmness; and on extraordinary occasions, it might be perfidiously abused. May not this defect of an absolute negative be supplied, by some qualified connection between this weaker department, and the weaker branch of the stronger department, by which the latter may be led to support the constitutional rights of the former, without being too much detached from the rights of its own department?

If the principles on which these observations are founded be just, as I persuade myself they are, and they be applied as a criterion, to the several state constitutions, and to the federal constitution, it will be found, that if the latter does not perfectly correspond with them, the former are infinitely less able to bear such a test.

There are moreover two considerations particularly applicable to the federal system of America, which place that system in a very interesting point of view.

First. In a single republic, all the power surrendered by the people, is submitted to the administration of a single government; and usurpations are guarded against by a division of the government into distinct and separate departments. In the compound republic of America, the power surrendered by the people, is first divided between two distinct governments, and then the portion allotted to each, subdivided among distinct and separate departments. Hence a double security arises to the rights of the people. The different governments will control each other; at the same time that each will be controlled by itself.

Second. It is of great importance in a republic, not only to guard the society against the oppression of its rulers; but to guard one part of the society against the injustice of the other part. Different interests necessarily exist in different classes of citizens. If a majority be united by a common interest, the rights of the minority will be insecure. There are but two methods of providing against this evil: The one by creating a will in the community independent of the majority, that is, of the society itself; the other by comprehending in the society so many separate descriptions of citizens, as will render an unjust combination of a majority of the whole, very improbable, if not impracticable. The first method prevails in all governments possessing an hereditary or self appointed authority. This at best is but a precarious security; because a power independent of the society may as well espouse the unjust views of the major, as the rightful interests, of the minor party, and may possibly be turned against both parties. The second method will be exemplified in the federal republic of the United States. While all authority in it will be derived from and dependent on the society, the society itself will be broken into so many parts, interests and classes of citizens, that the rights of individuals or of the minority, will be in little danger from interested combinations of the majority. In a free government, the security for civil rights must be the same as for religious rights. It consists in the one case in the multiplicity of interests, and in the other in the multiplicity of sects. The degree of security in both cases will depend on the number of interests and sects; and this may be presumed to depend on the extent of country and number of people comprehended under the same government. This view of the subject must particularly recommend a proper federal system to all the sincere and considerate friends of republican government: Since it shows that in exact proportion as the territory of the union may be formed into more circumscribed confederacies or states, oppressive combinations of a majority will be facilitated; the best security under the republican form, for the rights of every class of citizens, will be diminished; and consequently, the stability and independence of some member of the government, the only other security, must be proportionally increased. Justice is the end of government. It is the end of civil society. It ever has been, and ever will be pursued, until it be obtained, or until liberty be lost in the pursuit. In a society under the forms of which the stronger faction can readily unite and oppress the weaker, anarchy may as truly be said to reign, as in a state of nature where the weaker individual is not secured against the violence of the stronger: And as in the latter state even the stronger individuals are prompted by the uncertainty of their condition, to submit to a government which may protect the weak as well as themselves: So in the former state, will the more powerful factions or parties be gradually induced by a like motive, to which for a government which will protect all parties, the weaker as well as the more powerful. It can be little doubted, that if the state of Rhode Island was separated from the confederacy, and left to itself, the insecurity of rights under the popular form of government within such narrow limits, would be displayed by such reiterated oppression of factious majorities, that some power altogether independent of the people would soon be called for by the voice of the very factions whose misrule had proved the necessity of it. In the extended republic of the United States, and among the great variety of interests, parties and sects which it embraces, a coalition of a majority of the whole society could seldom take place on any other principles than those of justice and the general good; and there being thus less danger to a minor from the will of the major party, there must be less pretext also, to provide for the security of the former, by introducing into the government a will not dependent on the latter; or in other words, a will independent of the society itself. It is no less certain that it is important, notwithstanding the contrary opinions which have been entertained, that the larger the society, provided it lie within a practicable sphere, the more duly capable it will be of self government. And happily for the *republican cause*, the practicable sphere may be carried to a very great extent, by a judicious modification and mixture of the *federal principle*.

JAMES MADISON

ANTI-FEDERALIST PAPER
OCTOBER 18, 1787

To the Citizens of the State of New-York.

When the public is called to investigate and decide upon a question in which not only the present members of the community are deeply interested, but upon which the happiness and misery of generations yet unborn is in great measure suspended, the benevolent mind cannot help feeling itself peculiarly interested in the result.

In this situation, I trust the feeble efforts of an individual, to lead the minds of the people to a wise and prudent determination, cannot fail of being acceptable to the candid and dispassionate part of the community. Encouraged by this consideration, I have been induced to offer my thoughts upon the present important crisis of our public affairs.

Perhaps this country never saw so critical a period in their political concerns. We have felt the feebleness of the ties by which these United-States are held together, and the want of sufficient energy in our present confederation, to manage, in some instances, our general concerns. Various expedients have been proposed to remedy these evils, but none have succeeded. At length a Convention of the states has been assembled, they have formed a constitution which will now, probably, be submitted to the people to ratify or reject, who are the fountain of all power, to whom alone it of right belongs to make or unmake constitutions, or forms of government, at their pleasure. The most important question that was ever proposed to your decision, or to the decision of any people under heaven, is before you, and you are to decide upon it by men of your own election, chosen specially for this purpose. If the constitution, offered to your acceptance, be a wise one, calculated to preserve the invaluable blessings of liberty, to secure the inestimable rights of mankind, and promote human happiness, then, if you accept it, you will lay a lasting foundation of happiness for millions yet unborn; generations to come will rise up and call you blessed. You may rejoice in the prospects of this vast extended continent becoming filled with freemen, who will assert the dignity of human nature. You may solace yourselves with the idea, that society, in this favored land, will fast advance to the highest point of perfection; the human mind will expand in knowledge and virtue, and the golden age be, in some measure, realized. But if, on the other hand, this form of government contains principles that will lead to the subversion of liberty—if it tends to establish a despotism, or, what is worse, a tyrannic aristocracy; then, if you adopt it, this only remaining asylum for liberty will be shut up, and posterity will execrate your memory.

Momentous then is the question you have to determine, and you are called upon by every motive which should influence a noble and virtuous mind, to examine it well, and to make up a wise judgment. It is insisted, indeed, that this constitution must be received, be it ever so imperfect. If it has its defects, it is said, they can be best amended when they are experienced. But remember, when the people once part with power, they can seldom or never resume it again but by force. Many instances can be produced in which the people have voluntarily increased the powers of their rulers; but few, if any, in which rulers have willingly abridged their authority. This is a sufficient reason to induce you to be careful, in the first instance, how you deposit the powers of government.

With these few introductory remarks, I shall proceed to a consideration of this constitution:

The first question that presents itself on the subject is, whether a confederated government be the best for the United States or not? Or in other words, whether the thirteen United States should be reduced to one great republic, governed by one legislature, and under the direction of one executive and judicial; or whether they should continue thirteen confederated republics, under the direction and control of a supreme federal head for certain defined national purposes only?

This enquiry is important, because, although the government reported by the convention does not go to a perfect and entire consolidation, yet it approaches so near to it, that it must, if executed, certainly and infallibly terminate in it.

This government is to possess absolute and uncontrollable power, legislative, executive and judicial, with respect to every object to which it extends, for by the last clause of section 8th, article 1st, it is declared "that the Congress shall have power to make all laws which shall be necessary and proper for carrying into execution the foregoing powers, and all other powers vested by this constitution, in the government of the United States; or in any department or office thereof." And by the 6th article, it is declared "that this constitution, and the laws of the United States, which shall be made in pursuance thereof, and the treaties made, or which shall be made, under the authority of the United States, shall be the supreme law of the land; and the judges in every state shall be bound thereby, any thing in the constitution, or law of any state to the contrary notwithstanding." It appears from these articles that there is no need of any intervention of the state governments, between the Congress and the people, to execute any one power vested in the general government, and that the constitution and laws of every state are nullified and declared void, so far as they are or shall be inconsistent with this constitution, or the laws made in pursuance of it, or with treaties made under the authority of the United States.—The government then, so far as it extends, is a complete one, and not a confederation. It is as much one complete government as that of New York or Massachusetts, has as absolute and perfect powers to make and execute all laws, to appoint officers, institute courts, declare offenses, and annex penalties, with respect to every object to which it extends, as any other in the world. So far therefore as its powers reach, all ideas of confederation are given up and lost. It is true this government is limited to certain objects, or to speak more properly, some small

degree of power is still left to the states, but a little attention to the powers vested in the general government, will convince every candid man, that if it is capable of being executed, all that is reserved for the individual states must very soon be annihilated, except so far as they are barely necessary to the organization of the general government. The powers of the general legislature extend to every case that is of the least importance—there is nothing valuable to human nature, nothing dear to freemen, but what is within its power. It has authority to make laws which will affect the lives, the liberty, and property of every man in the United States; nor can the constitution or laws of any state, in any way prevent or impede the full and complete execution of every power given. The legislative power is competent to lay taxes, duties, imposts, and excises;—there is no limitation to this power, unless it be said that the clause which directs the use to which those taxes, and duties shall be applied, may be said to be limitation: but this is no restriction of the power at all, for by this clause they are to be applied to pay the debts and provide for the common defence and general welfare of the United States; but the legislature have authority to contract debts at their discretion; they are the sole judges of what is necessary to provide for the common defence, and they only are to determine what is for the general welfare; this power therefore is neither more nor less, than a power to lay and collect taxes, imposts, and excises, at their pleasure; not only [is] the power to lay taxes unlimited, as to the amount they may require, but it is perfect and absolute to raise them in any mode they please. No state legislature, or any power in the state governments, have any more to do in carrying this into effect, than the authority of one state has to do with that of another. In the business therefore of laying and collecting taxes, the idea of confederation is totally lost, and that of one entire republic is embraced. It is proper here to remark, that the authority to lay and collect taxes is the most important of any power that can be granted; it connects with it almost all other powers, or at least will in process of time draw all other after it; it is the great mean of protection, security, and defence, in a good government, and the great engine of oppression and tyranny in a bad one. This cannot fail of being the case, if we consider the contracted limits which are set by this constitution, to the late [state?] governments, on this article of raising money. No state can emit paper money—lay any duties, or imposts, on imports, or exports, but by consent of the Congress; and then the net produce shall be for the benefit of the United States: the only mean therefore left, for any state to support its government and discharge its debts, is by direct taxation; and the United States have also power to lay and collect taxes, in any way they please. Every one who has thought on the subject, must be convinced that but small sums of money can be collected in any country, by direct taxe[s], when the federal government begins to exercise the right of taxation in all its parts, the legislatures of the several states will find it impossible to raise monies to support their governments. Without money then cannot be supported, and they must dwindle away, and, as before observed, their powers absorbed in that of the general government.

It might be here shewn, that the power in the federal legislative, to raise and support armies at pleasure, as well in peace as in war, and their controul over the militia, tend, not only to a consolidation of the government, but the destruction of liberty.—I shall not, however, dwell upon these, as a few observations upon the judicial power of this government, in addition to the preceding, will fully evince the truth of the position.

The judicial power of the United States is to be vested in a supreme court, and in such inferior courts as Congress may from time to time ordain and establish. The powers of these courts are very extensive; their jurisdiction comprehends all civil causes, except such as arise between citizens of the same state; and it extends to all cases in law and equity arising under the constitution. One inferior court must be established, I presume, in each state, at least, with the necessary executive officers appendant thereto. It is easy to see, that in the common course of things, these courts will eclipse the dignity, and take away from the respectability, of the state courts. These courts will be, in themselves, totally independent of the states, deriving their authority from the United States, and receiving from them fixed salaries; and in the course of human events it is to be expected, that they will swallow up all the powers of the courts in the respective states.

How far the clause in the 8th section of the 1st article may operate to do away all ideas of confederated states, and to effect an entire consolidation of the whole into one general government, it is impossible to say. The powers given by this article are very general and comprehensive, and it may receive a construction to justify the passing almost any law. A power to make

all laws, which shall be *necessary and proper*, for carrying into execution, all powers vested by the constitution in the government of the United States, or any department or officer thereof, is a power very comprehensive and definite [indefinite?], and may, for ought I know, be exercised in a such manner as entirely to abolish the state legislatures. Suppose the legislature of a state should pass a law to raise money to support their government and pay the state debt, may the Congress repeal this law, because it may prevent the collection of a tax which they may think proper and necessary to lay, to provide for the general welfare of the United States? For all laws made, in pursuance of this constitution, are the supreme law of the land, and the judges in every state shall be bound thereby, any thing in the constitution or laws of the different states to the contrary notwithstanding.—By such a law, the government of a particular state might be overturned at one stroke, and thereby be deprived of every means of its support.

It is not meant, by stating this case, to insinuate that the constitution would warrant a law of this kind; or unnecessarily to alarm the fears of the people, by suggesting, that the federal legislature would be more likely to pass the limits assigned them by the constitution, than that of an individual state, further than they are less responsible to the people. But what is meant is, that the legislature of the United States are vested with the great and uncontrollable powers, of laying and collecting taxes, duties, imposts, and excises; of regulating trade, raising and supporting armies, organizing, arming, and disciplining the militia, instituting courts, and other general powers. And are by this clause invested with the power of making all laws, *proper and necessary*, for carrying all these into execution; and they may so exercise this power as entirely to annihilate all the state governments, and reduce this country to one single government. And if they may do it, it is pretty certain they will; for it will be found that the power retained by individual states, small as it is, will be a clog upon the wheels of the government of the United States; the latter therefore will be naturally inclined to remove it out of the way. Besides, it is a truth confirmed by the unerring experience of ages, that every man, and every body of men, invested with power, are ever disposed to increase it, and to acquire a superiority over every thing that stands in their way. This disposition, which is implanted in human nature, will operate in the federal legislature to lessen and ultimately to subvert the state authority, and having such advantages, will most certainly succeed, if the federal government succeeds at all. It must be very evident then, that what this constitution wants of being a complete consolidation of the several parts of the union into one complete government, possessed of perfect legislative, judicial, and executive powers, to all intents and purposes, it will necessarily acquire in its exercise and operation.

Let us now proceed to enquire, as I at first proposed, whether it be best the thirteen United States should be reduced to one great republic, or not? It is here taken for granted, that all agree in this, that whatever government we adopt, it ought to be a free one; that it should be so framed as to secure the liberty of the citizens of America, and such an one as to admit of a full, fair, and equal representation of the people, The question then will be, whether a government thus constituted, and founded on such principles, is practicable, and can be exercised over the whole United States, reduced into one state?

If respect is to be paid to the opinion of the greatest and wisest men who have ever thought or wrote on the science of government, we shall be constrained to conclude, that a free republic cannot succeed over a country of such immense extent, containing such a number of inhabitants, and these encreasing in such rapid progression as that of the whole United States. Among the many illustrious authorities which might be produced to this point, I shall content myself with quoting only two. The one is the baron de Montesquieu, spirit of laws, chap. xvi. vol. I [book VIII]. "It is natural to a republic to have only a small territory, otherwise it cannot long subsist. In a large republic there are men of large fortunes, and consequently of less moderation; there are trusts too great to be placed in any single subject; he has interest of his own; he soon begins to think that he may be happy, great and glorious, by oppressing his fellow citizens; and that he may raise himself to grandeur on the ruins of his country. In a large republic, the public good is sacrificed to a thousand views; it is subordinate to exceptions, and depends on accidents. In a small one, the interest of the public is easier perceived, better understood, and more within the reach of every citizen; abuses are of less extent, and of course are less protected." Of the same opinion is the marquis Beccarari.

History furnishes no example of a free republic, any thing like the extent of the United States. The Grecian republics were of small extent; so also was that of the Romans. Both of these, it is true, in process of time, extended their conquests over large territories of country; and the consequence was, that their governments were changed from that of free governments to those of the most tyrannical that ever existed in the world.

Not only the opinion of the greatest men, and the experience of mankind, are against the idea of an extensive republic, but a variety of reasons may be drawn from the reason and nature of things, against it. In every government, the will of the sovereign is the law. In despotic governments, the supreme authority being lodged in one, his will is law, and can be as easily expressed to a large extensive territory as to a small one. In a pure democracy the people are the sovereign, and their will is declared by themselves; for this purpose they must all come together to deliberate, and decide. This kind of government cannot be exercised, therefore, over a country of any considerable extent; it must be confined to a single city, or at least limited to such bounds as that the people can conveniently assemble, be able to debate, understand the subject submitted to them, and declare their opinion concerning it.

In a free republic, although all laws are derived from the consent of the people, yet the people do not declare their consent by themselves in person, but by representatives, chosen by them, who are supposed to know the minds of their constituents, and to be possessed of integrity to declare this mind.

In every free government, the people must give their assent to the laws by which they are governed. This is the true criterion between a free government and an arbitrary one. The former are ruled by the will of the whole, expressed in any manner they may agree upon; the latter by the will of one, or a few. If the people are to give their assent to the laws, by persons chosen and appointed by them, the manner of the choice and the number chosen, must be such, as to possess, be disposed, and consequently qualified to declare the sentiments of the people; for if they do not know, or are not disposed to speak the sentiments of the people, the people do not govern, but the sovereignty is in a few. Now, in a large extended country, it is impossible to have a representation, possessing the sentiments, and of integrity, to declare the minds of the people, without having it so numerous and unwieldy, as to be subject in great measure to the inconveniency of a democratic government.

The territory of the United States is of vast extent; it now contains near three millions of souls, and is capable of containing much more than ten times that number. Is it practicable for a country, so large and so numerous as they will soon become, to elect a representation, that will speak their sentiments, without their becoming so numerous as to be incapable of transacting public business? It certainly is not.

In a republic, the manners, sentiments, and interests of the people should be similar. If this be not the case, there will be a constant clashing of opinions; and the representatives of one part will be continually striving against those of the other. This will retard the operations of government, and prevent such conclusions as will promote the public good. If we apply this remark to the condition of the United States, we shall be convinced that it forbids that we should be one government. The United States includes a variety of climates. The productions of the different parts of the union are very variant, and their interests, of consequence, diverse. Their manners and habits differ as much as their climates and productions; and their sentiments are by no means coincident. The laws and customs of the several states are, in many respects, very diverse, and in some opposite; each would be in favor of its own interests and customs, and, of consequence, a legislature, formed of representatives from the perspective parts, would not only be too numerous to act with any care or decision, but would be composed of such heterogenous and discordant principles, as would constantly be contending with each other.

The laws cannot be executed in a republic, of an extent equal to that of the United States, with promptitude.

The magistrates in every government must be supported in the execution of the laws, either by an armed force, maintained at the public expense for that purpose; or by the people turning out to aid the magistrate upon his command, in case of resistance.

In despotic governments, as well as in all the monarchies of Europe, standing armies are kept up to execute the commands of the prince or the magistrate, and are employed for this purpose when occasion requires: But they have always proved the destruction of liberty, and [are] abhorrent to the spirit of a free republic. In England, where they depend upon the parliament for their annual support, they have always been complained of as oppressive and unconstitutional, and are seldom employed in executing of the laws; never except on extraordinary occasions, and then under the direction of a civil magistrate.

A free republic will never keep a standing army to execute its laws. It must depend upon the support of its citizens. But when a government is to receive its support from the aid of the citizens, it must be so constructed as to have the confidence, respect, and affection of the people. Men who, upon the call of the magistrate, offer themselves to execute the laws, are influenced to do it either by affection to the government, or from fear; where a standing army is at hand to punish offenders, everyman is actuated by the latter principle, and therefore, when the magistrate calls, will obey: but, where this is not the case, the government must rest for its support upon the confidence and respect which the people have for their government and laws. The body of the people being attached, the government will always be sufficient to support and execute its laws, and to operate upon the fears of any faction which may be opposed to it, not only to prevent an opposition to the execution of the laws themselves, but also to compel the most of them to aid the magistrate; but the people will not be likely to have such confidence in their rulers, in a republic so extensive at the United States, as necessary for these purposes. The confidence which the people have in their rulers, in a free republic, arises from their knowing them, from their being responsible to them for their conduct, and from the power they have of displacing them when they misbehave: but in a republic of the extent of this continent, the people in general would be acquainted with very few of their rulers: the people at large would know little of their proceedings, and it would be extremely difficult to change them. The people in Georgia and New Hampshire would not know one another's mind, and therefore could not act in concert to enable them to effect a general change of representatives. The different parts of so extensive a country could not possibly be made acquainted with the conduct of their representatives, nor be informed of the reasons upon which measures were founded. The consequence will be, they will have no confidence in their legislature, suspect them of ambitious views, be jealous of every measure they adopt, and will not support the laws they pass. Hence the government will be nerveless and inefficient, and no way will be left to render it otherwise, but by establishing an armed force to execute the laws at the point of the bayonet—a government of all others the most to be dreaded.

In a republic of such vast extent as the United States, the legislature cannot attend to the various concerns and wants of its different parts. It cannot be sufficiently numerous to be acquainted with the local condition and wants of the different districts, and if it could, it is impossible it should have sufficient time to attend to and provide for all the variety of cases of this nature, that would be continually arising.

In so extensive a republic, the great officers of government would soon become above the controul of the people, and abuse their power to the purpose of aggrandizing themselves, and oppressing them. The trust committed to the executive offices, in a country of the extent of the United States, must be various and of magnitude. The command of all the troops and navy of the republic, the appointment of officers, the power of pardoning offenses, the collecting of all the public revenues, and the power of expanding them, with a number of other powers, must be lodged and exercised in every state, in the hands of a few. When these are attended with great honor and emolument, as they always will be in large states, so as greatly to interest men to pursue them, and to be proper objects for ambitious and designing men, such men will be ever restless in their pursuit after them. They will use the power, when they have acquired it, to the purposes of gratifying their own interest and ambition, and it is scarcely possible, in a very large republic, to call them

to account for their misconduct, or to prevent their abuse of power.

These are some of the reasons by which it appears, that a free republic cannot long subsist over a country of the great extent of these states. If then this new constitution is calculated to consolidate the thirteen states into one, as it evidently is, it ought not to be adopted.

Though I am of opinion, that it is a sufficient objection to this government, to reject it, that it creates the whole union into one government, under the form of a republic, yet if this objection was obviated, there are exceptions to it, which are so material and fundamental, that they ought to determine every man, who is a friend to the liberty and happiness of mankind, not to adopt it. I beg the candid and dispassionate attention of my countrymen while I state these objections— they are such as have obtruded themselves upon my mind upon a careful attention to the matter, and such as I sincerely believe are well founded. There are many objections, of small moment, of which I shall take no notice—perfection is not to be expected in any thing that is the production of man—and if I did not in my conscience believe that this scheme was defective in the fundamental principles—in the foundation upon which a free and equal government must rest—I would hold my peace.

Brutus.

Presidents of the United States

	Party	Term
1. George Washington (1732–1799)	Federalist	1789–1797
2. John Adams (1735–1826)	Federalist	1797–1801
3. Thomas Jefferson (1743–1826)	Democratic-Republican	1801–1809
4. James Madison (1751–1836)	Democratic Republican	1809–1817
5. James Monroe (1758–1831)	Democratic-Republican	1817–1825
6. John Quincy Adams (1767–1848)	Democratic-Republican	1825–1829
7. Andrew Jackson (1767–1845)	Democratic	1829–1837
8. Martin Van Buren (1782–1862)	Democratic	1837–1841
9. William Henry Harrison (1773–1841)	Whig	1841
10. John Tyler (1790–1862)	Whig	1841–1845
11. James K. Polk (1795–1849)	Democratic	1845–1849
12. Zachary Taylor (1784–1850)	Whig	1849–1850
13. Millard Fillmore (1800–1874)	Whig	1850–1853
14. Franklin Pierce (1804–1869)	Democratic	1853–1857
15. James Buchanan (1791–1868)	Democratic	1857–1861
16. Abraham Lincoln (1809–1865)	Republican	1861–1865
17. Andrew Johnson (1808–1875)	Union	1865–1869
18. Ulysses S. Grant (1822–1885)	Republican	1869–1877
19. Rutherford B. Hayes (1822–1893)	Republican	1877–1881
20. James A. Garfield (1831–1881)	Republican	1881
21. Chester A. Arthur (1830–1886)	Republican	1881–1885
22. Grover Cleveland (1837–1908)	Democratic	1885–1889
23. Benjamin Harrison (1833–1901)	Republican	1889–1893
24. Grover Cleveland (1837–1908)	Democratic	1893–1897
25. William McKinley (1843–1901)	Republican	1897–1901
26. Theodore Roosevelt (1858–1919)	Republican	1901–1909
27. William Howard Taft (1857–1930)	Republican	1909–1913
28. Woodrow Wilson (1856–1924)	Democratic	1913–1921
29. Warren G. Harding (1865–1923)	Republican	1921–1923
30. Calvin Coolidge (1871–1933)	Republican	1923–1929
31. Herbert Hoover (1874–1964)	Republican	1929–1933
32. Franklin Delano Roosevelt (1882–1945)	Democratic	1933–1945
33. Harry S. Truman (1884–1972)	Democratic	1945–1953
34. Dwight D. Eisenhower (1890–1969)	Republican	1953–1961
35. John F. Kennedy (1917–1963)	Democratic	1961–1963
36. Lyndon B. Johnson (1908–1973)	Democratic	1963–1969
37. Richard M. Nixon (1913–1994)	Republican	1969–1974
38. Gerald R. Ford (b. 1913)	Republican	1974–1977
39. Jimmy Carter (b. 1924)	Democratic	1977–1981
40. Roland Reagan (b. 1911)	Republican	1981–1989
41. George Bush (b. 1924)	Republican	1989–1993
42. Bill Clinton (b. 1946)	Democratic	1993–

GLOSSARY

administrative adjudication   The quasijudicial powers delegated to executive agencies to try individuals or organizations that have violated legally binding agency rules.

administrative state   A national government involved in regulating or supporting almost every form of social activity by means of a large, complex, and diverse bureaucracy.

affirmative action   Positive steps taken to award educational opportunities or jobs to racial minorities or women because these groups have been the victims of prior discrimination.

agenda setting   The media's ability to determine what issues are considered legitimate, or even worthy of discussion, within the political arena.

agent provocateur   A person employed, usually by the government, to incite other people to break the law and thus make them liable to punishment.

American Civil Liberties Union (ACLU)   An organization that defends the civil liberties and civil rights of many individuals and groups in court challenges.

Anti-federalist   Opponent of the Constitution during the ratification debates of 1787–1788.

appellate court   A court that possesses the power to review the decisions of lower courts.

Articles of Confederation   The first written U.S. Constitution, ratified by the states in 1781, establishing a loose confederation among the former colonies under a weak national government.

autonomy   Greater freedom on the part of executive agencies from control by external forces.

Bill of Rights   The first ten amendments to the Constitution, which spell out the basic rights to which Americans are entitled.

block grant   The consolidation of a number of related categorical grants into one larger grant that provides recipients with the ability to spend the money as they see fit within the broad purposes of the grant.

Brown* v. *Board of Education of Topeka   The 1954 case in which the Supreme Court rejected the separate but equal doctrine in the field of education and thereby began the end of legal racial segregation.

Buckley* v. *Valeo   A 1976 U.S. Supreme Court ruling that struck down federal limits on overall campaign contributions by individuals. The decision also allowed interested citizens to spend unlimited amounts of money to support candidates independently of a campaign organization.

Budget and Impoundment Control Act of 1974   A law that reasserted congressional authority in budget making by creating new budget committees and the Congressional Budget Office and requiring annual timelines for the budgetary process.

bureaucracy   Units of the executive branch, organized in a hierarchical fashion, governed through formal rules, and distinguished by their specialized functions.

bureaucratic politics   The conflict that arises when an agency seeking to carry out its core mission is threatened by another agency promoting its core mission.

business confidence factor   The extent to which political officials anticipate and consider the future investment and spending habits of corporations when making political decisions.

bystander   A citizen who lacks consistent views about political issues, is generally uninterested in political events, and generally does not vote or participate in public affairs.

cabinet departments   The fourteen major divisions of the executive branch, each responsible for a broad area of governmental operations.

candidate-centered campaign Election contests in which candidates base their support on their personality, distinctive record, and self-developed organization rather than on their party affiliations.

capitalism An economic system in which individuals and corporations, not the government, own the principal means of production and accrue profits.

capital mobility The ability of investments to move around the globe seeking the highest return, regardless of national boundaries and the effect of investment and disinvestment on local communities.

casework The help given individual constituents by congressional staffs.

casino economy An economy prevalent since the 1980s, characterized by a high number of speculative sales, purchases, and mergers of corporations.

categorical grant Federal money to state and local governments that requires recipients to apply for funding under specific categories, detailing exactly how the money will be spent, and subject themselves to strict monitoring.

Central Intelligence Agency (CIA) The chief government intelligence-gathering agency, which has two primary functions: espionage and covert action.

civic journalism A tendency within contemporary journalism to concentrate on news coverage of issues of most concern to citizens rather than issues designated by news reporters as the most important.

civil disobedience The deliberate violation of the law by persons willing to accept the law's punishment in order to dramatize a cause.

civil liberties The basic freedoms embodied in the Bill of Rights, such as speech and religion, which individuals enjoy and government cannot invade.

civil rights Constitutional guarantees, such as the right to vote and equal treatment under the law, that belong to people because of their status as citizens.

Civil Rights Act of 1964 A law that made racial discrimination in public accomodations (hotels and restaurants) and employment illegal.

civil society The public space between the formal realm of government and the private realm of the family in which people form voluntary ties to each other.

Civil War amendments The Thirteenth, Fourteenth, and Fifteenth Amendments to the Constitution, which extended the Bill of Rights to and emphasized equality in the treatment of the former slaves.

clear and present danger test A Supreme Court standard stating that the government can prohibit political speech only if it can bring about an immediate evil that Congress has a right to prevent.

client politics The politics of policy making in which relatively small groups receive the benefits of the policy and the costs are borne by the public at large.

cloture A Senate procedure for terminating debate and ending a filibuster, which requires a three-fifths vote of the membership.

Cold War A worldwide political, economic and ideological struggle between the United States and the Soviet Union that lasted from 1945 to 1989.

collective action problem The difficulty in getting individuals to act collectively to obtain a common good when everyone in a group will benefit regardless of whether she or he contributes to the collective action.

committee system The division of the legislative workload among several congressional bodies assigned specific issues.

concurrent powers The constitutional authority granted to both the federal and state governments, such as the authority to tax.

concurring opinion A written statement by a Supreme Court justice about why he or she agrees with the decision reached in a case by the majority of the Court but not with the majority reasoning.

confidence and trust gap The decline in favorable popular opinion about the behavior and performance of government and social institutions, such as organized religion, corporations, and unions. Most observers date such decline from the late 1960s and early 1970s.

conservatism A political ideology emphasizing streamlined government, low taxes, and a business sector generally free from government regulation and interference. Conservative ideology also stresses traditional social values, such as a father-centered family, and a priority for military spending over social spending.

containment   A Cold War policy, also known as the Truman Doctrine, of a global American struggle to restrict the spread of communism.

core beliefs   The long-standing, consistent general attitudes that Americans share, such as support for freedom of speech and democracy.

corporate capitalism   The developed or advanced stage of capitalism in which large corporations dominate the means of production and often the political system as well.

corporate center strategy   An urban development strategy that focuses on downtown, transforming the industrial city into a center of high-level, corporate, professional service functions.

corporate image advertising   The promotion of a company's public persona rather than its products in order to create favorable public opinion about the role of the company in society.

corporate oligopoly   The current tendency for a few large corporations to control markets and investment capital in a particular area of economic production.

corporate welfare   Government subsidies, tax breaks, and tax expenditures that directly aid corporations.

cost-benefit analysis   A method of determining if the dollar benefits of proposed government regulation are greater than the dollar costs.

Council of Economic Advisers   A body of professional economists who provide the president with regular assistance.

court-packing plan   A failed attempt by President Franklin Roosevelt in 1937 to change the direction of the Supreme Court, by giving the president the power to name one new justice to the Court for each current justice over the age of seventy.

covert action   Secret CIA activities that cannot be traced to the U.S. government.

creative federalism   The attempt by President Lyndon Johnson to solve the problems of urban poverty by having the federal government bypass state and city governments and give grants directly to community and nonprofit organizations in the ghettos.

critical (realigning) election   An election that shapes entire electoral eras; it features increased voter turnout and a reshuffling of the social groups that support each party, resulting in the domination of one party in succeeding elections.

Declaration of Independence   The document written by Thomas Jefferson and adopted by the Continental Congress on July 4, 1776, in which the American colonies announced themselves to be free and independent from Great Britain and set forth the revolutionary principle of democracy.

deliberative poll   A new type of survey in which a representative selection of the population is brought together, presented with objective information about certain public questions, discusses the issues, and is then surveyed for their opinions.

Department of Defense   The cabinet department that coordinates and controls American military activities and is headed by a civilian secretary.

Department of State   The cabinet department that is the traditional organ of American diplomacy and is headed by a secretary.

deregulation   The reduction or elimination of government control of the conduct or activities of private citizens and organizations.

direct democracy   The face-to-face meeting of all citizens in one place to vote on all important issues.

discretion   The latitude that administrators have in carrying out their agency's mission.

disinformation campaign   CIA activity to disseminate misleading or false reports about opponents of the U.S. government's activities.

dissenting opinion   A written statement by a Supreme Court justice about why he or she disagrees with the decision reached in a case by the majority of the Court.

downsizing   Reducing the numbers of employees of a company by a conscious strategy of layoffs, firings, and retirements.

Dred Scott* v. *Sandford   The infamous 1857 case in which the Supreme Court decided that blacks were not citizens and that slaves were property protected by the Constitution.

dual federalism   The system created at the founding of the Constitution in which the national and state governments each have separate spheres of authority and are supreme within their own sphere.

economic cycles   The tendency of the world and national economy to vacillate between periods of economic expansion and recession or economic booms and busts.

economic individualism   The belief that hard work is the major determining factor in individual economic success and that economic opportunities are widely available to individuals who seek them.

economic planning   Long-term decisions by either government or corporations about what and how much to produce.

Economic Recovery Tax Act of 1981   Reagan administration legislation that dramatically cut taxes to encourage capital investment and economic growth.

economic regulation   Control by an independent regulatory commission of a specific industry that focuses on prices, quality of services, and the ability to enter or leave the industry.

electoral college   The body of electors, whose composition is determined by the results of the general election in each state, that chooses the president and vice president of the United States. Winning candidates must garner a majority of the 540 electoral votes.

electoral dealignment   The weakening of the party system caused by growing popular indifference to the parties themselves.

elite democracy   A political system in which the privileged classes acquire the power to decide by a competition for the people's votes and have substantial freedom between elections to rule as they see fit.

employee stock ownership plan (ESOP)   A legal arrangement, encouraged by federal legislation, which enables workers to gradually acquire shares of the companies they work for.

Employment Act of 1946   A law giving the federal government responsibility to promote free enterprise, avoid economic fluctuations, and maintain jobs, production, and purchasing power.

enterprise webs   The synergy created between different companies in selected industries when they are located in the same geographical area. California's Silicon Valley represents an enterprise web in the computer industry; the Los Angeles area is an enterprise web for the entertainment industry.

entitlement   A social benefit, such as Social Security, in which all who pay into it have a right to the benefits; you do not have to apply for the program or prove that you deserve help.

enumerated powers   The authority specifically granted to the federal government in the Constitution under Article I, section 8.

equality of condition   The idea that income and wealth should be leveled so that nobody is either very rich or very poor.

equality of opportunity   The idea that there should be no discriminatory barriers placed on an individual's access to economic success.

Establishment Clause   That part of the First Amendment that forbids Congress to make any law instituting a religion; the central component of the separation of church and state.

exclusionary rule   A doctrine, based on the Fourth Amendment's guarantee against unreasonable searches and seizures, in which the Supreme Court established that material seized in an illegal search cannot be introduced as evidence in a criminal case.

Executive Office of the President (EOP)   The complex of support agencies designed to assist the chief executive, including the White House staff, the Office of Management and Budget, the Council of Economic Advisers, and the National Security Council.

expansion   Nineteenth-century activities by the United States to extend the nation to the Pacific Ocean and to gain territorial acquisitions in Latin America and Asia.

expertise   The specialized knowledge of admistrators about their particular areas of responsibility.

Fairness Rule   An FCC regulation requiring broadcasters to provide reasonable time for expression of opposing views on controversial issues.

Federal Communications Commission (FCC)   The governmental regulatory agency charged with implementing laws and developing regulations for radio and television. The FCC licenses these media and regulates the private ownership of broadcast stations.

federal foundation or endowment   Organization that enables the federal government to sponsor scientific and cultural activities.

federalism   A system in which power is divided between the central government and the states.

Federalist   Supporter of the Constitution during the Constitutional Convention of 1787 and the ratification debates of 1787–1788.

Federal Register   The daily government publication of all national administrative regulations.

Federal Reserve   The main institution responsible for monetary policy in the United States. Created in 1913 to regulate banks and adjust the money supply, thus controlling inflation, its seven-member board of governors is appointed by the president with the consent of the Senate.

feminization of poverty   The increased proportion of women, especially single women with children, who fall below the poverty line.

filibuster   The Senate tradition whereby a senator can try to delay or defeat a vote on legislation by talking the bill to death.

fiscal policy   The manipulation of components of the national budget, taxes, and spending to regulate the economy.

5-5-10 rule   A Federal Communications Commission regulation, now defunct, requiring broadcasters to devote a minimum of 5 percent of airtime to local affairs, 5 percent to news and public affairs, and 10 percent to nonentertainment programming.

flexible specialization   An innovative form of production that enables companies to develop new products and produce them in smaller batches to respond to specialized niches in the market system.

focus and dial group   A selected sample of voters intensively interviewed by campaign consultants to gain knowledge about reactions to particular candidates and their campaign messages and themes.

footnote 4   A footnote in a 1938 Supreme Court decision that sets out three conditions under which the Court will not grant government action the presumption of constitutionality: when the action falls under the prohibitions of the Bill of Rights or Fourteenth Amendment, when the action restricts the democratic process, or when the action is harmful to particular religions or national or racial minorities.

franking privilege   The benefit enjoyed by members of Congress of free postage to send mass mailings to their constituents.

Freedom Summer   A intensive campaign of direct action launched in the summmer of 1964 by major civil rights organizations to press for federal intervention to eliminate racial segregation and discrimination in the southern states.

Free Exercise Clause   That part of the First Amendment that states that Congress shall make no law prohibiting the practice of religion.

frontloading   The decisions made by state governments to move their presidential primaries to dates earlier in the election year in order to increase their influence on presidential candidates.

gender gap   Distinctions between the attitudes, voting behavior, and political outlooks of men and women.

general revenue sharing   Federal grants to states and localities without the stringent requirements associated with categorical grants.

Gibbons v. *Ogden*   The 1824 case in which the Supreme Court broadly defined the congressional power to "regulate commerce among the states," thereby establishing the supremacy of the federal government over the states in matters involving interstate commerce.

grant-in-aid   Money provided by one level of government to another to perform certain functions.

grassroots campaign   A run for office that emphasizes volunteer efforts, person-to-person contact, and voter organization over paid advertising, extensive polling, and other costly activities managed by a central staff.

Great Compromise   An agreement, also known as the Connecticut Compromise, in which the Constitutional Convention of 1787 resolved that Congress would be bicameral, with the Senate composed of two members from each state and the House of Representatives apportioned according to each state's population.

growth machine   A local political coalition, centered on urban real estate interests, that pushes public policies designed to maximize economic growth that supposedly benefits all elements of the population.

horse race journalism   The tendency of the media to report election campaigns in terms of who is winning and losing rather than in terms of what issues are at stake.

ideological bloc   A group of two or more Supreme Court justices who vote the same way with a high degree of regularity on the basis of a shared legal philosophy.

ideology   A specific set of beliefs for making sense of issues and actions; a consistent pattern of opinion used to justify political behavior.

income inequality   The gap in yearly earnings between those groups and individuals with the highest and those with the lowest incomes.

incorporation   The doctrine that the Supreme Court used to apply the Bill of Rights to the states under the 14th Amendment Due Process Clause.

incumbent   The person who currently holds an office.

independent agency   An executive branch organization that stands outside of and generally handles more narrow areas of governmental operation than the cabinet departments.

independent regulatory commision   A governmental body that controls a sector of the economy and is directed by commissioners who are appointed by the president, have long terms, and are exempt from presidential removal so that the agency is distanced from political pressures.

information-based economy   Economic growth based on the generation of new ideas and services rather than the production of manufactured goods.

information superhighway   New technology allowing individuals and institutions with computers to communicate directly with each other and with commercial, educational, and other institutions via the Internet and profit-making operations such as Prodigy and America OnLine.

insider strategy   The use by an interest group of face-to-face, one-on-one persuasion to convince decision makers in Washington that the interest group's position makes sense.

interest group politics   Any attempt by an organization to influence the policies of government through normal extra electoral channels, such as lobbying, writing letters, testifying before legislative committees, or advertising.

intergovernmental relations   The modern system of federalism in which relations between the different levels of government are worked out by specific legislation and negotiations, rather than through the formal distinction of separate spheres of authority that characterized dual federalism.

invisible primary   The pre-election year competition for money, support, and media attention among potential presidential candidates.

iron triangle   An alliance between a congressional committee, an interest group, and an executive agency that serves each one's interest, often at the expense of the general public.

isolationism   The idea that apart from commercial relations, the United States should stay out of the political and military quarrels of the rest of the world; the core principle of American foreign and defense policy from the founding until World War II.

issue advocacy ad   Political advertising that avoids endorsements of specific candidates for office in order to escape campaign finance regulations.

Jim Crow laws   A series of measures, instituted by Southern state governments around the turn of the century, enforcing strict racial segregation as well as exclusion of African Americans from political participation by means of literacy tests, poll taxes, and "whites only" party primary contests. "Jim Crow" was struck down by a series of Federal civil rights acts in the 1960s.

Joint Chiefs of Staff (JCS)   A body composed of the commanding officer of each military service, and headed by a chair, that conveys the military's point of view to the president and the secretary of defense.

judicial review   The power of the courts to invalidate legislative or executive actions because they conflict with the Constitution.

jurisprudence of original intention   The argument that Supreme Court justices should restrict their constitutional interpretation to the precise words of the Constitution and the known intentions of the men who drafted it.

Laffer curve   The representational graph that argues that decreasing tax rates below a certain point will actually increase total tax revenues.

laissez-faire   The idea that government should not be involved in running the private economy.

legislative liaison staff   The group of people responsible for keeping the president informed of the political maneuvering and likely vote lineup in

Congress for important bills and for providing small favors to members of Congress in the hopes that they will later return these favors to the president with their votes.

Lemon test   The standard used by the Supreme Court in cases involving government aid to religion, which states that government assistance is constitutional only if it has a secular purpose, its effect does not advance or inhibit religion, and it does not entangle government and religious institutions in each other's affairs.

liberalism   A political ideology stressing the necessity of active government for the achievement of some measure of social and economic equality within the corporate capitalist system. Liberalism stresses the preservation of individual and group rights and liberties, and toleration for social change and ethnic and religious diversity. Historically, American liberals have usually placed a priority on social over military spending.

line-item veto   A recent grant of authority to the president to reject particular appropriations and narrowly targeted tax breaks while signing a budget bill.

macroeconomic policy   Economic policy that influences the performance of the economy as a whole and is not designed to have direct effects on different sectors or on the distribution of economic opportunities among different groups in the population.

mail order politics   The modern tendency for some to participate in politics through monetary contributions to Washington lobbying groups.

majoritarian politics   The politics of policy making in which all, or nearly all, citizens receive some benefits of the policy and pay the costs.

majority leader   The head of the majority party in the House of Representatives or Senate.

Marbury v. *Madison*   The 1803 case in which the Supreme Court established that it had the right to exercise judicial review even though that power was not stated in the Constitution.

market competition   The process in which markets become decentralized arenas where many producers and consumers make free choices among a wide range of products and services.

mass movement   The participation of large num-

bers of previously passive bystanders in a political protest action.

matching grant   Money given by the federal government to lower levels of government to fulfill certain functions, requiring that the recipients put up some of their own money and meet minimal federal standards for the program.

McCarthyism   The practice, named after Senator Joseph McCarthy, of falsely accusing individuals of being disloyal or subversive in order to gain publicity or suppress opposition.

McCulloch v. *Maryland*   The 1819 case in which Justice Marshall emphasized the constitutional supremacy of the federal government in striking down Maryland's attempt to tax the Bank of the United States.

means–tested benefits   The method of granting public assistance that forces people to prove their inability to support themselves in order to secure that assistance.

military-industrial complex   The network of ties among large corporations, the Department of Defense, the armed services, and their key political supporters in Congress and the executive branch.

minority leader   The head of the minority party in the House of Representatives or Senate.

Miranda warnings   The requirement that police inform all criminal suspects of their rights before taking them into custody.

mission   The central task to which the members of a government agency are committed.

monetarism   An economic philosophy that believes steady growth can be achieved if the money supply grows only as fast as the economy's productivity.

monetary policy   A method of economic management that regulates the supply of money in the economy.

most favored nation (MFN)   A trading partner of the United States who is accorded the best terms of trade available to any nation with which the U.S. does business.

Motor Voter bill   Legislation passed in 1993 that allows people to register to vote when they apply for a driver's license, thereby making voter registration easier and more accessible.

name recognition   The extent to which a candidate's or potential candidate's name is known by voters.

National Association for the Advancement of Colored People (NAACP)   An organization that fights for the rights of black Americans.

national entertainment state   Term used to describe the increasing concentration of ownership and control of new and old media by a few media conglomerates.

national party convention   Meetings held every four years to determine a political party's national platform and presidential and vice presidential candidates. Generally, convention delegates are selected through primaries and caucuses held in every state during election years.

national security adviser   The personal counselor to the president in foreign policy and defense matters.

National Security Council (NSC)   A governmental body created in 1947 to advise the president and coordinate foreign and defense policy.

national security state   A complex of executive, military, and secret powers that shaped American international relations in the Cold War and largely excluded Congress and the public from decisions about the country's security.

Necessary and Proper (or Elastic) Clause   The clause in the U.S. Constitution at the end of Article I, Section 8 that says that Congress has all powers that are required for it to execute its other powers. The Elastic Clause has been used by the Supreme Court to expand the powers of the federal government.

New Deal Democratic coalition   The Democrats' alliance of the Solid South, organized labor, Catholics, and urban ethnic groups stemming from Franklin Roosevelt's policies of the 1930s.

new federalism   The attempt by President Richard Nixon to weaken the power of liberal political lobbies in Washington and reverse the trend toward centralization of authority and control in Washington by placing more power, monies, and responsibility for government programs in the hands of the states.

New Jersey Plan   The proposal submitted by the New Jersey delegation at the Constitutional Convention of 1787 to reform the Articles of Confederation but maintain most governmental power in the states.

new working class   Those who make wages and labor in subordinate positions in the service industries that have grown rapidly in the past two decades.

North Atlantic Treaty Organization (NATO)   The military alliance among the United States, Canada, and the Western European states, created to oppose Soviet aggression in the Cold War period.

nullification   The doctrine that the states have the right to declare invalid any federal legislation that they believe violates the Constitution.

obscenity   Sexually explicit material that lacks serious literary, artistic, political, or scientific value and that appeals to a "prurient" interest; one of the categories of unprotected speech.

Office of Management and Budget (OMB)   The agency responsible for preparing the annual presidential budget and for scrutinizing legislative proposals originating in the agencies of the executive branch to ensure that these proposals are in accord with the president's legislative program.

oral argument   The spoken presentation of each side of a case to the justices of the Supreme Court.

original jurisdiction   The power of a court to hear a case at its inception.

outsider strategy   The mobilization by an interest group of forces outside Washington to put pressure on decision makers to act in ways favorable to the interest group.

outsourcing   The ability of large companies to avoid wage and benefit costs by contracting out many of their operations to smaller companies that hire cheaper, often part-time labor.

oversight   Congressional attempts to exercise control over the activities of executive branch agencies through a variety of techniques, including hearings and investigations.

pack journalism   The development by a group of reporters of similar views after receiving the same information and insights from the same sources.

paper entrepreneur   A person who makes his or her fortune by managing mergers or speculating in stocks.

party caucus   A public meeting held within a political party to select delegates pledged to the nomination of a particular candidate.

party identification   A person's psychological identification with or tie to a particular political party.

party system   Long-lasting themes and rules that dominate interparty competition and dialogue, usually established by realigning elections and usually featuring a dominant issue.

patronage   The power of elected officials to increase their political strength by appointing people of their choice to governmental or public jobs; one of the methods that political machines use to guarantee loyalty.

permanent campaign   The process by which incumbent officeholders are constantly gearing their official actions toward their reelection prospects.

personal registration   The practice, introduced in the Progressive era of the early twentieth century, whereby individual citizens are given the responsibility to register to vote. In most countries, the government itself assumes the responsibility of registering citizens.

Personal Responsibility Act of 1996   The act passed by Congress and signed into law by President Clinton in August 1996 that did away with the federal entitlement to welfare and replaced it with a block grant to the states that requires the states to move half of the people on welfare into jobs by 2002. The new program, called Temporary Assistance to Needy Families (TANF), replaces Aid for Families with Dependent Children (AFDC).

pluralism   The elite democratic theory that views the interest group system as a political marketplace in which power is dispersed among many interest groups competing for influence through a process of bargaining and compromising.

political action committee (PAC)   A voluntary organization that funnels monies from individuals in corporations, trade associations, labor unions, and other groups into political campaigns under Federal Election Commission laws.

political culture   The political values shared by the vast majority of citizens in a nation despite disagreements about their precise meanings.

political efficacy   The extent to which citizens believe that their participation in politics makes a difference for what government does.

political independent   A citizen who identifies with no political party.

political machine   An organization of political professionals able to win elections through intensive organization and voter loyalty, usually garnered by providing jobs and services to followers and denying them to opponents.

political socialization   The ways in which individuals obtain their ideas about human nature, politics, and political institutions.

poll bias   Conscious or unconscious mistakes in sampling technique or question wording that serve to mischaracterize or misinterpret public opinion.

popular democracy   A political system in which the citizens are involved as much as possible in making the decisions that affect their lives.

populism   A political doctrine advocating the regulation of excessive concentration of economic and political power, and the redistribution of power and wealth towards ordinary people. Populism stresses the importance of a common social morality over the claims of social and cultural minorities.

Populist party   The political party formed by southern and western farmers in the late 1880s to rally against the alleged advantages given to big business and banking interests.

precedent   A previous decision by a court that is treated as a rule for future cases.

preemption   The ability of the federal government to assume total or partial responsibility for a function where there is concurrent authority for both the federal government and the states to act.

presidential power of secrecy   The ability of the chief executive to make foreign policy and national security decisions that are not subject to public scrutiny.

president's cabinet   The executive body composed of the appointed heads of the fourteen major executive departments, plus any others designated by the chief executive.

primary   An election in which voters decide which of a party's candidates will be nominated to run for office in the general election. Closed primaries permit only those requested in a particular party to participate. Open primaries leave the balloting open to non–party registrants.

prior restraint   The First Amendment prohibition against government officials preventing information from being published.

privatization   The turning over of governmental functions to the private sector when it can perform functions more cheaply than government agencies.

privileged position of business   The idea that business has the advantage in most political disputes because of its power to threaten "disinvestment" when government proposes regulations and/or taxation.

productivity   The amount of labor or of labor time required to produce a commodity.

progressive tax   A tax that takes a higher proportion of income as income increases.

Progressivism   An early twentieth-century American reform doctrine that advocated limits to the power of political machines, expert and efficient bureaucracies, and a politics free of allegedly corrupt influences from party politicians, especially those representing urban immigrants.

protest politics   Political actions designed to broaden conflicts and activate outside parties to pressure the bargaining process in ways favorable to the protestors.

public corporation   A government agency that engages in business activities.

public interest group   Any association seeking government action, the achievement of which will not principally benefit the members of the association.

public opinion   The average person's ideas and views on political issues.

racial redistricting   The redrawing of congressional districts to redress past patterns of racial discrimination by creating new districts with "majority minority" populations. In the mid-1990s, however, the Federal courts ruled that race could not be the sole criteria for redistricting.

regulation   A process by which the government imposes restrictions on the conduct of private citizens and organizations.

"reinventing government" plan   An initiative of President Clinton and Vice President Gore to reform the federal bureaucracy by making executive agencies more entrepreneurial and by empowering civil servants.

relative deprivation   The theory that people mobilize politically not when they are worst off, but when they perceive that they are deprived unjustly, relative to other groups in the population.

republicanism   The eighteenth-century body of political thought, based on the ideas of liberty versus power, legislatures versus executives, civic virtue, and the small republic, that shaped the political activities of colonial Americans and infused them with the revolutionary "Spirit of '76."

reserved powers   The authority not given to the federal government and left to the states by the Tenth Amendment.

responsible two-party system   A scholarly ideal in which parties fulfill their democratic character by forming consistent and meaningful ideologies and programs that become well known to the voters and in which the winning party is held accountable by voters for implementation of programs and their consequences.

retrospective voting   The tendency of voters to cast ballots on the basis of the perceived performance of the incumbent while in office or the condition of the economy, rather than on the candidates' policy positions or voters' traditional allegiances.

revolving door   The phenomenon whereby people working in Congress or in an executive branch agency become lobbyists or journalists once they leave government service, using their experience and knowledge for the benefit of their clients.

right of privacy   The freedom to be left alone implied in the Constitution.

Roe v. *Wade*   The 1973 Supreme Court case that established a woman's right to choose abortion and rendered unconstitutional all state laws that made abortion a crime.

rule   A statement issued by the House Rules Committee indicating how much time will be devoted to floor debate on a particular bill and what kinds of amendments will be allowed on the floor.

rule-making authority   The power of an executive agency to issue regulations that carry the force of law.

rule of four   An informal Supreme Court standard whereby if any four justices vote that a case deserves consideration, the Court will grant certiorari.

salience   An issue's perceived degree of significance in public opinion.

satyagraha   "Truth Force"; or the belief of the Indian pacifist Mahatma Gandhi that a carefully orchestrated civil disobedience plan can persuade one's opponents of the justice of one's cause.

senatorial courtesy   The Senate's withholding of consent to the nomination of a district court judge if the senior senator of the president's party from the nominee's state objects to that nomination.

seniority   The congressional norm that dictates that the member from the majority party who has the most years of continuous service on a committee becomes its chair.

separate but equal   The doctrine established by the Supreme Court in the 1896 case of *Plessey* v. *Ferguson*, that separate equivalent facilities for whites and blacks did not violate the Fourteenth Amendment's guarantee of equal protection of the laws, thereby providing the legal basis for segregation of the races.

shareholder democracy   The idea that corporations are held accountable to the public through the power of shareholders over corporate policies.

Shays's Rebellion   A 1786 upheaval by desperate small farmers in Massachusetts that alarmed conservative republicans and thereby set the stage for the Constitutional Convention of 1787.

single-member district system   A type of representation that allows the person who wins the most votes in a district's election to represent the entire district.

smokestack chasing   The effort by state and local officials to offer deeper and deeper subsidies to entice industrial jobs into their jurisdiction.

social class   A group differentiated from others by occupation, income, wealth, power, and social and cultural outlook.

social mobility   The ability of a group or individual to move from one social class to another, thereby achieving greater or lesser income, wealth, or power.

social regulation   Executive agency rules that cover all industries and focus on such matters as environmental protection, safety, health, and non-discrimination.

social rights   The popular democratic belief that all citizens should be entitled to basic educational and health services and minimum income benefits.

soft money   Campaign funds raised legally by national political parties and used to influence federal elections, while often circumventing federal restrictions on campaign spending.

sound bite   A very short, supposedly representative quote from a public official presented in advertising or the news.

source bias   The tendency of modern journalists to seek a limited range of opinions and views from certain groups and institutions as they report the news.

Speaker of the House of Representatives   The presiding officer of the House of Representatives, who is chosen by the majority party in the House and is second, after the vice president, in the line of presidential succession.

split-ticket voting   The tendency of many voters to vote for the candidate of one party for a particular office and that of another party for other offices in the same election.

spoils system   The awarding of political jobs to political supporters and friends.

strict scrutiny   A Supreme Court standard in civil liberties or civil rights cases of striking down a law unless the government can demonstrate a "compelling interest" that necessitates such a law.

supply-side economics   The economic theory used by the Reagan administration to justify reducing taxes on investment, profits, and income and reducing government regulation of industry to promote economic prosperity.

Supremacy Clause   Article VI of the Constitution, which states that when the national and state governments conflict, the national laws shall supersede the state laws.

symbolic speech   Protected political expression that communicates with visual symbols instead of words.

system of 1896   The electoral era initiated by Republican William McKinley's defeat of Democrat/Populist William Jennings Bryan in 1896. The system featured Democratic control of southern state governments, Republican control of the big states and the national government, as well as low voter turnout and the initiation of restrictions on voter registration based on race.

tax expenditures   Defined in the 1974 Budget Act as "revenue losses attributable to provisions of the federal tax laws which allow a special exemption, exclusion, or deduction." Tax expenditures are calculated by subtracting what the government actually collects in taxes from what it would have collected had the special exemptions not been in place.

Telecommunications Act of 1996   Sweeping Federal legislation that abolishes many of the Federal Communications Commission's previous restrictions on radio and television ownership by individuals and corporations. The Telecommunications Act ostensibly promotes competition between different parts of the telecommunications and media industries, but has prompted new corporate mergers and concentration.

think tank   A nonprofit institution, funded primarily by foundations and corporate grants, that conducts public policy research.

transactional leader   A party or interest group leader whose leadership is based on brokering beneficial exchanges with followers, such as patronage jobs for votes.

transforming leader   A mass movement leader who engages the full personalities of followers, helping them to go beyond self-interest and participate in direct political action.

unitary government   A system in which all significant powers rest in the hands of the central government.

unprotected speech   Communication that is not protected by the First Amendment either because its social value is insignificant or because it verges on conduct that is harmful to others.

upscale demographics   The tendency of advertisers and media outlets to appeal to high-income, big-spending consumers.

veto   The constitutional power of the president to reject legislation passed by Congress, subject to a two-thirds override by both houses.

Virginia Plan   The proposal submitted by the Virginia delegation at the Constitutional Convention of 1787, to create a strong national government.

virtual democracy   The idea that the information superhighway created by the Internet and the World Wide Web will initiate new debates and discussions between citizens and officeholders.

Voting Rights Act of 1965   The law that removed the barriers that southern officials had placed in the way of African Americans who sought to register to vote, and involved federal supervision of the voting process.

Wagner Act   Also known as the National Labor Relations Act of 1935 and named for its sponsor, New York Senator Robert Wagner; legislation affirming the rights of workers to form unions and bargain with employers. The act established the National Labor Relations Board (NLRB).

War Powers Resolution of 1973   An attempt by Congress to reassert its constitutional authority in the area of war making.

wealth inequality   The gap in net money worth among various population groups.

wedge issue   A topic used to divide and split off one formerly loyal constituency of a political party from other groups in that party's coalition.

welfare state   The array of social policies in advanced industrial countries designed to redistribute wealth and assist those who cannot support themselves in the private marketplace.

White House staff   The president's personal aides and advisers along with their numerous assistants.

whip   The representative or Senator who assists a party's leaders in the House and Senate by gathering information about how party members plan to vote on forthcoming issues and by encouraging partisan loyalty through persuasion and personal attention.

yellow journalism   A form of reporting pioneered in the late nineteenth century by the Hearst and Pulitzer newspaper chains, emphasizing entertaining and often lurid scandals as news.

ENDNOTES

CHAPTER 1

1. Joseph A. Schumpeter, *Capitalism, Socialism and Democracy*, 3rd ed. (New York: Harper & Row, 1950), p. 269. In Part IV Schumpeter makes one of the classic defenses of elite democracy. For critiques of the elite theory of democracy from a popular democratic viewpoint, see Jack L. Walker, "A Critique of the Elitist Theory of Democracy," *American Political Science Review*, 60 (1966): 285–95; and Peter Bachrach, *The Theory of Democratic Elitism: A Critique* (Boston: Little, Brown, 1967).

2. The most influential political scientist who has written on the ideas of elite and popular democracy is Robert A. Dahl. Dahl began his career by defending a version of elite democracy in *A Preface to Democratic Theory* (Chicago: University of Chicago Press, 1956); and *Who Governs? Democracy and Power in an American City* (New Haven, Conn.: Yale University Press, 1961). In his later works, Dahl shifted dramatically to a more popular democratic position. See *A Preface to Economic Democracy* (Berkeley: University of California Press, 1985); and *Democracy and Its Critics* (New Haven, Conn.: Yale University Press, 1989).

3. See Ralph Ketcham, ed., *The Anti-Federalist Papers and the Constitutional Convention Debates* (New York: New American Library, 1986), p. 213.

4. We are not the first to present a cyclical view of American politics in which participatory upsurges are followed by periods of elite consolidation. See Arthur M. Schlesinger, Jr., *Paths to the Present* (New York: Macmillan, 1949); Arthur M. Schlesinger, Jr., *The Cycles of American History* (Boston: Houghton Mifflin, 1986); and Albert O. Hirschman, *Shifting Involvements: Private Interest and Public Action* (Princeton: Princeton University Press, 1982).

5. George Will, "In Defense of Nonvoting," *Newsweek*, October 10, 1983, p. 96.

CHAPTER 2

1. Gordon S. Wood, *The Radicalism of the American Revolution* (New York: Alfred A. Knopf, 1992), pp. 11–92.

2. For an excellent account of this political dynamic, see Pauline Maier, *From Resistance to Revolution: Colonial Radicals and the Development of American Opposition to Britain, 1765–1776* (New York: Vintage Books, 1974).

3. Sidney Hook, ed., *The Essential Thomas Paine* (New York: New American Library, 1969), pp. 48, 33.

4. On republicanism and the origins of the American Revolution, see Bernard Bailyn, *The Ideological Origins of the American Revolution* (Cambridge: Harvard University Press, 1967); and Gordon S. Wood, *The Creation of the American Republic: 1776–1787* (New York: W. W. Norton, 1972), pp. 3–124.

5. On the place of the Declaration of Independence in American political thought, see especially two books by Garry Wills: *Inventing America: Jefferson's Declaration of Independence* (New York; Vintage Books, 1978); and *Lincoln at Gettysburg: The Words that Remade America* (New York: Simon & Schuster, 1992).

6. Roy P. Basler, ed., *The Collected Works of Abraham Lincoln*, vol. 3 (New Brunswick, N.J.: Rutgers University Press, 1953), p. 375.

7. The Declaration of Independence was creatively used by Elizabeth Cady Stanton to advance the cause of women and by Frederick Douglass, W. E. B. DuBois, and Martin Luther King, Jr., to promote equality for African Americans.

8. On the state constitutions of 1776, see Wood, *Creation of the American Republic*, pp. 127–255.

9. On the economic legislation of the 1780s, see Merrill Jensen, *The New Nation: A History of the United States During the Confederation, 1781–1789* (New York: Vintage Books, 1950), pp. 302–26.

10. Jackson Turner Main, "Government by the People: The American Revolution and the Democratization of the Legislatures," in Jack P. Greene, ed., *The Reinterpretation of the American Revolution, 1763–1789* (New York: Harper & Row, 1968), pp. 322–38.

11. Marvin Meyers, ed., *The Mind of the Founder: Sources of the Political Thought of James Madison*, rev. ed. (Hanover, N.H.: University Press of New England, 1981), p. 62. For a penetrating analysis of Madison as an elite democratic thinker, see Richard K. Matthews, *If Men Were Angels: James Madison and the Heartless Empire of Reason* (Lawrence: University Press of Kansas, 1995). For an impressive presentation of the opposing position that Madison was something of a popular democrat, see Lance Banning, *The Sacred Fire of Liberty: James Madison and the Founding of the Federal Republic* (Ithaca, N.Y.: Cornell University Press, 1995).

12. Among the many treatments of the Constitutional Convention and the political system it shaped, one of the richest in insights is Jack N. Rakove, *Original Meanings: Politics and Ideas in the Making of the Constitution* (New York: Alfred A. Knopf, 1996).

13. Alfred A. Young, "Conservatives, the Constitution, and the 'Spirit of Accommodation,'" in Robert A. Goldwin and William A. Schambra, eds., *How Democratic Is the Constitution?* (Washington, D.C.: American Enterprise Institute, 1980), pp. 118, 138.

14. Max Farrand, ed., *The Records of the Federal Convention of 1787*, vol. 1 (New Haven, Conn.: Yale University Press, 1937), pp. 65, 66.

15. Charles A. Beard, *An Economic Interpretation of the Constitution* (New York: Macmillan, 1913).

16. Farrand, ed., *Records of the Federal Convention*, vol. 2, p. 370.

17. See Michael Allen Gillespie and Michael Lienesch, eds., *Ratifying the Constitution* (Lawrence: University Press of Kansas, 1989).

18. Herbert J. Storing, *What the Anti-Federalists Were For* (Chicago: University of Chicago Press, 1981), p. 72. An even more sympathetic treatment of the Anti-federalist perspective than Storing's is Christopher M. Duncan, *The Anti-Federalists and Early American Political Thought* (DeKalb: Northern Illinois University Press, 1995).

19. Clinton Rossiter, ed., *The Federalist Papers* (New York: New American Library, 1961), p. 79.

20. Ibid., p. 54.

21. Ibid., p. 346.

22. Ibid., p. 414.

23. On the Anti-federalist conception of virtue, see Storing, *What the Anti-Federalists Were For*, pp. 19–23.

24. Ralph Ketcham, ed., *The Anti-Federalist Papers and the Constitutional Convention Debates* (New York: New American Library, 1986), p. 202.

25. Rossiter, ed., *Federalist Papers*, p. 83.

26. See Storing, *What the Anti-Federalists Were For*, pp. 16–23.

27. Herbert J. Storing, ed., *The Anti-Federalist* (Chicago: University of Chicago Press, 1985), p. 116.

28. Rossiter, ed., *Federalist Papers*, p. 82.

29. Storing, ed., *The Anti-Federalist*, p. 340.

30. Rossiter, ed., *Federalist Papers*, p. 322.

31. Ibid., p. 423.

32. Ketcham, ed., *Anti-Federalist Papers*, p. 213.

33. Rossiter, ed., *Federalist Papers*, p. 78.

34. Ibid., p. 88.

35. Ketcham, ed., *Anti-Federalist Papers*, pp. 207–8.

36. Rossiter, ed., *Federalist Papers*, p. 314.

37. Merrill D. Peterson, ed., *The Portable Thomas Jefferson* (New York: Penguin, 1975), p. 417. For an excellent discussion of the conflicting perspectives on stability and change, see Michael Lienesch, *New Order of the Ages: Time, the Constitution, and the Making of Modern American Political Thought* (Princeton, N.J.: Princeton University Press, 1988), pp. 63–81.

38. Jackson Turner Main, *The Anti-Federalists: Critics of the Constitution, 1781–1788* (New York: W. W. Norton, 1974), p. 133.

39. On Madison and the Bill of Rights, see Robert A. Rutland, *James Madison: The Founding Father* (New York: Macmillan, 1987), pp. 59–65.

CHAPTER 3

1. Robert Nisbet, "Public Opinion versus Popular Opinion," in Bruce Miroff, Raymond Seidelman, and Todd Swanstrom, eds. *Debating Democracy* (Boston: Houghton Mifflin, 1997), p. 117. Phillip Converse, "The Nature of Belief Systems in Mass Publics," in David Apter, ed., *Ideology and Discontent* (New York: Free Press, 1964), pp. 243–45. Hamilton quoted in Clinton Rossiter, ed., *The Federalist Papers* (New York: New American Library, 1961), p. 432.

2. Benjamin Ginsberg, *The Captive Public* (New York: Basic Books, 1986). See also Walter Lippmann, *The Phantom Public* (New York: Harcourt, Brace, Jovanovich, 1925), pp. 15, 155; Thomas Dye and Harmon Ziegler, *The Irony of Democracy* (Monterey: Brooks/Cole, 1987), p. 145; Anthony King *Running Scared* (Cambridge: Harvard University Press, 1997) Michael Delli Carpini and Scott Keeter, "The Public's Knowledge of Politics," in David Kennamer, ed., *Public Opinion, The Press and Public Policy* (Westport, Conn.: Praeger, 1992).

3. C. Wright Mills, *The Power Elite* (New York: Oxford University Press, 1956), pp. 298–304; John Dewey, *The Public and Its Problems* (Athens, Oh.: Swallow Press, 1954). For a discussion of Dewey's views, see Robert Westerbrook, *John Dewey and Democracy* (Ithaca, N.Y.: Cornell University Press, 1991).

4. Robert Cirino, *Don't Blame the People* (New York: Basic Books, 1971). For a brilliant account of public opinion during the Vietnam War, see Godfrey Hodgson, *America in Our Time*, (New York: Pantheon, 1976).

5. This view of political culture is argued persuasively in David Croteau, *Politics and the Class Divide* (Philadelphia: Temple University Press, 1994), pp. 44–46. See also Robert Bellah et al., *Habits of the Heart* (New York: Harper/Collins, 1995).

6. James Davison Hunter and Carl Bowman, "The State of Disunion," Post-Modernity Project, University of Virginia, 1997. See also Herbert McCloskey and John Zaller, *The American Ethos* (Cambridge: Harvard University Press, 1984).

7. Kenneth Dolbeare and Linda Medcalf, *American Political Ideas in the 1980s* (New York: Random House, 1985). John Sullivan, James Pierson, and George E. Marcus, *Political Tolerance and American Democracy* (Chicago: University of Chicago Press, 1982).

8. See Jennifer Hochschild, *What's Fair: American Beliefs About Distributive Justice* (Cambridge: Harvard University Press, 1981); James Kluegel and Eliot Smith, *Beliefs About Inequality* (New York: Aldine de Gruyter, 1986). See also William Jacoby, "Public Opinion and Economic Policy in 1992," in Barbara Norrander and Clyde Wilcox, *Understanding Public Opinion* (Washington, D.C.: Congressional Quarterly Press, 1997).

9. Kluegel and Smith, *Beliefs*, pp. 135–43; Roper Center for Public Opinion Research "Change

and Persistence in American Ideas," *The Public Perspective* (April/May 1995): 14.

10. Bellah et. al., *Habits*, chaps. 1, 10–11; Robert Putnam, "The Strange Disappearance of Civic America," *The American Prospect*; Joel Rifkin, *The End of Work* (New York: Putnam/Tarcher, 1995), pp. 236–74.

11. Hunter and Bowman, "The State", pp. 1–6; Andrew Greeley, "The Other Civic America: Religion and Social Capital," *American Prospect* (May/June 1997): 68–74. The best source on the subject of participation is Sidney Verba, Kay Schlozman, and Henry Brady, *Voice and Equality: Civic Voluntarism in American Politics* (Cambridge: Harvard University Press, 1995).

12. See John Zaller and Stanley Feldman, "A Simple Theory of the Survey Response: Answering Questions and Revealing Preferences," *American Journal of Political Science* 36 (1992): 579–616. See John Zaller, *The Nature and Origins of Mass Opinion* (Cambridge: Cambridge University Press, 1992). See also Paul Sniderman et. al., "Principle Tolerance and the American Mass Public," *British Journal of Political Science* (February 1989): 25–45.

13. Dye and Ziegler, *Irony*, pp. 137–43; Samuel Stouffer, *Communism, Conformity and Civil Liberties* (New York: Doubleday, 1955).

14. Robert Erikson and Kent Tedin, *American Public Opinion* (Boston: Allyn and Bacon, 1995), pp. 155–59; James Gibson, "Political Intolerance and Political Repression During the McCarthy Red Scare," *American Political Science Review* (June 1988): 512–29; Michael Rogin, *The Intellectuals and McCarthy* (Cambridge: M.I.T. Press, 1970).

15. For this period, see Jonathan Schell, *The Time of Illusion* (New York: Pantheon, 1985). See also Mary Jackman and Michael Mulha, "Education and Intergroup Attitudes: Moral Enlightenment, Superficial Democratic Commitment or Ideological Refinement," *American Sociological Review* (August 1984): 753–73.

16. Zaller, *Nature*, pp. 1–32; Erikson and Tedin, *American Public Opinion*, p. 100; Dennis Chong, "How People Think, Reason, and Feel About Civil Liberties," *American Journal of Political Science* (August 1993): 867–99.

17. Seymour Martin Lipset and William Schneider, *The Confidence Gap* (New York: Free Press, 1983). Arthur Miller and Stephen Borelli, "Confidence in Government in the 1980s," *American Politics Quarterly* (April 1991): 147–75.

18. Harold Stanley and Richard Niemi, *Vital Statistics on American Politics* (Washington, D.C.: Congressional Quarterly Press, 1993), p. 169.

19. Times Mirror Center for the People and the Press, *Voter Anxiety Dividing GOP* (Washington, D.C.: Times/Mirror Center, 1995), p. 12.

20. National Opinion Research Center, *1994 Report*, in Roper Center, "Change and Persistence," *The Public Perspective* (April/May 1995): 2.

21. Roper Center, "Change," p. 16; "The Lost Job," *New York Times*, March 3, 1996 p. A1; Pew Center for the People and the Press, press release, April 13, 1995, p. 49.

22. Kluegel and Smith, *Beliefs*, chaps. 3–4; See also J. Huber and W. H. Form, *Income and Ideology* (New York: Free Press, 1973). Times/Mirror Center for the People and the Press, *The Generations Divide* (Washington, D.C.: Times/Mirror Center, July 1992), pp. 23–32.

23. Leon Baradat, *Political Ideologies: Their Origins and Impact* (Englewood Cliffs, N.J.: Prentice-Hall, 1979), pp. 30–37.

24. Kathleen Knight and Robert Erikson, "Ideology in the 1990s," in Norrander and Wilcox, *Understanding*, p. 107.

25. Pamela Conover and Stanley Feldman, "The Origins and Meaning of Liberal and Conservative Self-Identifications," *American Journal of Political Science* (November 1981): 617–45. Knight and Eriksen, "Ideology," in Norrander and Wilcox, pp. 107–10. M. Kent Jennings, "Ideological Thinking Among Mass Publics and Political Elites," *Public Opinion Quarterly* (Winter 1992): 419–41.

26. See Sidney Blumenthal, *Pledging Allegiance: The Last Campaign of the Cold War* (New York: Harper/Collins, 1989) for accounts of the withering of liberalism. For the 1990s, see Dick Morris, *Behind the Oval Office* (New York: Random House, 1997); Stanley Greenberg, "After the Republican Surge," *American Prospect* (Fall 1979): 6–13. Knight and Erikson, "Ideology," p. 104.

27. E. J. Dionne, *Why Americans Hate Politics* (New York: Simon & Schuster, 1993), p. 14.

28. Dionne, *Why Americans Hate Politics*, p. 323.

29. M. Kent Jennings and Richard Niemi, *The Political Character of Adolescence* (Princeton: Princeton University Press, 1974).

30. Alexander Astin, *The American Freshman: Twenty-Five Year Trends* (Los Angeles: Higher Education Institute, University of California, Los Angeles, 1991).

31. See Croteau, *Politics*, chaps. 1–3.

32. See Charles Lindblom, *Politics and Markets* (New York: Harper & Row, 1978).

33. M. R. Jackman and R. W. Jackman, *Class Awareness in the United States* (Berkeley: University of California Press, 1983); Sidney Verba, Kay Lehman Schlozman, and Henry Brady, "The Big Tilt," *American Prospect* (May/June 1997): 74–88.

34. See William Julius Wilson, *When Work Disappears* (New York: Alfred Knopf, 1996); Lawrence Bobo and James Kluegel, "Opposition to Race Targetting," *American Sociological Review*, 58 (1993): 443–64; and James Stimson and Edward Carmines, *Issue Evolution: The Racial Transformation of American Politics* (Princeton: Princeton University Press, 1988).

35. Lawrence Bobo, Charlotte Steen, and Howard Schuman, *Racial Trends in America* (Cambridge: Harvard University Press, 1985), p. 133, chap. 4. For updates, see same authors, *Racial Attitudes in America* (Cambridge: Harvard University Press, 1990).

36. Steven Tuch and Lee Sigelman, "Race, Class and Black White Differences in Social Views," in Norrander and Wilcox, *Understanding*, pp. 48–49. See also "Whites Retain Negative Views of Minorities," *New York Times*, January 14, 1991, p. B10.

37. Kluegel and Smith, *Beliefs*, pp. 135–43; Lee Sigelman and Susan Welch, *Black Americans' Views of Racial Inequality* (Cambridge: Harvard University Press, 1991), p. 59.

38. Tuch and Sigelman, "Race," pp. 41–47. See also Andrew Hacker, *Two Nations* (New York: Ballantine, 1992), pp. 50–60.

39. Sue Tolleson Rinehart, *Gender Consciousness and Politics* (New York: Routledge, 1992); Susan Carroll, "Women's Autonomy and the Gender Gap," in Carol Mueller, *Politics of the Gender Gap* (Beverly Hills, Calif.: Sage, 1988), pp. 235–57; Pamela Johnston Conover and Virginia Sapiro, "Gender, Feminist Consciousness and War," *American Journal of Political Science* 37 (1993): 1079–99.

40. See Kristi Andersen, "Gender and Public Opinion," in Norrander and Wilcox, *Understanding*, pp. 19–36; Scott Keeter, "Public Opinion and the Election," in Gerald Pomper, ed., *The Election of 1996* (Chatham, N.J. Chatham House, 1997).

41. Ted Jelen, "Religion and Public Opinion in the 1990s," in Norrander and Wilcox, *Understanding*, p. 63. General overviews include Clyde Wilcox, *God's Warriors: The Christian Right in Twentieth Century America* (Baltimore: Johns Hopkins University Press, 1991); and Mark Rozell and Clyde Wilcox, *God at the Grassroots* (Lanham, Md.: Rowman and Littlefield, 1995); C. Everett Ladd, "The Status Quo Election," *Public Perspective* (December/January 1997).

42. Quoted in Christopher Hitchens, "Voting in the Passive Voice," *Harper's*, April 1992, p. 46.

43. Susan Herbst, *Numbered Voices* (Chicago: University of Chicago Press, 1993), p. 2.

44. Hitchens, "Voting," p. 52.

45. James Fishkin, *We the People* (New Haven: Yale University Press, 1995); Herbst, *Numbered Voices*, chaps. 1–2.

46. Noam Chomsky and Edward Herman, *Manufacturing Consent* (New York: Pantheon, 1989); John Mueller, *Policy and Opinion in the Gulf War* (Chicago: University of Chicago Press, 1992), chap. 5; Michael Margolis and Gary Mauser, eds., *Manipulating Public Opinion* (Pacific Grove, Calif.: Brooks/Cole, 1987).

47. See the discussion in Benjamin Page and Robert Shapiro, *The Rational Public* (Chicago: University of Chicago Press, 1992).

48. Times Mirror Center for the People and the Press, "The New Political Landscape" (Washington, D.C.: Times Mirror Center, 1994), p. 2; Richard Berke, "Asked to Place Blame, Voters Name All of the Above," *New York Times*, November 10, 1994, p. B1.

49. Bruce Miroff, Raymond Seidelman, and Todd Swanstrom, *The Election of 1994: Revolution or Reaction* (Boston: Houghton Mifflin, 1995); Keeter, "Public Opinion", pp. 107–34; Benjamin Page and Robert Shapiro, "Effects of Public Opinion on Policy," *American Political Science Review* (March 1983): 175–90.

CHAPTER 4

1. David Korten, *When Corporations Rule the World* (New York: Kumarian Press, 1995; David Harris, *The Last Stand* (New York: Times Books, 1995).

2. Roger E. Alcaly, "Reinventing the Corporation," *The New York Review of Books*, April 10, 1997, pp. 38–45.

3. Louis Uchitelle, "Puffed up by Prosperity, U.S. Struts Its Stuff," *New York Times*, April 27, 1997, sec. 4.

4. The classic defense of free markets is Milton Friedman, *Capitalism and Democracy* (Chicago: University of Chicago Press, 1964).

5. Milton and Rose Friedman, *Free to Choose* (New York: Harcourt Brace Jovanovich, 1980), p. 6.

6. Mickey Kaus, *The End of Equality* (New York: Basic Books, 1992); Charles Murray and Richard Herrnstein, *The Bell Curve* (New York: The Free Press, 1994).

7. See Bill Gates, *The Road Ahead* (New York: Penguin, 1995).

8. The range of critiques is vast. For good recent ones, see Frances Moore Lappé, *Rediscovering America's Values* (New York: Ballantine Books, 1989); Barry Bluestone and Bennett Harrison, *The Great U-Turn* (New York: Basic Books, 1989); Samuel Bowles and Richard Edwards, *Understanding Capitalism: Competition, Command and Change in the U.S. Economy* (New York: HarperCollins, 1993).

9. See Barry Bluestone, "The Inequality Express," *American Prospect* (Winter, 1994): pp. 81–88.

10. See Kenneth Dolbeare, *Democracy at Risk* (Chatham, N.J.: Chatham House, 1988).

11. Michael Sandel, *Democracy and Its Discontents* (Cambridge: Harvard University Press, 1996), chap. 5. For a history of the emergence of the modern corporation, see Martin Sklar, *The Corporate Reconstruction of American Capitalism, 1890–1916* (Cambridge: Cambridge University Press, 1988); R. Jeff Lustig, *Corporate Liberalism: The Origins of Modern American Political Theory 1890–1920*) (Berkeley: University of California Press, 1982); Alfred Chandler, *The Visible Hand: The Managerial Revolution in American Business* (Cambridge: Belknap Press, 1977).

12. Charles Lindblom, *Politics and Markets* (New York: Basic Books, 1977), p. 356.

13. Nancy Folbre, *The New Field Guide to the U.S. Economy* (New York: The New Press, 1995), sec. 1; for recent figures, see Arthur Kennickell, Martha Starr McCluer, and Annika Sunden, "Family Finances in the U.S.: Recent Evidence from the Survey of Consumer Finances," *The Federal Reserve Bulletin* (January 1997): 5–9.

14. Michael Lind, "To Have and Have Not," *Harper's* (May 1996):35–49. Edward Wolff, "How the Pie is Sliced," *American Prospect* (Spring 1995). Lawrence Mishel, "Capital's Gain," *American Prospect* (July/August 1997): 71–73.

15. See Jeremy Rifkin and Randy Barber, *The North Will Rise Again: Pensions, Power and Politics in the 1980s* (Boston: Beacon Press, 1979); Richard Ippolito, *Pensions, Economics and Public Policy* (Homewood, Ill.: Dow Jones–Irwin, 1986).

16. Two of the most important works on the function of the modern corporation are Gardiner Means and Adolph Berle, *The Corporation and Private Property* (New York: Macmillan, 1948) and John Kenneth Galbraith, *The New Industrial State* (Boston: Houghton Mifflin, 1985).

17. Arlie Hochschild, *The Managed Heart* (Berkeley: University of California Press, 1983).

18. For accounts of postwar American oligopoly, see Robert Reich, *The Work of Nations* (New York: Random House, 1991); Jeremy Rifkin, *The End of Work* (New York: Tarcher/Putnam, 1995); Donald Barlett and James Steele, *America: What Went Wrong?* (Kansas City: McMeel and Andrews, 1993).

19. See Richard Barnet and John Cavanagh, *Global Dreams* (New York: Simon & Schuster, 1994), pp. 3–21.

20. See Louis Uchitelle and N. R. Kleinfield, "On the Battlefields of Business, Millions of Casualties," *New York Times*, March 3, 1996, p. A1; Rifkin, *The End of Work*, part II.

21. Korten, *When Corporations Rule*, pp. 216–18; Uchitelle, "On the Battlefields," p. 27.

22. David Sanger and Steve Lohr, "A Search for Answers to Avoid Layoffs," *New York Times*, March 9, 1996, p. A1; Alan Downs, *Corporate Executions* (New York: American Management Association, 1996)

23. Korten, *When Corporations Rule*, p. 223.

24. See Bennett Harrison, *Lean and Mean: The Changing Landscape of Corporate Power* (New York:

Basic Books, 1993). Marc Cooper, "Class War in Silicon Valley," *The Nation*, May 3, 1996, p. 12. Bob Herbert, "A Job Myth Downsized, *New York Times*, March 8, 1996, p. A31.

25. Barnet and Cavanagh, *Global Dreams*, p. 19; the term *casino society* is Susan Strange's in *The Casino Society* (London: Basil Blackwell, 1984). For figures on mergers, see Folbre, *New Field Guide*, table 9.9.

26. For a vivid account of union decline, see Thomas Geoghegan, *Which Side Are You On?* (New York: Plume, 1991). See also Michael Goldfield, *The Decline of Organized Labor in the United States* (Chicago: University of Chicago Press, 1987).

27. Robert B. Reich, *Locked in the Cabinet* (New York: Alfred A. Knopf, 1997), pp. 280–81. For articles about the revival of unions, see David Moberg, "Can Labor Change?" *Dissent* (Winter 1996): 16. See also Steven Greenhouse, "A Union Comeback? Tell it to Sweeney," *New York Times*, June 6, 1997, p. 4; Roger Waldinger et. al., "Justice for Janitors: Organizing in Difficult Times," *Dissent* (Winter 1997): 37–47.

28. Ann Markusen, "How We Lost the Peace Dividend," *American Prospect* (July-August 1997): 86–89; John Alic, Lewis Bramscomb, Harvey Brooks, Ashton Carter, and Gerald Epstein, *Beyond Spinoff: Military and Commercial Strategies in a Commercial World* (Cambridge: Harvard Business School Press, 1992); Ann Markusen and Joel Yudken, *Beyond the Cold War Economy* (New York: Basic Books, 1992).

29. Robert Hershey, Jr., "A Hard Look at Corporate Welfare," *New York Times*, March 7, 1995, p. D1.

30. See Lindblom, *Politics*, final chapter. Perhaps the best general account of the role of government in relation to the market economy is Ralph Miliband, *The State in Capitalist Society* (New York: Oxford University Press, 1977).

31. It is probably unnecessary to list a specific source here; the reader should consult any major business magazine for this position. Good candidates include *Forbes: Capitalist Tool;* the editorial page of the *Wall Street Journal, The Economist, Money,* or *Fortune. Business Week* is probably the best magazine for objective reporting of business news.

32. Deborah Lutterbeck, "Falling Wages," *Common Cause Magazine* (Winter 1995): 13; Lawrence Mishel, "Rising Tide, Sinking Wages," *American Prospect* (Fall 1995): pp. 60–72.

33. Keith Bradsher, "Rich Control More of U.S. Wealth," *New York Times,* June 22, 1996, pp. 31–32; Edward Wolff, *Top Heavy* (New York: Twentieth Century Fund, 1995).

34. Rohatyn quoted in Simon Head, "The New Ruthless Economy," *New York Review of Books,* February 29, 1996, p. 47. See also "Inequality," *The Economist* November 5, 1995, p. 20.

35. Lutterbeck, "Falling," p. 14; Herbert Stein and Murray Foss, *The New Illustrated Guide to the American Economy* (Washington, D.C.: American Enterprise Institute, 1995, pp. 126, 130, 132); Steven Greenhouse, "Minimum Wage Maximum Debate," *New York Times,* March 31, 1996, p. 3.

36. John Byrne, "How High Can CEO Pay Go?" *Business Week,* April 22, 1996, pp. 100–22. See also Robert Frank and Philip Cook, *The Winner Take All Society* (New York: Martin Kessler Books/ The Free Press, 1995).

37. Richard Freeman, ed., *Working Under Different Rules* (New York: Russell Sage, 1995); Aaron Bernstein, "Inequality: How the Gap Between Rich and Poor Hurts the Economy," *Business Week,* August 15, 1994, pp. 78–83; William Julius Wilson, *When Work Disappears* (New York: Alfred A. Knopf, 1997).

38. Folbre, *Field Guide,* tables 3.5, 4.10, 4.11.

39. Randy Albelda, *Real World Macro,* 12th ed. (Somerville, Mass.: Dollars and Sense, 1995); Margery Turner et. al., *Opportunities Denied, Opportunities Diminished: Racial Discrimination in Hiring* (Washington, D.C.: Urban Institute, 1992).

40. Folbre, *Field Guide,* table 3.7; U.S. Department of Labor, *Employment and Earnings Report,* 40 (January 1993): 231.

41. Two recent works argue persuasively that strong civil societies are necessary for effective democratic participation. Robert D. Putnam, *Making Democracy Work: Civic Traditions in Modern Italy* (Princeton, N.J.: Princeton University Press, 1993) and Verba, Schlozman, and Brady, *Voice and Equality.*

42. Verba, Schlozman, and Brady, *Voice and Equality,* chap. 3.

43. Robert D. Putnam, "Tuning In, Tuning Out: The Strange Disappearance of Social Capital in America," *PS: Political Science and Politics* (December 1995): 666.

44. Robert D. Putnam, "Bowling Alone," *Journal of Democracy* (January 1995): 69.

45. William Julius Wilson, *The Truly Disadvantaged: The Inner City, The Underclass, and Public Policy* (Chicago: University of Chicago Press, 1987) and *When Work Disappears.*

46. Verba, Schlozman, and Brady, *Voice and Equality,* p., 315. The poor are defined as having family incomes below $15,000, the rich, at $125,000 and over.

47. Juliet B. Schor, *The Overworked American: The Unexpected Decline of Leisure* (New York: Basic Books, 1992), p. 81.

48. Verba, Schlozman, and Brady, *Voice and Equality,* p. 378.

49. Uchitelle, "On the Battlefields," p. A1.

50. John Cassidy, "Who Killed the Middle Class?" *The New Yorker,* October 16, 1995, pp. 113–26.

51. Reported in Schor, *The Overworked,* p. 22.

52. Schor, *The Overworked,* p. 29.

53. Quoted in Schor, *The Overworked,* pp. 123–24.

CHAPTER 5

1. For figures, see "The Republican Primary Vote", *Congressional Quarterly Weekly Report*, August 3, 1996, p. 63.

2. See Todd Swanstrom and Edward Sauerzopf, "Urban Electorates," unpublished paper, SUNY/Albany, 1995.

3. Comparisons of New York's 19th C.D. and 11th C.D. from Michael Barone and Grant Ujifusa, *The Almanac of American Politics* (Washington, D.C.: The National Journal), 1995.

4. See Robert Wiebe, *Self-Rule* (Chicago: University of Chicago Press, 1996); Paul Kleppner, *Who Voted? The Dynamics of Electoral Turnout 1870–1980* (New York: Harper & Row, 1983).

5. George F. Will, "In Defense of Non-Voting," *Newsweek*, October 10, 1983, p. 96.

6. Two founding works in this tradition are Anthony Downs, *An Economic Theory of Democracy* (New York: Harper & Row, 1978); V. O. Key *The Responsible Electorate* (New York: Cambridge University Press, 1966). Modern accounts include Morris Fiorina, *Retrospective Voting in American National Elections* (New Haven, Conn.: Yale University Press, 1981). See also Ruy Teixeira, *The Disappearing Voter* (Washington, D.C.: the Brookings Institution, 1992).

7. See Michael Barone, "The Road Back to Tocqueville," *Washington Post*, January 7, 1996, pp. C1–2, and George Will, *Statecraft as Soulcraft* (New York: Simon & Schuster, 1983), p. 16. For a refutation, see Theda Skocpol, "Unravelling from Above," *The American Prospect*, March, 1996, pp. 20–24. Anthony King, *Running Scared*, (Cambridge: Harvard University Press, 1997).

8. See Will, *Statecraft*, p. 16. See also the discussion in Sidney Verba, Kay Schlozman, and Henry Brady, *Voice and Equality: Participation in American Politics* (Cambridge: Harvard University Press, 1996), p. 508, and King, Chap. 1.

9. See Frances Fox Piven and Richard Cloward, *Why Americans Don't Vote* (New York: Pantheon, 1987); see also Steven Rosenstone and John Mark Hansen, *Mobilization, Participation and Democracy in America* (New York: Macmillan, 1993).

10. Frances Fox Piven, personal communication, July 17, 1996; Frances Fox Piven and Richard Cloward, "Northern Bourbons: A Preliminary Report on the National Voter Registration Act", *PS*, March 1996, pp. 39–41; R. Drummond Ayres, "Laws to Ease Voter Registration Has Added 5 Million to the Rolls," *New York Times*, September 5, 1995, p. A1; and Human SERVE, "1995: The First Year" (New York: Human SERVE, March, 1996).

11. See G. Bingham Powell, "Voter Turnout in Comparative Perspective," *American Political Science Review*, 80 (March 1986): 1; Raymond Wolfinger and Steven Rosenstone, *Who Votes?* (New Haven, Conn.: Yale University Press, 1978), pp. 61–88; and Walter Dean Burnham, "The Appearance and Disappearance of the American Voter," in Walter Dean Burnham, *The Current Crisis in American Politics* (New York: Oxford University Press, 1982).

12. Ruy Teixeira, "Voter Turnout: Ten Myths," in Bruce Miroff, Raymond Seidelman, and Todd Swanstrom, *Debating Democracy: A Reader in American Politics* (Boston: Houghton Mifflin, 1997), pp. 164–69.

13. See Hanes Walton, *Black Politics* (New York: Lippincott, 1972); Manning Marable, *Black American Politics* (London: Verso, 1985); Allen Matusow, *The Unraveling of America* (New York: Harper & Row, 1984), chaps. 3, 7. See also Robert Scher, *Politics in the New South* (Armonk, N.Y.: M. E. Sharpe, 1997), pp. 193–265.

14. See Roman Hedges and Carl Carlucci, "The Implementation of the Voting Rights Act: The Case of New York," unpublished paper, SUNY/Albany, 1986; Jim Sleeper *The Closest of Strangers* (New York: W.W. Norton, 1990).

15. See David Montgomery, *The Fall of the House of Labor* (New York: Oxford University Press, 1988) for an account of the richness of late nineteenth-century labor associations. For the Alliance and populism, see Lawrence Goodwyn, *The*

Populist Moment in America (New York Oxford University Press, 1976). See also Michael McGerr, *The Decline of Mass Politics* (New York: W.W. Norton, 1992) and Wiebe, *Self-Rule*, chaps. 4–7. For a brilliant analysis of public "third places" in America, see Ray Oldenburg, *The Great Good Place* (New York: Paragon House, 1989).

16. Robert Putnam, "Bowling Alone: America's Declining Social Capital," *Journal of Democracy* (January, 1995): 34–35; and Robert Putnam, "The Strange Disappearance of Civic America," *The American Prospect* (Winter 1996): 34–48. For a brilliant extension of the idea that working class people are shut out of politics, see David Croteau *Politics and the Class Divide* (Philadelphia: Temple University Press, 1995). For an alternative view—that associational decline hasn't happened—see Roper Center for Public Opinion Research, *Public Perspective*, June/July, 1996. See also Robert Samuelson, "Join the Club," *Washington Post National Weekly Edition*, April 15–21, 1996, p. 5.

17. Verba et. al., *Voice and Equality*, p. 532. See also Evan MacKenzie, *Privatopia* (Berkeley: University of California Press, 1995); and Robert Reich, "Secession of the Successful," *New York Times Magazine*, January 20, 1992, p. 18.

18. This perspective is suggested by Howard Reiter, *Parties and Elections in Corporate America* (New York: St. Martin's 1987) chap. 8. See also Raymond Seidelman, "A Weak Democracy," in Miroff et. al., *Debating*, pp. 170–80. For accounts of this dimension in working class life, see Jonathan Rieder's *Canarsie* (Cambridge: Harvard University Press, 1989); Lillian Rubin, *Worlds of Pain* (New York: Harper & Row, 1976); and most especially Croteau, *Politics*, chap. 5. Quotation from Oldenburg, *Great Good Place*, p. 163.

19. Richard Vallely, "Response to Putnam," *The American Prospect* (March/April, 1996): 26. For evidence that low political efficacy is crucial in determining who votes and who doesn't, see League of Women Voters, "Mellman Group and Wirthlin Worldwide Survey of Nonvoters," press release, May 29, 1996. See also Campaign Study Group, *No-Show '96: Americans Who Don't Vote* (Evanston, Ill.: Northwestern University, Medill School of Journalism, 1996).

20. University of Michigan, Center for Political Studies, American National Election Studies, 1984; CBS New York Times Poll, *New York Times*, November 21, 1988, p. A5; League of Women Voters, "Mellman/Wirthlin," pp. 4–7. For diversity among the attitudes of nonvoters, see Campaign, *No-Show '96*, pp. 1–8.

21. William Maddox and Stuart Lilie, *Beyond Liberal and Conservative: Reassessing the Political Spectrum* (Washington, D.C.: The Cato Institute, 1984).

22. Kenneth Dolbeare, *Democracy at Risk*, (Chatham, N.J.: Chatham House, 1989), pp. 209–25.

23. The definitive account is Paul Kleppner, *Chicago: The Making of a Black Mayor* (DeKalb, Ill.: Northern Illinois University Press, 1984).

24. Kleppner, *Chicago*, chaps. 4–6.

25. For 1984, see Thomas Cavanagh and Lorn Foster, *Jesse Jackson's Campaign: The Primaries and the Caucuses* (Washington, D.C.: Joint Center for Political Studies, Report 2, 1984); for 1988, see Paul Abramson, John Aldrich, and David Rohde, *Change and Continuity in the Election of 1988* (Washington, D.C.: Congressional Quarterly Press, 1990), chap. 1.

26. The best accounts of the 1992 election are Gerald Pomper, ed., *The Election of 1992* (Chatham, N.J.: Chatham House, 1993). Data from Gerald Pomper, "The Presidential Election," in Pomper, ed., *Election*, pp. 140–42. See also Howard Fineman, "Ross Perot's New Army: How He's Building His Army Behind the Scenes," *Newsweek*, June 7, 1993, pp. 24–25; Jack Germond and Jules Witcover, "Perot Is Expanding His Local Base," *National Journal*, June 5, 1993, p. 1371. See also Michael Nelson, ed., *The Elections of 1992* (Washington, D.C.: Congressional Quarterly Press, 1993).

27. U.S. Census Bureau, *Voting and Registration in the Election of 1994;* Curtis Gans, "Report on the Election of 1994" (Washington, D.C.: Committee for the Study of the American Electorate, 1995). See also Ruy Teixeira, "The Economics of the 1994 Election and U.S. Politics Today," *Challenge* (January 1996): 26.

28. See Human SERVE, "National Voter Registration Act Adds Millions to Voter Rolls," press release, October 15, 1996.

29. See Jean Bethke Elshtain and Christopher Beem, "Issues and Themes: Economics, Culture and 'Small Party' Politics," in Michael Nelson, ed., *The Elections of 1996* (Washington, D.C.: Congressional Quarterly Press, 1997), pp. 106–20.

30. Scott Keeter, "Public Opinion and the Election," in Pomper, ed., *Election*, pp. 112–15. See also Pew Research Center for the People and the Press, "Voter Typology: Dole Fails with Populists, GOP Moderates, Clinton Unites Dems," press release, October 25, 1996. See also David Moore, "Low Turnout Helped GOP," *Polling Report*, November 18, 1996.

31. B. Drummond Ayres, "The Expanding Hispanic Vote Shakes Republican Strongholds," *New York Times*, pp. 1, 27.

32. Rosenstone and Hansen, *Mobilization and Participation*, p. 229.

CHAPTER 6

1. It shouldn't be surprising that cheerful accounts abound among media celebrities. See Jim Lehrer, *A Bus of My Own: A Memoir* (New York: New American Library, 1992); Dan Rather and Mickey Herskowitz, *The Camera Never Blinks Twice: Adventures of a TV Journalist* (New York: Ballantine Books, 1987).

2. Quote from William Greider, *Who Will Tell The People?* (New York: Simon & Schuster, 1992), pp. 306–7. For searing critiques of the mass media's role in American society, see C. Wright Mills, *The Power Elite* (New York: Oxford University Press, 1956), pp. 298–305; Ben Bagdikian, *The Media Monopoly* (Boston: Beacon Press, 1992).

3. "Nothing Against Your Baby, Mrs. Brown," *New York Times*, September 21, 1992, p. A14; Michael Wines, "Appeal of Murphy Brown Now Clear at the White House," *New York Times*, May 21, 1992, p. A1; Robert Lichter, Linda Lichter and Stanley Rothman, *The Media Elite* (Washington, D.C.: Regnery Publishers, 1991).

4. Thomas C. Leonard, *The Power of the Press* (New York: Oxford University Press, 1986).

5. Michael Schudson, *Discovering the News* (New York: Basic Books, 1978).

6. Frank Luther Mott, *American Journalism: 1660–1960* (New York: Macmillan, 1962), p. 529. For an account of Hearst's life, see W. A. Swanberg, *Citizen Hearst* (New York: Scribner's, 1961).

7. See the account in Ronald Berkman and Laura Kitch, *The Politics of the Mass Media* (New York: St. Martin's Press, 1990), p. 42. See also Pew Research Center for the People and the Press, "TV Viewership Declines," press release, May 16, 1996; "Newspapers Seek New Audiences," *New York Times*, May 21, 1997, p. D1.

8. For Murrow's story at CBS, see Alexander Kendrick, *Prime Time: The Life of Edward R. Murrow* (Boston: Little Brown, 1969).

9. Reuven Frank, *Out of Thin Air: The Invention and History of TV Network News* (New York: Simon & Schuster, 1991).

10. On TV coverage of the 1960s, see Edward Epstein, *News from Nowhere* (New York: Random House, 1973); Michael Arlen, *The Living Room War* (New York: Viking, 1969).

11. Pew Research Center for the People and the Press, *TV News*, May 13, 1996, appendix.

12. Daniel Weintraub, "The Technology Connection," *State Legislatures* (June 1993): 44. A number of works herald the growth of the Internet or warn about its possible misuse and commercialization. See Bill Gates, *The Road Ahead* (New York: Penguin, 1996); Richard Sclove, *Democracy and Technology* (New York: Five Walls Four Windows, 1996); Leonard Grossman, *The Electronic Republic* (New York: Viking, 1995).

13. Among the most critical accounts is Clifford Stoll, *Silicon Snake Oil* (New York: Doubleday, 1995).

14. Pew Research Center, "TV News," p. 4. See also Jarol Manheim, *All of the People, All of the Time* (Armonk: M.E. Sharpe, 1991). For distinctions between the print and electronic media, see W. Russell Neuman, Marion Just, and Ann Crigler, *Common Knowledge: News and the Construction of Political Meaning* (Chicago: University of Chicago Press, 1992).

15. For the 1940s, see Paul Lazarsfeld, Bernard Berelson, and Hazel Gaudet, *The People's Choice* (New York: Columbia University Press, 1948). For the 1970s, see Thomas Patterson and Robert McClure, *The Unseeing Eye: The Myth of Television Power in National Elections* (New York: G. P. Putnam, 1976), p. 90.

16. Shanto Iyengar and Donald Kinder, *News that Matters: The Agenda Setting Functions of the Press* (Chicago: University of Chicago Press, 1987); S. Iyengar, M. Peters, and D. Kinder, "Experimental Demonstrations of the 'Not so Minimal' Consequences of Television News Programs," *American Political Science Review* (Winter 1980).

17. The standard source on corporate control is Ben Bagdikian, *The Media Monopoly*, 4th ed. (Boston: Beacon Press, 1992). For more updated accounts, see Lance Bennett, *News: The Politics of Illusion*, 3rd ed. (White Plains, N.Y.: Longman, 1996). See also Doug Underwood, *When MBAs Rule the Newsroom* (New York: Columbia University Press, 1993).

18. *Morning Edition*, National Public Radio, July 31, 1996. See Mark Crispin Miller, "Free the Media," *The Nation*, June 3, 1996, pp. 9–15.

19. Edmund Andrews, "ABC Pulls Plug on a Texas Populist," *New York Times*, October 9, 1995, p. D7.

20. Peter Phillips, *Censored 1996* (New York: Seven Stories Press, 1996). See also "Comment by Leonard Grossman on the National Entertainment State," *The Nation*, June 6, 1996, p. 22.

21. Miller, "The National Entertainment State", p. 10. "Superbowl Advertising," *Media Week*, January 6, 1996, p. 3. See the intelligent discussion in Doris Graber, *The Mass Media in American Politics* (Washington, D.C.: Congressional Quarterly Press, 1996), pp. 50–52.

22. See Herbert Schiller, *Culture, Inc.: The Corporate Takeover of Public Expression* (New York: Oxford University Press, 1989); Martin Lee and Norman Solomon, *Unreliable Sources* (New York: Carol Publishing Group, 1991).

23. Robert McChesney, *Telecommunications, Mass Media and Democracy* (New York: Oxford University Press, 1993), chaps. 1, 6.

24. Susan Douglas, "Nobility of Capitalism," *The Progressive* (April 1966: pp. 16–18); "Telecommunications Bill," *New York Times*, August 4, 1995, p. D4. See Robert McChesney, "Digital Highway Robbery," *The Nation*, April 21, 1997, pp. 22–24.

25. See Fred Landis, "El Mercurio and the CIA," *Covert Action Information Bulletin* (March 1982); See also Lee and Solomon, *Unreliable*, pp. 117–20; Martha Honey, "Contra Coverage: Paid for by the CIA," *Columbia Journalism Review* (March/April 1987).

26. Athan Theoharis, *The Boss: J. Edgar Hoover and the Great American Inquisition* (Philadelphia: Temple University Press, 1988); Nelson Blackstock, *COINTELPRO: The FBI's Secret War on Press Freedom* (New York: Vintage, 1976).

27. For excellent accounts of the corrosive effects of celebrity journalism on the political agenda, see James Fallows, *Breaking the News: How the Media Un-*

dermine *American Democracy* (New York: Pantheon Books, 1995). See also William Hoynes and David Croteau, "Are You on the Nightline Guestlist?" *Extra!* (Winter 1990); pp. 12–16.

28. Special Issue on the Gulf War, *Extra!* (May 1991): 3–25. See W. Lance Bennett and David Paletz, *Taken by Storm: The Media, Public Opinion, and U.S. Foreign Policy in the Gulf War* (Chicago: University of Chicago Press, 1994).

29. Lichter et al., *The Media Elite*, final chapter.

30. David Weaver and G. Cleveland Wilhoit, "The American Journalist in the 1990s," (Arlington, Va.: Freedom Forum, 1992), p. 7.

31. Fallows, *Breaking the News*, pp. 33, 80.

32. Weaver and Wilhoit, "The American," pp. 12–13.

33. See Herbert Gans, *Deciding What's News* (New York: Vintage Press, 1980); Noam Chomsky and Edward Herman, *Manufacturing Consent: The Political Economy of the Mass Media* (New York: Pantheon Books, 1988).

34. Robert Entman, *Democracy Without Citizens: Media and the Decay of American Politics* (New York: Oxford University Press, 1989).

35. Bennett, *News: The Politics*, pp. 37, 120.

36. Ray Suarez, *Talk of the Nation*, National Public Radio, Thursday, March 13, 1997.

37. Timothy Crouse, *The Boys on the Bus* (New York: Random House, 1973), p. 44.

38. See Manheim, *All of the People*, chap. 3; W. Lance Bennett and Timothy Cook, "Journalism Norms and News Construction," *Political Communication* (Winter 1996); Graber, *Mass Media*, pp. 44–45.

39. Studies include Thomas Patterson, *Out of Order* (New York: Alfred Knopf, 1993); Matthew Robert Kerbel, *Remote and Controlled* (Boulder, Colo.: Westview Press, 1996); Larry Sabato, *Feeding Frenzy* (New York: Free Press, 1992).

40. Matthew Kerbel, "Viewing the Campaign Through a Strategic Haze," in Michael Nelson, ed., *The Elections of 1996* (Washington, D.C.: Congressional Quarterly Press, 1997); Marion Just, "Candidate Strategies and the Media Campaign," in Gerald Pomper, ed., *The Election of 1996* (Chatham, N.J.: Chatham House, 1997).

41. Fallows, *Breaking*, pp. 22–23; Kerbel, "Viewing the Campaign," p. 85; Marion Just et al. *Crosstalk: Citizens, Candidates and the Media in Presidential Campaigns* (Chicago: University of Chicago Press, 1996).

42. Center for Media and Public Affairs, *Media Monitor* (November/December, 1996): pp. 1–4.

43. Just, "Candidate Strategies," p. 90.

44. NBC *Nightly News*, January 6, 1996.

45. See James Carville and Mary Matalin, *All's Fair* (New York: Random House, 1994).

46. James Boylan, "Where Have All the People Gone," *Columbia Journalism Review* (May/June 1991): pp. 31–38.

47. See Sabato, *Feeding*, Wilson Carey McWilliams, "The Meaning of the Election," in Gerald Pomper, ed., *The Election of 1992* (Chatham, N.J.: Chatham House, 1993; Thomas Rosenstiel, *Strange Bedfellows* (New York: Hyperion Press, 1993).

48. Jarol Manheim, "Packaging the People," in Miroff, et al., eds., *Debating Democracy* (Boston: Houghton Mifflin, 1997), p. 146.

49. Fairness and Accuracy in Reporting's magazine is called *Extra!* See also the World Wide Web site of the Media Access Project, www.map.org.

50. See Michael Kelly, "Media Culpa," *The New Yorker*, November 4, 1996; Fallows, *Breaking the News*, pp. 189–97.

51. See "Freeing the Media: Proceedings of a Two Day Gathering to Strengthening Democracy in Media" (New York: The Learning Alliance, 1997).

CHAPTER 7

1. *Topeka Advocate*, 1892; cited in Michael McGerr, *The Decline of Popular Politics* (New York: Oxford University Press, 1986), p. 216; David Rosenbaum, "Campaign Finance: Developments So Far", *New York Times*, April 3, 1997, p. B9.

2. Lawrence Goodwyn, *The Populist Moment in America*, (New York: Oxford University Press, 1976).

3. This point is best made in Maurice Duverger's classic *Political Parties* (New York: Wiley and Sons, 1954); Max Weber, "Politics as a Vocation," in Hans Gerth and C. Wright Mills, *From Max Weber* (New York: Oxford University Press, 1958), pp. 77–128. See also E. E. Schattschneider, *Party Government* (New York: Holt, Rinehart and Winston, 1942). See also Walter Dean Burnham, "The End of American Party Politics," *Transaction*, December, 1969. pp. 16–36.

4. Overviews include Ronald Formisano, *The Transformation of Political Culture: Massachusetts Parties, 1790–1840* (New York: W. W. Norton, 1983); Paul Kleppner, ed., *The Evolution of American Electoral Systems* (Westport, Conn.: Greenwood Press, 1981); Everett Carll Ladd, *American Political Parties* (New York: W. W. Norton, 1970); James Sundquist, *Dynamics of the Party System* (Washington, D. C.: Congressional Quarterly, 1983).

5. Samuel Huntington, "The Visions of the Democratic Party," *The Public Interest* (Spring, 1985): 64.

6. Angus Campbell, Phillip Converse, Warren Miller, and Donald Stokes, *The American Voter* (New York: Wiley and Sons, 1960).

7. Walter Dean Burnham and William Nisbet Chambers, eds., *The American Party Systems* (New York: Oxford University Press, 1967); Paul Kleppner, *Who Voted? The Dynamics of Electoral Turnout 1870–1980* (New York: Harper & Row, 1983).

8. William Riordon, *Plunkitt of Tammany Hall* (New York: Dutton, 1963); Milton Rakove, *Don't Make No Waves . . . Don't Back No Losers: An Insider's Account of the Daley Machine* (Bloomington: Indiana University Press, 1975); Steven Erie, *Rainbow's End* (Berkeley: University of California Press, 1988).

9. This is somewhat less true of current European parties. See Joel Krieger and Mark Kesselman, eds., *European Politics in Transition* (Boston: D. C. Heath, 1993), especially Stephen Hellman's chapter on Italy.

10. See the discussion in Walter Dean Burnham, *The Current Crisis in American Politics* (New York: Oxford University Press, 1983). See also Howard Reiter, *Parties and Elections in Corporate America* (New York: St. Martin's Press, 1987).

11. See Douglas Amy, *Real Choices / New Voices: The Case for Proportional Representation* (New York: Columbia University Press, 1993).

12. Giovanni Sartori, *Parties and Party Systems* (Cambridge: Cambridge University Press, 1976), p. 42.

13. Walter Dean Burnham, *Critical Elections and the Mainsprings of American Politics* (New York: W. W. Norton, 1967). See also John Aldrich, *Why Parties?* (Chicago: University of Chicago Press, 1995).

14. See Jerome Clubb, Nancy Zingale, William Flanigan, *Partisan Realignment: Voters, Party, and Government in American History* (Beverly Hills, Calif.: 1980).

15. See Richard Jensen, *The Winning of the Midwest: Social and Political Conflict 1888–1896* (Chicago: University of Chicago Press, 1971). See also Walter Dean Burnham, "The Appearance and Disappearance of the American Voter," in Walter Dean Burnham, *The Current Crisis in American Politics* (New York: Oxford University Press, 1982), pp. 142–60.

16. For accounts of the period, see Robert Wiebe's two works, *The Search for Order* (New York: Hill and Wang, 1967) and *Self-Rule* (Chicago: University of Chicago Press, 1996). See also McGerr, *Decline*, pp. 211–19

17. Samuel P. Hays, *The Response to Industrialism* (Chicago: University of Chicago Press, 1957),

p. 156; see also Frances Fox Piven and Richard Cloward *Why Americans Don't Vote* (New York: Pantheon, 1987); Eldon Eisenach, *The Lost Promise of Progressivism* (Lawrence: University Press of Kansas, 1995).

18. V. O. Key, *Southern Politics* (New York: Alfred Knopf, 1949), final chapter.

19. See Steve Fraser and Gary Gerstle, eds., *The Rise and Fall of the New Deal Order, 1930–1980* (Princeton: Princeton University Press, 1989); Stephen Skowronek, *The Politics Presidents Make* (Cambridge: Harvard University Press, 1993); Sidney Milkis, *The Modern Presidency and the Transformation of the American Party System* (New York: Oxford University Press, 1993).

20. E. E. Schattschneider, quoted in Leon Epstein, *Political Parties in the American Mold* (Madison: University of Wisconsin Press, 1986), p. 32; Clinton Rossiter, *Parties and Politics in America* (Ithaca: Cornell University Press, 1957), p. 64.

21. Two good accounts of this period are Godfrey Hodgson, *America in Our Time* (New York: Pantheon, 1976) and Taylor Branch *Parting the Waters* (New York: Simon & Schuster, 1988). See also John Petrocik, *Realignment and the Decay of the New Deal System* (Chicago: University of Chicago Press, 1981).

22. Norman Mailer's *Miami and the Siege of Chicago* (New York: Harper & Row, 1970) remains a brilliant account of the 1968 election.

23. One account of cultural and racial divides is Thomas and Mary Edsall, *Chain Reaction* (New York: W. W. Norton, 1991). See also James Davison Hunter, *Culture Wars: The Struggle to Define America* (New York: Basic Books, 1990).

24. See Barry Bluestone and Bennett Harrison, *The Great U-Turn* (New York: Basic Books, 1989).

25. See Kevin Phillips, *The Emerging Republican Majority* (New Rochelle, N.Y.: Arlington House, 1969). See also Thomas Byrne Edsall, *The New Politics of Inequality* (New York: W. W. Norton, 1984).

26. A good account of the "revolution from above" is Thomas Ferguson and Joel Rogers, eds., *The Hidden Election* (New York: Pantheon, 1981) and Edsall, *New Politics*, chap. 3.

27. Byron Shafer, "The Notion of an Electoral Order: The Structure of Electoral Politics at the Accession of George Bush," in Byron Shafer, ed., *The End of Realignment* (Madison: University of Wisconsin Press, 1991); John Aldrich and Richard Niemi, "The Sixth American Party System," in Stephen Craig, ed., *Broken Contract* (Boulder, Colo.: Westview Press, 1995); Thomas Ferguson and Joel Rogers, *Right Turn: The Decline of the Democrats* (New York: Hill and Wang, 1986).

28. A general account of party decline and dealignment is A. James Reichley, *The Life of the Parties: A History of American Political Parties* (New York: Macmillan, 1992). See also Martin Wattenberg, *The Decline of American Political Parties 1952–1988* (New York: Oxford University Press, 1990). See also Walter Dean Burnham, "The Future of American Politics," in E. Sandoz and C. Crabb, eds., *The Election of 1984* (New York: The New American Library, 1985).

29. See Walter Dean Burnham, "Bill Clinton: Riding the Tiger," in Gerald Pomper, ed. *The Election of 1996: Reports and Interpretations* (Chatham, N. J.: Chatham House, 1997).

30. See Paul Allen Beck, *Party Politics in America*, 8th ed. (New York: HarperCollins, 1996).

31. For data on the low turnout in primary contests, see "Guide to the 1996 Republican National Convention," *Congressional Quarterly Weekly Report*, August 3, 1996, pp. 62–163. For other views of the party nomination process, see William Mayer, ed., *In Pursuit of the White House: How We Choose Our Presidential Nominees* (Chatham, N. J.: Chatham House, 1996).

32. See Michael Nelson, ed., *Congressional Quarterly's Guide to the Presidency* (Washington, D. C.: Congressional Quarterly Press, 1989). See also Michael Nelson, "The Election: Turbulence and Tranquility," in Michael Nelson, ed., *The Elec-*

tions of 1996 (Washington, D. C.: Congressional Quarterly Press, 1997), pp. 52–62. See also Michael Beschloss, "Let's Have Conventions with Cliffhangers," *New York Times*, August 11, 1996, p. E13.

33. See William Mayer, "The Presidential Nominations," in Pomper, ed., *Elections*, pp. 21–77.

34. Stephen Engelberg, Jeff Gerth, and Katherine Seelye, "Gingrich's Blueprints for a Revolution," *New York Times*, December 3, 1995, p. 26. See also Kenneth Weine, "Campaigns Without Human Faces," *Washington Post National Weekly Edition*, November 4–10, 1996, p. 24.

35. The story comes from William Greider, *Who Will Tell the People?* (New York: Simon & Schuster, 1993), pp. 246–48. For a contrasting view, see Daniel Shea and John Green, eds., *The State of the Parties: The Changing Role of Contemporary American Parties*, (Lanham, Md.: Rowman and Littlefield, 1996).

36. Sidney Verba, Kay Schlozman, and Henry Brady, *Voice and Equality* (Cambridge: Harvard University Press, 1995), chap. 7. See also Wattenberg, *Decline*.

37. Richard Berke, "Asked to Place Blame, Voters Name All the Above," *New York Times*, November 10, 1994, p. B1. Marjorie Randon Hershey, "The Congressional Election," in Pomper, ed., *Election*, pp. 212–17.

38. See Morris Fiorina, *Retrospective Voting in American National Elections* (New Haven, Conn.: Yale University Press, 1981). For analysis of recent elections, see Scott Keeter, "Public Opinion and the Election," in Pomper, ed., *The Election*, pp. 107–33.

39. See Martin Shefter and Ben Ginsberg, *Politics by Other Means*, (New York: W. W. Norton, 1991). For figures on split ticket voting, see Harold Stanley and Richard Niemi, *Vital Statistics on American Politics*, 2nd ed. (Washington, D. C.: Congressional Quarterly Press, 1990), p. 132.

40. Data found in Paul Abramson, John Aldrich, and David Rohde, *Change and Continuity in the 1992 Election* (Washington, D. C.: Congressional Quarterly Press, 1993). For 1994, see Clyde Wilcox, *The Latest American Revolution* (New York: St. Martin's Press, 1995). For 1996, see Pew Research Center for the People and the Press, *Post Election Survey*, November 9, 1996.

41. See "Portrait of the Electorate," *New York Times*, November 10, 1996, p. 28.

42. "Portrait," *New York Times*, p. 28; "The House Vote," *New York Times*, November 7, 1996, p. B3.

43. "Portrait " *New York Times*, p. 28. See Alison Mitchell, "Clinton Campaign Puts an Emphasis on Female Voters," *New York Times*, October 28, 1996. See also Keeter, "Public Opinion" and Pomper, "The Presidential Election," in Pomper, ed., *Elections of 1996*. An interesting work on the gender gap is Carol Mueller, ed., *Politics of the Gender Gap* (Beverly Hills, Calif.: Sage, 1988).

44. "Partisan Instability in the 1996 Campaign," *Public Perspective* 7 (October / November 1996), p. 3. Michael Golay and Carl Rollyson, *Where America Stands 1996* (New York: John Wiley, 1996), p. 172; Pew Research Center for the People and Press, *Survey*, February 29, 1996, p. 38.

45. Pomper, "The Presidential," in Pomper, ed., *Elections of 1996*, p. 196. Pomper's is among the most comprehensive short accounts of the 1996 presidential vote. See also two other insightful articles: Jean Bethke Elshtain and Christopher Beem, "Issues and Themes: Economics, Culture and Small Party Politics," in Nelson, ed., *The Elections*, pp. 106–21; Wilson Carey McWilliams, "The Meaning of the Election," in Pomper, *Elections of 1996*, pp. 241–74.

46. See Gary Jacobson, "The 105th Congress: Unprecedented and Unsurprising," in Nelson, *Elections*; pp. 143–66; Marjorie Randon Hershey, "The Congressional Elections," in Pomper, ed., *The Elections of 1996*, pp. 205–40; Larry Sabato, "The November Vote—A Status Quo Election," in Larry Sabato, ed., *Toward the Millennium* (Boston: Allyn and Bacon, 1997).

47. Times Mirror Center for the People and the Press, *The New Political Landscape* (October 1994): 5, 22, 42; Kevin Phillips, "Under the Electoral Volcano," *New York Times*, November 7, 1994, p. A19.

48. See E. J. Dionne, *They Only Look Dead* (New York: Simon & Schuster, 1996).

CHAPTER 8

1. Martin Wattenberg, *The Rise of Candidate-Centered Politics* (Cambridge: Harvard University Press, 1991).

2. Gary Jacobsen, *The Politics of Congressional Elections* (New York: St. Martin's Press, 1996).

3. William Mayer, ed., *In Pursuit of the White House: How We Choose Our Presidential Nominees* (Chatham, N.J.: Chatham House, 1996).

4. Harold Stanley, "The Nominations: Republican Doldrums, Democratic Revival," in Michael Nelson, ed., *The Elections of 1996* (Washington, D.C.: Congressional Quarterly Press, 1997) pp. 14–44; William Mayer, "The Presidential Nominations," in Pomper, ed., *The Election of 1996* (Chatham, N.J.: Chatham House, 1997), pp. 21–76.

5. See Gerald Pomper, "The Presidential Election," and Ross Baker, "The Congressional Elections," in Gerald Pomper, ed., *The Election of 1988*, (Chatham, N.J.: Chatham House, 1989).

6. Matthew Kerbel, "Viewing the Campaign Through a Strategic Haze," in Nelson, *Elections*, pp. 81–106. Howard Fineman and Thomas Rosenstiel, "The Last Insider," *Newsweek*, March 11, 1996, p. 32.

7. Sidney Blumenthal, *The Permanent Campaign* (New York: Harper & Row, 1981); David Mayhew, *Congress: The Electoral Connection* (New Haven: Yale University Press, 1974).

8. Figures taken from Federal Election Commission data, press release, November 24, 1996 and calculated by the authors.

9. Calculated from FEC data, November 24, 1996. Anthony Corrado, "Financing the 1996 Election," in Pomper, ed., *Election of 1996*, p. 151.

Brooks Jackson, "Financing the 1996 Election: The Law of the Jungle," in Larry Sabato, ed. *Towards the Millennium* (Boston: Allyn and Bacon, 1997) pp. 225–60.

10. Herbert Alexander and Anthony Corrado, *Financing the 1992 Election* (Armonk, M. E. Sharpe, 1995); Clyde Wilcox, The Revolution of 1994 (New York: St. Martin's Press, 1995); Bruce Miroff, Raymond Seidelman, and Todd Swanstrom, *The 1994 Elections: Revolution or Reaction?* (Boston: Houghton Mifflin, 1995).

11. Calculated from FEC data, November 4, 1994.

12. Jennifer Babson and Kelly St. John, "Momentum Helps GOP Collect Record Amounts from PACs," *Congressional Quarterly Weekly Report*, December 3, 1994, pp. 3456–59; Federal Election Commission, *Report*, March 31, 1995, p. 1; "Spending Soars for '94 Races," FEC press release, November 4, 1994.

13. James Caesar and Andrew Busch, *Losing to Win: The 1996 Elections and American Politics* (Lanham, Md.: Rowman and Littlefield, 1997); Common Cause, "1994 Incumbent Re-election Rates," press release, November 10, 1994.

14. Baker, "The Congressional Elections," in Pomper, ed., *The Election of 1988*, p. 167. See also Gary Jacobson, *The Politics of Congressional Elections* (New York: Harper/Collins, 1992), pp. 47–48. Alan Abramowitz, "Incumbency Campaign Spending and the Decline of Competition in U.S. House Elections," *Journal of Politics* (February 1991): pp. 47–49.

15. Richard Scher, *Politics in the New South* (Armonk, N.Y.: M. E. Sharpe, 1997); Peter Kostmayer, "The Price of Politics," *Korea Herald*, May 31, 1993, p. 6. For a similar and more recent account, see Dan Hamburg, "Inside the Money Chase," *The Nation*, May 5, 1997, p. 23.

16. See Dan Clawson, Alan Neustadt, and Denise Scott, *Money Talks: Corporate PACs and Political Influence* (New York: Basic Books, 1992). See also Frank Sorauf, *Inside Campaign Finance: Myths* *and Realities* (New Haven: Yale University Press, 1992).

17. For this line of analysis, see James Q. Wilson, *American Government* (Lexington, Mass.: D. C. Heath, 1990), p. 231.

18. Thomas Byrne Edsall, *The New Politics of Inequality* (New York: W. W. Norton, 1984), p. 104.

19. See Brooks Jackson, *Honest Graft* (New York: Alfred Knopf, 1988); William Greider, *Who Will Tell the People?* (New York: Simon & Schuster, 1992), pp. 65, 253; Harper's Index, *Harper's*, July, 1992.

20. Federal Elections Commission, *Contributions to Federal Candidates*, 1990.

21. Common Cause, "1994 Incumbent Reelection Rate," November 10, 1994; FEC press release, November 4, 1994, p. 1.

22. Corrado, "Financing," in Pomper, ed., *Election of 1996*, p. 157.

23. Ronald Dworkin, "The Curse of American Politics," *New York Review of Books*, October 17, 1997, pp. 19–23.

24. Corrado, "Financing," in Pomper, *Election of 1996*, pp. 152–53. Ken Silverstein, "My Life as an Undercover PAC," *The Nation*, May 5, 1997, p. 18.

25. David Stout, "GOP Fundraising," *New York Times*, March 11, 1997, A7, A21; Lynn Sweet, "Clinton Orders Donor Perk Review," *Chicago Sun Times*, June 30, 1995, p. 1; Center for Responsive Politics, *A Brief History of Money in Politics* (Washington, D.C.: CRP, 1995); Katherine Seelye, "GOP Rewards for Top Donors: Three Days With Party Leaders," *New York Times*, February 26, 1997, p. B9.

26. Center for Responsive Politics, *Report on Soft Money* (Washington, D.C.: CRP, 1996). FEC reports, November 25, 1996; Brooks Jackson and James Bovard, "Tithing at the Church of Subsidy" (Washington, D.C.: Cato Institute, September 26, 1995). R. W. Apple, "Money Politics and Its Suckers," *New York Times*, February 9, 1997, sec. 4,

pp. 1–3. Jeff Gerth, "Business Gains with Democrats," *New York Times*, December 25, 1996, p. B7.

27. Sidney Verba, Kay Schlozman, and Henry Brady, *Voice and Equality: Civic Voluntarism in American Politics* (Cambridge: Harvard University Press, 1995), pp. 49–87.

28. "Banners from a Survey of 200 Political Contributors," Lake Research paper, July 17–23, 1996; Robert Borosage and Ruy Teixeira, "The Politics of Money," *The Nation*, October 21, 1996, pp. 21–24; Verba, Schlozman, Brady, *Voice*, pp. 515–17.

29. David Rosenbaum, "Memos to Clinton," *New York Times*, April 3, 1997, p. A7.

30. Dick Morris *Behind the Oval Office* (New York: Random House, 1997), pp. 93, 141.

31. Rosenbaum, "Memos," *New York Times*, April 3, 1997; Tim Weiner, "Files Detail," *New York Times*, February 27, 1997, p. B8.

32. Larry Sabato, *The Rise of Political Consultants* (New York: Basic Books, 1981).

33. See Matthew McCubbins, ed., *Under the Watchful Eye: Managing Presidential Campaigns in the Television Era* (Washington, D.C.: Congressional Quarterly Press, 1992).

34. Christopher Hitchens, "Voting in the Passive Voice: What Polling Has Done To American Democracy," *Harper's* (April 1992): pp. 42–54.

35. Marion Just, "Candidate Strategies and the Media Campaign," in Pomper, ed., *The Election*, pp. 77–106; Darrell West, *Air Wars: Television Advertising in Election Campaigns, 1952–1992* (Washington, D.C.: Congressional Quarterly Press, 1993).

36. Recorded in Sabato, *Rise*, p. 149.

37. Steven Salmore and Barbara Salmore, *Candidates, Parties, and Campaigns* (Washington, D.C.: Congressional Quarterly Press, 1990).

38. See Christopher Arterton, "Campaign '92," in Gerald Pomper, ed., *The Election of 1992* (Chatham, N.J.: Chatham House, 1993).

39. For a defense, see James Carville and Mary Matalin, *All's Fair* (New York: Random House, 1994); David Runkel, ed., *Campaign for President: The Managers Look at '88* (Dover, Mass.: Auburn House Publishing, 1989).

40. See Sidney Blumenthal, *Pledging Allegiance: The Last Campaign of the Cold War* (New York: Harper/Collins, 1990).

41. See Paul Harrison and Clyde Wilcox, "The 1996 Presidential Election: A Tale of a Campaign That Didn't Seem to Matter" and Richard Cohen, "Campaigning for Congress: The Echo of '94," both in Sabato, *Toward the Millennium*, pp. 121–42, 163–88.

42. See Wilson Carey McWilliams, "The Meaning of the Election" in Pomper, *Election of 1988*, p. 191. See also Kathleen Hall Jamieson, *Dirty Politics* (New York: Oxford University Press, 1992).

43. Steven Ansolabehere and Shanto Iyengar, *Going Negative: How Political Advertisements Shrink and Polarize the Electorate* (New York: Free Press, 1995).

44. Kenneth Weine, "Campaigns Without Human Faces," *Washington Post National Weekly Edition*, November 4, 1996, p. 24.

45. "60 Seconds to Victory: Six Political Ad Men in Search of a Willie Horton in '92," *Harper's* (July 1992): 36–37.

46. See Paul Quirk and Jon Dalager, "A New Democrat and a New Kind of Political Campaign," in Nelson, *Elections*. See also Times/Mirror Center for the People and the Press, "Voters Say Thumbs Up to Campaign Process and Coverage," news release, November 15, 1992, pp. 3–4.

47. Ellen Miller, "Clean Elections, How To," *American Prospect* (January/February 1997): 56–59; Jamin Raskin, "Dollar Democracy," *The Nation*, May 5, 1997, pp. 11–15; Francis Clines, "Most Doubt a Resolve to Change Campaign Financing," *New York Times*, April 8, 1997, pp. A1–B8.

48. Adam Clymer, "Many Proposals, Few Supporters," *New York Times*, April 6, 1997, p. A1.

49. Ellen Miller, "Laundering Money for Real," *The Nation*, May 5, 1997, pp. 25–26.

50. Francis Clines, "Pursuing Campaign Overhaul, Advocates Shifts Fight to States," *New York Times*, April 6, 1997, p. 24.

51. William Greider, *Who?*, pp. 12–23.

CHAPTER 9

1. Data from the Roper Center for Public Opinion Research, as reported in Theda Skocpol, *Boomerang: Health Care Reform and the Turn Against Government* (New York: W. W. Norton, 1996), p. 75.

2. Based on research by Darrell M. West and Diane J. Heith of Brown University, as reported in Robin Toner, "The Art of Reprocessing the Democratic Process," *New York Times*, September 4, 1994.

3. Quoted in Robert Pear, "Doctors Rebel Over Health Plan in Major Challenge to President," *New York Times*, September 30, 1993.

4. Office of the Clerk, U.S. House of Representatives, as cited in W. Lance Bennett, *Inside the System: Culture, Institutions, and Power in American Politics* (Fort Worth, Tex.: Harcourt Brace, 1994), pp. 8–44. Eric Schmitt, "Order for Lobbyists: Hold the Gravy," *New York Times*, February 11, 1996.

5. Cited in Mark P. Petracca, "The Rediscovery of Interest Group Politics," in Mark P. Petracca, ed., *The Politics of Interests: Interest Groups Transformed* (Boulder, Colo.: Westview Press, 1992), p. 14.

6. See Ester R. Fuchs, *Mayors and Money: Fiscal Policy in New York and Chicago* (Chicago: University of Chicago Press, 1992), esp. chap. 7.

7. Quoted in Jeffrey H. Birnbaum and Alan S. Murray, *Showdown at Gucci Gulch: Lawmakers, Lobbyists, and the Unlikely Triumph of Tax Reform* (New York: Random House, 1987), pp. 178–79.

8. Kay Lehman Schlozman and John T. Tierney, "More of the Same: Washington Pressure Group Activity in a Decade of Change," *Journal of Politics* 45 (1988): 351–75.

9. Quoted in Kay Lehman Schlozman and John T. Tierney, *Organized Interests and American Society* (New York: Harper & Row, 1986), p. 85.

10. In 1993 for the top 1,100 employees in the executive branch, President Clinton raised the ban on lobbying their former agencies to five years.

11. Schlozman and Tierney, *Organized Interests*, p. 75.

12. Allen J. Cigler and Burdett A. Loomis, "The Changing Nature of Interest Group Politics," in William Lasser, ed. *Perspectives on American Government: A Comprehensive Reader* (Lexington, Mass.: D.C. Heath, 1992), pp. 305–06.

13. See David Truman, *The Governmental Process* (New York: A. A. Knopf, 1951); Robert Dahl, *A Preface to Democratic Theory* (Chicago: University of Chicago Press, 1956); and Dahl, *Who Governs? Democracy and Power in an American City* (New Haven: Yale University Press, 1961). Since *Who Governs?* Dahl has shifted from an elite democratic to a more popular democratic analysis of American politics. See his *A Preface to Economic Democracy* (Berkeley: University of California Press, 1985).

14. The survey did not include unions, which in 1990 represented about 16 percent of workers.

15. Sidney Verba, Kay Lehman Schlozman, and Henry E. Brady, *Voice and Equality: Civic Voluntarism in American Life* (Cambridge: Harvard University Press, 1995), p. 190.

16. E. E. Schattschneider, *The Semi-Sovereign People: A Realist's View of Democracy in America* (New York: Holt, Rinehart and Winston, 1960), p. 35. For critiques of pluralist theory as a form of democratic elitism, see Jack Walker, "A Critique of the Elitist Theory of Democracy," *American Political Science Review* 60 (1966): 285–95; and Peter Bachrach, *The Theory of Democratic Elitism: A Critique* (Boston: Little, Brown and Company, 1967).

17. Robert D. Putnam, "Tuning In, Tuning Out: The Strange Disappearance of Social Capital in America," *PS: Political Science and Politics* (December 1995): 664–83. See also his "Bowling Alone," in *Journal of Democracy* 6, no. 1 (December 1995): 65–78.

18. See Mancur Olson, Jr., *The Logic of Collective Action: Public Goods and the Theory of Groups* (New York: Schocken Books, 1968).

19. The following account of Nader's life and accomplishments relies on Robert F. Buckhorn, *Nader: The People's Lawyer* (Englewood Cliffs, N.J.: Prentice-Hall, 1972); Jay Acton and Alan LeMond, *Ralph Nader: A Man and a Movement* (New York: Warner Books, 1972); and Charles McCarry, *Citizen Nader* (New York: Saturday Review Press, 1972).

20. Buckhorn, *Nader*, p. 36.

21. Ralph Nader, *Unsafe at Any Speed: The Designed-in Dangers of the American Automobile* (New York: Grossman, 1966).

22. From court documents filed when Nader sued GM. Quoted in Nader, *Unsafe*, p. 14.

23. Quoted in *ibid.*, p. 36.

24. Ralph Nader, "How to Put the Punch Back in Politics," *Mother Jones* (July/August 1990): 26.

25. Jeffrey M. Berry, *Lobbying for the People* (Princeton, N.J.: Princeton University Press, 1977).

26. William Greider, *Who Will Tell the People: The Betrayal of American Democracy* (New York: Simon & Schuster, 1992), p. 48.

27. Schlozman and Tierney, *Organized Interests*, pp. 77–78.

28. Greider, *Who Will Tell*, p. 50.

29. Samuel Huntington called this the "democratic distemper." See his article, "The United States," in Michel J. Crozier, Samuel Huntington, and Joji Watanuki, *The Crisis of Democracy: Report on the Governability of Democracies to the Trilateral Commission* (New York: New York University Press, 1975), pp. 59–118.

30. House Government Operations Committee, Subcommittee on Commerce, Consumer and Monetary Affairs, as reported in Thomas Byrne Edsall, *The New Politics of Inequality* (New York: W. W. Norton, 1984), p. 116.

31. Advertisement, "Progress and the Environment," *New York Times*, December 3, 1981; quoted in Jeffrey M. Berry, *The Interest Group Society* (Boston: Little, Brown, 1984), p. 140.

32. James A. Smith, *The Idea Brokers: Think Tanks and the Rise of the New Policy Elite* (New York: Free Press, 1991), xiv.

33. Edsall, *New Politics*, p. 117

34. Jean Stefancic and Richard Delgado, *No Mercy: How Conservative Think Tanks and Foundations Changed America's Social Agenda* (Philadelphia: Temple University Press, 1996), p. 53.

35. Quoted in Smith, *Idea Brokers*, p. 195.

36. Quoted in *ibid.*, p. 20.

37. R. Kenneth Godwin, *One Billion Dollars of Influence: The Direct Marketing of Politics* (Chatham, N.J.: Chatham House, 1988), p. 2.

38. Schlozman and Tierney, *Organized Interests*, pp. 94–95.

39. Cited in *ibid.*, p. 22.

40. Hugh Heclo, "Issue Networks and the Executive Establishment," in Anthony King, ed., *The New American Political System*, (Washington, D.C.: American Enterprise Institute, 1978), pp. 87–124.

41. Stephen Englemberg, "A New Breed of Hired Hands Cultivates Grass-Roots Anger," *New York Times*, March 17, 1993.

42. Quoted in Greider, *Who Will Tell*, p. 38.

43. Quoted in Elizabeth Kolbert, "Special Interests' Special Weapon," *New York Times*, March 26, 1995.

44. Schlozman and Tierney, *Organized Interests*, p. 115.

CHAPTER 10

1. The following account of the Montgomery bus boycott is based on Taylor Branch, *Parting the Waters: America in the King Years 1954–63* (New York: Simon & Schuster, 1988); and Juan Williams, *Eyes on the Prize: America's Civil Rights Years 1954–1965* (New York: Penguin, 1987).

2. Michael Lipsky, *Protest in City Politics: Rent Strikes, Housing and the Power of the Poor* (Chicago: Rand McNally, 1970), p. 2. We draw freely in this chapter on Lipsky's analysis of protest as a political resource.

3. Charles C. Euchner, *Extraordinary Politics: How Protest and Dissent Are Changing American Democracy* (Boulder, Colo.: Westview Press, 1996).

4. Quoted in Williams, *Eyes on the Prize*, p. 78.

5. Euchner, *Extraordinary Politics*; Craig A. Rimmerman, *The New Citizenship: Unconventional Politics, Activism, and Service* (Boulder, Colo.: Westview Press, 1997).

6. Paul Kleppner, *Who Voted? The Dynamics of Electoral Turnout* (New York: Praeger, 1982), p. 116; as cited in Frances Fox Piven and Richard A. Cloward, *Why Americans Don't Vote* (New York: Pantheon, 1989), p. 144.

7. T. R. Gurr, *Why Men Rebel* (Princeton: Princeton University Press, 1970).

8. John D. McCarthy and Mayer N. Zald, "Resource Mobilization and Social Movements: A Partial Theory," *American Journal of Sociology*, 82, no. 6 (1977): 1212–41.

9. Sara M. Evans and Harry C. Boyte, *Free Spaces: The Sources of Democratic Change in America* (Chicago: University of Chicago Press, 1992).

10. For an insightful account of the populist movement that stresses the formation of a movement culture, see Lawrence Goodwyn, *The Populist Moment* (New York: Oxford University Press, 1978).

11. Quoted in Sara Evans, *Personal Politics: The Roots of Women's Liberation in the Civil Rights Movement and the New Left* (New York: Vintage Books, 1980), p. 87.

12. Quoted in Williams, *Eyes on the Prize*, p. 76.

13. The concepts of transactional and transformational leaders are developed in James MacGregor Burns, *Leadership* (New York: Harper & Row, 1978).

14. For an analysis of Stanton as a dissenting movement leader, see Bruce Miroff, *Icons of Democracy: American Leaders as Heroes, Aristocrats, Dissenters, & Democrats* (New York: Basic Books, 1993), chap. 4.

15. Saul D. Alinsky, *Reveille for Radicals* (New York: Random House, 1969), p. 132.

16. Henry David Thoreau, "Civil Disobedience," in Milton Meltzer, ed., *Thoreau: People, Principles, and Politics* (New York: Hill and Wang, 1963), p. 38.

17. Frances Fox Piven and Richard A. Cloward, *Poor People's Movements: Why They Succeed, How They Fail* (New York: Pantheon, 1977).

18. *Report of the National Advisory Commission on Civil Disorders* (New York: Bantam Books, 1968).

19. Murray Edelman, *The Symbolic Uses of Politics* (Urbana, Ill.: University of Illinois Press, 1967); see also Edelman's *Constructing the Political Spectacle* (Chicago: University of Chicago Press, 1988).

20. See Alan Wolfe, *The Seamy Side of Democracy* (New York: David McKay, 1978); David Caute, *The Great Fear* (New York: Simon & Schuster, 1978); and Robert Justin Goldstein, *Political Repression in Modern America* (Cambridge: Schenkman, 1978).

21. Quoted in William Greider, *Who Will Tell the People? The Betrayal of American Democracy* (New York: Simon & Schuster, 1992), p. 17.

22. For a contemporary elite democratic critique of mass politics, see Samuel P. Huntington, *American Politics: The Promise of Disharmony* (Cambridge: Harvard University Press, 1981).

23. For a critique of the populist / progressive movements along these lines, see Richard Hofstadter, *The Age of Reform: From Bryan to F.D.R.* (New York: Vintage, 1955).

24. Michael Paul Rogin, *The Intellectuals and McCarthy: The Radical Specter* (Cambridge: M.I.T. Press, 1967). Rogin's book is a carefully researched popular democratic defense of mass movements.

25. Merrill D. Peterson, ed., *The Portable Thomas Jefferson* (New York: Penguin, 1975), p. 417.

26. Tom Wolfe, *Radical Chic and Mau-Mauing the Flak Catchers* (New York: Bantam Books, 1971), pp. 117–18.

27. "No Guardrails," editorial, *Wall Street Journal*, March 18, 1993.

28. Samuel P. Huntington, "The United States," in Michael J. Crozier, Samuel P. Huntington, and Joji Watanuki, *The Crisis of Democracy: Report on the Governability of Democracies to the Trilateral Commission* (New York: New York University Press, 1975), pp. 59–118.

29. See Richard Rose, ed., *Challenge to Governance: Studies in Overloaded Politics* (Beverly Hills, Calif.: Sage, 1980).

30. Samuel P. Huntington, *American Politics: The Promise of Disharmony* (Cambridge: Harvard University Press, 1981), p. 219.

31. Thomas R. Dye and Harmon Ziegler, *The Irony of Democracy: An Uncommon Introduction to American Politics*, 9th ed. (Belmont, Calif.: Wadsworth, 1993), p. 17.

32. In 1977 a federal district court ordered all tapes, transcripts, and other FBI information on King's private life to be impounded for fifty years under the seal of secrecy. Branch, *Parting the Waters*, p. 872.

33. Euchner, *Extraordinary Politics*, p. 221.

34. For a gripping account of the events in Chicago, see James Miller, *"Democracy Is in the Streets": From Port Huron to the Siege of Chicago* (New York: Simon & Schuster, 1987), chap. 12.

35. *Rights in Conflict: The Violent Confrontation of Demonstrators and Police in the Parks and Streets of Chicago During the Week of the Democratic National Convention of 1968*, report submitted by Daniel Walker, director of the Chicago Study Team, to the National Commission on the Causes and Prevention of Violence, 1968.

36. Most Americans—57 percent, according to one poll—felt that the police had used the right amount of force or too little. John P. Robinson, "Public Reaction to Political Protest: Chicago 1968," *Public Opinion Quarterly* 34 (Spring 1970): 1–9.

37. U.S. Bureau of the Census, *Statistical Abstract of the United States 1996* (Washington, D.C.: U.S. Government Printing Office, 1996), p. 284. Joint Center for Political and Economic Studies, *Black Elected Officials: A National Roster* (Washington, D.C.: Joint Center for Political and Economic Studies, 1990), p. 10.

38. Jeffrey M. Berry, Kent E. Portney, and Ken Thomson, *The Rebirth of Urban Democracy* (Washington, D.C.: The Brookings Institution, 1993).

39. Jo Freeman, *The Politics of Women's Liberation* (New York: David McKay, 1975), p. 53.

40. Ethel Klein, *Gender Politics: From Consciousness to Mass Politics* (Cambridge: Harvard University Press, 1984), p. 30.

41. Figures on salaries and political representation computed from U.S. Bureau of the Census, *Statistical Abstract of the United States: 1989* (Washington, D.C.: U.S. Government Printing Office, 1989), pp. 448, 511; *Statistical Abstract of the United States: 1996* (Washington, D.C.: U.S. Government Printing Office, 1996), p. 468.

42. In 1992, Clinton did 5 percent better among women than among men (46 percent versus 41 percent); in 1996, the gender gap was 11 percent (54–43 percent). CBS News–*New York Times* polls based on a nationwide sample of voters leaving the polls on election day; as reported in the *New York Times*, November 5, 1992 and November 10, 1996.

43. For evidence on the personal effects of participation in protests, see Euchner, *Extraordinary Politics*, pp. 232–33.

44. Rufus P. Browning, Dale Rogers Marshall, and David H. Tabb, *Protest Is Not Enough: The Struggle of Blacks and Hispanics for Equality in Urban Politics* (Berkeley: University of California Press, 1984).

CHAPTER 11

1. Ronald M. Peters, Jr., "The Republican Speakership," paper delivered at the Annual Meeting of the American Political Science Association, San Francisco, August-September 1996, p. 20.

2. Gary C. Jacobson, *The Politics of Congressional Elections*, 4th. ed. (New York: Longman, 1997), p. 69.

3. Ibid., pp. 19–28.

4. David R. Mayhew, *Congress: The Electoral Connection* (New Haven, Conn.: Yale University Press, 1974); Morris P. Fiorina, *Congress: Keystone of the Washington Establishment*, 2nd ed. (New Haven, Conn.: Yale University Press, 1989); Richard E. Fenno, Jr., *Home Style: House Members in Their Districts* (Boston: Little, Brown, 1978).

5. John W. Kingdon, *Congressmen's Voting Decisions*, 3rd ed. (Ann Arbor: University of Michigan Press, 1989).

6. See Burdett Loomis, *The New American Politician: Ambition, Entrepreneurship, and the Changing Face of Political Life* (New York: Basic Books, 1988).

7. Michael J. Malbin, *Unelected Representatives: Congressional Staff and the Future of Representative Government* (New York: Basic Books, 1980).

8. Steven S. Smith and Christopher J. Deering, *Committees in Congress*, 2nd ed. (Washington, D.C.: CQ Press, 1990), p. 216.

9. Norman J. Ornstein, Thomas E. Mann, and Michael J. Malbin, *Vital Statistics on Congress, 1993–1994* (Washington, D.C.: CQ Press, 1994), pp. 201–2.

10. John R. Hibbing and Elizabeth Theiss-Morse, *Congress as Public Enemy: Public Attitudes Toward American Political Institutions* (New York: Cambridge University Press, 1995), p. 49.

11. John C. Berg, *Unequal Struggle: Class, Gender, Race, and Power in the U.S. Congress* (Boulder, Colo.: Westview Press, 1994), pp. 37–47.

12. See Barbara Sinclair, "The Emergence of Strong Leadership in the 1980s House of Representatives," *Journal of Politics* 54 (August 1992): 657–84.

13. Hibbing and Theiss-Morse, *Congress as Public Enemy*.

14. C. Lawrence Evans and Walter J. Oleszek, *Congress Under Fire: Reform Politics and the Republican Majority* (Boston: Houghton Mifflin, 1997), pp. 2–3.

15. Peters, "The Republican Speakership"; Daniel J. Stid, "Transformational Leadership in Congress?" paper delivered at the Annual Meeting of the American Political Science Association, San Francisco, August-September 1996.

16. Evans and Oleszek, *Congress Under Fire*, p. 120.

17. Peters, "The Republican Speakership," pp. 10–17.

18. David S. Cloud, "Speaker Wants His Platform to Rival the Presidency," *Congressional Quarterly* (February 4, 1995); 331–35.

19. Katharine Q. Seelye, "He's Top Man in the House, But Not in the Nation," *New York Times*, March 19, 1995.

20. Norman J. Ornstein, Robert L. Peabody, and David W. Rohde, "The U.S. Senate: Toward the Twenty-First Century," in Lawrence C. Dodd and Bruce I. Oppenheimer, eds., *Congress Reconsidered*, 6th ed. (Washington, D.C.: CQ Press, 1997), pp. 18–19.

21. Cited in Bruce I. Oppenheimer, "Abdicating Congressional Power: The Paradox of Republican Control," in Dodd and Oppenheimer, *Congress Reconsidered*, p. 376.

22. Jeffrey H. Birnbaum, "The Thursday Regulars," *Time*, March 27, 1995, pp. 30–31.

23. Quoted in Evans and Oleszek, *Congress Under Fire*, p. 134.

24. Evans and Oleszek, *Congress Under Fire*, pp. 122–23.

25. Steven S. Smith and Eric D. Lawrence, "Party Control of Committees in the Republican Congress," in Dodd and Oppenheimer, *Congress Reconsidered*, p. 163.

26. Janet Hook, "Conservative Freshman Class Eager to Seize the Moment," *Congressional Quarterly* (January 7, 1995): 47–49.

27. Chester B. Rogers, "The Decline of the Entrepreneurial Culture in Congress," paper delivered at the Annual Meeting of the American Political Science Association, San Francisco, August-September 1996.

28. R. W. Apple, Jr., "Back, Yes, But Subdued," *New York Times*, January 8, 1997.

29. Adam Clymer, "G.O.P. Effort to Halt Rumors of Unrest Just Causes More," *New York Times*, June 23, 1997.

30. Jackie Koszczuk and Donna Cassata, "From Revolution to Realism," *Congressional Quarterly* (October 5, 1996): 2832–39.

31. Michael Wines, "House Freshmen Label Themselves Pragmatic," *New York Times*, November 16, 1996.

32. C. Lawrence Evans and Walter J. Oleszek, "Congressional Tsunami? The Politics of Committee Reform," in Dodd and Oppenheimer, *Congress Reconsidered*, p. 209.

33. Lawrence C. Dodd and Bruce I. Oppenheimer, "Congress and the Emerging Order: Conditional Party Government or Constructive Partisanship?," in Dodd and Oppenheimer, *Congress Reconsidered*, pp. 390–413.

34. On heightened warfare between the branches under Reagan and Bush, see Benjamin Ginsberg and Martin Shefter, *Politics by Other Means: The Declining Significance of Elections* (New York: Basic Books, 1990). For a contrary view, see David Mayhew, *Divided We Govern: Party Control, Lawmaking, and Investigations, 1946–1990* (New Haven, Conn.: Yale University Press, 1991).

35. James A. Thurber, "The Impact of Budget Reform on Presidential and Congressional Governance," in James A. Thurber, ed., *Divided Democracy: Cooperation and Conflict Between the President and Congress* (Washington, D.C.: CQ Press, 1991).

36. For a dramatic account of these events, see Elizabeth Drew, *Showdown: The Struggle Between the Gingrich Congress and the Clinton White House* (New York: Simon & Schuster, 1996), pp. 300–77.

37. Eileen Burgin, "Assessing Congress's Role in the Making of Foreign Policy," in Dodd and Oppenheimer, *Congress Reconsidered*, pp. 293–324. Also see James M. Lindsay, *Congress and the Politics of U.S. Foreign Policy* (Baltimore: The Johns Hopkins University Press, 1994).

38. See Stephen R. Weissman, *A Culture of Deference: Congress's Failure of Leadership in Foreign Policy* (New York: Basic Books, 1995).

39. Joel D. Aberbach, *Keeping a Watchful Eye: The Politics of Congressional Oversight* (Washington, D.C.: The Brookings Institution, 1990), pp. 191–93.

40. Evans and Oleszek, *Congress Under Fire*, pp. 176–79. On congressional deliberation, see Joseph M. Bessette, *The Mild Voice of Reason: Deliberative Democracy and American National Government* (Chicago: University of Chicago Press, 1994).

CHAPTER 12

1. Alexander Hamilton et al., *The Federalist Papers* (New York: New American Library, 1961), p. 423. For a recent Hamiltonian argument, see Terry Eastland, *Energy in the Executive: The Case for the Strong Presidency* (New York: Free Press, 1992).

2. Ibid., p. 424.

3. Ralph Ketcham, ed., *The Anti-Federalist Papers* (New York: New American Library, 1986), p. 211.

4. Max Farrand, ed., *The Records of the Federal Convention of 1787*, vol. 1 (New Haven, Conn.: Yale University Press, 1937), p. 112.

5. Michael Weisskopf and Charles R. Babcock, "Washington's Priciest B & B: Big Donors Get First Class Treatment in the Clinton White House," *Washington Post National Weekly Edition*, January 6, 1997, pp. 6–7.

6. Bob Woodward, *The Agenda: Inside the Clinton White House* (New York: Simon & Schuster, 1994), p. 84.

7. Ibid., p. 239.

8. Ibid., p. 165.

9. Precise numbers for the White House staff are difficult to determine. See John Hart, *The Presidential Branch: From Washington to Clinton* (Chatham, N.J.: Chatham House, 1995), pp. 112–25.

10. See Thomas E. Cronin, *The State of the Presidency*, 2nd ed. (Boston: Little, Brown, 1980), pp. 223–51.

11. Quoted in "Be Resolute, Mr. Clinton. Here's How," *New York Times*, December 31, 1996.

12. See George E. Reedy, *The Twilight of the Presidency* (New York: New American Library, 1971).

13. See Hugh Heclo, "OMB and the Presidency: The Problem of 'Neutral Competence,'" *The Public Interest*, vol 11 (1975): 80–98.

14. Cronin, *State of the Presidency*, pp. 276–78.

15. For a hilarious and insightful view of life in President Clinton's outer cabinet, see Robert B. Reich, *Locked in the Cabinet* (New York: Alfred A. Knopf, 1997).

16. Quoted in Richard E. Neustadt, *Presidential Power and the Modern Presidents* (New York: Free Press, 1990), p. 10.

17. Richard P. Nathan, *The Administrative Presidency* (New York: Wiley, 1983). Also see Terry M. Moe, "The Politicized Presidency," in James P. Pfiffner, ed., *The Managerial Presidency* (Pacific Grove, Calif.: Brooks / Cole, 1991), pp. 135–57.

18. For the story of the Reagan administration and OSHA, see William F. Grover, *The President as Prisoner: A Structural Critique of the Carter and Reagan Years* (Albany, N.Y.: SUNY Press, 1989), pp. 112–23.

19. Hamilton et al., *Federalist Papers*, p. 322. For a view of legislative-executive relations that stresses cooperation as well as conflict, see Mark A. Peterson, *Legislating Together: The White House and Capitol Hill From Eisenhower to Reagan* (Cambridge: Harvard University Press, 1990).

20. George C. Edwards III and Stephen J. Wayne, *Presidential Leadership: Politics and Policy Making*, 4th ed. (New York: St. Martin's Press, 1997), pp. 311–12.

21. *Washington Post*, November 18, 1993.

22. On presidential resources and constraints in economic policy making during the Clinton administration, see M. Stephen Weatherford and Lorraine M. McDonnell, "Clinton and the Economy: The Paradox of Policy Success and Political Mishap," *Political Science Quarterly* 111 (Fall 1996): 403–36.

23. See Bruce Miroff, *Icons of Democracy: American Leaders as Heroes, Aristocrats, Dissenters, and Democrats* (New York: Basic Books, 1993), pp. 294–300.

24. Cited in Robert Reno, "Clinton Looks Golden From Where Business is Mining," *Newsday*, October 17, 1994.

25. Quoted in Leslie Wayne, "Yes, Even Now, There Are Clinton C.E.O.'s," *New York Times*, December 4, 1994.

26. Arthur Schlesinger, Jr., *The Imperial Presidency* (Boston: Houghton Mifflin, 1973).

27. *United States* v. *Curtiss-Wright Corp.*, 299 U.S. 304 (1936).

28. For an example, see Theodore Lowi, *The End of Liberalism*, 2nd ed. (New York: W. W. Norton, 1979), pp. 127–63.

29. Quoted in Louis Fisher, "President Clinton as Commander in Chief," in James A. Thurber, ed., *Rivals for Power: Presidential-Congressional Relations* (Washington, D.C.: CQ Press, 1996), p. 222.

30. Fisher, "President Clinton as Commander in Chief," p. 214.

31. See Christopher Andrew, *For the President's Eyes Only: Secret Intelligence and the American Presidency from Washington to Bush* (New York: HarperCollins, 1996).

32. For a vivid account of repression in the Nixon administration, see Jonathan Schell, *The Time of Illusion* (New York: Vintage, 1976).

33. For a good analysis of the framers' view of the president, see Jeffrey K. Tulis, *The Rhetorical Presidency* (Princeton, N.J.: Princeton University Press, 1987), pp. 25–45.

34. Samuel Kernell, *Going Public: New Strategies of Presidential Leadership*, 2nd ed. (Washington, D.C.: CQ Press, 1993), pp. 90–91.

35. See Stephen J. Wayne, "Great Expectations: What People Want from Presidents," in Thomas E. Cronin, ed., *Rethinking the Presidency* (Boston: Little, Brown, 1982), pp. 185–99.

36. See John Anthony Maltese, *Spin Control: The White House Office of Communications and the Management of Presidential News*, 2nd ed. (Chapel Hill: University of North Carolina Press, 1994).

37. *New York Times*, January 31, 1993.

38. *New York Times*, January 24, 1993.

39. See Bruce Miroff, "The Presidency and the Public: Leadership as Spectacle," in Michael Nelson, ed., *The Presidency and the Political System*, 5th ed. (Washington, D.C.: CQ Press, 1998).

40. See Steven Stark, "The First Post-Modern Presidency," *Atlantic Monthly* (April 1993).

41. Bruce Miroff, "Monopolizing the Public Space: The President as a Problem for Democratic Politics," in Cronin, ed., *Rethinking the Presidency*, pp. 218–32.

42. Material in the following paragraphs is adapted from Miroff, *Icons*, pp. 300–05.

43. Quoted in Miroff, *Icons*, p. 304.

CHAPTER 13

1. *The Congressional Record—House*, March 1, 1995, pp. H2402, H2407.

2. Clinton Rossiter, ed., *The Federalist Papers* (New York: New American Library, 1961), p. 174.

3. On the administrative apparatus under Washington and Hamilton, see Leonard D. White, *The Federalists: A Study in Administrative History, 1789–1801* (New York: Free Press, 1948).

4. Quoted in James A. Morone, *The Democratic Wish: Popular Participation and the Limits of American Government* (New York: Basic Books, 1990), p. 87.

5. Matthew A. Crenson, *The Federal Machine: Beginnings of Bureaucracy in Jacksonian America* (Baltimore, Md.: Johns Hopkins University Press, 1975), p. 4.

6. On late nineteenth-century state builders, see Stephen Skowronek, *Building a New American State: The Expansion of National Administrative Capacities, 1877–1920* (New York: Cambridge University Press, 1982), esp. pp. 42–45.

7. Morone, *Democratic Wish*, p. 98.

8. George McJimsey, *Harry Hopkins* (Cambridge: Harvard University Press, 1987), p. 114.

9. Quoted in McJimsey, *Hopkins*, p. 63.

10. Quoted in McJimsey, *Hopkins*, p. 97.

11. Quoted in McJimsey, *Hopkins*, p. 66.

12. Quoted in Charles T. Goodsell, *The Case for Bureaucracy*, 2nd ed. (Chatham, N.J.: Chatham House, 1985), p. 166.

13. Goodsell, *Case for Bureaucracy*, 2nd ed., p. 166.

14. Data on government employment are taken from Harold W. Stanley and Richard G. Niemi, *Vital Statistics on American Politics*, 5th ed. (Washington, D.C.: CQ Press, 1995).

15. Goodsell, *Case for Bureaucracy*, 2nd ed. p. 83.

16. B. Guy Peters, "Public Bureaucracy in the American Political System," in Gillian Peele, Christopher J. Bailey, and Bruce Cain, eds., *Developments in American Politics* (New York: St. Martin's Press, 1992), p. 170.

17. Charles T. Goodsell, *The Case for Bureaucracy*, 3rd ed. (Chatham, N.J.: Chatham House, 1994), p. 130.

18. Ibid., pp. 25–39.

19. See James Q. Wilson, *Bureaucracy: What Government Agencies Do and Why They Do It* (New York: Basic Books, 1989), pp. 179–95.

20. Ibid., pp. 113–36.

21. See John A. Rohr, *To Run a Constitution: The Legitimacy of the Administrative State* (Lawrence: University Press of Kansas, 1986), pp. 59–89.

22. Francis E. Rourke, *Bureaucracy, Politics, and Public Policy*, 2nd ed. (Boston: Little, Brown, 1976), p. 16.

23. Kenneth J. Meier, *Politics and the Bureaucracy: Policymaking in the Fourth Branch of Government*, 3rd ed. (Pacific Grove, Calif.: Brooks / Cole, 1993), pp. 68–72.

24. Rourke, *Bureaucracy, Politics, and Public Policy*, p. 46.

25. Wilson, *Bureaucracy*, p. 251.

26. David J. Garrow, *The FBI and Martin Luther King, Jr.* (New York: Penguin Books, 1983), pp. 125–34.

27. Charles H. Levine, B. Guy Peters, and Frank J. Thompson, *Public Administration* (Glenview, Ill.: Scott Foresman, 1990), pp. 52–53.

28. Morton H. Halperin, *Bureaucratic Politics and Foreign Policy* (Washington, D.C.: The Brookings Institution, 1974), p. 43.

29. Wilson, *Bureaucracy*, p. 257. For a historical account of this rivalry, see Skowronek, *Building a New American State*, pp. 165–292.

30. Michael D. Reagan, *Regulation: The Politics of Policy* (Boston: Little, Brown, 1987), p. 15.

31. The most famous—and controversial—of the revisionist histories is Gabriel Kolko, *The Triumph of Conservatism* (Chicago: Quadrangle Books, 1967).

32. For a critique of the capture thesis, see Wilson, *Bureaucracy*, pp. 83–88.

33. Adam Bryant, "On a Wing and a Fare," *New York Times*, Nov. 5, 1995.

34. Bob Benenson, "House Easily Passes Bill to Limit Regulations," *Congressional Quarterly*, March 4, 1995, p. 680.

35. Al Gore, *Report of the National Performance Review* (New York: Times Books, 1994), p. 43.

36. Ibid., p. 71.

37. Donald F. Kettl, "Building Lasting Reform: Enduring Questions, Missing Answers," in Donald F. Kettl and John J. DiIulio, Jr., eds., *Inside the Reinvention Machine: Appraising Governmental Reform* (Washington, D.C.: The Brookings Institution, 1995), p. 9. For a more skeptical view of the NPR, see Gerald Garvey, "False Promises: The NPR in Historical Perspective," in ibid., pp. 87–106.

38. Kettl, "Building Lasting Reform," pp. 14–23.

39. See E. S. Savas, *Privatizing the Public Sector: How to Shrink Government* (Chatham, N.J.: Chatham House, 1982).

40. William T. Gormley, Jr., *Taming the Bureaucracy: Muscles, Prayers, and Other Strategies* (Princeton: Princeton University Press, 1989), p. 71.

41. Ibid., p. 89.

42. Charles Noble, *Liberalism at Work: The Rise and Fall of OSHA* (Philadelphia: Temple University Press, 1986), p. 34.

43. Ibid., p. 201.

44. Barbara Priestly Noble, "Breathing New Life into OSHA," *New York Times*, Jan. 23, 1994.

CHAPTER 14

1. David M. O'Brien, *Storm Center: The Supreme Court in American Politics*, 3rd ed. (New York: W. W. Norton, 1993), p. 14.

2. The Constitution, ostensibly an expression of the will of the people, has become a lawyers' document. See John Brigham, *The Cult of the Court* (Philadelphia: Temple University Press, 1987).

3. For an illuminating treatment of the conflicting theories of democracy that have been utilized by different justices on the modern Supreme Court, see Martin Edelman, *Democratic Theories and the Constitution* (Albany: State University of New York Press, 1984).

4. Edwin Meese, address to the D.C. Chapter of the Federalist Society Lawyers Division, November 15, 1985, in Paul G. Cassell, ed., *The Great Debate: Interpreting Our Written Constitution* (Washington, D.C.: Federalist Society, 1986), p. 37.

5. Edwin Meese, address to the American Bar Association, July 9, 1985, in Cassell, *Great Debate*, p. 9.

6. Ibid.

7. Ibid., p. 1.

8. Ibid., p. 10.

9. Robert H. Bork, *The Tempting of America: The Political Seduction of the Law* (New York: The Free Press, 1990), p. 130.

10. Justice William Brennan, Jr., address to the Text and Teaching Symposium, Georgetown University, October 12, 1985, in Cassell, *Great Debate*, p. 14.

11. Ibid., p. 15.

12. Ibid., p. 17.

13. Ibid., p. 11.

14. Mark Tushnet, "The Politics of Constitutional Law," in David Kairys, ed., *The Politics of Law: A Progressive Critique* (New York: Pantheon Books, 1990), p. 230.

15. Duncan Kennedy, "Legal Education as Training for Hierarchy," in Kairys, *Politics of Law*, p. 38.

16. Gerald N. Rosenberg, *The Hollow Hope: Can Courts Bring About Social Change?* (Chicago: University of Chicago Press, 1991).

17. Ibid., p. 12.

18. Kermit L. Hall, *The Magic Mirror: Law in American History* (New York: Oxford University Press, 1989), pp. 78–79.

19. *Marbury* v. *Madison*, 1 Cranch 137 (1803).

20. Robert G. McCloskey, *The American Supreme Court* (Chicago: University of Chicago Press, 1960), p. 57.

21. *Dred Scott* v. *Sandford*, 19 How. (60 U.S.) 393 (1857).

22. Michael Les Benedict, "History of the Court: Reconstruction, Federalism, and Economic Rights," in Kermit L. Hall et al., eds., *The Oxford Companion to the Supreme Court of the United States* (New York: Oxford University Press, 1992), p. 388.

23. Linda Greenhouse, "Blowing the Dust Off the Constitution that Was," *New York Times*, May 28, 1995; Linda Greenhouse, "Taking States Seriously," *New York Times*, April 14, 1996.

24. O'Brien, *Storm Center*, p. 107.

25. Ronald Stidham, Robert A. Carp, and Donald R. Songer, "The Voting Behavior of President Clinton's Judicial Nominees," *Judicature* 80, no. 1 (July-August 1996): 16–20.

26. Joan Biskupic, "Making a Mark on the Bench," *Washington Post National Weekly Edition*, December 2–8, 1996, p. 31.

27. Ibid.

28. On the difference a single new appointee can make, see Laurence H. Tribe, *God Save This Honorable Court: How the Choice of Supreme Court Justices Shapes Our History* (New York: New American Library, 1986), pp. 36–48.

29. O'Brien, *Storm Center*, p. 92.

30. See Tribe, *God Save This Honorable Court*, pp. 60–92.

31. See John Massaro, *Supremely Political: The Role of Ideology and Presidential Management in Unsuccessful Supreme Court Nominations* (Albany: State University of New York Press, 1990).

32. *Brown* v. *Allen*, 344 U.S. 443 (1953).

33. For scathing portrayals of Chief Justice Burger, see Bob Woodward and Scott Armstrong, *The Brethren: Inside the Supreme Court* (New York: Avon Books, 1981), esp. pp. 27–29, 179–81, 199–201, 220–23, 303–304, 372–73; and Bernard Schwartz, *Decision: How the Supreme Court Decides Cases* (New York: Oxford University Press, 1996), pp. 120–54.

34. Bernard Schwartz, *A History of the Supreme Court* (New York: Oxford University Press, 1993), pp. 364–76.

35. See Walter Murphy, *Elements of Judicial Strategy* (Chicago: University of Chicago Press, 1964).

36. See Phillip J. Cooper, *Battles on the Bench: Conflict Inside the Supreme Court* (Lawrence: University Press of Kansas, 1995).

37. Lawrence Baum, "Membership Change and Collective Voting Change in the United States Supreme Court," *Journal of Politics* 54, no. 1 (February 1992): 3–24.

38. See Lawrence Baum, *The Supreme Court*, 4th ed. (Washington, D.C.: CQ Press, 1992), pp. 144–56.

39. Stephen L. Wasby, *The Supreme Court in the Federal Judicial System*, 4th ed. (Chicago: Nelson-Hall, 1993), p. 349.

40. See Gregory A. Caldeira, "Neither the Purse Nor the Sword: Dynamics of Public Confidence in the Supreme Court," *American Political Science Review* 80, no. 4 (December 1986): 1209–26.

CHAPTER 15

1. Joel Blau, *The Visible Poor: Homelessness in the United States* (New York: Oxford University Press, 1992), pp. 129–31; Peter Dreier and W. Dennis Keating, "The Limits of Localism: Progressive Housing Policies in Boston, 1984–1989," in Roger W. Caves, ed., *Exploring Urban America: An Introductory Reader* (Thousand Oaks, Calif.: Sage, 1995), pp. 360–81.

2. Blau, *Visible Poor*, pp. 117–18.

3. Mike Davis, *City of Quartz: Excavating the Future of Los Angeles* (New York: Verso, 1990), p. 233.

4. Edward S. Corwin, "The Passing of Dual Federalism," *Virginia Law Review* 36, no. 1 (1950): 4.

5. Justice William J. Brennan, Jr., "Federal Judges Properly and Inevitably Make Law Through 'Loose' Constitutional Construction," in Peter Woll, ed., *Debating American Government*, 2nd ed. (Glenview, Ill.: Scott, Foresman, 1988), p. 338.

6. Clinton Rossitor, ed., *The Federalist Papers* (New York: New American Library, 1961), no. 33.

7. *Dred Scott* v. *Sandford*, 19 How. 393 (1857). Discussed in more detail in Chapter 14.

8. *Munn* v. *Illinois*, 94 U.S. 113 (1877).

9. *Wabash, St. Louis and Pac. Ry.* v. *Illinois*, 118 U.S. 557 (1886).

10. Gabriel Kolko, *Railroads and Regulation: 1877–1916* (Princeton: Princeton University Press, 1965), p. 232.

11. *Pollock* v. *Farmers' Loan and Trust Co.*, 157 U.S. 429 (1895).

12. *Cincinnati N.O. & T.P. Railway Co.* v. *Interstate Commerce Commission*, 162 U.S. 184 (1896).

13. *Hammer* v. *Dagenhart*, 247 U.S. 251 (1918).

14. James A. Maxwell, *The Fiscal Impact of Federalism in the United States* (Cambridge: Harvard University Press, 1946), p. 135.

15. Josephine Chapin Brown, *Public Relief 1929–1939* (New York: Henry Holt, 1940), pp. 14–15; as cited in Francis Fox Piven and Richard A. Cloward,

Regulating the Poor: The Functions of Public Welfare (New York: Random House, 1971), p. 47.

16. In fact, in 1929 ten states authorized no outdoor relief at all. (Outdoor relief allows people to stay in their homes while they receive aid, like the present welfare system.) Advisory Commission on Intergovernmental Relations (ACIR), *The Federal Role in the Federal System: The Dynamics of Growth, Public Assistance: The Growth of a Federal Function*, (Washington, D.C.: ACIR, 1980), p. 7.

17. Piven and Cloward, *Regulating the Poor*, p. 60.

18. Mark I. Gelfand, *A Nation of Cities: The Federal Government and Urban America 1933–1965* (New York: Oxford University Press, 1975), pp. 32–33.

19. *Congressional Record*, vol. 75, p. 11597; as quoted in Maxwell, *Fiscal Impact*, p. 138.

20. *Schechter Poultry Corp.* v. *United States*, 295 U.S. 495 (1935).

21. David B. Robertson and Dennis R. Judd, *The Development of American Public Policy: The Structure of Policy Restraint* (Glenview, Ill.: Scott, Foresman, 1989), p. 105.

22. *The United States* v. *Butler et al.*, 297 U.S. 1 (1936).

23. *New State Ice Company* v. *Liebmann*, 285 U.S. 262 (1932).

24. *Massachusetts* v. *Mellon* (1923); as quoted in Robertson and Judd, *American Public Policy*, p. 138.

25. Maxwell, *Fiscal Impact*, p. 26.

26. The classic statement of American federalism as regulated by political processes is Herbert Wechsler, "The Political Safeguards of Federalism: The Role of the States in the Selection of the National Government," *Columbia Law Review* 54 (1954): 543–60.

27. Judge John F. Dillon was chief justice of the Iowa Supreme Court and wrote an influential *Treatise on the Law of Municipal Corporations* stressing that cities derived all their powers from states.

28. Piven and Cloward, *Regulating the Poor*, p. 295.

29. Not all federal grant programs targeted the poor. Many large federal grants, such as those for interstate highways and the construction of sewer and water systems, primarily benefitted the suburban middle class.

30. Thomas Byrne Edsall and Mary D. Edsall, *Chain Reaction: The Impact of Race, Rights, and Taxes on American Politics* (New York: W. W. Norton, 1991), p. 106.

31. Ibid., pp. 75–76.

32. Quoted in Timothy Conlan, *New Federalism: Intergovernmental Reform from Nixon to Reagan* (Washington, D.C.: The Brookings Institution, 1988), p. 31.

33. David B. Walker, *Toward a Functioning Federalism* (Cambridge, Mass.: Winthrop, 1981), p. 193.

34. Jeffrey L. Pressman and Aaron Wildavsky, *Implementation*, 3rd ed. (Berkeley: University of California Press, 1984).

35. Conlan, *New Federalism*, p. 154.

36. Joseph F. Zimmerman, *Contemporary American Federalism: The Growth of National Power* (New York: Praeger, 1992), p. 67.

37. U.S. Advisory Commission on Intergovernmental Relations (ACIR), *ACIR News: Negative Opinions of Federal Government Increase in 1992 ACIR Poll* (Washington, D.C.: ACIR, 1992); as reported in Frank J. Thompson, ed., *Revitalizing State and Local Public Service: Strengthening Performance, Accountability, and Citizen Confidence* (San Francisco: Jossey-Bass, 1993), p. 11.

38. Survey by CBS News / *New York Times*, February 22–25, 1995; as reported in *Rockefeller Institute Bulletin* (1996), p. 15.

39. *United States* v. *Lopez*, 115 S. Ct. 1624 (1995).

40. *U.S. Term Limits* v. *Thornton* (1995) and *Seminole Tribe* v. *Florida* (1996), U.S. Lexis 2165.

41. Richard P. Nathan, "The 'Devolution Revolution:' An Overview," *Rockefeller Institute Bulletin* (1996): 5–13.

42. See Grant McConnell, *Private Power and American Democracy* (New York: Random House, 1966) and Theodore J. Lowi, *The End of Liberalism: The Second Republic of the United States*, 2nd ed. (New York: W. W. Norton, 1979).

43. E. E. Schattschneider, *The Semisovereign People: A Realist's View of Democracy in America* (New York: Holt, Rinehart and Winston, 1960).

44. Larry C. Ledebur and William R. Barnes, *City Distress, Metropolitan Disparities and Economic Growth* (Washington, D.C.: National League of Cities, 1992), p. 2 and appendix.

45. *Serrano* v. *Priest*, 5 Cal.3d 584 (1971).

46. Ralph Nader, Mark Green, and Joel Seligman, *Taming the Giant Corporation* (New York: W. W. Norton, 1976), p. 37. The following account, unless otherwise noted, is based on this useful book.

47. Quoted in Nader, Green, and Seligman, *Taming the Giant*, p. 43.

48. Subsequently, Delaware surpassed New Jersey, passing "enabling acts" that allowed corporations to do as they pleased without interference from state regulation. William L. Cary, *Corporations: Cases and Materials*, 4th ed. (Mineoloa, N.Y.: Foundation Press, 1970), p. 10. By 1988, nearly eighteen thousand corporations were chartered in the tiny state of Delaware. Robertson and Judd, *The Development of American Public Policy*, p. 45.

49. Quoted in Nader, Green, and Seligman, *Taming the Giant*, p. 44.

50. Raymond T. Zillmer, "State Laws: Survival of the Unfit," *University of Pennsylvania Law Review*, 62 (1914): 509–24. To rein in corporate power, a Ralph Nader group proposed that the largest 700 corporations be required to obtain federal charters that would enforce basic rights for shareholders, employees, consumers, and neighboring communities.

51. "A Counterattack in the War Between the States," *Business Week*, June 21, 1976.

52. Council of State Governments, *The Book of the States, 1986–87* (Lexington, Kentucky: Council of State Governments, 1986).

53. Bryan D. Jones and Lynn W. Bachelor, *The Sustaining Hand: Community Leadership and Corporate Power*, 2nd ed. (Lawrence: University Press of Kansas, 1993), p. 80.

54. Ibid., p. 215.

55. Paul Brace, *State Government and Economic Performance* (Baltimore, MD: John Hopkins University Press, 1993), p. 128.

56. Quoted in Charles J. Spindler, "Winners and Losers in Industrial Recruitment: Mercedes-Benz and Alabama," *State and Local Government Review* 26, no. 3 (Fall 1994): 192.

57. Irene S. Rubin and Herbert J. Rubin, "Economic Development Incentives: The Poor (Cities) Pay More," *Urban Affairs Quarterly* 23, no. 1 (September 1987): 37–62.

58. Robert Dahl, *Who Governs? Democracy and Power in an American City* (New Haven, Conn.: Yale University Press, 1961).

59. G. William Domhoff, *Who Really Rules: New Haven and Community Power Reexamined* (Santa Monica, Calif.: Goodyear Publishing Company, 1978).

60. Norman I. Fainstein and Susan S. Fainstein, "New Haven: The Limits of the Local State," in Susan S. Fainstein et al., *Restructuring the City*, rev. ed. (New York: Longman, 1986), pp. 47–49.

61. Robert Dahl and Charles E. Lindblom, *Politics and Economics: Planning and the Politico-Economic Systems Resolved into Basic Social Processes* (Chicago: University of Chicago Press, 1976), preface, xxxvii.

62. Stephen Elkin, *City and Regime in the American Republic* (Chicago: University of Chicago Press, 1987), p. 100.

63. The term was coined in Harvey Molotch, "The City as a Growth Machine," *American Journal of Sociology* (September 1976): pp.309–32. See also John R. Logan and Molotch, *Urban Fortunes: The Political Economy of Place* (Berkeley: University of California Press, 1987).

64. Richard Child Hill, "Crisis in the Motor City: The Politics of Economic Development in Detroit," in Susan S. Fainstein et al., *Restructuring the City: The Political Economy of Urban Redevelopment*, rev. ed. (New York: Longman, 1986), p. 105.

65. Quoted in Tony Hiss, "Annals of Place: Reinventing Baltimore," *New Yorker* (April 29, 1991), p. 62. The following account of Baltimore is based on Dennis Judd and Todd Swanstrom, *City Politics: Private Power and Public Policy* (New York: HarperCollins, 1994), pp. 346–50.

66. Quoted in Hiss, "Annals of Place," p. 41.

67. For Hamilton's arguments for a strong executive with expert administration, see James Madison, Alexander Hamilton, and John Jay, *Federalist Papers*, ed. by Isaac Kramnick (New York: Penguin Books, 1987), *Nos.* 67–77.

68. Figures on the extent of structural reforms are taken from Terry Christenson, *Local Politics: Governing at the Grassroots* (Belmont, Calif.: Wadsworth, 1994), ch. 6.

69. Carl Abbott, *The New Urban America: Growth and Politics in Sunbelt Cities* (Chapel Hill: University of North Carolina Press, 1987).

70. Dennis R. Judd and Todd Swanstrom, *City Politics: Private Power and Public Policy* (New York: HarperCollins, 1994), pp. 97–100.

71. See Robert R. Alford and Eugene C. Lee, "Voter Turnout in American Cities," *American Political Science Review* 62 (September 1968): 796–813;

and Albert R. Karnig and B. Oliver Walter, "Decline in Municipal Voter Turnout: A Function of Changing Structure," *American Politics Quarterly* 11, no. 4 (October 1983): 491–505.

72. Judd and Swanstrom, *City Politics*, pp. 102–04.

73. Jonathan Rabinovitz, "States Are Arenas on Minimum Wage," *New York Times*, April 18, 1996; Louis Uchitelle, "Some Cities Pressuring Employers to Raise Wages of Working Poor," *New York Times*, April 9, 1996.

74. Ann O'M. Bowman and Richard C. Kearney, *State and Local Government*, 2nd ed. (Boston: Houghton Mifflin, 1993), pp. 12–13.

75. Robert S. Erickson, Gerald C. Wright, and John P. McIver, *Statehouse Democracy Public Opinion and Policy in the American States* (New York: Cambridge University Press, 1993).

76. V. O. Key, Jr., *Southern Politics in State and Nation*, new ed. (Knoxville, Tenn.: University of Tennessee Press, 1984).

77. Richard P. Nathan, et al., *Reagan and the States* (Princeton: Princeton University Press, 1987), chap. 5.

78. Peter K. Eisinger, *The Rise of the Entrepreneurial State: State and Local Economic Development Policy in the United States* (Madison: University of Wisconsin Press, 1988). See also David Osborne, *Laboratories of Democracy* (Boston: Harvard University Press, 1988).

79. For a full discussion of Chicago's democratic development plan, see Robert Mier, *Social Justice and Local Development Policy* (Newbury Park, Calif.: Sage, 1993).

80. Alexis de Tocqueville, *Democracy in America*, vol. 1 (New York: Schocken Books, 1961), p. 55.

81. John E. Schwarz, *America's Hidden Success: A Reassessment of Public Policy from Kennedy to Reagan*, rev. ed. ((New York: W. W. Norton, 1988).

82. This point is made in Jeffrey M. Berry, Kent E. Portney, and Ken Thomson, *The Rebirth of Urban Democracy* (Washington, D.C.: The Brookings Institution, 1993), chap. 2.

83. For an early account of this movement, see Harry C. Boyte, *The Backyard Revolution: Understanding the New Citizen Movement* (Philadelphia: Temple University Press, 1980).

84. Berry, Portney, and Thomson, *Rebirth of Urban Democracy*.

85. Barbara Ferman, *Challenging the Growth Machine: Neighborhood Politics in Chicago and Pittsburgh* (Lawrence, Kansas: University Press of Kansas, 1996), p. 151.

86. Robertson and Judd, *American Public Policy*, p. 380.

CHAPTER 16

1. *West Virginia State Board of Education* v. *Barnette*, 319 U.S. 624 (1943).

2. *Texas* v. *Johnson*, 491 U.S. 397 (1989).

3. See Samuel Walker, *In Defense of American Liberties: A History of the ACLU* (New York: Oxford University Press, 1990).

4. Actually, twelve amendments passed Congress. One was rejected by the states; the other, which required that congressional pay raises not take effect until after an election, did not receive enough state ratifications to pass. Resurrected in the early 1980s, this amendment finally was passed by enough states to become the Twenty-seventh Amendment in 1992—over two hundred years after it was originally proposed!

5. *United States* v. *Carolene Products Co.*, 304 U.S. 144 (1938).

6. On the double standard, see Henry J. Abraham and Barbara A. Perry, *Freedom and the Court: Civil Rights and Liberties in the United States*, 6th ed. (New York: Oxford University Press, 1994), pp. 9–29.

7. *Palko* v. *Connecticut*, 302 U.S. 319 (1937).

8. See Alan Wolfe, *The Seamy Side of Democracy: Repression in America* (New York: David McKay, 1973).

9. *Schenck* v. *United States*, 249 U.S. 47 (1919).

10. *Brandenburg* v. *Ohio*, 395 U.S. 444 (1969).

11. *Tinker* v. *Des Moines Independent Community School District*, 393 U.S. 503 (1969).

12. Owen M. Fiss, *Liberalism Divided: Freedom of Speech and the Many Uses of State Power* (Boulder, Colo.: Westview Press, 1996), pp. 9–30, 49–66.

13. *United States* v. *Kokinda*, 497 U.S. 720 (1990).

14. Fiss, *Liberalism Divided*, p. 5.

15. *Roth* v. *United States*, 354 U.S. 476 (1957).

16. *Miller* v. *California*, 413 U.S. 15 (1973).

17. *F.C.C.* v. *Pacifica Foundation*, 438 U.S. 726 (1978).

18. Garry Wills, *Under God: Religion and American Politics* (New York: Simon & Schuster, 1990), p. 16.

19. See the classic account by Anthony Lewis, *Gideon's Trumpet* (New York: Vintage Books, 1964).

20. See Thomas Y. Davies, "Exclusionary Rule," in Kermit L. Hall et al., eds., *The Oxford Companion to the Supreme Court of the United States* (New York: Oxford University Press, 1992), pp. 264–66.

21. See Yale Kamisar, "*Miranda* v. *Arizona*," in Hall et al., *Oxford Companion to the Supreme Court*, pp. 552–55.

22. Davies, "Exclusionary Rule," p. 266.

23. *Jencks* v. *United States*, 353 U.S. 657 (1957).

24. *Olmstead* v. *United States*, 277 U.S. 438 (1928).

25. *Griswold* v. *Connecticut*, 381 U.S. 479 (1965).

26. See Barbara Hinkson Craig and David M. O'Brien, *Abortion and American Politics* (Chatham, N.J.: Chatham House, 1993), pp. 35–68.

27. *Bowers* v. *Hardwick*, 478 U.S. 186 (1986).

28. Robert G. McCloskey with Sanford Levinson, *The American Supreme Court* (Chicago: University of Chicago Press, 1994), p. 169.

29. *Romer* v. *Evans*, 116 S. Ct. 1620 (1996).

30. *Plessy* v. *Ferguson*, 163 U.S. 537 (1896).

31. For the story of the NAACP campaign against school segregation, see Richard Kluger, *Simple Justice* (New York: Alfred A. Knopf, 1976).

32. *Brown* v. *Board of Education of Topeka*, 347 U.S. 483 (1954).

33. For a brief and vivid account of these struggles, see Juan Williams, *Eyes on the Prize: America's Civil Rights Years, 1954–1965* (New York: Penguin Books, 1988).

34. Barbara Bergmann, *In Defense of Affirmative Action* (New York: Basic Books, 1996), p. 16.

35. Terry Eastland, *Ending Affirmative Action: The Case for Colorblind Justice* (New York: Basic Books, 1996), p. 8.

36. *Adarand Constructors* v. *Peña*, 115 S. Ct. 2097 (1995).

CHAPTER 17

1. Quoted in Alfred L. Malabre, *Lost Prophets: An Insider's History of the Modern Economists* (Boston: Harvard Business School Press, 1994), p. 183. See Jude Wanniski, *The Way the World Works* (New York: Basic Books, 1978).

2. William A. Niskanen, *Reaganomics: An Insider's Account of the Policies and the People* (New York: Oxford University Press, 1988), p. 4.

3. See Barry Bosworth, *Tax Incentives and Economic Growth* (Washington, D.C.: The Brookings Institution, 1984); and Charles R. Hulten and Isabel V. Sawhill, eds., *The Legacy of Reaganomics: Prospects for Long-Term Growth* (Washington, D.C.: Urban Institute Press, 1984).

4. Krugman, *The Age of Diminished Expectations: U.S. Economic Policy in the 1990s* (Cambridge, Mass.: MIT Press, 1992), pp. 66–67.

5. For a detailed discussion of the 1992 Clinton plan for public investments, see Bill Clinton and Al Gore, *Putting People First: How We Can All Change America* (New York: Random House, 1992).

6. See Bryan Snyder, "Pop Austerity: Clinton Talks Populism But His Program Thrills Wall Street," in Randy Albeda et al., eds., *Real World Macro*, 12th ed. (Somerville, Mass.: Dollars and Sense, 1995), pp. 63–65.

7. Cited in Harold W. Stanley and Richard G. Niemi, *Vital Statistics in American Politics* 4th ed. (Washington, D.C.: Congressional Quarterly Press, 1994), p. 20.

8. A group of 1,100 economists, including eleven Nobel Prize winners, signed a petition calling the Balanced Budget Amendment "unsound and unnecessary."

9. The proposed Balanced Budget Amendment did permit escape hatches but they require "super-majorities" (3/5ths) to, for example, adopt an unbalanced budget or raise the debt ceiling.

10. Quoted in Bob Woodward, *The Agenda: Inside the Clinton White House* (New York: Simon & Schuster, 1994), p. 126. Woodward's book tells the story of how Clinton shifted from the popular democratic promises of the 1992 campaign to elite democratic deficit reduction.

11. The wholesale price index dropped an astonishing 65 percent between 1864 and 1890.

Robert B. Reich, *The Work of Nations* (New York: Vintage Books, 1992), p. 27.

12. Quoted in David E. Rosenbaum, "Critics Want Fed's Power Under More Accountability," *New York Times*, November 14, 1991.

13. The Federal Reserve reports are cited in William Greider, *Secrets of the Temple: How the Federal Reserve Runs the Country* (New York: Simon & Schuster, 1987), p. 39.

14. Quoted in ibid., p. 47.

15. Quoted in ibid.

16. See Milton Friedman, *Capitalism and Freedom* (Chicago: University of Chicago Press, 1982).

17. Quoted in Greider, *Secrets of the Temple*, p. 217.

18. Ibid., p. 593.

19. Quoted in Greider, *Secrets of the Temple*, p. 676.

20. Ibid., p. 682.

21. Ibid., p. 579.

22. Richard W. Stevenson, "It's Heresy at the Fed But Critics Say: Step on the Gas," *New York Times* (June 7, 1996).

23. Donald F. Kettl, *Leadership at the Fed* (New Haven, Conn.: Yale University Press, 1986).

24. Greider, *Secrets of the Temple*, p. 313.

25. Curt Anderson, "Federal Reserve Urged Not to Raise Interest Rates," *Albany Times Union* (April 26, 1997).

26. Quoted in Gwen Ifill, "Clinton Offers Plan for Overhaul of Welfare, with Stress on Work," *New York Times*, September 10, 1992.

27. Charles Murray, *Losing Ground: American Social Policy, 1950–1980* (New York: Basic Books, 1984).

28. Milton Friedman and Rose Friedman, *Free to Choose* (New York: Avon Books, 1981), p. 98.

29. Robert C. Lieberman, "Race and the Organization of Social Policy," a paper presented at the Annual Meeting of the American Political Science Association, Chicago, Illinois, September 3–6, 1992.

30. U.S. Bureau of the Census, *Statistical Abstract of the United States: 1996* (Washington, D.C.: U.S. Government Printing Office, 1996), p. 382.

31. Paul E. Peterson and Mark C. Rom, *Welfare Magnets: A New Case for a National Standard* (Washington, D.C.: The Brookings Institution, 1990).

32. The official poverty line is established by the federal government based on the amount of money needed to purchase an "emergency" diet (a diet that provides minimal adequate nutrition). This amount is then multiplied by 3, based on the assumption that food takes about one-third of the average family's budget. The poverty threshold undoubtedly underestimates the amount of poverty because most people spend less than one-third of their income on food. Other items, such as housing and transportation, have become more expensive.

33. Jason DeParle, "Why Marginal Changes Don't Rescue the Welfare System," *New York Times*, March 1, 1992.

34. U.S. Bureau of the Census as cited in Theresa Amott, "The Disenfranchised: Eliminating Poverty," in Richard Caplan and John Feffer, eds., *State of the Union 1994* (Boulder, Colo.: Westview Press, 1994), p. 171.

35. Kathryn Edin and Laura Lein, *Making Ends Meet* (New York: Russell Sage Foundation, 1997); as reported in Jason DeParle, "Learning Poverty Firsthand," *New York Times Magazine* (April 27, 1997).

36. Cited in John E. Schwarz, *America's Hidden Success: A Reassessment of Public Policy from Kennedy to Reagan*, rev. ed. (New York: W. W. Norton, 1993), p. 32.

37. For a review of the evidence on the relationship between welfare and the rise of single-parent families, see William Julius Wilson, *The Truly Disadvantaged: The Inner City, the Underclass, and Public Policy* (Chicago: University of Chicago Press, 1987), chap. 3.

38. DeParle, "Marginal Changes."

39. Wilson, *Truly Disadvantaged.*

40. Theresa Funiciello, *Tyranny of Kindness: Dismantling the Welfare System to End Poverty in America* (New York: Atlantic Monthly Press, 1993), p. 285.

41. Funiciello, *Tyranny of Kindness*, p. 268.

42. See Frances Fox Piven and Richard A. Cloward, *Regulating the Poor: The Functions of Public Welfare* (New York: Random House, 1971).

43. Quoted in Jonathan Rieder, *Canarsie: The Jews and Italians of Brooklyn Against Liberalism* (Cambridge: Harvard University Press, 1985), p. 102.

44. *Time*/CNN poll of 600 adults conducted by Yankelovich Partners, Inc. with a sampling error of plus or minus 4 percent. Reported in Nancy Gibbs, "The Vicious Cycle," *Time* (June 20, 1994), p. 26.

45. Jason DeParle, "A Sharp Decrease in Welfare Cases is Gathering Speed," *New York Times*, February 2, 1997.

46. Quoted in Jason DeParle, "Cutting Welfare Rolls but Raising Questions," *New York Times*, May 7, 1997.

47. Estimate is by Professor Harry Holzer of Michigan State University, as reported in "Welfare Reform's Other Victims," editorial, *New York Times*, April 6, 1997.

48. Urban Institute study as reported in Peter Edelman, "The Worst Thing Bill Clinton Has Done," *Atlantic Monthly* (March 1997): 46.

49. Theda Skocpol, "Targeting Within Universalism: Politically Viable Policies to Combat Poverty in the United States," in Christopher Jencks and Paul E. Peterson, eds., *The Urban Underclass* (Washington, D.C.: The Brookings Institution, 1991), p. 425.

50. U.S. Bureau of the Census, *Statistical Abstract of the United States 1996* (Washington, D.C.: U.S. Government Printing Office, 1996), p. 473.

51. Stanley S. Surrey and Paul R. McDaniel, *Tax Expenditures* (Cambridge: Harvard University Press, 1985), p. 34.

52. U.S. Bureau of the Census, *Statistical Abstract of United States 1996* (Washington, D.C.: U.S. Government Printing Office, 1996), table 518.

53. Michael Peter Smith, *City, State, and Market: The Political Economy of Urban Society* (Cambridge: Basil Blackwell, 1988).

54. *Housing at a Snail's Pace: The Federal housing Budget: 1978–1997* (Washington, D.C.: U.S. Government Printing Office, 1996), pp. 9, 75.

55. Timothy Smeeding, "Why the U.S. Antipoverty System Doesn't Work Very Well," *Challenge* (January-February 1992): 33.

56. Arnold J. Heidenheimer, Hugh Heclo, and Carolyn Teich Adams, *Comparative Public Policy: The Politics of Social Choice in America, Europe, and Japan*, 3rd ed. (New York: St. Martin's Press, 1990), p. 249.

57. In 1973, the Supreme Court ruled that education is not right guaranteed equal protection under the U.S. Constitution. See *Rodriguez* v. *San Antonio Independent School District*, 411 U.S. 1 (1973). Many state constitutions, however, do guarantee equal educational opportunity, and lawsuits have successfully forced changes in the unequal funding of schools in many states.

58. Jonathan Kozol, *Savage Inequalities: Children in America's Schools* (New York: HarperCollins, 1991).

59. U.S. Bureau of the Census, *Statistical Abstract of the United States 1996* (Washington, D.C.: U.S. Government Printing Office, 1996), p. 371.

60. Quoted in Robert Suro, "Duke Campaigns on Distorted Facts Despite Rebuttals and Clarifications," *New York Times*, November 12, 1991.

61. See Funiciello, *Tyranny of Kindness*.

62. See Barbara Ehrenreich, "The New Right Attack on Social Welfare," in Fred Block et al., eds., *The Mean Season: The Attack on the Welfare State* (New York: Pantheon Books, 1987), pp. 161–95.

63. Quoted in Jill Smolowe, "Ripped from the Womb," *Time*, December 4, 1995, p. 61.

64. Yankelovich poll, as reported in *U.S. News and World Report*, October 5, 1992, p. 40.

CHAPTER 18

1. The story of CIA plots against Castro is drawn from U.S. Senate, Select Committee to Study Governmental Operations with Regard to Intelligence Activities, *Alleged Assassination Plots Involving Foreign Leaders* (Washington, D.C.: U.S. Government Printing Office, 1975).

2. See especially Hamilton's arguments in *Federalist No. 6* and *No. 11*.

3. Clinton Rossiter, ed., *The Federalist Papers* (New York: New American Library, 1961), p. 424.

4. Richard H. Kohn, *Eagle and Sword: The Federalists and the Creation of the Military Establishment in America, 1783–1802* (New York: Free Press, 1975).

5. Ibid., p. 9.

6. Richard J. Barnet, *The Rockets' Red Glare: When America Goes to War—The Presidents and the People* (New York: Simon & Schuster, 1990), p. 82.

7. Ibid., pp. 111–15, 125–38; Bruce Miroff, *Icons of Democracy: American Leaders as Heroes, Aristocrats, Dissenters, and Democrats* (New York: Basic Books, 1993), pp. 182–87.

8. Roy P. Basler, ed., *The Collected Works of Abraham Lincoln* (New Brunswick, N.J.: Rutgers University Press, 1953–55), vol. 3, p. 357.

9. Quoted in Barnet, *Rockets' Red Glare*, p. 15.

10. Quoted in Ralph B. Levering, *The Cold War, 1945–1987* (Arlington Heights, Ill.: Harlan Davidson, 1988), p. 30.

11. Of all the Cold War presidents, Eisenhower probably had the deepest interest in peace. See Robert A. Divine, *Eisenhower and the Cold War* (New York: Oxford University Press, 1981), pp. 105–55.

12. George C. Herring, *America's Longest War: The United States and Vietnam, 1950–1975*, 2nd ed. (New York: Alfred A. Knopf, 1986).

13. John Prados, *Presidents' Secret Wars: CIA and Pentagon Covert Operations Since World War II* (New York: William Morrow, 1986), pp. 91–98.

14. Seymour M. Hersh, *The Price of Power: Kissinger in the Nixon White House* (New York: Summit Books, 1983), pp. 258–96.

15. Quoted in Divine, *Eisenhower and the Cold War*, p. 108.

16. James M. McCormick, *American Foreign Policy and Process*, 2nd ed. (Itasca, Ill.: Peacock, 1992), pp. 377–80.

17. Ibid., pp. 361–69.

18. Loch K. Johnson, *America's Secret Power: The CIA in a Democratic Society* (New York: Oxford University Press, 1989), pp. 16–17.

19. Prados, *Presidents' Secret Wars*, pp. 402–13.

20. Johnson, *America's Secret Power*, p. 10.

21. Ibid., pp. 107–10, 118–29, 207–33.

22. Tim Weiner, "CIA Hired Suspected Assassins, Panel Says," *New York Times*, June 29, 1996.

23. Charles W. Kegley, Jr., and Eugene R. Wittkopf, *World Politics*, 4th ed. (New York: St. Martin's Press, 1993), pp. 214–50.

24. Richard J. Barnet, *Roots of War* (New York: Penguin Books, 1973), pp. 179–82.

25. Johnson, *America's Secret Power*, p. 22.

26. See Thomas W. Graham, "Public Opinion and U.S. Foreign Policy Decision Making," in David A. Deese, ed., *The New Politics of American Foreign Policy* (New York: St. Martin's Press, 1994), pp. 190–215.

27. McCormick, *American Foreign Policy and Process*, pp. 498–505.

28. Robert Y. Shapiro and Benjamin I. Page, "Foreign Policy and Public Opinion," in Deese, *The New Politics of American Foreign Policy*, pp. 229–33.

29. Ibid., p. 220.

30. Ronald Steel, *Temptations of a Superpower* (Cambridge: Harvard University Press, 1995), p. 1.

31. James Schlesinger, "Quest for a Post–Cold War Foreign Policy," *Foreign Affairs* (January / February 1993): 17–28.

32. Samuel Huntington, "Why International Primacy Matters," *International Security*, Spring 1993: 68–83.

33. Larry Diamond, "Promoting Democracy," in Bruce Miroff, Raymond Seidelman, and Todd Swanstrom, eds., *Debating Democracy: A Reader in American Politics* (Boston: Houghton Mifflin, 1997), p. 367.

34. Patrick Buchanan, "America First—and Second, and Third," in ibid., p. 360.

35. Steel, *Temptations of a Superpower*, p. 5.

36. Ibid., p. 137.

37. See, for example, Michael Mandelbaum, "Foreign Policy as Social Work," *Foreign Affairs*, (January / February 1996): 28.

38. Tim Weiner, "Clinton as a Military Leader: Tough On-the-Job Training," *New York Times*, October 28, 1996.

39. John Stremlau, "Clinton's Dollar Diplomacy," *Foreign Policy* (Winter 1994–95): 18–35.

40. Jeffrey E. Garten, "Is America Abandoning Multilateral Trade?" *Foreign Affairs* (November/December 1995): 50–62.

41. Tom Masland, "How Did We Get Here?," *Newsweek*, September 26, 1994, pp. 26–31.

42. See Robert I. Rotberg, "Clinton Was Right," *Foreign Policy* (Spring 1996): 135–41.

43. Quoted in Elizabeth Drew, *On the Edge: The Clinton Presidency* (New York: Simon & Schuster, 1994), p. 162.

44. Drew, *On the Edge*, p. 283.

45. *New York Times*, November 22, 1995.

46. *New York Times*, November 28, 1995.

INDEX

CREDITS